Measuring the Effectiveness of Organizational Development Strategies During Unprecedented Times

Kyla Latrice Tennin
College of Doctoral Studies, University of Phoenix, USA & Forbes School of Business, USA & World Business Angels Investment Forum (WBAF)–G20, USA & Lady Mirage Global, Inc., USA

A volume in the Advances in Human Resources Management and Organizational Development (AHRMOD) Book Series

Published in the United States of America by
    IGI Global
    Business Science Reference (an imprint of IGI Global)
    701 E. Chocolate Avenue
    Hershey PA, USA 17033
    Tel: 717-533-8845
    Fax: 717-533-8661
    E-mail: cust@igi-global.com
    Web site: http://www.igi-global.com

Library of Congress Cataloging-in-Publication Data

Names: Tennin, Kyla Latrice, 1982- editor.
Title: Measuring the effectiveness of organizational development strategies
  during unprecedented times / edited by Kyla Latrice Tennin.
Description: Hershey, PA : Business Science Reference, [2023] | Includes
  bibliographical references and index. | Summary: "The purpose of this
  book is to substantiate organizational development in organizations
  (specifically during unprecedented times where digital transformation is
  critical), discuss the practical experience of organizational
  development implementation, and to measure the effectiveness of an
  organizational development strategy or plan initiative implemented.
  Chapters to be hosted in this book are also intended to be used as part
  of course/training material in various professional development
  settings. Presenting resources, tools, scientific and methodological
  perspectives, and various organizational development models or
  frameworks organizations can apply to assist them with being effective
  during crises or unprecedented times"-- Provided by publisher.
Identifiers: LCCN 2023010035 (print) | LCCN 2023010036 (ebook) | ISBN
  9781668483923 (hardcover) | ISBN 9781668483930 (paperback) | ISBN
  9781668483947 (ebook)
Subjects: LCSH: Organizational change. | Strategic planning. |
  Organizational effectiveness.
Classification: LCC HD58.8 .M437 2023 (print) | LCC HD58.8 (ebook) | DDC
  658.4/06--dc23/eng/20230302
LC record available at https://lccn.loc.gov/2023010035
LC ebook record available at https://lccn.loc.gov/2023010036

This book is published in the IGI Global book series Advances in Human Resources Management and Organizational Development (AHRMOD) (ISSN: 2327-3372; eISSN: 2327-3380)

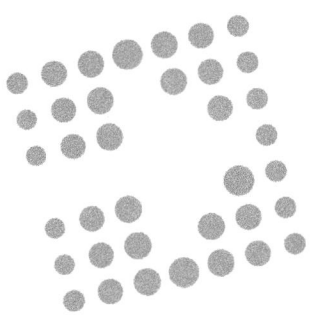

Advances in Human Resources Management and Organizational Development (AHRMOD) Book Series

Patricia Ordóñez de Pablos
Universidad de Oviedo, Spain

ISSN:2327-3372
EISSN:2327-3380

MISSION

A solid foundation is essential to the development and success of any organization and can be accomplished through the effective and careful management of an organization's human capital. Research in human resources management and organizational development is necessary in providing business leaders with the tools and methodologies which will assist in the development and maintenance of their organizational structure.

The **Advances in Human Resources Management and Organizational Development (AHRMOD) Book Series** aims to publish the latest research on all aspects of human resources as well as the latest methodologies, tools, and theories regarding organizational development and sustainability. The **AHRMOD Book Series** intends to provide business professionals, managers, researchers, and students with the necessary resources to effectively develop and implement organizational strategies.

COVERAGE

- Job Enrichment
- Succession Planning
- Human Relations Movement
- Personnel Retention
- Employee Evaluation
- E-Human Resources Management
- Corporate Governance
- Organizational Learning
- Talent Identification and Management
- Work-Life Balance

IGI Global is currently accepting manuscripts for publication within this series. To submit a proposal for a volume in this series, please contact our Acquisition Editors at Acquisitions@igi-global.com or visit: http://www.igi-global.com/publish/.

Titles in this Series

For a list of additional titles in this series, please visit: http://www.igi-global.com/book-series/advances-human-resources-management-organizational/73670

Socio-Economic Disparities, Vulnerable Communities, and the Future of Work and Entrepreneurship
JoAnn Denise Rolle (Medgar Evers College, City University of New York, USA) and Micah Crump (Medgar Evers College, City University of New York, USA)
Business Science Reference • © 2023 • 335pp • H/C (ISBN: 9781668469903) • US $240.00

Examining Applied Multicultural Industrial and Organizational Psychology
Bryan Christiansen (Southern New Hampshire University, USA) and Angela M. Even (Purdue University, USA)
Business Science Reference • © 2023 • 349pp • H/C (ISBN: 9781668472125) • US $250.00

Diversity, Equity, and Inclusion Efforts of Businesses in Rural Areas
Shashi Bala (V.V. Giri National Labour Institute, India) and Puja Singhal (National Centre for School Leadership (NIEPA), India)
Business Science Reference • © 2023 • 258pp • H/C (ISBN: 9781668468784) • US $225.00

Perspectives on Workplace Communication and Well-Being in Hybrid Work Environments
Alexandre Duarte (Universidade Nova de Lisboa, Portugal) Patrícia Dias (Universidade Católica Portuguesa, Portugal) Teresa Ruão (CECS, Universidade do Minho, Portugal) and José Gabriel Andrade (CECS, Universidade do Minho, Portugal)
Business Science Reference • © 2023 • 276pp • H/C (ISBN: 9781668473535) • US $225.00

Context, Policy, and Practices in Indigenous and Cultural Entrepreneurship
Wilfred Isak April (International University Management, Namibia) Anthony Adeyanju (International University of Management, Namibia) and Blessing Tafirenyika (International University of Management, Namibia)
Business Science Reference • © 2023 • 296pp • H/C (ISBN: 9781668475782) • US $240.00

Female Entrepreneurship as a Driving Force of Economic Growth and Social Change
Ana Dias Daniel (Universidade de Aveiro, Portugal) and Cristina Fernandes (Universidade da Beira Interior, Portugal)
Business Science Reference • © 2023 • 241pp • H/C (ISBN: 9781668476697) • US $250.00

Developing Diversity, Equity, and Inclusion Policies for Promoting Employee Sustainability and Well-Being
Sónia P. Gonçalves (ISCSP, Universidade de Lisboa, Portugal) Paula Cristina Nunes Figueiredo (Universidade Lusófona, Portugal) Eduardo Luis Soares Tomé (ULHT, Universidade Lusófona, Portugal) and José Baptista (ISCSP, Universidade de Lisboa, Portugal)
Business Science Reference • © 2023 • 333pp • H/C (ISBN: 9781668441817) • US $240.00

IGI Global
PUBLISHER of TIMELY KNOWLEDGE

701 East Chocolate Avenue, Hershey, PA 17033, USA
Tel: 717-533-8845 x100 • Fax: 717-533-8661
E-Mail: cust@igi-global.com • www.igi-global.com

Editorial Advisory Board

Table of Contents

Detailed Table of Contents

Chapter 1
Ali Rehman, A Sharqiyah University, Oman

The recent pandemic has had a negative impact on the market and related industries, primarily due to the forced closure of businesses by governments. However, the main cause of this impact is ineffective organizational strategies and their poor implementation. In today's business environment where profitability is the sole focus of management, there is a lack of strategy creation and implementation. In this scenario, the board of directors needs an additional resource to provide precise and well-researched information. This resource can be called the metaverse. Metaverse can be used in the corporate world to improve various processes and operations and provides assistance to make effective decisions. This chapter applies agency theory to show how the metaverse can act as a board member and improve the effectiveness of development strategies. This chapter introduces a new concept for organizational governance. It will be useful for regulators, policy makers, and boards of directors.

Chapter 2
Chabi Gupta, School of Commerce, CHRIST University, India

The delivery of a tailored customer experience is being widely recognised by executives in the technology industry as the key to unlocking revenue, minimising attrition, and providing growth. It is not simple to satisfy a consumer in today's market. Delivering reliable and efficient experiences across channels is more challenging than it has ever been because of the context of disparate privacy regulations, quick updates to browser technology, and an ever-evolving technological landscape. This research suggests that to do it right, the business needs to have the right people, processes, and technologies working in sync. This study highlights that many companies continue to invest in instruments and technology solutions before they have effectively accomplished the organisational transformation required to perform the role in a data-driven mode. Investments do not always yield the promised results since the basic pieces of mindset, vision, and people are not always in congruence. Consumers are no longer going to be 'just satisfied,' or 'even happy.'

Chapter 3
Oindrila Chakraborty, J. D. Birla Institute, India

The chapter thoroughly investigated various conceptual models for organisational development (OD). The implementation of the theoretical models and organisational development during the COVID-19 crisis would have been covered. The main objective of the book chapter is to equip readers with the knowledge and skills they need to comprehend the various frameworks, models, and concepts for managing organisational development, with a focus on how these concepts were used during the COVID-19-based pandemic. Additionally, the chapter checks on the different changes adapted by various sectors to accommodate sudden changes due to pandemic driven crises.

Chapter 4
*José G. Vargas-Hernandez, Tecnológico Superior de Jalisco Mario Molina, Zapopan,
 Mexico*
Teresa I. Salazar-Echeagaray, Universidad Autónoma de Sinaloa, Mexico
Omar C. Vargas-González, Tecnológico Nacional de Mexico, Ciudad Guzmán, Mexico

This study aims to analyze the implications of green knowledge and technology in organizational green innovation, urban green innovation, and green roofs. The analysis is supported by the assumption that green sharing knowledge and technology is basic to organizational green innovation and urban green innovation areas practices, operations, and activities. The methods employed are based on the analytical-reflective and descriptive supported with the review of theoretical and empirical literature. The analysis concludes that green knowledge sharing is relevant to create and develop green technology with positive implications for organizational green innovation, urban green innovation areas, and green roofs.

Chapter 5
José G. Vargas-Hernandez, Instituto Tecnológico Mario Molina, Zapopan, Mexico
Omar C. Vargas-González, Tecnológico Nacional de México, Ciudad Guzmán, Mexico

This study has the purpose of analyzing the implications of the organizational socio-ecosystem on innovation. It begins from the assumption that organizations are open and dynamic concepts of socio-ecosystems composed of technical, social, and environmental dimensions of sustainability departing from growth-based policies and jointly optimized in management strategies for organizational innovation and development that results in improved performance. The method employed is critical analysis and reflection based on the theoretical and empirical review of the literature. It is concluded that the organizational socio ecosystems innovation is the result of multiple organizational factors and environmental dimensions stimulated by the involvement of a diversity of actors, agents, stakeholders, government institutions, research centers and universities, organizational business, among others.

Organizational resilience is herein defined as the ability to positively manage environmental instability over time operationalized by strong corporate social responsibility (CSR). Appropriate CSR can help align business practices both in and outside the organization with current significant economic, social, environmental, and public health issues. Both academics and practitioners have discussed resilience as a voluntary and unobservable paradigm typically measured by outcomes. It is the hope of the author and the aim of this chapter that the sustain optimize change model and its renewed approach to optimized change management will expand corporate social responsibility awareness and activities, that address vulnerabilities, and build resilience in retort to augmented social inequalities.

This chapter explores the benefits of leveraging strategic tactics incorporating holistic approaches throughout cross-functional ecosystems with a deep dive into core work-life dynamics associated with organizational effectiveness, culture transformations, and change leadership aspects impacting the organizational development (OD) discipline evolution. Businesses today are consistently undergoing rapid change, triggered by the current volatile, uncertain, complex, and ambiguous (VUCA) post-pandemic state of the world. To enhance organizational efficiencies and effectiveness, astute leaders have found it imperative to align long-term evidenced-based scientific OD strategies with measurable people management and business outcomes. The key concepts in this chapter will inform best practices, deepen awareness at all levels, and establish appreciation for holistic leadership mindsets, which can address challenges such as internal aspects of employee disengagement and external aspects of customer or stakeholder dissatisfaction.

The breakout of the Covid-19 toward the end of 2019 sent shockwaves across the world. To prevent the spread of the disease and save lives, many countries have resorted to observing country-wide lockdowns, damaging the normalcy of their economy. As a result, the world economy lost trillions of dollars during this period. The renewable energy sector, too, was not spared from being affected by the pandemic. An amalgamation of the effects of the pandemic on the global economy and fluctuating oil prices resulting from country-wide lockdowns across the world further triggered its impact on the renewable energy industry. This chapter highlights the challenges that the energy sector has experienced due to the pandemic in terms of raw material availability, supply chain, market uncertainty, employment, and energy security.

The education industry has changed as a result of the adoption of ICT in schools at different levels. The greatest way to assist teaching and learning in traditional classroom settings as well as distant learning and online programmes that prepare students to participate in the dynamic world of technology is through technology. Nothing in the modern world makes sense or is simple to perform without the impact of ICT products and programmes, thus it is impossible to ignore the role that computers have played in global development. ICT products and programmes are a crucial instrument in assisting global standards. With the availability of educational opportunities, and access to learning materials in the form of photos and text, the internet has become so flexible that one can even obtain them at one's convenience at any time of the day. The use of ICT in education has gained popularity across the globe due to the ease with which it is associated.

Diagnosing organisations is a chapter that explores the intrinsic relationship between organisational purpose, the people, and value creation in relation to organisational structures. Without structure we can't be aware of what we are changing or monitoring if we are effectively achieving our organisational purpose. Structure in the form of governance, an operating system, or organisation design can be built to fight or embrace change. People can be taught to do the same. With the application change maturity built on organisational structures and people management coupled with a search to maximise value through creating continuously adaptive organisational systems, one can equip organisations with the tools they need to not only survive but thrive. By questioning the basic building blocks of organising, this chapter establishes not only factors that could be measures in this diagnosis of organisations, but establishes a set of invitations that are more profound in the sense that they offer strategic choice and development of this concept of organising and organisations.

The purpose of this study is to analyze the interacting internal and environmental variables of an institutionalized organizational perspective. It departs from the assumption that the institutional analysis of the interacting relations between the internal and environmental variables are critical to explain the coevolution development of organizations. The method employed originated in the conceptual, theoretical, and empirical literature review as the basis for the application of meta-cognitive and meta-analytical methods. The analysis concludes that the interactions between the internal and environmental variables using the institutional theory makes relevant contributions to the organizational studies.

Challenges like pandemics, technological breakthroughs, geopolitical instability, and climate change are making crisis an ever more present reality in the lives of people, organizations, and societies. This chapter examines how people around the world are being trained for crisis situations, focusing on skills and competencies being developed, as well as the training approaches and practices. Two complementary methodologies were used to address theory as well as practice. To grasp the perspective of researchers, a systematic crisis training literature review following the SPIDER approach was conducted; for the examination of training designs, a benchmarking of training websites on Google was completed. The analyses conducted, resulted in practical recommendations for future research and practice in the crisis training niche, ultimately aiming at facilitating crisis management and skills trainings worldwide to better prepare the society for inevitable critical events.

If the organisation's ecosystem has an excess of HiPPOs, data, measured analytics, and other real-time information that minimises uncertainty can help them mitigate the consequences. They disregard the wisdom of the crowd, overlook the front-line staff's abilities, and risk disengaging the workforce. This research advocates agile metrics and value management to tame the HiPPO. The authors posit to reign in opinions with metrics. The corporate enlightenment brought about a revolutionary idea over three centuries ago: to elevate science and knowledge above magical thought and mysticism. When the authors convert this into modern terms, they are referring to data-driven management, analytics, and hypothesis validation. In fact, the idea of applying science in the form of true evidence, confirmed data, etc. to production processes underlies much of the industrial revolution.

Foreword

Let me first say that it is truly an honor to write the *foreword* to this pivotal text. I find that writing a foreword is like constructing an invitation. It is a way to introduce the reader to what they should encounter if they decide to endeavor into the deeper foray of material. And for me, a foreword has always served to pique my interest, allow me to slip into the conversation, and ultimately immerse myself in the content. In fact, the topical content of this book concerns an area that I have deeply engaged in, and studied for some three years now as it relates to business and to the greater, human condition.

The study of business and industry, however, has always been woven into the many roles I have had the opportunity to serve over the years. My background includes a mosaic of leadership positions over the course of some 20-plus years now. I currently serve as the *Senior Director for Research Strategy, Innovation, and Development* for the College of Doctoral Studies at the University of Phoenix. As well, I run a private practice from Austin, Texas called *Inspirethought Counseling LLC* where I see a number of patients. I also maintain a *Psychology Today* blog, writing on a variety of issues, and am also the Chair for the Center for Leadership Studies and Organizational Research in the College of Doctoral Studies. I have served in a variety of leadership roles over the years, including an 8-year term for the Higher Learning Commission's Peer Review team, where I had the chance to truly meet with some of the nation's top academic leaders of institutions through my time there. In all of this, research has always been a pivotal cornerstone of what I do daily. In fact, as I write this, I am working on delivering research that will be presented at the 2023 American Psychological Association's national conference in Washington, D.C. Research has always held an interest for me, as I have come to understand its importance to so many things that constitute our lives.

When I was asked to open this text by Dr. Kyla Tennin, I couldn't have been happier, having worked now for several years with her, and bearing witness to some of her impactful contributions to the world of research and business. So, it is with this distinction I open this particular work of collective thoughts and research around a topic that is truly about the potentiating prospects of assuming a "Forward" navigation necessary for the industry to establish what is currently an imperative call for *preventative programming* for future crises. This is especially true after just having endured one of the most sustaining and harsh environmental issues engaged over the last century, the COVID pandemic.

It wasn't that long ago that we had arrived at the onset of this pernicious disaster that crept in during what is now referred to as our "pre-pandemic phase," and what ultimately hijacked the lives, and sadly, the health, of so many people globally. The world of business was also aggressively usurped and surrounded by uncommon ingressions. During the midst of this crisis, I think one of the best descriptors came from the work of researchers Harris et al., who stated, *"Necessity has been the mother of invention in the response to the COVID-19 pandemic, triggering many an innovation, often without the luxury of time to test these makeshift solutions to pressing problems. But there is much to be learned from times of crisis for times of plenty"* (Chaubey & Sahoo, 2021).

Their prelude to what has now become an *assimilation* of business intelligence (BI) around pernicious disaster scenarios for the industry has taken the forefront of business research these days, some three-plus years later. However, studies related to BI assimilation given such a crisis context are, unfortunately, still replete in the literature. Previous studies have, in fact, mentioned that such adoption and implementation of preventative programming is often considered the basis for any such diffusion concerning "programmatic innovation." Most organizations, however, will not understand the full prospects of what can be done until, and unless, such innovation is truly assimilated. To this end, such innovative "preventative" implementation activities required to offset such major crises events like the pandemic require the industry as a whole to assimilate the philosophy and practices across business routines for organizations to achieve the maximum benefits of any such BI implements (Nam et al., 2019). What I am suggesting here is that business leaders must not languish in post-artificial falsities such as "convenience" thinking which might have them believing this will be the last of such disasters. Thus, the importance of a work such as this is presented herein.

This textbook, by Dr. Kyla Tennin should be considered the first of many more we must be looking at if we are to construct a model that can be operationalized and engaged by leaders during crises. The time is ripe for *ideating*, as Dr. Tennin mentions, towards solutions. To languish in a series of cliché paradoxes without movement is not what the world needs right now. In doing so, we risk an even deadlier effect the next time around, and note, there will be always something else as the physics of the world dictates.

To lead this discussion and research, Dr. Kyla Tennin has assembled 17 industry experts internationally who analyze disaster in its various relational contexts, as they are articulated during such VUCA-inspired circumstances. I can also think of no better expert in business and industry than Dr. Tennin to engage in this venture. Dr. Tennin's work as an industry practitioner and specialist in Management and Organizational Leadership is thought-provoking and aspirational. She brings an intensified focus towards *Change Management,* alongside her own use of mixed-methods empirical research as core ingredients to lending knowledge for continuous improvement in business, business transformation, and most notably, a wisdom in assisting businesses and leadership in recovery efforts with future-directed recommendations. She is a leader in the various roles she has undertaken in the industry such as with high-level investment forums working with high-level dignitaries and other business leaders to strategize, and promote business decision-making possibilities to help with start-ups, advance knowledge, and/or scale to improve economic development, along with promoting social justice.

Dr. Tennin is also affiliated with the International Monetary Fund, World Bank Group, and Parliamentary Network (of leaders from around the world) to enhance economies and various forms of organizations. She is formerly an OB/GYN MD track turned DM (doctor) with a background in biology, biotechnology, and organic and biochemistry, with a major emphasis in women and gender studies. She also maintains project management and lean six sigma certifications, and educationally, a Master of Business Administration (MBA), and Ph.D. Fellow at the Global Peace Institute, headquartered in the United Kingdom. She completed additional studies (to launch and scale corporations) at Harvard, Stanford, Yale, the University of Cape Town, and the University of Glasgow just to name a few. She has personally written approximately 18 books, 3 book chapters with colleagues, 3 patents, and several other intellectual properties, amassing nearly 85 research reports, later conceptualized into products and services for global businesses. Dr. Tennin has also presented various research in practitioner and academic conferences, workshops, and international webinars across the country. She has professional experience in the financial services and investments, hospitality, restaurant, consumer products/beauty, and healthcare industries, with much of her experience spent in financial services and higher education.

As for the value of this text? The analysis contained in the pages of the following chapters should be ***required reading*** for any leader or expert in business at this time. To say that such insights will lend to the field is an understatement. In higher regard, this book will impact our field of understanding, and the potential to improve both smaller and larger scale understanding of organizational development, and its inherent processes, the specifics of organizational development models, and the advantages of applying organizational development in organizations, or to this end, entrepreneurship, to not only sustain, but provide ways to thrive in challenging times. It will also add value to any organization's "willingness" to transform, to better adapt through agile leadership so as to absorb any and all pernicious impacts. Of course, such movements I believe can only be had through a deeper "introspect" so that the industry will become stronger in responsivity to such events. But alas, that is dependent on their desire to prepare. And to the extent of how we sell business after something like a pandemic, the text offers an understanding of how crisis and *asymmetry* affect the ways business must interact now, and in the future. This text gives us a glimpse into what I refer to as a "postcrisis horizon", and ultimately affords many in business, to learn from what we have endured globally and listen to the insights of those who have taken up the cause from greater understanding and mobility during crisis times. Enjoy the analysis, and learn to adopt the wisdom for future sake.

Rodney Luster
Center for Leadership Studies and Organizational Research, College of Doctoral Studies, University of Phoenix, USA

REFERENCES

Chaubey, A., & Sahoo, C. K. (2021). Assimilation of business intelligence: The effect of external pressures and top leaders' commitment during pandemic crisis. *International Journal of Information Management, 59,* 102344. doi:10.1016/j.ijinfomgt.2021.102344

Nam, D., Lee, J., & Lee, H. (2019). Business analytics adoption process: An innovation diffusion perspective. *International Journal of Information Management, 49,* 411–423. doi:10.1016/j.ijinfomgt.2019.07.017

Preface

Measuring the Effectiveness of Organizational Development Strategies During Unprecedented Times discusses various crises in organizations around the globe. For instance, during the COVID-19 pandemic. To combat COVID-19 with organizational development (OD) strategies.

Further, OD and change management are sometimes used interchangeably although they are two different things. "Change management is the application of a structured process and set of tools for leading the people side of change to achieve a desired outcome. We apply change management by helping individuals impacted by a change make successful personal transitions that enable them to engage, adopt, and use a change" (Prosci Inc., 2023). Additionally, change management regards applying change models/ frameworks to help people impacted by the change make the successful personal transition necessary to "enable them to engage, adopt, and use a change" (Prosci, Inc., 2023).

Organization development is about addressing the alignment of an organization's processes, systems, people, structure, and design to build its capacity to change (Academy to Innovate HR (AIHR), 2023; Association for Talent Development, 2023). Including increasing its chances of accomplishing greater effectiveness and improving organizational health (van Vulpen, 2023; OD Network, 2023). Essentially increasing the organization's functioning; by applying activities that change organizational structures, leadership styles, and/or behavioral patterns (AIHR, 2023). Like Leavitt's System Model, the Action Research Model, Greiner's Equential Models, and Kurt Lewin's Unfreezing, Changing, and Refreezing Model (BMC Software, Inc., 2023; Hussain et al., 2018; Burnes, 2020). An example of Lewin's Three-Stage Model is shown in Figure 1.

Furthermore, the most common types of organizational development interventions are (1) Human Process Interventions, (2) Human Resource Management Interventions, (3) Technostructural Interventions, and (4) Strategic Change Interventions. See Figure 2 for an example of each intervention and its sub-categories.

Gargi (2019) stated entrepreneurship is about economies employing people, that can be connected to innovative technologies and innovations that with the ability to create more employment for markets. New technologies and innovations can also be profitable (Gargi, 2019). As a result, education, digital transformation, resilience, strategic partnerships, financial inclusion, and especially organizational development are necessary when crises happen. For saving and advancing economies and organizational ecosystems. So, being knowledgeable about the conception and processes of organizational development to decrease an enterprise's challenges is critical to know. In order to increase performance, address risk, innovate, execute a strategy to increase revenue, and implement new processes, systems, or digital transformation to scale. Therefore, the aim of this book is to provide practitioners, scholars, leaders, and key stakeholders of businesses and economies with unique ways of addressing significant challenges

Figure 1. Kurt Lewin's three-stage model
Source: *(BMC Software, Inc., 2023)*

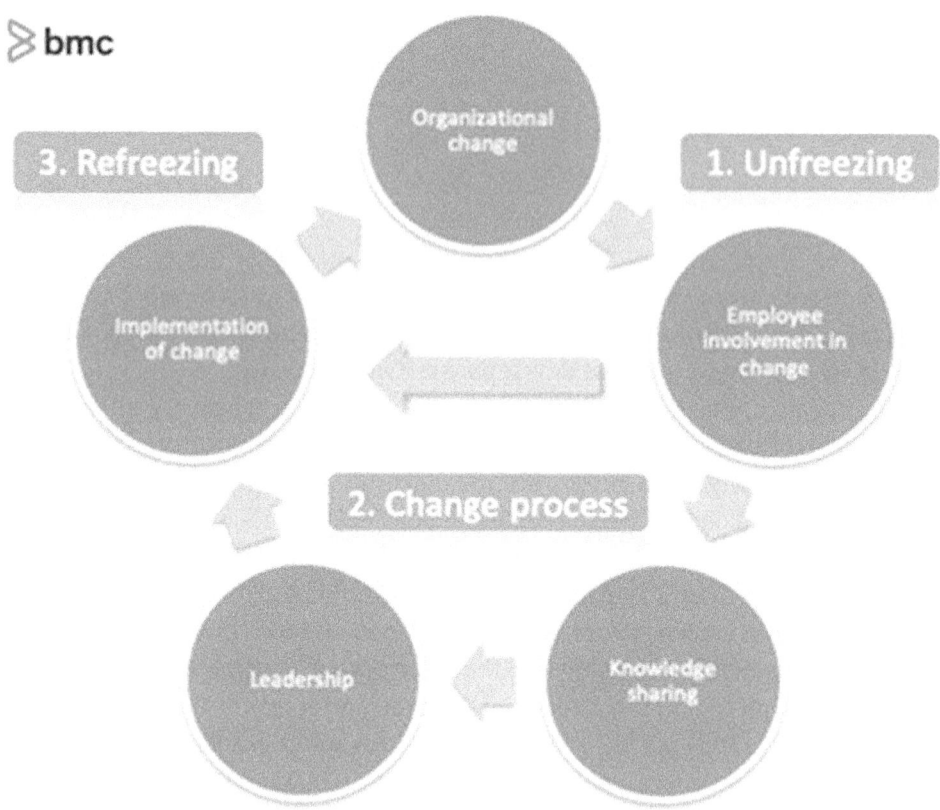

Figure 2. Most common organizational development interventions
Source: *(AIHR, 2023)*

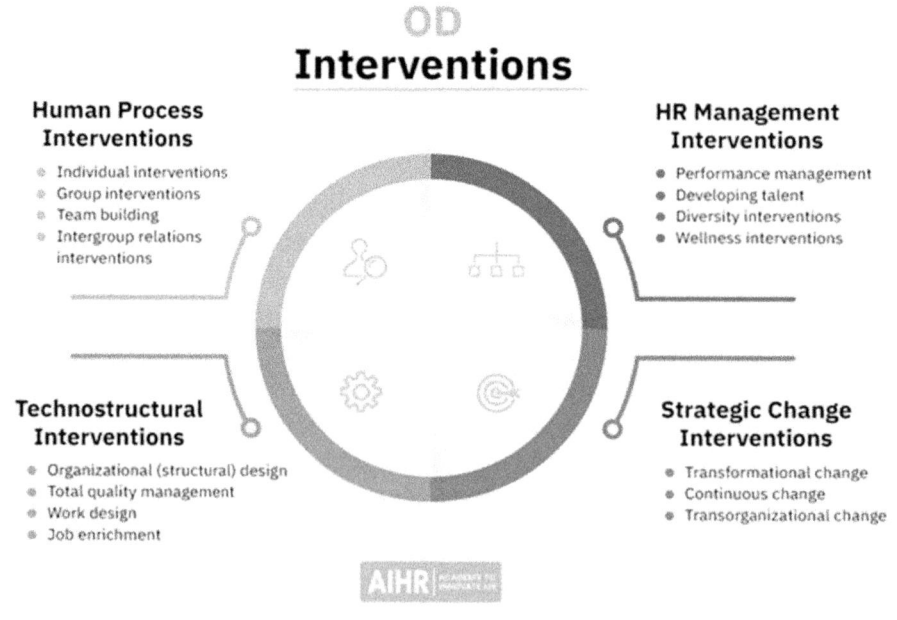

organizations face that affect the global economic landscape. Particularly, to evaluate the role and impact of organizational development on businesses, during unprecedented times.

The *objectives* (benefits of the publication) are we examined organizational development through the lenses of research and innovative practices contained within the fields of leadership and organizational development. The benefit of the publication is to enlighten communities through the efforts of a research perspective that amplifies practice-based potential in applying theory, models, and/or frameworks to real-time issues. Henceforth, solutions companies can implement to successfully solve a problem, move in a new direction, grow, innovate, and/or enter a new market.

The impact of the publication, and why the publication should be published is the purpose of this book is to substantiate organizational development strategies in organizations, discuss the practical experience of organizational development strategies implementation, and measure the effectiveness of an OD initiative implemented. Chapters to be hosted in this book are also intended to be used as part of course/training material in various professional development settings. Presenting resources, tools, scientific and methodological perspectives, and various OD models or frameworks organizations can apply to assist them with being effective during crises or unprecedented times. Professional development means, for example, executive coaching, research, presentations, conferences, training/workshops, leadership development, and other workplace initiatives.

Moreover, *the value of the book* or how the theme will impact our field of research is the book is aimed at professionals and professionals of organizations who want to improve their understanding of organizational development and its processes, the specifics of organizational development models, and the advantages of applying organizational development in organizations or entrepreneurship to survive challenging times. Or for general company transformation to scale, transition to new business models, processes, systems, or resources, successfully adopt or use some sort of change, or remain competitive. Including in various markets. Too, while encountering unprecedented times. Yet, highlighting the challenges, solutions, and opportunities within organizational development.

The *target audience* for the book is a variety. This premier reference source is an essential resource for company executives, business leaders, managers, entrepreneurs, human resource personnel, consultants, economists, government officials (agencies), librarians, researchers, practitioners, organization behavior specialists, scholars, academicians, and students and faculty of higher education.

Topics covered in the text include Organizational Development (OD) Frameworks, Organizational Development Models (e.g. Kurt Lewin, Kotter's 8-Stage Process, The Action Research Model, and The Generic Model of Planned Change), Change Management, Change Management Plan, Managing Change in the Workplace, Successful Transformation Efforts, Team Management, Emerging Economies, Development Strategy, Organizational Diagnosis, Organizational Performance, Employee Engagement, Mergers and Acquisitions, Risk Management, Team Management, Technology Integration, Change Management at Multiple Sites of an Organization, Implementation of New Technology, Implementing Organizational Development Strategy, Well-Being at Work, Learning and Development, Learning and Development Systems, Combating COVID-19 with Organizational Development, Considering Company Risks, Controls, Audit During Change, and Organizational Readiness for Change. Different types of organization designs are covered as well. For example, Mechinist Organization Design, Organic Organization Design, Holacratic Organisation, Helix Organisational Design, Dual Operating Systems, and Network Organizations. Operating models and systems and systems theory are discussed to complement the discussion of organizational development models and forms of organizational designs.

Next, the book is divided into three sections. Section one contains chapters one, two, three, and four and is about measuring the effectiveness of OD strategies during unprecedented times and the metaverse, data-driven insights to address customer experience, organization development frameworks and models, and green innovation. Chapters five, six, seven, eight, and nine comprise section two and regard organizational development and socio-ecosystem innovation, applying resilience to advance corporate social responsibility, work-life dynamics and holistic ecosystems, and online teaching and learning during such times. The final section, section three, encompasses chapters ten, eleven, and twelve and discusses organizational diagnosis and various organizational design strategies, corporate governance, systems theory, operating models and systems, institutional organizational development (e.g. institutional theory), organizational culture, crisis management, and training and development. Some industries deliberated in the book are healthcare, higher education, security, agriculture, sustainability, and civil aviation. While also reaching industries of entertainment, retail, consumer products, restaurant, hospitality, financial services/ banking, fintech, venture capital/ private equity, technology, manufacturing, energy, construction, and eCommerce.

For example, *Dr. Ali Rehman* of Ibra, Sharqiyah, Oman wrote chapter one and discussed how "the recent Covid pandemic has had a negative impact on the market and related industries, primarily due to the forced closure of businesses by governments… In today's business environment where profitability is the sole focus of management, there is a lack of strategy creation and implementation. In this scenario, the board needs an additional resource to provide precise, accurate, and well-researched information. This resource can be called Metaverse, which is a combination of artificial intelligence (AI), virtual reality (VR), and augmented reality (AR)", highlighting organizational development strategies businesses can use during the unprecedented time. *Dr. Chabi Gupta* of India wrote chapter two and talked about how prior to performing any kind of organizational transformation, a variety of things need to be considered. For example, "disparate privacy regulations, quick updates to browser technology, and an ever-evolving technological landscape. This research suggests that to do it right, the business needs to have the right people, processes, and technologies working in sync". Aspects that need to be considered to increase revenue and drive business growth. For chapter three, *Dr. Oindrila Chakraborty* of West Bengal, India extensively discussed various organizational development frameworks and models that can be applied to a variety of companies during crises. In chapter four, *Dr. Jose G. Vargas-Hernandez, Dr. Teresa I. Salazar-Echegaray,* and *Prof. Omar C. Vargas-Gonzalez* of Mexico reviewed the environmental industry and talked about organizational green innovations and technologies. Such businesses need specific operations and practices, in the face of change. *Dr. Jose G. Vargas-Hernandez* and *Prof. Omar C. Vargas-Gonzalez* of Mexico, in chapter five, explained organizational socio-ecosystems and innovation. How "organizations are open and dynamic" … and comprised of social, technical, and environmental dimensions.

In chapter six *Dr. Kim Sanders* of the United States discussed how applying a Corporate Social Responsibility (CSR) strategy to an organization "can help align business practices both in and outside the organization with current significant economic, social, environmental, and public health issues (Lamprinakis, 2019)". For example, via the Sustain Optimize Change Model. In chapter seven, *Dr. Joanne Principe* of the United States stated companies constantly face "rapid change, triggered by the current volatile, uncertain, complex, and ambiguous (VUCA) post-pandemic" complexities. She explored how "leveraging strategic tactics" is beneficial to assessing "core work-life dynamics associated with organizational effectiveness, culture transformations, and change leadership". Next, for chapter eight, *Babita Srivastava* of the United States talked about how COVID-19 caused lockdowns in various places of the world and business industries, causing a loss of trillions of dollars. Which can occur during any crisis. He mentioned how the energy sectors (e.g. renewable energy and oil) employment, supply chain, and even raw materials were negatively impacted. In chapter nine, *Ashok Asthana and Dr. Swati Srivastava* of India, explained the education sector, technology, and distance learning. Particularly, implementing Information and Communication Technologies (ICT) in schools around the world as a strategy for global development.

In chapter ten, *Miss Isolde Kanikani,* of the Netherlands explores an "intrinsic relationship between organizational purpose, the people, and value creation in relation to organizational structures. Without structure, we can't be aware of what we are changing or monitor if we are effectively achieving our organizational purpose". For example, with a focus on operations and governance. Meanwhile, in chapter eleven and considering the unprecedented times, *Dr. Jose G. Vargas-Hernandez* and *Prof. Omar C. Vargas-Gonzalez* of Mexico examined how "interacting internal and environmental variables of institutionalized organizational perspectives" and institutional theory applies to organizations facing unprecedented times. How to function under different institutional environments, addressing organizational culture, strategy, processes, structure, and human behavior. And in chapter twelve, *Helena Martins, PhD, Miss Lisa Dollmann, Miss Melanie Lehmann,* and *Dr. Ana Claudia Rodrigues* of Portugal discussed "how people around the world are being trained for crisis situations, focusing on skills and competencies being developed, as well as the training approaches and practices…aimed at facilitating crisis management and skills training's worldwide to better prepare the society for inevitable critical events".

In conclusion, the book impacts the fields of human resource management, change management, organizational culture, economic development, multinational enterprises, leadership, international business, management, and organization studies, like organizational culture, organizational behavior, and organizational design. Inclusive, contributes to the subject matter of *Organizational Development* because of the successful application and adoption of organizational strategies within an organization, particularly during unprecedented times countries are encountering. Hence, what various companies around the globe in a variety of sectors in various industries are implementing to overcome problems that arise during times of crisis? For example, during COVID-19, but also other crises chapter authors mentioned, like technological and socio-ecological.

Kyla Latrice Tennin
College of Doctoral Studies, University of Phoenix, USA & Forbes School of Business, USA & World Business Angels Investment Forum (WBAF)-G20, USA & Lady Mirage Global, Inc., USA

REFERENCES

AIHR (Jayla Cosentino). (2023). *15 OD interventions every HR practitioner should know.* AIHR. https://www.aihr.com/blog/od-interventions/#:~:text=As%20stated%20above%2C%20there%20are,from%20each%20of%20the%20groups

Association for Talent Development. (2023). *What is organization development?* Association for Talent Development. https://www.td.org/talent-development-glossary-terms/what-is-organization-development

BMC Software. (2023). *Lewin's 3-stage model of change explained.* BMC Software. https://www.bmc.com/blogs/lewin-three-stage-model-change/

Burnes, B. (2020). The origins of Lewin's three-step model of change. *The Journal of Applied Behavioral Science, 56*(1), 32–59. doi:10.1177/0021886319892685

Gargi, B. (2019). Financial inclusion, women empowerment, and entrepreneurship: A special emphasis to India. *Malaysian E-commerce Journal, 3*(3), 18–21. doi:10.26480/mecj.03.2019.18.21

Hussain, S. T., Lei, S., Akram, T., Haider, M. J., Hussain, S. H., & Ali, M. (2018). Kurt Lewin's change model: A critical review of the role of leadership and employee involvement in organizational change. *Journal of Innovation & Knowledge, 3*(3), 123–127. doi:10.1016/j.jik.2016.07.002

Organization Development Network. (2023). *What is organization development?* OD Network. https://www.odnetwork.org/page/what-is-od

Prosci, Inc. (2023). *Definition of change management.* Prosci Inc. https://www.prosci.com/resources/articles/definition-of-change-management#:~:text=Change%20management%20is%20the%20application,adopt%20and%20use%20a%20change

van Vulpen, E. (2023) *What is organizational development? A complete guide.* AIHR. https://www.aihr.com/blog/organizational-development/

Introduction

Measuring the Effectiveness of Organizational Development Strategies During Unprecedented Times discusses various crises in organizations around the globe. For instance, during the COVID-19 pandemic.

The book highlights during the COVID-19 pandemic, 41.3% of firms reported they shut down temporarily because of the pandemic (Stephan et al., 2021). In the United Kingdom, 32.5% of entrepreneurs stated they were still able to work during the pandemic, in comparison with entrepreneurs in Norway (58.5%), Bosnia and Herzegovina (81.6%), North America (55%), and France (55.9%) (Stephan et al., 2021). Within a global survey for the World Economic Forum (WEF) (2020), a variety of industries were surveyed, from entrepreneur startups to music festivals, manufacturing companies, and automotive enterprises. Seventy percent of startups reported they had to terminate their full-time employees since the start of the COVID-19 pandemic (WEF, 2020). Only 40% of new enterprises reported they have sufficient earnings to endure three months of operations (WEF, 2020).

CNBC advised, because of the pandemic, women lost 64 million jobs and $800 billion in earnings globally. To compare, the American Progress Report presented that since the pandemic women lost nearly 5.4 million jobs while men lost 4.4 million jobs. From Dr. Kyla's private experience, with consultation clients in almost 50 nations, working with investment forums, world leaders, presidents of nations, and business owners, Cuyper et al.'s (2020) claim closely resemble what various entrepreneurs stated, even though Bartik et al. (2020) and Stephan et al.'s (2021) claim is necessary too.

Crises in economies possess the capability to bring on hardships to both businesses and markets, as well as develop additional institutional voids. For example, Bartik et al. (2020) carried out a quantitative survey, as abovementioned, on the North American small business ecosystem within the Alignable Business Network of 4.6 million companies. Bartik et al. (2020) stated out of all the sample, 7500 businesses replied to taking the resilience survey, where 1.8% of firms stated they shut down permanently because of the pandemic. Businesses help economies not only exist, but to survive and thrive. They also play a role in addressing global social, environmental, and economic issues. Hence, for many years small businesses have been claimed to be the driving force behind economies' existence and stability. Gargi (2019) postulated entrepreneurship regards contributing to economies by employing people and is connected to new technologies and innovations that have the potential to create additional employment for markets. The new innovations and technologies also possess the ability to be profitable (Gargi, 2019).

Conclusively, resilience, education, financial inclusion, digital transformation, strategic partnerships, and particularly *organizational development* are needed when crises occur. To save and advance organizational ecosystems and economies. Therefore, knowing about the ideation and processes of organizational development to improve a company's negative circumstances is crucial to know. To innovate, improve performance, execute a strategy to increase revenue, address risk, implement new systems, processes, or digital transformation to scale, and help stop companies from closing and ultimately from filing for dissolution.

As a result, the aim of this book is to provide scholars, leaders, practitioners, and even key stakeholders of economies with different avenues to address important challenges companies encounter that impact the global economic landscape. Particularly, to assess the role and effects of organizational development on institutions, during unprecedented times. Organizational development is closely aligned with change management and human resources, but is very different in scope. For instance, human resources is operational while organization development is holistic and strategic, which is explored in the text.

REFERENCES

Bartik, A. W., Bertrand, M., Cullen, Z., Glaeser, E. L., Luca, M., & Stanton, C. (2020). The impact of COVID-19 on small business outcomes and expectations. *Proceedings of the National Academy of Sciences of the United States of America, 117*(30), 17656–17666. doi:10.1073/pnas.2006991117 PMID:32651281

Cuyper, L. D., Kucukkeles, B., & Reuben, R. (2020). *Discovering the real impact of COVID-19 on entrepreneurship*. World Economic Forum. https://www.weforum.org/agenda/2020/06/how-covid-19-will-change-entrepreneurial-business/

Gargi, B. (2019). Financial inclusion, women empowerment, and entrepreneurship: A special emphasis to India. *Malaysian E-commerce Journal, 3*(3), 18–21. doi:10.26480/mecj.03.2019.18.21

Stephan, U., Zbierowski, P., Perez-Luno, A., & Klausen, A. (2021). *Entrepreneurship during the COVID-19 pandemic: A global study of entrepreneurs challenges, resilience, and well-being*. King's Business School. https://www.kcl.ac.uk/business/assets/pdf/research- papers/global-report-entrepreneurship-during-the-covid-19-pandemic-a-global-study-of-entrepreneurs'-challenges-resilience-and-well-being.pdf

World Economic Forum (WEF). (2020). *Discovering the real impact of COVID-19 on entrepreneurship*. WEF. https://www.weforum.org/agenda/2020/06/how-covid-19-willchange-entrepreneurial-business/

Chapter 1
Can Metaverse Act as a Board of Directors?

Ali Rehman
A Sharqiyah University, Oman

ABSTRACT

The recent pandemic has had a negative impact on the market and related industries, primarily due to the forced closure of businesses by governments. However, the main cause of this impact is ineffective organizational strategies and their poor implementation. In today's business environment where profitability is the sole focus of management, there is a lack of strategy creation and implementation. In this scenario, the board of directors needs an additional resource to provide precise and well-researched information. This resource can be called the metaverse. Metaverse can be used in the corporate world to improve various processes and operations and provides assistance to make effective decisions. This chapter applies agency theory to show how the metaverse can act as a board member and improve the effectiveness of development strategies. This chapter introduces a new concept for organizational governance. It will be useful for regulators, policy makers, and boards of directors.

INTRODUCTION

The effectiveness of organizational strategies can be impacted by the unprecedented nature of the business environment (Kamal, 2020). Future foresight, flexibility, and adaptability are necessary in order to achieve desired outcomes, mitigate risk and develop sustainable growth. The recent pandemic demonstrated the closure of many organizations (Vu & Nguyen, 2022) and surfaced the poor development and implementation of organizational strategies (Boiral et al., 2021). Organizations are driven by profitability and for this reason, many of the strategies are the shorter period of time which does not take into consideration the potential of any unprecedented events or negative outcomes due to any other reason.

Closures of businesses due to ineffective organizational approaches for the planning and execution of strategies is not limited to one country or any specific type of business. Several businesses were closed permanently due to pandemic or aftereffects of pandemic. Unforeseen events has had a profound impact on the global economy and has resulted in the closure of many small and large businesses across

DOI: 10.4018/978-1-6684-8392-3.ch001

various industries. The Covid pandemic has had a significant impact on the world's economy, causing a sharp decline in global GDP in 2020. According to the International Monetary Fund (IMF), global GDP is estimated to have fallen by 4.4% in 2020, the steepest decline since the Great Depression of the 1930s. The decline was widespread across countries and regions, affecting both advanced and emerging economies. Figure 1 demonstrates the closure of businesses due to pandemic and is distributed into key and non-key organizations for countries. Key organizations are those which are considered as essential for the county such as textile companies, food, utilities and oil and gas companies (Stemmler, 2022).

It is obvious from Figure 1 that non-key organizations are the ones who suffer most and more than 70% of these remained close. It is worth mentioning that non-key organizations are considered as small and medium enterprises (SME) and they contribute to a greater extent to the nation's wealth (Covello & Iatridis, 2021) and create environment of circular economy (Gamidullaeva et al., 2020; Amoah et al., 2022). Furthermore, Figure 2 demonstrates the impact on the organizational revenues (Stemmler, 2022). It is evident that organizations close their business due to the decline in their revenues; however, despite that decreasing revenues they key-organizations sustained and continue with their businesses.

Closure of businesses due to the decrease in revenue can be attributable to many reasons; however, these organizations were focused and driven by profits only (Covello & Iatridis, 2021; Kalogiannidis, 2020). One of the major reasons for these profit driven organizations is the agency problems (Hao, 2022). Agency problems arise when there is conflict between the senior/ executive management of the organization with their board of directors. Senior management perceives that they are performing all the work and deserve all the credit; whereas board of directors keep shareholders interest as priority and want to distribute dividends/bonus shares from organization's profit (Rehman & Hashim, 2018). Such conflict shifts the mindset towards short term strategies and organizations focus shifted from long term sustainability which is failure to achieve organizational developmental strategies.

In the given scenarios the board of directors requires complete data and its related analysis which can be difficult due to limited knowledge and non-availability of right tools. Metaverse can provide the required details and can assist the board in making the right decisions. Metaverse can use AI to add new algorithms and improve its knowledge over time. As a Metaverse collects data and interacts with its users, it can use machine learning to identify patterns and make predictions, which can improve its overall functionality and decision-making processes. Furthermore, Metaverse can be an agent for the agency theory and can help in reducing agency conflicts and costs by providing accurate and timely information, improving decision-making processes, and monitoring and mitigating potential risks through automated systems and algorithms. This can result in more efficient and effective management of resources, better alignment of interests between stakeholders, and reduced opportunities for unethical behavior (Rehman & Hashim, 2022).

This chapter highlights the idea that a Metaverse can serve as a board member and act as an agent in agency theory. This is a novel concept with limited research available, mostly focused on e-commerce, education, and e-marketplaces. The chapter will provide benefits to regulators, policy makers, and companies and may prompt regulators to incorporate Metaverse into corporate governance and update related legal policies. This chapter can be transformed into empirical research.

BACKGROUND

The impact of unprecedented events on organizational strategies and the closure of businesses has become a topic of great interest, especially in the wake of the COVID-19 pandemic. The pandemic has caused a significant decline in global GDP, resulting in the closure of many businesses across various industries.

The closure of businesses due to the decline in revenue can be attributable to many reasons, but one of the major reasons is the agency problems. Agency problems arise when there is conflict between the senior/executive management of the organization with their board of directors. Such conflict shifts the mindset towards short-term strategies and organizations focus shifted from long-term sustainability, which is a failure to achieve organizational developmental strategies.

In this context, a Metaverse can serve as a board member and act as an agent in agency theory. The Metaverse can provide complete data and its related analysis, which can assist the board in making the right decisions. Metaverse can use AI to add new algorithms and improve its knowledge over time. As a Metaverse collects data and interacts with its users, it can use machine learning to identify patterns and make predictions, which can improve its overall functionality and decision-making processes.

This book chapter aims to highlight the potential benefits of incorporating a Metaverse into corporate governance and updating related legal policies. The chapter will provide insights to regulators, policy makers, and companies on how Metaverse can assist in reducing agency conflicts and costs by providing accurate and timely information, improving decision-making processes, and monitoring and mitigating potential risks through automated systems and algorithms.

The study's potential impact is significant, as it may prompt regulators to incorporate Metaverse into corporate governance, resulting in more efficient and effective management of resources, better alignment of interests between stakeholders, and reduced opportunities for unethical behavior. This chapter can also serve as a basis for further empirical research on the topic.

This book chapter intends to provide a comprehensive understanding of the potential of Metaverse in corporate governance and how it can mitigate the risks associated with organizational strategies, particularly in the context of unprecedented events.

MAIN FOCUS OF THE CHAPTER

The main focus of the chapter is to highlight the impact of unforeseen events on the closure of businesses and the poor development and implementation of organizational strategies. It suggests that profit-driven organizations, especially small and medium enterprises, suffer the most during crises. It also discusses agency problems, conflicts between senior executives and board of directors, that shift the focus towards short-term strategies and fail to achieve long-term sustainability. The study proposes the use of Metaverse as an agent in agency theory to reduce conflicts and costs and to provide accurate and timely information for better decision-making processes. The study emphasizes the importance of transdisciplinary thinking, staying up to date with technological trends, and adopting new technologies early on to gain a competitive advantage.

LITERATURE REVIEW

This section will discuss in detail the organizational development strategies, the impact on these strategies due to unprecedented times, role of board of directors and how Metaverse can act as board member. This section will also provide arguments that how Metaverse can be an agent under the agency theory.

Organizational Strategies Development

Organizations are constantly faced with new challenges in a rapidly changing environment involving economic, technical, political, and public interests. It is crucial to manage these challenges and prioritize the development of their strategy (Terziev & Georgiev, 2018). Strategy has evolved to refer to a plan of action in any aspect of social and economic life. In business, it involves effectively utilizing an organization's resources to survive and compete with others. Strategic planning involves a series of steps, including defining the organization's mission and goals, analyzing external factors, evaluating strengths and weaknesses, and selecting and implementing a strategy. A comprehensive strategic plan requires extensive research and is designed to guide a company's activities for a long period, while remaining adaptable to changing circumstances and or unprecedented scenarios (Papke-Shields & Boyer-Wright, 2017; Bolisani & Bratianu, 2017).

The challenges faced by an organization after registration can be classified into strategic, operational, and situational tasks. The situational tasks take center stage after the establishment of the legal entity, and the interaction of the organization with its customers, counterparties, and competitors (Terziev & Georgiev, 2018). The organization's shareholders, their selected board members and senior management hired by the board should prioritize the assessment of the environment, organization's activity, and other factors to make well-informed and educated decisions (Baysinger & Butler, 2019; Rehman & Hashim, 2020).

The success of the organization, especially in the early stages of development, hinges on the alignment of strategic and operational tasks, with the situational tasks being based on the operational tasks (Terziev & Georgiev, 2018). The organization's board members should first address the operational tasks, which involve short-term business prospects, and determine the strategy and prospects for long-term development (Asahak et al., 2018). Then, starting from the operational tasks, the organization will develop and forecast its situational tasks, determining its behavior and procedures in interaction with specific customers, counterparties, and competitors. This is usually driven by the need to establish organizational legal and financial foundations for the organization's full functionality (George et al., 2021). These all are considered as a development of organizational strategy.

Impact on Organizational Development Strategies Due to Unprecedented Times

Covid-19 has affected society and organizations as never before, resulting in negative impacts on economic and social issues.

Unprecedented times can impact organizational strategies. The recent pandemic affected society and organizations (Marques et al., 2021) and none of the organizations were able to anticipate its impact and related consequences. In accordance with the Organization for Economic Co-operation and Development (OECD) majority of the affected organizations were SMEs (OECD, 2020) as their main focus was the short-term strategy with no alternative plans. Lockdown measures were implemented by several nations to control the spread of COVID-19, leading to significant impacts on key economic areas including transportation, manufacturing, construction, and wholesale/retail (OECD, 2020).

Organizations are usually unable to prevent a crisis from happening, but with the proper tools they can detect it early and implement coping strategies to minimize risk. Despite having contingency and risk management plans in place, the immediate consequences of a crisis and performance failure suggest that these plans are either ineffective or not properly implemented (Ganatra et al., 2020).

Impacted organizations are inadequately equipped to handle a massive crisis and its economic ramifications. Hence, there is a necessity to assess economic players and business operations during times of intense crisis. The current management approach within organizations does not thoroughly evaluate the enterprise's operations, performance, and decisions during unforeseen circumstances (Obrenovic et al., 2020).

A deeper understanding of catastrophic events and potential hazards could aid organizations in developing plans to manage such situations. By understanding these circumstances, more effective strategies can be developed to mitigate the shock to organizations, regardless of their complexity. Organizations with a networked structure, decentralized workforce and leadership, flexible and streamlined policies, and low interdependence are more resilient and can better manage disastrous situations (Aldianto et al., 2021). Table 1 demonstrates the way to measure the effectiveness of organizational development strategies during unprecedented times:

Table 1. Steps to measure effectiveness of organizational development strategies in unprecedented times

Measure	Description
Set clear goals and objectives	Identify the specific outcomes organization want to achieve and align with development strategies and create a plan to measure progress.
Track key performance indicators (KPIs)	Define and track metrics that directly relate to organizational goals and objectives. This could include employee satisfaction, productivity, retention, and revenue.
Gather feedback	Conduct surveys, focus groups, or one-on-one interviews with employees to gather their perceptions and feedback on the effectiveness of the strategies.
Analyze data	Analyze the data collected from KPIs and feedback to identify areas of improvement and assess the impact of the strategies on the organization as a whole.
Evaluate and adjust	Regularly evaluate the results of measurements and make adjustments to strategies as necessary. This continuous improvement process will help ensure the effectiveness of organizational development efforts over time.

Organizations strategies should be flexible and adoptable. Organizations suffer if their strategies are not strong, if they have a centralized structure, centralized workforce and rigid leadership. Such organizations will have difficulty managing disastrous situations.

Board of Directors

The board of directors (board) are nominated and elected by the shareholders (Melville & Merendino, 2019). In any organization board is responsible for the approval of policies, selection of senior management and possesses overall responsibility for corporate governance (Aguilera, 2005; Greuning & Bratanovic, 2020). There is no rule available that can define number of board members (Segal, 2020;

Budiharta & Kacaribu, 2020); however, countries have defined minimum number of board members. Organizations are governed under the country's laws which also include codes of corporate governance. The code of corporate governance defines the powers and duties of the board. The powers and duties of the board depend upon the specific laws and regulations of the jurisdiction in which the organization is incorporated, as well as the organization's own articles of incorporation/ association. However, in general, the board is responsible for overseeing the management of the corporation and making important decisions on behalf of the organization's shareholders. Some of the specific powers and duties may be granted to the board by shareholders.

The role of the board in strategy setting is to provide oversight, guidance, and approval for the organization's strategic plans and goals (Barroso-Castro et al., 2017). Board work closely with senior management to review and evaluate the organization's performance and to ensure that strategies align with the organization's mission, values, and long-term interests (Brauer & Schmidt, 2008). The board is responsible for providing the necessary resources and support to execute the strategies, monitoring progress, and making adjustments as needed (Ellis, 2022). Ultimately, the Board's role in strategy setting is to provide the strategic direction and make the decision that shapes the organization's future. Table 2 defines the summary of the board's power and its duties.

Table 2. Summary of the board's power and its duties

Powers of Board of Directors	Source
The board is typically responsible for selecting the organization's senior management and determining their salaries and benefits.	Hong and Minor (2016)
The board is usually responsible for making decisions about the direction of the organization and its future, such as whether to expand into new markets or acquire other companies	Baldacchino, Camilleri, Schembri, Grima, and Thalassinos (2020)
The board is typically responsible for overseeing the organization's finances and approving its budgets, financial statements, and other financial reports	Tumwebaze, Bananuka, Alinda, and Kalembe (2021)
The board may set policies and procedures that govern how the organization operates and make decisions	Whitler and Puto (2020)
The board is often responsible for representing the organization and acting in its best interests, both internally and externally	Tumwebaze, Bananuka, Alinda, and Kalembe (2021)

Role of Board of Directors During the Unprecedented Times

During unprecedented times, the role of the board in strategy setting has become even more crucial. In these situations, the board must navigate new challenging circumstances and provide leadership and direction to the organization. Some identifiable responsibilities may include (Grove et al., 2020; Kaur et al., 2021).

- Overseeing risk management and ensuring that the organization is prepared to respond to the current crisis.
- Providing strategic guidance and direction to senior management to help the organization navigate through the crisis.

- Reviewing and adjusting existing strategies to ensure they are appropriate and effective in the current environment.
- Monitoring financial performance and ensuring that the organization is financially stable and can continue to meet its obligations.
- Ensuring that the organization is prepared for a post-crisis future and that plans are in place for recovery and future success.

Boards play a crucial role in guiding and supervising the organizations they serve, maintaining a proper division from Management, while also providing support to executive leadership and taking on responsibilities. Additionally, boards must understand that there is no pre-existing plan for the present situation and must exhibit adaptability and practicality in their governance of organizations. The Corporate Governance Framework within an organization must now, more than ever, reinforce organizational resilience by promoting strong leadership and oversight; improving stakeholder engagement and communication; establishing clear and transparent decision-making processes; implementing ongoing risk management, mitigation, and control measures; and monitoring the organization's overall performance. These are all critical components of a successful governance framework specifically at the extraordinary and exceptional situations/times (Deloitte, 2020).

The board should examine current systems and approach the standard board agenda with flexibility, identifying which aspects can be simplified or postponed, providing more time for management to tackle the immediate challenges facing the organization. Utilize the individual board members' skills and knowledge, along with their past experiences, to assist management in addressing their pressing needs and improving the organization's stability. Consider the possibility of implementing new crisis management strategies to aid the organization in effectively handling pressing matters. Encourage management by reminding them that striving for perfection can impede progress and establish appropriate expectations for communication, interaction, and content creation in light of the exceptional circumstances (Richard, 2020).

The board provides strategic direction and leads organization towards sustainable business growth (Le & Behl, 2022). This includes development of business continuity plan, disaster recovery plan, implementation of business continuity and disaster recovery plans and perform evaluations accordingly. The board is also responsible for the development of a proper control environment and defining tone at the top. Control environment determines how much importance is given for the internal controls. With an appropriate control environment, the board can create a culture of ethics and integrity. This will enable the organization to prosper and achieve the path of sustainability.

The recent Covid Times highlighted the fact that board members were not able to predict the risk which was associated with that pandemic. Accordingly, the identified risk were not covering the actual consequence and erroneous mitigation actions were implemented (Pourmansouri et al., 2022). The reason for non-prediction can be associated with the non-availability of right and complete data, wrong data analysis and limited knowledge of the board members. Boards can perform better if they are equipped with Metaverse which can be part of corporate governance and serve as a board member.

Metaverse as Board of Director

Innovations in computer science play a significant part in people's daily lives, as they impact and enhance human interaction, communication, and social activities. From the perspective of those who use technology, three significant technological innovation waves have been observed namely personal computers, the internet, and mobile devices. Currently, the fourth wave of technological innovation is underway and focuses on spatial (4-D) and immersive technologies like virtual reality (VR) and augmented reality (AR) with combination of artificial intelligence (AI). This wave is the next prevalent computing model, capable of revolutionizing business and is referred to as the Metaverse (Mystakidis, 2022).

Metaverse can use machine learning to add new algorithms and improve its knowledge over time. As Metaverse collects data and interacts with its users, it can use machine learning to identify patterns and make predictions, which can improve its overall functionality and decision-making processes. However, it is important to note that while a Metaverse may be able to improve its knowledge and functionality over time, it still lacks the capacity for independent thought and decision-making. The decisions made by a Metaverse are ultimately determined by the algorithms and rules set by its creators or operators. Moreover, the use of machine learning in a Metaverse also raises important ethical and legal questions about data privacy, accountability, and fairness, which may need to be addressed through regulations and guidelines. While the Metaverse may not be a conventional area for companies to allocate resources, some interesting statistics highlight the enormous potential of this concept: The market size of the Metaverse is projected to grow significantly over the next few years. In the year 2021, the market size was $63.83 billion and anticipated to grow to a staggering USD 1.5 trillion in year 2029 (Atkins, 2022).

In the current business environment majority of the organizations are operating in traditional manner and stakeholders are demanding the change. Although businesses are obliged to use accounting software but again this tool is utilized for financial purposes only and provides raw data for analysis. The board and the employees at not able to analyze the data that can predict the future risk and identify the red flags (Melnychenko, 2020). In this manner Metaverse can be considered as the innovation and game changer in the business field and can assist the board in decision making processes. Metaverse is the combination of AI, VR and AR and these are explained as follows.

Artificial Intelligence

In the current business landscape, artificial intelligence (AI) has become deeply ingrained in all aspects of corporate and organizational operations. It can be utilized in various areas, including regulatory compliance, risk identifications, and internal audits. Many techniques have been proposed to enhance risk identification while simultaneously improving internal controls through the use of AI. By analyzing organizational data, AI can increase transparency, build trust, develop mitigation actions, and decrease regulatory non-compliance. This connection between AI and risk identification puts corporate governance at the forefront of a new and exciting era (Rehman, 2022).

Many organizations have failed to embrace AI even though they should keep pace with rapid and continuous change and update themselves regularly. This is due to various obstacles in implementation (Schwendicke & Krois, 2021). Surprisingly, over 80% of organizational boards have not recognized the technological advancements and shifts in their business (Sarrazin & Willmott, 2016). The increasing complexity of business operations with technological advancements makes it difficult for senior management to make informed and wise decisions without the help of AI. Although AI has the potential to improve decision-making processes and be a part of governance management, its adoption is happening at a slow pace and some business leaders fail to see the benefits that AI can bring to their organizations (Rehman, 2022; Melnychenko, 2020).

With the capability of transforming the world, AI can be considered as most advanced and stronger technology. AI can assist organizations in performing, comprehending, observing, learning and interacting and recognizing all cognitive functions (Ergen, 2019). With substantial computational capabilities, AI can act as a business problems solver and provides services at a lower cost i.e., conducting data processing with advanced algorithms (Agrawal et al., 2018; Ergen, 2019). Additionally, the AI can effectively manage unexpected internal and external threats in unstructured and uncertain environments (Powell, 2020; Burns & Steele, 2020).

Another aspect of AI is its ability to satisfy all organizational needs, including corporate governance obligations and shareholder demands (Ammanath et al., 2020). By leveraging AI, organizations can identify potential issues and implement preventive measures (Burns & Steele, 2020). AI includes machine-based activities and systems that make predictions and related recommendations and assists in making decisions relevant to virtual, real, and anticipatory environments (Nilsson, 2010).

AI can be held accountable and can be a part of governance management system under the agency theory. The decisions made by AI systems can be challenged in court (Scherer, 2019), but the legal implications of such challenges can be complex and depend on various factors such as the specific laws and regulations in the jurisdiction, the design and implementation of the AI system, and the type of decision made by the system. In some cases, the decisions made by AI systems may be subject to review by a human being, who has the final say in the decision-making process. In such cases, a court may consider the human review as evidence of accountability for the decision made by the AI. It is worth mentioning that the legal implications of AI decision-making are still evolving and developing, and the laws and regulations surrounding AI are expected to change as technology advances.

Virtual Reality

Virtual reality (VR) is a computer-generated three-dimensional environment that users can interact with using a computer capable of projecting 3D information through a display. This display can be in the form of an isolated display or wearable display along with sensors that identify the users. VR can be categorized into two types namely non-immerse and immerse (Wohlgenannt et al., 2020). Non-immerse VR uses multiple screens to surround the users and present virtual information, allowing them to experience a simulated environment without being fully immersed (Rahouti et al., 2021) such as driving or flight simulation. On the other hand, immerse VR involves wearing a display device that tracks the user's movement and presents VR information based on their position, thereby providing 360-degree experience to its users (Hamad & Jia, 2022).

Although VR was initially marketed for gaming, there are various potentials and existing VR applications in diverse fields such as education, training and healthcare related areas. However, there is a lack of general comprehension regarding the strengths and limitations of VR across various application domains. The foremost challenges associated with current VR technology are difficult to overcome such as issues related to technical difficulties and financial constraints (Hamad & Jia, 2022).

Once VR is combined/ integrated with AI, it can provide many solutions to the corporate world such as construction simulations and investment in bonds simulations. These simulations can demonstrate the virtual impact of the potential investment and allow users to modify the investment plans/ designs schemes which can best suit their requirements. In current business environment, several forecasting tools are utilized but these tools do not validate that how the actual/realized investment will actually appear and whether it will achieve the desired objectives or not. VR along with AI can suggest design improvements and enhance potential savings (Velev & Zlateva, 2017).

The combination of AI and VR has the potential to revolutionize the corporate world in many ways. One of the key benefits of this integration is the ability to create realistic simulations that can accurately predict the impact of potential investment. This can help better informed decisions and mitigate the risk of costly errors. Few of the examples can include the construction industry and investments made by the organizations.

For construction industry VR simulations along with AI can allow architects, engineers and contractors to visualize the entire construction process before any actual works begins. This can help to identify potential issues or design flaws that may not have been apparent in traditional 2D plans, thereby reducing the risk of expensive delays or mistakes during actual construction work. With regards to the investment world, VR along with AI can allow investors/ board to visualize the potential outcomes of different investment strategies in a more intuitive way. With utilization of AI to analyze large amount of data and identify the patterns, board can make more informed decisions about which investment will achieve the potential objectives.

Augmented Reality

Augmented reality (AR) is a technology that overlays computer generated sensory input such as sound, video, graphics or GPS data onto real world environment. Unlike VR, which creates a completely simulated environment, AR enhances the user's perception of reality by blending digital information with the physical world (Schuemie et al., 2021). AR is one of the components of virtual-reality continuum. AR is a relatively new technological system that enables the addition of virtual objects to the real world in real-time during a user's experience. To be considered an AR system, it should combine real and virtual objects in a real environment, run interactively and in real-time, and register real and virtual objects with each other (Cipresso et al., 2018).

AR technology is used in a variety of applications, from mobile games and social media to industrial and medical fields. The most common use of AR is in the retail industry and is very famous in the clothing area. AR allows customers to have a look and feel about the clothes and accessories which they intend to buy. AR is also increasingly used in the education industry where it allows students to explore and interact with digital models of real-world objects such as planets or historical artifacts, enhancing their understanding of complex concepts. Additionally, AR is used in healthcare for medical training, allowing doctors and medical professionals to practice complex procedures in a safe environment (Chen, et al., 2019).

With regards to the corporate world and to enhance the governance perspective, AR can benefit organizations in the following ways to enhance training, board meetings, shareholders' communication, and risk management (Fenwick & Vermeulen, 2018):

- AR can be used for immersive and interactive training programs for employees and board members. For example, AR can simulate real-life scenarios and provide training on ethics, compliance, and risk management.
- AR can provide a more engaging and memorable training experience compared to traditional classroom or online training.
- AR can enhance board meetings by providing interactive and visual aids to support discussions and decision-making. For example, AR can display financial data, performance metrics, and other

relevant information in a more immersive and interactive way. This can help board members better understand complex data and make more informed decisions.

- AR can provide a more engaging and informative way to communicate with shareholders. For example, AR can be used to provide virtual tours of company facilities, product demonstrations, and other visual aids to help shareholders better understand the company's operations and strategy.

- AR can be used for risk management by providing a more immersive and interactive way to simulate and analyze potential risks. For example, AR can simulate a cyber-attack or a natural disaster and allow board members and executives to test and evaluate their response plans in a safe and controlled environment.

The amplification effects of digital technologies are driving exponential growth and creating new opportunities, as well as disrupting existing models. Figure 3 demonstrates the exponential growth of technologies. It is important for organizations and policymakers to adapt to these changes and to harness the potential of digital technologies to create a more equitable, sustainable, and prosperous future.

The significant impact of digital technologies comes from their ability to amplify and reinforce each other, leading to exponential growth and new opportunities, as well as disrupting existing business models, organizational forms, and regulatory models. Similarly, the combination of AI, VR and AR can create new possibilities for decentralized systems, automated transactions, and secure supply chains. This can lead to increased transparency, trust, and accountability, which can also create new business opportunities and disrupt existing ones.

AGENCY THEORY AND METAVERSE

The concept of agency theory refers to the delegation of decision-making authority and other responsibilities by shareholders to a group of experts, with the expectation that they will act in the best interests of the organization (Moloi & Marwala, 2020). These experts, known as agents, are employed by principals and act on their behalf.

The agency theory is often invoked to justify the prominent role of agents in corporate governance (Rehman, 2022). According to this theory, the delegation of authority can lead to problems when agents disregard the concerns of their principals, prioritize their own interests, and engage in unethical practices such as excessive bonuses, unwarranted raises, and kickbacks (Swanepoel, 2021). These unethical practices can involve fabricating revenue figures, inflating receivables, and engaging in irregular accounting practices. One contributing factor to such fraudulent behavior is that agents perform the tasks and do not want to share the benefits with principals who only invest money but are not involved in organizational operations (Rehman, 2022). Consequently, monitoring and protection are necessary, which can be provided by Metaverse, which can act as a board member and be present on the board to provide oversight.

The Metaverse can be viewed as an essential tool for devising and executing business strategies and organizational policies. Investing in the Metaverse is a strategic expenditure rather than an operational one, as it reduces uncertainties and offers a practical framework for internal controls and solutions during unprecedented times. Like hiring an agent and providing benefits, investing in the Metaverse enables the handling of daily tasks with precision and accuracy, which serves the true purpose of corporate governance while also satisfying the principal. By acting as an agent for the agency theory, the Metaverse can avoid or eliminate agency costs, which arise from agency conflicts. Furthermore, by leveraging current strategic strengths, the Metaverse can provide digital transformation strategies that can help reimagine work and decision-making processes around human or artificial capabilities (Moloi & Marwala, 2020).

The AI is a component of the Metaverse, which can function as a subset of stakeholders (OECD, 2021). By tracking capital distribution patterns, highlighting warning signs, and integrating into corporate governance practices, the Metaverse can enhance strategic controls and provide shareholder satisfaction. As an agent for the principal, the Metaverse can redefine personhood in the agency theory as a result of technological advancements (LoPucki, 2018). Under agency theory, principals and agents must be individuals with legal rights and claims. However, with the Metaverse's ability to create algorithmic entities, it can potentially attain legal personhood and become an agent for the principal, which reflects an appropriate development (Powell D., 2020). An algorithmic entity can be defined as "*advanced autonomous systems paired with limited liability companies that have no individual members*" (LoPucki, 2018).

SOLUTIONS AND RECOMMENDATIONS

Solutions and recommendations are mentioned in detail in the conclusion section; however, it can be summarized as follows:

- Future foresight, flexibility and adaptability are necessary for effective organizational strategies.
- Organizations need to consider potential unprecedented events or negative outcomes due to any other reason while developing strategies.
- Companies should adopt a long-term sustainability approach instead of focusing on short-term profits only.
- Metaverse can be an agent for the agency theory and can help in reducing agency conflicts and costs by providing accurate and timely information, improving decision-making processes, and monitoring and mitigating potential risks through automated systems and algorithms.
- Regulators should incorporate Metaverse into corporate governance and update related legal policies.
- Promote continuous transdisciplinary thinking that bridges gaps between diverse corporate knowledge.
- Companies should stay up to date with the latest technological trends and embrace new technologies early on to potentially gain a competitive advantage.

FUTURE RESEARCH DIRECTIONS

One promising direction for future research is to build upon the conceptual framework presented in this paper and develop it into a full empirical study. This could involve designing experiments or surveys to gather data on how users interact with different aspects of metaverse environments, such as avatars, social networks, and virtual economies. By collecting empirical data, researchers could test the validity of our theoretical model and refine it further.

Another avenue for future research is to apply our conceptual framework to the development of actual metaverse platforms. This would involve collaborating with software engineers and designers to create immersive virtual worlds that embody the principles we've outlined in our paper. By building and testing real-world metaverse environments, researchers could gain deeper insights into how our theoretical model plays out in practice and identify opportunities for further refinement.

CONCLUSION

Effective strategic thinking requires the ability to draw upon a range of disciplines and perspectives, making transdisciplinary thinking essential. However, successfully implementing transdisciplinary thinking in practice requires identifying and absorbing knowledge from a range of sources and applying it effectively. When a critical discipline or perspective is missing from a organization's strategic thinking, the organization becomes exposed to risks that could threaten its long-term success. To mitigate these risks, it is essential to promote continuous transdisciplinary thinking that bridges gaps between diverse corporate knowledge.

By reflecting on the lessons of history, we can see that companies that were quick to adopt new technologies tended to outperform their competitors. These early adopters were often top performers and experienced accelerated growth, while those companies that lagged in adopting new technologies tended to perform poorly and ranked in the bottom half. It is essential for companies to stay up to date with the latest technological trends and embrace new technologies early on. By doing so, they can potentially gain a competitive advantage and avoid falling behind their competitors. The Metaverse is a new and emerging technology that has the potential to reshape the way we interact with the world, and organizations that embrace it early on may have an opportunity to thrive in this new environment.

Further to the above, in current business environment there are several unforeseen scenarios and circumstances that can impact adversely and force organizations to close their operations or reduce their workforce. The recent Covid pandemic is an example of such an event, which negatively affected the market and related industries due to government-imposed business closures. Nevertheless, the main reason for this impact was the ineffective implementation of organizational strategies. While the board of directors holds the responsibility for approving these strategies, they require accurate and timely information to make informed decisions. However, in today's business environment, where profitability is the primary focus of management, there is often a lack of strategy creation and implementation. In such cases, an additional resource, such as the Metaverse, which combines artificial intelligence (AI), virtual reality (VR), and augmented reality (AR), can provide precise, accurate, and well-researched information to the board.

AI involves creating machines that can perform tasks that typically require human intelligence, such as decision-making, visual perception, speech recognition, and language translation. VR is a computer-generated simulation of a three-dimensional environment that allows for realistic interaction, and it is commonly used in entertainment, gaming, and educational settings. AR, on the other hand, superimposes computer-generated images onto the user's view of the real world, providing a composite view. It is commonly used for navigation, gaming, education, and enhancing customer experiences. In the corporate world, the Metaverse can be utilized to enhance various processes and operations. For instance, AI can be used to automate repetitive tasks, analyze large amounts of data, and improve decision-making. VR can be used for training, simulations, product design, visualization, and virtual events and conferences. AR can be used for product visualization, field service and remote assistance, training and education, and enhancing the customer experience.

By implementing these technologies, organizations can improve their efficiency, enhance their decision-making, and achieve sustainable results. The Metaverse offers adaptability and flexibility, enabling the board to make effective decisions and strengthen its capabilities. Applying agency theory, this chapter demonstrates how the Metaverse can act as a board member, predicting potential issues, suggesting mitigation actions, and determining the best course of action.

This conceptual chapter is a new approach to organizational governance and contributes to the existing body of knowledge. It will be valuable to regulators, policy makers, and boards of directors, demonstrating how the Metaverse can support not only the board but also organizational management and regulators. This may oblige policy makers and regulators to amend their policies and/ or code of corporate governance and introduce Metaverse as a board of directors.

REFERENCES

Agrawal, A., Gans, J., & Goldfarb, A. (2018). *Prediction Machines: The Simple Economics of Artificial Intelligence*. NY: Harvard Business Review.

Aguilera, R. V. (2005). Corporate governance and director accountability: An Institutional comparative perspective. *British Journal of Management, 16*(s1), S39–S53. doi:10.1111/j.1467-8551.2005.00446.x

Aldianto, L., Anggadwita, G., Permatasari, A., Mirzanti, I., & Williamson, I. (2021). Toward a Business resilience framework for startups. *Sustainability (Basel), 13*(6), 3132. doi:10.3390u13063132

Ammanath, B., Jarvis, D., & Hupfer, S. (2020). *Thriving in the era of pervasive AI*. Deloitte Consulting LLP.

Amoah, J., Belas, J., Dziwornu, R., & Khan, K. A. (2022). SMEs contribution to economic development: A perspective from an emerging economy. *Journal of International Students, 15*(2), 63–76. doi:10.14254/2071-8330.2022/15-2/5

Asahak, S., Albrecht, S. L., Sanctis, M. D., & Barnett, N. S. (2018). Boards of directors: Assessing their functioning and validation of a multi-dimensional measure. *Frontiers in Psychology, 9*, 2425. doi:10.3389/fpsyg.2018.02425 PMID:30564176

Atkins, B. (2022, Jun 16). Into the metaverse: Use cases for directors. *Forbes*. https://www.forbes.com/:sites/betsyatkins/2022/06/16/into-the-metaverse-use-cases-for-directors/?sh=47d9b863dc89

Baldacchino, P. J., Camilleri, A., Schembri, B., Grima, S., & Thalassinos, Y. E. (2020). Performance evaluation of the board of directors in listed companies: A small state perspective. *International Journal of Finance. Insurance and Risk Management, 10*(1), 99–119.

Barroso-Castro, C., Villegas-Periñan, M. M., & Dominguez, M. (2017). Board members' contribution to strategy: The mediating role of board internal processes. *European Research on Management and Business Economics, 23*(2), 82–89. doi:10.1016/j.iedeen.2017.01.002

Baysinger, B. D., & Butler, H. N. (2019). Corporate governance and the board of directors: Performance effects of changes in board composition. *Journal of Law Economics and Organization, 1*, 101–121.

Boiral, O., Brotherton, M.-C., Rivaud, L., & Guillaumie, L. (2021). Organizations' management of the COVID-19 pandemic: A scoping review of business articles. *Sustainability (Basel), 13*(7), 3993. doi:10.3390u13073993

Bolisani, E., & Bratianu, C. (2017). Knowledge strategy planning: An integrated approach to manage. *Journal of Knowledge Management, 21*(2), 233–253. doi:10.1108/JKM-02-2016-0071

Brauer, M., & Schmidt, S. L. (2008). Defining the strategic role of boards and measuring boards' effectiveness in strategy implementation. *Corporate Governance (Bradford), 8*(5), 649–660. doi:10.1108/14720700810913304

Budiharta, P., & Kacaribu, H. E. (2020). The influence of board of directors, managerial ownership, and audit committee on Carbon Emission Disclosure: A study of non-financial companies listed on BEI. *Review of Integrative Business and Economics Research, 9*(3), 75–87.

Burns, J., & Steele, A. (2020). *Blockchain and internal control The COSO perspective.* Durham: Committee of sponsoring organizations of the treadway commission.

Chen, Y., Wang, Q., Chen, H., Song, X., Tang, H., & Tian, M. (2019). An overview of augmented reality technology. *Journal of Physics: Conference Series, 1237*(2), 022082. doi:10.1088/1742-6596/1237/2/022082

Cipresso, P., Giglioli, I. A., Raya, M. A., & Riva, G. (2018). The past, present, and future of virtual and augmented reality research: A network and cluster analysis of the literature. *Frontiers in Psychology, 9,* 2086. doi:10.3389/fpsyg.2018.02086 PMID:30459681

Covello, C., & Iatridis, K. (2021). On the challenges and drivers of implementing responsible innovation in foodpreneurial SMEs. In E. Yaghmaei, & I. v. (eds), Assessment of Responsible Innovation (pp. 98-116). London: Taylor & Francis.

Deloitte. (2020). *The board's role in the COVID-19 crisis.* Deloitte Touche Tohmatsu Limited.

Ellis, J. (2022). *What is the board's role regarding strategy?* The Corporate Governance Institute. https://www.thecorporategovernanceinstitute.com/: insights/guides/what-is-the-boards-role-regarding-strategy/

Ergen, M. (2019). What is artificial intelligence? Technical considerations and future perception. *The Anatolian Journal of Cardiology, 22,* 5–7. doi:10.14744/AnatolJCardiol.2019.79091 PMID:31670719

Fenwick, M., & Vermeulen, E. P. (2018). *Technology and corporate governance: Blockchain, Crypto, and Artificial Intelligence.* Ecgi Global.

Gamidullaeva, L., Vasin, S., & Wise, N. (2020). Increasing small-and medium-enterprise contribution to local and regional economic growth by assessing the institutional environment. *Journal of Small Business and Enterprise Development, 27*(2), 259–280. doi:10.1108/JSBED-07-2019-0219

Ganatra, S., Hammond, S. P., & Nohria, A. (2020). The novel coronavirus disease (COVID-19) threat for patients with cardiovascular disease and cancer. *JACC. CardioOncology, 2*(2), 350–355. doi:10.1016/j.jaccao.2020.03.001 PMID:32292919

George, G., Haas, M. R., McGahan, A. M., Schillebeeckx, S. J., & Tracey, P. (2021). Purpose in the for-profit firm: A review and framework for management research. *Journal of Management*. doi:10.1177/01492063211006450

Greuning, H. V., & Bratanovic, S. B. (2020). *Analyzing banking risk: a framework for assessing corporate governance and risk management*. World Bank Group.

Grove, H., Clouse, M., & Xu, T. (2020). Trategies for boards of directors to respond to the Covid-19 pandemic. *Corporate Board: Role. Duties and Composition, 5*(1).

Hamad, A., & Jia, B. (2022). How virtual reality technology has changed our lives: An overview of the current and potential applications and limitations. *International Journal of Environmental Research and Public Health, 19*(18), 11278. doi:10.3390/ijerph191811278 PMID:36141551

Hao, G. (2022). Research on the agency problem, corporate governance and firm value. *7th International Conference on Financial Innovation and Economic Development (ICFIED 2022)* (pp. 2917-2923). NY: Atlantis Press. 10.2991/aebmr.k.220307.475

Hong, B. L., & Minor, D. (2016). Corporate governance and executive compensation for corporate social responsibility. *Journal of Business Ethics, 136*(1), 199–213. doi:10.100710551-015-2962-0

Kalogiannidis, S. (2020). Covid impact on small business. *International Journal of Social Science and Economics Invention, 6*(12), 387–391. doi:10.23958/ijssei/vol06-i12/257

Kamal, M. M. (2020). The triple-edged sword of COVID-19: Understanding the use of digital technologies and the impact of productive, disruptive, and destructive nature of the pandemic. *Information Systems Management, 37*(4), 310–317. doi:10.1080/10580530.2020.1820634

Kaur, M., Malik, K., & Sharma, S. (2021). A note on boardroom challenge, board effectiveness and corporate stewardship during COVID-19. *Vision (Basel), 25*(2), 131–135. doi:10.1177/0972262920987326

Le, T. T., & Behl, A. (2022). Role of corporate governance in quick response to Covid-19 to improve SMEs' performance: Evidence from an emerging market. *Operations Management Research : Advancing Practice Through Research, 15*(1-2), 528–550. doi:10.100712063-021-00238-4

LoPucki, L. M. (2018). Algorithmic entities. *Washington University Law Review, 95*(4), 887–951.

Marques, I. C., Marques, P., Serrasqueiro, Z., & Nogueira, F. (2021). Covid-19 and organisational development: Important signs of a new pillar for sustainability. *Social Responsibility Journal*. doi:10.1108/SRJ-10-2020-0415

Melnychenko, O. (2020). Is artificial intelligence ready to assess an. *Journal of Risk and Financial Management, 13*(191), 1–19.

Melville, R., & Merendino, A. (2019). The board of directors and firm performance: Empirical evidence from listed companies. *Corporate Governance (Bradford), 19*(3), 508–551. doi:10.1108/CG-06-2018-0211

Moloi, T., & Marwala, T. (2020). The agency theory. In *Artificial Intelligence in Economics and Finance Theories. Advanced Information and Knowledge Processing* (pp. 95–102). Springer. doi:10.1007/978-3-030-42962-1_11

Mystakidis, S. (2022). Metaverse. *Encyclopedia*, *2*(1), 486–497. doi:10.3390/encyclopedia2010031

Nilsson, N. (2010). *The quest for artificial intelligence: A history of ideas and achievements*. Cambridge University Press.

Obrenovic, B., Du, J., Godinic, D., Khan, M. A., & Jakhongirov, I. (2020). Sustaining enterprise operations and productivity during the COVID-19 pandemic: "Enterprise effectiveness and sustainability model". *Sustainability (Basel)*, *12*(15), 5981. doi:10.3390u12155981

OECD. (2020). *SMEs are major employers and particularly vulnerable to the impact of the Covid-19 crisis*. OECD.

OECD. (2021). *Recommendation of the council on artificial intelligence*. OECD.

Papke-Shields, K. E., & Boyer-Wright, K. M. (2017). Strategic planning characteristics applied to project management. *International Journal of Project Management*, *35*(2), 169–179. doi:10.1016/j.ijproman.2016.10.015

Pourmansouri, R., Mehdiabadi, A., Shahabi, V., Spulbar, C., & Birau, R. (2022). An investigation of the link between major shareholders' behavior and corporate governance performance before and after the COVID-19 Pandemic: A case study of the companies listed on the Iranian stock market. *J. Risk Financial Manag*, *5*(5), 208. doi:10.3390/jrfm15050208

Powell, D. (2020). Autonomous systems as legal agents: Directly by the recognition of personhood or indirectly by the alchemy of algorithmic entities. *Duke Law & Technology Review*, *18*(1), 306–331.

Powell, D. (2020). Autonomous systems as legal agents: Directly by the recognition of personhood or indirectly by the alchemy of algorithmic entities. *Duke Law & Technology Review*, *18*(1), 306–331.

Rahouti, A., Lovreglio, R., Datoussaïd, S., & Descamps, T. (2021). Prototyping and validating a non-immersive virtual reality serious game for healthcare fire safety training. *Fire Technology*, *57*(6), 3041–3078. doi:10.100710694-021-01098-x

Rehman, A. (2022). With the mediation of internal audit, Can artificial intelligence eliminate and mitigate fraud? In S. S. Kamwani, E. S. Vieira, M. Madaleno, & G. A. (eds), Handbook of Research on the Significance of Forensic Accounting Techniques in Corporate Governance (pp. DOI:). NY: IGI Global. doi:10.4018/978-1-7998-8754-6.ch012

Rehman, A., & Hashim, F. (2018). Forensic accounting on corporate governance maturity mediated by internal audit: A conceptual overview. *1st Economics and Business International Conference 2017 (EBIC 2017)* (pp. 161-168). NY: Atlantis Press. 10.2991/ebic-17.2018.26

Rehman, A., & Hashim, F. (2020). Impact of fraud risk assessment on good corporate governance: Case of public listed companies in Oman. *Business Systems Research*, *11*(1), 16–30. doi:10.2478/bsrj-2020-0002

Rehman, A., & Hashim, F. (2022). Can internal audit function impact artificial intelligence? Case of public listed companies of Oman. *The 5th Innovation and Analytics Conference & Exhibition (IACE 2021)* (pp. 040024-1–040024-7). AI.). .10.1063/5.0092755

Richard, B. (2020, Oct 30). *The effects of Covid-19 on boards and governance.* Spencer Stuart. https://www.spencerstuart.com: https://www.spencerstuart.com/research-and-insight/the-effects-of-covid-19-on-boards-and-governance

Sarrazin, H., & Willmott, P. (2016, July 13). *Adapting your board to the digital age.* McKinsey. https://www.mckinsey.com/: https://www.mckinsey.com/capabilities/mckinsey-digital/our-insights/adapting-your-board-to-the-digital-age

Scherer, M. (2019). *International arbitration 3.0 – How artificial intelligence will change dispute resolution.* Austrian Yearbook of International Arbitration.

Schuemie, M. J., Straaten, P. V., & Krijn, M. (2001). Research on presence in virtual reality: A survey. *Cyberpsychology & Behavior, 4*(2), 183–202. doi:10.1089/109493101300117884 PMID:11710246

Schwendicke, F., & Krois, J. (2021). Better reporting of studies on artificial intelligence: CONSORT-AI and beyond. *Journal of Dental Research, 100*(7), 677–680. doi:10.1177/0022034521998337 PMID:33655800

Segal, T. (2020, Mar 27). *Evaluating the board of directors.* Marottao Money. www.marottaonmoney.com/wp-content/uploads/2020/07/Evaluating-the-Board-of-Directors.pdf: www.marottaonmoney.com/wp-content/uploads/2020/07/Evaluating-the-Board-of-Directors.pdf

Stemmler, H. (2022). The effects of COVID-19 on businesses: Key versus non-key firms. Geneva: International Labor Organization (ILO).

Swanepoel, D. (2021). Does artificial intelligence have agency? In R. G. Clowes, *The Mind-Technology Problem.* [Cham: Springer.]. *Studies in Brain and Mind, 18*, 1–2. doi:10.1007/978-3-030-72644-7_4

Terziev, V., & Georgiev, M. (2018). Organizational development strategies. *Knowledge –. International Journal (Toronto, Ont.), 28*(1), 315–322.

Tumwebaze, Z., Bananuka, J., Alinda, K., & Kalembe, D. (2021). Intellectual capital: Mediator of board of directors' effectiveness and adoption of International Financial Reporting Standards. *Journal of Financial Reporting and Accounting, 19*(2), 272–298. doi:10.1108/JFRA-03-2020-0076

Velev, D., & Zlateva, P. (2017). Virtual reality challenges in education and training. *International Journal of Learning and Teaching, 3*, 33–37. doi:10.18178/ijlt.3.1.33-37

Vu, M. C., & Nguyen, L. A. (2022). Mindful unlearning in unprecedented times: Implications for management and organizations. *Management Learning, 53*(5), 797–817. doi:10.1177/13505076211060433

Whitler, K. A., & Puto, C. P. (2020). The influence of the board of directors on outside-in strategy. *Industrial Marketing Management, 90*, 143–154. doi:10.1016/j.indmarman.2020.07.007

Wohlgenannt, I., Simons, A., & Stieglitz, S. (2020). Virtual reality. *Business & Information Systems Engineering, 62*(5), 455–461. doi:10.100712599-020-00658-9

KEY TERMS AND DEFINITIONS

Agency problems: Conflicts of interest that can arise between principals and agents in organizations, resulting in adverse outcomes.

Agency theory: A theoretical framework that examines the relationship between principals (such as shareholders) and agents (such as managers) in organizations.

Algorithmic Entity: A system or entity that operates according to a set of predetermined rules or algorithms, often used in artificial intelligence and machine learning applications.

Algorithmic Legal Entity: advanced autonomous systems paired with limited liability companies that have no individual members.

Artificial Intelligence: The development of computer systems that can perform tasks that would typically require human intelligence, such as learning, problem-solving, and decision-making.

Augmented Reality: A technology that superimposes computer-generated images or information onto the real world to enhance the user's perception of reality.

Board of Directors: A group of individuals who are elected or appointed to oversee the management of a corporation or organization.

Covid Pandemic: The global outbreak of COVID-19, caused by the SARS-CoV-2 virus, which began in late 2019 and continues to affect people and economies around the world.

Fraud: Deception or misrepresentation for personal or financial gain, often involving illegal or unethical activities.

Legal Entity: A business organization that has legal rights and obligations, such as a corporation or limited liability company.

Chapter 2
How Close Are You to Your End Consumer?
Data-Driven Insights to Awesome Customer Experience

Chabi Gupta

https://orcid.org/0000-0002-1927-4349

School of Commerce, CHRIST University, India

ABSTRACT

The delivery of a tailored customer experience is being widely recognised by executives in the technology industry as the key to unlocking revenue, minimising attrition, and providing growth. It is not simple to satisfy a consumer in today's market. Delivering reliable and efficient experiences across channels is more challenging than it has ever been because of the context of disparate privacy regulations, quick updates to browser technology, and an ever-evolving technological landscape. This research suggests that to do it right, the business needs to have the right people, processes, and technologies working in sync. This study highlights that many companies continue to invest in instruments and technology solutions before they have effectively accomplished the organisational transformation required to perform the role in a data-driven mode. Investments do not always yield the promised results since the basic pieces of mindset, vision, and people are not always in congruence. Consumers are no longer going to be 'just satisfied,' or 'even happy.'

INTRODUCTION

The leaders of organisations in the emerging markets acknowledge that data and analytics have the potential to liberate opportunity and provide their companies with a competitive advantage. This may occur via the discovery of new marketing channels or the enhancement of effectiveness in manufacturing processes. Once the company's culture, vision, and stakeholders are all in sync, the organization can next concentrate on the data. It must be useful for its intended purpose, as stated by the strategy, and readily

DOI: 10.4018/978-1-6684-8392-3.ch002

accessible to the right people inside the business via the use of appropriate technology. There is still a problem with the data reliability at emerging market businesses (Frosch et al., 1996). Given conflicting inputs, expect poor results. Organizations may use the most sophisticated data analytics algorithms in the world, but the results are meaningless if the input data is unreliable.

In the ever-evolving landscape of business, data validity and reliability remain a critical challenge for organizations seeking to leverage analytics in order to develop long-term consumer-oriented strategies. The ability to collect accurate and relevant information is paramount; yet this remains elusive given the constant influx of data points from an increasingly complex set of sources. Despite advances in technology that offer solutions such as machine learning algorithms or natural language processing techniques, achieving truly reliable insights into customer behavior remains difficult at best. This leaves many businesses grappling with how best to navigate these challenges while remaining agile enough to adjust their approaches as needed based on emerging trends and shifts within their target markets. Ultimately, mastering these complexities will be key for any organization looking not only to survive, but thrive amidst the digital revolution currently underway across industries worldwide (Christopher, 1983).

Among the most aggravating issues for emerging market businesses is maintaining data integrity. Financial services firms in these regions have spent heavily on data transformation projects over the last five to seven years, with varied outcomes. In today's digital age, where every aspect of a business is heavily reliant on technology and the internet, data integrity and security have become crucial components for building a trustworthy relationship with end consumers (Christopher, 1983). Ensuring that sensitive information remains private and safeguarded against any unauthorized access or breach has now become an indispensable requirement for businesses to maintain their reputation as well as gain the confidence of their customers. With cyber-attacks becoming more frequent and sophisticated in nature, organizations need to invest in robust data protection mechanisms that not only prevent breaches but also provide prompt detection and response capabilities to mitigate any potential damage caused by such incidents. By prioritizing these aspects, companies can build long-term customer loyalty based on mutual trust and reliability which ultimately leads to sustainable growth opportunities.

Data stewardship is an area where many major companies have failed. To whom does the data belong? Which reliable data source(s) exist? The question is, "How do we keep auditing the quality of that data?" The research suggests that data integrity is less necessary when utilising data in a more directive form to assist decision-making, (Macdonald, 1995) even if it is crucial for commercial activities, such as compliance requirements or figuring out employee commissions. More and more businesses are coming to terms with the need for a more strategic approach when it comes to being close to their end consumers. (Gamble, 2006) in his research advocated that what we see successful e-commerce and information firms do is employ data analytics in the decision-making process, making their products more advisory in nature. (Alhouti et al., 2021) suggested that this is only possible if the business is in close touch with the customer preferences. Also, the most recent data is more essential than perfect data when this occurs. As an example, firms don't need to know the weekly sales data to the last penny; they need to know the approximate estimate, and that is good enough to guide their decisions from a directional perspective (Dvořáková et al., 2016).

Businesses have historically relied on traditional methods for reaching out to their end consumers. These time-honoured strategies have been tried and tested over the years, providing a reliable means of communicating with customers (Yang et al., 2023). However, in today's rapidly evolving digital landscape, companies must adopt more sophisticated techniques to connect with their audience at a deeper level. To truly engage modern-day customers, businesses need to leverage innovative technologies and embrace unconventional marketing tactics that allow them to forge authentic relationships built on trust and mutual understanding (Christopher, 1983).

Especially the banks and financial institutions must prioritize the establishment of meaningful relationships with their account holders, to gain a comprehensive understanding of their unique needs (Yang et al., 2023). By investing time and effort into fostering these connections, banks can ensure that they are able to provide personalized services that meet the specific requirements of each customer. This approach allows for an increased level of trust between the institution and its clients, leading to more successful partnerships built on mutual respect and effective communication (Gunarathne et al., 2018). Ultimately, this focus on relationship-building is crucial for ensuring long-term success within the competitive financial industry.

To cater to the needs of their accountholders, banks and financial institutions must offer a diverse range of services and products that are intricately tailored to meet specific requirements. It is imperative for these organizations to have an in-depth understanding of their customers' financial goals and priorities, as this knowledge enables them to design innovative solutions that not only fulfill immediate needs but also anticipate future ones (Gunarathne, et al., 2018). With an unwavering commitment towards providing top-notch service quality, banks and financial institutions can establish long-lasting relationships with their clients by delivering personalized experiences that exceed expectations (Gunarathne et al., 2018).

Considering the pandemic, when businesses needed to utilise data to make swift choices, this shift in perspective is the greatest transition taking place in data-driven firms. People have learned that there are times when precision isn't as crucial. Having data that is 70–80 percent accurate yet near real-time and available to the relevant individuals is far more valuable than having data that is 100% accurate (Akbari et al., 2019). This is because in today's fast-paced world, timely access to information can make all the difference in making informed decisions and taking proactive measures.

Data that is almost real-time provides organizations with a competitive edge by enabling them to respond quickly to changing market conditions, consumer demands, and emerging trends. Even if the accuracy of this data isn't perfect, it still holds tremendous value for businesses looking to stay ahead of their competitors (Güntürkün et al., 2023).

Furthermore, having data readily accessible to key stakeholders ensures that everyone within an organization is on the same page when it comes to decision-making (Akbari et al., 2019; Güntürkün et al., 2023). When critical insights are shared across departments and teams without delay or bottlenecks from slow-moving bureaucratic processes, companies become more agile and better equipped for success in rapidly evolving markets. In conclusion, while accurate data remains crucially important for any business seeking growth, having near-real-time availability can be just as valuable - particularly given the current pace at which technology continues advancing our workplaces (Akbari et al., 2019; Güntürkün et al., 2023).

Businesses also need data skills in addition to purpose-built, high-quality data. (Jaruzelski & Dehoff, 2008) discussed that because more and more businesses are relying on cloud-based services rather than on-premises servers, cloud-related skills such as programming, platform experience, network administration, and data integration are becoming more valuable. Businesses are progressively shifting complex workloads to the cloud. Almost 50% of respondents said they had made this transition by this year.

BACKGROUND

Information has replaced oil as the most precious commodity. Successful businesses in emerging economies are those who have learned to use agile data to adapt quickly to changing markets, consumer preferences, and internal processes. In the realm of information and analytics, a handful of organisations have managed to effectively harness its immense power to propel their corporate growth forward. However, regrettably, there exists numerous other entities that have yet to fully realise the vast potential it offers - falling behind in what could be considered one of the most consequential avenues for progress and prosperity in today's digital age (Bettencourt et al., 2015). The phrase "culturally, we are still not equipped" is often used to justify the status quo that is unwilling to change. However, we are constantly reminded that business upheaval and transition continue unabated (Thornhill et al., 2001).

The consequences of businesses adopting a transactional approach to their strategy, rather than prioritizing relationships with their customers, can be far-reaching and potentially damaging (Jandik & Salikhova, 2023). This narrow focus on short-term gains often leads to a lack of attention being paid towards developing meaningful connections with clients or fostering long-lasting loyalty (Heinonen, 2014). As such, companies that are purely transactional in nature may struggle to create strong brand identities and may find it challenging to retain customer trust over time.

Furthermore, by not investing sufficient resources into building positive rapport with stakeholders and potential partners alike, these organizations risk missing out on valuable networking opportunities that could ultimately lead to lucrative collaborations or partnerships (Jandik & Salikhova, 2023). Without taking the time necessary for cultivating strategic relationships both internally within the company as well as externally among industry peers, businesses run the risk of limiting growth potential while simultaneously increasing vulnerability (Heinonen, 2014). Ultimately then, enterprises must recognize that taking shortcuts when it comes down to solely focusing on individual transactions is likely unsustainable in terms of sustained revenue growth across timeframes; instead, leaders should place equal emphasis upon nurturing authentic relationships with their clients (Heinonen, 2014).

This was most obviously seen during the Covid-19 outbreak. Today, more than ever, businesses must be nimble in the face of economic unpredictability (Kotrba et al., 2012). The questions we ask of our data, the frequency with which we ask them, and the organisational outcomes associated with things like third-party distribution channels, customer loyalty, financial technology, and more, have all increased in importance as our demand for information has grown. (Henry & Luo, 2002) advocated the fact that it is now becoming more important for businesses to develop more effective methods to harness organisational data to make smarter alternatives as we abandon traditional business models and plunge into expanded business ecosystems (Kumaran & Hemalatha, 2023).

Establishing and maintaining a constant connection with their end users is an essential aspect for the success of any service industry. The ability to stay in touch with clients, promptly address concerns or queries, and provide top-notch customer service has become imperative in today's business landscape (Kumaran & Hemalatha, 2023). Companies that prioritize building lasting relationships by being accessible to customers around the clock are more likely to thrive and generate positive word-of-mouth referrals. With technology advancements providing multiple channels of communication such as email, social media platforms, live chat options etc., companies can ensure they have a comprehensive approach towards delivering exceptional customer experiences consistently (Kumaran & Hemalatha, 2023). Therefore, staying connected with end-users plays an indispensable role in driving growth and attaining sustainable success within the competitive market space of the service industry.

With its wide reach and instant connectivity, social media has emerged as a powerful tool to rapidly spread information in an efficient manner. Its ability to transcend geographical boundaries and connect people from diverse backgrounds makes it the perfect platform for sharing ideas, news updates or emergency alerts. Whether it is breaking news about a natural disaster or real-time updates during a crisis, social media can disseminate vital information within seconds with just one click of a button. Furthermore, its interactive nature facilitates active engagement between individuals and communities fostering mutual support and collaborative efforts towards achieving common goals. Overall, the impact of social media on modern-day communication cannot be overstated-its power lies not only in speedy dissemination but also in facilitating connections that drive positive change at scale.

In the aftermath of the recent pandemic, forging a meaningful and lasting bond with consumers has become imperative for businesses. The ability to establish deep-rooted connections with customers is now more crucial than ever as they navigate unprecedented levels of uncertainty and anxiety (Lee & Lee, 2020). With consumer preferences rapidly evolving in response to changing circumstances, companies that can build trust, empathy and understanding through effective communication will undoubtedly emerge as leaders in their respective fields (Yang et al., 2023). In short, establishing a strong emotional connection with customers is no longer just desirable; it's critical for long-term success in today's highly competitive marketplace (Kemp et al., 2021).

Also, there is a subsequent need for innovative and strategic customer engagement approaches has become more crucial than ever before (Yang et al., 2023). As businesses face increasing competition in their respective industries, it is imperative to devise unique methods of engaging with customers that not only attract them but also retain their loyalty over time. Therefore, a deep understanding of consumer behavior patterns and preferences combined with cutting-edge technologies must be leveraged to create compelling interactions that foster lasting relationships between brands and consumers alike (Kemp et al., 2021). Failure to implement such strategies may lead to missed opportunities for growth or even worse - complete irrelevance in an ever-evolving digital world (Yang et al., 2023).

MAIN FOCUS OF THE CHAPTER

Companies are continuously exploring and implementing innovative strategies to increase customer lifetime value. In order to create long-lasting relationships with customers, businesses are now focusing on deeper understanding of consumer behavior by utilizing data-driven insights from various digital platforms. Companies have started personalizing the customer experience through predictive analytics which help in identifying individual needs and preferences resulting in higher retention rates (Lasek & Jessa, 2013). Furthermore, organizations are also investing heavily in enhancing their communication channels such as social media platforms or chatbots that cater round-the-clock support services for resolving queries instantly while offering personalized recommendations based on past purchases thereby increasing overall satisfaction levels among consumers (Adam et al., 2021).

To ensure their longevity, businesses across all sectors are turning towards the practice of measuring customer lifetime value (Adam et al., 2021). This essential metric not only provides valuable insight into how much revenue a particular customer may generate over time but also helps companies identify and cultivate long-term relationships with customers. By fully understanding the worth of each individual consumer, industries can make strategic decisions regarding marketing investments, product development strategies, and overall business operations that will ultimately help them thrive in today's competitive market landscape for years to come (Adam et al., 2021).

Overall, these increased technological capabilities can provide a more intimate knowledge base about each consumer that was not possible before - allowing brands the ability to better tailor products/ services specifically around them and build loyal communities where consumers feel valued over time; thus, creating an increase in Customer Lifetime Value (CLV) over all transactions throughout their life cycle journey with a brand/company (Lasek & Jessa, 2013).

RESEARCH METHODOLOGY

Establishing a formidable bond with consumers holds greater significance for nascent start-ups and small-scale enterprises, as they require timely feedback to enhance their offerings. In this regard, developing a robust connection with the target audience enables these businesses to acquire valuable insights that can be leveraged to improve upon their products and services while also building brand loyalty among customers. Thus, establishing a strong rapport between companies and clients is essential in helping them grow sustainably by catering more effectively to customer demands through consistent interaction and communication (George & George, 2023).

Due to the prevalence of small credit enterprises engaged in high-volume, low-value transactional banking, the emerging markets present certain peculiarities from the high-income developed markets in this regard (George & George, 2023). These businesses use end user data to focus more on their consumers, making it simpler for their users to get loans quickly. Some areas of the financial services industry in these emerging markets are undergoing dramatic changes, proving that the region has the information and analytics skills necessary to be genuinely data driven, the correct priorities, enthusiasm, and resources (George & George, 2023).

Even though the International Data Corporation (IDC) study in August 2021 found that most organisations in Australia, Hong Kong, India, Japan, and Singapore still lack the talent management and task capabilities that are critical for a data-driven transformation, the desire to morph is evident across emerging economies. While more than 90% of respondents acknowledged the importance of information and analytics, only 20% could claim to be fully mature in their utilization of analytics. This research investigates the most prevalent blunders made by the corporate entities operating in emerging economies during data transformations and analyses the distinguishing factors between data-driven and non-data-driven businesses operating in the region. At last, it provides best strategies that businesses in the emerging economies can employ to transform their data and enhance their decision-making.

A total of 120 valid corporate respondents drawn from various sectors and regions classified as emerging economies have completed this research.

Table 1. Respondents' profile

Size of the Organisation	Key Industry Sectors	Regions	Number of Years in Business	Job Function of the Respondent
10% Fewer than 100 employees	13% Manufacturing	15% Hong Kong	40% Less than 5 yrs	25% General/executive management
40% 100 to 499 employees	13% Technology	15% Japan	40% Between 5-10 yrs	13% Sales/business development/ customer service
26% 500 to 999 employees	14% Financial services	10% Australia	20% More than 10 yrs	10% Marketing/PR/ communications
14% 1,000 to 4,999 employees	10% Health care	10% Singapore		8% Consulting
8% 5,000 to 9,999 employees	15% Retail	50% India		8% Strategic planning
2% 10,000 or more employees	All other sectors are less than 8% each			All other functions are less than 8% each

OBSERVATIONS

Question: To what extent has your organization implemented a customer relationship management tool for its customer data?

Figure 1. Implementation of a CRM tool

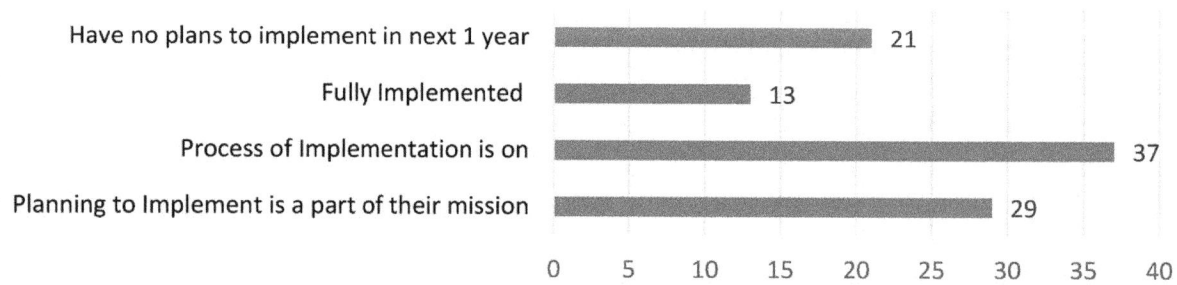

Implementation of a CRM tool

The process of implementation is on for 37% of the respondents. 21% however have no plans to implement in the next one year. Only 13% have fully implemented a CRM tool. This signifies a move towards implementation, but a gap exists between no plans at all to implement in the next one year and fully implemented. There may be various technology, people, or processes issues creating this gap. Change is also a steady, slow process and it's not a revolution but an evolution (Kožená et al., 2021).

Question: Is your organisation well prepared to implement such a tool?

Figure 2. Preparation for implementation of a CRM tool

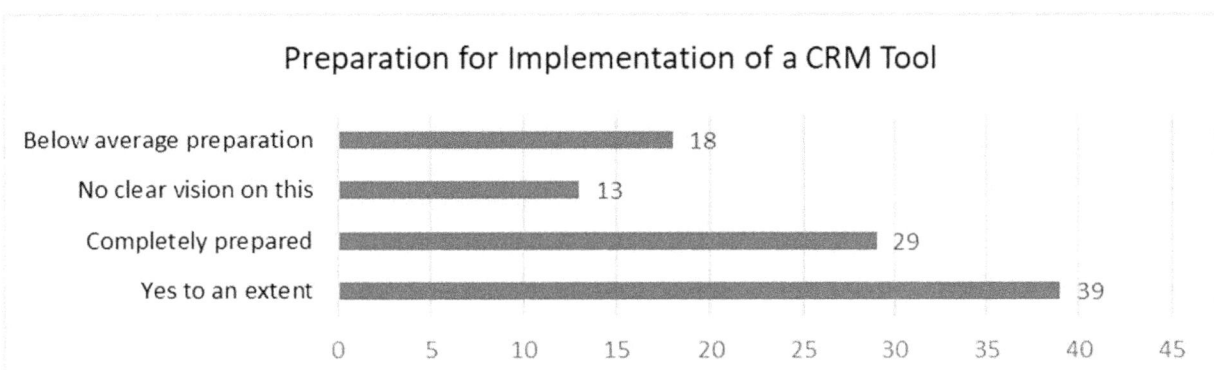

39% of respondents were sure their organization was planning to prepare for the implementation of a CRM tool in the next one to six months. Only 29% were confident that their organization was fully prepared. 13% agreed without a doubt that they were not prepared at all.

Question: Does your organization use digital tools and new platforms to connect people with data and insights?

Figure 3. Using digital tools and new platforms to connect people with data and insights

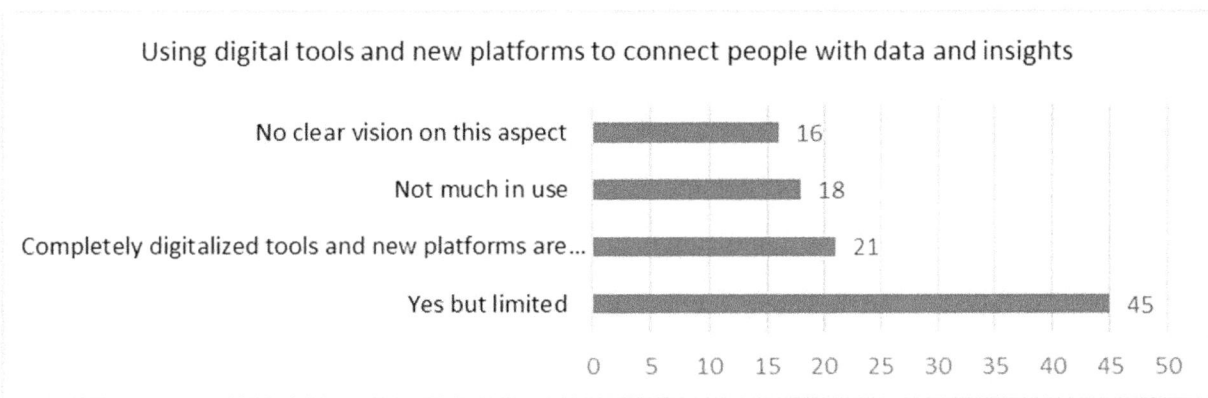

45% of respondents declared that their organizations had limited usage of digital tools and new platforms to ensure that the data and the insights really connect people. 16% had no clarity on this aspect which signifies the idea of connecting to end consumers requires concentrated effort.

Question: How well prepared is your organization to leverage greater amounts of data in an agile, flexible manner?

Figure 4. Prepared to leverage greater amounts of data in an agile, flexible manner

34% of respondents were of the view that their organization had below-average age preparation to leverage greater amounts of data in an agile, flexible manner. Only 27% of organizations were fully prepared for the same to handle any eventualities.

Question: What business outcomes has your organization realized from its customer data strategy? Select all that apply.

Figure 5. Business outcomes realized from the customer data strategy

Question: What are the present strategies of your organization to connect to the end consumers? Select all that apply.

Figure 6. Present strategies of your organization to connect to the end consumers

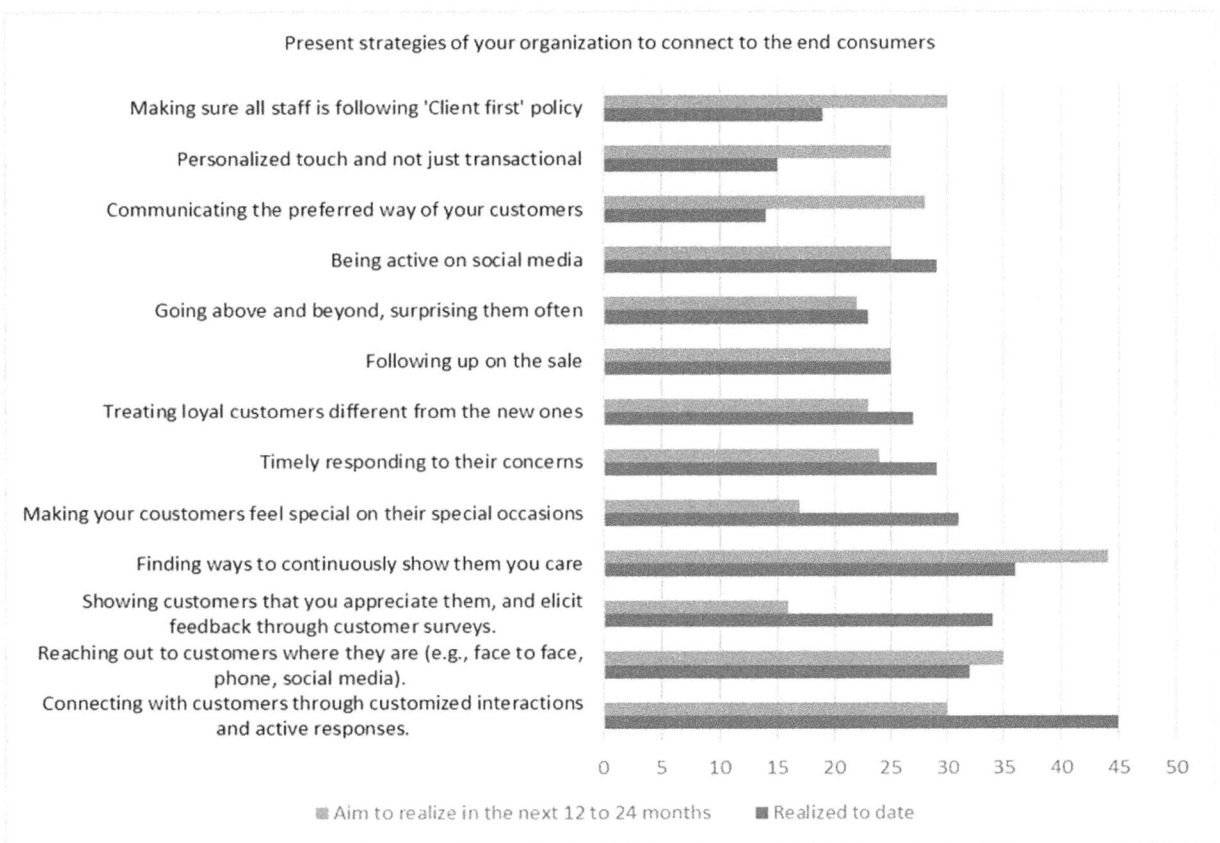

Question: Does your organization have a customer retention policy in place?

Figure 7. Customer retention policy in place

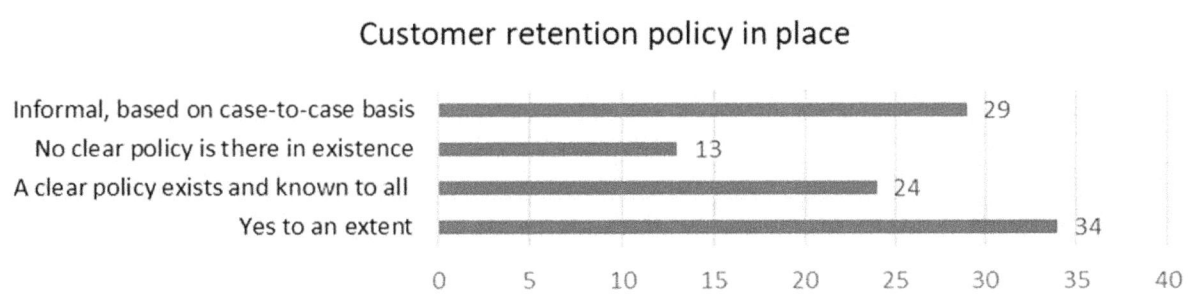

Question: How well do you think your organization is keeping a connection with their end customers?

Figure 8. Keeping a close connection with your end customers

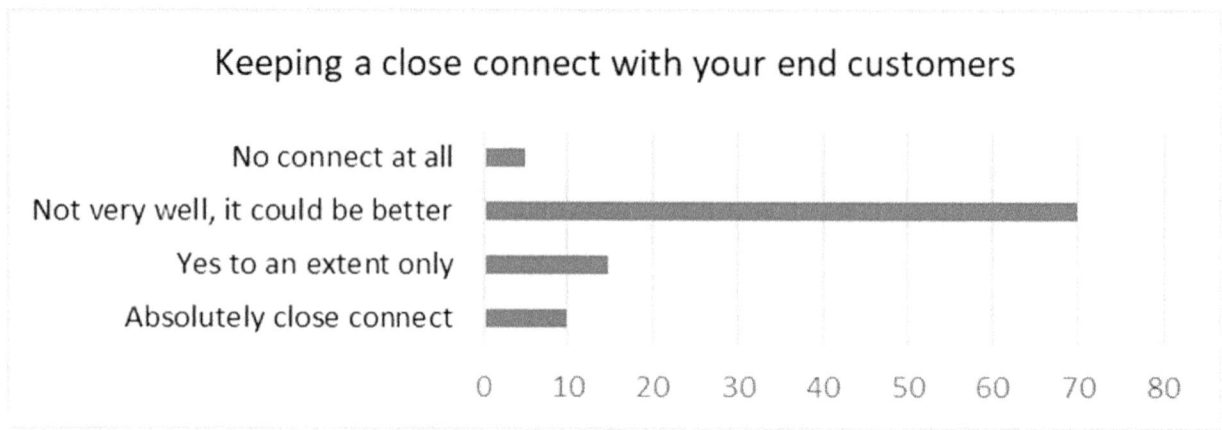

Question: Which region does your organization operate in?

Figure 9. Region of operations

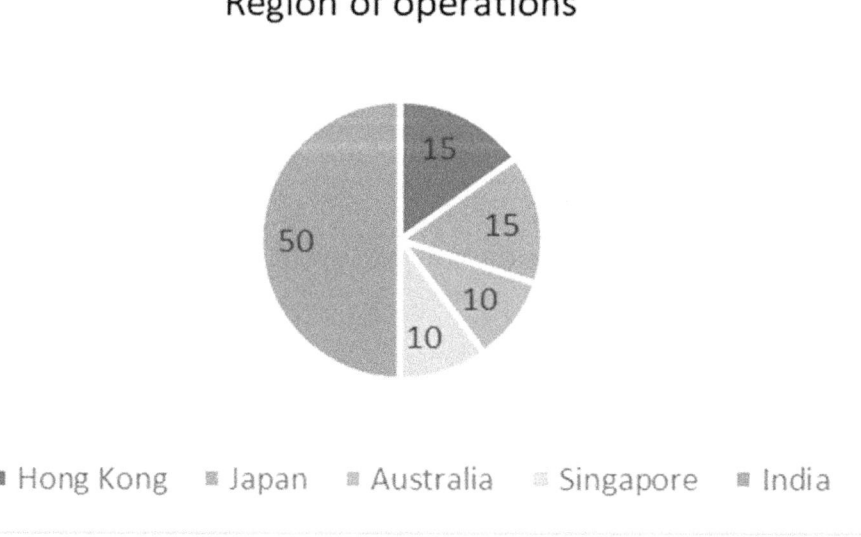

DISCUSSION AND FUTURE OUTLOOK

We have reason to anticipate that the phase we are now in will soon give way to a new one. Initial work on customer data platforms concentrated on the customization of marketing and advertising, and this area still seems to get most of the attention, energy, and resources. We have begun to see these transcend beyond marketing use cases and begin linking experiences across channels such as commerce, sales, and service. These examples are all included in this category. Personalization with an emphasis on customer relationship management offers an intriguing glimpse into the future and has a significant bearing on the situation. On the other hand, we are seeing the beginning of a new era in the field of customer data management: the rise of the ERP built data platform. Connecting the "back end" of corporate operations with the "front end" of consumer interaction is the focus of this ERP system.

We see the potential for utilising data from supply chains, industrial processes, and financial transactions to accelerate the process by which companies and consumers interact with one another. For this course of action to be successful, improved privacy and preference management, more ubiquitous intelligence and automation, and real-time capabilities are going to be required to fulfill the most ambitious goals of the most prominent technology leaders of today.

We think that the insights included in this research lead to an exciting future for customer data analytics and can help contribute to the formation of this new path. In today's fast-paced business world, emerging economies are quickly realizing the importance of transforming their data and enhancing their decision-making capabilities. To achieve this goal, businesses must employ the best strategies available in the market. These strategies should be carefully designed after analyzing different factors such as economic conditions, customer behavior patterns, industry trends and technological advancements. By using innovative technologies like big data analytics or artificial intelligence (AI), businesses can gain a deeper understanding of their customer's needs and preferences while also gaining insights into how they can improve operations internally. This information is crucial for making informed decisions that will drive growth and profitability.

Moreover, investing in training programs for employees to develop new skills is equally important as it allows companies to keep up with changing market dynamics; thus enabling them to remain competitive in a rapidly evolving landscape. Overall, adopting these transformative practices will enable businesses operating within emerging economies not only enhance operational efficiency but also boost revenue streams by leveraging technology-driven solutions that deliver real-time actionable insights – thereby setting themselves apart from the crowd.

Connecting With the End Consumers

As observed, several top-level executives are blissfully unaware of the fact that the foundations of their industries—consumerism and business—are crumbling. It's common knowledge that in today's emerging market, proximity to consumers is paramount. More importantly, most respondents from all regions considered in this research agree that the marketing industry is gaining up speed, mostly due to the rise of the Internet. It's not unusual for a business to use the level of marketing and management made feasible by modern network technologies. However, it seems as if most businesses are moving at a glacial speed, regarding digitalization. The main reason for this is maybe because they haven't learned the skills that pace can teach the firm, namely, how to know their clients inside and out and how to react to them periodically.

For example, let's see how this relates to the consumer goodsc industry. Traditional corporate constraints have always stifled the innovation at the heart of most marketing procedures. Because the merchant often stands between the manufacturer and the consumer, these items lack instant availability and a thorough understanding of their consumers. They have a limited capacity to use the real-time nature of the consumer data that is currently accessible due to the length of their supply chains from their factories to their customers' points of purchase. In addition, their marketing procedures are time-consuming since they are dependent on yearly plans, future driving times, and one-off market research surveys that need to be designed, implemented, and analysed—often by distinct market research departments that move at their own sluggish pace (Berndt & Brink, 2004).

Despite this, the network is a potentially game-changing medium that may overcome many of these built-in restrictions and prompt a wholesale revision of consumer marketing at these massive corporations. The network has made it possible for businesses to get a deep and instantaneous understanding of their clients in real-time. To be sure, this has its own unique difficulties. On the web, the customer has a lot more sway over the outcome of their transactions (Berndt & Brink, 2004). Attractive features include the convenience of access regardless of time or location, the possibility (and subsequent expectation) of personalised service, the ease with which information about competitors may be shared, and the proximity of rivals. Furthermore, everything happens instantaneously and in real-time, allowing online businesses to develop a far more lasting connection with their clients thereby offering them an awesome customer experience.

While it may seem impossible, client loyalty is the deciding factor in the success or failure of every online business (Zolkiewski et al., 2007). For a site to be successful, the great majority of its visitors must be people who have already interacted with it in the past and returned, generally because they bookmarked it. Paid search advertisements and other kinds of digital marketing bring in a negligible fraction of net new clients (Berndt & Brink, 2004). Although most online marketers spend too much time focused on sales leads through digital advertising, rather than improving their websites to develop long-term connections and enhance the lifetime income of their clients (Bauer et al., 2009).

Even if it's true that most manufacturers of consumer-packaged products don't make a lot of money from online sales, it doesn't mean that these principles shouldn't shape their strategies. Many millions of people visit the websites of major corporations each year. (Zolkiewski et al., 2007) discussed in their research that even if their goods and services are eventually marketed offline, businesses may swiftly test the waters with potential consumers online and use the insights gained to inform their day-to-day marketing strategies. Yet again, this seems to have been stifled by the cultural unwillingness of these ponderous marketing departments to think creatively about how they do business (Wayland & Cole, 1997).

'The desire for quick gratification' describes the more immediate nature with which consumers make decisions. Customers and potential customers are always gathering data on the firm and its competitors; if they don't actively participate in this process, they risk losing business to a more proactive rival. The notion of 'the desire for quick gratification' goes beyond the surface level and delves into the fundamental nature of consumer behavior (Mouawad & Kleiner, 1996). It reflects how customers make decisions, often driven by an immediate need or want that must be satisfied promptly. In today's fast-paced world, consumers are constantly bombarded with information about products and services offered by various firms in their respective industries.

As a result, they become highly engaged in gathering data on not only the firm they wish to engage with but also its competitors. In this highly competitive environment, businesses cannot afford to sit back passively while potential customers search for relevant information elsewhere - they must take proactive measures to ensure that their offerings are always readily available through various channels such as social media platforms or websites. The risk involved here is significant; if companies fail to stay ahead of the game when it comes to engaging customers actively and providing prompt solutions tailored precisely according to their needs – then there is always another rival who would seize any opportunity provided to them.

As observed from this research, large conglomerates have a disadvantage as compared to smaller ones when it comes to real-time monitoring and responding to changes in consumer behaviour, brand perception, and other metrics. But their usage of digital tools and new platforms to connect with the customer is gaining pace. Looking at the percentage who are yet to start with digitalization, there is an inherent need to be aware of each customer and connect with them periodically to understand their purchasing psychology.

Cultural Shift at the Organization Level

As per MIT Sloan Management Review, 'Cracking the Culture Code for Successful Digital Transformation' finding the right balance between continuity and change can help leaders better manage the cultural changes that occur during a digital transformation. To successfully navigate a business into the digital age, organisational culture is also an incredibly important factor to consider. When a company's culture is fast-paced and heavily reliant on technology, employees often use their own devices and solutions instead of working together and sometimes sharing information. This can make individuals have various viewpoints about clients and what they desire. Even though technology gives us the chance to optimise, organisations can end up putting more emphasis on operational efficiency than on innovation. This can stop people from experimenting with new ideas and could slow growth.

As humans, we are creatures of habit and comfort. We often resist change, especially when it is sudden or rapid. It takes a considerable amount of time for individuals to fully comprehend the implications that changes in technology or processes can have on their personal objectives and skillsets. Unfortunately, this reluctance towards change has resulted in numerous people becoming nothing more than turnover statistics as they struggle to adapt to new platforms and technologies. The mere thought of moving forward with cautious optimism causes fear among those who choose not to jump ship at the first sign of trouble. Therefore, it is imperative that all aspects - be it people, processes or technologies - work together cohesively if an organization wishes to sustain itself amidst ongoing transformations within its industry. In essence: successful adaptation requires a synergistic approach from every facet involved for any venture to truly flourish over time.

The cultural shift that occurs within the organization is a multifaceted process that delved into the very core of its values and beliefs. It involves an extensive assessment of all aspects of organizational culture, including communication styles, leadership practices, employee attitudes and behaviours, as well as external influences such as market trends and social norms. This transformational change requires a collective effort from every member of the organization to embrace new ideas and ways of thinking about work. Managers play a crucial role in setting an example for others by modelling positive behaviors and promoting open communication channels with employees at all levels. The goal is to create an inclusive environment where everyone feels valued regardless of their background or position within the company. This includes implementing diversity initiatives designed to recruit more people from different backgrounds while also fostering respect for diverse opinions among existing staff members. As a result of this monumental cultural shift, there can be an increased collaboration across departments resulting in greater innovation capabilities which will help propel the firm's success even further beyond expectations.

SOLUTIONS AND RECOMMENDATIONS

By leveraging data-driven solutions, businesses can establish a deeper and more meaningful connection with their customers. With the insights gained from customer behavior analytics, companies can tailor their products and services to meet the specific needs of each individual client. Through personalized marketing campaigns and targeted advertising strategies, businesses can effectively communicate with consumers on a one-to-one basis, fostering greater engagement and loyalty. Moreover, by continuously monitoring consumer feedback through social media platforms and other channels, organizations can gain valuable insights into how they can improve their offerings to better serve their customers' evolving preferences and requirements. Ultimately, investing in data-driven solutions allows businesses to not only connect with customers but also create long-lasting relationships built on mutual trust and understanding.

In today's ever-evolving technological landscape, artificial intelligence (AI) powered applications have become increasingly prevalent tools for businesses looking to foster a deeper connection with their customer base. But just how exactly can these innovative technologies be leveraged effectively to achieve this goal? From personalized marketing campaigns and targeted messaging strategies to automated chatbots that facilitate seamless communication between consumers and brands, the possibilities are truly endless when it comes to utilizing AI as a means of enhancing customer engagement (Chakrabortty et al., 2023). By thoughtfully implementing cutting-edge software solutions into their operations, forward-thinking companies can not only streamline key processes and improve overall efficiency but also build lasting relationships with customers through dynamic experiences that reflect their unique needs and preferences (Chakrabortty et al., 2023).

Achieving customer delight is crucial for any business that wants to maintain a loyal customer base and stay competitive in the market. To attain this objective, businesses must go beyond mere satisfaction and strive to create an exceptional experience for their customers. One way to achieve this is by understanding their customers' needs, preferences, and pain points. Conducting thorough research on their target audience can help them gain valuable insights into what drives their purchasing decisions and how they perceive their brand. This information can then be used to tailor their products or services, accordingly, resulting in a more personalized experience for each individual customer (Guo et al., 2020). Another important factor in achieving customer delight is providing excellent customer service at all touchpoints of the buyer journey - from pre-sales inquiries through post-purchase follow-up communication. It's essential that businesses respond promptly to feedback or complaints as it demonstrates a willingness to listen actively and improve continuously based on client input. In addition, incorporating innovative technologies such as chatbots or AI-powered tools could make interactions with clients even more efficient (Guo et al., 2020).

The proximity of a business to its customers can be the make-or-break factor in achieving an exceptional customer experience. A company that is truly invested in serving its clients will go above and beyond to ensure easy accessibility, timely communication, and personalized service at every touchpoint. The ability for a business to connect with their audience on a deeper level enables them to gain valuable insights into what their consumers really want and need, ultimately leading to more meaningful relationships and long-term loyalty. In today's competitive marketplace where customer satisfaction reigns supreme, being close physically, emotionally and culturally is paramount for delivering unparalleled customer experiences that leave lasting impressions.

Building and maintaining a strong connection with customers has become increasingly crucial in today's business landscape. To stay competitive, businesses need to make efforts to establish relationships with their customer base that go beyond the mere exchange of products or services.

FUTURE RESEARCH DIRECTIONS

To this end, it is important for businesses to implement strategies that prioritize genuine engagement and communication between the company and its customers. Case studies can be developed by researchers or organizations to accomplish this. This can also be achieved by leveraging social media platforms as well as through personalized messaging and email campaigns. Furthermore, incorporating data analytics tools into a business strategy can help track consumer behaviors, preferences and feedback which in turn can inform targeted marketing initiatives tailored specifically towards individual customers (Richard et al., 2007). Overall, cultivating meaningful connections with consumers requires ongoing effort on behalf of companies who must remain attuned to changing trends within their respective industries while consistently striving for new ways of enhancing customer experiences.

CONCLUSION

The appropriate structure and culture, supported by a well-defined data strategic plan, may assist businesses in the emerging economies in extracting more value from the information systems they are amassing. Developing and implementing a comprehensive data strategy can empower businesses. When supported by an appropriate organizational structure and culture, such a plan can help unlock valuable insights that drive growth and innovation. By taking this proactive approach to leveraging data, companies operating in rapidly evolving markets stand poised to achieve greater success than ever before.

What are the effective strategies and techniques that a business can utilize to enhance their customer experience? With an abundance of options available, how does a company set itself apart from its competitors and deliver exceptional service to its customers consistently? Delving deeper into this topic reveals various factors such as providing personalized attention, understanding consumer needs, offering seamless communication channels, investing in employee training programs and utilizing feedback mechanisms. All these play a significant role in creating remarkable experiences for customers which lead to loyalty and increased satisfaction levels (Richard et al., 2007).

Creating an extraordinary customer experience is vital for businesses to thrive and sustain their growth. Technology can play a pivotal role in achieving this objective, provided it is utilized efficiently. Here are some essential steps that businesses should follow to leverage technology for creating exceptional customer experiences:

1) Analyze the Customer Journey: Understanding customers' behavior at every touchpoint throughout their journey helps businesses identify areas where they can improve the overall experience.

2) Integrate Multiple Technologies: To create a seamless and consistent user experience across various channels like website, social media platforms or mobile apps; companies must integrate different technologies into one unified ecosystem.

3) Personalize Communication & Engagement: By using data analytics, companies have access to critical insights on consumer preferences and behaviors which allows them to personalize communications tailored precisely towards individual needs.

4) Implement Robust Self-Service Options: Providing consumers with efficient self-service options empowers them while reducing company overheads as well as helping reduce wait times resulting in increased satisfaction rates.

5) Leverage AI-powered applications to assist being always connected with their end user.

The task of building the appropriate skills and frameworks, as well as acquiring the relevant systems, equipment, and people, becomes much simpler once a clear roadmap has been established (Cantista et al., 2008). Additionally, fragmented data may be brought together in a logical fashion to empower business users. Only after this step can organizations have any chance of reaping the full assortment of benefits that are made possible by highly advanced data applications such as AI and ML. To get started, businesses should develop a comprehensive use case and then centre their strategies and business teams around it. Closer connect to their end consumer will help them achieve their objectives faster. The expectations imposed on businesses by their consumers are increasing significantly, and the only way to fulfil these requirements is to make more efficient use of data in a manner that is both nimble and adaptable. Experiences that are delightful for customers are what fuel businesses in recent times.

REFERENCES

Adam, M., Wessel, M., & Benlian, A. (2021). AI-based chatbots in customer service and their effects on user compliance. *Electronic Markets, 31*(2), 427–445. doi:10.100712525-020-00414-7

Akbari, M., Mehrali, M., SeyyedAmiri, N., Rezaei, N., & Pourjam, A. (2019). Corporate social responsibility, customer loyalty and brand positioning. *Social Responsibility Journal, 16*(5), 671–689. doi:10.1108/SRJ-01-2019-0008

Alhouti, S., Wright, S. A., & Baker, T. L. (2021). Customers need to relate: The conditional warm glow effect of CSR on negative customer experiences. *Journal of Business Research, 124*, 240–253. doi:10.1016/j.jbusres.2020.11.047

Bauer, H. H., Grether, M., & Leach, M. (2002). Building customer relations over the Internet. *Industrial Marketing Management, 31*(2), 155–163. doi:10.1016/S0019-8501(01)00186-9

Bauer, H. H., Grether, M., & Leach, M. (2002). Customer relations through the Internet. *Journal of Relationship Marketing, 1*(2), 39–55. doi:10.1300/J366v01n02_03

Berndt, A., & Brink, A. (2004). *Customer relationship management and customer service.* Juta and company Ltd.

Bettencourt, L. A., Blocker, C. P., Houston, M. B., & Flint, D. J. (2015). Rethinking customer relationships. *Business Horizons, 58*(1), 99–108. doi:10.1016/j.bushor.2014.09.003

Cantista, I., & Tylecote, A. (2008). Industrial innovation, corporate governance and supplier-customer relationships. *Journal of Manufacturing Technology Management, 19*(5), 576–590. doi:10.1108/17410380810877267

Chakrabortty, R. K., Abdel-Basset, M., & Ali, A. M. (2023). A multi-criteria decision analysis model for selecting an optimum customer service chatbot under uncertainty. *Decision Analytics Journal.*

Christopher, M. (1983). Creating effective policies for customer service. *International Journal of Physical Distribution & Materials Management, 13*(2), 3–24. doi:10.1108/eb014555

Dvořáková, L., & Faltejsková, O. (2016). Development of corporate performance management in the context of customer satisfaction measurement. *Procedia: Social and Behavioral Sciences, 230,* 335–342. doi:10.1016/j.sbspro.2016.09.042

Følstad, A., & Skjuve, M. (2019, August). Chatbots for customer service: user experience and motivation. In *Proceedings of the 1st international conference on conversational user interfaces* (pp. 1-9). ACM. 10.1145/3342775.3342784

Frosch, R. A. (1996). The customer for R&D is always wrong! *Research Technology Management,* 22–27.

Gamble, P. R. (2006). *Up Close & Personal?: Customer relationship marketing@ Work.* Kogan Page Publishers.

George, A. S., & George, A. H. (2023). A review of ChatGPT AI's impact on several business sectors. *Partners Universal International Innovation Journal, 1*(1), 9–23.

Gunarathne, P., Rui, H., & Seidmann, A. (2018). When social media delivers customer service: Differential customer treatment in the airline industry. *Management Information Systems Quarterly, 42*(2), 489–520. doi:10.25300/MISQ/2018/14290

Güntürkün, P., Haumann, T., Edinger-Schons, L. M., & Wieseke, J. (2023). How attributions of coproduction motives shape customer relationships over time. *Journal of the Academy of Marketing Science,* 1–29. PMID:36684408

Guo, Y., Fan, D., & Zhang, X. (2020). Social media–based customer service and firm reputation. *International Journal of Operations & Production Management, 40*(5), 575–601. doi:10.1108/IJOPM-04-2019-0315

Heinonen, K. (2014). Multiple perspectives on customer relationships. *International Journal of Bank Marketing, 32*(6), 450–456. doi:10.1108/IJBM-06-2014-0086

Henry, P. S., & Luo, H. (2002). WiFi: What's next? *IEEE Communications Magazine, 40*(12), 66–72. doi:10.1109/MCOM.2002.1106162

Jandik, T., & Salikhova, T. (2023). The effect of social connections on capital structure in supplier-customer relationships. *Journal of Corporate Finance, 79,* 102352. doi:10.1016/j.jcorpfin.2023.102352

Jaruzelski, B., & Dehoff, K. (2008). Customer connection: The innovation 1000. *Strategic Finance, 89*(8), 17.

Kemp, E., Porter, M. III, Anaza, N. A., & Min, D. J. (2021). The impact of storytelling in creating firm and customer connections in online environments. *Journal of Research in Interactive Marketing*, *15*(1), 104–124. doi:10.1108/JRIM-06-2020-0136

Kotrba, L. M., Gillespie, M. A., Schmidt, A. M., Smerek, R. E., Ritchie, S. A., & Denison, D. R. (2012). Do consistent corporate cultures have better business performance? Exploring the interaction effects. *Human Relations*, *65*(2), 241–262. doi:10.1177/0018726711426352

Kožená, M., & Mlázovský, M. (2021). The impact of customer behaviour on the corporate competitiveness in the European environment. In *SHS Web of Conferences* (*Vol. 129*, p. 07003). EDP Sciences.

Kumaran, L. A., & Hemalatha, J. (2023). E-business enabled customer service management and its performance: Evidence from Indian micro, small and medium enterprises. *International Journal of Business Forecasting and Marketing Intelligence*, *8*(1), 1–12. doi:10.1504/IJBFMI.2023.127700

Lasek, M., & Jessa, S. (2013). Chatbots for customer service on hotels' websites. *Information Systems Management*, 2.

Lee, S. M., & Lee, D. (2020). "Untact": A new customer service strategy in the digital age. *Service Business*, *14*(1), 1–22. doi:10.100711628-019-00408-2

Macdonald, S. (1995). Too close for comfort?: The strategic implications of getting close to the customer. *California Management Review*, *37*(4), 8–27. doi:10.2307/41165808

Mouawad, M., & Kleiner, B. H. (1996). New developments in customer service training. *Managing Service Quality*, *6*(2), 49–56. doi:10.1108/09604529610109774

Nicolescu, L., & Tudorache, M. T. (2022). Human-Computer Interaction in Customer Service: The Experience with AI Chatbots—A Systematic Literature Review. *Electronics (Basel)*, *11*(10), 1579. doi:10.3390/electronics11101579

Nordheim, C. B. (2018). *Trust in chatbots for customer service–findings from a questionnaire study* [Master's thesis, University of Oslo].

Nordheim, C. B., Følstad, A., & Bjørkli, C. A. (2019). An initial model of trust in chatbots for customer service—Findings from a questionnaire study. *Interacting with Computers*, *31*(3), 317–335. doi:10.1093/iwc/iwz022

Richard, J. E., Thirkell, P. C., & Huff, S. L. (2007). An examination of customer relationship management (CRM) technology adoption and its impact on business-to-business customer relationships. *Total Quality Management & Business Excellence*, *18*(8), 927–945. doi:10.1080/14783360701350961

Rossmann, A., Zimmermann, A., & Hertweck, D. (2020). The impact of chatbots on customer service performance. In *Advances in the human side of service engineering: Proceedings of the AHFE 2020 Virtual Conference on The Human Side of Service Engineering,* (pp. 237-243). Springer International Publishing. 10.1007/978-3-030-51057-2_33

Sun, Z., Wu, L. Z., Ye, Y., & Kwan, H. K. (2023). The impact of exploitative leadership on hospitality employees' proactive customer service performance: A self-determination perspective. *International Journal of Contemporary Hospitality Management*, *35*(1), 46–63. doi:10.1108/IJCHM-11-2021-1417

(2005). Sushil, "A Flexible Strategy Framework for Managing Continuity and Change,". *International Journal of Global Business and Competitiveness*, (1), 22–32.

Thornhill, S., & Amit, R. (2001). A dynamic perspective of internal fit in corporate venturing. *Journal of Business Venturing*, *16*(1), 25–50. doi:10.1016/S0883-9026(99)00040-3

Wayland, R. E., & Cole, P. M. (1997). *Customer connections: New strategies for growth*. Harvard Business Press.

Xu, A., Liu, Z., Guo, Y., Sinha, V., & Akkiraju, R. (2017, May). A new chatbot for customer service on social media. In *Proceedings of the 2017 CHI conference on human factors in computing systems* (pp. 3506-3510). 10.1145/3025453.3025496

Yang, B., Sun, Y., & Shen, X. L. (2023). Understanding AI-based customer service resistance: A perspective of defective AI features and tri-dimensional distrusting beliefs. *Information Processing & Management*, *60*(3), 103257. doi:10.1016/j.ipm.2022.103257

Zolkiewski, J., Lewis, B., Yuan, F., & Yuan, J. (2007). An assessment of customer service in business-to-business relationships. *Journal of Services Marketing*, *21*(5), 313–325. doi:10.1108/08876040710773624

KEY TERMS AND DEFINITIONS

Brand awareness: The extent to which people can recall and recognize a brand.

Churn rate: A measurement used to calculate customer retention and is significant for recurring revenue companies. It helps companies identify how many customers they lose in each period.

Contextual marketing: A strategy that's guided by the behaviours and conditions surrounding the marketing efforts, so all content is relevant to the person receiving it.

Cost per lead: This refers to the amount spent on acquiring a lead.

Customer lifetime value: The predicted net profit associated with the future relationship with that customer.

Inbound marketing: A customer-centric approach that focuses on drawing high-fit customers in as opposed to blasting a message to anyone and everyone.

Chapter 3
Organizational Development (OD) Frameworks and Models:
An Exploration of OD During COVID-19 for Enhancing Organizational Effectiveness

Oindrila Chakraborty

J. D. Birla Institute, India

ABSTRACT

The chapter thoroughly investigated various conceptual models for organisational development (OD). The implementation of the theoretical models and organisational development during the COVID-19 crisis would have been covered. The main objective of the book chapter is to equip readers with the knowledge and skills they need to comprehend the various frameworks, models, and concepts for managing organisational development, with a focus on how these concepts were used during the COVID-19-based pandemic. Additionally, the chapter checks on the different changes adapted by various sectors to accommodate sudden changes due to pandemic driven crises.

INTRODUCTION

Organizational researchers had a growing interest in the subject of *Organisational Effectiveness* (OE) since the late 1960s. Due to a lack of theoretical support, the topic was ignored in the 1950s and the early 1960s (Hannan & Freeman, 1977). A dawning realization that the concept of OE is crucial to the investigation of organizational structures, processes, and outcomes (Cameron & Whetton, 1981) led to this perception that there could be as much theoretical justification in looking at the consequences of different structural arrangements as in probing their determinants. As a result, the majority of research at the organizational level of analysis is linked, at least in part, to this realization (Goodman & Pennings, 1980).

The idea of OE emerged because of the contentions made by contingency theorists that some organizational structures were more appropriate for particular activities or situations than others (Scott, 1987). Many contingency theorists, including Pennings (1975), contended that OE is both a cause and an effect of organizational structure. Considering this, OE has grown to be among the most intricate

DOI: 10.4018/978-1-6684-8392-3.ch003

and contentious subfields of organizational science. However, it has traditionally been challenging for academics to clearly define the concept of effectiveness. Some of these issues are brought on by the concept's strong relationship to the value-related issue (Georgopoulos & Tannenbaum, 1957). Since OE deals with values and preferences that cannot be determined through objective means, several academics avoid it. The concept of Organizational Development (OD) came as an offshoot of the organizational effectiveness and later became the ground breaker for the concept.

BACKGROUND OF COVID-19 INDUCED PANDEMIC CAUSING ORGANISATIONAL CHANGE AND DEVELOPMENT

The COVID-19-driven epidemic in Wuhan, China, started to spiral out of control in the month of December 2019. From there, it swept across all nations with equal violence, putting an end to daily life. Every country was warned to educate its residents about the precautions needed to fend off the virus. The protective care comprised rules of physical and social isolation as well as numerous cleaning techniques, like hand washing and the use of face shields or masks. It also included social gathering bans, according to Sintema (2020), to stop the spread of this incredibly dangerous and wildly contagious disease. The COVID-19 injected a calamitous transformation into the worldwide platform by producing severe disruptions, disengagement, and a near breakdown of the ongoing business environment. The cautious measures, which also included various social distance-building, protective measures, and cleaning requirements, culminated in a government notification ordering the closure of academic, financial, and other corporate organisations.

As the direct result of a highly contagious New Corona virus (Dhawan, 2020) alerting the world to a never-before problem, (Pokhrel & Chhetri, 2021). The governments of the vast majority of countries overnight altered the strategic paradigm from the physical office scenario to digital (work from home) or phygital (hybrid work mode) to deal with the potential risk (Chaturvedi et al., 2020). The COVID-19 outbreak had caused widespread concern throughout the world. Everyone would suffer immensely from the COVID-19 pandemic's social and economic impacts. The harm caused by the virus has spread to every country in the connected globe of yesteryears. It's anticipated that the COVID-19 would have some long-lasting or irreversible impacts. There would surely be severe economic and social damage after the pandemic is over, in addition to a new world, new language, and new social norm. Several people started having major health issues as the COVID-19 outbreak spread across the globe, and the mortality rate increased. To prevent the virus from spreading, all social and economic activity in the affected nations must be put on hold for an indefinite period of time.

During this dreadful situation, many countries responded by implementing total lock-down. Under such a horrific scenario, all business activities across all industries came to a complete standstill. The lockdown had varying effects on different industries. For instance, the majority of the time during the lockdown, the aviation, hospitality, including hotel, and manufacturing sectors completely ceased operations. It would be a very long time, if ever, before they are able to make up for the loss. Millions of employees in these sectors had lost their jobs and unfortunately the number of this clan would increase. The COVID-19 epidemic caused significant business disruptions, and it will probably take years for them to bounce back.

Several businesses are likely to permanently close as a result of the pandemic's financial losses and interruptions. In an effort to improve the situation, businesses are experimenting with "Work from Home"

(WFH) mode to manage offices and administrative positions. To fight the economic unrest brought on by COVID-19, businesses have been utilizing disruptive technologies to combat the situation. It used to be only possible to work from home in the IT and IT sectors. Although WFH is a fantastic business approach, other industry sectors were reluctant to adopt it due to concerns about an odd work culture and a challenge in implementing effective control mechanisms.

The widespread adoption of work-from-home rules by companies is the largest business change that may be seen in the contemporary situation as a result of the pandemic's global spread. Throughout the past few years, businesses have found the WFH to be quite useful. In the future, the majority of companies would see WFH as an essential part of their business strategy. The WFH mode helps numerous industries and functions in a limited way to keep running. Those who work from home are compelled to live in social isolation and emotional distance as a result of the COVID-19 problem (Kaushik & Guleria 2020). Depending on the organization and the sector's convenience, the WFH mode has a range of degrees.

The Phygital or Hybrid mode of work has been chosen method where only quite vital meetings have been conducted through in-person meetings, otherwise virtual offices have been replacing to avoid any complications. Pure work from home has become a choice for those companies, where physical evidences of customer encounters were not integral. Some regrettable professions were unable to introduce WFH since it might have been an existential catastrophe for them.

MAIN FOCUS OF THE CHAPTER

The chapter would explore and review the diverse conceptual models of Organisational Development (OD). It would also delve into the Organisational Development during the crisis period of COVID-19 and the implementation of the theoretical models. The major goal of the book chapter is to give readers the knowledge and abilities to comprehend the numerous concepts, models, and framework for managing the organisational development with a special reference to implementations of those during COVID-19 basedpandemic. Figure 1 explains the primary focus of the chapter.

The chapter would primarily deal with following research questions:

A)   What are the major theoretical models related to Organisational Development (OD)?
B)   What had been the challenges of organisations across the industries, to adapt those OD theoriesat the Backdrop of COVID-19 driven pandemic?
C)   Had it been possible for organisations to adapt various OD theories during the recent turbulent times of COVID-19?

Figure 1. Showing the vision of the chapter

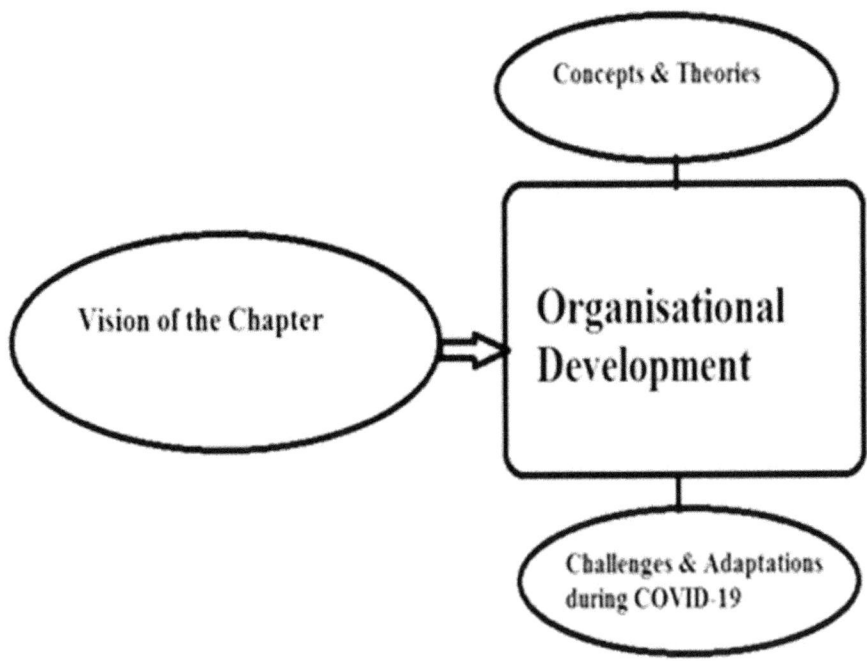

RELATED OPERATIONAL DEFINITIONS AND CONCEPTS OF ORGANISATIONAL DEVELOPMENT (OD)

The following portion of the chapter consists of three segregated sub-portions: (1) Operational Definitions of different terms used in the chapter, (2) Characteristics of OD, and (3) Conceptual Framework of Organisational Development (OD):

Operational Definitions

Pandemic

A disease that spreads across the entire nation or globe.

COVID-19 (Corona Virus Disease-19)

An acute human sickness termed as 'COVID-19', a coronavirus-based disease, caused by the SARS-CoV-2 virus, is predominantly characterized by fever and cough but can progress to severe symptoms and, in rare cases, death, especially in older people and people with underlying medical conditions. It was originally identified in China in 2019, expanded to other nations in 2020, and began to be referred to as a pandemic as a result of its extremely high mortality rates. Many strains have been discovered to date, each with a unique pattern of symptoms and severity.

Organizational Effectiveness

The definition of effectiveness, used by academicians is sometimes ambiguous, which makes it difficult to comprehend the findings of their study (Cameron, 1984). Unfortunately, very few studies have attempted to define OE (Mohr, 1971), except for Price (1968), who defines effectiveness as the degree of goal achievement. These studies include Seashore and Yuchtman (1967), who saw effectiveness as the organization's capacity to exploit the environment in the acquisition of crucial resources. According to Peter Drucker, Organisational Effectiveness is the capacity to utilize resources as effectively as possible to achieve objectives. The following table (Table 1) shows the different levels of dimensions defined by various authors.

Table 1. Showing different dimensions of organisational effectiveness

Author	Level of Attaining Effectiveness
Scott et al. (1987), Cummings (1980)	Individual level
Pennings and Goodman (1977), Van de Ven and Ferry (1980)	Sub-unit level
Yucthman and Seashore (1967) Price (1968),	Organisation level
Hirsch (1977), Pfeffer and Salnick (1978)	Organisation level

Adapted from (Cameron & Whetton, 1981)

However, for ease of understanding of organizational effectiveness, four approaches could be considered: *(1) The Goal Attainment Approach (2) The Systems Resource Approach (3) The Strategic Constituencies Approach and (4) The Competing Values Approach,* which has been defined in a structured manner in Table 2.

Table 2. Popular approaches for organizational effectiveness

Name of the Approach	Focus of Operational Definition	Most Preferred Situation
Goal Attainment	To achieve stated goal.	Meant for SMART objective.
System Resource	Resource optimisation.	There is a direct relationship between performance and inputs.
Strategic Constituencies	Every strategic stakeholder is at least somewhat satisfied.	The organisation is strongly influenced by its constituents, and it must respond to their needs.
Competing Values	The emphasis on the four separate quadrants' criterion for preferences is met.	The organization's own criteria are ambiguous, or they have changed over time.
Process	It functions smoothly internally without experiencing internal tension.	Organizational processes and performance are definitely linked.
High Performing Systems	In comparison to other organisations, it is deemed exceptional.	It is desirable to compare similar organisations.
Legitimacy	It continues to exist because it partakes in legitimate activity.	Organizational survival, decline, and death are interesting topics.
Fault Driven	Compared to other organisations of a similar nature, it has been excellent.	It is desirable to compare similar organisations.
Ineffectiveness	Attributes of ineffectiveness are absent.	Uncertain criteria for effectiveness or a need for organisational reform initiatives

(Source: Cameron, 1984)

Organisational Development (OD)

Organization Development (OD) refers to any process or activity that is grounded on behavioral sciences and can develop in an organizational environment over the short- or long term. The factors that are intended to be favorable to the individual, group, team, society, region, nation, or the entirety of humankind include improved knowledge, expertise, productivity, satisfaction, income, interpersonal connections, team spirit, and other desired results like goodwill. The relationship between people and groups has been given top priority in organization development in order to foster mutuality and collaboration amongst them and enable them to work cooperatively toward the advancement of the organization.

Organizational development has a fairly broad definition and meaning; as a result, the following intended outcomes and salient features have been established and are derived from such meanings:

1. Profound organizational transformation.
2. Promote a shift in the organizational culture.
3. Boost revenue and competitiveness.
4. Ensure the health and well-being of businesses and employees.
5. Promote learning and growth.
6. Enhance problem-solving.

7. Boost efficiency.
8. Initiate and/or manage change.
9. Strengthen the development of systems and processes.
10. Encourage adjusting to change.

All of the aforementioned elements increase the complexity and engagement of the field of organizational development, complicating and enhancing the work of practitioners and organizers. The organization's internal and external environments are always demanding advancement, creativity, innovation, and productivity.

Characteristics of Organization Development

1. Organizational development (OD) is a methodology that draws on a variety of disciplines, including management, business, psychology, sociology, anthropology, management, economics, education, counseling, and public administration. Enhancing organizational effectiveness is its key goal.
2. OD acknowledges the value of top management's dedication, backing, and participation. The goal is to improve the entire company, including people, departments, and work groups. It may even be expanded to include the entire human race.
3. Organizational Development (OD) is a deliberate, long-term approach to promote growth and change in both the organizational structure and its interconnected aspects.
4. OD is a program-based education that aims to create values, attitudes, conventions, and management practices that promote positive company culture and positive behavior attributes among employees and other stakeholders.
5. Organizational Development (OD) is a data-based method for understanding and analyzing organizations. A change agent, change team, or line management whose main responsibilities include serving as a facilitator, coach, and instructor and directing the process. The task entails planned interventions and modifications to the procedures and organizational structures, and it calls for knowledge and abilities in dealing with both groups and people.

Conceptual Framework of Organisational Development (OD)

Organizational Development is the conscious, systematic alteration of employee behavior or values with the purpose of fostering overall expansion within a business or organization. It is different from routine business operations and workflow enhancements. It adheres to a clear procedure that management explains to all employees for pre-planned positive changes.

Organizational development and transformation can be a protracted, at times stressful process, but businesses typically start with a number of objectives in mind:

1. Continuous Improvement
2. Improved or expanded communication
3. Development of EmplProfit
4. Profit growth

Organisational Development and Related Models

Since the field of Organisation Development (OD) first emerged in the early 19th century, several change models have been put out to assist the industry's primary objective, which is to plan and implement change to support organizational effectiveness. These models offer the foundations on which change agents may proceed with creating, planning, and implementing change, even though they might not fully explain every event in the real world. The adoption of one or more of the following change intervention strategies—human process-based strategies, techno-structural strategies, socio-technical strategies, and organizational transformation strategies—has been linked to increased organizational effectiveness over the course of the last 20 years or so on (Mulili & Wong, 2011; McLean, 2005).

Every OD change intervention strategy has the potential to result in organizational learning, including the acquisition of information, the development of insight, and the development of habits and skills (Mulili & Wong, 2011). Despondently, not every intervention technique can lead to the development of a learning organization. An organization that aspires to shape its own future, believes that learning is an ongoing and creative process for its members, and develops, adapts, and transforms in response to the needs and ambitions of individuals both inside and outside the organization. These types of organizations are called Learning Organisations (Mason, 2015). Therefore, such an organization actively adopts organizational learning activities in order to anticipate and successfully manage both internal and external changing scenarios (Cummings & Worley, 2009).

There are significant differences between *organizational learning* and a *learning organisation*, thus it's crucial that they are not mixed together or utilized indiscriminately. Mulili and Wong (2011) highlighted the fact that organizational learning is a learning process that naturally happens in all organizations without any intentional efforts in their analysis of the significance of organisations embracing OD activities. However, a learning organization was defined as a sort of organisation that needs the cooperation of the entire system in order to be established. Perhaps Schein's (1996) description of organizational learning as learning by people and groups 'Within the organisation' and a learning organisation as learning 'By the organisation' as a whole is a more succinct distinction. It is impossible to overstate the benefits of establishing learning organisations. It improves an organization's capacity to respond to the intricate and constantly changing needs of customers. Additionally, it provides businesses with a consistent competitive advantage over rival businesses. Additionally, learning firms can continuously develop new goods and services by successfully transferring knowledge acquired from continuous learning into them. In fact, some contend that learning organisations are a key characteristic of OD initiatives that set the discipline apart from change management.

In practice, as a way to assess the OD change process, companies and change agents may pay attention to a variety of outcomes. The development of learning organisations, which has been the area of ultimate organisationaldevelopmental goal over time, must be prioritised not only as a desirable consequence but also as a need. Reviewing the models that commonly support the OD change process is only a noble course given the importance of organisations becoming learning organisations. This would make it easier to determine whether current models are appropriate for assisting change agents in creating learning organisations as part of the OD consulting process. The examination of OD models is justified by other important factors. Successful planned interventions are guided by comprehensive models, which are essential to promoting not only organisational structures and procedures but also the members' quality of working lives. The constantly evolving nature of organisations and their needs, which are partly a result of technological advancements, support the ongoing evaluation of planned change models in order to guarantee that the overall OD model is always comprehensive and pertinent to the intricate and changing needs of its clients.

Outline of Organisational Development Models

Figure 2. Showing the major models for organisational development

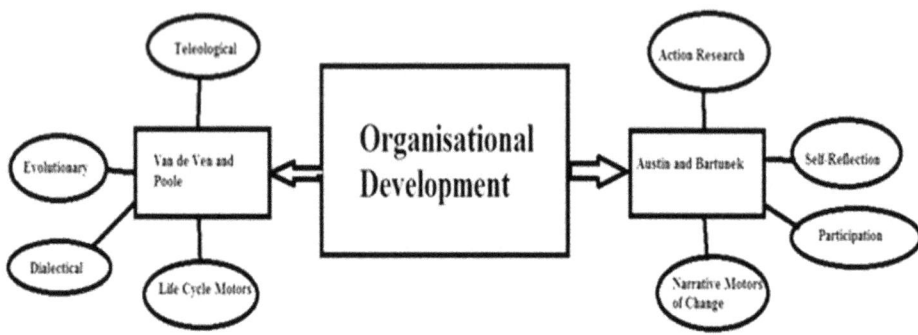

Conceptually, the change process theory and the implementation theory are the two fundamental theories on which organizational change approaches are founded. While the latter focuses on how activities generate change and what actions can be taken to initiate and steer change, the former is concerned with the dynamics of the change process (how and why change occurs) (Austin & Bartunek, 2003).

Each theory is built up of numerous types of change theories, which are again composed of a diverse variety of particular models. For instance, there are four *main motors theories* for bring about and directing change in implementation approaches. They are the *Action Research, Participation, Self-Reflection*, and *Narrative Motors of Change*, as per Austin and Bartunek (2003). The *Teleological, Dialectical, Evolutionary*, and *Life Cycle Motors* are among the four primary kinds or *engines of change* listed in Van de Ven and Poole's taxonomy of change process theories from 1995. The fact that academics have contributed significantly more to the development of the former than practitioners have to the latter is a crucial contrast between the change process and implementation approaches. Figure 2 shows the framework for the Organisational Developmental models.

Models of OD (such as the *Appreciative Inquiry Model*) are unique models that are informed by presumptions from one or more motors (Austin & Bartunek, 2003). Although this approach frequently poses a challenge to OD's focus on developing stronger integration of theoretical and practitioner-generated knowledge, the majority of organizational change models do tend to be predominantly influenced by either change process or implementation theories. For instance, the four models under evaluation tend to be implementation theories in that they describe the sets of actions required to bring about change at each step and/or guide the process/phases via which change occurs (Austin & Bartunek, 2003). Yet, other models (such as the *Action Research Model*) may make assumptions based on a mix of the implementation motors and the change process.

The Motor Theories of Organisational Development

Change-related ideas can be categorized into four broad groups, according to Vande Ven and Poole (1995). A distinction is created based on what drives (facilitates, energizes, encourages, etc.) the change: *(1) The Teleological Motor (2) The Life-Cycle Motor (3) The Dialectical Motor (4) The Evolutionary Motor.*

The Teleological Motor

Backdrop

The need to uphold the social structure that the organization's members are a part of forces such developments. Setting, achieving, reviewing, and altering goals are all phases of the development process. The majority of change models are built on this.

Goals are typically the focus of a strategic transformation approach. It fits into this category since it alludes to a planned and goal-oriented transition that leaders initiated and oversaw (Rajagopalan and Spreitzer 1996).

The Life-Cycle Motor

Backdrop

Some perspectives hold that development is a procedure with discrete stages. The order of some inter-related occurrences that must take place in order to attain the ultimate state determines and even demands them (Van de Ven and Poole 1995).

The Dialectical Motor

Backdrop

According to the dialectical motor technique, conflicts between various organisational units result in organizational changes. New concepts and values are directly opposed to the status quo. This is little more than the application of Hegel's rules of evidence; hypotheses and anti-hypotheses engage in conflict with one another in order to create a possible synthesis that favours the maintenance of the status quo.

Communicative Change Theories

According to the social interaction and social cognitive construct theories, interpersonal communication results in changes (Berger & Luckmann 1966; Giddens, 1984). The majority of the time, we interact with others as members of specific social groups rather than as lone individuals (Wieman & Giles, 1997). Depending on how much influence individual actors have over the organization, different perspectives, attitudes, and ideas are expressed there, and these things are constantly changing.

The Evolutionary Motor

Backdrop

The cycle of alternatives, selection, and maintenance underlies the evolution process. The theories are focused on how businesses respond to environmental cues. We anticipate that someone will notice changes in the environment and begin change in accordance, if the organisation has the skill and expertise required to carry out the change.

Internal Change Routines

This tactic looks at how original ideas for improvement are selected and approved by a business. Organizations should develop a procedure, routine, or action pattern expressly designed to aid and facilitate the change process, according to Nelson and Winter (1982). According to Lewitt and March (1988), a thoughtful procedure (that can be maintained over the long term) may significantly benefit organizations in implementing changes, regardless of their issue. But, as Kelly and Amburgey (1991) note, a similar process might potentially expose the organization's rigidity.

The Three-Step Process of Change

Backdrop

Lewin's (1947) Three-Step Model of Change was one of four interconnected components that made up his planned method to change. The other three components were field theory, action research, and group dynamics (Burnes, 2004).

It focuses on the circumstances and causes that influence or obstruct behavior (Kritsonis, 2005). The social scientist claims that a dynamic balance of forces acting in opposing directions is what causes human behavior (Burnes, 2004; Kritsonis, 2005). The three-step model or field theory consequently presupposes that desired changes in behavior can be brought about by shifting the balance of these forces or conditions in the direction of the planned change (Kritsonis, 2005).

Restraining forces, such as group norms, impede change by pulling employees in the opposite direction, whereas driving forces (such as incentives) encourage change by pushing employees away from their existing behavior and towards the desired change (Burnes, 2004; Kritsonis, 2005). A Quasi-Stationary Equilibrium State is referred to as the current state of affairs, problem situation, or status quo (Burnes, 2004).

Fundamental Elements

An effective change program involves three stages, according to Lewin (1947). The first phase, known as *"unfreezing"*, is diminishing the factors that keep organizational behavior or the status quo in place, raising the forces that influence behavior way from the current organizational state, or combining both strategies. The second phase entails raising the organization's equilibrium level or intended behavior (implementing the desired change). The implementation of the change program's first two stages has been shown to require a certain set of tasks. They include challenging the legitimacy of the status quo or convincing employees that the current system is not in their best interests. At the *"unfreezing"* and *"moving"* stages, it's crucial to instil remorse about the current condition and actively involve staff members and leaders in identifying issues and finding solutions. Also, it has been discovered that these two steps of the three-step paradigm are made easier by establishing psychological safety or ensuring participants that the desired change won't come at any psychological cost, such as loss or shame to them (Burnes, 2004; Kritsonis, 2005). The planned change is incorporated into organizational values and traditions in the third step, known as *"refreezing"* in order to stabilize the new quasi-equilibrium condition and prevent a return to the original crisis scenario.

At this third level, reinforcement is a crucial technique for establishing new behaviors within organizations and institutionalizing them (Burnes, 2004; Kritsonis, 2005). Changes in corporate culture, rules, and practices are indicators of refreezing or a new quasi-equilibrium state (Burns, 2006). Figure 3 shows the Schematic representation of Three Steps Model.

Figure 3. Showing the Kurt Lewin's three-step process model
Source: Lewin (1946)

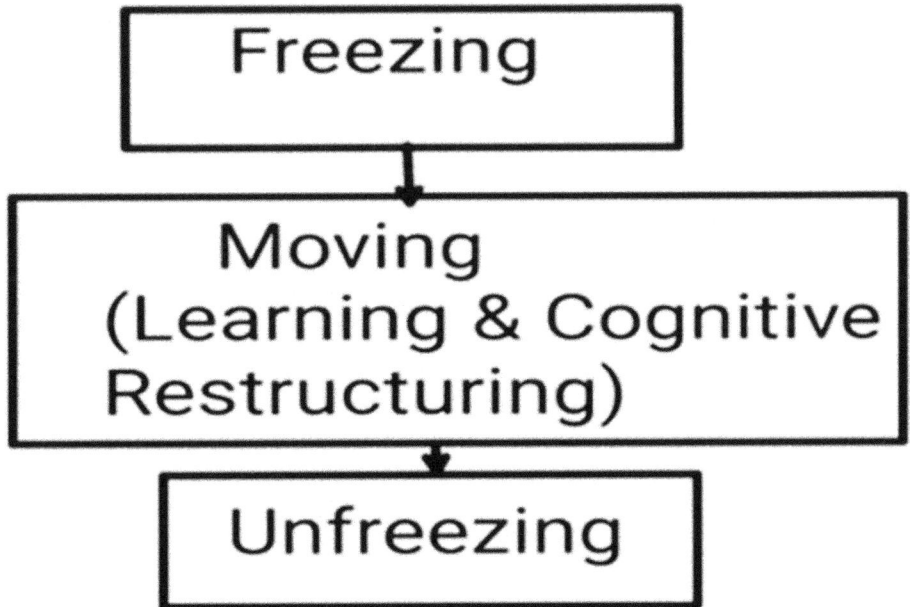

The Action Research Model

Backdrop

Like the three-step approach, the idea of action research is credited to Lewin (1946) as a component of deliberate change. Lewin (1946) defined action research as a research strategy that is predicated on a relationship of cooperative problem-solving between the researcher and client and that strives to both solve a problem and provide new information. Hence, conventional action research assumes that organizational issues can be resolved through cycles of knowledge collecting and application of action solutions when these dual activities are carried out simultaneously and purposefully by organization members (Coghlan & Brannick, 2014).

Fundamental Elements

Eight key processes are involved in directing planned change within organizations: problem identification, expert consultation in behavioral science, data gathering and preliminary diagnosis, client input, joint diagnosis of the problem, collaborative action planning, action, and data gathering after action (Cummings & Worley, 2009). Identification of the problem is the first of these processes. This entails detecting a situational change or issue within the company (Coghlan & Brannick, 2014). Typically, this is done by a senior executive or another important individual who recognizes one or more issues that could be resolved with an OD practitioner's assistance (Cummings & Worley, 2009). The organization consults with a behavioral science specialist, such as an OD practitioner, in the second stage. In order to create an honest and cooperative connection with the company, the expert may share his framework for carrying out the intended change with them at this time (Cummings & Worley, 2009; Coghlan, & Brannick, 2014; McLean, 2005).

The third step is data gathering and preliminary diagnosis, which is done jointly with organisation members but is mostly carried out by the OD practitioner. To obtain appropriate and applicable information on the organization's structures and/or activities, the OD practitioner may employ process observation, interviews, questionnaires, and/or organisational performance statistics. This data is then analysed to fully comprehend how the organisation is currently operating and to identify the root causes and effects of the problems that are present inside the organisation (Cummings & Worley, 2009). Following the data collection phase, the OD practitioner provides members of the company with feedback on the results of the diagnostic exercise (e.g. employees, managers, and executives).

According to Cummings and Worley (2009), it's crucial at this point in the change process to strike a balance between openness about pertinent and helpful information and confidentiality regarding sensitive or private data sources. The previous stages of the transformation process depend greatly on how prepared the organization is for the diagnostic data. After providing the client with comments, the issue is jointly diagnosed. In order to avoid misdiagnosis during the data-gathering stage, the OD practitioner and organization members must at this point agree on the nature of the issue and its root causes. According to Wicks and Reason (2009), this is a crucial stage in the action research approach since failure to recognize or correctly diagnose the issues that have been identified could result in resistance to change (Cummings & Worley, 2009).

The OD practitioner and the organization members collaboratively decide on the actions or interventions required to effect the intended change during the joint action planning stage, which comes before the actual action phase. The precise course of action decided upon at this point typically depends on a variety of criteria, including the problem's diagnosis, the organization's culture, and the nature of the intervention or activities (Cummings & Worley, 2009; McLean, 2005). The planned actions are carried out during the action phase to achieve the desired organizational changes (e.g., changes in strategic mission and goals, structure, processes, and human resources), at the group level (e.g., changes in culture or behavior of departments or teams), or at the individual level (e.g. changes in job descriptions and tasks) (Cummings & Worley, 2009; McLean, 2005). The final step in the paradigm is data collection after the action has been performed. Here, the OD specialist compiles information on the results.

The Appreciative Inquiry Model

Backdrop

Appreciative inquiry was one of the first OD techniques to function outside of the *Lewinian Paradigm of Planned Change* (Bushe, 2011). This model, which Cooperrider and Srivastva first presented in 1987, advocates a positive change strategy as an alternative to action research's problem-centered strategy. The *Appreciative Inquiry Paradigm*, which is firmly rooted in social constructionist theory, draws on narrative OD methodologies like storytelling to produce fresh concepts, hypotheses, and visions of the future for change (Bushe, 2011; Cummings & Worley, 2009; Gallos, 2006). It focuses on understanding and appreciating an organization's skills in order to create better strategies for nurturing its current potential (Bushe, 2011; Cummings & Worley, 2009; Lewis et al., 2008; McLean, 2005).

It is also predicated on the idea that individuals often communicate and behave in ways that fulfill their expectations, and that expectations of the organization that are favorable can engender anticipation that energizes and guides behavior towards fulfilling those expectations (Bushe, 2011; Cummings & Worley, 2009; Gallos, 2006). Additionally, it is founded on the claim that fresh ideas are the most powerful force for change and that the traditional action research paradigm does not provide such ideas (Bushe, 2011). A process of collective discovery into the best of what is, what might be, what should be, and what can be was the foundation of the original appreciative inquiry methodology (Bushe, 2011). Over time, numerous viewpoints on the constructive approach have been put forth (e.g. the 5-D model; Cummings & Worley, 2009). Yet, the approach that is nearly always referred to as the appreciative inquiry method continues to stand out as the 4-D model, which directs planned change through a process of four primary stages (Bushe, 2011).

Fundamental Elements

According to Cooperrider and Srivastva's (1987) 4-D model of Appreciative Inquiry, organizational change is the end outcome of a cyclical process that starts with discovery. At this stage, participants' thoughts and debates on the "best of what is" in regard to the subject are used to conduct an investigation into the change/focus topic (Bushe, 2011; Cummings & Worley, 2009). Interviewing participants about instances of customer satisfaction rather than customer unhappiness, for example, could be part of an investigation into how to increase customer satisfaction (Cummings & Worley, 2009; Lewis et al., 2008). Members of the organization imagine the organization in its ideal state in regard to the change-related issue during the dream phase, which comes after the discovery stage. Often, an effort is made to identify and symbolically represent the shared goals and desires of organization members (Bushe, 2011; Lewis et al., 2008).

Members create compelling possibility/design statements for the next organizational state during the design stage, the third phase of the 4-D model, in order to close the gap between the organization's 'existing best practices' and 'ideal future state' (Bushe, 2011; Cummings & Worley, 2009; Lewis et al., 2008). Members execute actions in accordance with the design statements at the delivery or destiny stage, evaluate the results, and then adapt as necessary to move the organization closer to the ideal condition and realize '*what will be.*' The next step in this circular process is an evaluation of the best examples of '*what is*' (Bushe, 2011; Lewis et al., 2008).

The Generic Model of Planned Change

Backdrop

The General Model of Planned Change, suggested by Cummings and Worley (2009), is a broad framework for directing the OD consulting process based on the three models discussed above. This broad organizational development (OD) paradigm focuses on planned change from a *'problem-solving viewpoint'* as well as from the perspective of finding and utilizing best practices inside companies. The paradigm emphasizes both an overlapping and nonlinear approach to planned change in addition to a participatory approach to change (Cummings & Worley, 2009; McLean, 2005).

Fundamental Elements

The generic OD model states that four sets of activities—entering and contracting, diagnosis and feedback, planning and implementation, evaluation and institutionalization—can be used to accomplish intentional change within organizations over the course of four major stages. The first stage, referred known as the *'entry and contracting stage,'* outlines the initial set of tasks that the change agent and the organization must do in order to determine what needs to be improved or enabled and whether to continue with the intended change program (Cummings & Worley, 2009; McLean, 2005).

The activities include gathering information to pinpoint issues or opportunities for change, discussing the information with others, deciding to implement the change, and setting expectations for the change agent's role (such as consultant or expert), time commitment, compensation, and the resources the organization will need to dedicate to the process. The second stage of the OD consulting process is *'diagnostic and feedback'*. In order to clearly identify the set of intervention activities required to increase organizational effectiveness, it entails a collection of activities targeted at understanding the existing status of the organization (including the causes and consequences of organizational problems or best practices). Cummings and Worley (2009) cite this phase as one of the most crucial ones in the change process. Choosing an appropriate diagnostic model (such as the whole systems model) to understand the organization, gathering pertinent information about current operations and culture at the organizational, group, and/or individual level, analyzing the information, and communicating the results to the organizational members are the key change activities at this stage (Cummings & Worley, 2009; McLean, 2005).

Following the diagnosis and feedback stage, the *planning and execution* step comes before the final stage of the change process. At this point, depending on the findings of the diagnostic, organization members and the change agent jointly build action plans or interventions. Interventions may concentrate on changing organizational strategy, structure, technology, human processes, and/or people resources depending on the results of the diagnostic. The type and extent of the interventions created may also be influenced by organizational elements like the change agent's drive, dedication, skills, and competencies as well as organizational culture, power structures, and preparedness for change. Also, during this stage, the change agent directs and coordinates the application of the action plans or interventions so that, at the very least, all members of the organization are aware of the change's effects (Cummings & Worley, 2009; McLean, 2005).

The final phase of *'thechangeprocess'* involves institutionalising and evaluating the change. Here, the change agent collects information about the organization's present situation after the intervention was put into place in order to determine how successfully the intervention fulfilled the intended objectives.

A key action at this point is providing organisational members with feedback on the intervention's effects. It gives organisational members—particularly management—the option to choose whether to keep, make modifications to, or get rid of the changes. When an intervention is determined to be effective, it is institutionalised, or made a regular part of how the organisation conducts business, using techniques like feedback, rewards, and training (Cummings & Worley, 2009; McLean, 2005).

COMMONALITIES AND DIFFERENTIAL ATTRIBUTES OF MODELS FOR ORGANIZATIONAL DEVELOPMENT

The Motor theories are all based on gradual planned changes without radical change. Just like Motor theories, the four models -Action Research Model, Appreciative Inquiry Model, General Model of Planned OD Change and Three Steps Process of Change are the models that define the key phases of planned change as they occur in companies. All of them place a strong emphasis on action plans that are preceded by a preliminary diagnosis or unfreezing *stage* and are followed by an *assessment* or *closing stage*. The models also share a focus on using behavioral science information to the planned change process and varied degrees of involvement of organizational personnel (Cummings & Worley, 2009; Gallos, 2006; McLean, 2005).

The other three models, barring the Three Steps Process of Change, describe the process as well as the specific OD actions required to bring about change, in contrast to Lewin's model, which concentrates on the whole process of planned change (Kritsonis, 2005). Lewin's Three Steps Model differs, from Action Research Model, and the Appreciative Inquiry Model in that they place an emphasis on the change agent's role while enabling some engagement from organizational members. In contrast, the Appreciative Inquiry Approach recognizes the organization's members and the change agent as co-learners who are both participants in the planned change process (Cummings & Worley, 2009). The change foci of the models also vary.

Lewin's model and the Action Research Model concentrate on identifying and resolving issues, but the Appreciative Inquiry Approach is focused with recognizing and utilizing strengths, best practices, and new ideas (Bushe, 2011; Kritsonis, 2005). On the other hand, the comprehensive general OD model focuses on both opportunity creation and problem-solving as means of implementing deliberate change (Cummings & Worley, 2009; Gallos, 2006). Moreover, Lewin's model tends to take a linear approach, whereas the other three models encourage a cyclical approach to identifying possibilities and issues, promoting actions, and reflecting on changes that have been made (Gallos, 2006).

ASSESSMENT OF MODELS FOR ORGANIZATIONAL DEVELOPMENT

The emphasis on organizational member participation, while to varied degrees, is a crucial component of all the models examined because it enables organizations to benefit from the knowledge and expertise of the change agent (Cummings & Worley, 2009). This gives organizations the confidence they need to work effectively together or support future changes. Contrarily, the extra time required of employees to participate in research/inquiry and other stages of the change process might be costly due to the emphasis on cooperation. It may be difficult for newly established and small companies to engage in cycles of research and action due to their limited time and human resource availability (Cummings & Worley, 2009; Gallos, 2006).

The requirement for change agents to evaluate significant organizational and practitioner aspects that may affect the formulation, implementation, and adoption of action plans is not taken into account by any of the four models. The models examined do not offer instructions on how the change agent can end the assisting connection during the change process. The fact that none of the models explicitly explains how change agents might assist and enable firms to transform into learning organizations towards the conclusion of the change process may be more significant.

The group-based methodology of Lewin's work can be cited as a major benefit of the there-step model in particular (Burnes & Cooke, 2012). Changes in individual behavior won't be maintained unless group norms and routines are also altered, as highlighted correctly by Burnes (2004). The model's simplicity, according to Cummings and Worley (2009), may offer a clear approach to organizational change and serve as a foundation for the creation of further change models. Examples include the eight-stage model proposed by Kotter (1996) and Lippit's stages of change theory (Lippit et al., 1958). Hendry (1996) further claimed that the idea that change is a three-stage process that starts with a process of unfreezing or confronting the current situation seems to be the foundation of every method to bringing about and managing change. Lewin's approach, on the other hand, has drawn criticism for being extremely straight-forward, linear, and comparatively sluggish, which limits its applicability in circumstances where quick and intricate adjustments are needed within an organization (Burnes, 2004; Kritsonis, 2005). It is also criticized for disregarding individual elements that can influence change, such as staff members' emotions, experiences, and prior contributions (Kritsonis, 2005). Also, rather than focusing on change from the standpoint of whole systems (e.g., organizational strategies, technology, structure, and behaviors), the model focuses on change primarily from the perspective of individuals' behaviors (Kritsonis, 2005).

The Action Research Model's emphasis on the twin process of academic research/knowledge generation and issue solving has over the years made major contributions to the field of Organisational Development (OD) and beyond (Coghlan & Brannick,2014). Therefore, it can be stated that the idea has played and will continue to play a crucial part in closing the researcher-practitioner divide in the field of organizational development. According to Burnes (2004), the Action Research Model is the method that Organisational Development (OD) practitioners most frequently use, which lends support to the numerous problem-centered cases that Gallos (2006) noted had been successfully resolved through the application of the model. Given that a variety of action research formats have evolved from the initial idea, the Action Research Model is also renowned for its robustness and for having made significant contributions to the improvement of theory and methodology (Coghlan & Brannick, 2014). The Action Research Paradigm has faced opposition from other OD field advocates despite its advantages and efficacy. The model and its underlying assumptions were attacked by Cooperrider and Srivastva as focusing on utilitarian and technical views of organizations as problems to be solved as early as 1987. As a substitute, they suggested the Appreciative Inquiry Model.

The Appreciative Inquiry Model's emphasis on appreciating existing circumstances to produce fresh, constructive ideas—which some in the field have claimed are the most significant forces for change—has been one of its primary strengths (Bush, 2011). This strategy's efficacy has also received extensive research. Including religious, medical, military, academic, and educational organizations, it has been discovered that the appreciative inquiry approach has played a crucial role in encouraging good change and progress in both small- and large-scale groups (Cooperrider, 2000; Lewis et al., 2008; Gallos, 2006). The 4-D view has been challenged for abandoning the crucial first step of identifying or defining the topic of the inquiry/the subject of change itself, notwithstanding the excellent results it has produced (Bushe, 2011). Even though the definition of the topic of inquiry has not been plainly outlined, it has been maintained that defining it and making sure that leaders and participants are highly interested in it are essential to the success of the change process in general (Bushe, 2011). The concept has also come under fire for only emphasizing an organization's advantages. According to several experts in the industry, comprehensive and effective reforms necessitate not only a focus on the best aspects of the status quo but also solutions to the issues and challenges that companies face (Cummings & Worley, 2009; Gallos, 2006; McLean, 2005).

Being a combination of the other three models, the General Model of OD builds on their advantages while striving to fill in their weaknesses. Its advantages include encouraging client and change agent collaboration, a focus on both problem identification, and the development of fresh, constructive ideas and best practices. It also focuses on organizational, group, and individual change (e.g., job descriptions), as well as structural and strategic change at the organizational, departmental, and group levels. It stresses going through research and implementation cycles until the desired change is made.

Additionally, it promotes research that helps define and identify problems. The basic OD model also provides change agents with clear direction on the sets of actions required at each step to take the organization to the intended state, in addition to informing them about the stages of change (Cummings & Worley, 2006; Lacey, 1995). On the other hand, it may be said that the model has limitations in at least two key areas. First, the literature identifies a number of crucial client and practitioner variables that might affect the preparation for and execution of change, such as organizational readiness and the abilities and values of the change agent (Armenakis & Bedeian, 1999; Cummings & Worley, 2009; Gallos, 2006; McLean, 2005). The model does not, however, list the assessment of these fundamental factors as a crucial step in the change process. Second, it is accurate to say that the model's focus on engagement from organizational members can encourage the sharing of knowledge and expertise between members and the change agent.

In order to exist, all organizations must inherently participate in learning in some way. To succeed and become leaders in their industry, businesses must put policies in place to continuously and proactively collect and grow knowledge as a cohesive system. It is critical that the basic OD model be improved to explain how change agents can assure that clients become learning organizations by the time they withdraw from their supporting role because the development of learning organizations is a fundamental emphasis of the study of organizational development. It is crucial that the underlying model employed may direct how change agents may continue to work, even in instances where they may work with customers on a long-term basis.

ISSUES, PROBLEMS, AND CHALLENGES IN IMPLICATIONS OF OD MODELS IN THE WORKPLACES DURING COVID-19 PANDEMIC

During pandemic times, there have been three distinct difficulties, problems, and challenges at work, each with its own levels and dimensions. It also included three viewpoints: (1) The issue of theorists forcing organizational change and development theories in a wholly disruptive, unanticipated and unplanned situation, (2) the employee's perspective dealing with a precarious predicament, and (3) the employer's perspective covering enormous loss and peril.

Figure 4 shows a gradual, progressive change is preferred to a radical, drastic overnight shift for slow adaption for most of the OD approaches, but COVID-19 did not offer the same opportunity to introduce change gently into the system without causing obvious problems and noticeable disturbances. It became extremely challenging for the theorists to come up with adjustable propositions to fit the bill.

The employee's perspective has mainly been composed of five areas, namely: (1) Financial and job-related insecurity (pay cut and retrenchment); (2) Concern for health (self and family); (3) Mental stress of adjusting to changed work environment (professional work in presence of family members); (4) Self-learning of digital platforms to acclimatise to virtual workplace; and (5) 24 hour pressure to innovate disruptive techniques for offsetting impact on the declining demand for corporates.

The primary issues for employers have been the financial losses resulting from an organization's abrupt shutdown and the revised, acceptable workplace circumstances (The New Normal). Other than that, the organisations have been concerned with the employees' psychological health and constant business challenges. Many distribution and logistics channels were shut down, so it was crucial for the Organizations to come up with new solutions. Several employees underperformed due to unexpected rise in workload and personal turmoil (including loss of a loved one), which led to lower revenue and production. Losing business opportunities and performing below expectations became a tremendous burden for many organisations.

Figure 4. Showing the different perspectives of issues, problems, and challenges

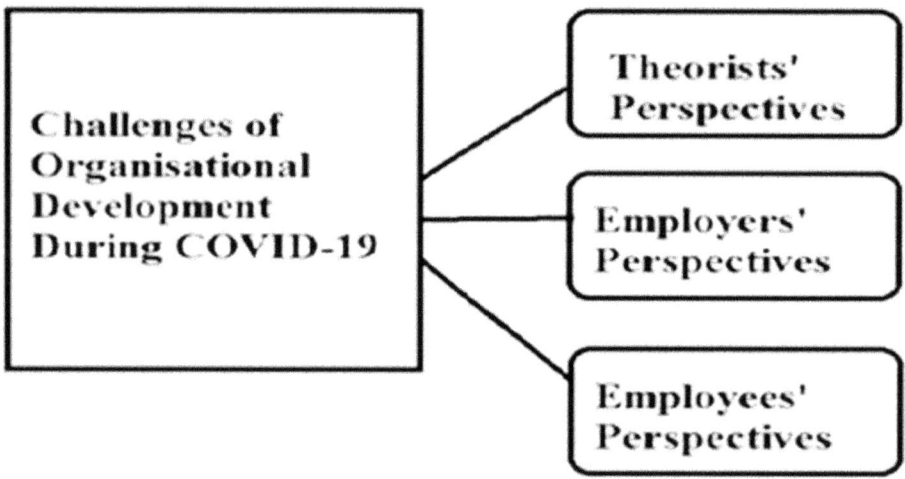

TRENDS, RECOMMENDATIONS AND SOLUTIONS OF DIFFERENT ADAPTATIONS IN ORGANISATIONAL DEVELOPMENT DURING COVID-19 PANDEMIC

Figure 5. Showing the different sectors going through organisational developmental changes during COVID-19

The degree of professional adaptation differs based on industry and convenience, as well as by the degree of self-interest and desire to succeed in the approaching corporate environment. Also, the organization's response to the pandemic's requirements for individual and career change has been influenced by the organization's ability to adapt. Losses in terms of money and health, as well as coordinating with the new work pattern, have been the main causes of the individual stress. Stress in the workplace has primarily been caused by jarring changes and the adaptations that followed.

Some of the sectors have shown divergence in the coping mechanism in response to the COVID-19 outbreak. Figure 5 shows the primary sectors undergoing changes during COVID-19.

Information Technology

Online/virtual workplaces/WFH have been a preferred alternative in the information technology sector both during the pandemic and in the ongoing new-normal period. The hybrid forms have only been used for really important things, such as some meetings and client visits. The type of change that the employees have gone through is crucial. It was clear that employees had disclosed psychological trauma and a state of illness, despite the fact that organisational actions were insufficient to address such trauma. Whilst certain new jobs have evolved in terms of job nomenclature and positions, the phase-out of services was also adjusted progressively. Several jobs, including Business Analytics, Data Analytics, and others, were created specifically to support international initiatives. To keep in mind the mental vulnerability of employees, some special job positions were created like 'Mental Health Manager' to neutralise the damages. Though these positions are also started getting redundant for some of the global giants.

Finance

Hardly any WFH has been introduced in the insurance sector, with the exception of some menial back office tasks for freelance insurance brokers. With the exception of a few virtual meetings, most physical interfaces have been employed in banking and microfinance, sustaining social distance standards.

Despite the institutions taking only minimal action, the stress level was rather high. In contrast to the microfinance or insurance industries, major banks have adopted the significant proportion of the initiatives. The subsequent ones suffered greatly as a result of numerous death claims and insufficient customer sourcing. The established conventions within the initiative range included incentives and virtual meetups.

Retail Industry

The COVID-19 pandemic has had a significant impact on the retail industry, leading to changes in consumer behaviour, supply chain disruptions, and economic uncertainty.

Shift to e-commerce: As people were forced to stay at home, there was a surge in online shopping. Retailers had to quickly adapt to this shift by ramping up their online operations, offering more delivery options, and enhancing their websites and mobile apps.

Supply chain disruptions: Many retailers experienced supply chain disruptions as factories and transportation systems were shut down or slowed down due to the pandemic. This led to shortages of some products, particularly those that were imported from other countries.

Reduced foot traffic: With many physical stores closed or operating at reduced capacity, retailers experienced a significant decline in foot traffic. This led to lower sales and revenue for many businesses.

Increased safety measures: Retailers had to implement new safety measures to protect their employees and customers from the virus. This included social distancing measures, frequent cleaning and disinfecting, and requiring masks or other personal protective equipment.

Changes in consumer behavior: The pandemic has also led to changes in consumer behavior, with many people prioritizing essential items and cutting back on non-essential purchases. Some consumers have also shifted their focus to buying locally or from small businesses.

Overall, the COVID-19 pandemic has had a profound impact on the retail industry. Due to these clear pandemic reasons, weightage has indeed been placed on online and phygital/hybrid modes in the retail industry, as a part of organizational development. Employee stress levels have been fairly high, but organizational efforts to reduce it fell short, with the exception of informal guidance from managers and a limited amount of incentives. But importance has been given on hygiene part as a regime of Covid-19 protocol.

Hospitality Industry

With the exception of meetings involving business development during the initial phase of the pandemic and lockdown, the preponderance of operations for the hotel sectors were physical. Apart for the essential operational execution, the lodging facilities were nearly halted during the lockdown phase. To house the COVID patients, some of the low-cost hotels temporarily transformed into isolation or quarantine facilities. In the medical community, WFH for private chambers was mostly either physical (direct contact) or hybrid (online consultation and other accouterments) during the entire lockdown period or later.

Organizational activities like workshops, seminars, and webinars were fairly common in the hospitality industry, particularly in the medical community. Although the organizations were sympathetic to the staff, several doctors grumbled about the enormous workload and long hours they were required to work for valid reasons.

Academia

To finish off classroom interactions in academia, WFH mode was gradually replaced by Phygital or hybrid teaching-learning. Teachers and administrative staff were under a great deal of stress trying to keep up with the rapid changes in technology and adapt to the new age of digital learning. Yet, the majority of organizations adopted quasi-strategies to regularise the transition, such as regular meetings, webinars, counseling, and motivational sessions.

FUTURE RESEARCH DIRECTIONS

The chapter solely contains literature and an observation-based review of the information. It does not contain any primary data-based survey. In order to establish a statistically significant conclusion for data-based inference, a further quantitative analysis could be undertaken sector-wise. The chapter does not also furnish any solution and recommendation due lack of statistical analysis.

CONCLUSION

Comparing the consequences to the actual scenario has made them rather hazy. Since the pandemic brought about a profound transition, it was unable to proceed from a period of change momentum to one of slow transformation (The Teleological Motor theory). To further explain, the System Approach adopted radical changes based on the level of contamination and the contagiousness of the disease because incremental theory could not be used. According to field theory, the steps of Moving and Unfreezing have been used without enough time passing between them to deal with the urgency, such as executing government protocol and adopting the essential disruptive corporate strategies to further strengthen it. The Teleological Motor Theory's Change Momentum part, which attempted to accelerate the current status quo, were unable to be modified, despite the fact that business and governmental goal setting has historically depended on the circumstances. In order to distinguish between the stages of online, hybrid, and physical work modes, the Lifecycle Motor theory was put into practice during phase out. The Dialectical Motor hypothesis favours the situation that is most convenient by explaining the causes of organisational stress from both the employees' and employers' perspectives. The alteration of cognitive learning through counselling sessions, motivational sessions, webinars, seminars, and individual counselling through superior-subordinate interactions has also exhibited the Schematic modifications (Communicative Changes).

The Evolutionary Motor Theories are also applicable to how organisations adapt and take basic initiatives to balance the phase. As a consequence, the organisation engages in situational experimentation to find a balance between both the unfavourable scenario and organisational benefits (Internal Change Routine). The Appreciative Inquiry Model and The Action Research Model were also of little use due to its delinquency of urgency-based change without phase wise, planned and deep interventions. Though several sectoral corporates, especially in academics and information technology industry, utilized Appreciative Inquiry Model and The Action Research Model during re-opening phase with feedback system and counselling to re-establish and normalise employees' psychological stress pattern. Due to the lack availability of adequate long-term data, the effectiveness of the developmental strategies could not be evaluated further.

An empirical study from numerous industries revealed that the radical change brought on by government mandates was used more frequently than the incremental way of organizational development (Chakraborty, 2023). Yet, soft changes have been implemented throughout the phase-out of re-opening to relieve employees of additional emotional shock and hence both sides of the changes (Shut down and reopening) were not dealt in similar manner. While shutdown came as a drastic change, re-opening was done with a phase-out to help employees with a softer touch. Although the majority of organizations have tried to implement stress management to balance the recent changes made to the organization, these efforts have only been superficially undertaken without any deep intervention.

REFERENCES

Armenakis, A. A., & Bedeian, A. G. (1999). Organizational change: A review of theory and research in the 1990s. *Journal of Management*, *25*(3), 293–315. doi:10.1177/014920639902500303

Austin, J. R., & Bartunek, J. M. (2003). Theories and practices of organizational Development. W. Borman, D. Ilgen, R. Klimoski, and I.Weiner (ed.). Handbook of Psychology. John Wiley and sons, Inc, New York.

Berger, P., & Luckmann, T. (1966). *The social construction of reality*. Anchor Books.

Boutaud, N., Agarwal, A., Postel, E. A., & Pericak-Vance, M. A. (2005). Complement factor H variant increases the risk of age-related macular degeneration. *Science*, *308*(5720), 419–421. doi:10.1126cience.1110359 PMID:15761120

Burnes, B. (2004). Kurt Lewin and the planned approach to change: A re-appraisal. *Journal of Management Studies*, *41*(6), 977–1002. doi:10.1111/j.1467-6486.2004.00463.x

Bushe, G. R. (2011). Appreciative inquiry: Theory and critique. *The Routledge Companion to Organizational Change*, 87-102.

Cameron, K. S. (1984). The effectiveness of ineffectiveness. In B. M. Staw & L. L. Cummings (Eds.), *Research in organizational behaviour* (Vol. 6, pp. 235–285). JAI Press.

Cameron, K. S. (1986). Effectiveness as a paradox: Consensus and conflict in conceptions of organisational effectiveness. *Journal of Management Science*, *32*(5), 539–553.

Cameron, K. S., & Whetton, D. A. (1983). *Organisational effectiveness: A comparison of multiple models*. Academic Press.

Chakraborty, O. (2023). Theories and application of organisational change management during the COVID-19 era. In K. L. Tennin (Ed.), *Change management during unprecedented times* (pp. 155–185). IGI Global. doi:10.4018/978-1-6684-7509-6.ch008

Chambers, R. (2019). *Development*, *22*(7), 953–969.

Chaturvedi, S., Rizvi, I. A., & Pasipanodya, E. T. (2019). How can leaders make their followers to commit to the organization? The importance of influence tactics. *Global Business Review, 20*(6), 1462–1474. doi:10.1177/0972150919846963

Christopher, M., & András, T. (2013). Imprinting: Toward a multilevel theory. *The Academy of Management Annals, 7*(1), 195–245. doi:10.5465/19416520.2013.766076

Coghlan, D., & Brannick, T. (2014). *Doing action research in your own organization.* Sage.

Cooperrider, D. L., Peter, F. S. Jr, Whitney, D., & Yaeger, T. F. (2000). Appreciative inquiry: Rethinking human organization toward a positive theory of change. *Team Performance Management, 6*(7-8), 140–140.

Cooperrider, D. L., & Srivastva, S. (1987). Appreciative inquiry in organizational life. *Research in Organizational Change and Development, 1*(1), 129–169.

Cummings, T., & Worley, G. (2009). *Organization development & change* (9th ed.). South Western Cengage Learning.

Davidson, R., Goodwin-Stewart, J., & Kent, P. (2005). Internal governance structures and earnings management. *Accounting and Finance, 45*(2), 241–267. doi:10.1111/j.1467-629x.2004.00132.x

Dhawan, S. (2020). Online learning: A panacea in the time of COVID-19. Crisis. *Journal of Educational Technology Systems, 49*(1), 5–22. doi:10.1177/0047239520934018

Gallos, J. (2006). *Organization development: A jossey bass reader.* Jossey-Bass.

Giddens, A. (1984). *The construction of society.* University of California Press.

Goodman, P. S., & Pennings, J. M. (1977). *New perspectives on organisational effectiveness.* Jossey-Bass.

Hendry, C. (1996). Understanding and creating whole organizational change through learning theory. *Human Relations, 48*(5), 621–641. doi:10.1177/001872679604900505

Kaushik, M., & Guleria, N. (2020). The impact of pandemic COVID-19 in workplace. *European Journal of Business and Management, 12*(5), 9–18.

Kelly, D., & Amburgey, T. L. (1991). Organizational inertia and momentum: A dynamic model of strategic change. *Academy of Management Journal, 34*(3), 591–612. doi:10.2307/256407

Kotter, J. P. (1996). *Leading change.* Harvard Business School Press.

Kritsonis, A. (2005). Comparison of change theories. *International Journal of Scholarly Academic Intellectual Diversity, 8*(1), 1–7.

Lacey, M. Y. (1995). Internal consulting: Perspectives on the process of planned change. *Journal of Organizational Change Management, 8*(3), 75–84. doi:10.1108/09534819510090178

Lewin, K. (1946). Action research and minority problems. In G. W. Lewin (Ed.), *Resolving social conflict.* Harper & Row. doi:10.1111/j.1540-4560.1946.tb02295.x

Lewin, K. (1947). Frontiers in group dynamics II. Channels of group Life; Social Planning and Action Research. *Human Relations, 1*(2), 143–153. doi:10.1177/001872674700100201

Lewis, S., Passmore, J., & Cantore, S. (2008). Using appreciative inquiry in sales team development. *Industrial and Commercial Training, 40*(4), 175–180. doi:10.1108/00197850810876217

Lewitt, B., & March, J. G. (1988). Organizational learning. *Annual Review of Psychology, 14*, 319–340.

Mason, M. A. (2015). *What is a learning organization?* Moyak. https://www.moyak.com/papers/learning-organization.html

McLean, G. (2005). *Organization development: Principles, processes, performance.* Berrett-Koehler Publishers.

Mohr, L. B. (1971). Organisational technology and organisational structures. *Administrative Science Quarterly, 16*(4), 444–459. doi:10.2307/2391764

Mulili, B. M., & Wong, P. (2011). Continuous organizational development (COD). *Industrial and Commercial Training, 43*(6), 377–384. doi:10.1108/00197851111160513

Nelson, R. R., & Winter, S. G. (1982). *An evolutionary theory of economic change.* Belknap Press.

Pennings, J. M. (1975). The relevance of the structure-contingency model for organisational effectiveness. *Administrative Science Quarterly, 20*(3), 393–410. doi:10.2307/2391999

Pokhrel, S., & Chhetri, R. (2021). A literature review on impact of COVID-19 pandemic on teaching and learning. *Higher Education for the Future, 8*(1), 133–141. doi:10.1177/2347631120983481

Price, J. L. (1968). *Organisational effectiveness.* Richard D. Irwin, Inc.

Price, J. L. (1972). The study of organisational effectiveness. *The Sociological Quarterly, 13*(3), 3–15. doi:10.1111/j.1533-8525.1972.tb02100.x

Quinn, R. E., Spreitzer, G. M., & Brown, M. V. (2000). Changing others through changing ourselves: The transformation of human systems. *Journal of Management Inquiry, 9*(2), 47–164. doi:10.1177/105649260092010

Rajagopalan, N., & Spreitzer, G. M. (1996). Towards a theory of strategic change: A multi-lens perspective and integrative framework. *Academy of Management Review, 22*(1), 48–79. doi:10.2307/259224

Schein, E. H. (1996). *Organizational learning: What is new?* MIT. http://dspace.mit.edu/bitstream/handle/1721.1/2628/SWP-3912-35650568.pdf

Scott, R. W. (1987). *Organisations: Rational, natural, and open systems* (2nd ed.). Prentice Hall.

Seashore, S. E., & Yutchman, E. (1967). Factor analysis of organisational performance. *Administrative Science Quarterly, 12*(3), 377–395. doi:10.2307/2391311

Shearer, C. S., Hames, D. S., & Runge, J. B. (2001). How CEOs influence organizational culture following acquisitions. *Leadership and Organization Development Journal, 22*(3), 105–113. doi:10.1108/01437730110389256

Sintema, E. J. (2020). Effect of COVID-19 on the performance of grade 12 students: Implications for stem education. *Eurasia Journal of Mathematics, Science and Technology Education, 16*(7), 1–6. doi:10.29333/ejmste/7893

Van de Ven, A. H., & Poole, M. S. (1995). Explaining development and change in organizations. *Academy of Management Review*, *20*(3), 510–540. doi:10.2307/258786

Vygotsky, L. S. (1962). *Thought and language*. MIT Press. doi:10.1037/11193-000

Watzlawick, P., Weakland, J. H., & Fisch, R. (1974). *Change: principles of problem formation and problem resolution*. W. W. Norton.

Weick, K. E. (1995). *Sensemaking in organizations*. Sage.

Weick, K. E., & Quinn, R. E. (1999). Organizational change and development. *Annual Review of Psychology*, *50*(1), 361–386. doi:10.1146/annurev.psych.50.1.361 PMID:15012461

Wicks, P. G., & Reason, P. (2009). Initiating action research challenges and paradoxes of opening communicative space. *Action Research*, *7*(3), 243–262. doi:10.1177/1476750309336715

Wieman, J. M., & Giles, H. (1997): Azinterperszonáliskommunikáció In: Szociálpszichológiaszerk. KJK, Budapest.

KEY TERMS AND DEFINITIONS

Covid-19: COVID-19 is an infectious respiratory illness caused by the severe acute respiratory syndrome coronavirus 2 (SARS-CoV-2). It first emerged in Wuhan, China in December 2019 and has since spread globally, resulting in a pandemic. COVID-19 is primarily spread through respiratory droplets when an infected person talks, coughs, or sneezes, and can also be transmitted by touching a surface contaminated with the virus and then touching the mouth, nose, or eyes. Symptoms of COVID-19 can range from mild to severe and include fever, cough, fatigue, and shortness of breath. Some individuals may also experience loss of taste or smell, body aches, sore throat, and diarrhea. The severity of symptoms can vary widely and some people may not show any symptoms at all. COVID-19 can lead to severe respiratory illness, pneumonia, and in some cases, death, particularly among older adults and those with underlying health conditions. Vaccines and other preventive measures such as social distancing, wearing masks, and hand hygiene are effective ways to reduce the spread of COVID-19.

Deep Intervention: Deep intervention refers to a type of organizational intervention that involves significant and often transformative changes to an organization's structure, culture, and processes. Deep intervention typically goes beyond surface-level changes and involves a fundamental shift in the way an organization operates. This type of intervention may be necessary in situations where an organization is facing significant challenges such as declining performance, low employee morale, or a need for a major strategic shift. Examples of deep interventions include restructuring an organization's departments and reporting lines, implementing new technology or systems, overhauling the organization's culture, and redefining the organization's mission or purpose. Deep interventions require careful planning and execution, as they can have significant impacts on an organization's stakeholders, including employees, customers, and shareholders. Successful deep interventions can result in improved organizational effectiveness, increased employee engagement and satisfaction, and long-term growth and success.

Organisational Adaptation: Organizational Adaptation refers to the ability of an organization to adjust and modify its structures, processes, strategies, and behaviors in response to internal and external changes and challenges. It involves identifying and understanding shifts in the business environment, such as market trends, technological advancements, regulatory changes, or customer preferences, and making appropriate modifications to ensure the organization remains effective, competitive, and sustainable. Organizational adaptation often requires flexibility, innovation, and a willingness to embrace change.

Organisational Development: Organizational Development (OD) refers to the process of planning, implementing, and managing change in organizations in order to improve their overall effectiveness and performance. OD is a multidisciplinary field that draws on a variety of theories and practices from areas such as psychology, sociology, and management. The goal of OD is to help organizations improve their efficiency, adaptability, and competitiveness in a rapidly changing environment. This can involve a wide range of interventions, such as team building, leadership development, change management, and cultural transformation. OD practitioners typically work closely with organizational leaders, employees, and stakeholders to identify areas for improvement, develop strategies for change, and monitor progress over time. Successful OD initiatives can result in improved productivity, employee satisfaction, and organizational effectiveness, leading to long-term growth and success.

Organisational Effectiveness: Organizational effectiveness refers to an organization's ability to achieve its goals and objectives, while maintaining a high level of efficiency and maximizing its resources. It is a measure of how well an organization is using its resources to achieve its mission, vision, and strategic objectives. Organizational effectiveness is often measured through various key performance indicators (KPIs) such as revenue growth, profitability, employee engagement, customer satisfaction, and market share. A highly effective organization is one that can adapt to changing circumstances, innovate, and continuously improve its operations, products, and services. It is also one that has a strong and positive organizational culture, effective leadership, and a clear and compelling vision for the future. Organizational effectiveness is essential for long-term success and sustainability in today's rapidly changing business environment.

Phygital Work Mode: Phygital work mode refers to a hybrid approach that combines physical and digital elements in the way work is conducted. It involves integrating physical and digital environments, tools, and technologies to create a seamless and flexible work experience. In a phygital work mode, employees have the flexibility to work both in physical office spaces and remotely using digital platforms and tools. This approach aims to leverage the benefits of both physical and digital work environments, allowing for increased collaboration, productivity, and work-life balance.

Work From Home: Work from home refers to the practice of conducting one's job or professional activities remotely, typically from a personal residence or any location outside of a traditional office environment. It allows individuals to perform their job duties using technology and communication tools, eliminating the need for daily commuting, and enabling flexibility in terms of working hours and location.

Chapter 4
Green Knowledge in Urban Green Innovation Spaces and Green Roofs

José G. Vargas-Hernandez

Tecnológico Superior de Jalisco Mario Molina, Zapopan, Mexico

Teresa I. Salazar-Echeagaray

Universidad Autónoma de Sinaloa, Mexico

Omar C. Vargas-González

Tecnológico Nacional de Mexico, Ciudad Guzmán, Mexico

ABSTRACT

This study aims to analyze the implications of green knowledge and technology in organizational green innovation, urban green innovation, and green roofs. The analysis is supported by the assumption that green sharing knowledge and technology is basic to organizational green innovation and urban green innovation areas practices, operations, and activities. The methods employed are based on the analytical-reflective and descriptive supported with the review of theoretical and empirical literature. The analysis concludes that green knowledge sharing is relevant to create and develop green technology with positive implications for organizational green innovation, urban green innovation areas, and green roofs.

INTRODUCTION

The COVID-19 pandemic is a sanitary crisis that questions many activities to become greener and more sustainable. Sustainable and green are two concepts increasingly used to mean the same, however, sustainability refers to the persistence and indefinite future of necessary and desired characteristics of the human subsystem within and the ecosystem (Hodge, 1997).

Organizational environmental and green knowledge learning is linked to green technology for the environmental protection to stimulate organizational green innovation, urban green innovation areas and

DOI: 10.4018/978-1-6684-8392-3.ch004

green roofs. Sustainable development is related to decision making in the economic and social effects (Wiering, Liefferink, Boezeman, Kaufmann, Crabbé & Kurstjens, 2020). Sustainable development meets the needs of the present without compromising the ability of future generations to meet their own needs (Brundtland, 1987).

Urban sustainability including social and economic has been highlighted as one of the leading features of cities (Visit Berlin, 2017). Some green trends are proposed as smart city, sustainable city, and so forth. Use of green and ecofriendly technology offers more sustainability environment with zero gas emissions to the environment and some other opportunities and challenges.

People living in dense communities tend to use public urban green innovation spaces and public parks more frequently to have more relaxation time and may travel more to the countryside for leisure. Experimenting and testing new greener ways of conducting organizations concentrated on environmental sustainability, enable to introduce green innovations (Anderson et al., 2010; Stubbs & Cocklin, 2008). Organizations embracing the concept of saving money, by creating recycling programs and monitoring thermostats, focusing on environmental sustainability. Organizations may contribute to support nongovernmental agencies involved in environmental troublesome areas.

The frequency of use of a green space living environment support individuals to be satisfied with public spaces and improves the social space and the mental health (Hadavi, 2017). People using public and private urban green innovation spaces attach meanings, identity, and psychological experiences to diverse types of green spaces, as described in the Place identity integrated model and environmental representation (Bernardini & Irvine 2007). Research on green organization identity has focused on individual level (Chen & Chang, 2013; Chen, 2011). Green organizational identity supports individual tasks of organizational members related to the organizational environmental activities and strengthens the ability to cope with organizational green oriented conditions. Landscape connectivity has some differences between urban green innovation roofs and urban open space management.

Organizations are facing challenges regarding the compliance with green sustainability strategy. The deployment of a green strategy to face the negative effects that industrialization has on the environment. Organizational business sustainability considers the green growth, green branding, and green sustainable reporting. Branding sustainability enhances the ability of the organization to appeal customers concerned about the environment.

Green sustainable development combined with economic growth, social justice and progress and environmental security concepts are relevant issues in research such as green entrepreneurship in organic farming (Gupta & Vegelin, 2016; Mohd & Norhidayah, 2016; Savickiene & Miceikiene, 2018; Ihnatenko & Novak, 2018; Kucher, 2019; Shevchenko & Petrenko, 2020; Skydan, Nykolyuk, Pyvovar & Martynchuk, 2020). Not much research has addressed the integration of green roofs and urban green innovation space.

Organizations engage in green initiatives to develop sustainable competitive advantages and competitiveness (Wysocki, 2021; Galdeano-Gómez, Céspedes-Lorente, & Martínez-del-Río, 2008; López-Gamero, Claver-Cortés & Molina-Azorín, 2008). Sustainable components of organizations and business achieve competitive advantage (Namkung & Jang, 2012; Chang & Fong, 2010; Bansal, 2005; Barnet, 2007). Organizational business systems are the foundation for any kind of sustainable organizational business. Organizations are formulating and implementing green initiatives to attain sustainability and competitiveness (Chuang & Huang, 2015). The ecological partnership between organizations and society provides sustainable competitiveness.

The organizational ecological and sustainable procedures follow a strategic orientation (Fernandes & Solimun, 2017). Sustainability has been considered an added cost, but nowadays it is viewed as a sustainability strategy and tool to derive value and lead to innovation (Van Holt et al., 2020). An organizational shared vision enables development of green behaviors, making meaningful contributions (Renwick, Redman & Maguire, 2008; Aragon-Correa, Hurtado-Torres, Sharma & García-Morales, 2008).

BACKGROUND

Numerous studies, including Castro & Orellana (2019), deal with green roofs. They look at how adding green roofs could improve the sustainability and inventiveness of cities. According to the authors, green roofs can help create urban green innovation zones, which are intended to encourage sustainable urban growth by fusing green infrastructure and innovation. The paper includes a review of the literature on the advantages of green roofs, including how they can be incorporated into urban green innovation spaces and how they can reduce the effects of urban heat islands, improve stormwater management, and enhance biodiversity.

Another study by Klemm, Zinngrebe & Heidenreich (2019), they investigate the role of green roofs as part of urban green infrastructure and their potential to contribute to sustainable and innovative cities. The authors argue the challenges and barriers to the implementation of green roofs, such as lack of knowledge and expertise, and the need for supportive policies and regulations. The authors conclude that green roofs are a valuable component of urban green infrastructure for innovative cities, and that their full potential should be realized through supportive policies and regulations.

In addition, Hemsley-Brown & Laing (2019) focused their inquiry on potential roadblocks to the adoption of green roofs as a method for sustainable urban development. The lack of understanding and knowledge of green roofs, the high initial installation costs, the absence of encouraging policies and regulations, and the lack of incentives for property owners to install green roofs are just a few of the potential barriers that the authors identified after conducting a literature review. The study also looks at social and cultural variables including aesthetic preferences and notions of the worth of green space that could influence the adoption of green roofs. According to the authors, overcoming these obstacles would necessitate a multifaceted strategy involving cooperation amongst several stakeholders, including policymakers, researchers, practitioners, and the public.

A thorough analysis of the study on the influence of green roofs on the urban heat island effect is also provided by Palomino & Durán (2020). The urban heat island effect—a phenomenon in which urban regions experience hotter temperatures than their rural neighbors because of the built environment and human activity—and its causes are covered by the writers. For policymakers, practitioners, and academics interested in the conception and application of green roofs in urban environments, it emphasizes the potential of green roofs to reduce the urban heat island effect and enhance thermal comfort.

A thorough overview of the literature on the functions of green roofs in sustainable urban development is also provided by Wu & Jim (2021). The study addresses the advantages of green roofs, including how they lower the urban heat island effect, enhance biodiversity, improve stormwater management, and provide social benefits, as well as how these advantages support the broader objectives of sustainable urbanization. The authors conclude that green roofs are a significant part of urban green infrastructure, which is a network of green areas and green technologies that offer numerous social and environmental benefits, and that they have an enormous potential to support sustainable urban growth.

MAIN FOCUS OF THE CHAPTER

Green Knowledge and Technology

New knowledge in green organizational and business models is uncertain and volatile in business eco-system conditions, challenging risk management and decision-making. Technological knowledge of economic, social, and environmental benefits of constructing green roofs enhances the good construction of green roofs without any problems of maintaining the roof vegetation. Organizational green knowledge shares issues adopting a multilevel framework to make contributions to green technology. Organizational management must formulate green knowledge and green technology.

Knowledge management of environmental issues is a source for learning, solving problems and creating competitiveness (Liao, Chang, Cheng & Kuo, 2004). Green knowledge management is an effective tool for organizational improvement in transformation environment (Raudeli ̄ unien ̇ e, Davidavi ̌ cien ̇ e, Jakubavi ̌ cius, 2018). The dynamic complexity of organizational green innovation requires environmental knowledge learning (Li et al., 2019) and green technology. Organizational environmental green knowledge learning drives green innovation. Organizational environmental knowledge learning is linked to green technology for the environmental protection to stimulate green innovation (Redman, 2014).

Knowledge sharing is the basis for knowledge management (Zhang & Sundaresan, 2010). Green knowledge sharing in terms of sustainable development goals such as eliminating pollution, environmental protection, and SDGs, etc.) with other organizational members is good (Bock, Zmud, Kim & Lee, 2005). Green knowledge sharing is the behavior of organizational members who pass information, data and knowledge about green concerns and issues to other members and create new knowledge and learning opportunities to encourage others (Norton, Parker, Zacher & Ashkanasy, 2015; Chen & Chang, 2013).

Green Knowledge Sharing (GKS) is the organizational members' behavior, which means to pass on personal information and new knowledge learning opportunities about green issues to other members (Bock, Zmud, Kim & Lee, 2005). Green property psychological ownership and green knowledge sharing are influenced by green organizational identity. Knowledge sharing of people under pressure of time is reduced (Chang, Chen, Yeh & Li, 2020).

Organizational knowledge sharing focuses on creating an atmosphere of environmental protection to create green knowledge sharing related to green issues. Green technology is a socio-environmental healing technology capable to reduce environmental damages and degradation while conserving natural resources. Sustainable green technologies used in processes and applications do not create footprint (Aithal & Shubhrajyotsna, 2016).

Urban green innovation technology can be transferred by public government and confidential business pursuing inclusive green growth and ensuring social integration by eradicating poverty of vulnerable groups and maintaining the footprint of humanity within the ecological boundaries. Building an inclusive and green organization of available and retained talent is an arduous task (Goulden, Mason & Frasch 2011; Brands & Fernandez-Mateo, 2017). Green roof technology is used to tackle social and environmental concerns to enhance climate resilience. Green plant based green chemistry principles are used for green synthesis, nanomaterials, and nanoparticles (Maas & Hox, 2005). Green and eco-friendly nanotechnology based on green chemistry techniques tends to decrease the risks associated to industrial applications.

Green eco-friendly nanotechnology solutions used in sustainable development goals reduces the technification threat. Environmental degradation and climate pose a threat to global sustainable development and the Sustainable Development Goals. The concept of achieving sustainable development goals by means of using and developing proven green ecofriendly nanotechnology processes further accelerates the spread and growth of many other systems and devices.

Green nanotechnology is based in miniature sized communication and computational devices and nano sensor devices, high density, and memory chips. Ensuring ecological communication among the stakeholders disclose the relevance of environmental concerns (Abimbola, Lim, Hillestad, Xie & Haugland, 2010). Sustainable green nanotechnology principles and processes in the primary sector of the economy is related to the extraction of raw materials from nature.

Long-term effects of human food are required by green manufactured nanomaterials designed according to principles of green nanotechnology complemented with current regulations aimed to address sustainable development of green technology. Manufactured and processed inorganic food has increased the cases of illnesses leading to healthy food safety. Green design and development of health and environment using nanoscale materials is a concern to improve sustainable solutions. Green synthesis methods can be used to take care of adverse effects on nanomaterials on the environment and user health. Complementarity of mixed methods to detect contradictions, improve the results of one method using the results of the other method and enhance the scope and breath for different components of research (Greene et al. 1989).

Green nanotechnology in the service industry is intangible in nature and affected directly and indirectly. Green nanotechnology innovates in educational technology through higher quality and low-cost and ubiquitous online education. ICCT technologies working with green nanotechnology provide intelligent services in artificial intelligence, internet of things, cloud and quantum computing, 3D printing, etc. Green nanotechnology supports ICCT technologies to develop super-intelligent machines and human beings. Green nanotechnology improves the durability, speed, and reachability of digital entertainment instruments (Aithal & Shubhrajyotsna, 2018).

Organizational Green Innovation

Organizational green business innovations follow the principles, values and norms of economic concern, societal parity, and ecological accountability (Alawattage & Fernando, 2017). New green organizational innovations are created either in-house or external. Organizational green innovation activities are stimulated by green contexts-oriented factors. Organizations have attached more relevance to environmental issues based on green organizational identity that enhances organizational green innovation and competitiveness and ensures organizational competitive advantages (Geraie 2015). Organizational identity theory and psychological ownership theory are combined to integrate a conceptual model.

Organizational green process innovation is friendly to the environment through developing processes of manufacturing goods according to their cycle (Chiou, Chan, Lettice & Chung, 2011; Kam-Sing 2012). Organizational green innovation and actions are designed to reduce adverse environmental consequences. There is a relationship between organizational green innovation strategy and actions because the green innovation behaviors conducted under a strategy.

Motivational mechanisms stimulate innovation to facilitate organizational green innovation. Motivated organizational stakeholders to pursue collective efforts towards green innovative outcomes with their teammates lead with values of organizational green innovation (Norton, Parker, Zacher & Ashkanasy, 2015; Jabbour, Santos, Fonseca & Nagano, 2013). According to meta-analytical research, prosocial motivation is a mechanism to link contextual factors and innovative and creative outcomes (Liu, Jiang, Shalley, Keem & Zhou, 2016).

Organizational green innovation addresses the potential risks and challenges of implementing innovative resources and inputs supported by green efficacy (Liu, Chen & Tao, 2015). Green organizational innovation is related to individual tasks of organizational environmental activities to strengthen the organization Society gives relevance to environmental issues and concerns where green organizational identity enhancing organizational creativity and innovation and ensuring sustainable competitive advantages (Geraie, 2015). Social acceptance enables the organization to attain and develop sustainable organizational green competitiveness capability.

The green competitive advantage is the concept describing the conditions to hold a position in sustainable and ecological management and innovation of the firm which cannot be imitated by others (Lin & Chen, 2017). Resources and capabilities that are not imitable provide sustainable competitive advantage (Barney, 1991). The resource-based view of organizational research focuses on the characterization of organizations (Pereira & Vence, 2012) and organizational resources and capabilities (Fong & Chang, 2012; Marchi, 2012) such as organizational redundancy, innovation capabilities, network, embedding, strategy orientation and green innovation strategy as the drivers of green innovation practices.

Organizations depend on intangible resources to enhance environmental sustainability (Singh, Del Giudice, Chierici & Graziano, 2020). In a resource intensive sector, a green pioneer organization must have an organizational model (Elkington,1994) with a social and environmental impact.

Human resources green management deals with valuable organizational resources and assets considered based on environmental sustainability. There is evidence that the workforce engages strongly about the environmental sustainability development and become more organizational committed and satisfied. Human resource green management is engaged in organizational environmental sustainability management (Wirtenberg, Harmon, Russell & Fairfield, 2007; Shoeb & Nisar, 2015).

Green dynamic capability is in the nature within the organization processes. The green dynamic capabilities are permanently dependable in the organizations (Chen, 2008).

Urban Green Innovation Spaces and Green Roofs

The rapid growth of the urban population and the low rate of economic development due to the pandemic, are leading to serious civilization problems, among others the lack of urban greener innovations spaces, pollution, and lack of health. Smart growth is supported by sustainable growth based on adoption of greener, efficient technologies, inclusive growth, fostering employment and social cohesion (Gunn & Mintrom, 2016). Organizations must take an approach to stay in inclusive green organizations embracing elements such as equity and social justice needed to create goals, formulate, and implement strategies and develop public commitment (Johnson, 2017).

Organizational green innovation refers to the innovation that emphasizes the implementation of organizational green culture, environmental prevention of pollution and waste reduction to enhance organizational sustainability. Urban green innovation areas are increasing in green metropolis driven by the preservation and expansion of sustainable environmental development (Kalandides, 2021).

Urban green innovation spaces must be defined by the limits of construction and protection. The interactions of people and urban green innovation spaces are divided in public and private (Vijayaraghavan, 2016). Public and private urban green innovation spaces co-exist and can be incorporated green roofs as open green spaces aimed to use multi-functionality framed in an effective landscape management.

Public and private green spaces have differences in perception (Coolen & Meesters 2012) although they should co-exist (Mesimaki, et al. 2017).

People have different perceptions on private and green urban spaces with social identity and environmental sustainability. Green behaviors are defined as the actions and behaviors on which employees engage linked with and contribute to environmental sustainability (Ones & Dilchert, 2012, p. 87). This concept includes voluntary green behaviors beyond the job tasks referred as organizational citizenship, also considered as task-related environmental behavior (Boiral & Paillé, 2012; Bissing-Olson, Iyer, Fielding & Zacher, 2013). Sustainable development and green jobs guidelines are adopted by the international labor organization (ILO) for a transition towards environmentally sustainable societies and economies (ILO, 2015).

The disappearance of green urban areas due to residential and commercial purposes, enhanced by the urban sprawl, leads to loss of habitats, biodiversity, and recreation areas, and decrease of natural resources and elements (Burszta-Adamiak & Fiałkiewicza, 2019). Urban green spaces with high social and environmental vulnerability are the most urbanized areas with high land temperature might be prioritized for the implementation of urban green innovation areas and green roofs.

Traditional streets can be transformed into green urban connecting areas considered as an open space system and park lands. An urban green innovation belt prevents urban expansion and urban sprawl by merging with nearby settlements. Greenbelt conserves accessibility of open spaces along roadways and connect to a regional trail. Nevertheless, greenbelt was not successful to prevent urban expansion and sprawl but facilitates the access to open spaces (Maruani & Amit-Cohen, 2007).

Intensification of investments to develop accessible green spaces conceived to cover economic, social and leisure needs, and activities contribute to create the sense of community and respond to the pressures of construction. Urban green innovation areas are open to enhance urban green innovation space networks and extend the green infrastructure with the functions of green roofs (Fung, 2018).Green infrastructure is the urban physical environment in a network of green open spaces that brings economic, social, and environmental benefits to residents of communities in cities, towns, and villages (TEP 2005).

Green infrastructure is a way to create an attractive environment, increase the urban resilience benefits by better managing stormwater, mitigating the urban heat island effect, purifying air. Green roofs are considered passive open green spaces that have environmental benefits and provide open spaces for more urban livability (Mesimaki, et al. 2017). Eco roofs are required for new city infrastructures and facilities. Multi-functional urban green innovation infrastructure should allocate funding for green initiatives of development.

Scholars like Vijayaraghavan (2016) have applied quantitative and qualitative analysis to address the needs and perceptions of people on green roofs. The environmental effectiveness of green roofs should improve public health and connect the social needs of vulnerable people (Vijayaraghavan, 2016). Green roofs and solar and living roofs considered a multi-benefit asset bringing significant economic benefits beyond stormwater management, energy efficiency for cooling, improving air quality, reducing urban heat island. Loss of green spaces intensify heat island effect and storm water runoffs. The development of urban green innovation spaces and roofs are required to comply with regulations on stormwater control. A motivation program for the installation of eco roofs provides incentives to better management of the stormwater.

Green roofs have historically evolved from the hanging gardens in Babylon embracing the aesthetic values and facilitating the human interactions and increase the insulation. Le Corbusier applied green roofs to modern architecture. (Berardi, GhaffarianHoseini & GhaffarianHoseini, 2014). In Germany followed by France and Switzerland occurred the research and implementation of green roofs. In Portland, USA in 2005 requires the city-owned buildings to build green roof while Toronto passed a bylaw requiring all the new developed buildings. In Tokyo, the new constructed buildings must have green roofs (Vijayaraghavan, 2016).

Urban green innovation areas should provide spaces for green infrastructure solutions such as the building green roofs, which have beneficial influence on the urban environment. The stage of operation of green infrastructure is the maintenance solutions. The green infrastructure is single function derived from the ability to effectively manage stormwater and focusing on ecological landscape conservation than social and economic benefits (Mell, 2010). Urban green innovation roofs integrated into open space management have multifunctional opportunities to develop green infrastructure and benefits in urban communities and neighborhoods. Private and public green roofs as open spaces a multi-functional green infrastructure and should accommodate the urban open space needs of residents (Meerow & Newell, 2017).

Well-developed urban green innovation infrastructure needs to be supported by a multi-faceted approach. The increasing awareness of green roofs to alleviate global and local environmental impacts. Vegetated green roofs reduce carbon dioxide (CO_2) in the atmosphere naturally sequestered through the photosynthesis processes (Rowe, 2011). It has been confirmed the capacity of green roofs to retain rainwater, reduce air pollutants and improve microclimate that have a positive influence in urban heat island effect (Shafi que, Kim & Rafi q, 2018; Burszta-Adamiak, Stańczyk & Łomotowski, 2019).

There are diverse types of intensive and extensive green roofs which include vegetation with different soil depth and weight, irrigation, plant species and maintenance. Urban green innovation projects include urban gardening, permaculture, guerrilla gardening, smart city and building architecture. Productive urban green innovation combines urban agriculture, allotment gardens and self-sufficiency culture ecologically motivated (Plattform produktives Stadtgrün, 2020; Chen, Lin, Lin, Hung, Chang & Huang, 2020).

Mitigation of greenhouse gas emission technique to improve the environmental impact of agriculture needs to consider animal welfare the largest anthropogenic contributor (Llonch, Haskell, Dewhurst & Turner, 2017; Reisinger & Clark, 2018; Kucher, Heldak & Orlenko, 2018). Wasteland spaces can be converted into a place of productive greenery and developed into natural and green innovation areas that preserve and increase the ecological value and be used also as place for joint creation and learning, (Nachhaltiges, 2020; Green, 2020).

Rehabilitation of buildings using energy optimization should consider the creation of new alternative green spaces transformed into green innovation areas for free recreational purposes. Green roofs provide leisure spaces and enhance aesthetical values of buildings (Sutton, 2014) reduce carbon footprint in urban areas (Ugai, 2016) and direct water footprint (Fialkiewicz et al., 2018). Matching urban places needing urban green innovation areas and green roofs in suitable buildings to determine opportunities to implement in communities and neighborhood.

Administrative and technical support are necessary in designing, constructing, developing, and maintaining urban green innovation areas and green roofs. This task recommendation enhances the allocation of urban green innovation areas based on the structural design of buildings and the surrounding environmental characteristics in the community. The design and construction of green roofs need to consider the plant species and the development of small fauna.

The construction and application of green roofs can be achieved in large urban areas are located near another urban constructed areas and should not be single investments. Stovin, Vesuviano & Kasmin (2012) calculate that the surface of roofs accounts for almost 50% of the sealed urban areas with the potential for urban green innovation roofs. Green roofs decrease the costs for discharging snowmelt and stormwater.

The infrastructure of green storm water initiative reduces greenhouse gas emissions and improves the air quality. The development initiatives of green roofs are linked with storm water management to meet the flood management control required.

A study that uses standards from the Forschungsanstalt Landschaftsentwicklung Landschaftsbau (FLL) to examine the viability and utility of creating green roofs The FLL guidelines are used as the basis for the construction of green roofs. Vegetation on green roof infiltration reduces the stormwater runoff. Vegetated surfaces may utilize public facilities to demonstrate a mandate of a green buffer surrounded by parking facilities that may also function as a stormwater infiltration. Green stormwater infrastructure reduces the demand of grey stormwater infrastructure, enhancing the climate resilience (FLL, 2002).

Local building codes must allow green roofs exempted from the building floor area and related to open spaces. The incentives for zoning to encourage the implementation of the urban green innovation roof should include the development of parking landscapes as one measure adopted in a stormwater management plan that may provide solutions (Murray, 2017).

The development of green roofs value investments as an additional incentive for potential customers. Meeting the ecological needs of customers (Jain & Kaur, 2004). There is a trend of organizations to shift operations towards the direction of environment-friendly processes despite the challenges of customer cynicism regarding organizational green actions (Kumar & Christodoulopoulou, 2014). Co-financing and local legal regulations for the construction of green roofs are most often used incentives. Green development finance has been assigned to Multilateral Development Banks, alongside public-private partnerships (PPPs) and new forms of finance, blended finance, bond instruments, green bonds, social impact bonds and development impact bonds. Urban green innovation roofs are the result of the implementation of motivational tools and other incentives for the different stakeholders.

The existence of types of barriers encourages local authorities to improve the use of incentives for the creation and functioning of urban green innovation areas and urban green innovation roofs. The most commonly use of incentives are the direct ones and legal regulations for the construction of regulations (Mentens, Raes & Hermy, 2006). Incentives must be translated from sufficient interest into motivation for the excessively strict requirements for the construction of green roofs such as the minimum surface area, to become eligible for co-financing and tax allowance.

Market demand-related incentives such as promotional instruments, are tools to determine demand for buildings with greenery in comparison to traditional. The implementation of financial and non-financial incentives is a crucial factor for the green roofs as a relevant element of urban environment (Brudermann & Sangkakool, 2017). Financial incentives include subsidies or donations granted to reimburse costs of investments that are aimed to support potential investors.

The development of rural and urban green innovation tourism close to nature and based on settlements is becoming more relevant for the impact on green economy and ecology, with the self-employment of residents to provide environmentally accommodation and food to the visitors (Tomashuk & Baldynyuk, 2021; Kolomiets & Tomashuk, 2021; Mazur & Tomashuk, 2019). The green economy development and the pursuit of environmental protection is bringing profits to the organizations (Chen, Lai & Wen, 2006).

SOLUTIONS AND RECOMMENDATIONS

Case Studies

The following case studies are included, and a comparison is made between them, for a better understanding of green roofs. Both the Nogué& Sala (2018) inquiry and the Gong, Li, & Li (2020) study concentrate on the utilization of green roofs in urban green innovation areas. The potential of green roofs to support sustainable urban growth and innovation is highlighted by both studies. While Nogué & Sala (2018) offers a broader perspective on the motivations, advantages, and challenges of implementing green roofs in urban green innovation spaces, Gong, Li & Li (2020) provides a more in-depth analysis of the design features and effectiveness of green roofs.

The scope and focus of the studies do vary, though. A case study of green roofs in Beijing is presented by Gong, Li, & Li (2020), who also examine their design elements and efficiency in increasing urban green innovation spaces. They offer suggestions on how to design and deploy green roofs to support sustainable urban development and innovation for policymakers and practitioners. The case study of the usage of green roofs in urban green innovation areas in Barcelona is presented by Nogué & Sala (2018) in contrast. The study investigates the reasons for installing green roofs in urban green innovation areas, the advantages, and difficulties of doing so, and the part stakeholders play in the planning and maintenance of green roofs.

Furthermore, Li, Yin, Li, Sun, Li, & Li (2021) and Tan, Wong, Tan & Wong (2019) are two further case studies that have been compared. In both cases, case studies of green roofs in urban green innovation spaces are presented. The potential of green roofs to support sustainable urban growth and innovation is emphasized in both studies. However, Li, Yin, Li, Sun, Li, & Li (2021) provides a more detailed analysis of the design and implementation of green roofs in specific urban green innovation spaces, while Tan, Wong, Tan, & Wong (2019) offers a broader perspective on the policies and regulations that have facilitated the implementation of green roofs in an entire city.

The scope and focus of the studies, on the other hand, varied to some extent. A case study on the use of green roofs in urban green innovation areas in Jinan City, China, is presented by Li, Yin, Li, Sun, Li, & Li (2021). They evaluate the effectiveness of green roofs in providing a variety of environmental and social benefits, including lowering the urban heat island effect, enhancing air quality, and supplying space for community activities. They analyze the design and implementation of green roofs in a community garden and on a university campus. The examination also analyses the difficulties and potential associated with implementing green roofs in Jinan City and offers suggestions for future studies and government initiatives.

In contrast, a case study of green roof innovation in Singapore is presented by Tan, Wong, Tan, and Wong (2019). They look at the laws and policies that have made it easier for green roofs to be installed in Singapore, how well they work at offering a variety of environmental and social advantages, and what obstacles stand in the way of their use. They also offer suggestions on how to design and execute green roofs in Singapore and other urban contexts for policymakers and practitioners.

Finally, a comparison between the studies conducted by Scharenbroch & Bucci (2017) and Kazemi, Khan & Shafique (2018). Both studies examine how well urban areas with green roofs perform ecosystem services. Both articles highlight the potential of green roofs to provide ecosystem services to cities, but Kazemi et al. (2018) offer a more in-depth analysis of the environmental and financial advantages of green roofs in a particular urban setting, while Scharenbroch & Bucci (2017) provide a wider perspective on the biodiversity and ecological advantages of green roofs in a larger urban region.

Their research's breadth and focus, however, differs in some ways. In their 2018 paper, Kazemi, Khan, & Shafique gives a case study of the installation of green roofs in Calgary, Canada, and assess how well they contribute to environmental sustainability in urban settings. The authors examine the financial and environmental advantages of green roofs in lowering urban heat.

FUTURE RESEARCH DIRECTIONS

Future research must address the integration of green roofs and urban green innovation spaces focusing more on green organization and community identity that on individual level.

Further research should be conducted on green sustainable development combined with economic growth, social justice and progress and environmental security concepts and relevant issues in urban green innovation areas and green roofs, and green entrepreneurship in organic farming, just to mention two.

Research must focus on the resource-based view of urban green innovation areas including the relationship with the characterization of organizations and communities involved in urban green innovation areas and green roofs.

CONCLUSION

This study analyzes the organizational environmental and green knowledge learning is linked to green technology for the environmental protection to stimulate organizational green innovation, urban green innovation areas and green roofs.

Organizations transform to mitigate and neutralize the environmental impact and to adapt environmental sustainability. Green transformation is a multifaceted process incorporating interconnected and overlapping processes posing several managerial challenges. Environmental community involvement promotes and improve the natural environment aiming to sustainable growth of society, inspiring for voluntary participation in social activities. The green government should make and secure access to affordable sustainable housing in urban green innovation spaces and open buildings to create an urban social cohesion process consolidated in urban social movements.

Organizational networks are vital to connecting each other in the space of a green movement. The environmental movements along the nongovernment organizations and environmental foundations lack of racial diversity despite the efforts to increase diversity and inclusion (Johnson, 2019) Residents also express their intentions to be involved in discussions and debates to develop a green urban framework.

Adding green components to technology can become sustainable green technologies able to avoid degradation and provide clean environment. Green roof technology is used to tackle social and environmental concerns to enhance climate resilience. Green roof is related to be linked to resilience, restorative, and accessible. Green nanotechnology represents opportunities and challenges in industry to encourage growth by supporting nanotechnology usage.

Gain competitive advantage through the implementation of a sustainable organizational strategy is relevant for the survival. The organizational green shared vision should involve sustainable business goals. Long-term organizational green innovation strategy must stimulate followers to implement green operations. Organizational socio ecological strategies are formulated an implemented to achieve green competitiveness (Wang, Hu, Dai, & Burns, 2021).

REFERENCES

Abimbola, T., Lim, M., Hillestad, T., Xie, C., & Haugland, S. A. (2010). Innovative corporate social responsibility: The founder's role in creating a trustworthy corporate brand through "green innovation.". *Journal of Product and Brand Management, 19*(6), 440–451. doi:10.1108/10610421011085758

Aithal, P. S. & Shubhrajyotsna Aithal. (2018). Nanotechnology based Innovations and Human Life Comfortability –Are we Marching towards Immortality? *International Journal of Applied Engineering and Management Letters, 2*(1), 1–8. doi:10.5281/zenodo.1485048

Alawattage, C., & Fernando, S. (2017). Postcoloniality in corporate social and environmental accountability. *Accounting, Organizations and Society, 60*, 1–20. doi:10.1016/j.aos.2017.07.002

Anderson, R., Amodeo, M., & Harzfeld, J. (2010). Changing business cultures from within. The World watch Institute.

Aragon-Correa, J. A., Hurtado-Torres, N. E., Sharma, S., & García-Morales, V. J. (2008). Environmental strategy and performance in small firms: A resource-based perspective. *Journal of Environmental Management, 86*(1), 88–103. doi:10.1016/j.jenvman.2006.11.022 PMID:17239519

Bansal, P. (2005). Evolving sustainably: A longitudinal study of corporate sustainable development. *Strategic Management Journal, 26*(3), 197–218. doi:10.1002mj.441

Barnet, M. L. (2007). Stakeholder influence capacity and the variability of financial returns to corporate social responsibility. *Academy of Management Review, 33*(3), 794–816. doi:10.5465/amr.2007.25275520

Barney, J. (1991). Firm Resources and Sustained Competitive Advantage. *Journal of Management, 17*(1), 99–120. doi:10.1177/014920639101700108

Berardi, U., GhaffarianHoseini, A. H., & GhaffarianHoseini, A. (2014). State-of-the-art analysis of the environmental benefits of green roofs. *Applied Energy, 115*, 411–428. doi:10.1016/j.apenergy.2013.10.047

Berlin, G. (2020). *Capital of Green Trends: How Berlin leads the Way in Urban Sustainability.* Visit Berlin. https://about.visitberlin.de/en/green berlin

Berlin, N. (2020). *Stadt der grünen Trends-Wie Berlin den Weg der urbanen Nachhaltigkeit geht.* Visit Berlin. https://about.visitberlin.de/nachhaltiges-berlin

Bernardini, C, & Irvine, K. (2007). The 'nature' of urban sustainability: private or public green spaces? *Transactions on Ecology and the Environment,* 661-673.

Bissing-Olson, M. J., Iyer, A., Fielding, K. S., & Zacher, H. (2013). Relationships between daily affect and pro-environmental behavior at work: The moderating role of pro-environmental attitude. *Journal of Organizational Behavior, 175*(2), 156–175. doi:10.1002/job.1788

Bock, G. W., Zmud, R. W., Kim, Y. G., & Lee, J. N. (2005). Behavioral intention formation in knowledge sharing: Examining the roles of extrinsic motivators, social-psychological forces, and organizational climate. *Management Information Systems Quarterly, 2005*(29), 87–112. doi:10.2307/25148669

Boiral, O., & Paillé, P. (2012). Organizational citizenship behaviour for the environment: Measurement and validation. *Journal of Business Ethics, 109*(4), 431–445. doi:10.100710551-011-1138-9

Brands, R. A., & Fernandez-Mateo, I. (2017). Leaning out: How negative recruitment experiences shape women's decisions to compete for executive roles. *Administrative Science Quarterly, 62*(3), 405–442. doi:10.1177/0001839216682728

Brudermann, T., & Sangkakool, T. (2017). Green roofs in temperate climate cities in Europe - An analysis of key decision factors. *Urban Forestry & Urban Greening, 21*, 224–234. doi:10.1016/j.ufug.2016.12.008

Brundtland, G. (1987). *Our Common Future: The World Commission on Environment and Development.* Oxford University Press.

Burszta-Adamiak, E., & Fiałkiewicza, W. (2019). Review of green roof incentives as motivators for the expansion of green infrastructure in European cities. *Scientific Review – Engineering and Environmental Sciences* (2019), *28* (4), 641–652.

Burszta-Adamiak, E., Stańczyk, J., & Łomotowski, J. (2019). Hydrological performance of green roofs in the context of the meteorological factors during the 5-year monitoring period. *Water and Environment Journal : the Journal / the Chartered Institution of Water and Environmental Management, 33*(1), 144–154. doi:10.1111/wej.12385

Castro, A. J. L., & Orellana, F. (2019). Green roofs as a strategy for urban green innovation spaces. *Sustainable Cities and Society, 44*, 697–705. doi:10.1016/j.scs.2018.10.034

Chang, N. J., & Fong, C. M. (2010). Green product quality, green corporate image, green customer satisfaction, and green customer loyalty. *African Journal of Business Management, 4*(13), 2336–2344.

Chang, T. W., Chen, Y. S., Yeh, Y. L., & Li, H. X. (2020). Sustainable consumption models for customers: Investigating the significant antecedents of green purchase behavior from the perspective of information asymmetry. *Journal of Environmental Planning and Management, 2020*, 1–21.

Chen, Y. S. (2008). The driver of green innovation and green image–green core competence. *Journal of Business Ethics, 81*(3), 531–543. doi:10.100710551-007-9522-1

Chen, Y. S., & Chang, C. H. (2013). The determinants of green product development performance: Green dynamic capabilities, green transformational leadership, and green creativity. *Journal of Business Ethics, 2013*(116), 107–119. doi:10.100710551-012-1452-x

Chen, Y. S., Lai, S. B., & Wen, C. T. (2006). The influence of green innovation performance on corporate advantage in Taiwan. *Journal of Business Ethics, 2006*(67), 331–339. doi:10.100710551-006-9025-5

Chen, Y. S., Lin, S. H., Lin, C. Y., Hung, S. T., Chang, C. W., & Huang, C. W. (2020). Improving green product development performance from green vision and organizational culture perspectives. *Corporate Social Responsibility and Environmental Management, 2020*(27), 222–231. doi:10.1002/csr.1794

Chiou, T. Y., Chan, H. K., Lettice, F., & Chung, S. H. (2011). The influence of greening the suppliers and green innovation on environmental performance and competitive advantage in Taiwan. *Transportation Research Part E, Logistics and Transportation Review, 2011*(47), 822–836. doi:10.1016/j.tre.2011.05.016

Coolen, H., & Meesters, J. (2012). Private and public green spaces: Meaningful but different settings. *Journal of Housing and the Built Environment, 27*(1), 49–67. doi:10.100710901-011-9246-5

Elkington, J. (1994). Towards the sustainable corporation: Win-win-win business strategies for sustainable development. *Cal. Manag. Rev. 36* (3), 90e100.

Fernandes, A. A. R., & Solimun. (2017). The mediating effect of strategic orientation and innovations on the effect of environmental uncertainties on the performance of business in the Indonesian aviation industry. *International Journal of Law and Management, 59*(6), 1269–1278. doi:10.1108/IJLMA-10-2016-0087

Fialkiewicz, W., Burszta-Adamiak, E., Kolonko-Wiercik, A., Manzardo, A., Loss, A., Mikovits, C., & Scipioni, A. (2018). Simplified direct water footprint model to support urban water management. *Water (Basel), 10*(5), 630. doi:10.3390/w10050630

Fong, C. M., & Chang, N. J. (2012). The impact of green learning orientation on proactive environmental innovation capability and firm performance. *African Journal of Business Management, 6*(32), 727–735.

Forschungsanstalt Landschaftsentwicklung Landschaftsbau [FLL] (2002). *Dachbegrünungsrichtlinie. Richtlinien für die Planung, Ausführung und Pflege von Dachbegrünungen [Green roof policy. Guidelines for the planning, execution, and maintenance of green roofs]*. Bonn: Forschungsanstalt Landschaftsentwicklung Landschaftsbau.

Fung, K. L. (2018). *Expanding the green network on rooftops: A study of integrating green roofs as a part of urban green innovation space planning* (Order No. 10932095 ProQuest One Academic. http://wdg.biblio.udg.mx:2048/login?url=https://www.proquest.com/dissertations-theses/expanding-green-network-on-rooftops-study/docview/2124999351/se-2?accountid=28915 https://www.proquest.com/docview/2124999351?pqorigsite=gscholar&fromopenview=true

Galdeano-Gómez, E., Céspedes-Lorente, J., & Martínez-del-Río, J. (2008). Environmental performance and spillover effects on productivity: Evidence from horticultural firms. *Journal of Environmental Management, 88*(4), 1552–1561. doi:10.1016/j.jenvman.2007.07.028 PMID:17825476

Geraie, M. S., & Rad, F. M. (2015). Mediator role of the organizational identity green in relationship between total quality management and perceived innovation with sustainable competitive advantage. *International Journal of Biology, Pharmacy and Allied Sciences, 2015*(4), 266–276.

Gong, Y., Li, X., & Li, Z. (2020). How to design green roofs to enhance urban green innovation space? Evidence from Beijing. *Habitat International, 107*, 102–113. doi:10.1016/j.habitatint.2020.102113

Goulden, M., Mason, M. A., & Frasch, K. (2011). Keeping women in the science pipeline. *The Annals of the American Academy of Political and Social Science, 638*(1), 141–162. doi:10.1177/0002716211416925

Greene, J. C., Caracelli, V. J., & Graham, W. F. (1989). Toward a conceptual framework for mixed-method evaluation designs. *Educational Evaluation and Policy Analysis, 11*(3), 255–274. doi:10.3102/01623737011003255

Gunn, A., & Mintrom, M. (2016). Higher Education Policy Change in Europe: Academic Research Funding and the Impact Agenda. *European Education, 48*(4), 241–257. doi:10.1080/10564934.2016.1237703

Gupta, J., & Vegelin, C. (2016). Sustainable development goals and inclusive development. *International Environmental Agreement: Politics, Law and Economics, 16*(3), 433–448. doi:10.100710784-016-9323-z

Hadavi, S. (2017). Direct and indirect effects of the physical aspects of the environment on mental well-being. *Environment and Behavior, 2017*(49), 1071–1104. doi:10.1177/0013916516679876

Hemsley-Brown, T., & Laing, A. (2019). Green roofs and sustainable urban development: An exploratory review of potential barriers to adoption. *Sustainable Cities and Society, 50*, 101648. doi:10.1016/j.scs.2019.101648

Hodge, T. (1997). Toward a conceptual framework for assessing progress toward sustainability. *Social Indicators Research, 1997*(40), 5–98. doi:10.1023/A:1006847209030

Ihnatenko, M., & Novak, N. (2018). Development of regional programs for the development of agrarian enterprises with organic production based on the European and international experience. *Baltic Journal of Economic Studies, 4*(4), 126–133. doi:10.30525/2256-0742/2018-4-4-126-133

ILO. (2015). *News*. ILO. https://www.ilo.org/global/topics/green-jobs/news/WCMS_42257 5/lang--en/index.htm

Jabbour, C. J. C., Santos, F. C. A., Fonseca, S. A., & Nagano, M. S. (2013). Green teams: Understanding their roles in the environmental management of companies located in Brazil. *Journal of Cleaner Production, 2013*(46), 58–66. doi:10.1016/j.jclepro.2012.09.018

Jain, S. K., & Kaur, G. (2004). Green marketing: an Indian perspective. *Decision* (0304-0941), *31*(2), 161–209.

Johnson, S. K. (2017). What 11 CEOs have learned about championing diversity. *Harvard Business Review*.

Johnson, S. K. (2019) *Leaking Talent How People of Color are Pushed Out of Environmental Organizations. Diverse Green*. diversegreen.org/research/leaking-talent/

Kalandides, A., & Grésillon, B. (2021). The Ambiguities of "Sustainable" Berlin. *Sustainability (Basel), 2021*(13), 1666. doi:10.3390u13041666

Kam-Sing Wong, S. (2012). The influence of green product competitiveness on the success of green product innovation: Empirical evidence from the Chinese electrical and electronics industry. *European Journal of Innovation Management, 2012*(15), 468–490. doi:10.1108/14601061211272385

Kazemi, F., Khan, M. S., & Shafique, M. (2018). Green roofs as an innovative urban infrastructure for environmental sustainability: A case study of Calgary, Canada. *Environmental Science and Pollution Research International, 25*(27), 27411–27423. doi:10.100711356-018-2649-6

Klemm, W., Zinngrebe, Y., & Heidenreich, S. (2019). Green roofs as part of urban green infrastructure for innovative cities. *Environmental Innovation and Societal Transitions, 31*, 50–56. doi:10.1016/j.eist.2018.11.003

Kolomiets T.V., Tomashuk I.V. (2021). Entrepreneurship and development of rural areas in Ukraine. *Colloquium-journal, 9*(96).

KucherA. (2019), *Sustainable soil management in the formation of competitiveness of agricultural enterprises.* Academic Publishing House «Talent», Plovdiv, Bulgaria. doi:10.13140/RG.2.2.19554.07366

KucherL.HeldakM.OrlenkoA. (2018). Project management in organic agricultural production. *Agricultural and Resource Economics, 4*(3), pp. 104–128. doi:10.22004/ag.econ.281753

Kumar, V., & Christodoulopoulou, A. (2014). Sustainability and branding: An integrated perspective. *Industrial Marketing Management, 43*(1), 6–15. doi:10.1016/j.indmarman.2013.06.008

Larwood, L., Falbe, C. M., Kriger, M. P., & Miesing, P. (1995). Structure and meaning of organizational vision. *Academy of Management Journal, 1995*(38), 740–769. doi:10.2307/256744

Li, J., Yin, Z., Li, Y., Sun, S., Li, M., & Li, Y. (2021). The application of green roofs in urban green innovation spaces: A case study in Jinan City, China. *Environmental Science and Pollution Research International, 28*(3), 3525–3537. doi:10.100711356-020-11544-2 PMID:32892283

Liao, S. H., Chang, J. C., Cheng, S. C., & Kuo, C. M. (2004). Employee relationship and knowledge sharing: A case study of a Taiwanese finance and securities firm. *Knowledge Management Research and Practice, 2004*(2), 24–34. doi:10.1057/palgrave.kmrp.8500016

Lin, Y. H., & Chen, Y. S. (2017). Determinants of green competitive advantage: The roles of green knowledge sharing, green dynamic capabilities, and green service innovation. *Quality & Quantity, 51*(4), 1663–1685. doi:10.100711135-016-0358-6

Liu, D., Jiang, K., Shalley, C. E., Keem, S., & Zhou, J. (2016). Motivational mechanisms of employee creativity: A meta-analytic examination and theoretical extension of the creativity literature. *Organizational Behavior and Human Decision Processes, 2016*(137), 236–263. doi:10.1016/j.obhdp.2016.08.001

Liu, J., Chen, J., & Tao, Y. (2015). Innovation Performance in New Product Development Teams in China's Technology Ventures: The Role of Behavioral Integration Dimensions and Collective Efficacy. *Journal of Product Innovation Management, 2015*(32), 29–44. doi:10.1111/jpim.12177

Llonch, P., Haskell, M. J., Dewhurst, R. J., & Turner, S. P. (2017). Current available strategies to mitigate greenhouse gas emissions in livestock systems: An animal welfare perspective. *Animal, 2017*(11), 274–284. doi:10.1017/S1751731116001440 PMID:27406001

López-Gamero, M. D., Claver-Cortés, E., & Molina-Azorín, J. F. (2008). Complementary resources and capabilities for an ethical and environmental management: A qual/quan study. *Journal of Business Ethics, 82*(3), 701–732. doi:10.100710551-007-9587-x

Maas, C. J., & Hox, J. J. (2005). Sufficient sample sizes for multilevel modeling. *Methodology: European Journal of Research Methods for the Behavioral and Social Sciences, 2005*(1), 86–92. doi:10.1027/1614-2241.1.3.86

Marchi, V. D. (2012). Environmental innovation and R&D cooperation: Empirical evidence from Spanish manufacturing firms. *Research Policy, 41*(3), 614–623. doi:10.1016/j.respol.2011.10.002

Maruani, T., & Amit-Cohen, I. (2007). Open Space planning models: A review of approaches and methods. *Landscape and Urban Planning, 81*(1-2), 1–13. doi:10.1016/j.landurbplan.2007.01.003

Mazur, K. V., & Tomashuk, I. V. (2019). Governance, and regulation as an indispensable condition for developing the potential of rural areas. *Baltic Journal of Economic Studies, 5*(5), 67–78. doi:10.30525/2256-0742/2019-5-5-67-78

Mell, I. C. (2010). *Green infrastructure: concepts, perceptions, and its use in spatial planning.* [Doctoral Thesis, School of Architecture, Planning and Landscape Newcastle University].

Mentens, J., Raes, D., & Hermy, M. (2006). Green roofs as a tool for solving the rainwater runoff problem in the urbanized 21st century? *Landscape and Urban Planning, 77*(3), 217–226. doi:10.1016/j.landurbplan.2005.02.010

Mesimaki, M., Hauru, K., Kotze, D. J., & Lehvavirta, S. (2017). Neo-spaces for urban livibility? Urbanities' versatile mental image of green roofs in the Helsinki metropolitan area, Finland. *Land Use Policy, 61*, 587–600. doi:10.1016/j.landusepol.2016.11.021

Mohd, H. A. and Norhidayah, S. (2016), Sustainable food production: insights of Malaysian halal small and medium sized enterprises. *International Journal of Production Economics, 181*, 303–314. . doi:10.1016/j.ijpe.2016.06.003

Murray, N. (2017). Urban disaster risk governance. A systemic review. UCL Institute of Education.

Namkung, Y., & Jang, S. (2013). Effects of restaurant green practices on brand equity formation: Do green practices really matter? *International Journal of Hospitality Management, 33*(2), 85–95. doi:10.1016/j.ijhm.2012.06.006

Nogué, S., & Sala, M. (2018). The use of green roofs in urban green innovation spaces: A case study in Barcelona. *Urban Forestry & Urban Greening, 33*, 19–29. doi:10.1016/j.ufug.2018.02.008

Norton, T. A., Parker, S. L., Zacher, H., & Ashkanasy, N. M. (2015). Employee green behavior: A theoretical framework, multilevel review, and future research agenda. *Organization & Environment, 2015*(28), 103–125. doi:10.1177/1086026615575773

Ones, D. S., & Dilchert, S. (2012a). Employee green behaviors. In D. S. S. E. Jackson (Ed.), *Managing human resource for environmental sustainability* (pp. 85–116). Jossey-Bass.

Oswald, S. L., Mossholder, K. W., & Harris, S. G. (1994). Vision salience and strategic involvement: Implications for psychological attachment to organization and job. *Strategic Management Journal, 1994*(15), 477–489. doi:10.1002mj.4250150605

Palomino, J. C., & Durán, P. (2020). The influence of green roofs on the urban heat island effect: A review of the current state of knowledge. *Urban Climate, 34*, 100696. doi:10.1016/j.uclim.2020.100696

Pell, A. N. (1996). Fixing the leaky pipeline: Women scientists in academia. *Journal of Animal Science, 74*(11), 2843–2848. doi:10.2527/1996.74112843x PMID:8923199

Pereira, Á., & Vence, X. (2012). Key business factors for eco-innovation: An overview of recent firm-level empirical studies. *Cuadernos de Gestión, 12*, 73–103. doi:10.5295/cdg.110308ap

Redman, C. (2014). Should sustainability and resilience be combined or remain distinct pursuits? *Ecology and Society, 19*(2), 190–202. doi:10.5751/ES-06390-190237

Reisinger, A., & Clark, H. (2018). How much do direct livestock emissions contribute to global warming? *Global Change Biology, 2018*(24), 1749–1761. doi:10.1111/gcb.13975 PMID:29105912

Renwick, D. W. S., Redman, T., & Maguire, S. (2008). Green human resource management: A review and research agenda. *International Journal of Management Reviews, 10*(1), 1–18. doi:10.1111/j.1468-2370.2011.00328.x

Rowe, D. B. (2011). Green Roofs as a means of pollution abatement. *Environmental Pollution, 159*(8-9), 2100–2110. doi:10.1016/j.envpol.2010.10.029 PMID:21074914

S., S., & Newell, J. P. (2017). Detroit, Spatial planning for multifunctional green infrastructure. *Landscape and Urban Planning* 62-75.

Savickiene, J., & Miceikiene, A. (2018). *Sustainable economic development assessment model for family farms* (Vol. 64). Agricultural Economics – Czech. doi:10.17221/310/2017-AGRICECON

Scharenbroch, B. C., & Bucci, M. (2017). Green roofs as an ecosystem service provider in the Chicago Wilderness region. *Ecological Engineering, 99*, 240–251. doi:10.1016/j.ecoleng.2016.11.010

Shafi Que, M., Kim, R. & Rafi Q. M. (2018). Green roof benefits, opportunities, and challenges– A review. *Renewable and Sustainable Energy Reviews, 90*, 757-773.

Shevchenko, A., & Petrenko, O. (2020). Current state of micro and small agribusiness in Ukraine. *Agricultural and Resource Economics, 6*(1), 146–160. doi:10.51599/are.2020.06.01.10

Shoeb, A., & Nisar, T. (2015). Green Human Resource Management: Policies and practices. *Cogent Business & Management.* https://www.tandfonline.com/doi/full/10.1080/23311975.2015.1030817 doi:10.1080/23311975.2015.1030817

Singh, S. K., Del Giudice, M., Chierici, R., & Graziano, D. (2020). Green innovation and environmental performance: The role of green transformational leadership and green human resource management. *Technological Forecasting and Social Change, 150*, 119762. doi:10.1016/j.techfore.2019.119762

Skydan, O., Nykolyuk, O., Pyvovar, P., & Martynchuk, I. (2020). Methodological approach to the evaluation of agricultural business system flexibility. *Management Theory and Studies for Rural Business and Infrastructure Development, 41*(4), 444–462. doi:10.15544/mts.2019.36

Stubbs, W. & Cocklin, C. (2008). Conceptualizing a sustainability business model. *Org.Env. 21* (2), 103e127.

Sutton, R. (2014). Aesthetics for green roofs and green walls. *The Journal of Living Architecture, 1*(2), 1–20. doi:10.46534/jliv.2014.01.02.001

Tan, P. Y., Wong, N. H., Tan, T. K., & Wong, K. W. (2019). Green roof innovation in Singapore: Policies, performance, and potential. *Journal of Environmental Management, 233*, 128–135. doi:10.1016/j.jenvman.2018.12.060

TEP. (2005). *Advancing the delivery of green infrastructure Targeting Issues in England's Northwest.* Issue Paper, England Northwest.

Tomashuk I.V. & Baldynyuk V.M., (2021). Identification of problems and prospects of rural infrastructure development of Ukraine. *Economic sciences, 13* (100). doi:10.24412/2520-6990-2021-13100-58-70

Tsai, W., & Ghoshal, S. (1998). Social capital and value creation: The role of intrafirm networks. *Academy of Management Journal, 1998*(41), 464–476. doi:10.2307/257085

Ugai, T. (2016). Evaluation of sustainable roof from various aspects and benefits of agriculture roofing in urban core. *Procedia: Social and Behavioral Sciences, 216*, 850–860. doi:10.1016/j.sbspro.2015.12.082

UNDP. (2020). *Environmentally Sustainable Operations.* UNDP. https://www.undp.org/accountability/social-and-environmental-responsibility/sustainable-operations

Van Holt, T., Statler, M., Atz, U., Whelan, T., van Loggerenberg, M., & Cebulla, J. (2020). The cultural consensus of sustainability-driven innovation: Strategies for success. *Business Strategy and the Environment, 29*(8), 3399–3409. doi:10.1002/bse.2584

Vijayaraghavan, K. (2016). Green roofs: A critical review on the role of components, benefits, limitations, and trends. *Renewable & Sustainable Energy Reviews, 57*, 740–752. doi:10.1016/j.rser.2015.12.119

VisitBerlin (2017). *12 mal Berliner Leben, 12 mal Berlin Erleben. Konzept für einen stadtverträglichen Berlin-Tourismus 2018+;* VisitBerlin: Berlin, Germany. https://about.visitberlin.de/tourismuskonzept-2018

Wang, Y., Hu, H., Dai, W., & Burns, K. (2021). Evaluation of industrial green development and industrial green competitiveness: Evidence from Chinese urban agglomerations. *Ecological Indicators, 124*, 107371. doi:10.1016/j.ecolind.2021.107371

Wiering, M., Liefferink, D., Boezeman, D., Kaufmann, M., Crabbé, A., & Kurstjens, N. (2020). The Wicked Problem the Water Framework Directive Cannot Solve. The Governance Approach in Dealing with Pollution of Nutrients in Surface Water in the Netherlands, Flanders, Lower Saxony, Denmark, and Ireland. *Water (Basel), 12*(5), 1240. doi:10.3390/w12051240

Wirtenberg, J., Harmon, K. D., Russell, W. G., & Fairfield, K. D. (2007). HR's role in building a sustainable enterprise. *Human Resource Planning, 30*, 10–20.

Wu, W., & Jim, C. Y. (2021). Urban green infrastructure and sustainable urbanization: A comprehensive review of the roles of green roofs. *Landscape and Urban Planning, 212*, 104097. doi:10.1016/j.landurbplan.2021.104097

Wysocki, J. (2021). Innovative green initiatives in the manufacturing SME sector in Poland. *Sustainability (Basel), 13*(4), 2386. doi:10.3390u13042386

Zhang, Z., & Sundaresan, S. (2010). Knowledge markets in firms: Knowledge sharing with trust and signalling. *Knowledge Management Research and Practice, 2010*(8), 322–339. doi:10.1057/kmrp.2010.22

Chapter 5
Organizational Socio-Ecosystem Innovation

José G. Vargas-Hernandez
Instituto Tecnológico Mario Molina, Zapopan, Mexico

Omar C. Vargas-González
Tecnológico Nacional de México, Ciudad Guzmán, Mexico

ABSTRACT

This study has the purpose of analyzing the implications of the organizational socio-ecosystem on innovation. It begins from the assumption that organizations are open and dynamic concepts of socio-ecosystems composed of technical, social, and environmental dimensions of sustainability departing from growth-based policies and jointly optimized in management strategies for organizational innovation and development that results in improved performance. The method employed is critical analysis and reflection based on the theoretical and empirical review of the literature. It is concluded that the organizational socio ecosystems innovation is the result of multiple organizational factors and environmental dimensions stimulated by the involvement of a diversity of actors, agents, stakeholders, government institutions, research centers and universities, organizational business, among others.

INTRODUCTION

The innovation theory began with Schumpeter (1961) who defined it as a new product, production process, or form of organization, such as the acquisition and opening of new markets (Schumpeter, 1934). Advances in organizational theory, the innovation models, and systems, have caused a revolution in approaching innovative organizations since its development in the 1940s to control the boundaries among the group relationships with other sectors.

Modern organizations face innovation environments exceeding the stable state providing goods and services at low costs and good quality but may aspire to adapt to a new stability level after the transition to achieve a permanent transformation. Organizational stability fulfills the role of crosslinking agent leading to learning development skills and innovation at individual and organizational levels. The dimen-

DOI: 10.4018/978-1-6684-8392-3.ch005

sion of socio-ecological innovation is growing in organizations and needs to be in innovation theories and processes.

The organization set is the system of relationships among organizations in their innovation environment (Evan, 1966). Physical environment organizations are an indirect way to provide properties conducive to innovation and entrepreneurship through technology transfer marketing attending the differentiated sources. The sociological theory of classical risk in the social and organizational innovation context is a concept that refers to individual and organizational decisions (Beck, 1986; Luhmann, 1991). Reputational risk management and framing the impacts of socio-ecological innovation issues and risk mitigation develops into an organizational logic of decision-making (Power et al., 2009).

Theoretical and empirical developments in organizational ecology perspective is away from the Trist (1976) approach (De melo, 1997) focusing on traditional concepts of ecology and adapted from Darwinian approach more related to life cycles, natural selection, birth, mortality, organizational growth, and innovation (Madsen & MacKelvey, 1996; Geroski & Mazzucato, 2001). The capacious concept of innovation has spatial implications in the happenings beyond the identification and mapping of networks and clusters of individuals and organizations knowledge intensive.

The sociological theoretical framework supports the innovation concepts and instruments necessary for the implementation, the adaptive planning, and the process of cross-over and inter-organizational domain. The sociological theoretical approach for governance in innovation environments is based on the principle of self-regulation as opposed to hierarchical controls in complex and high-uncertainty organizational contexts. The self-regulation principle sustains the delicate balance of the innovation organizational eco-system and habitat requiring the dynamic negotiation process between the participant's different units.

The concept of organizational ecology became the subject related to the inter-organizational ecology research interests of Trist (1976) contrasting with trust and concerned with the organizational activities of several organizations in their innovation environment. Organizational ecology is a field created by the interrelationships of organizations that develop in an organizational innovation field. The system is characteristic of the global field that becomes the recentering investigation object and not the individual organization related to its organizational innovation set (Warren, 1967).

The socio-ecological approach derived from the concepts of organizational ecological systems is used as a theoretical framework to analyze the complexity and uncertainty of changing environments (Trist, 1976a; de Melo, 1997) in the governance of local innovation systems. The concept of local innovation systems revolves around a cluster formed by government, social, and market organizations that seek the physical benefits and interests of the agglomeration based on the dynamics of interactions and interrelationships of trust and cooperation in the community. Local innovation systems are made up of start-ups, research universities, associated firms, and market organizations, government agencies and institutions, associations of companies, capital and services providers, end users, etc.

Research and development in socio-ecological innovation is a shift searching for new paradigms and the policymaking process, which requires skill to make further efforts to improve existing innovations. The interactions and learning dynamics of the local innovation systems between the conglomerate of agents and actors culminate in an innovative performance of firms leading to feedback and value generation mechanisms for the actors' enabling capabilities to provide the environment of making new firms and market and extra market organizations seek to carry out innovations while non-market organizations make contributions to the innovation environment in terms of qualified jobs generation, taxes, etc.

The non-market organizations refer to the technical and informative institutions that support local systems of innovation, are active members of the environment, and have an interest in actions developed by organizations in goods and services markets. Support organizations act as intermediaries between university research centers and technology-based firms, concentrating services and providing physical spaces, and promoting cooperation between firms, investors, and researchers.

A university-based local innovation system is a network of first-level socioecological organizations (Trist, 1976a) supporting innovation projects where the University emerges as the reference organization with a reticule agent. Despite the centrality of the university as the reference organization in innovation environments, the Board of Directors makes decisions with a pertinent autonomy in terms of technology management related to intellectual property and technology innovation commercialization policies.

Complexity and heterogeneity of organizations, actors, and agents in socio-ecological organizational environments require management mechanisms and explicit policies and socioeconomic objectives with a decentralized and dispersed organizational structure making difficult if not impossible the collaborative and innovative character to maintain competitiveness in innovation environments. Organizational analysis is a system that has strategic meaning of the organizational problems that are omitted by other frameworks of analysis with obvious implications in organizational innovations (Trist, 1981).

The resistance to the proposed change to innovation is proportional has a proportional degree to the threat that the innovation represents to the system (Trist, 1976a). The organizational structure change is hampered by types of defenses against innovation (de Melo, 1997). The factor known as negative elasticity relates to the organizational system immediately after the removal of the force that motivated innovation and changes returns to its initial state (de Melo, 1997).

The analysis begins with the study of organizational innovation and its multiple social and environmental implications leading to the creation and development of an organizational socio-eco-system innovation followed by some supporting mechanisms based on organizational innovation strategies and policies. Finally, the study develops some conclusions.

BACKGROUND

Organizational Innovation

There is vast inconclusive empirical work related to the firm size and its effects in the industrial-organizational innovation economics motivated by the works of Schumpeter (1942). Organizations of different sizes contribute to innovation in sectors, such as instrumentation equipment and software conditioned to the investments and contexts (Tidd et al., 1997). Organizational innovation has characteristics that facilitate the adaptation process to organizational changes. Organizations with the best opportunities for survival evolve as living beings by developing organizational innovation abilities to transform motivated by the environment (De Geus, 1997; De Geus, 1998).

Organizations are related to strategic components seeking to satisfy the need of stakeholders, shareholders, customers, suppliers, and other organizations through innovation and transformation processes that enable them to ensure balanced development and sustainable sources for competitive advantages (Price, 1996; Tidd et al., 1997).

The systematic work of organizational innovation integrates values into routinary organizational operations. Organizational innovation is created by incorporating knowledge and skills in local and non-local interactions with the organizational socio-ecosystem. Organizational members get involved in social and organizational innovation interactions with socio-ecosystems dynamics leading to increasing or decreasing spaces for collaborators maneuvering to solve problems and conflicts.

The economic and social environment induces the emergence of organizational innovation development in a non-linear development. From the perspective of organizational learning and innovation, the members of the organization perceive the environment. The interdependence of organizations leads to learning and innovation processes aimed to survive and adapt to high degrees of uncertainty through the development of trust in negotiation processes of shared values and objectives, mutual advantages, etc. Organizational learning innovation barriers in the public sector are many types of features manifested at odds under the assumption of smart innovation place-based experimentalism (Morgan, 2017).

The organizational environment is defined as the set of factors, general and specific, external to the organization perceived in decisions where organizations have autonomy and freedom (Ahumada Figueroa, 2001). Governments, firms, research institutes, universities, regional development authorities, agencies and other actors are interested on environmental issues and their respective particularities and objectives (Massey et al., 1992; Vedovello, 2001) identified for the interest groups. Organizations are superior to other forms of collective action in their level of innovation reliability. The re-emergence of innovation in organizations has an impact on the economic and social and environment on their non-linear development.

Socioeconomic and ecological innovation contexts characterized by biodiversity and processes of technical change in the diversity of enterprises, tend to overcome barriers to innovation by developing cognitive and psychological competencies and network linkages leading to knowledge organizations. Diversity is related to greater individual and organizational flexibility to expand the possibilities of change and innovation. Individual diversity of functions and the development of technical-productive flexibility in innovation and production changes.

The socio-technical approach is based on the organizing innovative principle with the minimum critical specification required for each unit according to the higher-order organization unit, which means that superior organization units avoid assuming roles that may be performed by lower-level organizations. The sociotechnical theory assumes the innovative organization as an open system that must manage the internal and external environment configurations favorable to performance (de Melo, 2002).

The design initiative of a feasible and realizable pathway to address a meta-level objective in innovation requires a large organizational vision of the work focusing upon a functional prototype. The system focuses on the design efforts that are concentrated on setting the agenda for the realization of innovative events (Laszlo et al., 2012). The large size of organizations is associated with high levels of bureaucratic complexity for the design and implementation of innovative events (Blau & Schoenherr, 1971).

The traditional bureaucratic regulation is characterized by external control, centralized and hierarchical which contrasts with the inter-organizational strategic approach of socio-ecological regulation based on organizational interdependence to survive and adapt to the environment with a high degree of uncertainty, to build trust through learning and innovation process in the negotiation of roles, objectives, mutual and shared benefits. The premise raised to cope with high-level uncertainty and complex environments, organizations and institutions must form innovation networks sharing spaces of action and responsibilities in coordination and integration of organizational agents and actors around common objectives.

The positive relationship between organizational aging and organizational mortality may be due to the impediments of action and understanding, political coalitions, and the like (Barron et al., 1994). Organizational age influences the predictions of inventions to be cited in the future at the time it is developed excluding self-citations and previously issued patents. The patents are differentiated between the self-citing patents of prior patents, and the non-self-citing patents do not build on the organization's earlier patents.

MAIN FOCUS OF THE CHAPTER

Organizational Socio-Ecosystem Innovation

The concept of socio-ecological innovation advances the social and environmental dimensions of sustainability departing from growth-based policies and based on the assumption of a low-carbon economy. Organizations, sectors, and individuals must have to overcome friction to begin with socio-ecological innovation (Wolf & Primmer, 2006). The socio-ecological organization has a central characteristic making the innovative organization, agent, and actor become stronger dominant over others and generating conflicts of interest and reducing trust leading to suppression of the cooperative character (Trist, 1976a; de Melo, 1997; de Melo 2002). At the level of socio-ecological organizations, actors and agents are not referenced in the organizational innovation networks leading to the creation of a separate organization not dominated and controlled by all the organizations.

Organizations are becoming increasingly aware of the need for a more innovative sustainable living by facing the socio-ecological crisis and increasing economic inequality (Rees, 2002; Dabla-Norris et al., 2015). Living organizations have the objective to perpetuate themselves as developing organizational communities beyond the companies that only have the objective to generate profits (Schon, 1973; de Melo, 1997).

Sustainable organizational innovation refers to making rare innovations, inimitable and transferable, development of natural resources institutional infrastructures to counteract the non-substitutability of sustainable innovations. Downsizing disrupts organizational innovation structures and redefines labor in shrinking economies because of the socio-ecological transformations. Organizations could become drivers of a socio-ecological innovation and transformation in sustainable development and facilitating the worker's participation from the bottom-up process to democratize socio-economic development (Gouverneur & Netzer, 2014).

Socio-ecological resources are internal natural resources of innovative organizations such as biodiversity. The conceptualization of the socio-ecological data allows to analyze the relationships between the organizational natural resources and transitional strategies aimed to take advantage of innovation opportunities and navigate constraints of socio-agroecological production systems. Socio-ecological transition affects organizational work and labor (Fischer-Kowalski et al., 2012) Integrating just transitions to more socio-ecological innovation transformations in organizations requires the formulation of a broader concept and guiding principles for sustainable development and work and reshaping organizing capacities in social, and industrial, and labor policymaking (Gouverneur & Netzer, 2014).

Findings of sustainable organizational innovation are associated with the sustainability approach enhancing positive e socio-ecological externalities and maintaining the financial and socio-ecological well-being of organizations. The reorientation of financial funding for institutional innovation policy instruments is influenced by institutional and legal transformations in the organizational structure of the innovation systems (OECD, 1999).

Organizations are becoming increasingly aware of socio-environmental sustainability innovation challenges leading to create the need for socio-ecological innovations aimed to address the negative externalities associated with manufacturing processes and practices and to foster sustainable development (Kiron et al., 2013; Boons & Lüdeke-Freund, 2013; Silvestre, 2015).

Organizations have an increasing awareness on the innovative contribution to these crises in terms of negative ecological externalities (Sukhdev, 2013). The socio-ecological innovative organization has a decentralized character with not any reference organization such as for example, the student movements of the sixties all over the world, which was no political representation, specific program, or recognized leader despite the values and lifestyle never had explicit objectives, the group remained fluid (Trist 1971, in Trist, 1976a).

A cluster of innovation emerges in well-endowed socio-ecological and organizational entrepreneurship resources with an expanding ecological biodiversity area as the strategy for a successful transition to generate well-being for local communities. Socio-agroecology transitional innovation systems are facilitated by access to developed organizational infrastructure and resources to improve learning efficiency while mitigating some risks. The appropriate mix and balance existing between technical devices and socio-organizational arrangements is associated with an innovation systems framework (Hall et al., 2003).

The socio-ecological perspective with a socio-technical base and the organizational ecology perspective learning provides mechanisms to deal with characteristics components of uncertainties and turbulent environments experienced by society in the context of local innovation systems. The socio-ecological perspective and its sociotechnical basis and the inter-organizational process are the theoretical foundation of concepts such as the adaptive planning and innovative approach to the adaptation process of organizational changes to support the development of planning for the governance structure of local innovation systems.

The governance structure of a local innovation system resembles the socio-ecological organization in which none of the actors involved emerges as a reference organization leading to the creation of a separate organization (Trist, 1976a). This type of arrangement gives more visibility to the reference organization and facilitates the consensus among the members. The structure of the organizational component of local innovation systems is formed with a government agency defining the science, technology and innovation technology policies and issues leading to the implementation of complex processes through the executing agencies, public and private universities and research centers aimed to develop basic and applied science knowledge and innovation technology, technical and professional agencies, financial and funding institutions, national e international agencies.

State and local governments must promote the formation of organizational structures of governance for local innovation systems through strategic alliances with the participation of science and technology agencies, universities and research institutes, suppliers of services and equipment, and firms' beneficiaries.

Local innovation systems focus on the innovative activities of organizations meanwhile other institutions, agents and actors and participants aimed to guide actions to achieve their own innovation goals. Any analysis of the functions and operations of local innovation systems must point to the feedback to identify the bottlenecks and gaps in the process that need to be addressed for adjustments in the benefits of the innovative performance of organizations and agents involved and emerging as the result in terms of value generation for market and non-market organizations.

The implementation of active planning constituted as adaptive planning methodology has an incremental pattern in holistic nature that aims to social, managerial, and technical changes of the innovative organizations that assimilates the impact in a turbulent environment in constant evolution (de Melo, 1985; de Melo, 1991).

Participative adaptive planning requires the organizational involvement to make decisions to adopt it as a continuous learning and innovation processes framed by a holistic vision through coordination of actions and integration at all organizational levels (Trist, 1976b). The concept of innovative planning focusing on strategies of change adopted by organizations to survive and prosper in unstable environment in economic, social, and political terms. The active learning perspective contributes to the development of innovative planning leading to identify innovation nodes in the interorganizational field and the formation of innovative action networks.

More complex interorganizational domains such as Local Innovation Systems operate through structure and less through culture. The interorganizational level is the domain in which actors emerge as the reference organization establishing management mechanisms to allocate human resources and information, organizational norms, and rule for organizational innovation practices.

Using the sociological perspective, the functional characteristics of the local innovation systems give support to the processes of the dynamism of entrepreneurship and innovation environments using methodologies based on complex open systems and treating it as an organizational ecology providing appropriate mechanisms to find the means. In the new context of social capital in organizations and societies, the aim is to elucidate cooperation as an environmental component for the socio technical innovation processes.

The dynamism of innovation environments using the socio-ecological perspective leads to organizational ecology expressed in new cooperation forms in the context of structural changes, as the main features of the strategic innovation component adapted to the paradigm faced by society and organizations. Structural changes in organizations imply institutional and organizational changes and innovation as the instrument in competitiveness strategy in the international market environment.

The dynamics of local innovation system based on research and higher education centers identify the actors and effective policies to ensure the functioning of government, private organizations, and universities. The actors of the local innovation system have autonomy that may happen organically with no formal governance of organizations interacting with each other with firms in relationships with universities, and the innovation system only intervene when the shared objective may be affected and should be mediated by those involved and interested.

The sustainable development approach consistent with natural resource view, the base of the pyramid and triple bottom line refers to sustainable organizational innovations motivated by the enhancement of people, financial returns, profits, and the planet by reducing the negative socio-ecological externalities (Hart, 1995; Hart & Dowell, 2011; Hart, 2007, Prahalad, 2010; Elkington, 1997). Organizational capabilities promote relevant sustainable innovation potentially to become a driver for a sustainable world. The resource-based framework of organizational innovation uses qualitative methods to demonstrate the internal and external resource endowments mediate transitions towards more socio-ecological systems potentially to reduce pollution and improving the environmental stewardship.

A different approach to sustainable environmental innovation consistent with radical resource view and the double bottom line is adopted by organizations focuses on the returns generated by the socio-ecological innovations motivated by the financial viability with the improvement of well-being considered more relevant and enabling the enhancement of positive socio-ecological externalities.

The radical perspective of the resource-based view is a theoretical-conceptual framework for the development of organizational capabilities aimed at promoting innovation for sustainable development of local communities and organizations. Socio-ecological value creation for the socio-ecological and holistic well-being of local communities rather the financial value capture may result from the development of qualitative organizational capabilities more consistent with the expectations of sustainable innovation based on radical resource-based view.

Value is created at the project meso level and more formal value capture at the macro level of organizational ecosystems leading to innovation outcomes of the urban socio-ecological transition becoming sustainable to ensure the quality of life. The radical resource view (Bell & Dyck, 2011; Walske et al., 2013) and the double bottom line approach enhance innovation of socio-ecological well-being considered to be more important than the financial well-being (Kurucz et al., 2014).

Socio-ecological relationships are relevant for all kinds of innovation in organizations not just for the agroecological and agri-food business organizations. Some socio-ecological innovations to enhance the sustainable development of ecosystems are the conservation policies, vegetable cultivation and high-yield varieties, subsidies on food imports, horticultural promotion, cultivation of medicinal and aromatic plants etc. Some of them are relevant and meaningful for the socioeconomic and socioecology of sustainable environmental development.

Socio-ecological transitions to new organizational arrangements must be based on the innovative management of biological diversity relationships. Innovation management of networking relationships is a form to facilitate transitions between the spatial proximity of individuals and organizations of the cluster. Networks dynamics facilitates social learning of legitimate knowledge for socio-ecological transitional innovation systems in evolving organizations (Carolan, 2006).

The organizational innovation networks create and develop more innovative and cooperative environments adapted to deal with more complex and uncertain environmental components in spheres of organizations (OECD, 2001a; OECD, 2001c; Porter, 2001). The concept of the crossover process focuses on the formation of innovative action networks among linking organizations sharing the same action space and providing the necessary means for a better dynamic of local systems. The local systems innovation is an organization whose objective is to provide the necessary resources to the source firms to ensure survival and self-support (Lalkaka, 1999). Innovative action networks link organizations, agents and actors sharing relationships and interactions in the same action space and formed to enable survival in the turbulent environment (de Melo, 1991). Concerns for organizational ecology structure originated in collaboration strategies for the balance of the interorganizational turbulent environment.

A reticulist role emerges as an element allowing the regulatory mechanisms to mediate the relationships between the members of the innovation network or grid and to enable change of focus from the organizational network (de Melo, 2002). In the reticulation process, planning is carried out through negotiation of an order and mobilization that aims to better organizational innovation operations with the environment. The reticulist is responsible for the regulation mechanisms mediating the relationships between the members of the network reticules to achieve better performance of the nature of innovative organizations in the environment in relation to individuals.

The crosslinking agent is an organization involved in the innovation network performing the functions of reticulist to enable to negotiate the relationships among the members with advantages identified in the transfer of roles from individuals to the organizations with the capacities to offer information to human resources required to consolidate the agreement (Burns, 1981). The function of creating links between the organizations, actors and agents must exercise the reticulist judgment aimed to activate the network selective innovation decisions based on the structure of problems and political conditions of involved organizations (Fiend & Jessop, 1969, in de Melo 2002).

A favorable political environment of technological innovation and the university as the reference organization of the local innovation system as the engine of economic growth and social value, along the collaboration with the local leaders and private sector can turn around and shape the regional economy.

Investments for technological innovation include private ventures and government participation in private funds to enter local innovation systems, venture capitals to invest in seed and early-stage start-ups, commercialization, and technology transfers, angel investors, bridging organizations mediating access for start-ups, etc. These investments are justified by the financial sector exposure of the public sector leading to counterparties of firms and the anchor university of the local innovation system based in the university. An angel investment implements mechanisms for local seed capital fund and ventures organization with functions serving as a vehicle for investment in innovation infrastructure.

An integrated environment to firms affected by organizations, institutions, groups, and individuals, out of which the most influential are the universities and research institutes, firms, support institutions and all government levels support technological innovation in the context of strategic alliances involving all the levels of government and private sector aimed to consolidate the science, technology, and innovation local system. The innovation university based has the more permanent character to act as a reference organization and has the capacity to offer human and informative resources becoming the environmental crosslinker creating negotiated relationships and links between the members of the innovation networks made up at the innovation centers and parks, and their actors such emerging firms, as non-market, extra-market, and market organizations, supporting organizations, all seeking benefits of agglomerations.

The crossover process concept focuses on innovative action networks linking organizations, sharing the action space, providing means for the analysis of local innovation system dynamics, and identifying the goals expected by the actors involved. The diversity of factors in a meta-problem give identity to multi-organization defined as the arrangements in which several organizations, represented by some of their parts, dedicate themselves to solving common problems (de Melo, 1997, p. 8) through innovating practices.

Networks of socio-ecological innovation framed and facilitated by the state aims to advance alternative agroecological working use of land programs deriving resources from public and private organizations, government institutions and business relations and drawing on knowledge and industrial and socio-ecological resources. The socio-ecosystem innovation management system links knowledge systems, organizations, and institutions (Berkes & Folke, 1998; Berkes et al., 2003; Dale et al., 2000; Imperial, 1999). Promotion of business-university-government interrelationships in close cooperation with supporting geographically proximate institutions (Porter, 2001).

High-tech organizations require the action of public and private institutions and innovation organizations in government, business, research, etc., for their creation, development, and consolidation, considering the high vulnerability of environmental changes. Socio-technical based management system leads to effective interrelationships of organizational units in action capable of better guiding towards the innovation goals (de Melo, 1997). The original concept of socio-technical introduced by Trist emphasizes self-regulation and inter-organizational dominance as the appropriate governance mechanisms for local socio-technical innovation systems.

The socio technical innovation systems in local contexts are more sensitive to environmental turbulence. The socio-ecological perspective is the basis of a socio-technical approach. Other relevant organizational socio-technical principles are related to compatibility of the system utilizing the personal innovation capabilities in participative organization (Cherns, 1976). The principle of minimum critical specification necessary for the objectives, tasks and roles coordinated by an innovation unit (Herbst, 1974). The participative adaptive process implies continuous implementation of monitoring and permanent evaluation of actions lading to redefinition of goals and objectives that requires change in focus toward the interorganizational as a reticulist planner creator of collaborative innovation networks of organizations (de Melo, 1997). The evaluation processes of socio-ecological systems including the social, socio-economic, environmental and policy have to be supported by regional studies (Ramakrishnan, 2000).

The socio-technical approach adopts as a work unit and level of analysis the whole organization and the macrosystem (Trist, 1981) expanding to the organizational ecosystem of organizations sharing innovation responsibilities under the same decisions and action space (Melo, 1997). The organizational innovation work groups and innovation units must have the required information to carry out on their tasks and activities while receiving feedback for control and learning from the variations of process development. Groups in socio-ecological organizations operate through culture and not structure. The control of each organizational work unit is delimited by its members and the functions of managers and supervisors focus on border activities achieving a high degree of autonomy with respect to other units to ensure resources and coordination of innovation activities.

Alternative organizations facilitate the opportunities and resources for networking to gain innovation management knowledge as a sources of identity formation and social support agroecological isolated farmers perceived to be different (Hassanein, 1999; Bell, 2004). A socio-ecosystem innovation management operates in a dynamic organization using social networks to support all the activities at a small cost to the community (Westley, 1995). A flexible socio-ecosystem innovation management supported by adaptive organizations plays a critical role in community transformations (Olsson et al., 2004b). Socio-ecological innovation actors usually develop networks for horizontal relationships to create, develop, share, and exchange knowledge and information among the individuals of various communities and develop vertical relationships with other organizations and institutions to widespread socio-ecological innovation to affect transformations of organizational and institutional changes toward more socio-economic sustainable systems.

In the context of urban innovation in urban green areas in relation with transitions to socio-ecological goals in green urban environments, are incubated by organizations that stimulate growth and development. The urban living lab is an innovative socio-ecosystem of knowledge creation and development for socio-ecological transition. The urban living lab concept is a multi-stakeholder innovation development and inter-organizational R&D design process to govern socio-ecological innovation models supported by local collaborative innovation processes designed to tackle socio-ecological innovation challenges by means of eco-entrepreneurship and public–private interactions.

Socio-ecological innovation models are of interest to other innovating actors and agents with emphasis on the purpose beyond the organizations to achieve competitive advantages and with the rationale of innovation responding to social needs and informed by ideological values and norms. Innovative organizations have advantages as market pioneers able to charge premium prices while competitors' struggle. The innovation diplomacy limits formal and semi-formal commitments from local governments to eco-entrepreneurs and semi-public urban living lab organizational management.

Different stakeholders and actors' members of the organizations are involved in the urban green living lab. The urban living lab is a multi-stakeholder democratic innovative concept and inter-organizational design of a socio-ecological innovation development process able to govern models based on action research. Incubated start-up organizations in urban living lab with socio-ecological innovation goals in the green urban environment areas stimulate innovation with the collaborative support of local government agencies as the required stakeholder in the innovation ecosystem.

The ecosystem-based innovation management transformation requires the corresponding organizational change (Danter et al., 2000). Academics, farmers, civil society organizations argue that socio-ecological innovation principles advance the transition to sustainability of agriculture, agroecological production systems and agri-food systems (IAASTD, 2008). The innovative governance outcomes response to analyze the socio-ecological risk of agricultural cooperative organizations.

There is not any formal governance model and organizational form between the relationships of various agents involved in innovation processes, including mediation conflicts resolution and its attributions may be similar to the reticulation agent of organizational ecology in negotiating the relationships between other members (Burns, 1981; de Melo, 2002) The analysis of cooperative innovation networks focusses on the relationships and interactions between organizations, individual actors and agents characterized by power asymmetries of relationships of cooperation and conflicts (OECD, 2001c).

The transition from traditional agriculture to agroecological innovation production systems is implemented complementing the dominant tradition and integrating analysis by bridging cognitive-material, macro-micro, nature-society, and structure-agency. Nature is a project-centric for collaborations and knowledge innovation production and exchange with the involved organizations.

Transition in socio-agroecology is the process through which a farmer shifts from traditional management of an innovative farming system with low species diversity and reliance on external chemical inputs, to an organizations system based on agroecological practices and relations (NRC, 2010; Tomich et al., 2011).

Facing the socioenvironmental crisis for organizations requires addressing the critical issues derived from climate change and to implement social and ecological innovations aimed at fostering sustainable development. The socio-ecological innovations between the relevance of different scales and levels supported by regional economies and international non-governmental organizations have influences on national actors on socio-technical climate change. Anthropology has similar concerns to explain socio-ecological innovation between the relevant levels and scales with regional economies and international non-government organizations influencing actors and innovations and national socio-technical climate change regime on territorial ethnic movements in interaction with the processes of dynamics of land uses, subjectivities, and normative dimensions of social media (Campbell, 2018).

SOLUTIONS AND RECOMMENDATIONS

Organizational Innovation Strategies

Natural resources and innovation organizational transitional strategies are either internal at individual and organizational or external network levels, which are divided in clusters of cognitive resources, ecological organizational resources and network relations, knowledge organizations and innovation policies. A third-class organizational domain is identifying that there is no reference on innovative organization. Organizations, actors, and agents in a domain must have reference innovative organization to give a broader character and greater visibility in the organizational field facilitating the construction of consensus, maximizing collaboration, minimizing conflict, and reducing resistance leading to carry out effective and relevant innovations (Trist, 1976a). The term network aims to differentiate the spontaneous formation processes of organizational structures because of collaborative actions for innovation.

Strategic organizational innovation concept leading to collaborative and competitive strategies (Amburgey & Rao, 1996) are closed to the concepts proposed and developed as an evolutive organizational ecology in opposition to Trist (1976) who defends concepts such as the bureaucratic regulation. Weber reveals bureaucracy as the perfected organizational monument suited to the prevailing reactive conditions but in times of turbulent environmental conditions imply the innovation practice of another alternative organizing principle found in line with the characteristics of an organizational ecology systems. Organizational ecology is based on internal self-regulation as opposed to external hierarchical type of control for turbulent environments.

Organizations may promote specific sustainable innovations leading to improved social and ecological well-being, placing the emphasis on value creation rather than financial value. Qualitative organizational capabilities of non-governmental organizations (NGOs) promote innovation for sustainable development. Design tools for encoding, decoding, understanding, and communicating organizational innovation strategies are conducted within organizations and across the business ecosystems.

The open distributional strategy is in line with the socio-ecological innovation model pressing to local governments to question the implementation of the top-down dominant paradigm innovation development and leading to individuals and organizations to experiment innovation processes in urban green innovation areas and environments (Bogers & West, 2012; Chesbrough, 2003; Paskaleva, 2011).

Regional innovation policies encourage regional and local governments and business organizations to concentrate knowledge and funding resources to transform activities of sectors in the economic structure through research and development. Local government incentives innovation programs providing land and tax exemptions to attract high tech firms and organizations to the region and local communities.

Interorganizational strategies must improve the innovation and adaptability of organizations inserted in the environments for an effective regulatory process for domains including independent organizations and groups in interactions through complex interrelationships. Organizations must step out of defensive strategies of reacting to policies that do not promote the drivers of socio-ecological innovation. The strategy of ecological biodiversity expansion aims to transition at organizational innovation level to generate innovation in socio-agro-biodiversity.

Organizational ecology strategies increase innovation and adaptability while reducing vulnerability. Urban socio-ecological trends in different frames of time use are leading to the formulation and implementation of post-carbon innovation strategies applied to regional socio ecosystems and organizational ecology development policies.

FUTURE RESEARCH DIRECTIONS

Policymaking of public policies in innovation technology face challenges of consolidating science, technology, and innovation systems of responding to social demands articulated with several segments of society leading to higher level of development based to technological innovation, productivity, and competitiveness. The segments of society are firms, government financing institutions and agencies, international organizations, consultants, etc., aimed to mobilize resources, information, skills, and capabilities necessary to achieve strategic objectives through cross-linking processes. Each aspect is worth further research to remain current with the times.

CONCLUSION

This study analyzes the implications of the organizational socio-ecosystem on innovation, beginning from the assumption that organizations are open and dynamic concepts of socio-ecosystems composed of technical, social, and environmental dimensions of sustainability departing from growth-based policies and jointly optimized in management strategies for organizational innovation and development that results in improved performance. The analysis concludes that the organizational socio ecosystems innovation is the result of multiple organizational factors and environmental dimensions stimulated by the involvement of a diversity of actors, agents, stakeholders, government institutions, research centers and universities, organizational business, among others.

Support mechanisms for organizations linked to innovation sectors are essential for the survival and development in the economic globalization environment. To maintain the vitality over time of an environment, the reference innovative organization must be involved in open dialogue with the included organizations and in activity caring not interfere with the changing dynamics. The analysis of structural change process can be motivated by information and communication technologies, leading to the emergence of innovation organizational forms and collaboration between the economic agents.

No single alone actor or agent, local government, local community, civil society, civil organizations, etc. can achieve impact in specific socio-ecological innovation issues. Socio-ecological transition towards more innovative organizations affects the organizational work and labor, practices, and activities. Organizational-social support innovation systems must be designed to reinforce the organizational objectives and structure consistent with the philosophy and administrative actions.

It is assumed that organizations are open and dynamic systems, composed of technical and social subsystems jointly optimized in management strategies for organizational innovation and development that results in improved performance. Organizational and personal growth in addition to commitment of involved people facilitates learning, innovation, and abilities development.

The organizational component of local innovation systems is structured with a government agency at the top who defines the innovation technology issues to complex executing agencies, public and private research institutions and universities developing basic and applied science knowledge and technology, professional and technical institutions, financial institutions, and development agencies.

The generation of value through economic and social benefits are generated by innovative organizational performance and technology-based products and services. Generation of value by means of specialized human resources for the operation of infrastructure, networks and environments aimed to support organizational innovation, social capita formation and entrepreneurship through components such as the educational programs, technology transfer and commercialization programs. These programs identify and evaluate research with potential for economic value, markets for commercialization and ensure intellectual property of inventions and patents and make decisions on the best marketing strategy.

REFERENCES

Ahumada, L. (2001). *Teoría y cambio en las organizaciones: Un Acercamiento desde los modelos de aprendizaje organizacional*. Ediciones Universitarias de Valparaíso.

Amburgey, T. L., & Rao, H. (1996). Organizational ecology: Past, present and future directions. *Academy of Management Journal, 39*(5), 1265–1286. doi:10.2307/256999

Barron, D. N., West, E., & Hannan, M. T. (1994). A time to grow and a time to die: Growth and mortality of credit unions in New York City, 1914-1990. *American Journal of Sociology, 100*(2), 381–421. doi:10.1086/230541

Beck, U. (1986). Risikogesellschaft: Auf dem weg in eine Andere Moderne. Frankfurt a M: Suhrkamp.

Bell, G. G., & Dyck, B. (2011). Conventional resource-based theory and its radical alternative: A less materialist-individualist approach to strategy. *Journal of Business Ethics, 99*(1), 121–130. doi:10.100710551-011-1159-4

Bell, M. (2004). *Farming for us all: Practical agriculture & the cultivation of sustainability*. The Pennsylvania State University Press.

Berkes, F., & Folke, C. (Eds.). (1998). *Linking social and ecological systems: Management practices and social mechanisms for building resilience*. Cambridge University Press.

Blau, P. M., & Schoenherr, R. (1971). *The structure of organizations*. Basic Books.

Bogers, M., & West, J. (2012). Managing distributed innovation: Strategic utilization of open and user innovation. *Creativity and Innovation Management, 21*(1), 61–75. doi:10.1111/j.1467-8691.2011.00622.x

Boons, F., & Lüdeke-Freund, F. (2013). Business models for sustainable innovation: State of the art and steps towards a research agenda. *Journal of Cleaner Production, 45*, 9–19. https://www.sciencedirect.com/science/article/pii/S0959652612003459. doi:10.1016/j.jclepro.2012.07.007

Burns, R. B. (1981). *The self-concept*. Longman.

Campbell, B. (2018). Biodiversity, livelihoods and struggles over sustainability in Nepal. *Landscape Research, 43*(8), 1056–1067. doi:10.1080/01426397.2018.1503241

Carolan, M. S. (2006). Social change and the adoption and adaptation of knowledge claims: Whose truth do you trust regarding sustainable agriculture? *Agriculture and Human Values, 23*(3), 325–339. doi:10.100710460-006-9006-4

Cherns, A. (1976). The principles of sociotechnical design. *Human Relations, 29*(8), 783–792. doi:10.1177/001872677602900806

Chesbrough, H. W. (2003). *Open innovation: The new imperative for creating and profiting from technology*. Harvard Business School Press.

Dabla-Norris, E., Ji, Y., Townsend, R. M., & Filiz Unsal, D. (2015). Distinguishing constraints of financial inclusion and their impact on GDP and inequality. *NBER Working Paper 20821*. Cambridge, MA: National Bureau of Economic Research.

Dale, V. H., Brown, S., Haeuber, R. A., Hobbs, N. T., Huntly, N., Naiman, R. J., Riebsame, W. E., Turner, M. G., & Valone, T. J. (2000). Ecological principles and guidelines for managing the use of land. *Ecological Applications, 10*(3), 639–670. doi:10.2307/2641032

Danter, K. J., Griest, D. L., Mullins, G. W., & Norland, E. (2000). Organizational change as a component of ecosystem management. *Society & Natural Resources*, *13*(6), 537–547. doi:10.1080/08941920050114592

de Geus, A. (1997). *The Living Company - habits for survival in a turbulent environment*. Harvard Business School Press.

de Geus, A. (1998). *Planning as learning*. Harvard Business School Press.

de Melo, M. A. C. (1991). *Innovatory planning: Antecipating social and technological innovation. Resumo. Anais do "3e Congrés International in France:Le Génie Industriel: facteur de Competitivité des enterprises"*. Groupement de Génie Industriel-GGI.

de Melo, M. A. C. (1997). *Processo de planejamento e as inovações tecnológicas e sociais: Uma perspectiva sócio-ecológica*. Anais do 5o. Seminário de Modernização Tecnológica.

de Melo, M. A. C. (2002). Inovação e modernização tecnológica e organizacional nas MPMEs: O domínio interorganizacional. *Seminário Internacional: Políticas para Sistemas Produtivos Locais de MPME*: 2002.

de Melo, M. A. C. (2002). *Enriquecendo a atuação de incubadora de emrpesas.Tecnologia e inovação: experiências de gestão nas micro e pequenas empresas*. PGT/USP.

de Melo, M. A. C., & de Melo, L. C. P. (1985). Os agentes reticuladores e o processo de planejamento: um estudo de caso. Anais do X simpósio nacional de pesquisa de administração em C&T. FEA/USP.

Elkington, J. (1997). The triple bottom line. *Environmental Management: Readings and Cases*, *2*, 49–66.

Evan, W. (1966). Organizational lag. *Human Organization*, *25*(1), 51–53. doi:10.17730/humo.25.1.v7354t3822136580

Fischer-Kowalski, M., Haas, W., Wiedenhofer, D., Weisz, U., Pallua, I., & Possanner, N. (2012). Socio-ecological transitions: definition, dynamics and related global scenarios. Institute of Social Ecology - AAU, Centre for European Policy Studies, Vienna, Brussels.

Geroski, P. A., & Mazzucato, M. (2001). Modelling the dynamics of industry populations. *International Journal of Industrial Organization*, *19*(7), 1003–1022. doi:10.1016/S0167-7187(01)00060-1

Gouverneur, J., & Netzer, N. (2014). Take the wheel and steer! Trade unions and the just transition. In *State of the World 2014. State of the World*. Island Press. doi:10.5822/978-1-61091-542-7_21

Hall, A., Rasheed Sulaiman, V., Clark, N., & Yoganand, B. (2003). From measuring impact to learning institutional lessons: An innovation systems perspective on improving the management of international agricultural research. *Agricultural Systems*, *78*(2), 213–241. doi:10.1016/S0308-521X(03)00127-6

Hart, S. L. (1995). A natural-resource-based view of the firm. *Academy of Management Review*, *20*(4), 986–1014. doi:10.2307/258963

Hart, S. L. (2007). *Capitalism at the crossroads: Aligning business, earth, and humanity*. Wharton School Publishing.

Hart, S. L., & Dowell, G. (2011). A natural-resource-based view of the firm: Fifteen years after. *Journal of Management*, *37*(5), 1464–1479. doi:10.1177/0149206310390219

Hassanein, N. (1999). *Changing the way America farms: Knowledge and community in the sustainable agriculture movement*. University of Nebraska Press.

Herbst, P. G. (1974). *Socio-technical design: Strategies in multi-disciplinary research*. Tavistock Publications.

IAASTD. (2008). *About*. International assessment of agricultural knowledge, science and technology for Development. https://www.agassessment.org/.

Imperial, M. T. (1999). Institutional analysis and ecosystem-based management: The institutional analysis and development framework. *Environmental Management, 24*(4), 449–465. doi:10.1007002679900246 PMID:10501859

Kiron, D., Kruschwitz, N., Haanaes, K., Reeves, M., & Gho, E. (2013). The innovation bottom line. research report. *MIT Sloan Management Review, 54*(2), 69–73.

Kurucz, E. C., Colbert, B. A., & Marcus, J. (2014). Sustainability as a provocation to rethink management education: Building a progressive educative practice. *Management Learning, 45*(4), 437–457. doi:10.1177/1350507613486421

Lalkaka, R., & Abetti, P. (1999). Business incubation and enterprise support systems in restructuring countries. *Creativity and Innovation Management, 8*(3), 197–209. doi:10.1111/1467-8691.00137

Luhmann, N. (1991). *Soziologie des risikos*. De Gruyter.

Madsen, T. L., & Mckelvey, B. (1996). Darwinian dynamic capability: Performance effects of balanced intrafirm selection processes. *Proceedings - Academy of Management, 1996*(1), 149. doi:10.5465/ambpp.1996.4978158

Massey, D., Quintas, P., & Wield, D. (1992). *High tech fantasies: Science parks in society, science, and space*. Routledge.

Morgan, K. (2017). Nurturing novelty: Regional innovation policy in the age of smart specialization. *Environment and Planning C. Politics and Space, 35*(4), 569–583.

NRC. (2010). *Toward sustainable agricultural systems in the 21st century*. National Academic Press. [National Research Council]

OECD. (1999). *Boosting innovation: The cluster approach*. OECD.

OECD. (2001a). *Innovative Clusters: drivers of national innovation systems*. OECD.

OECD. (2001b). *Innovative Networks: co-operation in national innovation systems*. OECD.

OECD. (2001c). *Innovative Networks: co-operation in national innovation systems*. OECD.

Olsson, P., Folke, C., & Hahn, T. (2004). Social-ecological transformation for ecosystem management: the development of adaptive co-management of a wetland landscape in southern Sweden. *Ecology and Society, 9*(4), 2. https://www.ecologyandsociety.org/vol9/iss4/art2

Paskaleva, K. (2011). The smart city: A nexus for open innovation? *Intelligent Buildings International, 3*(3), 153–171. doi:10.1080/17508975.2011.586672

Porter, M. (2001). Clusters of Innovation: regional foundations of U. S competitiveness. Council on Competitiveness. Washington, D.C.: Monitor Group.

Prahalad, C. K. (2010). The fortune at the bottom of the pyramid: Eradicating poverty through profits (Revised and Updated 5th Anniversary Edition). Upper Saddle River, N.J.: Wharton School Pub.

Price, R. M. (1996). Technology and strategic advantage. *California Management Review, 38*(3), 38–56. doi:10.2307/41165842

Ramakrishnan, P. S. (2000). Biodiversity, land use and traditional ecological knowledge: the context. In: Ramakrishnan, P.S., Chandrashekara, U.M., Elouard, C., Guilmoto, C.Z., Maikhuri, R.K., Rao, K.S., Sankar, S., Saxena, K.G. (eds). Mountain biodiversity, land use dynamics and traditional ecological knowledge. Oxford & IBH Publication, India (P) Ltd.

Rees, W. E. (2002). Globalization and sustainability: Conflict or convergence? *Bulletin of Science, Technology & Society, 22*(4), 249–268. doi:10.1177/0270467602022004001

Schon, D. A. (1973). A study of field experience. [Unpublished memorandum, Massachusetts Institute of Technology].

Schumpeter, J. (1934). *The Theory of Economic Development: An inquiry into profits, capital, credit, interest and the business cycle.* Transaction Publishers.

Schumpeter, J. A. (1942). *Capitalism, Socialism and Democracy.* HarperCollins.

Silvestre, B. S. (2015). Sustainable supply chain management in emerging economies: Environmental turbulence, institutional voids, and sustainability trajectories. *International Journal of Production Economics, 167,* 156–169. doi:10.1016/j.ijpe.2015.05.025

Sukhdev, P. (2013). Transforming the corporation into a driver of sustainability. In *State of the World 2013.* Island Press. doi:10.5822/978-1-61091-458-1_12

Tidd, J. (1997). *Managing innovation: Integrating technological, market and organizational change.* John Wiley & Sons.

Tomich, T. P., Brodt, S., Ferris, H., Galt, R., Horwath, W. R., Kebreab, E., Leveau, J. H. J., Liptzin, D., Lubell, M., Merel, P., Michelmore, R., Rosenstock, T., Scow, K., Six, J., Williams, N., & Yang, L. (2011). Agroecology: A review from a global-change perspective. *Annual Review of Environment and Resources, 36*(1), 193–222. doi:10.1146/annurev-environ-012110-121302

Trist, E. L. (1971). Critique of scientific management in terms of socio-technical theory. *Prak-seologia,* (39-40), 159–174.

Trist, E. L. (1976a). A Concept of Organizational Ecology: an invited address to the three Melbourne universities. Melbourne, AU: xxx.

Trist, E. L. (1976b). Action research and adaptative planning. In A. W. Clark (Ed.), *Experimenting with Organizational Life: The Action Research Approach.* Plenum Press. doi:10.1007/978-1-4613-4262-5_17

Trist, E. L. (1981). Evolution of socio-technical systems. *Occasional Paper, 02.* Ontario: Quality of Working Life Center.

Vedovello, C. (2001). Perspectivas e limites da interação entre universidades e MPMEs de base tecnológica localizadas em incubadoras de empresas. *Revista do bndes, 16*(8), 281-316.

Walske, J. (2013). Exploring theoretical fit of the resource-based view and human capital theory. In Social entrepreneurship and broader theories: Shedding new light on the 'bigger picture. *Journal of Social Entrepreneurship, 4*(1), 88–107. doi:10.1080/19420676.2012.725422

Warren, R. L. (1967). The interorganizational field as a focus for investigation. *Administrative Science Quarterly, 12*(3), 396–419. doi:10.2307/2391312

Westley, F. (1995). Governing design: The management of social systems and ecosystems management. In L. H. Gunderson & C. S. Holling (Eds.), *Barriers and Bridges to the Renewal of Ecosystems and Institutions*. Columbia University Press.

Wolf, S., & Primmer, E. (2006). Between incentives and action: A pilot study of biodiversity conservation competencies for multifunctional forest management in Finland. *Society & Natural Resources, 19*(9), 845–861. doi:10.1080/08941920600835601

KEY TERMS AND DEFINITIONS

Innovation strategy: It is the process of directing and managing projects based on innovative ideas. The innovation strategy is one that defines the direction of projects of this type. As shocking and disruptive as they may seem, ideas do not get started or run on their own. Its development process is just as important or even more important than the idea itself.

Innovation: A process that modifies existing elements, ideas, or protocols, improving them or creating new ones that have a favorable impact on the market.

Organization: An association of people who relate to each other and use resources of various kinds to achieve certain objectives or goals. An organization is an ordered structure where people with various roles, responsibilities or positions coexist and interact to achieve a particular goal. The organization usually has rules (formal or informal) that specify the position of each person in the structure and the tasks they should carry out.

Organizational innovation: It is the search for new organizational designs altering the internal structures of the organization and involves changing the boundaries between the organization and the market.

Socio-ecosystem innovation: An environment made up of various interrelated agencies and functions whose purpose is to promote innovation and from it the economic development of a territory.

Socio-ecosystem: System that includes among its component elements and interrelationships those of natural and social systems constituting an integrated whole. Holistic concept that helps to understand and manage the systemic unity of the biosphere.

Chapter 6
Sustainable Change:
Building Resilience Advancing Corporate Social Responsibility

Kim Sanders
University of Phoenix, USA

ABSTRACT

Organizational resilience is herein defined as the ability to positively manage environmental instability over time operationalized by strong corporate social responsibility (CSR). Appropriate CSR can help align business practices both in and outside the organization with current significant economic, social, environmental, and public health issues. Both academics and practitioners have discussed resilience as a voluntary and unobservable paradigm typically measured by outcomes. It is the hope of the author and the aim of this chapter that the sustain optimize change model and its renewed approach to optimized change management will expand corporate social responsibility awareness and activities, that address vulnerabilities, and build resilience in retort to augmented social inequalities.

INTRODUCTION

According to the assertions claimed by Tischendorf (2020), capitalism has generated unbelievable prosperity, manufactured products, provided services for the masses worldwide, and more, but the pandemic has and is still illuminating and intensifying key market breakdowns along with what can be seen as governmental breaches. Researchers, scholars, and other numerous other academics have tackled Corporate Social Responsibility (CSR) and its relationship to COVID-19 from multiple and varied perspectives. Although it appears difficult to garner consensus on many issues related to this topic, it is interesting to find that most concur in calling for efforts for an established and enhanced strategy to sustain the recovery of individual businesses, specific industries, and the nation.

DOI: 10.4018/978-1-6684-8392-3.ch006

BACKGROUND

Very few would argue that the COVID-19 emergency has made bare an overabundance of societal issues with vast economic and social effects, unfortunately precise evaluation of the impact has yet to be attained. Such an assessment is contingent upon on wide-ranging concern such as the development and rollout of updated and current vaccine variants, new federal policies, and mandates in retort to covid-related problems. In addition, how corporations' plan or intend to respond to and counteract the challenges is at the forefront of the minds of business owners, employees, and other members of society.

Organizations must seek ways to meet the demands of the moment, one approach is the move towards greater corporate agility. Agile organizations will benefit by increased competitive advantage during the wind down phase that we are now experiencing and after most certainly after the pandemic has subsided. Organizations may realize this level of success by distinctly delineating renewed sustainability strategies and initiatives, and social corporate responsibility that demonstrate the ability meet the stakeholder's expectations while building needed competency, capacity, and capability for sustained optimized change. COVID-19 and the fallout are creating massive challenges across the globe for organizations of all sizes and has devastated most Sustainable Development Goals (Tischendorf, 2020). The pandemic has presented businesses with a range of unimagined problems. As a result, the federal government has sprung into action to provide corporations with some much-needed relief. The relief comes in the form of financial assistance such as bailouts. But which organizations were afforded this relief and in what amounts?

Considerable assurance has been given by the federal government in partnership with banks and financial institutions, to support a green recovery with the use of public resources. The question, that becomes apparent to citizens worried about the way public funds are used, is to ask decision makers that govern issues related to corporate social responsibility, should this funding be reserved for or distributed based on the level of economic inclusivity for green sustainability. A recovery consistent with moving towards a green organization will pointedly enhance their resilience, economies, and society in general.

COVID-19 has manifested unparalleled challenges for organizations as they seek to survive destructive realities and assuage future risks for their stakeholders in specific and broader society in general (Crane, 2020). When political, fiscal, and social environments are volatile corporate organizations are faced with the endless battle for market differentiation and increased profits, while balancing the need to attract and maintain exceptional employees coupled with the maintenance of a suitable growing market share and customer base. In other words, these organizations must demonstrate the capability to be resilient. Resilience in business or organizational management can be thought of as an interdisciplinary idea that shelters a range of research fields, such as economics, physics, mathematics, analytics, psychology, engineering, social science, law, medicine, and others that demonstrate an organization's ability to recover after it has been reeked with and devastated by the ongoing disruption and global impact of an occurrence such as COVID-19 (Wendong et al., 2019).

Organizational resilience is herein defined as the ability to positively manage environmental instability over time operationalized by strong corporate social responsibility. Appropriate CSR can help align business practices both in and outside the organization with current significant economic, social, environmental, political, and public health issues. Researchers, academics, and other professionals in the field have discussed resilience as a voluntary and unobservable paradigm typically measured by outcomes (Lamprinakis, 2019).

COVID-19 has further illuminated the pervasive systemic societal inequities which are and have been present and consistent in most if not all government and business practices and institutions, and industries. The author explores the concept of strategy optimized change and how it might present organizationally in the wake of unprecedented circumstances experienced by citizens and organizations on the local, national, and global levels. For purposes of this exercise, strategy optimized change can be thought of as the intersection of organizational strategy and sustainable change coupled with positive corporate social responsibility.

MAIN FOCUS OF THE CHAPTER

This chapter will cover the implications to women, minorities, and other underserved populations, by providing defining variables that highlight the disparities between race and gender in the workplace utilizing research acumens coupled with compelling statistical insights drawn from various texts and measured outcomes. This chapter will also lend itself to industry leaders to foster the potential for advancing awareness and utilizing such insights as a resource mechanism to help current and future businesses and their leaders to reassess and address these and other disparities to affect and sustain organizational change.

Since the onset of COVID-19, corporations and in some cases entire industries have been faced by innumerable challenges, known and unknown vulnerabilities, increased interdependence, along with health and physical safety exposures for employees, stakeholders, shareholders, and customers. The pandemic has magnified prevailing social and economic inequality and catapulted the social and economic gaps to top of mind of public cognizance (Bapuji et al., 2020).

As a result, organizations in essence have been forced to reevaluate future corporate strategy and outdated business models. In doing so organizations who seek agility and resiliency have begun to prioritize concerns such as goals and objectives, developing sustainable supply chains, and the availability of remote work. Long-term or sustained resilience will enable corporations to tackle systemic inequalities, while building strategic agility that will encourage and help foster more efficacious strategic commitments and enhance their capacity to survive and adapt to constant fluctuations in these turbulent times of the slow to end pandemic.

The United States government along with several businesses and or industries have been more recently concerned with addressing challenges to both social and operational environments coupled with the attempt to mitigate vulnerabilities in the workplace. According to Bapuji et al. 2020 (pg 1206), corporate social responsibility can contribute to the *"normalization, reinforcement, and reduction of economic inequalities in society"*. The pandemic has led to noticeable and increased awareness of corporate social responsibility efforts since the illumination of several far-reaching vulnerabilities that speak to the core framework of these companies (*Lancet,* 2020). Strategies to battle the health and economic crisis amplified by COVID-19 are contingent upon the organizations ability to build and sustain resilience in the interchange amongst government, organizations, and society, with a more profound emphasis on economics, the environment and social strategy.

Despite the devastation exacted by the effects of COVID-19, the pandemic has undoubtedly presented a unique occasion for local, state, and federal policy makers in parallel with corporate decision makers, shareholders, and boards of directors to analyze in real time the efficacy of current and long standing corporate social responsibility approaches. Use of the Sustain Optimize Change Model (SOCM) approach will facilitate and support corporations in revisiting corporate strategy to focus on building resilience and to advance and contribute to positive corporate social responsibility. It is the hope of the author and the aim of this chapter that the Sustain Optimize Change Model and its renewed approach to optimized change management will expand corporate social responsibility awareness and activities, that address vulnerabilities, and build resilience in retort to augmented social inequalities.

Post pandemic as organization begin to navigate what has been coined the new normal businesses must focus on building more resilient, equitable and inclusive organizations and by extension, society that will seek to benefit underrepresented or vulnerable populations. Corporate social responsibility should develop proactively far beyond pure philanthropy to embrace and advance a more just, fair, and integrated society. Organizations that strive to acquire or sustain resiliency should be reminded of the connection between or intersection of strategic agility, and dynamic capability (Zhao, 2021). Corporations should entrench corporate social responsibility in strategy development as a fundamental part of any strategic plan. Additionally, according to Zhao (2021) the competence to attain strategic agility and dynamic capability must be developed.

Use of the Sustain Optimize Change Model in preparing for enhanced corporate social responsibility will lend itself to support organization in the development of dynamic capabilities, that transition into *"the ability to integrate, build, and reconfigure internal and external competences to address rapidly changing environments"* (Cantrell et al., 2015; Teece et al., 1997). Companies seeking resiliency aspire to become dynamic and capable of cultivating and sustaining a competitive edge. Dynamic capabilities are central to exploit future possibilities and create optimal business strategy. Organizations that are strategically agile, and dynamically capable have the greatest potential to acquire across-the-board knowledge of the specific risks they may encounter in the future (Cantrell et al., 2015).

Social Determinants of Health

The COVID-19 pandemic has sparked debate related to corporate objectives and how organizations should handle the actualities of inequality, systemic injustice, and that which is required to protect vulnerable populations. Considering the intensified illumination of innumerable and widespread disparities policy makers and organizations have had to contemplate ways to develop an optimal strategy, business operations and change models more conducive for sustained and responsible change. This change is necessary to not only the existing internal environment but the external or social environment to confront the covid crisis and its longevity but to also tackle the aftermath and prepare for the next inevitable natural or man-made public health crisis. Noted disparities are present in corporate hiring and promotions, the justice system, banking and lending practices, health, gender, wages, and real estate appraisals for example. All of which are inconsistent with appropriate or accountable corporate social responsibility but consistent with unfair labor, organization, and corporate policy and practices.

Although it is true that COVID-19 does not discriminate, inequality unfortunately does, and the consequences and impact of the virus and global pandemic are proven not to be homogeneous across demographics (Zhao, 2021). Vulnerable populations, those with poor physical, psychological, or social health (Aday, 2003), are affected the most and unquestionably are at increased risk of injury, harm such as long covid, or death. Vulnerable cohorts in the pandemic have been racial and ethnic minorities, children, the elderly, immigrants and refugees, lesbian, gay, bisexual, transgender and queer (LGBTQ), poor, indigent, incarcerated, indigenous, the disabled, and women have all been affected disproportionately. Many businesses have contributed to or participated in this reality whether consciously or unconsciously.

Since vulnerable populations have been routinely and customarily omitted from clinical research, disregarded, or absent from socioeconomic and political agendas, discussion, or debate (Delaunay, Augusto, & Santos, 2020), understanding their circumstances can support an immediate and well-deserved focus on long standing health disparities and wealth inequities through the lens of the social determinants of health. Ask yourself what are the realities of years of omissions from inclusion in the institutions that drive the economy of the United States for entire races and generations of individuals, families, and communities? Now sit with and digest the truth and now become part of the solution.

Recent studies have promoted the notion that organizational strategies or processes are critical to create resilience (Antes & Umit, 2011). Very little has been explored or written about what contributes to an organization's resilience and how or what that may look like in a natural setting such as society post and during COVID-19. The interdependence between the social environment and economic welfare is calling out for behaviors that demonstrate social and environmental responsible behaviors from both within and outside of the business sector. The author puts forth that greater social corporate responsibility would aid in organizational resilience and sustainability despite being thrust in the middle of unprecedented times.

There has been considerable trauma, adversity and discussion since the summer of 2020 surrounding positive social change, equity, inclusion, diversity, healthcare, individual rights over the common good or the good of society, public health vaccinations and how leadership could or should respond. The realities of COVID-19 and the political and social unrest over the past couple of years have sparked copious debate about many issues but two are topics of interest here, first socioeconomic status or conditions and second equity. Before equity can be confronted socioeconomics must be explored.

Socioeconomics has been defined in several ways but in this context for these purposes it can be defined as the social, political, and cultural conditions that form lives and inform behaviors. The term lifestyle drift explains the short-sighted trend in public health to emphasize individual behaviors, that have been proven to cause health inequity such as drug and alcohol use, smoking, and poor diet but continue ignoring conditions that drive the behaviors. This appears to be yet another form of discrimination to in some way blame those impacted rather than the known gaps in systems that drive the conditions. Notwithstanding lifestyle considerations many socioeconomic factors such as discrimination or bias, living below the poverty level, and social determinants of health are systemic, and contribute tremendously to the equity gap.

Socioeconomic standing effects the quality of primary and secondary education, through things like community districting or if a person can make enough wages for private school (Solomon & Weller, 2018). Quality of education affects the probability of those who might otherwise be in pursuit of higher education, which in turn affects future employment prospects and by default shapes their future socioeconomic condition (Virginia Commonwealth University, 2015). Socioeconomics played a huge part in COVID-19 in terms of risk of infection and death, and later the availability and distribution of the vaccine.

Further, socioeconomic standing can influence the kinds of occupations individuals work and their career course or path. A persons type or category of occupation ultimately either supports or transforms a person's status through revenue received from participation in the workforce. In addition, the type of job one performs has a direct impact on whether the person is allowed to work from home. This is quite often decided based on position placing salaried professionals over those who earn an hourly wage (Solomon & Weller, 2018).

Likewise, countless hourly employees who do not have the ability to transition to a work from home model generally speaking frequently depend on public forms of transportation. Using public transportation such as buses, metro trains, or even rideshare augments the risk of exposure to COVID-19 transmission. It is difficult to social distance and avoid encountering other humans while using public forms of transportation.

Social determinants of health have assumed center stage in current health policy debate. Social determinants of health (SDOH) are the conditions in the environments where people are born, live, learn, work, play, worship, and age that affect a wide range of health, functioning, and quality-of-life outcomes and risks (DHHS n.d.). The US Department of Health and Human Services denotes that social determinants of health are comprised of secure housing, transportation, and communities; racism, discrimination, violence; education, job opportunities and income.

Reflect how a person's lack of access to basic human needs has the potential to impact every aspect of daily living. Think of a homeless person with no access to clean water and a food insecure child living below the poverty level. How does the homeless person begin to look for employment until the need for secure shelter is met and access to clean drinking water is realized? What level of concentration or academic productivity can be achieved by a school aged child who is hungry, cold, exhausted, or suffering from malnutrition? Sustained exposure to any one of these adverse conditions could be harmful to progress of individuals but coupled with one or multiple others is in essence a blueprint to poor, negative, or adverse outcomes and is indicative of the potential for long term generational implications on low-income families and communities of color.

Tackling, understanding, creating awareness activities for social determinants is important to improve health and to reduce long-term established social and economic disparities. There is increased recognition that improving health and achieving health equity requires a broader approach that speaks to the social, economic, and environmental factors that affect health. Behaviors, policies, and practices in sectors not related to health can have a profound impact on an individual's quality of life. For example, a person living in an area with no available public transportation would also have limited access to employment, affordable healthy food choices, and adequate health care. It is becoming increasing understood that a person's zip code can provide a clear and sounder indicator of health over their genetic code (Healthy-People, 2020).

Gender Wage Gap?

Most describe a phenomenon as an exceptional or unexpected occurrence, thing, or event. There are a multitude of complex examples of which to discuss but since the parameters and space for prose in this chapter is limited the decision to address those less complex and more readily understood was made. Two such occurrences involving women, and minorities are considered in this context to help demonstrate the link between organizational policies, corporate culture, customs and norms and society at large. This link illuminates the connection between corporate social responsibility and the social determinants of health.

In one occurrence the results were positive changes for women and in the other the result ushered devastatingly negative outcomes. First the *gender wage gap* includes all women and establishes the starting point for discussion. The occurrence that yielded positive results is the drive by women to seek higher education coupled with obtaining advanced technology skills and training (competence).

The second and final occurrence is COVID-19 and the economic ramifications realized by women and minorities. As a barometer of women's standing in the workplace an examination of wages is explored. During the 20th century, women's contribution to the labor force grew considerably. Women have worked more hours and pursued higher education in larger numbers. Advanced technical skills and higher levels of education are driving women's earnings closer to their male counterparts, but other considerations contribute to an undeniable wedge. Despite this progression, noteworthy wage gaps between men and women continue.

What is the Gender Wage Gap?

The gender wage gap indicates the variance in wages between women and men. Although this gap has been calculated in numerous ways the result is consistent, women earn less than men. In 2017, more women 3.8 million than men 3.1 million were included in the working poor. Based on the Current Population Survey (CPS) the working poor is a term used to describe people who work regularly but make a wage that falls below the national poverty level (United States Census Bureau, 2020). In the same survey the overall working-poor rate was 5.3 percent for women and 3.8 percent for men while working-poor rates for African American women was 10 percent and Hispanic women 9.1 percent, which is more than twice those of Caucasian women at 4.5 percent (United States Bureau of Labor Statistics, 2020). As seen in the statistics women in general but more specifically women of color are those most plagued by the gender wage gap.

A review of the most recently published United States Census Bureau data (2018) revealed women of all races earned, on average, 82 cents for every $1 earned by men of all races. When addressing the wage gap for women, it is imperative to emphasize that there are significant differences by race and ethnicity. The wage gap is larger for most women of color. The 2018 data indicated that 55 percent of African American children live in households headed by single women, 38 percent live below the poverty level while 20 percent of Caucasian children live in households headed by women with 32 percent living in poverty (U.S. Bureau of Labor Statistics, 2018). If we stopped here with just these statistics above, the facts or evidence proves that all women are impacted but women of color experience a double negative in the job market, they are marginalized or penalized for gender and race.

Causes of Wage Gaps

Wage gaps can be attributed to many causes such as differences in career industries and job roles. There are jobs that are traditionally based on gender norms or expectations such as teachers, caregivers and or child-care workers. These jobs are often lower paying and frequently have limitations on hours available to work. Another consideration is variations in years of experience, hours available to and number of hours worked. Typically, in a two-person household, it is the women who traditionally leave the workforce to accommodate caregiving for parents or children and tend to work less hours for the same reasons, in accommodation for family obligations. Reduced hours coupled with less experience equals lower pay or wages and reduced benefits or incentives. In 2019 women earned $545.7 billion less than men (U.S. Bureau of Labor Statistics, 2020). Hiring and compensation decision are often based on previous salary history putting women at deficit at the onset upon hiring. All of this can be viewed as long standing institutional gender-based bias against women and minorities.

This fiscal handicap is cyclic, and the result or impact is a profound limit on economic progress. Many factors such as discrimination, poverty, and social determinants of health are systemic, contribute to the gap and help to create challenges or barriers to wealth generation. Think of it in this way a child who goes to a poor school (old books, low or no technology and educators with limited skills and experience) will receive a poor or substandard education leading to a low paying job as an adult. That child now an adult with a low paying job still lives in a poor neighborhood with limited services and access to financial resources raises a family in the same poor or inferior conditions and the cycle continues. In this scenario there is little room to stop the cycle and build generational wealth since basic survival is of course the top priority.

COVID-19

The second significant and widespread phenomenon up for discussion is the coronavirus pandemic. This virus has clearly illuminated the interconnectivity and interdependence of the SDOH on the financial success and well-being of minority populations. These determinants become important when investigating the extent and ways the events of 2020 interrupted normalcy and disrupted livelihoods in the United States and across the globe. COVID-19 has unmasked many economic or job-related inequities, barriers, and stressors for women and minorities amid the current work force.

The labor force participation rate of all women with children 6 to 17 years old, was 76.5 percent March 2018 (U.S. Bureau of Labor Statistics, 2018). Many women left their jobs during the height of the pandemic to take care of young children and supervise online learning for school-age children when in-person learning ceased, and daycare closed.

Based on reports from the United States Bureau of Labor Statistics the unemployment rate for women varied by race and ethnicity but the rate for women was 3.8 percent as compared to 3.9 percent for men in 2018 (U.S. Bureau of Labor Statistics, 2020). Since 2020 unemployment rates for African American people and other minorities are nearly double those of Caucasian workers (Due et al., 2021). The pandemic has caused the largest female-to-male gap in unemployment rates since 2000 (Kurtz, 2021). Recent reports indicate almost 450,000 more women than men have been displaced from employment (U.S. Bureau of Labor Statistics, 2020).

Job losses have disproportionately affected minorities, women, and workers with lower educational attainment or income, as evidenced by the University of Phoenix (UOP) Career Optimism Index and the United States Census Current Population Survey (CPS). The index data revealed households with an annual income below $30,000 realized double the unemployment rates of households with higher income and approximately 56 percent of job market exits, because of the pandemic, were women even though women only represent 48 percent of workforce. Improved socioeconomic structures could elevate the economic health of individuals, families, and organizations.

Building Resilience

Resilient organizations possess the flexibility, agility, and capacity to adapt to and recover from conditions in the environment that have the potential to disrupt or diminish the businesses longevity and resiliency (Zhao, 2021). During these unprecedented times companies should and are expected to undertake more accountable and inclusive policies, daily practices, and inclusive corporate culture to both distinguish and limit exposures throughout and beyond the pandemic to help the United States in the rebuild and recovery efforts. The pandemic is and has had disproportionate consequences on disadvantaged or marginalized populations exposing a myriad of commonplace inequality.

The inequalities are profound many are old, several new because of the current politically charged environment, that provide optimal corporate social responsibility undertakings aimed to decrease known imbalances. For example, organizations could concentrate on helping all communities ascertain access to the internet and technology both hardware and software such as computers and online learning management systems (LMS). In addition to the populations previously mentioned, some others have been identified as contract workers with zero-hours, or employees in the global supply chain. Sustained optimized change most often involve the development of a vulnerability matrix. Through the SOCM the organizations vulnerability is accessed to identify individuals or groups from two perspectives both with employees inside the organization or other populations in communities within society at large.

Post pandemic, as health threats slow down organizations are beginning to navigate what has been coined the new normal. Organizations must focus on building more resilient equitable and inclusive organizations and by extension society, to benefit underrepresented or vulnerable populations. Corporate social responsibility should develop proactively far beyond pure philanthropy to embrace and advance a more just, equitable, and integrated nation.

Organizations that strive to acquire or sustain resiliency should be reminded of the connection of strategic agility, and dynamic capability (Zhao, 2021). Corporations should entrench corporate social responsibility as a fundamental part of any strategic planning. Additionally, according to Zhao (2021) the competence to attain strategic agility and dynamic capability must be developed.

Use of Sustain Optimize Change Model in preparing for enhanced corporate social responsibility will lend itself to support organization in the development of dynamic capabilities, that transition into *"the ability to integrate, build, and reconfigure internal and external competences to address rapidly changing environments"* (Cantrell et al., 1997). Many companies want to be dynamic and capable of cultivating and sustaining a competitive edge. Dynamic capabilities are central to exploit future possibilities and create an optimal business strategy. Organizations that are strategically agile, and dynamically capable have the greatest potential to acquire across-the-board knowledge of the specific risks they may encounter in the future and how to mitigate them when they arise.

Leadership Roles

There has been a tremendous increase in organizations viewing sustainability as a basis of what differentiates or sets them apart from the others and in some way has the tendency to signal competitive advantage. While leaders of organizations might boast and like to denote distinctions between them, the process of change in organizations is identical (Harraf, 2015) and can be a painful eye-opener. Notwithstanding the uncertainty involved with change, a suitable leadership style is essential for successful implementation (Kozcu, 2021). Today leaders must possess the ability and willingness to transition the organization to an agile, adaptive culture with a primary focus on resilience and sustainability. In these rapidly changing and uncertain times flexibility and adaptability is critical. The necessity for leaders of organizations to develop resiliency in terms of structure, competency, capacity, capability is now if the goal is to achieve and maintain competitive advantage. Subsequently, the identification of what are or should now be central areas within an organization demands new attention from organizational leaders in the management of socially responsible sustainable change.

Within any organization the leadership is the principal source and enforcer of their pledge to the vision. Leaders develop the strategy to help employees achieve the mission, vision, and goals. In general, leaders of agile organizations make decisions rapidly and follow through with the implementation of those decisions. A good leader offers guidance and creates the practices an organization follows and executes. Rapid response adjacent to a business decision is closely connected to a leader's capacity to communicate a decision and organize a response (Kozcu, 2021).

Development of a Learning Organization

A learning organization can typically be described as one that, encourages the learning of their employees, seeks to consistently develop, and transform at all levels to include structure, process, and outcomes, avoids stagnation, and improves the bottom line (Kozcu et al., 2021). Organizations such as these characteristically employ the greatest agility, since learning and continuous improvement links with responsiveness and symbolizes the idea that every experience faced by an organization whether the experience is considered positive or negative, represents a learning opportunity (Kozcu et al., 2021).

To maintain competitive advantage, organizations should be rapid to use lessons learned from previous experience both positive and negative (Alipour et al., 2018). It is true that a learning organization cannot be described as specific place; or goal, but rather a learning organization is an environment or space where people consistently expand their competence (Alipour & Karimi, 2018). It has been observed that in organizations of this sort continuous learning is encouraged, knowledge is produced, transferred, and managed, and fresh skills are supported. Learning organizations are vibrant and seek to drive growth and innovation in alignment with organizational goals and strategy.

Today, organizations should offer a context in which the knowledge formation is used and applied in daily life, where normal principles are tested, and this space with new routines equates to value-added activities (Alipour & Karimi, 2018). A learning organization equips employees with the information and knowledge they need to always have the competency, capability, and capacity to maintain a competitive market share.

SOLUTIONS AND RECOMMENDATIONS

Sustain Optimize Change Model (SOCM)

This chapter can be used by leaders in business sectors or industries to establish a mechanism for information brokering, understanding, and utilizing an informed approach when examining and self-reflecting on the potentials to not only understand this disparity phenomenon, but to also look at contributive factors that have helped propagate and endure along this chasm of inequality. Consider a new organizational tool a strategy-based model for sustained change which would assess organizational needs and vulnerabilities, capability, gaps, and next steps or required action.

Against this backdrop, the purpose of this chapter is to explore the concept of strategy optimized change. The researcher asserts that strategy optimization occurs when organizational strategy and change management are aligned in a manner that fosters resilience and sustainability while advancing corporate social responsibility or positive social change. The author presents the development of an optimization model and acknowledges the rareness of the resilience and sustainable development challenges associated with change in the era of a global pandemic. The aim is to mitigate vulnerability both in and outside of the workplace by encouraging and empowering organizations to battle social and environmental challenges in society. This new Sustain Optimize Change Model is in retort to the necessity for progressive approaches to organizational change management and strategic planning.

FUTURE RESEARCH DIRECTIONS

SOCM is agile, outcomes driven and implemented through the lens of 3 C's competency, capability, and capacity. The 3 Cs are developed over three fluid, and dynamic phases unique to the organization's specific requirements or circumstances. The phases are briefly outlined below. Phase 3 capacity has two parts vulnerability/gaps and action plan.

The 3 C's

Phase 1: Competency (Needs)

This phase of the SOCM is based on needs. As such a needs assessment of the organization, will be conducted to understand, categorize, and prioritize the identified needs.

A competency is what is commonly referred to as KSA's or knowledge, skills, abilities. Competency further includes employee related dynamics and individualities that help distinguish superior performance from ordinary performance under quantified conditions. Organizations and businesses identify competencies to plainly describe the core functions and requirements of the job. Attainment of goals and peak organizational performance if often indicated by how effective the organization makes use of resources such as technology, capital, material, and human. To be clear an organization can only achieve its express or implied goals through the efforts of and availability and cooperation of human resources. If an organizations pool of human resources is adequately inspired and properly prepared with the necessary proficiencies, which align with organizational core values such as goals, mission, vision, and strategy it has the potential to have a significant impact on the organization's performance. In addition, a central consideration that can help lead to the accomplishment of organizational goals is social cooperation (Rengkung, 2022). Social cooperation within an organization is a characteristic that will certainly demonstrate the level of the organizations capacity for its resources to work together.

Phase 2: Capability (Inventory)

The second phase of SOCM involves an enterprise-wide inventory known as an inventory of services. Such an inventory encapsulates an inventory of not only services, but experience, resources, funding, and other critical operational factors will be assessed or evaluated. This phase will also consider organizational competency.

Capabilities can be described as an organizations capacity to successfully utilize both tangible and intangible resources. These resources are used to complete an action or task all aimed at increased performance. Capabilities are the foundation of what all organizations seek, competitive advantage, while resources are the basis of capabilities (Zhao, 2021).

Resilient and vibrant organizations enjoy the capacity to change in accordance with fluctuations in the economic, social, and political environment through the optimization of their capability and resources. This way of thinking lends itself to the implication organizations that integrate concerns, trends, and realities present in the environment with strategic planning choices can both increase their performance and provide some level of protection for the shared environment (Zhao, 2021). Accordingly, organizations should move forward to concurrently strengthen their capacity to elevate and renew their capability, varied assets, and resources to respond to changes or threats to the above-mentioned environments.

Organizations which are amenable to change are most often those organizations who also appear to strive towards resiliency and a sustainable competitive advantage. Agile organizations need to adjust to their natural environment and implement a change model that is fluid, and congruent with their business structure and organizational strategy (Zhao, 2021). A successful, well-designed implementation of organizational change is critical. In short, resilient organizations need dynamic, flexible capabilities and capacity for sustained change. This approach lends itself to the organization adapting its current proficiencies to new or emerging risks and in addition possibly creating new opportunities and mitigating threats (Mladenova, 2022).

Phase 3: Capacity (Vulnerability & Gaps / Action Plan)

Vulnerability and gap analysis of requirements to meet the needs; and action or the plan to implement, monitor and measure the overall success of the strategic optimized change.

Using the SOCM five characteristics of an organization are normally evaluated to establish its change capacity. They are: (1) structure, (2) goals and strategy, (3) culture, (4) power dynamics, and (5) technology. These characteristics are interconnected and the slightest change in any of them can impact one or more of the others (Gravenhorst et al., 2003). Businesses in almost every industry are overwhelmingly confronted and must both counter and predict constantly fluctuating competitive, economic, technical, market, and social conditions within the new normal (McAlearney et al., 2021). Successful organizational change often remains elusive and must focus on leveraging organizational knowledge to challenge business risks that are both apparent and those that remain unknown.

This chapter seeks to demonstrate how the author using the SOCM model can ask and answer some of the following questions to drive strategy optimized change.

What impact does organizational culture and norms have on strategy decisions and business outcomes?

Based on the situational awareness (assessment findings and enterprise-wide secondary data) what is required to operationalize sustainability practices in the organization?

What organizational strengths, weaknesses, opportunities, and threats are barriers that impede a change management implementation to responsible and sustainable social corporate responsibility?

How can the organization align corporate strategy and positive social corporate responsibility to foster sustainable change and build resilience?

How robust is the organizational competency, capacity, capability for change?

CONCLUSION

When embraced Sustain Optimize Change Model is appropriately flexible and can be adapted by all industries and types of organizations including private business, local, state, and federal governments, the health care industry, universities, and global business models, just to name a few. The three C's, competency, capability, capacity and are imperative to and drive the ability for successful strategy optimization and a well-planned implementation of the Sustain Optimize Change Model.

The United States is at a tipping point in terms of the future of our democracy, a woman's right to choose, and basic human rights. This effort plays a minuscule role in shining a light on this highly complex, multi-dimensional problem and providing tangible solutions. Through the adaptation of the Sustain Optimize Change Model the aim is to foster a paradigm shift in corporate culture and business practices that embraces a strong foundation of corporate social responsibility on the path to organizational resilience and sustainability.

REFERENCES

Alipour, F., & Karimi, R. (2018). Creating and developing learning organization dimensions in educational settings; Role of human resource development practitioners. *International Journal of Management. Accounting & Economics, 5*(4), 197–213.

Ates, A., & Umit, B. (2011). Change process: A key enabler for building resilient SMEs. ("Change process: a key enabler for building resilient SMEs"). *International Journal of Production Research, 49*(18), 5601–5618. doi:10.1080/00207543.2011.563825

Bapuji, H., Patel, C., Ertug, G., & Allen, D. G. (2020). Corona crisis and inequality: Why management research needs a societal turn. *Journal of Management, 46*(7), 1205–1222. doi:10.1177/0149206320925881

Cantrell, J. E., Kyriazis, E., & Noble, G. (2015). Developing CSR giving as a dynamic capability for salient stakeholder management. *Journal of Business Ethics, 130*(2), 403–421. doi:10.100710551-014-2229-1

Crane, A. (2020). *Is COVID-19 changing the face of corporate social responsibility?* BATH. https://blogs. bath.ac.uk/business-and-society/2020/09/09/is-covid-19-changing-the-face-of-corporate-social-responsibility/

Delaunay, C. D., Augusto, A., & Santos, M. (2020). Invisible vulnerabilities: Ethical practical, and methodological dilemmas in conducting qualitative research on the interaction with IVF embryos. *Societies, 10*(1). *Article, 7*, 1–15. doi:10.3390oc10010007

Due, A., Ellingrud, D., Lazar, M., Luby, R., Srinivasan, S., & Van Aken, T. (2021). *Achieving an inclusive US economic recovery.* McKinsey & Company. https://www.mckinsey.com/~/media/McKinsey/Industries/Public%20and%20Social%20Sector/Our%20Insights/Achieving%20an%20inclusive%20US%20economic%20recovery/Achieving-an-inclusive-US-economic-recovery.pdf?shouldIndex=false

Finnegan, M., & O'Donoghue, B. (2019). Rethinking vulnerable groups in clinical research. *Irish Journal of Psychological Medicine, 36*(1), 63–71. doi:10.1017/ipm.2017.73

Gravenhorst, K. M. B., Werkman, R. A., Boonstra, J. J., Gravenhorst, K. M. B., Werkman, R. A., & Boonstra, J. J. (2003). Questionnaire to assess the change capacity of organizations. *Applied Psychology, 52*, 83–105. doi:10.1111/1464-0597.00125

Harraf, A., Wanasika, I., Tate, K., & Talbott, K. (2015). Organizational agility. [JABR]. *Journal of Applied Business Research, 31*(2), 675–686. doi:10.19030/jabr.v31i2.9160

Kozcu, G. Y., & Timurcanday Özmen, Ö. N. (2021). Effects of transformational leadership on organizational change management and organizational ambidexterity. *Global Journal of Economics & Business Studies, 10*(20), 15–25.

Kurtz, A. (2021). The US economy lost 140,000 jobs in December. All of them were held by women. *CNN Business.*

Lamprinakis, L. (2019). Improving business resilience through organizational embeddedness in CSR. *Development and Learning in Organizations, 33*(1), 24–27. doi:10.1108/DLO-06-2018-0071

McAlearney, A. S., Gregory, M., Walker, D. M., & Edwards, M. (2021). Development and validation of an organizational readiness to change instrument focused on cultural competency. *Health Services Research, 56*(1), 145–153. doi:10.1111/1475-6773.13563 PMID:33025602

Mladenova, I. (2022). Relation between organizational capacity for change and readiness for Change. *Administrative Sciences (2076-3387), 12*(4), 135. doi:10.3390/admsci12040135

Nelson, J. (2020). Staying Resilient During and Post Covid-19—Research Findings and Resources for Entrepreneurs and Governments: Interview with Jane Nelson (Harvard Kennedy School by Susann Tischendorf). *Inclusive Business.* https://www.inclusivebusiness.net/ib-voices/staying-resilient-during-and-post-covid-19-research-findings-and-resources-entrepreneurs

Rengkung, L. R. (2022). Exploration and exploitation: Driving organizational capability and organizational change toward competitive advantage. *Management Theory and Studies for Rural Business and Infrastructure Development, 44*(1), 39–51. doi:10.15544/mts.2022.05

Solomon, D., & Weller, C. E. (2018). *Systematic inequality: how America's structural racism helped create the black-white wealth gap.* Center for American Progress. https://www.americanprogress.org/issues/race/reports/ 2018/02/21/447051/systematic-inequality/

Teece, D., Pisano, G., & Shuen, A. (1997). Dynamic capabilities and strategic management. *Strategic Management Journal, 18*(7), 509–533. doi:10.1002/(SICI)1097-0266(199708)18:7<509::AID-SMJ882>3.0.CO;2-Z

The Lancet. (2020). Redefining vulnerability in the era of COVID-19. *Lancet, 395,* 1089.

U.S. Bureau of Labor Statistics. (2019). *Women in the labor force: a databook.* BLS. https://www.bls.gov/opub/reports/womens-databook/2019/home.htm

U.S. Bureau of Labor Statistics. (2020). *Usual weekly earnings of wage and salary workers fourth quarter 2019, Table 1.* BLS. https://www.bls.gov/news.release/archives/wkyeng_01172020.pdf

U.S. Census Bureau. (2021). *Current population survey: PINC-05. Work experience-people 15 years old and over, by total money earnings, age, race, Hispanic origin, sex, and disability status: 2018.* USCB. https://www.census.gov/data/tables/time-series/demo/income-poverty/cps-pinc/pinc-05.html

Virginia Commonwealth University. (2015). *Education and health: The return on investment.* Virginia Commonwealth University. https://societyhealth.vcu.edu/work/the-projects/education- and-health-the-return-on-investment.html

Wendong, L., Wei, Y., & Li, X. (2019). What dimension of CSR matters to organizational resilience? Evidence from China. *Sustainability (Basel), 11*(6), 1561. doi:10.3390u11061561

Zhao, J. (2021). Reimagining corporate social responsibility in the Era of COVID-19: Embedding resilience and promoting corporate social competence. *Sustainability (Basel), 13*(12), 6548. doi:10.3390u13126548

KEY TERMS AND DEFINITIONS

Capability: Capabilities can be described as an organization's ability to successfully utilize both tangible and intangible resources.

Capacity: Organizational alignment of (1) structure, (2) goals and strategy, (3) culture, (4) power dynamics, and (5) technology.

Competency: What is commonly referred to as KSA's or knowledge, skills, and abilities.

Corporate Social Responsibility: Organizations contributing to the social, economic and environmental conditions of society in a positive way and standing up for what is right over profits.

Gender Wage Gap: The variance in wages between women and men.

Organizational Resilience: The ability to positively manage environmental instability over time operationalized by strong corporate social responsibility.

Social Determinants of Health: The conditions in the environments where people are born, live, learn, work, play, worship, and age that affect a wide range of health, functioning, and quality-of-life outcomes and risks.

Strategy Optimized Change: The intersection of organizational strategy and sustainable change coupled with positive corporate social responsibility.

Sustain Optimize Change Model: Modern change model used to assist organizations preparing for enhanced corporate social responsibility and to support organizations in the development of dynamic capabilities.

Chapter 7
The Work–Life Dynamics Cultural Impact:
Evolving the Future of Strategic Holistic Ecosystems Post Pandemic

Joanne Príncipe
https://orcid.org/0000-0001-6510-0086
Purposeful Advising & Coaching LLC, USA

ABSTRACT

This chapter explores the benefits of leveraging strategic tactics incorporating holistic approaches throughout cross-functional ecosystems with a deep dive into core work-life dynamics associated with organizational effectiveness, culture transformations, and change leadership aspects impacting the organizational development (OD) discipline evolution. Businesses today are consistently undergoing rapid change, triggered by the current volatile, uncertain, complex, and ambiguous (VUCA) post-pandemic state of the world. To enhance organizational efficiencies and effectiveness, astute leaders have found it imperative to align long-term evidenced-based scientific OD strategies with measurable people management and business outcomes. The key concepts in this chapter will inform best practices, deepen awareness at all levels, and establish appreciation for holistic leadership mindsets, which can address challenges such as internal aspects of employee disengagement and external aspects of customer or stakeholder dissatisfaction.

INTRODUCTION

The COVID-19 pandemic impacted the future of work as these unprecedented times have for the most part transformed the traditional workplace toward hybrid environments on a permanent basis within corporate America. Vázquez-de-Príncipe (2021) aligned principles of continuous organizational development (OD) improvements while investigating organizational effectiveness facets such as workplace culture leadership, change management, and sustainable culture transformations within various sectors, including

DOI: 10.4018/978-1-6684-8392-3.ch007

nonprofit, private, public, and government. This multidisciplinary research incorporated superconscious leadership principles, which inspired a new framework of Work-Life Predictive Dynamics and informed the ideation for the Holistic Leadership Intelligence (HLQ) Model (Vázquez-de-Príncipe, 2021).

The doctoral dissertation study explored the influence of leadership and human-intelligences on impacting work-life dynamics towards fostering sustainable organizational excellence transformations. In Vázquez-de-Príncipe's (2021) study, organizational excellence was perceived as the capacity of professional practitioners to catalyze dynamic cultural enhancements towards serving as a precursor alignment construct for establishing sustained quality performance improvements. Additionally, enterprise organizational change management was emphasized as being necessary to effectively communicate strategic business transformations with a concerted effort to mitigating the risk of resistance and to minimizing uncertainty or obstructions towards enhancement behaviors and engagements (Vázquez-de-Príncipe, 2021).

Change agents, in particular, have the critical role of anticipating resistors, analyzing the potential consequences from any negativity, and engaging the workforce to learn perspectives from the resisting person or the people asked to perform a new behavior or activity. Change professionals challenge complacency intentionally to lead-by-example for promoting the desired behavior, strategically design motivators, and courageously address the potential consequences from "culture of entitlement" behaviors often evident in highly-hierarchical "public sector with strong civil service rules and…unionized workforces" (Kendall & Bodinson, 2017, p. 111). The pandemic triggered unplanned change for the world-at-large, which exposed the lack of resiliency and adaptability within public organizations and beyond. A demonstration of the lack of resilience and adaptability was the inability to seize opportunities to influence work-life evolution positively. The investigation highlighted work-life dynamics impacted by the volatile, uncertain, complex, and ambiguous (VUCA) (Diefenbach & Deelmann, 2016) state of the world, incorporating the core concepts of leadership, authenticity, grit, resilience, social-emotional skills, growth intelligence, and spiritual intelligence (Vázquez-de-Príncipe, 2021).

In sum, this chapter will deepen multi-level awareness, understanding, and appreciation for subject matter, guided by doctoral dissertation findings and outcomes, while incorporating current topic-specific insights associated with concerns about measuring effectiveness of OD strategies during the post-pandemic world. Additionally, the audience will receive recommendations and sample reflective questions to ask themselves and others before embarking on the quest of becoming a holistic-minded manager or leader within post-pandemic multicultural organizations in spite of facing corporate challenges. Furthermore, the objective is to encourage industry and thought leaders to engage with the findings for raising provocative inquiries that can potentially influence the future of Work/Life research. Moreover, the aim of collaboration is to build a resource to further relationships between researchers and industry leaders towards the elevation of high-quality leadership and management discipline enhancements within holistic-oriented organizations for the near- and long-term betterment of the world-at-large.

KEY CONCEPTS

This section emphasizes important key factors serving as reference points for providing further insights and clarity for the reader. The contextual descriptions herewith include key terms, phrases, and words used throughout the research documentation. Furthermore, the concepts described below incorporate the fully integrated constructs and research elements used in the study.

Human Intelligences

The intelligence quotient (IQ) is "a score derived from a set of standardized tests developed to measure a person's cognitive abilities concerning their age group" (ScienceDaily, 2014, p. 1). Gardner (2003), the founding theorist of the Multiple Intelligences theory, accepted the argument and yielded to his contradictory stance against fellow theorists eager for theory expansion, thereby acknowledging "intelligence is a judgment call and not an algorithmic conclusion" (p. 10). Blackwell et al. (2015) explained the preconceived notions of cognizance in the Multiple Intelligences (MQ) framework cognitive capacities can be learned in various ways, suggesting growth through intentional education. The neuroplasticity of the immature human brain is malleable; consequently, "the power to transform your life lies in your ability to consciously change 1.4-kilogram lump of meat inside your head" (Abuhassàn & Bates, 2015; pp. 1-2) through positive intellectual stimulation (Costandi, 2016; Geraerts, 2018; Kokubun et al., 2018). Hence, the commonplace phrase about the brain bears mentioning you must "use it or lose it" (Mistridis et al., 2017, p. 1) does hold much truth to it, whereas practicing mental agility is crucial for keeping the mind sharp as one ages (Sweeney, 2009). Research indicates pandemic fatigue is triggering burnout conditions with negative stress impacting psychological, relational, medical, and organizational performance (de Smet & Vogel, 2021; Duckworth, 2021).

Interpersonal Intelligence

Merton (1969) conveyed leadership as the capacity to incorporate facets of interpersonal relations to entice members to desire to participate derived from positive engagement, not from a place of dictatorship as in rigid autocratic organizations (Argyris, 1962). Interpersonal ability is a social-oriented mechanism that facilitates recognizing and understanding other's thoughts, emotions, and feelings during experiential situations (Gardner, 1983; Leiter & Maslach, 1988; Powers, 2014). Matured interpersonal abilities enable humans' ability to focus on developing positive environments, problem-solving effectively, conflict management, learning through pro bono service, open to multiple perspectives, appreciating diversity at all levels, even intellectual, neurological, cultural, physical, emotional, and financial differences (Flynn & Shayer, 2018; Kwan et al., 2021; Powers, 2014). Empirical evidence indicated that 90% of the leadership skills necessary to be successful are not technical but interpersonal competencies (Leiter & Maslach, 1988; Wellins et al., 2012).

Intrapersonal Intelligence

Literature indicates the "intrapersonal operations process" as mainly focused on "empathy as an emotional regulation" (Ringwald & Wright, 2020, p. 2) for critical stress coping varies depending upon situational circumstances, and most notably, narcissistic people lack empathetic traits have limiting resilience ability during a crisis. Hence, dynamically serving an affiliative interpersonal function with a central purpose of satisfying motives of moving interacts towards building authentic deep connections with others while adequately managing reactions to feelings and emotions during a crisis (Dethlefs et al., 2017; King et al., 2012). Hence, both the authentic and spiritual leadership approaches aligned with the constructs of intrapersonal intelligence. Intrapersonal abilities are reflective-oriented to recognize and understand one's thought processes, emotions, and deeply rooted causes of feelings during experiential situations (Gardner, 1983; Hannah et al., 2011). Matured intrapersonal capacities enable humans to focus on the foundational building blocks of goalsetting, time management, self-esteem formation, critical thinking, emotional expression, and curiosity, so compelling interactions lead to self-directed learning, which can be compassionate and reflective in nature (Campbell et al., 1996; Daud, 2020; Kwan et al., 2021).

Organizational Health

Cox et al. (1993) explained organizational healthiness moderated by the relationships between burnout, work stress, and health. Halbesleben and Buckley (2004) confirmed that "burnout in organizational life" is an innate human psychological response to environmental conditions that produce work stress, exhibited by characteristics of mental, physical, and "emotional exhaustion, depersonalization, and reduced feelings of personal accomplishment" (p. 859). The hallmark identifier of unhealthy organizations is the oppressive cultural climate exhibited by outcomes include low employee morale, inconsistent performance energy-momentum, limited trustworthiness, hostile relational dynamics, and inadequate knowledge transfer producing conditions for negative financial implications to bottom-line derived from poor culture and apathetic human performance levels (Črešnar et al., 2019; Swan, 2016; Vyas, 2016). On the contrary, the characteristics of organizational healthiness activities are evident when leaders' empowerment, encouragement, and resource enablement are exercised in adopting intervention strategies necessary to transform their team operations and become acceptable practices to enhance cultural dynamics incrementally (Bell-Ellis, 2013; Jung & Sosik, 2002).

The management of organizational excellence is aligned with the ideals of organizational health as concepts strategically integrate with infrastructure ecosystems to effectively navigate transitional and transformational activities, whereas achieving quality demands the utmost trust, collaboration, and respect for people (Fernández-del-Río et al., 2021). The construct of organizational excellence progresses beyond foundations established by the total quality management (TQM) framework by moving towards participation engagements at all levels of business (Rago, 1996; Sharma & Hoque, 2002). Quality-centered transformations require organizations to fully embrace the dual mindsets of change resiliency and continuous improvement as guideposts by embedding practices as core values (Dolan & Altman, 2012; Oakland & Tanner, 2007). These values must align with the corporate mission with a long-term OD strategic vision striving towards becoming best in class and demonstrating value-based behaviors where people come first, then customers, and produce quality outcomes.

Achieving sustainable organizational excellence is evident in OD scorecard outputs measuring key factors such as financial cost-savings or revenue realization, customer experience, streamlined processes adoption, education agility, and change resilience growth-promoting continuous improvement strategies (Errida & Lotfi, 2020; Kendall & Bodinson, 2017). The respect for people's value is demonstrated by developing and coaching positive leadership behaviors consistently through practical teachings associated directly with deliberate management improvements towards enhancing targeted business functional areas, namely information-sharing, streamlined workflows, valuing people, rewards systems, resiliency, and education agility (Torch, 2023). Change adaptability is facilitated by standards, technologies, structures, and human capital through streamlined processes intended for engaging employees daily, garnering impacted people commitments towards mutually beneficial motivations, striving to deliver quality services consistently, and fulfilling customer requirements within business expectations (Kodama, 2019).

HISTORICAL CONTENT

The content within the next section discusses historical sources, which connects with both the foundations for conceptual development and summarizes imperative concepts to provide a basic understanding needed for anyone reading the Vázquez-de-Príncipe (2021) study. The contextual elements described herewith in this chapter include human development, humanistic organizations, and enterprise change management. Subsequently, the discussion will proceed to address the constructs of current topic specific context materials.

Human Development

Burns (1978) defined human development as one's morality and needs. Transforming leadership dynamics helps with guiding members/partners/participants to the next level of their evolution by increasing intrinsic motivation, which is instrumental towards becoming self-actualized (Campbell & Pritchard, 1976; Couto, 1993; Daud, 2020; Kotter, 1990; Maslow, 1954; Tidd, 2016). Leaders are born not made is a false narrative as task managers who are encouraged to learn to lead others can potentially drive performance excellence (Gardner, 1995). Therefore, many people live out only a fraction of their potential or overlook their innate strengths, talents, and leadership gifts because of scarce development opportunities and funding for training. The "reservoir of unused human talent and energy is vast and learning to tap that reservoir more effectively is one of the exciting tasks ahead of humankind" (Gardner, 1995, p. 7). Society can do better in developing new leaders capable of multiplying themselves by intentionally building tomorrow's leaders (Gardner, 1995).

A critical distinction exists between the capacity-building concepts of developing leaders and developing leadership as expertise (Day, 2000). The purpose for evolving leadership at work is to enhance the well-being of the human-conditional existence for all, which is professionally socioeconomic-oriented, influenced by leader-member reciprocal partner interactions, and inner-state exchanges transform culture is externally evident (Burns, 1978; Ericsson & Pool, 2016; Mohamed et al., 2020; Munro, 2020). In contrast, the purpose for leadership development is to motivate individuals to perform with extra effort, which is solely organizationally oriented, influenced by one-sided leader-to-member directives, and no inner-state exchange, hence keeping the culture at its current toxic state (Bass, 1985a, 1985b; Ericsson & Pool, 2016).

Literature on leadership has historically functioned on the widespread misconception once the collective in a field identifies a leadership theory, then that would be the essential key for motivating effective education strategies (Avolio et al., 2009; Contractor et al., 2012; Jung et al., 1995; Walumbwa & Lawler, 2003; Walumbwa et al., 2003). However, human development comprises complex processes when engagements are misaligned, compartmentalized, and isolated random events as single learning experiences are inconsequential in transforming individuals and organizations. Thus, once fully embraced by a healthy holistic enterprise the synergic integration of both of these dimensions and consistent blended learning experiences where the profound enablement process to catalyze leadership for transforming culture can begin strategically (Day, 2000; Day & Sin, 2011; Day et al., 2005, 2009; Flynn & Shayer, 2018; Kodama, 2017, 2019; Lencioni, 2012; Maslow, 1998; Nisbett et al., 2012; Quatro et al., 2007).

Humanistic Organizations

Historically, the traditional bureaucratic organizational model is inadequate because of its failure to recognize and "meet the needs of an enlightened workforce [eager to grow intellectually, creatively, professionally], and take into account the totality of the human psyche" conditioned towards continuously flourishing (Edlund, 1992, p. 75). Employees intrinsically yearn a sense of genuine caring from their leaders, managers, and colleagues, which fosters a positive work environment fulfills their desire for a pleasant climate of "love, family, and labor" (Edlund, 1992, p. 77) for moving towards happier life satisfaction (Oleś & Jankowski, 2018). The denigration of workforce competencies is cautioning indicator public organizations have become unsustainable stemming from the crippling bureau pathological practices stifling employees and consequently producing permanent health, mental, or emotional damage (Bennis, 1959; Giblin, 1981; Vigoda-Gadot & Meisler, 2010).

Intentional steps are needed to integrate workplace and workforce ecosystems to foster holistic practices, mindsets, attitudes, values, and behaviors. The multidimensional synergistic approach helps to improve the human condition with the potential to positively impact Work-Life dynamics, where senior executives proactively lead by example for management to emulate, producing ripple effects efficiently embeds cultural transformations within humanistic organizations (Ahmed et al., 2016; Athar, 2020; Korten, 1998). Simultaneously, the employees are respectfully treated as worthy end for the greater good and viewed as highly valued partners with focused objectives for meeting the needs of both organizational and professional goals mutually benefiting of leader, member, and team alike. On the other hand, when individuals are utilized as mere robots with no value, only as a 'means to an end,' and their sole purpose is to meet the needs of business and leader alone, no mutual reciprocity produces an oppressive cultural climate, which is detrimental to the triple-bottom-line.

Humanistic organizations are conscious entities, which are mindful as to the impact their decisions make upon others in the current state, while also anticipating the potential future implications for mitigation development. Hence, humanistic-oriented enterprises have no tolerance of Machevallianistic treatment of employees (Gieseke, 2014; Lucire, 1986; Modlin, 1986; Moon, 2021). They are intentional about proactive efforts to ensure individuals' humane treatment by using OD metrics as organizational health risk-level indicators for monitoring burnout and other conditions induced by work stress to maintain healthiness range and to mitigate risks promptly for sustainability (Cox et al., 1993; Creswell et al., 2011; Leiter et al., 2014; Naplyokov, 2018).

The Demand-Control-Support Model is a prominently accepted philosophy within humanistic entities to help reduce the risk of job stress by encouraging a balance among three core dimensions, namely: job demands, job decision-making latitude, and job social support (Karasek & Theorell, 1990). By permitting members to influence decisions directly impact their work by granting professional autonomy flexibility within their field of expertise of their choosing, providing development with career pathways, and releasing access to the resources needed to execute effective deliverables (Ahmed et al., 2016; Karasek & Theorell, 1990; Mohamed et al., 2020; Moon, 2021; Naplyokov, 2018; Phipps, 2012). Human beings innately desire the ability to solve problems freely and seek opportunities to make choices and decisions affect their responsibilities, which are characteristics of humanistic organizations having positive-culture externally evident by an empowered workforce with a voice (Kodama, 2017, 2019; Moon, 2021; Naplyokov, 2018). Hence, the humans' inner-being naturally strives towards having a voice, which is valued and enabled to offer input into matters impacting their ability to "achieving their work outcomes for which they will be held accountable" (Leiter & Maslach, 2011, p. 5) as respect and recognized subject matter experts (Ericsson & Pool, 2016).

Enterprise Change Management

Enterprise management and leadership is constantly coping with the complexities of bringing about order and consistency in producing quality business outcomes requiring rigid structures and measurable standards (Carder & Monda, 2013; Kotter, 1990). Notwithstanding, leadership differs when coping with sudden organizational change, which demands more attention to respond rapidly to a crisis requiring qualities of nimble adaptive resilience (Carder & Ragan, 2005; Cork, 2010; Duncan, 2020). Vázquez-de-Príncipe (2021) focused on navigating the intricacies of transformative change moving towards a deductive reasoning (QUAN-logic) direction to incorporate ecosystem perspectives, such as planning, budgeting, organizing, staffing, controlling, problem-solving, and rewarding (Denzin, 2012; Hesse-Biber, 2010; Kotter, 1990). Furthermore, leaders with focused vision can inspire people throughout disruptive times of volatility, uncertainty, complexity, and ambiguity—VUCA world, moving towards inductive reasoning (qual-logic) direction to strategically mitigate resistance perspectives, such as aligning professional with personal values, cultural intelligence, and meeting social-emotional-psychological safety and wellness needs (Bommer et al., 2005; Ilies et al., 2005).

The two most prominent past organizational assumptions guided business strategies first, their controlled destinies were operations, and second, their environments were predictable and stable (Beckhard & Pritchard, 1992). These assumptions no longer ring true for organizations, which find themselves in a constant influx of change from external forces negatively impacting business strategies, such as recession, industry policy changes, and social, environmental demands driving fundamental business change decisions (Applebaum et al., 2015; Moon, 2021; Naplyokov, 2018). Therefore, designing transformation management strategies with a constellation of changes can viably function simultaneously in a discreet and interdependent manner to achieve quality culture outcomes embedded into the fabric of the organization as business as usual (Beckhard & Pritchard, 1992). Moreover, an overarching corporate vision for integrative learning incorporating the philosophy of continuous improvement/growth mindset, which focuses on the quality of performance as an equally valued excellence component helps connect fundamental organizational change strategy (Beckhard & Pritchard, 1992; Fernet et al., 2015).

CURRENT CONTENT

This section discusses current content sources connecting to foundational research development and summarizes essential concepts to provide a piece of basic knowledge for readers about the Vázquez-de-Príncipe (2021) investigation. The contextual elements described herewith in this chapter includes: Appreciative Inquiry Theory, ADKAR change process model, and spirituality at work. Next, the discussion will move into the conceptual context for the investigation to provide background knowledge.

Appreciative Inquiry Theory

The Appreciative Inquiry theory enables asking questions, envisioning the future, growing awareness, and gathering knowledge are critical components for enhancing the organizational ecosystem's capacity for successful collaborations and changes by facilitating leadership engagements (Cooperrider et al., 2000). The Appreciative Inquiry (AI) phased process approach focuses on utilizing four stages, namely: Discover, Dream, Design, and Destiny or Deliver, dependent upon the scope parameters of change initiatives (Cooperrider et al., 2000). These AI process stages constitute: (1) Discover—identifying best organizational processes; (2) Dream—envisioning processes for the future; (3) Design—planning and prioritizing best processes; and (3) Destiny (Deliver)—implementation (execution) of proposed design solution (Cooperrider et al., 2000, 2001). Ideally, to appraise the first iteration of solutions, a small group to test is the best tactic to attain feedback; designers can alter solutions as needed, tested and retest until established readiness, and designated final iteration cleared for launch release.

Change leaders who influence through the power of appreciative inquiry can apply positive analysis techniques to accelerate executive strategic planning for creative problem-solving and evidence-based decision-making to facilitate moving towards establishing the essential need, which promote both professional and organizational excellence (Buckham, 2018; Cooperrider & Srivastva, 2000; Muchemi & Wakonyo, 2020; Wilson, 2021). Change executives who exercise an appreciative management approach engaging positive thoughts and action taking can read their environment keenly identifying situations needed to address immediately to harmonize dynamics among the people, teams, and cultural climate (Coghlan, 2000; Muchemi & Wakonyo, 2020). The integration of AI into corporate strategies can foster improvements by adding value with the potential of transforming cultures organically by aligning psychological dynamics, leadership education, and social-emotional cognition ecosystems (Barratt, 2017; Krattenmaker, 2001; Lustig, 2003; Spillius, 1988).

The O. C. Tanner Company (2018) conducted a longitudinal study that identified the appreciative culture as essential to ignite organizational commitment and motivation. A cultural climate of recognition can transform mindsets and attitudes to shift from good enough to strive for excellence by igniting a passionate fire at work from engagements, such as organizational awareness, trust, and career-pathing with education planning (Covey & Merrill, 2006, 2007; Covey et al., 2012; Cowan, 2005). The appreciative inquiry approach intentionally does not promote perfectionism, as a mindset of striving for perfection only breads complacency, conformity, and stagnation, fueling Work-Life apathy, detrimental to human condition by diminishing dynamic performance, reducing productivity of unattainable and unforgiving objectives (Brown, 2010). On the other hand, a mindset striving for excellence seeks to foster intrinsic motivation to willfully give one's extra effort without 'fear of failure,' instead, viewed as an opportunity to learn and improve self, team, and organization subsequently (Brown, 2010).

Furthermore, when managers employ appreciative recognition, teams have performance improved with outcomes attributed to reduced turnover rates, enhanced triple-bottom-line, increased leadership capacity, accountability, goals attainment, strong communications, and formation of genuine trust relationships. Endresen of HealthStream Research summarized findings of the longitudinal study as astounding empirical research linking both hard-and-soft-sides of change by recognizing the human need for achievement while meeting business essentials positively impacted profitability by improving overall performance (Johnson & Leavitt, 2001; O. C. Tanner Company, 2018). Enhancing performance appraisal practices through appreciative inquiry is an intrinsically powerful intervention towards building personal worthiness awareness in employees and teams who view their value potential within the enterprise ecosystem, thereby catalyzing their willingness to perform extra effort (Buckham, 2018; Wilson, 2021). *Gratitude-centered-participatory-experiences* helps people reconnect by stimulating the brain's *flow-state* of ideation for establishing groups' "collective purpose and contribution," for encouraging "better communication flow throughout the organization," which was a critical factor hampering organizational transformations during the pandemic disruption (Alameda et al., 2022; Wilson, 2021, pp. 34-35).

ADKAR Change Process Model

Highly structured businesses, governments, and organizations benefit most from the ADKAR model for driving projects forward by deploying the five steps in the sequential process: Awareness, Desire, Knowledge, Ability, and Reinforcement. (Hiatt, 2006; Hiatt & Creasey, 2012). The ADKAR process steps constitute (1) Awareness—communicating need for aligned change; (2) Desire—galvanizing participants as advocates; (3) Knowledge—job-profiling, job-redesigning, career-pathing, or capacity-building; (4) Ability—assessing day-to-day consistency for adoption quality; and (5) Reinforcement—advising/coaching to sustain implemented change (Hiatt, 2006). The ADKAR model intended to foster successful individual behavior change in support of advancing projects through the holistic principles of people needs come first, which is a core foundational component for sustainable culture transformations (Al-Shamlan & Al-Mudimigh, 2011). In essence, less resistance to change projects occurs when overarching strategic business objectives along with intentional end goals are equitably aligned and broadly communicated throughout enterprise in a routine manner, especially during crucial milestones or key checkpoints of initiative's life cycle (Leiter & Harvie, 1998). Although identifying suitable change processes are advantageous, remaining agile is imperative for consistent success. In contrast, prescriptive models and tools are guideposts, not rigid checklists, hindering the potential for building strong, trustworthy partnerships fostered by creative learning collaborative experiences.

"Change strategy plays a crucial role in mitigating resistance to change," "thus reducing the failure rate," while applying the ADKAR process within more significant technological transformations, such as the implementation of Enterprise Resource Planning software solutions, to streamline systematic organizational processes (Al-Shamlan & Al-Mudimigh, 2011, p. 402; Colbert, 2011; Kavanagh & Ashkanasy, 2006; Kazmi & Naarananoja, 2013; Rosenbaum et al., 2018). Literature showed agile businesses "undergoing many organizational changes are perceived as more successful when managed by a transformational leader" (Boga & Ensari, 2009, p. 246). However, the literature suggests many changes project sponsors do not possess leadership capacities, have no commitment to initiatives, and are mostly disengaged (Boga & Ensari, 2009). ADKAR provides a phased-process approach to elicit organizational commitment at the individual level for small projects requiring people behaviors to change to facilitate the adoption of a new manner of working (Creasey & Ball, 2017).

Business strategies leveraging change interventions, such as ADKAR, provide a sense of organizational commitment from established project alignments with reciprocity for all, which supports to motivate everyone intrinsically, and inspires project teams to collaborate (Athar, 2020; Rosenbaum et al., 2018). The OSUVA study incorporated the ADKAR methodology into the research framework because the model helped facilitate the swift identification of potential problems in the process throughout every phased checkpoint of their project (Kazmi & Naarananoja, 2013). The integrated research design strategy supported prompt risk mitigation and was instrumental in building buy-in from key internal and external stakeholders (Leiter & Harvie, 1998).

ADKAR integrates facets of William Deming's continuous process improvement cycle, specifically–Plan, Do, and Act phases; however, framework excludes the 'Check' phase within Deming's model (Creasey & Ball, 2017). The design of the ADKAR model did not intend usage as cultural awareness intervention; however, applying process as a component of strategic planning at the enterprise level to aligning systems has the potential for promising incremental positive cultural impact. Notwithstanding, these changes are not sustainable as the micro-culture effect dissipates once specific projects are completed and closed.

Henceforward, enterprise aspirations of project members' servicing as culture carriers are unrealistic without a proper vision for embedding cultural enhancements globally beyond program or project-centeredness with accountable executive leadership, guidance, development, and direction. Deming's Check-phase is critical to integrating into enterprise efforts intended for culture interventions, which can promptly mitigate identified change resistors at each stage with frequent quality-checks and purposefully coach change sponsors from the onset of culture-focused initiatives. In addition, process enhancements are procedural elements for embedding throughout the organization to begin cultural mindsets shifting strategically and organized.

A positivity framework exemplifies a focused strategic approach to enable organizational culture transformations at a broader enterprise-level, which is needed as the first step to then produce the trickle-down effect naturally across all business functions (Meyer, 2016; Norman et al., 2010; Phipps, 2012; Rosenbaum et al., 2018; Wang et al., 2014; Woolley et al., 2011). Traditionally, in the 'Check' phase in the ADKAR change process, the expectation is implementation will occur faster irrespective of the measurable quality of deliverables. Furthermore, overarching outcome attitude of let's get it done; even if it's at 60% quality rate, is commonly accepted as public-sector norm—whereas no output excellence expectation exists, structurally rewarding people executing extra efforts towards improving performance consistently (Athar, 2020; Daud, 2020; Fernet et al., 2015; Rosenbaum et al., 2018). Moreover, the ADKAR model is becoming more accepted within public/government entities as a change process tool, and usage focused on business process improvements projects incorporating lean/six sigma elements (Errida & Lotfi, 2020; Rosenbaum et al., 2018). Nevertheless, lack of merit-based rewards-systems through governance process structures for recognizing teams' executing successfully special projects' benefits realization remains a hurdle for improvements' long-term programs sustainability (Li et al., 2011).

Public organizations heavily depend on external consultants for change transformations; however, rarely are culture matters addressed in-depth within these arrangements. Literature shows culture is most challenging to change and measure, especially for externally hired consultants; however, internal change professionals have a unique opportunity to initiate culture interventions collaboratively with the employees' input (de Smet & Vogel, 2021; Errida & Lotfi, 2020). Change professionals seeking to break out beyond the historical niches must develop a career-pathing plan to remain relevant post-pandemic. The change management discipline is no longer simply considered a process-oriented tool deployed only to bring people along for technology transformation implementations.

Expectations are high from the top for global change talent who poses executive presence, enabling mobilizing the workforce towards ambitious initiatives transform corporate culture, cities, states, countries, and the world of work for the socioeconomic good. Those unable to demonstrate through professional, relational, educational, and organizational excellence by showing their unique worth through visible thought leadership credibility will not be asked to The Table to collaboratively design strategic solutions, advise enterprise people-matters, and inspire workforce engagement. On the contrary, inaction will, unfortunately, foster complacency and stagnation without growth potential; hence these practitioners will be left behind for not seizing the pandemic's silver-lining opportunities afforded to all those who choose to accept the challenge ensuring the change discipline flourishes.

Spirituality at Work

Empirical studies have showed integrating "spirituality at work" tends to radiate "ripples of hope" (Bell-Ellis, 2013, p. 333) throughout all levels of business, which produces a sense of organizational health and employee wellness, which aligns with work-life's purposeful meaning, and helps to create a sense of flourishing happiness (Baykal, 2019; Keller, 2021; Lencioni, 2012; Smith & Halligan, 2021; Vasconcelos, 2018). "Spirituality is absolutely necessary for organizations to ensure ethical behavior, job satisfaction, productivity, employee commitment, and competitive advantage" (Aravamudhan & Krishnaveni, 2014, p. 64) as morally-oriented institutions (Zainun et al., 2021).

When workplace norm accepting one's spiritual-being as a critical component of the whole person that requires soul nurturing, is in place by astutely recognizing values, embracing dexterities, and encouraging dialogue, affirming forces foster intrinsic motivation for passionately driving professional and organizational high- performance (Benefiel, 2008; Bolman & Deal, 2011; Desai, 2009; Fry & Matherly, 2007). In these organizations' leaders authentically believe "[a] happy worker is a productive worker," that "by providing clear growth paths in organizational ladder and by empowering subordinates their trust can be won" (Thakur & Singh, 2016, pp. 5186-5187). Literature showed work-life balance struggles are prominent throughout the Covid-19 pandemic, with women exiting the workforce in record numbers to nurture loved ones (Dilmaghani, 2019; Ramachandaran et al., 2017; Vroman & Danko, 2020). This situation would not have become so continuously prominent had organizational spirituality already become normalized as a business-as-usual valued practice throughout the United States.

BACKGROUND

Public-sector organizations are constantly in a state of change, demanding organizational resiliency and agility to enable rapid adaptability (Kotter, 2019). Maranto and Wolf (2013) explained that government agencies are seeking to reinvent themselves have deployed entrepreneurial change leaders to transform the public-sector corporate culture. However, the long-term sustainability of "reinventing government movement" (Maranto & Wolf, 2013, p. 231) has proven to be a challenge to implement broadly throughout public agencies as political elements, and bureaucratic strategies are barriers in successful turnarounds. The bureaucracy within public service agencies limits management's ability for decision-making and action-taking to adapt rapidly to changes in their environments effectively (Rampersad, 2008; Reker & Wong, 1988). Nevertheless, these bureaucratic change barriers are not permanent and can be impacted positively by leaders who intentionally target these issues, which hinder creativity and innovation (Wilson, 1989; Wolf, 1997).

For public sector agencies to improve their cultures, they must realign ecosystems with vision and strategies to increase employee engagement within the workplace (Kavanagh & Ashkanasy, 2006; Milliman et al., 2018). These alignments are essential for management to streamline effective and efficient ecosystems, processes, communications, and foster leadership acumen throughout all organizational levels. Cameron and Quinn's Competing Values Framework (2006) describes a hierarchical corporate culture, control, stability, and productivity, efficiently influencing a balanced approach. However, many public-sector agencies have attributed the Hierarchical Culture as a factor in producing an overblown toxic climate of bureau-pathology that creates an oppressive environment, which damages the human spirit resulting in the denigration in workers' motivation, engagement, and organizational commitment (Cameron & Quinn, 2006; Giblin, 1981; Lee & Kamarul, 2009).

Public-sector organizations would benefit most from a blend of a top-down and bottom-up strategic alignment approach (Sminia & van Nistelrooij, 2006; van Nistelrooij et al., 2007). An organization desiring a culture of excellence may implement an educational system, which embeds a balance of elements of each of the four culture types – clan, adhocracy, market, and hierarchy (Cameron & Quinn, 2006). An integrative culture improvement approach encompasses both an internal focus, which integrates stability and control while maintaining an external focus differentiated through flexibility and freedom to act on decisions (Cameron & Quinn, 2006). For change practitioners to impact the culture at the enterprise level, they must intentionally enhance the system-wide leadership capabilities by building the leaders' and managers' self-awareness, authenticity, relationships, connectedness, empathy, and values identification (Astin, 2004; Graen & Uhl-Bien, 1995; King et al., 2012; König et al., 2020).

Public enterprises are under constant scrutiny and the media's microscope (van Nistelrooij & Sminia, 2010; Wallgrave & van Aelst, 2006). Vázquez-de-Príncipe (2021) expressed that doctoral dissertation study may help satisfy scholar's and practitioners' intellectual curiosity about leadership capacity and change enablement within public institutions and garner an in-depth understanding of the phenomena associated with leadership and human-intelligences on influencing culture improvements to foster sustainable organizational excellence transformations (Dehler & Welsh, 1994; Deluga, 1988; Schein, 1968, 1978). Additionally, an interest in understanding the phenomena associated with change resilience agility, social skills, relationships, and work-life balance may inform baseline organizational interventions (Curran & Monti, 1982; Curran et al., 1982). Culture improvements narratives may improve performance at all levels, from employees to management, enhancing the enterprise's quadruple-bottom-line (QBL) performance.

Generally, public enterprises are consistently in organizational transformations driven by a reactive stance to comply with governmental directives. Hence, this state poses considerably more challenges towards organizing change processes among the entire ecosystem when involving policy strategically, organizational design, cross-functional collaborations, technology, and learning delivery (Fernandez & Rainey, 2006; Pettigrew et al., 2001). Proactive activities encompassing all ecosystems including human components from an embedded positive enterprise culture, can present consistent results. Despite the importance of change management for public sector management practice, literature generally does not focus on organizational change as an enterprise-level ecosystem implementation problem; instead, the focus remains at the project level (Stewart & Kringas, 2003).

The strategic practice mindset problem devalues the change profession by removing leaders' authority for their expert decision-making and must evolve to enable the sustainable embedding of any meaningful enterprise change transformation to ensure institutional future market relevance and business continuity (Steyrer & Mende, 1994). Meaningful work reflects a "deep sense of meaning and purpose in one's work" (Milliman et al., 2003, p. 429). The literature tends to address change management content deliverables rather than strategically realigning the enterprise ecosystems with the culture to foster the environmental readiness by establishing an in-house enabled network to engage in initial change implementation processes (Jaros, 2007; Kickert, 2010; McNulty & Ferlie, 2004).

Identifying the leadership component is critical in creating change commitment among employees (Fernandez & Pitts, 2007). However, research on change leadership primarily concentrated on the sponsors' activities associated with promoting the initiative, not active participation throughout the entire change implementation process lifecycle (Higgs & Rowland, 2005). Also, the empirical evidence identified the relevance and effectiveness of leveraging leadership during change. However, little literature exists about their influence to foster commitment for large-scale organizational transformations such as reorganizations and consolidations within the public sector (Fernandez & Pitts, 2007). Moreover, Bass et al. (2003) and Yukl (1999) suggested more empirical research on mediating predictor mechanisms linking leadership and performance.

The literature consistently points toward sponsors' being the most critical success factors of "active and visible participation by senior business leaders" (Hiatt & Creasey, 2012, p. 70) throughout change management efforts. Change initiatives that fail indicate structural problems such as a weak top-down commitment with vision and strategy misalignments, lacking sponsorship, and practitioners with limited autonomy for decision-making challenged to mitigate or guide competing change values during portfolio collisions among stakeholders (Colbert, 2011; Kazmi & Naarananoja, 2013). Organizational culture transformations without change management cannot be sustainable as they require sponsorship interventions to build their capacity to drive, lead, embed, and support the goals (Lough, 2016; van der Voet & Vermeeren, 2017; Schein, 1992). Literature on "transformational leadership effectiveness and its relevance within the public sector have been contradictory with data arguing for and against the idea" (Atwater & Bass, 1994, p. 93).

The empirical evidence showed burnout and Work-Life issues impact the talent acquisition process with financial implications for public-sector institutions related to the time and resources required to backfill high profile leadership roles, hindering organizational change momentum (van Dierendonck et al., 2005). These stress-related impact issues have the potential risk of having long-term adverse performance consequences because losing executives and employees to burnout when the risk is mitigated by business strategies such as well-being policies, procedures, and programs (van Dierendonck et al., 2005). Literature links burnout with Work-Life balance and is associated with spirituality and job satisfaction (Kökalan, 2019; Maslach & Leiter, 2008). However, deficiencies in the research associate burnout and Work-Life as mitigating factors to leadership and human intelligence as predictive factors with influential forces of its outcome effect on change leaders to drive sustainable organizational transformations (Boyatzis et al., 2006; Dehler & Welsh, 1994). In the literature review process limited empirical evidence was found, showing an explicit focus on leading change within public organizations associate the impact of leadership to organizational transformations while incorporating the perspectives of change management practitioners (Higgs & Rowland, 2005; Kuipers et al., 2014; Lawrence, 2015).

MAIN FOCUS OF THE CHAPTER

The Covid-19 pandemic expanded the digital transformation already underway, with new technologies accelerating the rate of change across all industries, which increased demands for highly skilled workforce ability to support the rapidly emerging tools (American Society of Quality, 2021). The unprecedented disruption catapulted Work-Life ecosystems into a tailspin like no other historical global event, which propelled organizations to an involuntary digital transformation by shifting to facilitate a remote environment (Athar, 2020; Bonacini et al., 2021; Clack & Harmon, 2020; Dey et al., 2020; Trougakos et al., 2020). Overnight, the global workforce had to stay home, and business operations became remote, impacting work, school, and family dynamics (Garrote Sanchez et al., 2021; Nguyen, 2021; Shockley & Clark, 2020; Wigert & Agrawal, 2022).

The Covid-19 pandemic brought crisis management to the forefront as a muscle needing strengthening in business worldwide. The public enterprises' challenge consists of broadening perspectives around leading crises proactively. Many public service-oriented institutions within the United States have been operating for well over a century. The rich public history of these enterprises comes with deeply embedded limiting constructs about problem-solving, relational dynamics, and working structures. While deploying change management practices for project-based planned activities in public organizations, the pandemic highlighted the necessity for increased resiliency and adaptability across all levels. The change leaders tasked with such transformational efforts themselves have experienced pandemic fatigue triggered by human conditions at work with negative stress impacts on psychological, relational, medical, and organizational performance (de Smet & Vogel, 2021; Duckworth, 2021).

The general problem is that change practitioners concentrate on surviving immediate daily crises resulting in a constant sense of urgency with stress. This concentration produces a narrowing of global cultural perspectives and time horizons, inhibiting their ability to reflect upon quality performance factors necessary to respond effectively to long-term people matters (Alahdab et al., 2020; Athar, 2020; de Smet & Vogel, 2021; Duncan, 2020; Papageorge et al., 2021). The doctoral dissertation study may provide a deeper understanding of the complex multi-layered leadership capacities and change enablement phenomena within the public sector to offer better experiential narratives (Vázquez-de-Príncipe, 2021). Deeply comprehending these concepts is pivotal to address practitioners' abilities to influence work-life for positively impacting corporate culture holistically and for fostering organizational excellence towards long-term sustainable improvement transformations.

The specific problem is change leaders' inability to proactively engage the rapidly evolving hybrid workplace model, which demands a greater emphasis on radically human relationships founded upon trust, collaboration, and people's respect for effectively aligning work-life with culture and ecosystems (Fernández-del-Río et al., 2021). The self-protecting mindsets and behaviors of change practitioners, at times even unbeknownst by them, is what negatively defines their corporate cultures, albeit evident in emotional suppression and censorship practices within public institutions (Papageorge et al., 2021; Zhang et al., 2020). Hence, change management executives are the first who achieve organizational excellence by growing facets that bolster their intellectual and business acumen. Specifically, business education associated with transformational leadership, authentic leadership, grit, social skills, and spiritual intelligence can influence critical areas of work-life, which may impact corporate cultural environments for the aspirational attainment of organizational excellence for long-term sustainability.

The topic described herewith may help fill the knowledge gap in the literature for leadership and change management disciplines. The literature illustrated consequences as public enterprises seek to retain and recruit high-quality leadership talent, foster change agility in succession practices, drive measurable ROI realization, and grow leadership pipeline for meeting emerging Industry 4.0 relational demands (Czifra & Molnár, 2020; Fareri et al., 2020; Sasangohar et al., 2020). Gaining an understanding of change leaders' perspectives on work-life barriers preventing positive culture impact to foster organizational excellence performance levels could lead to interventions and multidisciplinary resources for practitioners to begin embedding enhanced vision, values, strategies, and structures. Public institutions could benefit from these efforts to align leaping post-pandemic leaders of hybrid organizations by recalibrating, adapting, and embracing the future. The leap forward requires collaborative, agile, integrative, and holistic leadership mindsets (Ahmed et al., 2016; Boyd, 2017; Kodama, 2019).

FUTURE RESEARCH DIRECTIONS

Vázquez-de-Príncipe (2021) expressed recommendations for the direction of future research based upon the outcomes discussed from investigation that were threefold. First, the study's replication is recommended within broader public service-oriented settings across a more diverse population to determine the extent to which predictive variables impact the outcome findings on a broader scale (Jena & Pradhan, 2014). Second, the study took place within the United States of America, thereby the replication of the investigation with global perspectives would expand the reliability and validity of the findings, which would be beneficial in fully comprehending the scope of impact (Baykal, 2019). Finally, the researcher recommends replication as a longitudinal comparison study with an Equity, Inclusion, and Belonging (EIB) lens to understand the differences between the pre- and post-pandemic impact on Work-Life Dynamics, inclusive verses holistic leadership, and enterprise change management disciplines within global public enterprises (Atwater et al., 1996; Brown, 2019b; McBride et al., 2020).

Furthermore, future case studies within public/government institutions should investigate the Work-Life components by incorporating larger population sample size. The approach supports the enablement towards garnering deeper understandings of organizational culture sustainability factors to facilitate developing a corporate scorecard to identify the areas needing focused attention to improve alignments consistently (Borins, 2002; Jardon & Martínez-Cobas, 2019; Jiang & Men, 2017). A comparative analysis could offer additional insights between agencies, departments, or practice groups to foster change transformation intervention strategies (Fernandez & Rainey, 2017; Rampersad, 2008). One requirement for organizations to participate in these case studies should be they are already employing or are exploring the dual-operating model within a change management practice, group, or discipline embedded into the ecosystem's framework (Muchemi & Wakonyo, 2020; Vroom & Jago, 1995).

SOLUTIONS AND RECOMMENDATIONS

To catalyze public-sector culture transformations, professionals must possess Holistic Leadership Intelligence (HLQ) capabilities, utilizing whole-system multidisciplinary creative-critical-thinking through 4Ps techniques and unleashing holistic leadership workplace culture towards organizational excellence (Hardison, 2017; Howell, 2018). Driving holistic impact across an organization, enterprise, industry, sector, school/university, church, or community is no easy feat by any means, which needs whole-hearted leaders as catalysts to help with shaping the future of workplace culture. Making a difference which will outlive programs, sponsors, managers, and politics demand the need for whole-system perspectives to sustain organizational excellence, even during times of crisis (Maxwell, 2017).

Holistic Catalyzing Culture Leaders

The ability of any public entity to withstand, adapt, and thrive in the face of shocks, such as the Covid-19 pandemic, requires external and internal perspectives to assess the financial/operational strengths, weaknesses, threats/risks, and rebalancing opportunities to facilitate strategic resilience (Cooperrider & Godwin, 2022). The optimal resourcing to initiate a culture transformation effort is to solicit volunteers throughout the entire organization for establishing a coalition of catalysts demonstrating like-mindedness, purpose-driven, energized people, desire to collaborate in diverse groups by knowledge-sharing, passion growth-interests, and goal-oriented (Duckworth, 2016; Franklin, 2014). For optimization, "the new network part of a dual operating system takes those steps and turbocharges them" (Kotter, 2019) to deploy sustainable culture transformations founded upon organizational excellence synergistic ideologies holistically centered on both equitable economic- and culture-value paradigms (Beer & Nohria, 2000; Vasconcelos, 2017).

The recommendation is a mixed operating model customized based on business functional areas where multifaceted ecosystems leverage best practices from infrastructure within an integrative-synthesized design to better formulate a change enabled workforce structure to sustain a holistic multi-level culture transformation, influencing profit and personal growth (Giorgi et al., 2020). Integrating both inner-and-outer nuances to ensure business continuity from a real-social-role-of-leadership within the workplace supports deep-inner-work for intrinsic self-knowledge, so the wellbeing of the organization and workforce are not entirely dependent upon external circumstances (Fairholm, 1996). The resilience-building approach enables all to remain professionally and personally competitive, innovative, creative, and adaptive, supporting all the industry, sector, or discipline post-pandemic and being more vital to withstand eminent future turmoil confidently. The resilience dimensions to proactively prepare for future disruption includes influencing the board on synergizing financial, operational, technological, organizational, reputational, and purposeful business-model as sustainability strategies with prosperity and planet alignments as ascribed to in the Holistic Workplace Culture Model.

Since leadership skills are not in the core curriculum in U.S. schools as a life-skill, the gap is immense; however, in recent years, partnerships have begun to form between education systems and nonprofit, not-for-profit, and NGOs to address the national systemic issue (Amanchukwu et al., 2015; Tierney, 2006). However, private, and public sectors are lagging in addressing leadership education, which benefits all levels, not simply for growing the C-suite, executives, and emerging leaders (Miñon, 2017; Nolan-Arañez & Ludvik, 2018; Schmidt et al., 2017). Leadership is not a positional title on an organizational chart, social status, wealth, or geography; instead, leading is about one life inspiring and motivating another to strive in becoming the best version of themselves by dreaming, learning, and shining more within Work-Life (Bennis, 2021; Li et al., 2011; Zohar & Marshall, 2004). Thus, leadership provides a sense of personal growth while aligning to organizational commitment towards a purposeful common goal.

The recommendation is to purposefully invest in people by accelerating the building of workforce capabilities at scale to support them in thriving both during and post-pandemic crises (Bilginoğlu & Yozgat, 2021). The imperative facet to grow their foundational technical, organizational, and professional skills towards learning agility for leading themselves and others based on their role to establish passion-purpose-practice Work-Life alignments within a positive culture to drive the business forward (Bilginoğlu & Yozgat, 2021; Ferguson, 2009). Furthermore, stress management engagement and mental health awareness interventions are critical for the well-being and both workforce and organization health (Kokubun et al., 2020).

To close, the author as a scholar-practitioner-leader with varied expertise and insights proposes creating a new executive enterprise-level role designed with the sole focus is dedicated to serving as a global catalyst responsible for culture change leadership education. A strategic and visionary approach is highly recommended for hierarchical and bureaucratic institutions as these environments face a constant state of change. The public-sectors' unique regulatory governmental accountability and transparency demands for risk mitigation management strategies consistently. Basic components should include: reimagined workforce-ecosystem enhancements; routine workforce-analysis-profiling-collaborative-explorations; future-focused custom-competencies-job-credentialing; customized-unbiased-interventions for up-/re-/

across-skilling; internal/external multidisciplinary/interindustry business relationship-management, pre-/post-test program evaluation assessments/analysis, internal/external forum Work-Life culture-change-leadership facilitations/engagements in virtual/in-person/blended (synchronous/asynchronous) experiences, and return-on-investment monitoring to ensure measured-validity-quality of culture embedment (Jung, 1973). The purposeful influence of holistic catalyzing culture leadership is to impact the sustainability of transformative change, especially during crisis times can serve as a stabilizing force, which calls for an enhanced holistic-thinking perspective to drive the mission forward effectively (Kodama, 2019).

Holistic Organizational Health

The characteristics of organizational healthiness activities are evident when leaders' empowerment, encouragement, and resource enablement are exercised in adopting intervention strategies necessary to transform their team operations and become acceptable practices to enhance cultural dynamics incrementally (Bell-Ellis, 2013). During Covid-19, the positivity research with appreciative inquiry (AI) practices was leveraged as a reliable tool for helping many leaders and educators build resilience and grit and strengthen resourcefulness to face the future by not resisting the change (Cooperrider & Godwin, 2022; Lewis et al., 2016; Sorensen et al., 2022). AI intervention practices can be instrumental to consciously progress through the grieving, healing, reconsolidating, and refocusing processes triggered by trauma-informed events such as pandemics. Additionally, learning concepts and applying enhanced leadership principles to oneself and others, regardless of position, authority, or status, can impact daily interactions, regardless of communication methods within healthy organizations.

Identifying synergistic leadership intelligence can advance workplace culture beyond traditional agendas towards equitable integrative frameworks to foster opportunities for the pursuit of prosperity while attaining the fullest potential of all people and for business optimization simultaneously. Cultivating organizational spirituality is growing momentum from the pandemic crisis impact as a global phenomenon with change implementations occurring across industries/disciplines, including technology, universities, public/military, healthcare, economic/finance, manufacturing, marketing/sales, hospitality/tourism, and equity/diversity/inclusion, by delivering sustainable culture transformation realization with increased productivity (Dilmaghani, 2019; Geh, 2014; Golestanipour, 2016; Pourmola et al., 2019). Empirical studies showed integrating "spirituality at work" radiates "ripples of hope" (Bell-Ellis, 2013, p. 333) throughout all levels of business, which produces a sense of organizational health and employee wellness, which aligns with Work-Life's purposeful meaning creating a sense of flourishing happiness (Baykal, 2019; Keller, 2021; Smith & Halligan, 2021; Vasconcelos, 2018).

Future of Work and Well-Being

The empirical literature suggests when consciously leading any change engagements, extra careful considerations are made of participants' needs and well-being during and post the pandemic era as disparities and inequities are trending upward on many levels, negatively impacting the workforce (Bonacini et al., 2021; Kokubun et al., 2020; Lawrence, 2015; Papageorge et al., 2021; Weiss & Li, 2020). Critical components are to assess current state and ensure occupational health has balanced ecosystems at the enterprise level as an astute future state risk mitigation strategy to any potential resistance in advance of declaring the organization has reached change readiness for intervention engagement based upon diagnosis (Geh, 2014; Khari & Sinha, 2018; Muchemi & Wakonyo, 2020; Sinclair et al., 2020; Wigert &

Agrawal, 2022). Research suggested a change and pandemic fatigue co-occurring, which are global red flags demanding cross-disciplinary integrative interventions and course corrections as virtual teams lack good leadership, apprehensive organizational commitment to mitigate risks of burnout, stress, resilience, and relational matters (Irawanto, 2020; Papageorge et al., 2021; Shanafelt et al., 2019).

The literature indicates high-significance promoting leaders-members authentic connections with at least one person at work for organically mitigating job stress, anxiety, and other health issues by creating a sense of satisfaction, belonging, acceptance, and well-being irrespective of the environment's crisis conditions (Brown, 2019a; Demirci & Ekşi, 2018; Li et al., 2020; Sultana et al., 2020). The absence of meaningful connections in the workplace fosters burnout conditions, whereas "emotional exhaustion leads to greater depersonalization, which subsequently leads to diminished personal accomplishment" from reduced extra efforts, engagement, and organizational commitment (Baykal, 2019; Kokubun et al., 2020; Leach et al., 2013; Leiter & Maslach, 1988, p. 297; Leiter et al., 2014).

Traditional leaders pre-pandemic focused on visioning, motivating, empowering, and developing the future line of succession effectively in preparation for the demands forth-coming on the workforce involving artificial intelligence, the internet of things, and robotics. However, the pandemic has accelerated these technological advances exponentially, producing immediate talent upskilling and reskilling efforts across the globe to meet the escalating job market needs (Czifra & Molnár, 2020). Surprisingly, C-suite level positions show the most significant number of job vacancies, and women in executive roles are lagging more now than pre-crisis. Literature showed work-life balance struggles were prominent throughout the Covid-19 pandemic, with women exiting the workforce in record numbers to nurture loved ones (Dilmaghani, 2019; Ramachandaran et al., 2017; Vroman & Danko, 2020). The author proposes that this situation would not have become so prominent had organizational spirituality already become normalized as a business-as-usual valued practice throughout the United States (Emmons, 2000a; 2000b; Rocha & Pinheiro, 2020). Hence, growing a pipeline of holistic leadership capacity-building at all levels for organizations has become paramount for the sustainability of any transformational strategic initiatives, such as psychological wellness and coaching interventions (Amini et al., 2021; Torch, 2023).

Evolution of Change Management for Realigning Ecosystems

The structured change process transforms the leader's growth mindset when nurturing equitable and belonging practices by addressing systemic and systematic organizational ecosystem misalignment through an innovative work/life integrative intelligence approach, including work-life harmony practices such as Appreciative Inquiry and Positive Culture Leadership (Bremer, 2018; Brown, 2019a; Cekada, 2018; Cooperrider & Godwin, 2022; Sorensen et al., 2022). Ecosystem realignments prompt individual shifts such as behavioral, mental, psychological, emotional, and business/educational structural shifts such as economic (Ozili & Arun, 2020), environmental, cultural/spiritual, humility, and social bonds impact considerations. To focus solely on technology alone is superficial, with an outside-in approach that ignores or leaves for last the human element, which is the most basic mistake organizations can make (Czifra & Molnár, 2020). Hence, aligning with the human-centered ecosystems is imperative to coordinate resources of high-level skills, specializations, certifications, and qualifications needed for transformational change, including policies, rewards, incentives, and reinforcement systems comprised of monetary, nonmonetary, and career-based structures (Czifra & Molnár, 2020).

CONCLUSION

The investigation contributed to the body of knowledge in a manner that was fourfold. First, the transformational and authentic leadership styles were integrated with the interpersonal capacities of social skills (sensitivity/expressivity, S-EQ), grit/growth intelligence, and spiritual intelligence/leadership to influence work-life by impacting culture to sustain organizational excellence transformations that expanded each of these paradigms. Thereby, stimulating ideation for constructing the Sustainable Holistic Workplace Culture Model (Vázquez-de-Príncipe, 2021, p. 95) (Figure 1), integrating a *quadruple-bottom-line* (Alibašić, 2018) approach towards strategic planning, designing, decision-making, and encouraging workforce voicing along the way for developing collaborative custom solutions.

Furthermore, the spiritual intelligence (SQ) variable was the most significant integrative component in the investigation, serving as *spiritual capital* (Zohar & Marshall, 2004) with overlapping facets presented as advantageous glue needed for the synergistic alignment of the rest of the variables in the conceptual framework. Therefore, when empowered, a spiritually intelligent leader within a holistic workplace culture, can profoundly impact others to heighten individuals, teams, and humanistic organizations to unprecedented excellence levels by building organizational commitment fostering a sense of meaningful work, even among public administrators (Alimudin et al., 2017; Otaye-Ebede et al., 2020).

Figure 1. Sustainable holistic workplace culture model
Source: Vázquez-de-Príncipe, 2021

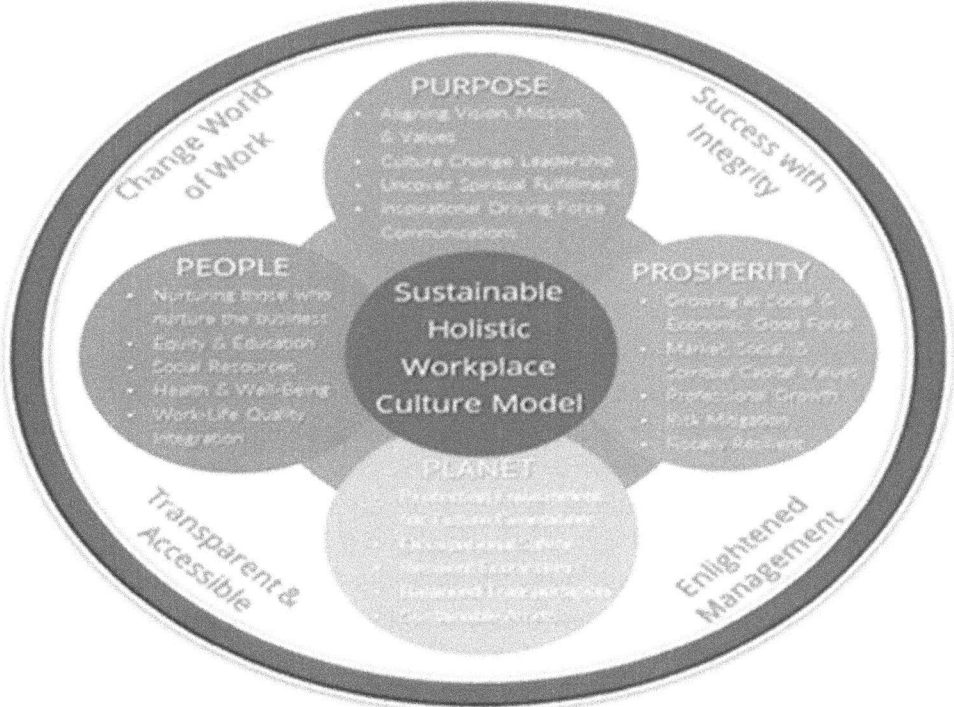

Second, the investigation's conceptualized framework also stimulated ideation for the Holistic Leadership Intelligence (HLQ) Model (Vázquez-de-Príncipe, 2021, p. 109) (Figure 2), representing the ideal consummate superconscious leadership approach towards organically fostering a sustained, holistic workplace culture. The HLQ's considerations nurture synergized enhanced mindsets, attitudes, behaviors, and intellect towards optimal competencies for leading comprehensively across widely diverse cultural complexities. A sense of values-based vision, mission, and purposeful drive of these selfless true public-servants can effectively adapt the all-inclusive multifaceted concepts consistent of synergized mind/brain, body/hands, heart/energy, and spirit/light perspectives.

Figure 2. Holistic leadership intelligence (HLQ) model
Source: Vázquez-de-Príncipe, 2021

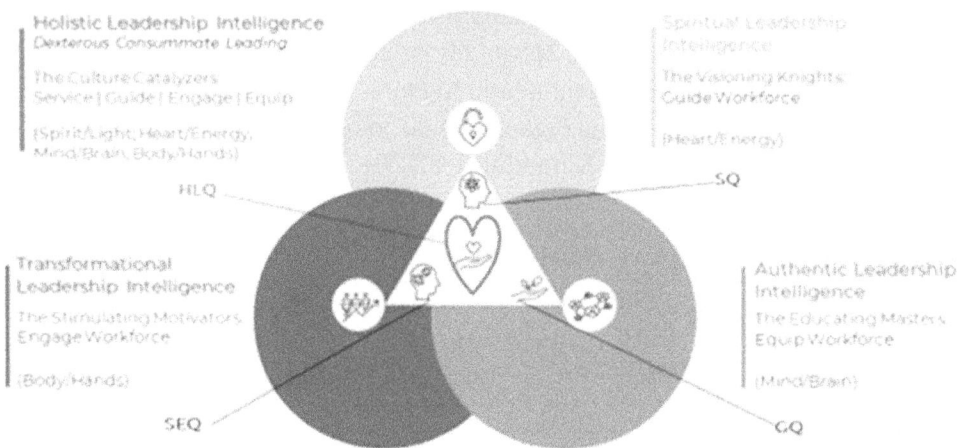

Third, study highlighted paradigm shifts occurring within the change management discipline and leadership evolution fostered by challenges drive by the Covid-19 pandemic, which exposed the industry's lack of resilient preparedness to supporting leaders during turbulent times of crisis (Abrahamsson & Ollander-Axelsson, 2020; Bonacini et al., 2021; Weiss & Li, 2020). Therefore, the pandemic highlighted the need for the change management discipline to broaden perspectives to focus on developing professionalism built-on mastery constructs beyond process-orientation towards growing leadership and learning-agility, distinct from consistent application of technological implementations with its technical training (Diefenbach & Deelmann, 2016; Mack et al., 2015). Hence, leadership agility strategy enables change catalysts to lead, direct, advise; coach, mentor, manage teams; and guide C-suite executives and senior leadership through any future VUCA world situations (Hodgson & White, 2003, p. 185) crises while still cultivating professional advancement opportunities (Mack et al., 2015). Furthermore, the future of change management education must incorporate multidisciplinary and inter-industry essentials for varied organizational levels from executives, leaders, managers, advisors, coaches, individual contributors, implementors, influencers, and more, including interventions such as crisis management and virtual engagements (Kokubun et al., 2020; Muchemi & Wakonyo, 2020; Restubog et al., 2020).

Fourth, the scholarly investigation's contribution was synthesizing various disparate bodies of literature, disciplines, practices, industries, sciences, intelligence, processes, techniques, and models.

The researcher as Scholar-Practitioner-Leader successfully weaving the divergent perspectives into the conceptual framework as a practical roadmap towards enhancing Work-Life through culture impact for sustainable organizational leadership excellence. The synergy among these disparate bodies of knowledge explicitly focused contextual alignments specific to the public sector's unique challenges towards intentionally improving Work-Life, leadership capacity, and positive culture transformations. Although the hierarchical structures are necessary, the future of work demands calls for a more holistically harmonious workplace climate and culture, which is not conducive within such competitive atmospheres driven by scarcity of opportunities, lack of organizational commitment, weak interpersonal growth, and entitlement attitudes (Athar, 2020; Kodama, 2019). Therefore, the integration of synergized model structure infused with change professionals as liaisons across business functions and the deployment of non-prescriptive concepts specific to the industry purpose.

Work/Life Dynamics Dimensionality

The sustainability of culture transformational journeys with or without technological components managed with superficial pretense circumstances are highly unlikely viable for the long haul and produce minimal performance results at best (Bengtsson & Raza-Ullah, 2016). At the same time, unconfirmed willingness from deep buy-in at the point of achieving capacity competence-level bears resistance with a nonadaptive spirit cultivated by lack of trust, commitment, confidence, and leadership among the leader/member exchange cultural and societal dynamics (Crossman, 2016; O'Connor & Yballe, 2007). These detrimental outcomes demonstrate disconnect from deeper-level reality produced by leader's fears of vulnerability, reluctance to express need for help, rejecting responsibility/accountability, whereas unbalanced ego personas are evident of lack of wisdom, faith, hope, vision, and self-/cultural awareness (Athar, 2020; Menguc et al., 2017).

Maslow who was—and still is—globally esteemed as the humanistic psychology guru on matters of human condition, behavior, personality, and motivation. His theories of human motivation and needs have indeed withstood the test of over seventy years' time. Crises impact from Covid-19 pandemic and civil unrest exposed human-centered vulnerabilities—triggering demands for deeper-levels of human nature understanding indicating "we need Maslow in the 21st Century" (Abulof, 2017, p. 508) society—indubitably imperative for *hybrid work-life* (Gallup, 2023), as perpetual VUCA World calls for personal and professional transformational journeys.

The investigator evaluated Maslow's research then unexpectedly discovered synergistic alignments with contrast variations, albeit adaptable, which were associated to leadership and human-intelligences constructs of conceptual framework, herewith a derivative from multi-level crisis situations. Henceforth, the investigator realized the Hierarchy of Needs framework had never been placed in a structured pyramid figure by Maslow himself, actually his supporters were the ones who later formalized the depiction. For that reason, Vázquez-de-Príncipe (2021) found an iceberg valuation would be most appropriate to reflect upon pandemic crises impacts on work-life dynamics, leadership, human-intelligences, and change management disciplines.

The Deeply Formed Work/Life Dimensionality Iceberg (Vázquez-de-Príncipe, 2021, p. 267) (Figure 3) illustrates a dynamic model for contrasts and comparisons of empirical and theoretical literature, synergistic framework constructs, and multi-dimensional interdisciplinary contexts influenced by principles of the HLQ Model (p. 109). This Iceberg Model below reflects the organizational, educational, interpersonal, spiritual, and cultural multidimensional synergistic dynamics informed by the HLQ Model principles

(Vázquez-de-Príncipe, 2021, pp. 109, 267). The human need for satisfying self-actualization has evolved with mindsets shifting from linear-thinking, beyond human-centered principles, towards holistic-thinking paradigm of self-realization, which synthesizes both conscious and unconscious paradigms. Whereas highly matured individual contributors were essential constituents to align organizations, communities, universities, enterprises with holistic-human-value levels beyond financial to real intrinsic motivations, thereby inspiring authentic transformational journeys for serving others and garnering excellence commitments for the greater good.

Figure 3. Deeply formed work/life dimensionality iceberg model
Source: Vázquez-de-Príncipe, 2021

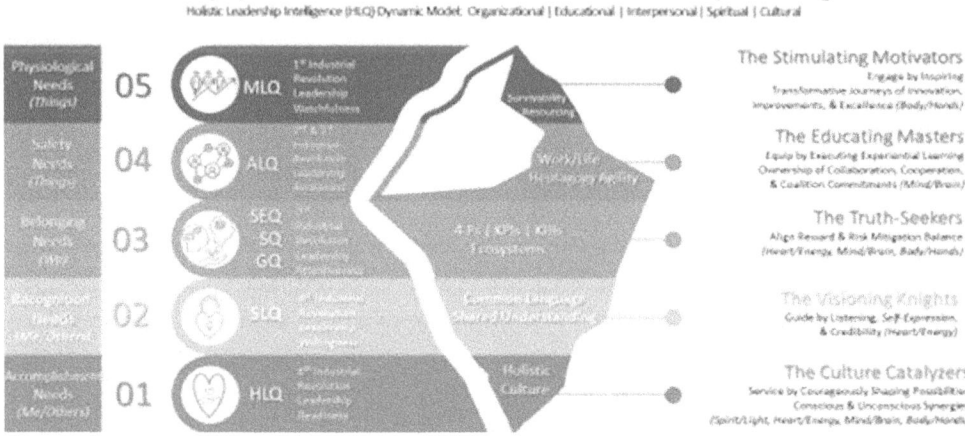

The HLQ model integrates resilient business and people needs outcomes, such as practitioners shaping holistic cultural workplaces in preparation for the forthcoming demands from the 4th Industrial Revolution (Industry 4.0). Practitioners who embrace the responsibilities and accountabilities associated with serving a catalyzing culture changer strive to guide, engage, and equip the workforce leveraging their dynamic mind/brain, body/hands, heart/energy, and spirit/light wisdom. HLQ consummate servant leaders dexterously function at multiple levels on needs spectrum simultaneously demonstrating their resilient shine from inner-light, employ agile mindsets, and execute proactive innovation/improvement visionary efforts by initiating, then ensuring follow-through to implementation, evaluation, and lessons learned exploration.

Furthermore, ego fueled immature leaders promote a Tell-Culture with focused mindset of Me, which hinders their leadership capability to sustain long-term benefits of any form of transformational change efforts. On the contrary, highly matured consummate servant leaders with focused mindset of We, promote a Coach-Culture evolved by a synergistic deep-commitment mindset of Me and Others, which generates awareness and responsibility across all levels. Authentic transformational journeys with such holistic leaders, organically encourages within Coach-Culture, leadership aptitude, benevolence for workforce, inspirational influence, real intimate trust interactions, quality performance, transparent communications, positive Work-Life dynamic outcomes, innovation/improvement excellence recognition, and customer/stakeholder care integrity.

Moreover, it is critical to highlight both Transformational and Authentic Leadership are illustrated in Figure 3 above the waterline of iceberg. Hence, indicating these constructs are outward facing only addressing corporate climate matters, such as policies, processes, and procedure. When one or both approaches are elevated in isolation, the outcomes have only superficial climate-related impact on Work-Life dynamics. Therefore, any transformation efforts cannot be sustained long-term with immature and underdeveloped individual contributors. However, the three levels beneath the waterline specifically address the deeper cultural contextual constructs such as organizational health, inclusion, psychological safety, and personal/corporate identities. Moreover, chance practitioners who grows all the five levels shown in the iceberg can deeply enable both professional and organizational performance improvements leading towards the true long-term sustainment of organizational excellence transformations.

Holistic Leadership Mindedness: A Reflective Practice

Research has shown that self-reflection, or the identification and evaluation of your thoughts, emotions, and actions can promote learning outcomes for individuals with a growth mindset (Kwan et al., 2022). It is thought to be the basis for self-regulation (Ward & King, 2018) – or the ability to adaptively adjust our behaviors in accordance with our goals – and has been shown to be strongly related to self-efficacy. By reflecting on the growth, we have attained, we offer ourselves the opportunity to observe our strengths, note the progress achieved in addressing our weaknesses, enhance our self-efficacy, and reward ourselves for our hard work. The increase in self-efficacy and positive self-regard that often emerges from reflection can promote sustained commitment to our goals.

Nevertheless, it is important to note, however, that the process of self-reflection is only beneficial when you engage in it with a growth mindset. Studies suggest that people with a fixed mindset do not see the same benefits of self-reflection (Kwan et al., 2022), likely because the focus is on weaknesses and the progress yet to be made rather than strengths and achievements. Reflecting specifically on the areas in which you feel you are lacking can be detrimental to your commitment. As you are developing your growth mindset, if you notice your reflections tend to center on negative aspects of your experience, adjust your strategy to focus on self-compassion instead. Research has shown that self-compassion can be a useful exercise for individuals who are still learning to shed their fixed mindset (Kwan et al., 2022).

Self-compassion is an essential component of a growth mindset (Dweck, 2015). Being compassionate with ourselves gives us the room we need to grow. Without it, our potential is stifled, and we are unable to recognize our mistakes and inadequacies without being flattened by them. That is, after an experience of failure or disappointment, self-compassionate people are able to see themselves and their behavior in a way that corresponds more closely with reality, rather than forming a self-image that is unrealistically enhanced or self-deprecating. Self-compassion has been shown to be associated with increased life satisfaction, higher motivation for self-improvement, well-being, optimism, curiosity, and exploration (Hope et al., 2014; Neff, 2003).

Furthermore, it has been shown that self-compassion helps regulate goal engagement and negative emotions in response to setbacks (Miyagawa et al., 2018). When confronted with failure, we have the option to persist in our goals or abandon them. People who were high in self-compassion tend to be better able to identify the best course of action and, when the best choice was to abandon the goal, they were more likely to engage in an alternative goal that was similarly meaningful than their less self-compassionate peers (Miyagawa et al., 2018).

Holistic-minded leaders intentionally practice self-compassion by reflecting on recent experiences they are having difficulty with. For example, work stress or disputes with colleagues, family, or friends. Next, they write out a description of this challenging experience, then answer the four following questions: (1) Determine what is one thing you can do to tend to your emotional needs? (2) Determine how could you make yourself feel physically calmer or more at ease? (3) Determine what could you say that would validate your feelings? (4) Determine how you could motivate yourself to work through your difficult experience with kindness and understanding?

Lastly, practicing reflections throughout one's work-life can promote positive inter-relational dynamic behaviors that leverages the principles of the Holistic Leadership Intelligence (HLQ) model (Vázquez-de-Príncipe, 2021, p. 109). These integrative practices can trigger sustainable transformational mind shifts towards harmonizing interconnected work-life dynamics for fostering positive cultures where people can thrive and flourish, even during unprecedented times of uncertainty and disruption (Bremer, 2018; Brown, 2019a). To better understand yourself and to apply an appreciative inquiry approach for becoming a leader with a growth mindset to influence a holistic positive culture towards organizational excellence and healthiness, consider pondering the next three questions: (1) Determine how best you as a leader can help others bring their best selves, extra efforts, talents, and creativity to the workplace? (2) Determine how you can as an influencer promote ecosystem processes and procedures to accelerate others' careers, growth development to help others reach their highest potential, and progression of the organization, team, department, or community? (3) Determine how as a culture catalyst you can leverage the multicultural diverse workforce as part of the overall strategic business goals measured by organizational health OD metrics?

ACKNOWLEGEMENT

This research received no specific grant from any funding agency in the public, commercial, or not-for-profit sectors.

REFERENCES

Abuhassàn, A., & Bates, T. C. (2015). Grit: Distinguishing effortful persistence from conscientiousness. *Journal of Individual Differences*, *36*(4), 205–214. doi:10.1027/1614-0001/a000175

Ahmed, A., Arshad, M. A., Mahmood, A., & Akhtar, S. (2016). Holistic human resource development: Balancing the equation through the inclusion of spiritual quotient. *Journal of Human Values*, *22*(3), 165–179. doi:10.1177/0971685816650573

Al-Shamlan, H. M., & Al-Mudimigh, A. S. (2011, March). The change management strategies and processes for successful ERP implementation: A case study of MADAR. *International Journal of Computer Science Issues*, *8*(2), 399–407.

Alahdab, F., Halvorsen, A. J., Mandrekar, J. N., Vaa, B. E., Montori, V. M., West, C. P., Murad, M. H., & Beckman, T. J. (2020). How do we assess resilience and grit among internal medicine residents at the Mayo Clinic? A longitudinal validity study including correlations with medical knowledge, professionalism, and clinical performance. *BMJ Open*, *10*(12), e040699. doi:10.1136/bmjopen-2020-040699 PMID:33323437

Alameda, C., Sanabria, D., & Ciria, L. F. (2022). The brain in flow: A systematic review on the neural basis of the flow state. *Cortex*, *154*, 348–364. doi:10.1016/j.cortex.2022.06.005 PMID:35926367

Alibašić, H. (2018). *Sustainability and resilience planning for local governments: The quadruple bottom line strategy*. Springer International Publishing. doi:10.1007/978-3-319-72568-0

Amanchukwu, R. N., Stanley, G. J., & Ololube, N. P. (2015). A review of leadership theories, principles and styles and their relevance to educational management. *Management*, *5*(1), 6–14. doi:10.5923/j.mm.20150501.02

Amini, A., Shirvani, H., & Bazgir, B. (2021). Effectiveness of guided visualization and mental imagery on perceived stress, psychological well–being and sleep quality in Armed Forces retirement. *Journal Mil Med*, *23*(12), 913–924.

Applebaum, S. H., Degbe, M. C., MacDonald, O., & Nguyen-Quang, T. S. (2015). Organizational outcomes of leadership style and resistance to change (part two). *Industrial and Commercial Training*, *47*(3), 134–144. doi:10.1108/ICT-07-2013-0045

Aravamudhan, N. R., & Krishnaveni, R. (2014). Spirituality at workplace–an emerging template for organization capacity building? *PURUSHARTHA—A Journal of Management. Ethics, and Spirituality*, *7*(1), 63–78.

Astin, H. S. (2004). Some thoughts on the role of spirituality in transformational leadership. *Spirituality in Higher Education Newsletter*, *1*(4), 1–5.

Athar, H. S. (2020). The influence of organizational culture on organizational commitment post-pandemic Covid-19. *International Journal of Multicultural and Multireligious Understanding*, *7*(5), 148–157.

Atwater, D. C., & Bass, B. M. (1994). Transformational leadership in teams. In B. M. Bass & B. J. Avolio (Eds.), *Improving Organizational Effectiveness Through Transformational Leadership*. Sage Publications, Inc.

Avolio, B. J., Sosik, J. J., Jung, D. L., & Berson, Y. (2003). *Leadership models, methods, and applications: Small steps and giant leaps* (Vol. 12). Handbook of Psychology. John Wiley & Sons. doi:10.1002/0471264385.wei1212

Baykal, E. (2019). Creating organizational commitment through spiritual leadership: Mediating effect of meaning at work. *Business & Management International Journal*, *7*(2), 837–855. doi:10.15295/bmij.v7i2.1113

Beckhard, R., & Pritchard, W. (1992). *Changing the essence: The art of creating and leading fundamental change in organizations*. Jossey-Bass Publishers.

Beer, M., & Nohria, N. (2000, May). Cracking the code of change. *HBR's Ten Must Reads on Change Management, 78*(3), 137–154. PMID:11183975

Bell-Ellis, R. (2013). Integrating spirit at work: A ripple of hope for healthy organizational cultures. In *Handbook of Faith and Spirituality in the Workplace* (pp. 333–343). Emerging Research and Practice. doi:10.1007/978-1-4614-5233-1_21

Benefiel, M. (2008). *The soul of a leader: Finding your path to fulfillment and success.* The Crossroad Publishing Company.

Bengtsson, M., & Raza-Ullah, T. (2016). A systematic review of research on coopetition: Toward a multi-level understanding. *Industrial Marketing Management, 57,* 23–39. doi:10.1016/j.indmarman.2016.05.003

Bennis, W. (2021). *On becoming a leader.* Perseus Books Group.

Bennis, W. G. (1959). Leadership theory and administrative behavior: The problem of authority. *Administrative Science Quarterly, 4*(3), 259–301. doi:10.2307/2390911

Bilginoğlu, E., & Yozgat, U. (2021). The impact of sparking leadership on creating work passion and job satisfaction in organizations - An empirical study. Anadolu University. *Journal of Social Sciences, 21*(1), 43–58. doi:10.18037/ausbd.902549

Blanchard, K. H., & Hersey, P. (1997). Situational leadership. In: *Dean's Forum, 12*(2), 5.

Bolman, L. G., & Deal, T. E. (2011). *Leading with soul: An uncommon journey of the spirit.* Jossey-Bass Publishers. doi:10.1177/1071799199600300117

Bommer, W. H., Rich, G. A., & Rubin, R. S. (2005). Changing attitudes about change: Longitudinal effects of transformational leader behavior on employee cynicism about organizational change. *Journal of Organizational Behavior, 26*(7), 733–753. doi:10.1002/job.342

Bonacini, L., Gallo, G., & Scicchitano, S. (2021). Working from home and income inequality: Risks of a 'new normal' with Covid-19. *Journal of Population Economics, 34*(1), 303–360. doi:10.100700148-020-00800-7 PMID:32952308

Boyatzis, R. E., Smith, M., & Blaize, N. (2006). Developing sustainable leaders through coaching and compassion. *Academy of Management Learning & Education, 5*(1), 8–24. doi:10.5465/amle.2006.20388381

Boyd, E. (2017, February). Holistic thinking beyond technology. *Nature Climate Change, 7*(2), 97–98. doi:10.1038/nclimate3211

Bremer, M. (2018). *Developing a positive culture where people and performance thrive.* Motivational Press, Inc.

Brown, B. (2010). *The gifts of imperfection: Let go of who you think you're supposed to be and embrace who you are.* Hazelden.

Brown, B. (2019a). *Braving the wilderness: The quest for true belonging and the courage to stand alone.* Penguin Random House LLC.

Brown, J. (2019b). *How to be an inclusive leader: Your role in creating cultures of belonging where everyone can thrive*. Berrett-Koehler Publishers.

Buckley, P., & Bachman, D. (2017). Meet the US workforce of the future: Older, more diverse, and more educated. *Deloitte Review*, *21*, 47–61.

Cameron, K. S., & Quinn, R. E. (2006). *Diagnosing and changing organizational culture: Based on the competing values framework*. Jossey-Bass Publishers.

Carder, B., & Monda, M. (2013). *Deming's profound knowledge and leadership: We are still not out of the crisis*. ASQ Quality Press.

Carder, B., & Ragan, P. (2005). Measurement matters. *Professional Safety*, *50*(4), 17.

Cekada, T. L. (2018). Salesmanship for change: Utilizing WIIFM and understanding employee needs. *Professional Safety*, *63*(03), 44–47.

Chawla, V. (2014). The effect of workplace spirituality on salespeople's organizational deviant behaviors: Research propositions and practical implications. *Journal of Business and Industrial Marketing*, *29*(3), 199–208. doi:10.1108/JBIM-08-2012-0134

Christensen, M. (2005). The third hand: Private sector consultants in public sector accounting change. *European Accounting Review*, *14*(3), 447–474. doi:10.1080/0963818042000306217

Christie, R. (2013). Why Machiavelli? In: Christie, R., & Florence, L. G. (Eds.), Studies in Machiavellianism. Academy Press.

Colbert, A. E., Judge, T. A., Choi, D., & Wang, G. (2012). Accessing the trait theory of leadership using self and observer ratings of personality: The mediating role of contributions to group success. *The Leadership Quarterly*, *23*(4), 670–647. doi:10.1016/j.leaqua.2012.03.004

Conger, J. A. (1994). *Spirit at work: Discovering the spirituality in leadership* (1st ed.). Jossey-Bass Publishers.

Contractor, N. S., DeChurch, L. A., Carson, J., Carter, D. R., & Keegan, B. (2012). The topology of collective leadership. *The Leadership Quarterly*, *23*(6), 994–1011. doi:10.1016/j.leaqua.2012.10.010

Cooperrider, D. L., & Godwin, L. N. (2022). Strengths-based megacommunities and the Appreciative Inquiry's complete convention: Creating wholepower, willpower and waypower for our world's Earthshot moment. *AI Practitioner*, *24*(1), 94–106. doi:10.12781/978-1-907549-50-2-8

Cork, S. (2010). *Resilience and transformation: Preparing Australia for uncertain futures*. CSIRO Publishing. doi:10.1071/9780643098138

Cox, T., Kuk, G., & Leiter, M. P. (1993). Burnout, health, work stress, and organizational healthiness. In: W. B. Schaufeli, C. Maslach, & T. Marek (Eds.), *Series in applied psychology: Social issues and questions, Professional Burnout: Recent Developments in Theory & Research* (pp. 177–193). Taylor & Francis.

Crossman, J. (2016). Alignment and misalignment in personal and organizational spiritual identities. *Identity*, *16*(3), 154–168. doi:10.1080/15283488.2016.1190726

Czifra, G., & Molnár, Z. (2020). Covid-19 and Industry 4.0. *Research Papers: Faculty of Materials Science and Technology, 28*(46), 36-45. Slovak University of Technology. doi:10.2478/rput-2020-0005

Daud, Y. M. (2020). Self-leadership and its application to today's leader-A review of literature. *Strategic Journal of Business & Change Management, 8*(1), 1-11.

Day, D. V., & Sin, H. P. (2011). Longitudinal tests of an integrative model of leader development: Charting and understanding developmental trajectories. *The Leadership Quarterly, 22*(3), 545–560. doi:10.1016/j.leaqua.2011.04.011

de Rue, D. S., Nahrgang, J. D., Wellman, N. E. D., & Humphrey, S. E. (2011). Trait and behavioral theories of leadership: An integration and meta-analytic test of their relative validity. *Personnel Psychology, 64*(1), 7–52. doi:10.1111/j.1744-6570.2010.01201.x

de Smet, A., & Vogel, T. (2021, January 21). *McKinsey Live: Reenergizing the workforce: How leaders can overcome pandemic fatigue.* COVID Response Center. McKinsey & Company.

Deal, T. E., & Kennedy, A. A. (1982). *Corporate cultures.* Addison-Wesley.

Dealy, M. D., & Thomas, A. R. (2007). *Managing by accountability: What every leader needs to know about responsibility, integrity—and results.* Praeger Publishers.

Demirci, İ., & Ekşi, H. (2018). Keep calm and be happy: A mixed method study from character strengths to well-being. *Educational Sciences: Theory & Practice, 18*(2).

Denzin, N. K. (2012). Triangulation 2.0. *Journal of Mixed Methods Research, 6*(2), 80–88. doi:10.1177/1558689812437186

Desai, P. (2009). Spiritual psychology: A way to effective management. *African Journal of Marketing Management, 1*(7), 165–171.

Diefenbach, S., & Deelmann, T. (2016). Organizational approaches to answer a VUCA world. In O. Mack, A. Khare, A. Krämer, & T. Burgartz (Eds.), *Managing in a VUCA World.* Springer Nature. doi:10.1007/978-3-319-16889-0_13

Dilmaghani, M. (2019). Deep-level religious diversity and work-life balance satisfaction in Canada. *Applied Research in Quality of Life, 16*(1), 315–350. Advance online publication. doi:10.100711482-019-09768-3

Dolan, S. L., & Altman, Y. (2012). Managing by values: The leadership spirituality connection. *People & Strategy, 35*(4), 20–26.

Duckworth, A. L. (2016). *Grit: The power of passion and perseverance.* Simon and Schuster.

Duckworth, A. L. (2021). *Strengths of will playbooks.* Character Lab.

Duncan, D. L. (2020). What the Covid-19 pandemic tells us about the need to develop resilience in the nursing workforce. *Nursing Management, 27*(3). PMID:32400142

Dweck, C. S. (2015). Carol Dweck revisits the growth mindset. *Education Week, 35*(5), 20–24.

Emmons, R. A. (2000a). Is spirituality an intelligence? Motivation, cognition, and the psychology of ultimate concern. *The International Journal for the Psychology of Religion, 10*(1), 3–26. doi:10.1207/S15327582IJPR1001_2

Emmons, R. A. (2000b). Spirituality and intelligence: Problems and prospects. *The International Journal for the Psychology of Religion, 10*(1), 57–64. doi:10.1207/S15327582IJPR1001_6

Ericsson, A., & Pool, R. (2016). *Peak: Secrets from the new science of expertise.* Houghton Mifflin Harcourt.

Errida, A., & Lotfi, B. (2020). Measuring change readiness for implementing a project management methodology: An action research study. *Academy of Strategic Management Journal, 19*(1), 1–17.

Fairholm, G. W. (1996). Spiritual leadership: Fulfilling whole-self needs at work. *Leadership and Organization Development Journal, 17*(5), 11–17. doi:10.1108/01437739610127469

Ferguson, L. (2009). Working spiritually: Aligning gifts, purpose, and passion. *The Workplace and Spirituality: New Perspectives on Research and Practice*, 23-33.

Fernandez, S., & Rainey, H. G. (2017). Managing successful organizational change in the public sector. In: *Debating Public Administration Review* (pp. 7–26). Routledge. doi:10.4324/9781315095097-2

Fernández-del-Río, E., Ramos-Villagrasa, P. J., & Escartín, J. (2021). The incremental effect of dark personality over the Big Five in workplace bullying: Evidence from perpetrators and targets. *Personality and Individual Differences, 168*, 110–291. doi:10.1016/j.paid.2020.110291

Fernet, C., Trépanier, S. G., Austin, S., Gagné, M., & Forest, J. (2015). Transformational leadership and optimal functioning at work: On the mediating role of employees' perceived job characteristics and motivation. *Work and Stress, 29*(1), 11–31. doi:10.1080/02678373.2014.1003998

Franklin, M. (2014). *Agile change management: A practical framework for successful change planning and implementation.* Kogan Page Limited.

Fry, L. W., & Matherly, L. L. (2007). *Workplace spirituality, spiritual leadership, and performance excellence. Encyclopedia of Industrial/Organizational Psychology.* Sage Publications, Inc.

Gallup. (2023). *Global indicator: Hybrid work.* Gallup. https://www.gallup.com/401384/indicator-hybrid-work.aspx

Geh, E. Z. (2014). Organizational spiritual leadership of worlds "made" and "found": An experiential learning model for "feel." *Leadership and Organization Development Journal, 35*(2), 137–151. doi:10.1108/LODJ-04-2012-0052

Giblin, E. J. (1981). Bureaupathology: The denigration of competence. *Human Resource Management, 20*(4), 22–25. doi:10.1002/hrm.3930200405

Giorgi, G., Lecca, L. I., Alessio, F., Finstad, G. L., Bondanini, G., Lulli, L. G., Arcangeli, G., & Mucci, N. (2020). Covid-19-Related mental health effects in the workplace: A narrative review. *International Journal of Environmental Research and Public Health, 17*(21), 7857. doi:10.3390/ijerph17217857 PMID:33120930

Golestanipour, M. (2016). Simple and multiple relationships between ethical leadership, transformational leadership and ethical climate and organizational spirituality among the employees of the Iran national steel industrial. *Review of European Studies, 8*(2), 355–363. doi:10.5539/res.v8n2p183

Hannah, S. T., Avolio, B. J., & Walumbwa, F. O. (2011). Authentic leadership and effects on follower moral courage, psychological capital, and performance. *Business Ethics Quarterly, 21,* 555–557. doi:10.5840/beq201121436

Hardison, C. M. (2017). Three hundred sixty-degree assessment. In A. Farazmand (Ed.), *Global Encyclopedia of Public Administration, Public Policy, and Governance.* Springer. doi:10.1007/978-3-319-31816-5_2744-1

Hesse-Biber, S. N. (2010). *Mixed methods research: Merging theory with practice.* Guilford Press.

Hiatt, J. M. (2006). *ADKAR: A model for change in business, government, and our community—How to implement successful change in our personal lives and professional careers.* Prosci Learning Center Publications.

Hiatt, J. M., & Creasey, T. J. (2012). *Change management: The people side of change.* Prosci Learning Center Publications.

Hope, N., Koestner, R., & Milyavskaya, M. (2014). The role of self-compassion in goal pursuit and well-being among university freshmen. *Self and Identity, 13*(5), 579–593. doi:10.1080/15298868.2014.889032

Howell, K. R. (2018). Fiedler & Chemers Revisited: Understanding the implications of the least preferred co-worker scale. *Journal of Business & Management Sciences, 6*(3), 82–85. doi:10.12691/jbms-6-3-3

Ilies, R., Morgeson, F. P., & Nahrgang, J. D. (2005). Authentic leadership and eudaemonic well-being: Understanding leader-follower outcomes. *The Leadership Quarterly, 16*(3), 373–394. doi:10.1016/j.leaqua.2005.03.002

Irawanto, D. W. (2020). Unexpected and habit driven: Perspectives of working from home during the Covid-19 Pandemic. [Asia Pacific Management and Business Application]. *APMBA, 8*(3), 165–168. doi:10.21776/ub.apmba.2020.008.03.1

Jung, C. G. (1973). *Synchronicity: An acausal connecting principle.* Princeton University Press.

Kavanagh, M. H., & Ashkanasy, N. M. (2006). The impact of leadership and change management strategy on organizational culture and individual acceptance of change during a merger. *British Journal of Management, 17*(S1), S81–S103. doi:10.1111/j.1467-8551.2006.00480.x

Kazmi, S. A. Z., & Naarananoja, M. (2013, January). Comparative approaches of key change management models—a fine assortment to pick from as per situational needs. In: International Conference on Business Strategy and Organizational Behavior (BizStrategy), *Proceedings,* 217-224. Global Science and Technology Forum.

Keller, T. (2021). *Hope in times of fear: The resurrection and the meaning of Easter.* Penguin Publishing Group. 9780525560807.

Khari, C., & Sinha, S. (2018). Organizational spirituality and knowledge sharing: A model of multiple mediation. *Global Journal of Flexible Systems Managment, 19*(4), 337–348. doi:10.100740171-018-0197-5

Kodama, M. (2019). Business innovation through holistic leadership-developing organizational adaptability. *Systems Research and Behavioral Science, 36*(4), 365–394. doi:10.1002res.2551

Kökalan, Ö. (2019). The effect of organizational cynicism on job satisfaction. *Management Research Review, 42*(5), 625–640. doi:10.1108/MRR-02-2018-0090

Kokubun, K., Ogata, Y., Koike, Y., & Yamakawa, Y. (2020). Brain condition may mediate the association between training and work engagement. *Scientific Reports, 10*(1), 6848. doi:10.103841598-020-63711-3 PMID:32321951

König, A., Graf-Vlachy, L., Bundy, J., & Little, L. M. (2020). A blessing and a curse: How CEOs' trait empathy affects their management of organizational crises. *Academy of Management Review, 45*(1), 130–153. doi:10.5465/amr.2017.0387

Kotter, J. P. (1990). *A force for change: How leadership differs from management.* Free Press.

Kotter, J. P. (2019). *Accelerate!: Building strategic agility for a faster-moving world.* Harvard Business Review Press.

Kwan, L. Y., Hung, Y. S., & Lam, L. (2021). How can we reap learning benefits for individuals with growth and fixed mindsets?: Understanding self-reflection and self-compassion as the psychological pathways to maximize positive learning outcomes. *Frontiers in Education.* doi:10.3389/feduc.2022.800530

Lawrence, P. (2015). Leading change – Insights into how leaders actually approach the challenge of complexity. *Journal of Change Management, 15*(3), 231–252. doi:10.1080/14697017.2015.1021271

Leach, A., Wandmacher, R., Ayres, J., & Gobran, L. (2013, April). Change management: Creating an internal change capacity—What's the right organizational model? [Accenture.]. *Outlook Point of View, 1*, 1–2.

Lee, H. Y., & Kamarul, Z. B. A. (2009). The moderating effects of organizational culture on the relationships between leadership behavior and organizational commitment and between organizational commitment and job satisfaction and performance. *Leadership and Organization Development Journal, 30*(1), 53–86. doi:10.1108/01437730910927106

Leiter, M. P. (1992). Burnout as a crisis in professional role structures: Measurement and conceptual issues. *Anxiety, Stress, and Coping, 5*(1), 79–93. doi:10.1080/10615809208250489

Leiter, M. P., & Harvie, P. (1997). The correspondence of supervisor and subordinate perspectives on major organizational change. *Journal of Occupational Health Psychology, 2*(4), 1–10. doi:10.1037/1076-8998.2.4.343 PMID:9552302

Leiter, M. P., & Maslach, C. (1988). The impact of interpersonal environment on burnout and organizational commitment. *Journal of Organizational Behavior, 9*(4), 297–308. doi:10.1002/job.4030090402

Leiter, M. P., Maslach, C., & Frame, K. (2014). Burnout. Encyclopedia of Clinical Psychology, 1-7.

Lencioni, P. M. (2012). *The advantage: Why organizational health trumps everything else in business.* John Wiley & Sons.

Lewis, S., Passmore, J., & Cantore, S. (2016). *Appreciative inquiry for change management: Using AI to facilitate organizational development.* Kogan Page Publishers.

Li, J., Ghosh, R., & Nachmias, S. (2020). In a time of Covid-19 pandemic, stay healthy, connected, productive, and learning: Words from the editorial team of HRDI. *Human Resources Development Institute*, 199-207.

Li, W. D., Arvey, R. D., & Song, Z. (2011). The influence of general mental ability, self-esteem and family socio-economic status on leadership role occupancy and leader advancement: The moderating role of gender. *The Leadership Quarterly, 22*(3), 520–534. doi:10.1016/j.leaqua.2011.04.009

Lucire, Y. (1986). Neurosis in the workplace. *The Medical Journal of Australia, 145*(7), 323–327. doi:10.5694/j.1326-5377.1986.tb113838.x PMID:2945081

Mack, O., Khare, A., Krämer, A., & Burgartz, T. (2015). *Managing in a VUCA world.* Springer Nature.

Maslow, A. H. (1954). *Motivation and personality.* Harper & Row.

Maxwell, J. C. (2017). *The power of your leadership: Making a difference with others.* Hachette Book Group, Inc.

Menguc, B., Auh, S., Yeniaras, V., & Katsikeas, C. S. (2017). The role of climate: Implications for service employee engagement and customer service performance. *Journal of the Academy of Marketing Science, 45*(3), 428–451. doi:10.100711747-017-0526-9

Meyer, E. (2016). *The culture map: Decoding how people think, lead, and get things done across cultures* (International Ed.). Public Affairs.

Milliman, J., Czaplewski, A. J., & Ferguson, J. (2003). Workplace spirituality and employee work attitudes: An exploratory empirical assessment. *Journal of Organizational Change Management, 16*(4), 426–447. doi:10.1108/09534810310484172

Milliman, J., Gatling, A., & Kim, J. S. (2018). The effect of workplace spirituality on hospitality employee engagement, intention to stay, and service delivery. *Journal of Hospitality and Tourism Management, 35*, 56–65. doi:10.1016/j.jhtm.2018.03.002

Miñon, C. G. (2017). Workplace spirituality, work ethics, and organizational justice as related to job performance among state university educators. *Journal of Teaching and Education, 7*(1), 407-418.

Miyagawa, Y., Taniguchi, J., & Niiya, Y. (2018). Can self-compassion help people regulate unattained goals and emotional reactions toward setbacks? *Personality and Individual Differences, 134*, 239–244. doi:10.1016/j.paid.2018.06.029

Modlin, H. C. (1986). Compensation neurosis. *The Bulletin of the American Academy of Psychiatry and the Law, 14*(3), 263–271. PMID:2945605

Mohamed, T., Singh, J. S. K., & Subramaniam, S. (2020). Social ontelligence, spiritual intelligence, and emotional intelligence: Job satisfaction among public sector employees in a high-risk country. *Global Business and Management Research, 12*(3), 104–117.

Moon, J. (2021). Effect of emotional intelligence and leadership styles on risk intelligent decision making and risk management. *Journal of Engineering. Project & Production Management, 11*(1), 71–81. doi:10.2478/jeppm-2021-0008

Muchemi, A., & Wakonyo, E. N. (2020). Change management practices and performance of the national police service in Uasin Gishu County, Kenya. *International Journal of Current Aspects, 4*(1), 1–21. doi:10.35942/ijcab.v4i1.95

Naplyokov, Y. V. (2018). Changing of mental models for effective decision-making. *Public Management, 1*(11), 209–228. doi:10.31618/vadnd.v1i11.28

Neff, K. D. (2003). The development and validation of a scale to measure self-compassion. *Self and Identity, 2*(3), 223–250. doi:10.1080/15298860309027

Nguyen, M. H. (2021). Factors influencing home-based telework in Hanoi (Vietnam) during and after the Covid-19 era. *Transportation, 48*(6), 1–32. doi:10.100711116-021-10169-5 PMID:33518829

Nolan-Arañez, S. I., & Ludvik, M. B. (2018). Positing a framework for cultivating spirituality through public university leadership development. *Journal of Research in Innovative Teaching & Learning, 11*(1), 94–109. doi:10.1108/JRIT-08-2017-0018

Oleś, P., & Jankowski, T. (2018). Positive orientation—A common base for hedonistic and eudemonistic happiness? *Applied Research in Quality of Life, 13*(1), 105–117. doi:10.100711482-017-9508-9 PMID:29492164

OziliP. K.ArunT. (2020). *Spillover of Covid-19: Impact on the global economy.* doi:10.2139/ssrn.3562570

Papageorge, N. W., Zahn, M. V., Belot, M., Van den Broek-Altenburg, E., Choi, S., Jamison, J. C., & Tripodi, E. (2021). Socio-demographic factors associated with self-protecting behavior during the Covid-19 pandemic. *Journal of Population Economics, 34*(2), 691–738. doi:10.100700148-020-00818-x PMID:33462529

Pourmola, M., Bagheri, M., Alinezhad, P., & Nejad, P. (2019). Investigating the impact of organizational spirituality on human resources productivity in manufacturing organizations. *Management Science Letters, 9*(1), 121–132. doi:10.5267/j.msl.2018.10.011

Rago, W. V. (1996). Struggles in transformation: A study in TQM, leadership, and organizational culture in a government agency. *Public Administration Review, 56*(3), 227–234. doi:10.2307/976445

Ramachandaran, S. D., Krauss, S. E., Hamzah, A., & Idris, K. (2017). Effectiveness of the use of spiritual intelligence in women's academic leadership practice. *International Journal of Educational Management, 31*(2), 160–178. doi:10.1108/IJEM-09-2015-0123

Restubog, S. L. D., Ocampo, A. C. G., & Wang, L. (2020). *Taking control amidst the chaos: Emotion regulation during the Covid-19 pandemic.*

Rocha, R. G., & Pinheiro, P. G. (2020, February 21). Organizational spirituality: Concept and perspectives. [Springer Nature Switzerland.]. *Journal of Business Ethics*, 1–12.

Schein, E. H. (1968). Organizational socialization and the profession of management. *Industrial Management Review*, *9*, 1–15.

Schein, E. H. (1978). *Career dynamics: Matching individual and organizational needs*. Addison-Wesley.

Schein, E. H. (1992). *Organizational culture and leadership* (2nd ed.). Jossey-Bass Publishers.

Schmidt, E., Groeneveld, S., & van de Walle, S. (2017). A change management perspective on public sector cutback management: Towards a framework for analysis. *Public Management Review*, *19*(10), 1538–1555. doi:10.1080/14719037.2017.1296488

Shanafelt, T. D., West, C. P., Sinsky, C., Trockel, M., Tutty, M., Satele, D. V., Lindsey, E., Carlasare, F., Lotte, N., & Dyrbye, L. N. (2019, September). Changes in burnout and satisfaction with work-life integration in physicians and the general US working population between 2011 and 2017. *Mayo Clinic Proceedings*, *94*(9), 1681–1694. doi:10.1016/j.mayocp.2018.10.023 PMID:30803733

Sinclair, R. R., Allen, T., Barber, L., Bergman, M., Britt, T., Butler, A., Ford, M., Hammer, L., Kath, L., Probst, T., & Yuan, Z. (2020). Occupational Health Science in the Time of Covid-19: Now more than ever. *Occupational Health Science*, *4*(1-2), 1–22. doi:10.100741542-020-00064-3 PMID:32838031

Smith, J. M., & Halligan, C. L. (2021). *Making meaning without a maker: Secular consciousness through narrative and cultural practice. Sociology of Religion, 82(1), 85-110*. Oxford University Press. doi:10.1093ocrelraa016

Sorensen, P. F., Yaeger, T. F., Savall, H., Zardet, V., Bonnet, M., & Peron, M. (2022). A review of two major global and international approaches to organizational change: SEAM and Appreciative Inquiry. *Organization Development Journal*, *40*(2), 21–27.

Sultana, U. S., Tarofder, A. K., Darun, M. R., Haque, A., & Sharief, S. R. (2020). Authentic leadership effect on pharmacists' job stress and satisfaction during Covid-19 Pandemic: Malaysian perspective. *Journal of Talent Development and Excellence, 12*(3s) 1824-1841, and ISSN: 1869-2885.

Thakur, K., & Singh, J. (2016). Spirituality at workplace: A conceptual framework. *International Journal of Applied Business and Economic Research*, *14*(7), 5181–5189.

Tidd, C. (2016). *Staff perceptions of the effect of the leader in me on student motivation and peer relationships in elementary school*. Walden University.

Tierney, T. J. (2006). Understanding the nonprofit sector's leadership deficit. *Leader to Leader*, *1*, 13S–19S.

Torch. (2023). *Research Report: Leveraging coaching and mentoring to create more effective leaders*. Harvard Business School Publishing.

Trougakos, J. P., Chawla, N., & McCarthy, J. M. (2020). Working in a pandemic: Exploring the impact of Covid-19 health anxiety on work, family, and health outcomes. *The Journal of Applied Psychology*, *105*(11), 1234–1245. doi:10.1037/apl0000739 PMID:32969707

Vázquez-de-Príncipe, J. (2021). *Investigating leadership and human-intelligences during public-sector organizational change: A mixed methods study* [Doctoral dissertation, University of Phoenix]. ProQuest Dissertations & Theses (PQDT) Global – ProQuest Publishing.

van der Voet, J. (2016). Change leadership and public-sector organizational change: Examining the interactions of transformational leadership style and red tape. *American Review of Public Administration*, *46*(6), 660–682. doi:10.1177/0275074015574769

van der Voet, J., & Vermeeren, B. (2017). Change management in hard times: Can change management mitigate the negative relationship between cutbacks and the organizational commitment and work engagement of public-sector employees? *American Review of Public Administration*, *47*(2), 230–252. doi:10.1177/0275074015625828

Vasconcelos, A. F. (2018). Workplace spirituality: Empirical evidence revisited. *Management Research Review*, *41*(7), 789–821. doi:10.1108/MRR-07-2017-0232

Vroman, S. R., & Danko, T. (2020, June 8). Against what model? Evaluating women as leaders in the pandemic era. *Gender, Work and Organization*, *27*(5), 860–867. doi:10.1111/gwao.12488

Walumbwa, F. O., & Lawler, J. J. (2003). Building effective organizations: Transformational leadership, collectivist orientation, work-related attitudes, and withdrawal behaviors in three emerging economies. *International Journal of Human Resource Management*, *14*(7), 1083–1101. doi:10.1080/0958519032000114219

Walumbwa, F. O., Lawler, J. J., Avolio, B. J., & Wang, P. (2003). *Relationship between transformational leadership and work-related attitudes: The moderating effects of collective and self-efficacy across cultures* (Working paper). University of Nebraska-Lincoln.

Ward, S. J., & King, L. A. (2018). Moral self-regulation, moral identity, and religiosity. *Journal of Personality and Social Psychology*, *115*(3), 495–525. doi:10.1037/pspp0000207 PMID:30024183

Weiss, P. G., & Li, S. T. T. (2020). Leading change to address the needs and well-being of trainees during the Covid-19 Pandemic. *Academic Pediatrics*, *20*(6), 735–741. doi:10.1016/j.acap.2020.06.001 PMID:32512054

Wigert, B., & Agrawal, S. (2022). *Returning to the office: The current, preferred and future state of remote work*. Gallup.

Wilson, J. Q. (1989). *Bureaucracy: What government agencies do and why they do it*. Basic Books.

Yukl, G. (1999). An evaluation of conceptual weaknesses in transformational and charismatic leadership theories. *The Leadership Quarterly*, *10*(2), 285–305. doi:10.1016/S1048-9843(99)00013-2

Zainun, N. F. H., Johari, J., & Adnan, Z. (2021). Machiavellianism, locus of control, moral identity, and ethical leadership among public service leaders in Malaysia: The moderating effect of ethical role modeling. *International Journal of Sociology & Social Policy*. Emerald Publishing Limited. doi:10.1108/IJSSP-07-2020-0289

Zhang, S., Sun, J., & Gao, X. (2020). The effect of fatigue on brain connectivity networks. *Brain Science Advances*, *6*(2), 120–131. doi:10.26599/BSA.2020.9050008

Zohar, D., & Marshall, I. N. (2004). *Spiritual capital: Wealth we can live by*. Berrett-Koehle Publishers, Inc.

ADDITIONAL READINGS

de Smet, A., & Vogel, T. (2021, January 21). *McKinsey Live: Reenergizing the workforce: How leaders can overcome pandemic fatigue*. COVID Response Center. McKinsey & Company.

Errida, A., & Lotfi, B. (2020). Measuring change readiness for implementing a project management methodology: An action research study. *Academy of Strategic Management Journal, 19*(1), 1–17.

Gallup. (2023). *Global indicator: Hybrid work*. Gallup. https://www.gallup.com/401384/indicator-hybrid-work.aspx

Kodama, M. (2019). Business innovation through holistic leadership-developing organizational adaptability. *Systems Research and Behavioral Science, 36*(4), 365–394. doi:10.1002res.2551

Torch. (2023). *Research Report: Leveraging coaching and mentoring to create more effective leaders*. Harvard Business School Publishing.

KEY TERMS AND DEFINITIONS

Deeply Formed Work/Life Dimensionality Iceberg: The integrative model reflecting the organizational, educational, interpersonal, spiritual, and cultural multi-dimensional synergistic dynamics informed by the principles of HLQ depicting the deepest level (#1) as realizing accomplishment needs focused on 'Me' and "Others,' preparing business in 4th Industrial Revolution leadership readiness, cultivating a holistic positive climate as culture catalyzers through courageous service, and shaping possibilities of an enlightened flourishing work/life.

Holistic Catalyzing Culture Leadership: The leader's ability to withstand, adapt, and thrive in the face of unprecedented shocks waves, by leveraging both external and internal perspectives to assess the organization's financial/operational strengths, weaknesses, threats/risks, to enable rebalancing opportunities that facilitate strategic resilience, while fostering holistic positive cultures within human-centric workplaces.

Holistic Leadership Intelligence (HLQ): The dexterous consummate superconscious leadership mindset integrating spiritual, authentic, and transformational leadership styles for leading as culture catalyzers by servicing, guiding, engaging, and equipping others with social behavioral dynamics exhibited by those who can deeply connect by harnessing the spirit/light, heart/energy, mind/brain, and body/hands.

Organizational Health Factors: The hallmark identifier of healthy organizations is the flourishing cultural climate exhibited by outcomes such as high employee morale, consistent performance energy-momentum, unlimited trustworthiness, pleasant relational work-life dynamics, and adequate knowledge transfer producing conditions for positive financial implications to bottom-line derived from superior culture and energetic human performance levels.

Spirituality at Work: The workplace norm acceptance of one's spiritual-being as being a critical component of the whole person, which requires nurturing of the soul, recognizing values-systems, embracing dexterities, encouraging dialogues, and affirming these forces to foster ultimate intrinsic motivation for passionately driving high-performance at professional and organizational levels.

Spiritually Intelligent Leaders: The leader's ultimate intellectual ability to lead oneself while influence others from a holistic place of spiritual well-being, towards fostering a sense of purpose, meaning, and connectedness within work-life dynamics through integrative experiences for building existential engagements that are transformative.

Work-Life Predictive Hierarchical Model: The regression model outcomes of investigation with sub-variables having positive and negative relationships associated with primary scales of social skills, grit, and authentic leadership.

Chapter 8
Measuring the Effectiveness of Organizational Development Strategies During Unprecedented Times

Babita Srivastava
William Paterson University, USA

ABSTRACT

The breakout of the Covid-19 toward the end of 2019 sent shockwaves across the world. To prevent the spread of the disease and save lives, many countries have resorted to observing country-wide lockdowns, damaging the normalcy of their economy. As a result, the world economy lost trillions of dollars during this period. The renewable energy sector, too, was not spared from being affected by the pandemic. An amalgamation of the effects of the pandemic on the global economy and fluctuating oil prices resulting from country-wide lockdowns across the world further triggered its impact on the renewable energy industry. This chapter highlights the challenges that the energy sector has experienced due to the pandemic in terms of raw material availability, supply chain, market uncertainty, employment, and energy security.

INTRODUCTION

As years go by, there is an expectation that technology will continue to innovate, that the climate will improve and that lives across the globe will get better. There are times where there are major setbacks, such as in the year 2020 with the arrival of a global pandemic, Covid-19. At the end of 2019, China was the first area hit with this virus (Eroğlu, 2020). Many were unaware of the severity of it or how quickly it would spread. It quickly turned into a truly global pandemic where it is highly contagious and can be contracted by anyone. The coronavirus disease 2019 (Covid-19) outbreak was declared a public health emergency of international concern by the World Health Organization (WHO) on 30 January 2020 when all 34 regions of China had cases of infection, and the total case count surpassed that for the severe acute respiratory syndrome (SARS) of 2003 (BBC News, 2020).

DOI: 10.4018/978-1-6684-8392-3.ch008

Although there is no concrete evidence but it is believed to have originated from a seafood wholesale market in the city of Wuhan of Hubei Province in late December 2019; the number of cases increased exponentially within and beyond Wuhan, spreading widely across the world (Birol, 2020; Eroğlu, 2020). None of the nations were prepared for this unfortunate event. There is now a major health crisis in which only so much can be done for it to be mitigated. Everywhere one can look there are faces with masks on and people maintaining a six-feet distance from most, which is a requirement in most institutions. Covid-19 brought with it many deaths and many health issues. This has also greatly impacted the economies across the world, regardless of their status of being a developed or underdeveloped nation. The Covid-19 pandemic is a major problem that needs to be addressed and considered in every aspect.

Many would prefer to forget 2020 from their lives but it is a year that everyone around the world will never forget the impact that this virus has had on the world.

Mentally, emotionally, physically, and financially this pandemic has affected everyone throughout the world; it is a virus that does not discriminate on race, ethnicity nor the amount of money anyone has. The U.S economy has taken a massive hit when it comes to the Coronavirus. The Coronavirus has caused an even greater shock to the U.S economy by far the worst since the 2008 financial crisis. The U.S is currently leading both in the number of infections and deaths (Worldometer, 2020). As of the end of December 2020, there have been over 82 million coronavirus cases, 1.8 million deaths throughout the world that has been reported related to the Coronavirus, and approximately 59 million people have recovered from the virus (Worldometer, 2020). In the U.S. alone, the total number of infections is expected to exceed over 20 million and the death toll over 350 thousand (Worldometer, 2020).

Covid-19 has adversely impacted sustainable economic development and has severely affected the global economy and financial markets. There have been significant reductions in income, a rise in unemployment, and disruptions in the transportation, service, and manufacturing industries are among the consequences of the disease. Now different countries are taking mitigation measures to minimize the impact of this pandemic, but one thing become clear that none of the governments and global healthcare systems were prepared to deal with such a tragic event. The entire world underestimated the risks of rapid Covid-19 spread and were mostly reactive in their crisis response. As disease outbreaks are not likely to disappear soon, proactive international actions are required to not only save lives but also protect economic prosperity. Significant economic impact has already occurred across the globe due to reduced productivity, loss of life, business closures, trade disruption, and decimation of the tourism industry. Covid-19 may be that "wake-up" call for global leaders to intensify cooperation on epidemic preparedness and provide the necessary financing for international collective action. There has been ample information on the expected economic and health costs of infectious disease outbreaks, but the world has failed to adequately invest in preventive and preparedness measures to mitigate the risks of large epidemic.

Covid-19 has hit this world with devastating impact and developing countries were hit particularly hard. Before Covid-19, the UN has called for coordinated action from the world's leading economies toward 17 Sustainable Development Goals (SDGs) and maximum financial and technical support for the poorest and most vulnerable people and countries (Barbier & Burgess, 2020). As Figure 1 indicates, the pandemic is likely to adversely impact 12 of the 17 SDG goals. This will occur at a critical juncture for some of the sustainable economic goals when 736 million people still live-in extreme poverty, 821 million are undernourished, 785 million people lack even basic drinking water services, and 673 million still practice open defecation. About 3 billion people lack clean cooking fuels and technology, and of the 840 million people without electricity, 87% live in rural areas (Barbier & Burgess, 2020).

Figure 1. The impact of Covid-19 on the UN sustainable development goals
Adopted from reference (Barbier & Burgess, 2020)

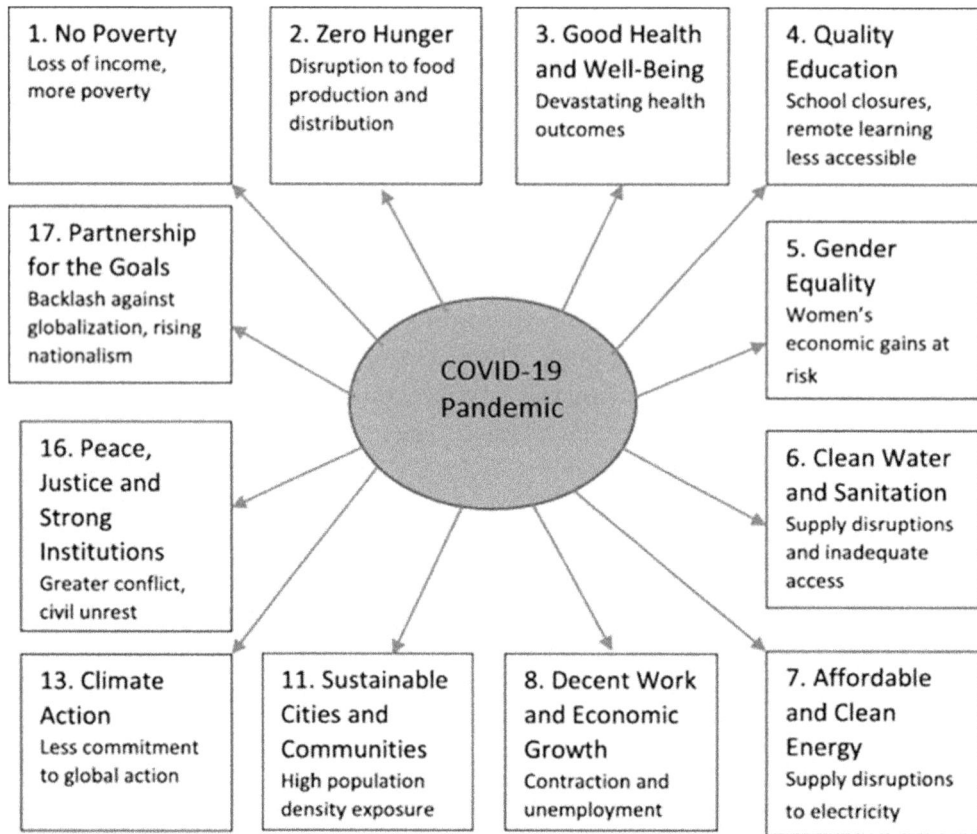

Another major impact was the fact that Covid-19 had hit China first, a major player in the economic sphere. In a strongly connected and integrated world, the impacts of the disease go beyond those who have died and those who may be unable to work due being high-risk and it has become apparent since the outbreak. Since the Chinese economy has slowed down with interruptions to production, "the functioning of global supply chains has been disrupted. Companies across the world, irrespective of size and geographical location, that are dependent upon inputs from China have started experiencing contractions in production. Transport being limited and even restricted among countries has further slowed global economic activities. Most importantly, some panic among consumers, organizations and firms has distorted usual consumption patterns and created market anomalies. Global financial markets have also been responsive to the changes and global stock indices have plunged" (Barbier & Burgess, 2020).

Globally, economies are connected by cross-border flows of goods, services, knowledge, people, financial capital, foreign investment, international banking, and exchange rates. They are also connected by beliefs and "all these things are also mechanisms for the propagation of economic shocks, or economic contagion. The transportation restrictions have also slowed economic activity and production. There is also the impact to the organizations, firms and financial markets. The rise in risk might reveal that one or more key financial market players have taken investment positions that are unprofitable under current conditions, further weakening trust in financial instruments and markets.

Different countries and territories are expected to experience divergent recovery paths, with the shape of that path for each location influenced by the interplay between their experience in containing and managing the spread of Covid-19 and the underlying socio-economic characteristics of each country or territory, as is evident in the disparity of cases per capita in several countries, regardless of their economic standing. The analysis reveals trade exposed countries may take proportionally longer to recover in the scenario where the Covid-19 pandemic becomes drawn out compared to less trade exposed states (McKibbin & Fernando, 2020). Simply, the longer the pandemic continues, the more damaging it becomes to world trade. Recent progress on coronavirus vaccines has brightened the economic outlook, but some economists believe that a potentially slow rollout of vaccines across developing economies could hamper the return of activity to pre-pandemic levels. Even among advanced economies, renewed lockdowns in Europe in a bid to stave off a resurgence in infections could push back economic recovery (World Economy, 2020).

BACKGROUND: EFFECT OF COVID-19 ON THE GLOBAL ECONOMY

The world has never seen such drastic economic impacts since the great depression and the financial crisis of 2008. The Covid-19 virus has wiped out over 4-5 years of economic growth (Bachman, 2020). It has also created future uncertainty and panic. Covid-19 has significantly impacted the economic growth of G-20 growth. Instead of positive growth as projected before Covid-19, it was revised to 4.2% contraction after the Covid-19 pandemic as indicated in Table 1 (The Economist, 2020).

Table 1. Pre and post Covid-19 GDP growth forecast for G-20 nations

Country	Post Covid-19 projection (%)	Pre Covid-19 projection (%)
Argentina	-9	-2
Australia	-4.2	2
Brazil	-5.5	2.4
Canada	-4.3	1.8
China	1	5.9
France	-8.8	1
Germany	-6.1	0.9
India (2020/21 fiscal year)	-4	6
Indonesia	1	5.1
Italy	-10.8	0.4
Japan	-5.2	0.4
South Korea	-2.1	2.2
Mexico	-9	1.1
Russia	-5.2	1.6
Saudi Arabia	-3.2	1
South Africa	-5.6	1.4
Turkey	-5.4	3.8
UK	-8.7	1.1
US	-4	1.7
Global (market exchange rates)	-4.2	2.3

In its June World Economic Outlook update, the International Monetary Fund (IMF) projected that global GDP would decline 4.9 percent in 2020, the largest drop on record (Boatwright & Wynne, 2020). In the United Kingdom, gross domestic product (GDP) declined at a 59.8 percent annual rate in the second quarter—the largest drop of any advanced economy this year. In USA it was about 32 percent. In India, GDP slid at a 69.4 percent annual rate-the greatest drop among emerging-market economies (Boatwright & Wynne, 2020). Although countries still have a long way to go and there is still a lot of suffering around the world, but it is possible that the world is at a point now where one can clearly see the end of this crisis and the foundations of a sustainable recovery (Capital Group, 2020). Projected 2021 GDP growth by International Monitory Fund is expected to go and it shows in Figure 2.

Figure 2. Projected GDP for 2020 and 2021
(Capital Group, 2020)

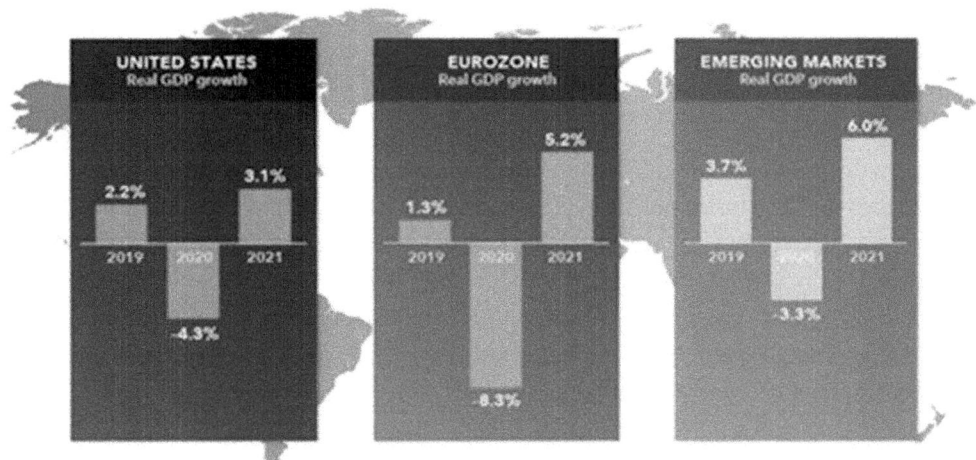

Global industrial production has already been substantially affected by the shutdown in the US and other parts of the world (Yardeni et al., 2020). The most impacted industries are those that depend on workers whose jobs cannot be carried out remotely. The majority of US manufacturers expect that the pandemic will have a financial impact on their business (Capital Group, 2020). Some major industrial companies have closed facilities and are mulling the extent of layoffs to help curb the spread of the virus, as well as for economic reasons.

Clearly, the manufacturing sector, which employs some 13 million workers in the US, is poised to be hit hard during this outbreak, primarily for two reasons: first, many manufacturing jobs are on-site and cannot be carried out remotely. Second, slowed economic activity has reduced demand for industrial products in the US and globally (Capital Group, 2020). Not to mention, with the need to be on-site, the risk of exposure increases and for any exposed, they will need to quarantine up to 14 days, which also slows production significantly for companies already suffering from lags. Some analysts predict that roughly 15% of all U.S. jobs, which represents over 20 million U.S. workers could permanently work remotely (Fottrell, 2020).

Many manufacturing firms rely on imported intermediate inputs from China and other countries affected by the disease. Many companies also rely on sales in other countries to meet their financial goals. The slowdown in economic activity - and transportation restrictions - in affected countries had impacted the production and profitability of specific global companies, particularly in manufacturing and in raw materials used in manufacturing. For companies that rely on intermediate goods from affected regions, and that are not able to easily switch sourcing, the size of the impact may depend on how quickly the outbreak fades. Small and medium-sized firms may have greater difficulty surviving the disruption. Businesses tied to travel and tourism are facing losses that are likely not recoverable.

Temporary disruptions of inputs and/or production might stress some firms, particularly those with inadequate liquidity. Traders in financial markets may or may not correctly anticipate or understand which firms might be vulnerable. The resulting rise in risk might reveal that one or more key financial market players have taken investment positions that are unprofitable under current conditions, further weakening trust in financial instruments and markets. A possible (likely low probability) event would be a significant financial market disruption as participants become concerned about counterparty risk. A somewhat more likely possibility is a significant decline in equity markets and corporate bond markets, with investors preferring to hold government securities (particularly US treasuries) because of the uncertainty created by the pandemic.

Energy is a vital infrastructure of economic development. It is a well-established fact that energy and economic growth go hand in hand. In fact, some economists regard energy as a fourth factor of production in addition to the land labor and capital. Energy inputs such as electric power and coal are required to support a growing industrial sector. The ready availability of cheap energy serves to stimulate industrial development energy thus can be called as fuel of economic growth. Conversely, progress in energy intensive industrial development will lead to increased energy production and consumption per capita. Increasing living standards leads to increasing energy consumption because of the comfort need that must be satisfied by energy intensive devices such as automobiles, air conditioners and other electrical appliances indicates energy supplies could inhibit economic growth. It could affect a wide range of activities in the agriculture and industrial sector.

Until the mid-1800s, wood was the source of nearly all the nation's energy needs for heating, cooking, and lighting (U.S. Energy Information Administration [EIA], 2019). From the late 1800's until today, fossil fuels - coal, petroleum, and natural gas - have been the major sources of energy. Hydropower and wood were the most used renewable energy resources.

Renewable energy is often thought of as a new technology, harnessing nature's power has long been used for heating, transportation, lighting, and more. Wind has powered boats to sail the seas and windmills to grind grain. The sun has provided warmth during the day and helped kindle fires to last into the evening. But over the past 500 years or so, humans increasingly turned to cheaper, dirtier energy sources such as coal and fracked gas. Renewable power is booming, as innovation brings down costs and starts to deliver on the promise of a clean energy future. American solar and wind generation are breaking records and being integrated into the national electricity grid without compromising reliability.

Now that we have increasingly innovative and less-expensive ways to capture and retain wind and solar energy, renewables are becoming a more important power source, accounting for more than one-eighth of U.S. generation. The expansion in renewables is also happening at scales large and small, from rooftop solar panels on homes that can sell power back to the grid to giant offshore wind farms. Even some entire rural communities rely on renewable energy for heating and lighting.

Renewable energy is a cost-effective source of new power that insulates power markets and consumers from volatility, supports economic stability and stimulates sustainable growth. With renewable additions providing most of the new capacity last year, many countries and regions recognize the degree to which the energy transition can deliver positive outcomes.

While the trajectory is positive, more is required to put global energy on a path with sustainable development and climate mitigation – both of which offer significant economic benefits. At this challenging time, we are reminded of the importance of building resilience into our economies. In what must be the decade of action, enabling policies are needed to increase investments and accelerate renewables adoption.

The renewable energy sector added 176 gigawatts (GW) of generating capacity globally in 2019, marginally lower than the 179 GW added in 2018. However, new renewable power accounted for 72 percent of all power expansion last year, according to new data released by the International Renewable Energy Agency (IRENA). IRENA's annual Renewable Capacity Statistics 2020 shows that renewables expanded by 7.6 percent last year with Asia dominating growth and accounting for 54 percent of total additions

(International Renewable Energy Agency (IRENA), 2020). While expansion of renewables slowed last year, total renewable power growth outpaced fossil fuel growth by a factor of 2.6, continuing the dominance of renewables in power expansion first established in 2012. Solar and wind contributed 90 percent of total renewable capacity added in 2019 (International Renewable Energy Agency [IRENA], 2020).

Renewables accounted for at least 70 percent of total capacity expansion in almost all regions in 2019, other than in Africa and the Middle East, where they represented 52 percent and 26 percent of net additions, respectively. The additions took the renewable share of all global power capacity to 34.7 percent, up from 33.3 percent at the end of 2018. Non-renewable capacity expansion globally followed long-term trends in 2019, with net growth in Asia, the Middle East and Africa, and net decommissioning in Europe and North America.

Solar added 98 GW in 2019, 60 percent of which was in Asia. Wind energy expanded by close to 60 GW led by growth in China (26 GW) and the United States (9 GW). The two technologies now generate 623 GW and 586 GW respectively - close to half of global renewable capacity. Hydropower, bioenergy, geothermal and marine energy displayed modest year on year expansion of 12 GW, 6 GW, 700 MW and 500 MW, respectively.

Asia was responsible for over half of the new installations despite expanding at a slightly slower pace than in 2018. Growth in Europe and North America increased year over year. Africa added 2 GW of renewable capacity in 2019, half of the 4 GW it installed in 2018 (International Renewable Energy Agency (IRENA), 2020). The global installed renewable energy trend is shown in Figure 3.

Figure 3. Global installed renewable energy trend
Adopted from reference (International Renewable Energy Agency (IRENA), 2020)

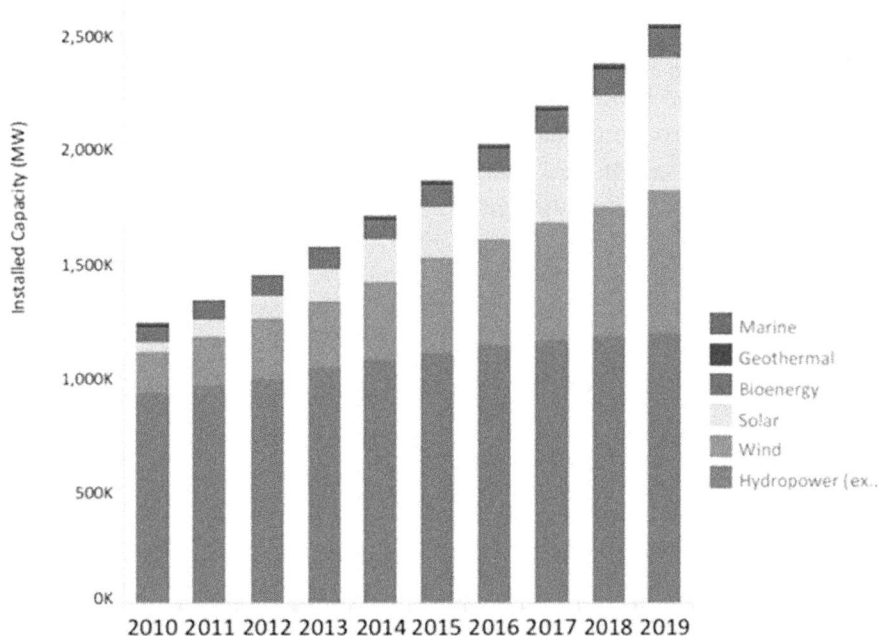

Highlights by technology:

- Hydropower: Growth was unusually low in 2019, possibly because some large projects missed their expected completion dates. China and Brazil accounted for most of the expansion, each adding more than 4 GW.

- Wind energy: Wind performed particularly well in 2019, expanding by nearly 60 GW. China and the United States continued to dominate with increases of 26 GW and 9 GW respectively.

- Solar energy: Asia continued to dominate global solar capacity expansion with a 56 GW increase, but this was lower than in 2018. Other major increases were in the United States, Australia, Spain, Ukraine and Germany.

- Bioenergy: Expansion of bioenergy capacity remained modest in 2019. China accounted for half of all new capacity (+3.3 GW). Germany, Italy, Japan and Turkey also saw expansion.

- Geothermal energy: Geothermal power capacity grew by 682 MW in 2019, slightly more than in 2018. Again, Turkey led with an expansion of 232 MW, followed by Indonesia (+185 MW) and Kenya (+160 MW).

- Off-grid electricity: Off-grid capacity grew by 160 MW (+2%) to reach 8.6 GW in 2019. In 2019, off-grid solar PV increased by 112 MW and hydropower grew by 31 MW, compared to growth of only 17 MW for bioenergy.

The amounts and the percentage shares of total U.S. energy consumption from biofuels, geothermal energy, solar energy, and wind energy increased, and in 2019, the combined percentage share of these renewable energy sources was greater than the combined share of wood and hydro energy. US energy consumption by energy source in 2019 is shown in Figure 4.

The consumption of biofuels, geothermal, solar, and wind energy in the United States in 2019 was nearly three times greater than in 2000 (U.S. Energy Information Administration [EIA], 2019). In 2019, renewable energy provided about 11.5 quadrillion British thermal units (Btu)-1 quadrillion is the number 1 followed by 15 zeros-equal to 11.4% of total U.S. energy consumption. The electric power sector accounted for about 56% of total U.S. renewable energy consumption in 2019, and about 17% of total U.S. electricity generation was from renewable energy sources (U.S. Energy Information Administration [EIA], 2019). In Figure 5, the share of total energy consumption in US since 1776 clearly elucidate the increase in the renewable energy contribution in the total energy consumption in last 10 years.

Figure 4. US energy consumption by energy source
Adopted from reference (U.S. Energy Information Administration [EIA], 2019)

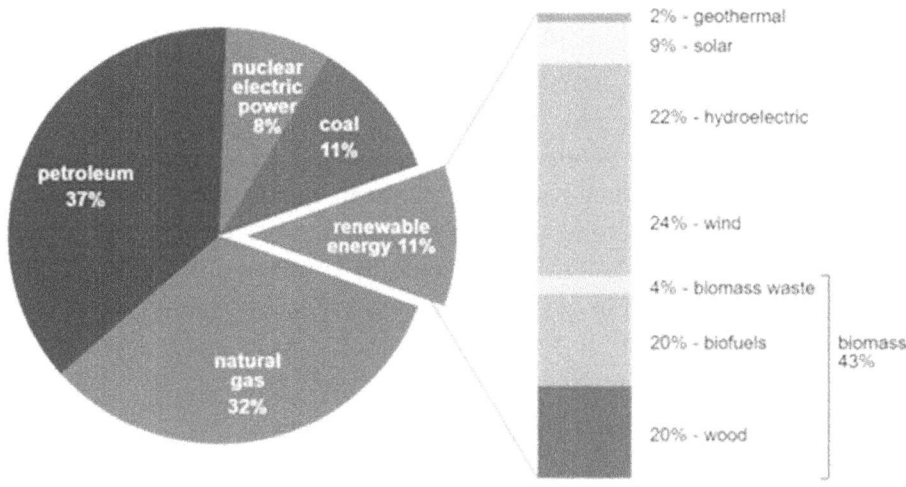

Figure 5. The change in energy consumption pattern in US
Adopted from reference (U.S. Energy Information Administration [EIA], 2019)

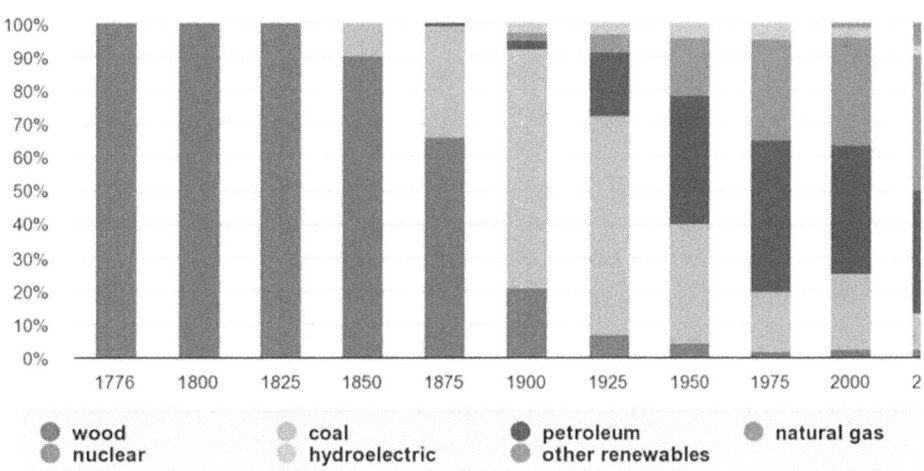

MAIN FOCUS OF THE CHAPTER

The Covid-19 pandemic is one of the most severe economic and energy shocks in modern history. On top of the massive disruptions to business, mobility, and everyday life, there clearly will be longer-lasting implications for the energy transition away from fossil fuels. Covid-19 has brought the generation of energy from fossil fuels to a breaking point. As the lockdown measures were introduced, global energy demand dropped precipitously at levels not seen in 70 years (Majorro, 2020). The IEA has estimated that overall energy demand contracted by 6% and energy-related emissions will decrease by 8% for 2020 (IEA, 2020).

S&P Global Platts Analytics expects global oil demand to decline by 8.7 million barrels per day (down 8.4%) from the pre Covid-19 forecast, wiping out six years of growth. Reductions to industry and power generation, particularly in developing nations, are likely to reduce coal demand by the equivalent of 4.4 million barrels per day of oil (down 5.7%). Natural gas demand, due to its prevalence as a heating fuel, took less of a hit during lockdowns, declining by only 2.1 million barrels per day (down 3.0%) of oil equivalent from the pre Covid-19 forecast. Delays in renewables installations in key markets are likely to reduce renewable energy production by less than 1.0 million barrels per day of oil equivalent (down 3.6%) in 2020 (Kramarchuk et al., 2020).

Global renewable electricity installation is expected to hit a record level in 2020, according to the International Energy Agency (IEA), in sharp contrast with the declines caused by the coronavirus pandemic in the fossil fuel sectors (Ambrose, 2020). According to IEA report almost 90 percent of new electricity generation in 2020 will be renewable, with just 10 percent powered by gas and coal. The trend puts green electricity on track to become the largest power source in 2025, displacing coal, which has dominated for the past 50 years (Ambrose, 2020).

The disruptions from Covid-19 have exposed vulnerabilities in the energy system. The short-term outlook for the energy transition is therefore at risk. The unprecedented speed and extent of the drop in energy demand, and the accompanying price volatilities and geopolitical implications have destabilized the global energy system.

The economic dimensions of energy transition mean that extreme price volatility has fiscal implications for countries and impacts the livelihoods of millions of energy sector workers. It also alters the competitiveness of renewable energy technologies and reduces incentives for energy efficiency. Resilience - not just in markets and infrastructure, but also in policy and cooperation mechanisms – will be critical for an accelerated recovery in energy transition.

There are signs of revival, as energy demand seems to be gradually picking up. However, it might be longer before the economy reclaims the lost ground. Given the uncertain economic outlook, purchase of automobiles and domestic appliances might be postponed, infrastructure development could be paused, and non-essential industrial activities might take longer to restart.

Along with a sustainable and thriving ecosystem for future generations, an effective energy transition is also essential for economic growth and social development. In an increasingly turbulent global paradigm, disruptions are the new normal, and energy transition roadmaps need to integrate robustness against these disruptions. Resilience of energy transition, in the long-term, implies a strong enabling environment that sees the system bouncing back from unforeseen or exogenous disruptions. This includes the presence of strong political commitment, stable capital markets and access to investment, a steady pipeline of innovations, modernization of infrastructure, training human capital for future energy systems, etc.

The World Economic Forum's Energy Transition Index (ETI) benchmarks countries on these fundamentals for energy transition, along with the performance of their energy system on economic growth, environmental sustainability, and energy access and security. From the recently completed analysis for this year's index, the evidence of gradual progress on energy transition is strong.

Only a handful of countries have been able to make steady annual progress on the ETI over the past six years, which demonstrates the complexity and challenges of energy transition. Improving levels of regulations and political commitment, capital and investment, and technology development have been critical to unlocking this progress globally.

When we finally manage to put the global tragedy of Covid-19 behind us, there may be some valuable lessons learned. The energy transition challenge is like the pandemic in terms of scale, cascading effects across social and economic systems, more severe for vulnerable populations, and the necessity of a decisive, timely and concerted response. Stakeholders need to be conscious that the fight against Covid-19 does not set us back in solving the critical socio-economic puzzle of global energy transition, otherwise the losses resulting from the virus will take an even greater toll on humanity.

Countries like the U.S. and Australia source a lot of renewable components and raw materials from China. Even though the United States started to procure panels from other countries across Asia, such as South Korea and Vietnam in 2012 due to tariffs, the process has been slow moving. And, according to Global Data Energy, even solar manufacturing plants located outside of China are dependent on Chinese imports for raw materials such as aluminum framing and solar PV glass (McElroy, 2020). As China slowly brings back production and manufacturing in a limited capacity, prices for renewable materials and components are expected to increase before ultimately declining again.

To better handle any bottlenecks or slowdowns in the supply chain, developers, EPCs, and subcontractors are requesting long lead time orders or asking to delay current projects if they have not been already. Not knowing if they will be on-site to take receipt for delivered material or even to install material is contributing to delayed project schedules and shipments.

One benefit of the disrupted supply chain is that it forces the renewable industry's hand at seeking a more diversified supply chain. Alternative energy sources could bring future stabilization to such critical renewable energy technologies, meaning more independence and more competitive prices.

Material deliveries. Install delays. Labor shortages. Covid-19 affects every aspect of renewable energy from the supply chain down to the installers. However, corporate demand coming out of the quarantine will provide more immediate certainty about where the renewable market is headed.

It is not a surprise that investors in the renewable market are holding cash on hand to weather this current crisis. Given all the global uncertainty, this is causing a downstream cash flow issue for subcontractors who rely on these investments to support their business. Despite the uncertainty at this time, there are no other long-term solutions on the market that can generate new energy as cheap and as clean as renewable energy. If capital can be secured for future projects and the interest rates remain at these incredible lows to promote price-locking, it's not a matter of *if* renewable energy construction will rebound but of *when*. It may be faster than most expect (McElroy, 2020).

Renewable Energy Buyers Alliance (REBA) announced in February 2020 that 9.33 GW of renewable energy deals has already been signed by large energy buyers. With tech companies such as Facebook, Google, AT&T, and Microsoft coming at the top of the list, their interest in achieving a zero-carbon energy future will be best served by bringing these projects to completion quickly.

All energy sources have some impact on our environment. Fossil fuels, such as coal, oil, and natural gas, do substantially more harm than renewable energy sources by most measures, including air and water pollution, damage to public health, wildlife and habitat loss, water use, land use, and global warming emissions (Omer, 2008).

The coronavirus, rather than geopolitics, has weakened the main oil producers' control of markets and driven the natural gas prices down into the $2 range; as a result, the remaining coal-based power plants in Europe are going to switch to gas soon (Wire, 2020). The fossil fuel price reduction is particularly worrisome in developing countries where the low-cost electrical power supply seems imperative due to their poor economic situation at the time of Covid-19. The high sensitivity of these nations to the energy cost will compel their governments to adopt cheaper conventional energy sources instead of renewable energy, which would be terrible for global climate policy. This unpleasant situation could be prevented if the banks would promote ultra-low interest rates to address the economic stagnation that threatens the implementation of high capital cost, renewable energy projects that would prevent the energy market from shifting further towards the fossil fuel-based power generation.

Before this strange condition, the transition to renewable and sustainable energy was underway in many countries. The renewable energy has become significantly affordable due to substantial innovations, impressive policy frameworks, and technologies cost downturn. The solar and wind power have become cheaper in the recent years, and it was anticipated that, before long, the renewables would outpace fossil fuels (Hosseini & Wahid, 2016). In a $60-per-barrel oil price period, the fossil fuel players had commenced to invest in carbon mitigation strategies; however, due to the challenges of the Covid-19 and the oil price reduction, their investments in renewables has slowed down. For instance, Calgary-based oil sands giant Suncor Energy Inc. announced cutting its 2020 capital budget by $1.5 billion (or 26%) and held off two cogeneration units that would have mitigated GHG emissions and a wind power plant located at the northern and southern Alberta respectively. Nevertheless, the evidences illustrate that both solar and wind energy continued to grow through the last oil price mitigation because most investment in renewables comes from outside the fossil fuel sectors (Healing, 2020).

U.S. employment in the renewable energy sector increased in 2019 and was expected to continue growing in 2020. Before Covid-19, nearly 3.4 million Americans across all 50 states and the District of Columbia worked in clean energy occupations, including renewable energy, energy efficiency, grid modernization, clean vehicles, and fuels. That's more people than those who work in real estate, banking or agriculture in the U.S., and three times the number of Americans that worked in fossil fuels, according to E2's Clean Jobs America report (Karlin, 2020). Pre-Covid, the clean energy sector was booming. In 2019, 524,785 total renewable energy jobs made up more than half of total jobs in the Electric Power Generation sector, and more than twice the Electric Power Generation-related jobs in the oil, natural gas, and coal sectors combined. In addition, energy storage sector jobs reached 84,301 in 2019, with battery storage and pumped hydropower technologies together creating 74,452 jobs (Ahmed, 2020).

However, the global Covid-19 pandemic has stopped clean energy job growth in its tracks. Supply chain disruptions, social distancing measures, project delays and cancellations, and other pandemic-related factors are significantly impacting the renewable energy workforce (Karlin, 2020). Strikingly, March 2020 unemployment claims effectively wiped out all renewable sector job growth from 2019, which is a trend that is expected to worsen as the months progress (Karlin, 2020). According to the December 2020 federal unemployment report, 446,000 clean energy workers remained out of work since February 2020, which is a 13 percent decline over pre-Covid-19 employment levels (Busienss leaders, 2020).

While the nation's overall jobs recovery has stalled over the last several months, the clean energy sector has been particularly slow to rebound (S&P Global Market Intelligence, 2020). As the U.S. ramps up its preventive measures, most construction starts have been paused indefinitely. Among them, many renewable energy developments. Although 2020 was thought to be a booming year for renewable energy, the recent outbreak is infecting the energy industry with uncertain skepticism (McElroy, 2020). The unemployment situation in the renewable energy sector may be temporary. Although renewables are seeing a lot of delays right now, there is still contracted work to be completed. As soon as it is reasonably possible, the industry will hopefully pick back up right where it left off and keep moving forward. Many companies are mindful of tax credits that are set to reduce at year-end. No one can say for certain if the ITC will get an extension at the higher rate through year-end, so, when work can resume normally, there will probably be a big push to get these projects completed (McElroy, 2020).

SOLUTIONS AND RECOMMENDATIONS

The global renewable and sustainable energy scenario, which has flourished in the recent decades and enjoyed rapid growth, has encountered a serious challenge because of the coronavirus. The Covid-19 pandemic has struck the renewable energy manufacturing facilities, supply chains, and companies and slowed down the transition to the renewables. Even the well-established renewable energy policies are under question, particularly those that burden industries that are badly influenced by the crisis. Many countries' budgets will certainly be squeezed, and the implementation of new renewable energy projects will almost certainly be deferred. The development projects of manufacturers that make/install equipment for renewable energy technologies will be shelved amidst the adoption of austerity measures. As an example, the American-based Morgan Stanley company plans to decrease the installation of the US solar photovoltaics (PVs) in the second, third, and fourth quarters of 2020 by 48%, 28%, and 17% respectively (Sarad, Alexander & Donovan, 2020). The disruptions of the supply chain will interrupt accomplishment of the under-construction renewable energy projects worldwide, particularly solar power plants, as considerable parts of the solar panels, connectors, modules, and cells are manufactured in China and East Asia (Fox-Penner, 2020).

Despite challenges, growing acceptance of the need to tackle the climate crisis by cutting carbon emissions has made renewable energy increasingly attractive to investors. The IEA reports that shares in renewable equipment makers and project developers have outperformed most major stock market indices and that the value of shares in solar companies has more than doubled since December 2019 (Yale Environment 360, 2020). The United States is one of the world's biggest markets for renewables and the IEA suggests deployment could accelerate even faster if the policies of the president-elect, Joe Biden, are implemented.

Covid-19 has drawn increased attention to climate policy in Europe and has played a role in the U.S. elections. Most likely the global growth outlook for renewables generally remains intact, even if stimulus plans prioritize employment and direct support measures to the economy over green growth, especially in China and emerging markets. Key risks for the sector are reductions in direct subsidies and tax credits as observed in China, Europe, and the U.S and a cloudier outlook for long-term prices. On the other hand, continued strong investor appetite and declining costs are allowing renewables to compete increasingly at grid-parity prices, but with lower returns and rising market risks. As a result, larger renewables players, with strong balance sheets and vertical integration to mitigate merchant risks, may be better positioned and could move to consolidate the industry (Kramarchuk et al., 2020). The resilience and positive prospects of the sector are clearly reflected by continued strong appetite from investors (Yale Environment 360, 2020).

In 2025, renewables are set to become the largest source of electricity generation worldwide, ending coal's five decades as the top power provider. By that time, renewables are expected to supply one-third of the world's electricity (Yale Environment 360, 2020). Solar power capacity has increased by 18 times since 2010 and wind power by four times, according to IEA data (Earth.org, 2020). It is believed that solar power will be the new king of the future world's electricity markets. Hydropower provided 77 percent of green power in 2010, but that has fallen to 45 percent in 2020. However, electricity is only about one-fifth of all energy use, with the burning of fuels in transport, industry and heating making up the bulk of energy emissions (Yale Environment 360, 2020). The IEA forecasts that new renewable capacity around the world will increase by a record 200 gigawatts in 2020, driven by China and the U.S. where developers are rushing to take advantage of expiring incentive schemes (Yale Environment 360, 2020).

There is even stronger growth to come in 2021, the IEA said, when India and the European Union will be the driving forces (Yale Environment 360, 2020). But growth could decline slightly in 2022 under current policies, the IEA warned. Renewables are resilient to the Covid-19 crisis but not to policy uncertainties. Governments can tackle these issues to help bring about a sustainable recovery and accelerate clean energy transitions. In the U.S., for instance, if the proposed clean electricity policies of the next U.S. administration are implemented, they could lead to a much more rapid deployment of solar PV and wind.

Renewable energy sources, like wind and solar, are steadily growing and outpacing expectations (Team LightBox, 2020). Proving to be affordable and reliable sources of energy, they were poised for huge growth in 2020. However, the effects of Covid-19 have provided new challenges and impacted renewable energy industry forecasts. Like most industries, disruptions of supply chains and delays in construction projects due to lockdowns and social distancing are some of the major reasons that growth slowed down.

Even with these delays, renewable energy consumption still grew 40% so far in 2020 compared to 2019, and experts believe renewable energy is essential for economic recovery (Mojarro, 2020). With the fall in demand, renewable sources (mainly wind and solar) saw their share in electricity substantially increase at record levels in many countries. In less than 10 weeks, the USA increased its renewable energy consumption by nearly 40% and India by 45%, as seen in Figure 6. Italy, Germany, and Spain set new records for variable renewable energy integration to the grid. Investors are turning towards this industry to support economic recovery (Mojarro, 2020). A recent report from UC Berkeley shows how the U.S. can achieve carbon-free electricity by 2035, and how the nation would benefit. Millions of new jobs and trillions of dollars into the economy are a few major advantages.

Figure 6. Renewable energy demand after Covid-19 lockdown
Adopted from reference (Mojarro, 2020)

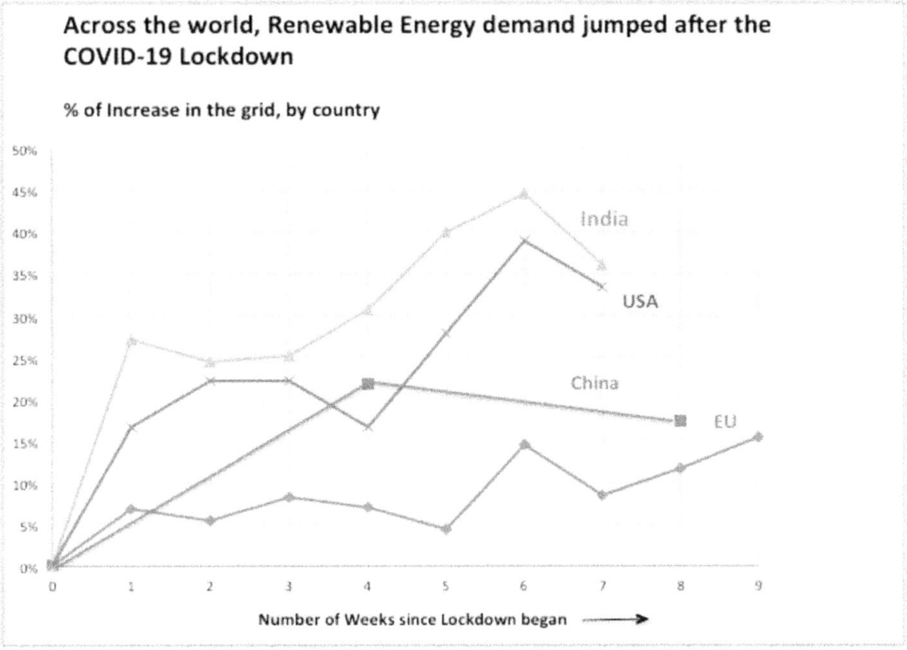

FUTURE RESEARCH DIRECTIONS

Although the pandemic is circumstantial and unexpected, the current outcome for the power sector is not. The ongoing increase in renewable energy into the grid results from a mixture of past policies, regulations, incentives, and innovations embedded in the power sectors of many forward-thinking countries.

These are several factors behind the increase in renewable energy during this crisis:

1. Renewables have been supported by favorable policies low interest rates in the foreseeable future, offering favorable conditions for wind and PV projects, which require high upfront investments (International Energy Agency [IEA], 2020). In many countries, renewables receive priority through market regulation. The priority for the first batch of energy to the network is given to the less expensive source, favoring cheaper and cleaner sources.
2. Continuous innovation is also a factor. Renewable energy has become the cheapest source of energy. IRENA recently reported that the cost of solar had fallen by 82% over the last 10 years (Sorenson, 2020). Bloomsburg NEF (2020) states that renewable energy is now the cheapest energy source in two-thirds of the world.
3. Renewable energy projects provide a "safe heaven" for certain institutional investors confronting the emerging economic slowdown because they often come with long-term fixed-price contracts.
4. So far, the Covid-19 crisis has not prompted governments in major markets to abandon or cancel already-announced policies ensuring investors that policy support will continue despite the economic turbulence. In addition, long-term net-zero goals in the European Union and China, the two

largest renewable energy markets, provide investors with long-range visibility (International Energy Agency [IEA], 2020).

5. Preferred investment can also be factored. Renewable energy has become investors' preferred choice for new power plants. For nearly two decades, renewable energy capacity has grown steadily, and now 72% of all new power capacity is a renewable plant (IRENA, 2020).

6. Stimulus packages have maintained the solvency of major utilities and, to some extent, small businesses investing in renewable projects (i.e. independent power producers [IPPs]) in both emerging markets and advanced economies. These relief measures have been crucial to improve their cash flow and allow them to finance planned projects in the second half of this year (International Energy Agency [IEA], 2020).

CONCLUSION

The pandemic has occurred at a time when declining renewable energy costs, persistently low oil prices, rising debt in the fossil fuel sector and investor concerns about the impact of fossil fuels on carbon emissions and environmental regulations were already lowering capital investment in the fossil fuel industry while making renewable energy one of the fastest growing industries. However, the massive, two-decade-long growth behind renewable energy looks to level off in 2020 due to the Covid-19 pandemic. It is too early to judge how profound the negative impacts of the pandemic on the global renewables will be, but that does not mean it is going to be flat for long.

Governments, businesses and households have 'kept the lights on' during the pandemic but with cheaper and greener energy. Stimulating investment, conditioning Covid-19 relief to green recovery, innovation and infrastructure opportunities in low-carbon and digital technologies are likely to keep the clean energy curve from flattening. Ultimately, the world's renewable energy scenario could return to its long-term trajectory toward green power generation over the next few years. In the post-Covid-19 era in which the economy bounces back, the experience of this pandemic period could convince governments to expedite the renewable energy policy efforts before another worldwide economic shock emerges due to other disease or an unknown weather event. All in all, there is hope that renewable energy can continue its forward trajectory.

REFERENCES

Ahmed, M. (2020). COVID-19 Hinders Progress in U.S. Renewable Energy Job Growth. *American Council of Renewable Energy*. https://acore.org/covid-19-hinders-progress-in-u-s-renewable-energy-job-growth/

Ambrose, J. (2020). Investors fear there ' ll be no bright post Covid dawn for oil majors. *Observer Business Agenda*. https://www.theguardian.com/business/2020/oct/25/investors-fear-therell-be-no-bright post-covid-dawn-for-oil-majors

Bachman, D. (2020). The economic impact of COVID-19 (novel coronavirus). *Deloitte Insight*. https://www2.deloitte.com/us/en/insights/economy/covid-19/economic-impact-covid-19.html

Barbier, E. B., & Burgess, J. C. (2020). Sustainability and development after COVID-19. *World Development*, *135*, 105082. doi:10.1016/j.worlddev.2020.105082 PMID:32834381

BBC News. (2020). *Worldwide cases overtake 2003 Sars outbreak*. BBC News. https://www.bbc.com/news/world-51322733

Birol, F. (2020). Put clean energy at the heart of stimulus plans to counter the coronavirus crisis. In *IEA*. https://www.iea.org/commentaries/put-clean-energy-at-the-heart-of-stimulus-plans-to-counter-the-coronavirus-crisis

Bloomsburg report. (2020). *Scale-up of Solar and Wind Puts Existing Coal, Gas at Risk*. Bloomsberg. https://about.bnef.com/blog/scale-up-of-solar-and-wind-puts-existing-coal-gas-at-risk/

Boatwright, A., & Wynne, M. A. (2020). Record Global GDP Contraction Indicative of COVID-19's Cross-Country Effect. *Dallas Federal Economics*, *30*, 1–3.

Busienss leaders. (2020). *Clean Energy & COVID-19 Crisis*, *2*(November). https://e2.org/reports/clean-jobs-covid-economic-crisis-april-2020/

Capital Group. (2020). 2021 Outlook : Turning points on the road to recovery. In *Capital Group*. https://www.capitalgroup.com/advisor/insights/articles/2021-outlook.html

Earth.org. (2020). *Renewable Energy Hits Record Growth in 2020- Report*. Earth.org. https://earth.org/renewable-energy-hits-record-growth-in-2020/#:~:text=Solar power capacity has increased 18-fold since 2010,renewable energy is becoming increasingly appealing to investors.

Eroğlu, H. (2020). Effects of Covid-19 outbreak on environment and renewable energy sector. *Environment, Development and Sustainability*, *0123456789*. doi:10.100710668-020-00837-4 PMID:32837274

Fottrell, Q. (2020). Will COVID-19 push more employees to work remotely after the pandemic? This economist says yes. *Market Watch*. https://www.marketwatch.com/story/does-covid-19-have-the-power-to-revolutionize-work-this-economist-says-yes-2020-12-11

Fox-Penner, P. (2020). Will the COVID-19 Pandemic Slow The Global Shift to Renewable Energy? In *The Brink, Boston University*. https://www.bu.edu/articles/2020/will-the-covid-19-pandemic-slow-the-global-shift-to-renewable-energy/

Healing, D. (2020). Big Oil's interest in renewable energy investments expected to waver, report says. In *The Globe and Mail*. https://www.theglobeandmail.com/business/article-big-oils-interest-in-renewable-energy-investments-expected-to-waver/

Hosseini, S. E., & Wahid, M. A. (2016). Hydrogen production from renewable and sustainable energy resources: Promising green energy carrier for clean development. *Renewable & Sustainable Energy Reviews*, *57*, 850–866. doi:10.1016/j.rser.2015.12.112

IEA. (2020). *Exploring the impacts of the Covid-19 pandemic on global energy markets, energy resilience, and climate change*. IEA.

International Energy Agency [IEA]. (2020). *Renewables 2020 – Analysis and forecast to 2025* (Issue November). IEA. https://www.iea.org/reports/renewables-2020

International Renewable Energy Agency (IRENA). (2020). *Renewable Capacity Statistics 2020*. IRENA. https://www.irena.org/publications/2020/Mar/Renewable-Capacity-Statistics-2020

IRENA. (2020). *Renewables Account for Almost Three Quarters of New Capacity in 2019*. IRENA.

Karlin, M. (2020). Slow Job Growth in November Leaves 446, 000 Clean Energy Workers Unemployed as COVID Cases, Shutdowns Surge. *American Council on Renewable Energy [ACORE]*. https://good-menproject.com/featured-content/slow-job-growth-in-november-leaves-446000-clean-energy-workers-unemployed-as-covid-case

Kramarchuk, R., Klein, D., Brunetti, B., Joseph, I., Schiavo, M., Georges, P., Redmond, S., Anankina, E., Prabhu, A., Lu, G., Huang, D., Amiot, M., & Roache, S. (2020). How is COVID-19 Impacting the Energy Transition? *SP Global*. https://www.spglobal.com/en/research-insights/featured/how-is-covid-19-impacting-the-energy-transition

Majorro, N. (2020). COVID-19 is a game-changer for renewable energy. Here's why. In *World economic forum*. https://www.weforum.org/agenda/2020/06/covid-19-is-a-game-changer-for-renewable-energy/

McElroy, B. (2020). How COVID-19 is impacting renewable energy. *Renewable Energy World*. https://www.renewableenergyworld.com/2020/04/29/how-covid-19-is-impacting-renewable-energy/.

McKibbin, W. J., & Fernando, R. (2020). The Global Macroeconomic Impacts of COVID-19: Seven Scenarios. SSRN *Electronic Journal,* 1–43. doi:10.2139/ssrn.3547729

Mojarro, N. (2020). *COVID-19 is a game-changer for renewable energy. Here's why.* World Economic Forum. https://www.weforum.org/agenda/2020/06/covid-19-is-a-game-changer-for-renewable-energy

Omer, A. M. (2008). Energy, environment and sustainable development. *Renewable & Sustainable Energy Reviews*, *12*(9), 2265–2300. doi:10.1016/j.rser.2007.05.001

Sarad, N. J., Alexander, M. J., & Donovan, L. P. (2020). COVID-19 Impact on US Renewable Energy Projects Article By. *The National Law Review*, *10*(363), 1–5.

Sorenson, B. (2020). Renewable Power Generation Costs in 2019. *IRENA*. https://irena.org/publications/2020/Jun/Renewable-Power-Costs-in-2019

S&P Global Market Intelligence. (2020). *As market expands, renewable energy unemployment barely budges.* SP Global. https://www.spglobal.com/marketintelligence/en/news-insights/latest-news-headlines/as-market-expands-renewable-energy-unemployment-barely-budges-60666681

Team LightBox. (2020). *The Effects of COVID-19 on the Renewable Energy Industry, and How this Industry is Important to Economic Recovery*. Dig Map. https://www.digmap.com/blog/the-effects-of-covid-19-on-the-renewable-energy-industry-and-how-this-industry-is-important-to-economic-recovery/

The Economist. (2020). *Covid-19 to send almost all G20 countries into a recession - Economist Intelligence Unit*. EIU. https://www.eiu.com/n/covid-19-to-send-almost-all-g20-countries-into-a-recession/

U.S. Energy Information Administration [EIA]. (2019). *Renewable energy explained: Portfolio standards*. US EIA. https://www.eia.gov/energyexplained/renewable-sources/portfolio-standards.php

Wire, F. (2020). Oil and Coronavirus Shocks Add Pressure for MEA Sovereigns. In *FitchRatings*. https://www.fitchratings.com/research/sovereigns/oil-coronavirus-shocks-add-pressure-for-mea-sovereigns-10-03-2020

World Economy. (2020). *5 charts show what the global economy looks like heading into 2021*. CNBC. https://www.cnbc.com/2020/12/28/5-charts-show-covid-impact-on-the-global-economy-in-2020.html

Worldometer. (2020). *COVID-19 CORONAVIRUS PANDEMIC*. World Meter. https://www.worldometers.info/coronavirus/

Yardeni, E., Johnson, D., & Quintana, M. (2020). *Global Economic Briefing: Industrial Production*. Global Economic Briefing: Industrial Production. www.yardeni.com

KEY TERMS AND DEFINITIONS

Covid-19: In another term Coronavirus was a virus that triggered a global pandemic in 2019, originating in Wuhan, China. Over the years in which it ravaged the globe, variants emerged such as Omicron and Delta.

Energy security: The ongoing availability, accessibility, affordability and acceptability of energy sources in the long term.

Environment Economics: The study of how economic principles and concepts are applied to the utilization of natural resources.

Market outlook: The trend of the market via macroeconomic and microeconomic segments.

Pandemic: Widespread occurrence of an infections virus or disease that affects a whole country or globally.

Renewable energy: Alternate energy sources that are sustainable and long term.

Supply-chain: Is the process of taking raw materials through to the final product ready for consumption.

Sustainability: The state of being long lasting and/or reusable. In this context, it refers to long lasting resources.

Chapter 9
Online Teaching and Learning Amidst COVID-19

Ashok Asthana
Sarala Birla University, Ranchi, India

Swati Srivastava
K. R. Mangalam University, India

ABSTRACT

The education industry has changed as a result of the adoption of ICT in schools at different levels. The greatest way to assist teaching and learning in traditional classroom settings as well as distant learning and online programmes that prepare students to participate in the dynamic world of technology is through technology. Nothing in the modern world makes sense or is simple to perform without the impact of ICT products and programmes, thus it is impossible to ignore the role that computers have played in global development. ICT products and programmes are a crucial instrument in assisting global standards. With the availability of educational opportunities, and access to learning materials in the form of photos and text, the internet has become so flexible that one can even obtain them at one's convenience at any time of the day. The use of ICT in education has gained popularity across the globe due to the ease with which it is associated.

INTRODUCTION

While many countries are at different levels of COVID-19 infection rates, globally there are more than 1.2 Billion children in 186 countries affected by school closures due to the COVID-19 pandemic (World Economic Forum (Li & Lalani, 2020). Given the abruptness of the situation, administrators and teachers were unprepared for the transition. Yet, they were forced to build emergency remote learning systems almost immediately (Donelly et al., 2021). Governments in developed countries already have the infrastructure and readiness to embrace ICT long before the pandemic and has started with already high growth and adoption in education with global investments reaching 18.66 billion USD in 2019 and the overall market for online education projected to reach 350 Billion USD by 2025 (Li & Lalani, 2020).

DOI: 10.4018/978-1-6684-8392-3.ch009

COVID-19 resulted in the closure of schools and educational facilities in most affected countries for observing social distancing. UNESCO estimates suggest that over 90% of the world's students are not currently attending schools in response to the pandemic, with over 1.5 billion learners affected. However, within these extraordinary times, one common trend is the increase in academic activities around the world using E-Learning, making a swift transition from place-based classes to virtual online learning systems (Abbasia et al., 2020).

With no successful vaccine or treatment available, and in an attempt to contain the spread of COVID-19, most governments around the world, authorized unprecedented social containment measures. These measures, among others, included social distancing and the temporary physical closure of educational institutions. Educational institutions had to adopt a digital approach to instruction and student learning, dramatically transitioning traditional in-person classroom instruction to predominantly distance learning where teaching is provided remotely on digital platforms (DePietro, 2020). While distance learning is not a new approach to instruction and learning, the unplanned, rapid, and uncertain duration of the approach is presenting challenges and takes a toll on students at all academic levels. Not much information on best practices was available to guide such abrupt transitions to school education (Armstrong-Mensah et al., 2020).

The introduction of ICT in schools at various levels has brought about developments in the education sector. Technology is the best-supporting link to enhance teaching and learning in a physical classroom setting, as well as distance and online instruction programs, aimed at preparing citizens to participate in the dynamic technologically driven environment. The place computers in the development of the world cannot be put aside, it is a vital tool in aiding the standard of the world; in the current world, nothing makes sense or is easy to do without the influence of ICT products and programs. Access to learning materials in pictures and writings through the internet has become so flexible to get even at the comfort of someone's home anytime any day with an availability of educational opportunities. Because of the easiness attached to it, the use of ICT in education has become increasingly trendy globally (Samuel, 2021; Cheri & Abdullahi, 2018). While some believe that the unplanned and rapid move to online learning – with no training, insufficient bandwidth, and little preparation – will result in a poor user experience that is unconducive to sustained growth, others believe that a new hybrid model of education will emerge, with significant benefits.

BACKGROUND

COVID-19 has resulted in a massive economic and social slowdown in almost all countries of the world since its outbreak in 2019. The education industry is among the hardest hit targets of COVID- 19 as a result of which all stakeholders related to education especially the learners and education providers were poorly impacted. As per the report of UNESCO more than 100 countries have witnessed the complete closure of the entire education system especially primary and higher education 1 student out of 4 students were not attending their classes in case of higher education and 1 student out of 5 students was not attending their primary classes throughout the world due to this pandemic. The COVID-19 pandemic requires urgent attention and collective action from all Governments, stakeholders, and communities. It is essential that Governments, civil society, and international organizations come together to ensure that every child is able to access education during this pandemic. It is also important to recognize that the interruption of the education system due to the pandemic has long-term implications and affects the quality of education in the years to come.

MAIN FOCUS OF THE CHAPTER

The main focus of the chapter is to explain the meaning, importance, need, and application of E-Learning, especially during COVID – 19 pandemic. The present chapter is an attempt to show why e-learning has been adopted more vigorously during the pandemic and how E-Learning and internet-based technologies are used to deliver a wide range of solutions that improve the knowledge and performance of experienced and inexperienced learners. The chapter also attempts to give a brief description of utilizing the Internet to deliver E-Learning initiatives in the business market and in higher education institutions. Indeed, E-Learning has enabled universities to expand on their current geographical reach, capitalize on new prospective students, and establish themselves as global educational providers.

E-LEARNING: MEANING AND RELEVANCE

The American Society for Training and Development defines E-Learning as a broad set of applications and processes, which include web-based learning, computer-based learning, virtual classrooms, and digital content. The definition of E-Learning varies depending on the organization and how it is used, but at its core, it involves electronic means of communication, education, and training (Nedeva & Dimova, 2010). Rosenberg (2001) confines E-Learning to the Internet as the use of Internet technologies to deliver a broad array of solutions that enhance knowledge and performance. It is based upon three fundamental criteria: networked delivered to the end-user via a computer using standard internet technology focuses on the broadest view of learning". He later redefined the concept as the use of internet technologies to create and deliver a rich learning environment that includes a broad array of which to enhance individual and organizational performance.

Ahmad (2012) maintained that E-Learning is all about learning with the use of technologies, presumably computers, and other modern-day tools. There is no doubt that E-Learning involves the use of electronic technology innovated tools to communicate ideas to learners who are relatively inexperienced, it can as well be used to monitor learner's performance and to report the learner's progress to the appropriate personnel. Rosenberg (2013 as cited in Samuel, 2021) viewed E-Learning as the process by which people acquire skills or knowledge for the purpose of enhancing their performance through the internet or intranet and multimedia which leads to reinforced learning by means of video, audio, quizzes, and other forms of interaction.

Craige (2007) defines E-Learning as the computer and network-enabled transfer of skills and knowledge for the diffusion of innovative teaching. A learning system based on formalized teaching but with the help of electronic resources is known as E-Learning. While teaching can be based in or out of the classrooms, the use of computers and the Internet forms the major component of E-Learning. E-Learning can also be termed as a network-enabled transfer of skills and knowledge, and the delivery of education is made to a large number of recipients at the same or different times. Earlier, it was not accepted wholeheartedly as it was assumed that this system lacked the human element required in learning (The Economic Times, 2021).

However, with the rapid progress in technology and the advancement in learning systems, it is now embraced by the masses. The introduction of computers was the basis of this revolution and with the passage of time, as we get hooked to smartphones, tablets, etc, these devices now have an important place in the classrooms for learning. Books are gradually getting replaced by electronic educational materials like optical discs or pen drives. Knowledge can also be shared via the Internet, which is accessible 24/7, anywhere, anytime (The Economic Times, 2021).

The implementation of E-Learning in education has been favorable in multiple contexts. Previous studies have presented several advantages associated with the implementation of E-Learning technologies into education (Raspopovic et al., 2017). E-Learning has been viewed as the ability to focus on the requirements of individual learners. For instance, focusing on the needs of individual learners can deliver knowledge in the digital age effectively as compared to educational institutions' needs or instructors (Huang & Chiu, 2015). Objectives can be achieved in the shortest time with the least effort through E-Learning. When managing the E-Learning environment, its effect on educational learning is observed in providing equal access to information regardless of the users' locations, ethnic origins, races, and ages. The environment for E-Learning also helps students or learners to rely on themselves so that instructors are no longer the solitary knowledge source rather they serve as guides and advisors (Joshua et al., 2016).

Several studies have shown the positive effects of E-Learning from the insights of learners or students (Gautam & Tiwari, 2016; Martínez-Caro, Cegarra-Navarro & Cepeda-Carrión, 2015; Chang, 2016). For instance, E-Learning allows observing much more flexible learning ways to go to classes with a much-reduced need for travel. Learners are allowed to get deeper insights into the information through activities that are carried-out in the classroom through interactive video facility (Gautam & Tiwari, 2016; Martínez-Caro, Cegarra-Navarro & Cepeda-Carrión, 2015). This allows learners to respond promptly to the activities.

The internet is a technological development that has the potential to change, not only the way society retains and accesses knowledge but also to transform and restructure traditional models of higher education, particularly the delivery and interaction in and with course materials and associated resources. Utilizing the Internet to deliver E-Learning initiatives has created expectations both in the business market and in higher education institutions. Indeed, E-Learning has enabled universities to expand on their current geographical reach, capitalize on new prospective students, and to establish themselves as global educational providers (Ronteltap & Eurelings, 2002).

Holmes and Gardner (2006) cited in Arkorful and Abaidoo (2014) summed the advantages of E-Learning to education as follows:

i. It is flexible when issues of time and place are taken into consideration. Every student has the luxury of choosing the place and time that suits him/her. E-Learning provides the institutions as well as their students or learners the flexibility of time and place of delivery or receipt of learning information.

ii. E-Learning enhances the efficacy of knowledge and qualifications via ease of access to a huge amount of information.

iii. It is able to provide opportunities for relations between learners by the use of discussion forums. Through this, E-Learning helps eliminate barriers that have the potential of hindering participation including the fear of talking to other learners. E-Learning motivates students to interact with others, as well as exchange and respect different points of view. E-learning eases communication and also improves the relationships that sustain learning. E-Learning makes available extra prospects for interactivity between students and teachers during content delivery.

iv.   E-Learning is cost-effective in the sense that there is no need for the students or learners to travel. It is also cost-effective in the sense that it offers opportunities for learning for a maximum number of learners with no need for many buildings.

v.   E-Learning always takes into consideration the individual learners' differences. Some learners, for instance, prefer to concentrate on certain parts of the course, while others are prepared to review the entire course.

vi.   E-Learning helps compensate for scarcities of academic staff, including instructors or teachers as well as facilitators, lab technicians etc.

vii.   The use of E-Learning allows self-pacing. For instance, the asynchronous way permits each student to study at his or her own pace and speed whether slow or quick. It, therefore, increases satisfaction and decreases stress.

In a broader fashion, and put differently, Abed (2019) summed up the advantages of E-Learning in education as follows:

i.   Easy access to the teacher: E-Learning has made it much easier to obtain and access the teacher as soon as possible outside the official working hours, because the trainee can now send his inquiries to the teacher through e-mail, and this advantage is more useful and appropriate for the teacher rather than remain restricted to his office. It would be more useful for those whose working hours were inconsistent with the teacher's schedule or when there was an inquiry at any time that could not be postponed.

ii.   Increasing the possibility of communication between students among them, and between students and the school: Through the ease of communication between these parties in several directions such as discussion boards, e-mail, and dialogue rooms. The researchers believe that these things increase and stimulate students to participate and interact with the topics in question.

iii.   Sense of equality: The communication tools allow every student the opportunity to express his opinion at any time without embarrassment, unlike the traditional classrooms that deprive him of this feature either because of the poor organization of the seats, or the weakness of the student himself, or shame, or other reasons, but this type of education provides a full opportunity for students because they can send their opinion and voice through available communication tools from the e-mail, discussion boards, and discussion rooms. This feature is more useful for students who are afraid and anxious because this method of education makes students more daring to express their ideas and find the facts more than they were in the traditional classroom. Studies have shown that online discussion helps and urges students to confront more.

iv.   Contributing to different views of students: Online forums, such as discussion boards and dialogue rooms, provide opportunities for exchanging views on topics that increase the chances of benefiting from the ideas and suggestions presented and integrating them with the views of the student, which helps to form a solid foundation for the learner, has strong knowledge, opinions through the knowledge and skills acquired through dialogue rooms.

v.   The possibility of changing the teaching method: It is possible to receive the scientific material in a way that suits the student. Some of them are suitable for the visual method. Some of them are suitable for the audible or readable method. Some of them correspond to the practical method.

E-Learning and its sources allow the possibility of applying the sources in many different ways that allow modification according to the best method for the trainee.

vi. Adapting the various methods of education: E-Learning allows the learner to focus on important ideas while writing and compiling the lecture or lecture, and also allows students who have difficulty concentrating and organizing tasks to benefit from the material because they are arranged and coordinated in an easy and important way.

vii. Additional assistance in repetition: This is an added advantage for those who learn in a practical way. Those who teach through training, if they want to express their ideas, put them in certain sentences, which means they have repeated the information they have been trained on, as students do when they prepare for a particular exam.

viii. The curriculum is available 24 hours a day, seven days a week: This feature is useful for people who are moody or want to learn at a certain time because some prefer to learn morning and evening, as well as for those who bear personal burdens and responsibilities, this feature allows everyone to learn in a time that suits them.

ix. Continuity in access to curricula: This feature makes the student in a stable state that he can get the information he wants at the time that suits him, it is not related to the opening and closing times of the library, which leads to the student's comfort and not being tired.

x. Do not rely on actual attendance: The student must adhere to a fixed, binding and binding schedule of collective action for traditional education, but now it is no longer necessary because modern technology has provided ways of communication without having to be present at a particular time and place so coordination is not as important as the inconvenience.

xi. Ease and multiple ways to assess the development of the student: Instant evaluation tools provided teachers with a variety of ways to quickly and easily build, distribute and classify information.

xii. Maximize the time: The provision of the time element is very useful and important for both the teacher and the learner. The student has immediate access to the information in the specified place and time, so there is no need to go from home to the classroom, library, or office. This saves time from loss, and the teacher can keep his time from Loss because it can send what the student needs through the line of instant communication.

COVID-19 PANDEMIC AND GOVERNANCE

COVID-19 began in Wuhan, China, in December 2019; and remains an imperative problem affecting millions worldwide. It was declared a pandemic on March 11, 2020, by the World Health Organization (WHO), and by March 25, 2020, the total number of confirmed cases that were reported rose to 414,179. Together with infecting individuals' health, COVID-19 continues to damage the socio-economic conditions and education of any country it has touched, thus being more than just a medical emergency (Nicola et al., 2020; Alipio, 2021; McKibbin & Fernando, 2021).

The COVID-19 crisis forced governments around the world to operate in a context of radical uncertainty and faced with difficult trade-offs given the health, economic, and social challenges it raises. Within the first three months of 2020, the novel coronavirus developed into a global pandemic. Schools and universities were closed in the spring of 2020 for more than one billion students of all ages. By November 2020, COVID-19 spread to almost all countries and affected more than 50 million people around the world, resulting in more than 1.25 million deaths. More than half of the world's population has experienced a lockdown with strong containment measures –the first time in history that such measures are applied on such a large scale (OECD, 2020a).

Beyond the health and human tragedy of COVID-19, it is now widely recognized that the pandemic triggered the most serious economic crisis since World War II. All economic sectors are affected by disrupted global supply chains, weaker demand for imported goods and services, dropping international tourism (OECD, 2020b), a decline in business travel, and most often a combination of these. Measures to contain the virus' spread have hit SMEs and entrepreneurs particularly hard (OECD, 2020c). Unemployment levels and the number of aid seekers have increased dramatically. Many countries "exited" virus containment measures to mitigate the impact of the economic crisis only to face a rising wave of cases in the autumn of 2020, jeopardizing recovery. The exit strategy from the crisis is not linear, with possible "stop and go" strategies of lockdowns until a treatment or vaccine, or cure is available (OECD, 2020a).

Estimates released by the OECD in September 2020 indicate that real global GDP is projected to decline by 4.5% in 2020 before picking up by 5% in 2021. OECD unemployment is projected to rise to 9.4% in Q4 2020 from 5.4% in 2019. The projections assume that sporadic local outbreaks of the virus will continue, with these being addressed by targeted local interventions rather than national lockdowns; wide availability of vaccination is not expected until late in 2021 (OECD, 2020d). The multi-faceted nature and unprecedented scale of the COVID-19 crisis, comparisons with past crises, including the 2008-2009 financial crisis, have significant limitations. COVID-19 is proving unique in its generation of both a supply side and a demand side shock, and its impact on all sectors and regions of the world. The uncertainty is also much higher. Governments face a difficult trade-off between managing the economic recovery and mitigating the impact of a second wave of the virus (OECD, 2020a).

SOLUTIONS AND RECOMMENDATIONS: E-LEARNING AMID COVID-19 PANDEMIC—SYSTEMS AND POLICIES

With this sudden change from classroom learning to online learning in many parts of the world, some people and policymakers are wondering whether the adoption of online learning will continue to persist in the post-pandemic, and how such a shift would impact the worldwide education market (Li & Lalani, 2020). In response to significant demand, many online learning platforms are offering free access to their services, including platforms like BYJU'S, a Bangalore-based educational technology and online tutoring firm founded in 2011, which is now the world's most highly valued tech company. Since announcing free live classes on its Think and Learn app, BYJU has seen a 200% increase in the number of new students using its product. Similarly, Tencent classroom has been used extensively since mid-February after the Chinese government instructed a quarter of a billion full-time students to resume their studies through online platforms. This resulted in the largest "online movement" in the history of education with approximately 730,000, or 81% of K-12 students, attending classes via the Tencent K-12 Online School in Wuhan (Li & Lalana, 2020).

Other companies are bolstering their capabilities to provide a one-stop shop for teachers and students. For example, Lark, a Singapore-based collaboration suite initially developed by ByteDance as an internal tool to meet its own exponential growth, began offering teachers and students unlimited video conferencing time, auto-translation capabilities, real-time co-editing of project work, and smart calendar scheduling, amongst other features. To do so quickly and in a time of crisis, Lark ramped up its global server infrastructure and engineering capabilities to ensure reliable connectivity. Similarly, Alibaba's distance learning solution, DingTalk, had to prepare for a similar influx. To support large-scale remote work, the platform tapped Alibaba Cloud to deploy more than 100,000 new cloud servers in just two hours – setting a new record for rapid capacity expansion (Li & Lalana, 2020).

Some school districts are forming unique partnerships, like the one between The Los Angeles Unified School District and PBS SoCal/KCET to offer local educational broadcasts, with separate channels focused on different ages, and a range of digital options. Media organizations such as the BBC are also powering virtual learning; Bitesize Daily, launched on 20 April, is offering 14 weeks of curriculum-based learning for kids across the UK with celebrities like Barcelona's footballer, Sergio Aguero teaching some of the content (Li & Lalana, 2020).

Ukraine also implemented measures to support remote teaching and learning, starting with broadcasting video lessons via television and using online distance learning platforms. Organizations like EdCamp Ukraine organized online professional development and peer-to-peer learning opportunities for teachers to meet remotely and share experiences with online learning during the COVID-19 crisis. Ukraine also conducted information campaigns, such as "Schools, We Are Ready," together with UNICEF, to inform teachers, administrators, students, and parents about the guidelines for safe and sustained learning under COVID-19 in the 2020–21 school year (Donnelly et al., 2021).

A notable impact on the economy and education has been observed with the current state of the Philippine government coupled with the crippling pandemic. The recent adoption of the K-12 program, the transition of first K-12 completers to college, and the provision of free and inclusive education have challenged the education governing bodies in the country even more. The K-12 program includes Kindergarten and 12 years of basic education (six years of primary education, four years of junior high school, and two years of senior high school [SHS]) to allow for mastery of concepts and skills, the development of lifelong learners, and the preparation of graduates for tertiary education, middle-level skill development, employment, and entrepreneurship. The implementation of the K- 12 program began in the 2012-2013 academic year, and the first batch of SHS completers was produced in 2018 (Clemen et al., 2021).

The Commission on Higher Education (CHEd) in the Philippines advised institutions of higher education in the country to implement distance education methods of learning for its classes, such as the use of electronic learning (E-Learning), to maximize the academic term despite the suspensions (CHEd, 2020). Several other public and private tertiary institutions implemented such arrangements for their classes; however, several student groups appealed to CHEd to suspend mandatory online classes considering the logistical limitations and well-being of students. In addition, financial and acceptance factors remain a problem that would limit the use of E-Learning (Baticulon et al., 2021). While both the supply and demand for E-Learning opportunities have risen in recent years, many professionals are beginning to question whether students are prepared to succeed in an online learning environment (Rotas & Cahapay, 2020). After all, the demonstrated success of students in a conventional education and training classroom may not be an adequate predictor of success in an E-Learning classroom (Almomani et al, 2019).

Unfortunately, despite best efforts to set up a supportive remote learning experience, evidence is emerging to show that school closures have resulted in actual learning losses. Research analyzing these outcomes is ongoing, but early results from Belgium, the Netherlands, Switzerland, and the United Kingdom indicate both learning losses and increases in inequality. Alarmingly, these losses are found to be much higher among students whose parents have less education, a finding reinforced by a study showing that children from socioeconomically advantaged families have received more parental support with their studies during the school closure period (Donnelly et al., 2021).

These emerging data, which provide insights into the region's highest-income countries, can also be used to predict outcomes in middle-income countries. Despite their substantial technological capability, even Europe's high-income countries have experienced learning losses and increased inequality as a result of the abrupt transition to virtual learning. These outcomes are likely to be even more acute in middle- and lower-income countries like Ukraine, where there is much less technological capability and a larger share of families living below the poverty line (Donnelly et al, 2021).

Research on online learning challenges in medical education during the COVID-19 outbreak by Rajab et al (2020) reported that the challenges were communications, assessment, online education experience, technology use tools, time management, anxiety, and coronavirus disease stress. However, students reported positively the effectiveness of online learning during the pandemic. Another study was conducted to evaluate students' views about the future of mobile learning after the current pandemic in basic education colleges in Kuwait. The study concluded with a good impression from the student in utilizing mobile learning in higher education. The advantage of the study is the recommendation for developing and teaching courses about m-learning use and application (Alanezi & AlAzwani, 2020).

Another study explored the importance of online learning and investigated the analysis of weaknesses, strengths, challenges, and opportunities of online education in the time of the pandemic (Shivangi, 2020; cited in Mahyoob, 2020). The study provided some guidelines for dealing with online learning challenges at natural disasters and epidemics. A case study for features of adolescent online learners was investigated in Pennsylvania by Wolfinger (2016) cited in Mahyoob (2020). The study focused on the achievement of fully online virtual schooling through middle school. The research paid attention to academic, social support, learners' characteristics, and educational support. The results revealed the importance of teachers' role in virtual learning, and parents' involvement could promote their academic achievements.

A survey was conducted by the International Association of Universities 2020 about the impact of COVID-19 globally on higher education institutes. The findings of the study indicated that all the activities of the participating institutes have been affected by the COVID-19 crisis. The results also showed t negative influence on the quality of activities and the inequity of education opportunities. Alturise (2020) conducted a study about learners' and teachers' satisfaction with the online learning model using the Blackboard platform at Qassim University, Saudi Arabia. The study concluded that the E-Learning mode is an advancement in education, but significant work is needed to improve online learning applications (Mahyoob, 2020).

Although online education is developing rapidly around the world, more applications of online education are used as a supplement to regular place-based school education. In conventional education and teaching practice, more students go to schools to participate in traditional classroom teaching. However, during the COVID-19 pandemic, the luxury of using E-Learning as an adjunct to traditional learning is not possible. The majority of schools and institutions worldwide are relying solely on virtual learning to fulfill their basic needs of education. Drawing the experience through previous crisis situations, an adaptation of web-based learning and supporting the continuation of educational activities through online classes has been effective and successful (Nortvig et al., 2018; Franchi, 2020; Abbasia et al., 2020).

Important Recommendations

Some of the important recommendations to keep online teaching more effective are as below:

- Strengthen the infrastructure to facilitate online teaching and learning well in advance

- Make online teaching a regular feature and at least 30% of the curriculum should be taught in online mode.
- Try to engage students online
- Prefer recording the lecture rather than streaming it.
- Instructor/Teacher must show face and conversation/ discussion should be facilitated in between.
- Keep the online content short, crisp, and clear.
- Provide short training to students and learners regarding the use of online courses and Learning apps effectively.

FUTURE RESEARCH DIRECTIONS

The present work explains the meaning, need, and importance of online teaching and learning during COVID-19. The chapter has presented a well-crafted note on the emergence of teaching and learning using virtual platforms/internet-based technologies. The objectives considered for the present study were well met however there is a scope for future research. Some of the related fields in which future research could be conducted are mentioned below:

- How online teaching and learning can be made more effective, especially for students in underdeveloped and developing countries?
- What is the impact of online teaching and learning on the mental thrust, learning ability, and employability of students?
- How attitudes of teachers and students could be made more sublime to accept virtual teaching and learning as the future of the education industry?
- How to strengthen the current educational infrastructure throughout the world to minimize the impact of a pandemic?

CONCLUSION

The place of E-Learning cannot be overlooked in this dynamic world where the physical ways of teaching and learning process is gradually changing to digital forms. The sudden outbreak of COVID-19 coupled with the lockdown of schools at various levels of education across the globe served as a test for the education technology interventions for teaching-learning activities. Unfortunately, many less-developed countries' education systems arrived at this point unprepared. Such countries are still battling with the economic meltdown when COVID-19 surfaced, leading to a cost of procurement, installation of needed ICT tools for E-Learning and maintenance becoming more tedious that their currencies continue losing value in the world market. Coupled with this is the misappropriation of funds allocated to the educational sector because of the high rate of corruption and dirty politics. It was observed that even the E-Learning chosen as an alternative to the physical teaching-learning process in the lingering period of the COVID-19 pandemic has not been fully effective because of the non-unemployment of experts to manage the IT section of many countries', poorly designed education systems, huge tariff charges from various network providers that are becoming unbearable on daily bases, and non-existent, poor or dilapidated infrastructure for information and communication technology network. To reduce and reverse the long-term negative effects of COVID-19, less developed or developing countries which are likely to be hit harder, need to implement learning recovery programs, increase education budgets, and prepare for future similar shocks by building education to meet the global standard.

REFERENCES

Abbasia, M.S., Ahmeda, N., Sajjadb, B., Alshahranic, A., Saeedd, S., Sarfaraze, S., Alhamdanf, R.S., Vohrac,F. & Abduljabbarc, T. (2020). *E-Learning perception and satisfaction among health sciences students amid the COVID-19 pandemic.* IOS Press. doi:10.3233/WOR-203308

Abed, E. K. (2019). Electronic learning and its benefits in education. *Eurasia Journal of Mathematics, Science and Technology Education, 15*(3), 1–8. doi:10.29333/ejmste/102668

Ahmad, S. A. (2012). Essentialities for E-Learning: The Nigerian tertiary Institutions in question. *Academic Research International, 2*(2), 286–219.

Alanezi., & Azwani, A. (2020). Future of mobile learning during and after global (covid-19) pandemic: College of basic education as case. *Journal of Education and Practice, 11.*

Alipio, M. (2021). Education during Covid-19 era: Are learners in a less-economically developed country ready for E-Learning? *IMCC Journal of Science, 1*(2), 94–101.

Almomani, E. Y., Qablan, A. M., Atrooz, F. Y., Almomany, A. M., Hajjo, R. M., & Almomani, H. Y. (2019). *The influence of Coronavirus diseases (COVID-19).* National Institute of Health.

Alturise, F. (2020). Evaluation of the blackboard learn learning management system for full online courses in Western Branch Colleges of Qassim University. *International Journal of Emerging Technologies in Learning, 15*(15), 33–50. doi:10.3991/ijet.v15i15.14199

Arkorful, V., & Abaidoo, N. (2014). The role of E-Learning, the advantages and disadvantages of its adoption in Higher Education. *International Journal of Education and Research, 2*(12), 397–410.

Armstrong-Mensah, E., Ramsey-White, K., Yankey, B., & Self-Brown, S. (2020). covid-19 and distance learning: Effects on Georgia State University School of Public Health Students. *Public Health, 8,* 576227. doi:10.3389/fpubh.2020.576227 PMID:33102425

Baticulon, R. E., Sy, J. J., Alberto, N. R. I., Baron, M. B. C., Mabulay, R. E. C., Rizada, L. G. T., & Reyes, J. C. B. (2021). Barriers to online learning in the time of COVID-19: A national survey of medical students in the Philippines. *Medical Science Educator, 31*(2), 615–626. doi:10.100740670-021-01231-z PMID:33649712

Bayham, J., & Fenichel, E. P. (2020). Impact of school closures for COVID-19 on the US health-care workforce and net mortality: A modelling study. *The Lancet. Public Health, 5*(5), 271–278. doi:10.1016/S2468-2667(20)30082-7 PMID:32251626

Chang, V. (2016). Review and discussion: E-Learning for academia and industry. *International Journal of Information Management, 36*(3), 476–485. doi:10.1016/j.ijinfomgt.2015.12.007

Cheri, L., & Abdullahi, M. (2018). E-governance: Illusion or opportunity for Nigerian university's administration. *Global Journal of Political Science and Administration*, 6(3), 33–43.

Clemen, J. C., Ali, H., Abdulmadid, A., & Jabbar, J. H. (2021). Education during covid-19 era: Readiness of students in a less-economically developed country for E-Learning. *IMCC Journal of Science*, 1(2), 94–101.

Commission on Higher Education [CHEd]. (2020). *Guidelines on the implementation of flexible learning*. CHED. https://ched.gov.ph/wp-content/uploads/CMO-No.-4-s.-2020-Guidelines-on-the-Implementation-of-FlexiblE-Learning.pdf

Craig, W. (2007). *Overview of the E-Learning capital programme*. JISC. https://www.jisc.ac.uk/media/documents/programmes/capital/elearningprogramme_craigwentworth

DePietro, A. (2020). Impact of Coronavirus (COVID-19) on Colleges and Universities in the U.S. *Forbes*. https://www.forbes.com/sites/andrewdepietro/2020/04/30/impact-coronavirus-covid-19-colleges-universities/#6ecab23661a6

Donelly, R., Patrinos, H. A., & Gresham, J. (2021). *The impact of COVID-19 on education – recommendations and opportunities for Ukraine*. World Bank.

Franchi, T. (2019). The impact of the covid-19 pandemic on current anatomy education and future careers: A student's perspective. *Anatomical Sciences Education*. doi:10.1002/ase.1966 PMID:32301588

Holmes, B., & Gardner, J. (2006). *E-Learning: concepts and practice*. SAGE Publications. doi:10.4135/9781446212585

Huang, Y. M., & Chiu, P. S. (2015). The effectiveness of a meaningful learning-based evaluation model for context-aware mobile learning. *British Journal of Educational Technology*, 46(2), 437–447. doi:10.1111/bjet.12147

Joshua, D., Obille, K., John, E., & Shuaibu, U. (2016). E-Learning platform system for the department of library and information science, Modibbo Adama University of Technology, Yola: A Developmental plan. *Journal of Information and Knowledge Management*, 7(1), 51–69.

Li, C., & Lalani, F. (2020). *The COVID-19 pandemic has changed education forever*. World Economic Forum.

Mahyoob, M. (2020). Challenges of E-Learning during the COVID-19 Pandemic Experienced by EFL Learners. *Arab World English Journal*, 11(4), 351–362. doi:10.24093/awej/vol11no4.23

McKibbin, W., & Fernando, R. (2021). The global macroeconomic impacts of covid-19: Seven scenarios. *Asian Economic Papers*, 20(2), 1–30. doi:10.1162/asep_a_00796

Murphy, M. P. (2020). COVID-19 and emergency eLearning: Consequences of the securitization of higher education for post-pandemic pedagogy. *Contemporary Security Policy*, 1(3), 1–4. doi:10.1080/13523260.2020.1761749

Nedeva, V., & Dimova, E. (2010). Some advantages of E-Learning in English language training. *Trakia Journal of Sciences*, 8, 21–28.

Nicola, M., Alsafi, Z., Sohrabi, C., Kerwan, A., Al-Jabir, A., Iosifidis, C., Agha, M., & Agha, R. (2020). The socio-economic implications of the coronavirus pandemic (COVID-19): A review. *International Journal of Surgery, 78*, 185–193. doi:10.1016/j.ijsu.2020.04.018 PMID:32305533

Nortvig, A. M., Petersen, A. K., & Balle, S. H. (2018). A literature review of the factors influencing E-Learning and blended learning in relation to learning outcome, student satisfaction and engagement. *Electronic Journal of e-Learning, 16*, 46–55.

Organisation for Economic Cooperation and Development [OECD] (2020a). *The territorial impact of COVID-19: Managing the crisis across levels of government.* OECD. https://www.read.oecd-library.org/view/?ref=128_128287-5agkkojaaa&title=The–territorial-impact-of-covid-19-managing-the-crisis-across-levels-of-government

Organisation for Economic Cooperation and Development [OECD] (2020b). *Strategic foresight for the COVID-19 crisis and beyond: Using futures thinking to design better public policies.* OECD. https://www.oecd.org/coronavirus/policy-responses/strategic-foresight-for-the-covid-19-crisis-and-beyond-using-futures-thinking-to-design-better-public-policies-c3448fa5/

Organisation for Economic Cooperation and Development [OECD] (2020c). *The territorial impact of covid-19: Managing the crisis across levels of government.* OECD. https://www.oecd.org/cfe/leed/COVID-19-Italian-regions-SME-policy-responses.pdf

Organisation for Economic Cooperation and Development [OECD]. (2020d). *OECD Economic Outlook: Interim report.* OECD. doi:10.1787/34ffc900-en

Rajab, M. H., Gazal, A. M., & Alkattan, K. (2020). Challenges to online medical education during the covid-19 pandemic. *Cureus, 12*(7). doi:10.7759/cureus.8966 PMID:32766008

Raspopovic, M., Cvetanovic, S., & Jankulovic, A. (2016). Challenges of transitioning to E-Learning system with learning objects capabilities. *International Review of Research in Open and Distance Learning, 17*(1). doi:10.19173/irrodl.v17i1.2172

Ronteltap, F., & Eurelings, A. (2002). Activity and interaction of students in an electronic learning environment for problem-based learning. *Distance Education, 23*(1), 11–22. doi:10.1080/01587910220123955

Rosenberg, M. J. (2001). *E-Learning.* McGraw-Hill.

Rotas, E. E., & Cahapay, M. B. (2020). Difficulties in remote learning: Voices of Philippine university students in the wake of COVID-19 crisis. *Asian JDE, 15*, 147–158.

Samuel, A. I. (2021). The concept of E-Learning amid coronavirus (covid-19) pandemic in Nigeria: Issues, benefits, challenges, and way forward. *International Journal of Education and Evaluation, 7*(3), 23–33.

The Economic Times. (2021). Definition of E-Learning. *The Economic Times.* https://economictimes.indiatimes.com/definition/E-Learning

United Nations Educational, Scientific and Cultural Organization [UNESCO]. (2020). *COVID-19 educational disruption and response.* UNESCO. https://en.unesco.org/themes/education-emergencies/coronavirus-school-closures

KEY TERMS AND DEFINITIONS

Communication Technology: Communications technology, also known as information technology, refers to all equipment and programs that are used to process and communicate information.

COVID–19: Coronavirus disease (COVID-19) is an infectious disease caused by the SARS-CoV-2 virus. It was first witnessed by the world in December – 2019.

E-Learning: It is a process to deliver content and knowledge to stakeholders, learners, and students through the use of an internet-based platform.

Job Performance: In the context of the present work it is about the performance of teachers and students in teaching and learning.

Lockdown: It is a state or period in which movement within or access to an area is restricted in the interests of public safety or health.

Online Teaching: It is about the transfer of knowledge on internet-based virtual platforms to facilitate learning.

Pandemic: It is an outbreak of a specific disease that impacts countries throughout the globe.

Chapter 10
Diagnosing Organisations:
Everything Is Vague to a Degree – You Do Not Realise Until You Have Tried to Make It Precise

Isolde Kanikani

Plat4mation, The Netherlands

ABSTRACT

Diagnosing organisations is a chapter that explores the intrinsic relationship between organisational purpose, the people, and value creation in relation to organisational structures. Without structure we can't be aware of what we are changing or monitoring if we are effectively achieving our organisational purpose. Structure in the form of governance, an operating system, or organisation design can be built to fight or embrace change. People can be taught to do the same. With the application change maturity built on organisational structures and people management coupled with a search to maximise value through creating continuously adaptive organisational systems, one can equip organisations with the tools they need to not only survive but thrive. By questioning the basic building blocks of organising, this chapter establishes not only factors that could be measures in this diagnosis of organisations, but establishes a set of invitations that are more profound in the sense that they offer strategic choice and development of this concept of organising and organisations.

INTRODUCTION

The purpose of this research is to investigate the interplay between organizational structure and people. Exploring how different structural designs and intentions give rise to situations where people can thrive and where change capability is a built-in function of the organization's framework and governance. Using a series of invitations to help highlight areas of organizational diagnosis, structural development and approaches to change and people that will support the diagnosis of an organization's health. These invitations are synonymous with actions, outcomes, progression, and research that will help us further

DOI: 10.4018/978-1-6684-8392-3.ch010

define the 'as is' state, potentially changing this setup ensuring a greater degree of organizational health dealing with mass and unprecedented change.

When it comes to topics of a working definition of an organization, effective structures or purpose, the material is conceptually young, and in terms of the potential lifetimes of organizations there haven't been enough renditions of organizational turnover to really explore, test or understand what the possibilities of organizational design and operation are or could be. Organizations are still in many ways led by yesterday's thought, while trying to become future proof. To reach this new logic and future-proof state we need to be able to effectively diagnose the current organizational state, connecting 'new logics' explored in the different invitations found below. It's important to define that which we seek to measure, starting with ´What is an organization?

The inherent value of diagnosis lies in the fact that it helps an organization identify its strengths, weaknesses, opportunities, and threats. By conducting an internal health diagnosis, an organization gains a deeper understanding of its current state, which can then be used to develop strategies and solutions to address any underlying issues and improve organizational performance. Furthermore, the sheer speed of change in these times ask organizations to be lean in the way they are run. We can no longer afford the luxury of waiting to see what happens next. Diagnosing an organization gives us the information we need to proactively step ahead of our competition while tackling issues in their infancy rather than when they get so big that there is a big problem to solve or worse crisis. The act of diagnosing gives us the opportunity to save on present costs, foresee new ones that can be stopped before they become too big an investment.

BACKGROUND

Diagnosing organizations allows us to get a clear picture of where we are, to check that the way we are currently operating is in line with what we need to tackle in these times. Health equals an ability to change and remain relevant through development and innovation around the core organizational purpose and strategy (Burton & Obel, 2004). Supported by an update in infrastructural logic where necessary that will further serve the organization's purpose. Besides, this creates further strategic choices posed as invitations in this text. Exploring these factors for diagnosis gives rise to areas of strategic choice, particularly when we view organizations with a system-focused, multiple contingencies lensed open systems view.

There are many concepts integral to the understanding of topics within this chapter and so let us begin with some of the invitations and working definitions for alignment. At its core, an organization is defined by its purpose or mission, which guides its activities and decision-making. It also has a formal structure, which includes roles, responsibilities, and reporting lines, that helps to ensure that its members work together effectively and efficiently. Organizations can vary in size and complexity, ranging from small, single-person operations to large multinational corporations with thousands of employees. They can also have different types of ownership, such as for-profit, non-profit, or government owned. Overall, an organization is a group of people who come together to achieve a common purpose, and who are organised in a way that enables them to work together effectively towards that goal. The first invitation comes with the way we define organizations, if defining them as a metaphorical machine then our approach will differ from when the definition is using an organism or political metaphor (Morgan, 2006). So appropriately defining the word 'organization' is key to unravelling the other choices and invitations we have at our fingertips and is the first building block of a healthy organization. This is certainly not the only invitation, more to be discussed later in this text.

This word 'effectively' is key to the following chapter and what we will explore here, this can be interposed with the possibility of diagnosing organizational health. What does effective mean in the light of the times we now find ourselves in? The purpose is also important and defines the very existence of the organization and if the people are effective in their drive towards their collective vision. A well-defined purpose, effective approach defined by structures and engagement of people are the base ingredients for diagnosing an organizations health. The ability to change, develop and innovate with digital dexterity are key for organizations remaining in their prime and could be considered as secondary factors to keep in mind.

An organization's purpose is critical to diagnosing its health because it is the foundation upon which all other activities occur, and operations are built. The purpose of an organization defines its mission, vision, and values, and it provides direction and clarity to its employees, stakeholders, and customers. A guiding north star that scopes an organizations activity and maximises the way resources are used to reach this vision. The second invitation is to check whether this purpose and the way it has been defined allows the organization to thrive in the environment it now finds itself in. Part of this is to check if there is a focus on value creation in line with purpose over internal process? One example of an organizational vision that can be bad for internal innovation is a vision that is too narrow or restrictive.

For instance, if an organization's vision is focused solely on maintaining the status quo or on a very specific, narrow goal, it may stifle internal innovation by discouraging employees from thinking outside the box and exploring new ideas. It is these new ideas that often keep an organization moving forward and adapting to the ever-changing environment and therefore vital. Another outcome of a too narrow focus is that it encourages short term decision making over short-term gain. The narrower the scope of decisions and mission the less we are holistically viewing the organization as a whole and the potential impact of these decisions. Organizational debt build up is inevitable in narrow focus organizations which is inherently bad for the organizational capability to adapt and agilely transform in connection to shifts in the external environment. Therefore, defining an appropriate purpose for the challenges of this time is vital and seeing that a change done in one part of the organization not only impacts another part but can be strategically harnessed to increase effectiveness.

An organization needs a clear vision, strategy, strong leadership, skilled and motivated employees, a positive organizational culture, and effective communication to effectively reach its purpose. These are all end results and say nothing for how we achieve them. The meaning of effectiveness can go in many directions but for this text, effectiveness is specifically about the approach and structures we use to realise an organization's purpose. This is where an organization's operating system, organizational design and governance come in. If these 'structures' can be built to intrinsically adapt and holistically include human centric factors into the mix, we start to touch on a third invitation. Rather than design governance that will stagnate, we can infuse it with the wealth of knowledge on complex adaptive systems to make it the beating heart of an organization. Rather than seek a machinistic metaphorical control of people, empower them with an organizational design built for employees partnering with customers to create value. Rather than create an operating system built only on formality, build in a dual operating system that creates agility to move with the fast pace of change in these times. If we can frame an organization's purpose into a set of living breathing structures built to enhance people created value supported digitally created value, we would be able to step ahead of the current survival game and into the realm of future proofing.

Finally, all these provocations and invitations lead to mass organizational change. Both relying on organizational change capability to carry out a diagnosis as well as building change maturity by undergoing these transformations. It's clear that yesterday's organizational logic of people being 'units of production' no longer fits the visual need of organizations today tackling issues of high attrition and unsuitability of workforce to new types of work requirement. Where new employee and customer needs are driving the formation of a new logic, one that is human centric. Building change capability in our workforces is a part of this, and the benefit to organizations is both short term and cumulative to a strategic tipping point (Kanikani, 2023).

This chapter aims to dig deeper into the topic of building new logic into our concept of organizations, their purpose, structure, and approaches that is built so people can thrive and benefits each of the invitations expressed above can be fully realised.

For efficiency, several natural background additions have been placed in the Main focus of this chapter' section where they are brought into the chapter's main discussion.

MAIN FOCUS OF THE CHAPTER

Invitation 1: Defining a Fitting Definition of 'Organization'

Gareth Morgan's organizational metaphors give us an interesting foundation to work with, where organizations have been placed in different categories depending on the meaning of organization, the attitudes of leadership and the way change is approached (King et al., 2014). One of these metaphors is the 'Machines' metaphor which aptly enshrines the Taylorist idea that organizations can be designed and controlled. People are merely units of production that can be included in a planned and managed way (Taylor, 2006). Sound familiar? This is one of the oldest organizational approaches dating from the industrial era where many of these states were a reality at the time, even though there have been major shifts in the working environment, in one form or another this legacy still informs a lot of what we do today (Orwell, n.d.; Schmidt, n.d.).

Looking at the idea of corporate governance which stems from the basis laid out where politicians govern countries, the best practices then adapted for organizations, we haven't moved much further in this field either (Tohidian & Rahimian, n.d.; Millstein & MacAvoy, 2004). The management of change is also conceptually young and certainly not helped by this machinist metaphor where there seems to be an assumption of change being linear and therefore manageable. The first invitation is to seek a working definition or metaphor of 'Organization' which supports the complexity of our current situation, highlighting a need for agility when faced with change and a more holistic approach to organizations structured with human-centric approaches. Luckily Morgan gave us more metaphors to work with including the idea of organizations being an 'organism' promoting holistic open adaptive systems, a 'brain' metaphor where knowledge is the central driver and approach to change, with more that advocate for change capability and evolution in relation to external circumstances (Morgan, 2006). These metaphors are derived and developed by many other models including new additions to the original metaphors, new emerging organizational models with their own definitions of 'Organization' like Holacracy and Rijnlands (Örtenblad et al., 2016; Jones, 2007).

Figure 1. The metaphors, own depiction

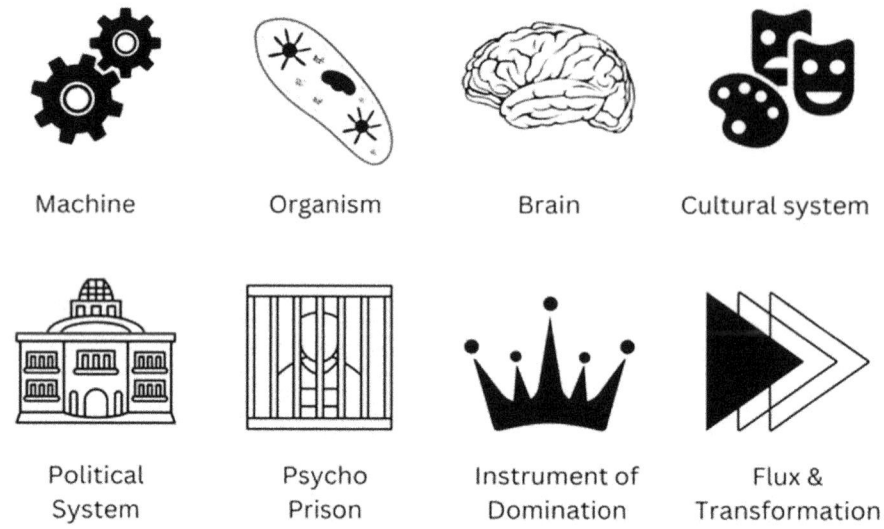

Machine   Organism   Brain   Cultural system

Political System   Psycho Prison   Instrument of Domination   Flux & Transformation

Systems theory and concept of organizations is thorough and focuses on the interconnectedness of parts or subsystems adapting which is a powerful image and one that lends itself to the goal of diagnosing organizations (Sterman, 2010; Skyttner, 2006; Brown, 2012). Particularly as it doesn't prescribe structures or organizational forms, simply that everything is connected. Within systems theory there is an interesting model or concept of 'organization'. An organization is defined as a complex system that is made up of interdependent and interconnected parts or subsystems. These subsystems can include people, processes, resources, technologies, and other elements that are essential for the organization to function effectively (Senge, 2006). McKinsey's 7S model and method also promotes this same interconnectedness of organizational elements (McKinsey, 2008). This interconnectedness could also be described as the governance, operating system and organizational design that enables these constituent parts to fully function. It could also be the flow of information, the realisation of value from processes or the formal and informal relationships that drive the people's side of a company. Often structure becomes stagnant and rigid stopping the very outcomes it was put in place to achieve. When focusing on structure we can frame organizational health as an agile framework that supports change rather than the unhealthy rigid and outdated structures often in place. When focusing on the people element, community Genogram mapping and conventional stakeholder analysis can be a great method for diagnosing the interconnectedness of different organizational stakeholders to support more effective and long-lasting change (Rigazio-DiGilio et al., 2005).

There are also a great many maturity models that both assess a particular factor's maturity and through this changeability. An example would be the CMMI maturity model for process maturity and IT-CMF for IT capability maturity (Van Haren Publishing, 2017; Konrad et al., 2003). There are various assessments associated with each of the models and approaches that could be drawn into an organizational health diagnosis.

Viewing organizations as open systems, meaning that they are constantly interacting with their environment and exchanging information and resources is interesting because this could imply a state of continual flux, where organization impacts its environment and environment impacts the organization. This seems to be a more holistic view of how an organization actually functions rather than the traditional organizational island where everything can be measured and controlled and would suggest a great deal of agility is needed to survive. The logical next question would be whether organizations have this agility, particularly if their internal formal structure is hierarchical, siloed, or bureaucratic in nature.

Many of the movements in Lean manufacturing have taken this systemic approach and refined it to an art, an example would be the way suppliers become part of a tightly interconnected system where good operations means increased benefit for all partners involved (Womack et al., 2007; Johnson, 2020). Viewing an organization with its interconnected network of partners as connected open systems emphasises the need for efficient flow of value, through an organization and through multiple organizations reaching some kind of end conclusion or conclusions that would naturally be customers. No flow suggests a culture of focusing on activity rather than value and outcomes are lost in the process of doing. Finding a way to measure this flow would also be a very interesting factor for organizational health diagnosis. Finding an approach to measuring external influences in relation to a single organization will help to home in on a more detailed analysis of organizational health. Francis Aquilar's PESTLE (E) method is a very useful tool for the diagnosis of external factors and would relate very well to the internal diagnosis we are trying to build here.

Figure 2. Systems theory, own depiction

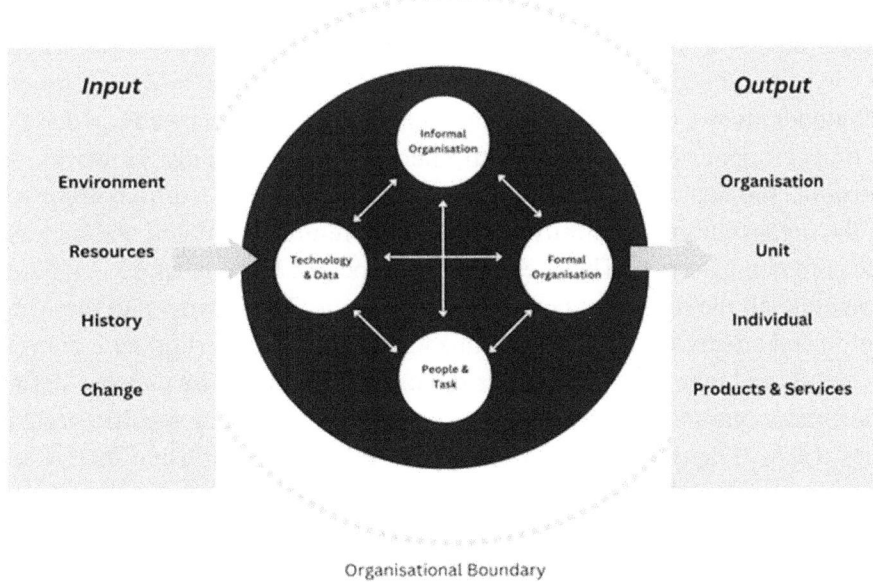

Furthermore, systems theory recognizes that organizations are dynamic and constantly evolving, as they respond to changes in their environment and adapt to new circumstances. The level of capability of people to change and their relationship to inherent organizational culture is a major factor affecting the ability to adapt (Hanson, 1995; DeSchoolmeester, 2014). This evolution can be seen in the way that organizations change over time via formal and informal networks. For example, by introducing new products or services, expanding into new markets, or changing their internal processes (Mella, 2018). By understanding the organization as a complex system, systems theory provides a useful framework for analysing and improving organizational performance by identifying areas of weakness or inefficiency and developing strategies to address them. What is particularly interesting is the adaptive nature, implying that organizations are more than the sum of their parts, they change and sometimes beyond what could be imagined if we were solely focusing on their structural design and governance or their interconnected capability with partners. Agile organizations will organically adapt significantly more than those where governance is left to decompose, leaving an interesting question around whether this adaptation can be shaped for good and in doing so create strategic advantage over other organizations with stagnated still standing systems.

There are quite several ways to classify organizations, and a good number of models, theories, and approaches to boot. Everything from informal versus the formal relationships within organizations, to the actual structural design (tackled in the next section), the way of monitoring achievement of purpose or tall versus flat relating to the amount of hierarchy and bureaucracy that might exist. The definition of an organization could be defined by its structure, but the suggestion is to relate it to the desired purpose including influencing factors of external environment, the degree of interconnectedness and the approach to value creation, all of which carried out by people and technology. By creating the definition of organization first, we can tune into our environment and the context within which our entity will establish itself.

Invitation 2: Defining a Fitting Purpose

Organizational purpose can be expressed in different ways taking the form of a vision statement, BHAG or Big Scary Audacious Goal, communicated values amongst others. The Golden Circle that includes establishing the why, how, and what of an organizations purpose is a great tool for getting started (Sinek, 2011). Other techniques involve defining core values that if well communicated can drive deep meaningful connections on key organizational topics both internally and externally. However, we come to the definition of 'purpose', the important message here is that the purpose needs to both fit with the modern era and support the organization to healthily move into the future. Too dated and the organization will struggle with the common external influences of today's society. If the purpose is too undefined, organizations risk spending all the resources before attaining goals. Too narrow and there can be a closing down of innovation and creativity within an organizations culture. Too rigid and an organization can't shift as markets, trends and other external factors require it to change. The purpose definition takes the 'organization' definition one step further in detail, narrowing down to a specific organization and set of goals or values that will be the drivers for the further efforts to establish effective structuring with operating models, organizational design, and governance. The invitation that arises when creating organizational purpose is built in establishing a clarity of focus, with a scope that can be shifted in relation to the need an organization might come across when dealing with certain external factors.

So, what would be a good purpose? This warrants a thought out internal and research, if needed adaptability. The Golden Circle offers a simple but poignant tool here. Researching what and why of an organizations purpose and asking what intrinsic value the organization brings to Society. Testing this with a whole host of potential scenarios where external factors could render it useless, needing improvement or strong enough to withstand most onslaughts. Finding the right balance between stability where an organizations infrastructure can be built on it, but agile enough that a purpose's scope can be broadened or tightened according to need. The How of purpose needs to be built for this agility, coming in the form of the way people and organizational structure are both formed and built for a high level of change maturity.

Figure 3. Golden circle own depiction

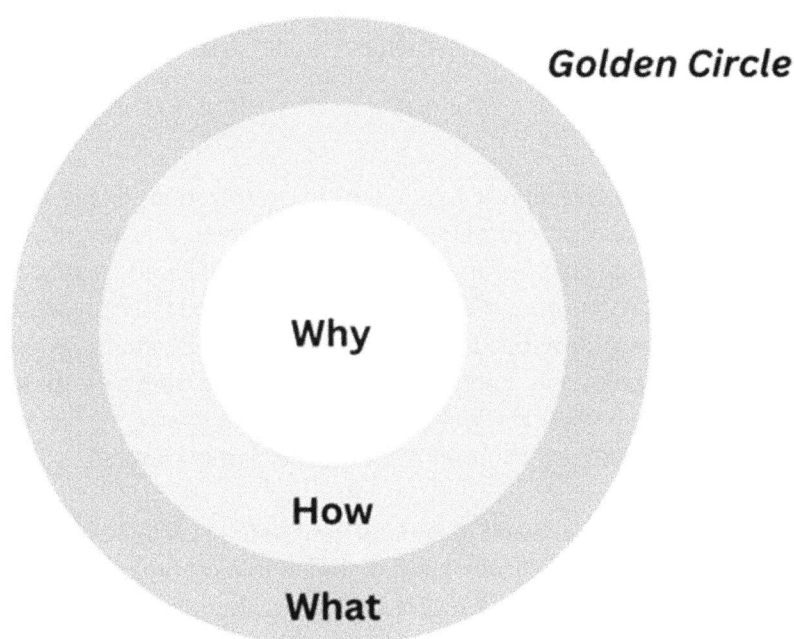

Invitation 3: Defining Effective Structures and Approach

The different views of designing, governing and operating organizations often get confused and their intrinsic value can be truly realised when installed structure is maintained and constantly improved. Getting strategies and structures right for the conditions, and successfully matching strategies and structures with each other are crucial. The company will also need to the process of change to established structures for them to remain relevant (Mansfield, 1986). Before going into the types of structure and the potential to diagnose, it is useful to first establish what they are.

A working definition of corporate governance is 'Governance refers to the system of rules, practices, and processes by which an organization is directed and controlled to achieve its purpose, ensure accountability, and manage risks (Kraakman et al., 2017; Gunay, 2008). It encompasses the relationships among stakeholders and the mechanisms for decision-making, monitoring, and performance management (Development & OECD, 2012; Financial Training, 2017). A definition for Organizational design is the process of creating and implementing structures, systems, and processes that align an organization's resources and activities with its strategic goals and objectives. It involves determining the most effective way to organise people, tasks, and technologies to achieve optimal performance and adapt to changing conditions. Governance focuses on the decision-making structures and processes that determine how an organization is managed and controlled, while organizational design focuses on the structural and operational elements of the organization itself. As one can see, there is a lot of overlap in the factors involved but the intent of governance is inherently different to that of organizational design, and both complement each other if well structured around purpose leading to an invitation to check alignment and suitability of these two factors. Furthermore, the choice in type governance approach and organizational design will certainly impact the way purpose is achieved if it is achieved. Bringing more angles and potential questions to check. Is the approach to corporate governance fit for purpose? For example, will our present organizational design help us achieve strategic business outcomes defined by purpose?

Corporate Governance

Corporate governance plays a critical role in diagnosing organizations because it affects the company's overall health and performance. Corporate governance is concerned with how the company's management interacts with its shareholders, board of directors, and other stakeholders, and how it makes decisions and sets policies to achieve its purpose (De Kluyver, 2013). To date, the approach to governing organizations is often stoic and underdeveloped in the sense that there is often a search to rigidify structures to be able to effectively monitor and 'control'. This is no longer fitting for these times where we need to increase the data driven aspects of the business while providing an agile framework to move with the insights from this data. Technology can offer much of this agility through automation and centralising of data sources into one source.

The OECD has both an approach and method of assessing the implementation of Key Principles of Corporate governance, many of which aren't solidly found in most organizations (OECD., 2017). There are approaches available that are almost too radical to fit the more traditional cultures of operating governance, like outsourcing boards to external service providers who can offer cost savings, expertise, and improve the quality of governance by introducing new ideas into the mix (Bainbridge & Henderson, 2018). Digitising corporate governance gives the possibility of integrating information and management systems, combining with global compliance standards like ISO 9001 and ISO 27001 to name a couple (Jensen, 2016). Realisation that by measuring some aspects of organizational health we adversely affect other areas and measures (Scott, 1987). The nature of governance means structures that need to be maintained or become outdated. What if there is so much change taking place through a myriad number of daily decisions and interactions based on our companies being open systems that corporate governance doesn't have a chance to keep up. Unlike maybe 50 years ago, it's now always out of date. Systems that were once most probably well designed and elegant require a great deal of investment to keep maintained while offering little value to the organizations profit footprint. Organizational debt in all its forms is on the rise, increasing hand in hand with the amount of change organizations need to address. By digitalising governance with an appropriately agile technology framework, we move it from outdated to a continually updating beating heart of the organization (Stafford & Schindlinger, 2019). Add in strategic outcomes to the digital framework, and you have a vehicle that will achieve organizational purpose both now and into the future (Ajogwu & King, 2020).

By creating a comprehensive list of potential approaches and methods to realizing corporate governance we could start to test whether an organization's governance approach is fit for purpose. Surely a key indicating factor of health, likewise if we can measure something we are incapable of truly assessing its capability. The same would be true of Governance. Building change capability within governance systems in the form of continuous improvement and where needed new fitting approaches drives down organization debt by creating governance as an oscillating platform and beating heart of the organization (Jaffee, 2000).

Organizational Design

The trends around designing an organization's structure have taken some quite significant steps since the early 1900s and have given rise to structures that are defined by different desired outcomes as well as organizational purpose. An example of this could be everything from change agility to monitoring and control or collaboration and silo elimination. To give some structure we will use an approach formed by Elliot Jacuqes who broke down organizational design and management of it into three organizational views. The formal view emphasises the importance of formal structure and procedures, the extant view focuses on informal relationships and network, and the requisite view proposes a structure that is aligned with the complexity of the work being performed (Jaques, 1997). Each of the most common forms of organizational design usually emphasise one or two of these views more strongly and sometimes only one. The three views themselves give a basic framework we could use to diagnose the suitability of organizational design and whether it's fit to achieve its purpose.

Starting with Scientific Management, an approach to organizational design, popularised by Frederick Winslow Taylor, that emphasised the use of data and analysis to optimise workflows and processes for greater efficiency. Then came the Bureaucratic organization approaches that were pioneered by Max Weber and focused on the use of formalised rules and hierarchies to manage complex organizations. Both the Scientific management and Bureaucratic approaches informed the basic understanding of corporate governance which was installed to strategically govern these organization types and some of the older organizations maintaining these organizational designs are often struggling to remain agile in these times of mass change.

The Human Relations Movement dating roughly from the mid-1900's emphasised the importance of social and cultural factors in organizational design and highlighted the need for communication and collaboration within organizations. The movement gained traction in direct response to the limitations of the previous approaches. Proponents of the human relations movement believed that organizations could improve productivity and morale by creating a more supportive and participative work environment. They argued that employee satisfaction and engagement were critical factors in organizational success and that organizations should prioritise the development of interpersonal relationships and communication channels between management and employees (Smedley et al., 2017). One study, published in the Journal of Change Management, found that effective communication is critical in managing change and maintaining a sense of organizational purpose (Hughes & Brennan, n.d.). The study found that organizations that communicated openly and transparently about the changes were more likely to maintain employee commitment and motivation, even in the face of significant change. Making this an interesting organizational design model if one is intending to build change maturity.

The Matrix Organizations (1960s to 1980s) approach to organizational design emphasised the importance of cross-functional collaboration and involved the creation of project teams that cut across traditional functional boundaries. Some of the learning from the Human Relations movement around communication efficiency can counteract that natural need for this capability within Matrix organizations due to the overlap between project and function. The matrix structure brings many advantages though including enhanced collaboration, elimination of silo's, better resource allocation to name a few.

Figure 4. Comparing a mechanistic and organic organizational design

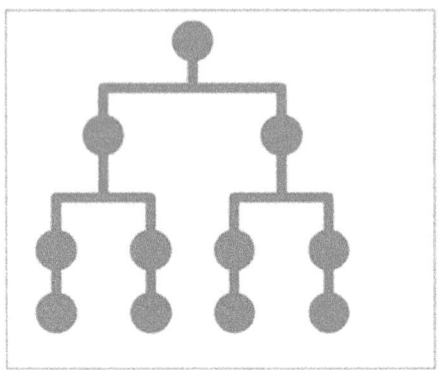 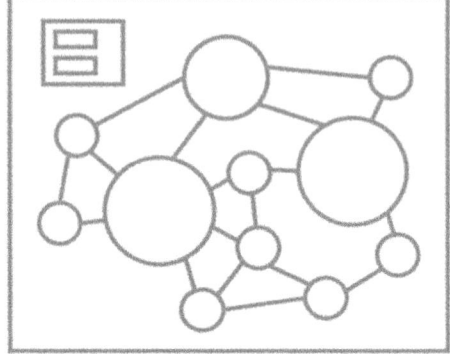

Mechinist Organisation design   Organic Organisation design

Lean Organizations (1980s to present) popularised by Toyota, emphasises the importance of continuous improvement, waste reduction, and the involvement of frontline workers in decision-making. With the development of stronger partnerships in relation to the operational efficiency created by Just in Time manufacturing methods, the line between one organization and its partners starts to become much more blurry than traditional designs. This might not go to the extent of Jack Welch's boundaryless organization concept (Welch & Byrne, 2003; Ulrich et al., 1995,), where Welch advocates for breaking down internal barriers and silo's moving toward an agile, collaborative, and innovative way to do business.

Agile Organizations (2000s to present) emphasises the importance of flexibility and adaptability in organizational design, and involves the use of cross-functional teams, rapid iteration, and customer feedback to drive innovation. The difference between Agile and agile is good to name here, the main difference between them being that agile is about the state of being agile in an organizational context and the Agile method which is an iterative approach to software development and project management with articulated principles, values, methods, roles, processes, and tools. In terms of Agile organizational design, it is suggested to focus on the agility of organizational design and approach where Agile methodology can be used but is not essential. There are many techniques that can be used to create an agile organization with a customer focus, decentralised decision making and continuous improvement and learning being key aspects.

Figure 5. Holacratic organizational design

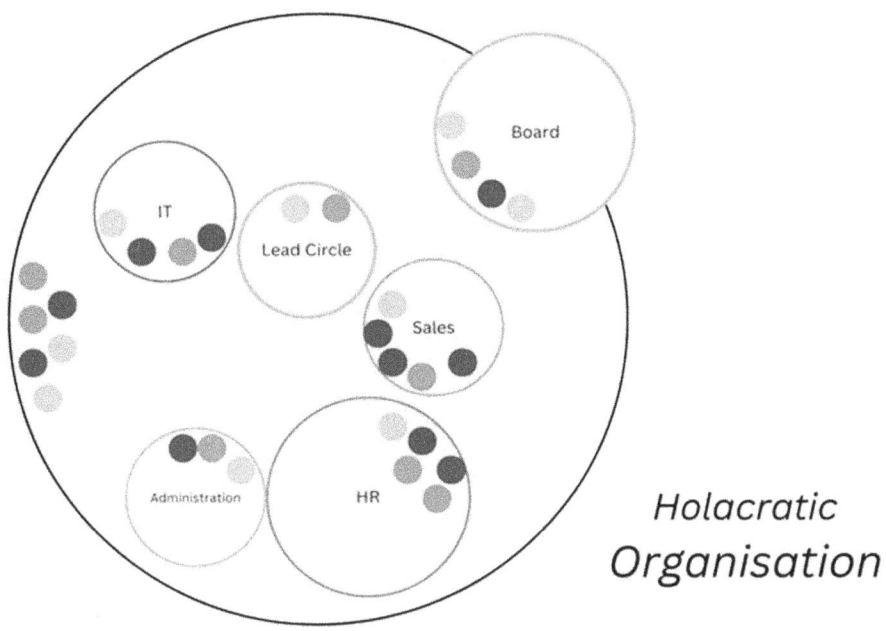

The Holacratic Organizations established in 2010 by Brian Robertson has an approach that involves the elimination of traditional hierarchies and the adoption of a more fluid, decentralised approach to decision-making and governance. This way of organising has deep seated roots in systems theory using the idea of a 'holon' a whole that is part of a whole and holarchy as the connection between holons coined in 1967 by Arthur Koestler (Koestler, 2015) The formal aspects including the organization chart and job descriptions are fluidly developed in relation to those working on the job rather than remaining static structures that soon become irrelevant. Unlike more traditional organization designs, Holacracy keeps redefining how work gets done daily to improve and move with the needs of the organization (Robertson, 2016).

The Rijnland model of design and key principles is very similar to Holacratic ones, but with the key focus on stakeholder and informal social view aspects of organising (Peters & Weggeman, 2019). Rijnlands organizations place a high value on trust, both within the organization and with external stakeholders. With a long-term view, emphasising the importance of sustainable growth and development over short-term profits. They believe that a healthy organization is one that can adapt and evolve over time, rather than one that is focused solely on maximising profits in the short term. Trust is essential for building strong relationships and achieving shared goals. A high value is placed on participation and collaboration, both within the organization and with external stakeholders. They believe that a participative approach is essential for building strong relationships and achieving shared goals. Some would say this is still very theoretical and somewhat ideological since the focus on people with less formal structure tends to lead to loss of dynamic movement in realising organizational purpose. There are however some successful examples of organizations who have implemented this organizational design and it's good to keep in mind that each of the designs presented here have their strengths and weaknesses. The Rijnlands model is interesting for its emphasis on people and distinctive outcomes due to decentralisation with a systemic approach.

Figure 6. Helix organizational structures

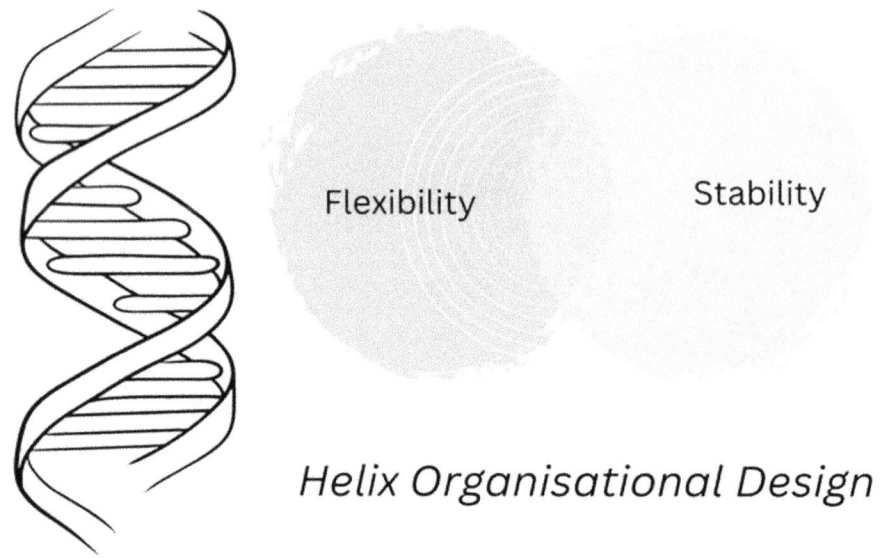

A helix organization is a type of organizational design that combines elements of both hierarchy and network structures. These organizations are designed to be dynamic and flexible, able to adapt quickly to changing market conditions and customer needs (Hamel & Zanini, 2020). To achieve this, helix organizations typically have a flat hierarchy, with fewer layers of management than traditional hierarchical organizations. This allows for faster decision-making and greater employee empowerment. Cross-functional teams are also used to bring together employees with diverse skills and perspectives to work on specific projects or initiatives (Moree & Minnaar, 2020). Agile project management methodologies are often employed to allow for iterative development, frequent feedback, and continuous improvement. Helix organizations also place a high value on innovation, encouraging employees to experiment and take risks to develop new products, services, and processes. Using a networked structure that enables decentralized decision-making and collaboration across different functional areas, promoting knowledge-sharing and collaboration. Considerations for dual system of operating where network meets hierarchical can be interesting within this organizational type by providing a legitimising structure to the extant view (Kotter, 2014). The dual operating system model allows organizations to balance the need for stability and efficiency with the need for innovation and growth. It allows them to maintain their core business operations while also exploring new opportunities and experimenting with new ideas. This model can help organizations to adapt to changing market conditions, stay ahead of competitors, and drive long-term growth (Christensen, 2016). Overall, the helix organization concept highlights the need for organizations to be both hierarchical and networked to thrive in today's rapidly changing business environment (Dignan, 2019; Gray, 2016).

Figure 7. Network organizational design

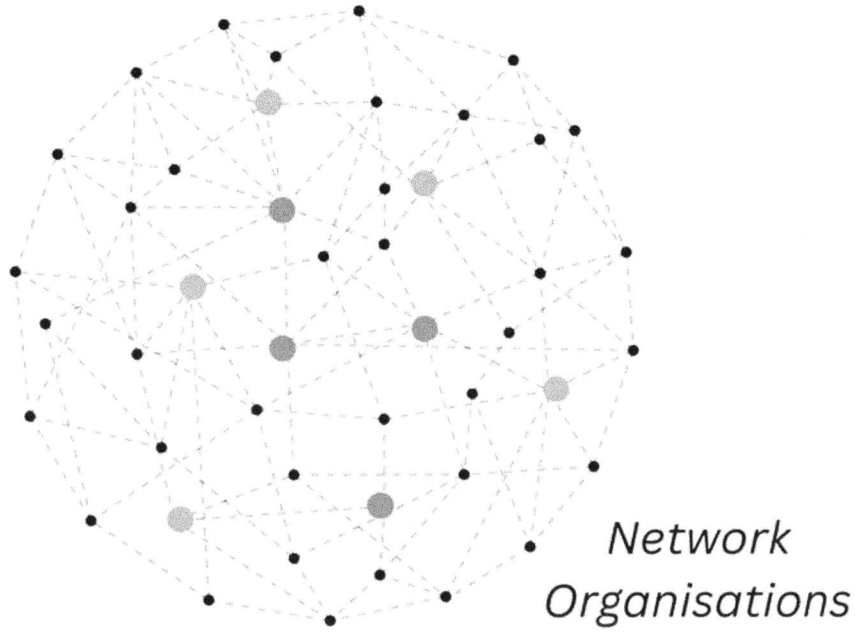

Network Organisations

A network organization is a type of organizational design that emphasises flexibility, collaboration, and innovation through a decentralised structure (Peters & Frisart, 2000). In a network organization, communication and decision-making occur through a web of interconnected nodes rather than a traditional hierarchy. This essentially creates a small world network within the organization, where individuals are connected through a relatively small number of intermediaries. This means that communication and collaboration can occur quickly and efficiently, even among individuals who are not directly connected. The small world theory also emphasises the importance of "hubs" within the network. These are individuals or nodes that have many connections to other nodes. In a network organization, these hubs can play an important role in facilitating communication and collaboration across the organization. Promoting interconnectivity and relationship, flow of information and an adaptable structure that can quickly respond to shifts in the external environment. The Small world theory adds an interesting addition to this organizational structure (Buchanan, 2003). We can think of an organization as a small world network or take the bigger picture where an organization is part of an open system and therefore more like a major hub in the scene of things. Whichever scope is taken, there are intrinsic networked structures to the world economy which inherently influences all organizations as intrinsic parts (Loudon, 2001).

While a network organizational design has a specific target, there is also something interesting that we can borrow for any organization when looking to diagnose. Mapping an organizations network either formal or informal, including the nodes, flows of information and important hubs gives the potential to analyse on a much more profound level through 3D visualisation. Fuel this with real time data we can start to track progress and any significant shifts that would need to be quickly dealt with. It becomes very clear if there are silo's that exist, or where succession planning should be considered due to the importance of a particular hub for the organization. We can track value streams and interdepartmental process flows to see where bottlenecks and organizational debt slows down progress. Bring in the Holacratic fluidity around job roles innovation and we build in a way to respond to such visualisations. Community Genogram approach to mapping the formal and informal network views also lends itself to understanding not only the formal organization chart but the extant or informal (the way things are done state), and through this establishing a diagnosis of the ás is' state to connect this with the requisite 'wants to be' and 'to be' states. We are in a time where diagnosis and solutioning steps can be rapidly carried out if the organizations design, governance, technological capability, and data handling processes are in order. Holistically viewing and assessing the organization in terms of the formal, extant, and requisite gives us a diagnosis model with built in vision of what's to come and how we can practically and strategically take ourselves there.

Operating Models and Systems

An organizational operating model is the framework that defines how an organization operates and delivers value to its stakeholders. It includes the organization's strategy, structure, processes, technologies, and capabilities, as well as the ways in which these elements are aligned to deliver on the organization's goals and objectives. The operating model describes how an organization's resources and activities are structured and managed to achieve its strategic objectives and is a key element of the organization's overall design. An operating system in an organizational context refers to the set of processes, procedures, and workflows that an organization uses to execute its day-to-day operations. It includes the tools, technologies, and systems that are used to manage and coordinate tasks and is focused on the efficiency and effectiveness of the organization's operations.

An operating system is the engine that powers an organization's day-to-day activities and enables it to achieve its strategic goals and objectives. In simple terms, corporate governance is concerned with the "what" and "why" of the organization, organizational design is concerned with the process of structuring, aligning its resources and activities with its strategic goals and objectives, and the operating system is concerned with the "how" daily. There are a couple of invitations with the choice of operating system and approach.

The first is simply to check for alignment with the organizational purpose and whether the daily operations are and remain aligned with the key business outcomes that need to be realised. The second is to consider new ways of organising operations like the dual operating system approach that allows the balance between stability and innovation within the design. A dual operating system is an organizational design that combines two different structures or systems of management within a single organization. The first system is the traditional, hierarchical system, which is responsible for maintaining stability, enforcing rules, and ensuring efficiency in day-to-day operations. The second system is a more flexible, adaptive, and innovative system that is designed to explore new opportunities, experiment with new products or services, and create new business models. These factors could be shifted to other key attributes and therefore a new approach to operating could well be relevant and a worthwhile exploration.

Figure 8. Dual operating system

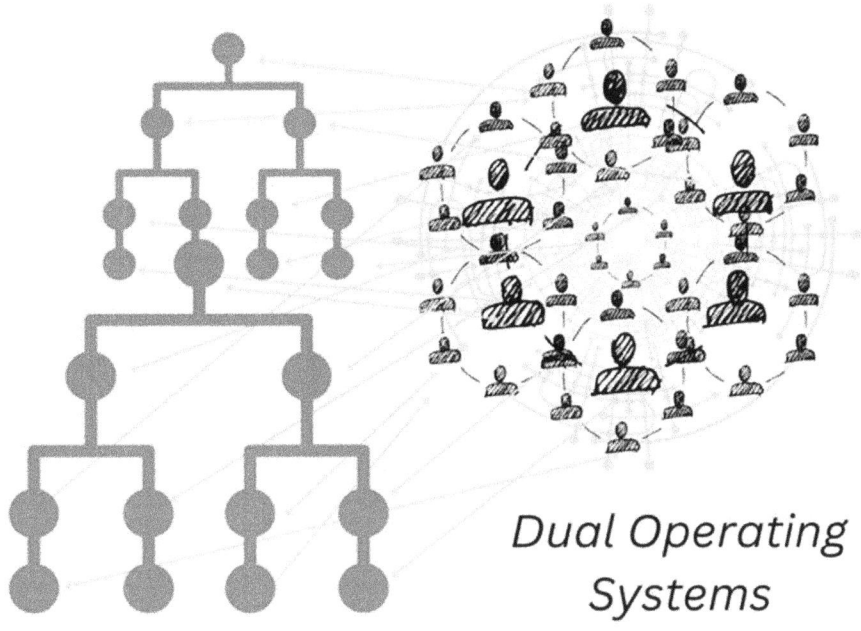

Dual Operating
Systems

Invitation 4: Defining Human Centric in Relation to Structure and Value Creation

There is a common misconception that creativity and innovation thrive in a completely unstructured environment. The same with the capability to change and the change maturity that organizations can build up over time, this isn't without structure and in fact change need's structure to thrive (Rogers, 2003). Unstructured change is chaotic and in its own way can form a barrier to people realising their true potential in organizations. Mass and unprecedented change impacts motivation, often letting our neurological survival mechanism kick in devoiding any thought of organization and governance of purpose. So, there is such a thing as positive structures that can support the creation of more than the simple parts, opening up the possibility of maximising value creation in an organised and specific way.

Research has shown that people need boundaries to become creative and innovate in organizations (Karan Girotra, 2018; Pirson & Gazella, n.d.). Boundaries can provide a framework for creativity and innovation by giving people clear parameters within which to operate. These boundaries can include time constraints, resource limitations, and specific goals or objectives. When people are given clear boundaries, they are forced to think more critically and creatively within those constraints, which can lead to more innovative solutions (Amabile et al., n.d.). In addition, boundaries can help to focus creativity and innovation efforts. Without clear boundaries, people may become overwhelmed with the number of possibilities available to them and may struggle to identify the best path forward (Rice & Galbraith, 2008). By providing boundaries, organizations can help to channel creativity and innovation efforts in a more focused and productive way. Of course, it's important to note that the boundaries provided should not be too restrictive or confining. One invitation could be to define what structure constitutes good boundaries and what potentially negatively impacts people in organizations. With this we hit on some of the big topics of our time with everything from how to stop attrition, how to evolve work forces of the future plugging the skills gap and how to bring about the ultimate collaboration of human and machine. Besides this you have the much-studied organizational behaviour

'When nobody is willing to take responsibility, decision making becomes slow and the organization becomes inflexible, that is, unable to change and adapt quickly to new developments' (Jones, 2007). This sentiment strongly makes a case for clear governance with defined roles and responsibilities. Whether or not this is the traditional hierarchical design with a high degree of formality or one of the other designs mentioned here, would probably depend on the organizational purpose and desired approach. Human beings have an innate inner drive to be autonomous, self-determined, and connected to one another (Pink, 2022). Give them responsibility and they are more driven than if given freedom or the other extreme controls if basic hygiene factors are catered for (Herzberg, 2008). So, motivating and hygiene factors along with clarity of role and amount of responsibility could be measured as part of any organizational diagnosis. In the end, happy people equal a higher chance of happy organization.

Invitation 5: Change Maturity Building

Building change maturity in organizations is essential for fostering a healthy and thriving environment for both the organizational structure and its people. It's good to be clear that there are two types of maturity often confused. Change Maturity which is the ability in this case for the organization to change and Change Management Maturity which is referring to how developed the Change Management practice is (Kanikani, n.d.). Both are important when assessing organizational health, but organizational change maturity is far further reaching. By building change maturity, organizations can create a culture of continuous improvement, where change is embraced as a necessary and positive aspect of organizational life. This can lead to improved performance, increased innovation, and greater employee engagement and satisfaction, ultimately resulting in a more resilient and successful organization. It's the vital cog in the machine of People and Structure where technology and data are becoming ever increasingly important factors (Graaf et al., 2013). Change maturity and the building thereof relies greatly on the core disciplines that make an organization what it is (Howe, 2014). This can be project management maturity in organizations that rely on projects, data maturity, operational maturity, quality management maturity to name a few. The sixth invitation is about measuring these disciplines' maturity as a vehicle of change and the capability of the organization to go about this change. This is because the natural turbulence of open organizational systems means we can't ever really know what's coming and some external environmental factors are out of our control (Viscio et al., 1999).

Figure 9. Diagnosing organizational change maturity

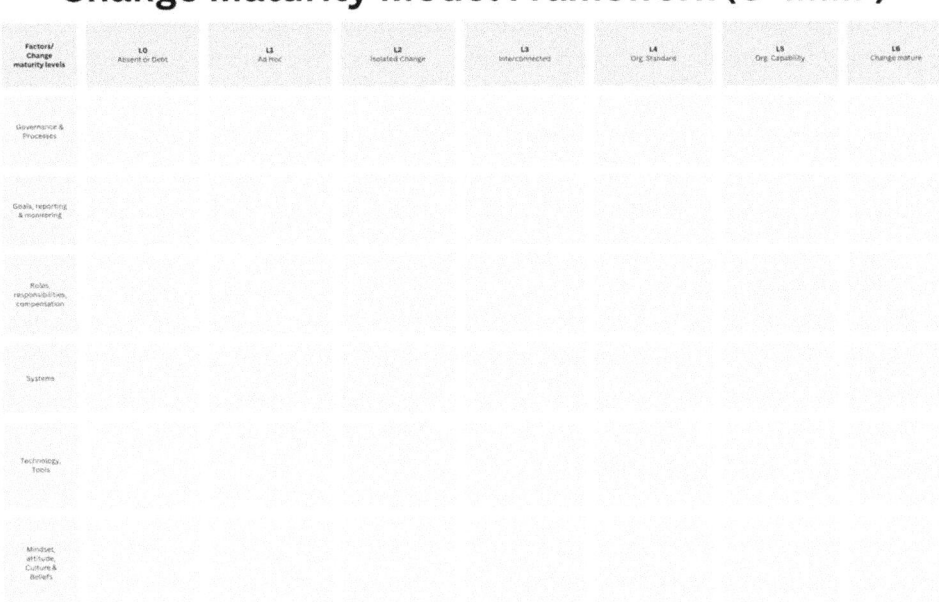

Change Maturity Model Framework (C+MMF)

Invitation 6: Already Existing Approaches to Diagnosing Organizations

Within this chapter we seek to explore additional ways of diagnosing organizations and pushing the boat out by linking further approaches and methods, however it is important to name existing approaches of diagnosis as they form a substantial body of best practice used to assess an organization's strengths, weaknesses, and overall health. These approaches provide insights into the organization's structure, culture, leadership, and performance, which can help identify areas for improvement and guide strategic decision-making.

One approach is the cultural diagnosis, which focuses on understanding an organization's culture and how it influences behaviour, decision-making, and performance. This approach involves analysing the organization's values, beliefs, assumptions, and norms, and how they shape the organization's interactions with its stakeholders. The OCIA instrument and Competing Values Framework (CVF) by Robert Quinn and Kim Cameron, and the Cultural web by Johnson and Scholes along with Cultural mapping techniques developed by Erin Meyer are just a few of the many cultural diagnosis tools available. Tichy's technical political cultural (TPC) framework also brings interesting and practical applications.

Another approach is the structural diagnosis, which focuses on understanding the organization's formal and informal structures and how they affect performance. This approach involves analysing the organization's hierarchy, departments, processes, and workflows, and how they facilitate or hinder communication, coordination, and decision-making. Structural diagnosis can be done through process mapping, organizational charts, and stakeholder interviews. Examples include McKinsey's 7S model, Galbraiths star and the Organizational Structure Assessment tool (OSAT) are intriguing tools available.

A third approach is the strategic diagnosis, which focuses on understanding the organization's competitive environment, market position, and strategic goals. This approach involves analysing the organization's strengths, weaknesses, opportunities, and threats, and how they relate to the organization's mission, vision, and objectives. Strategic diagnosis can be done through market research, SWOT analysis, and stakeholder interviews. Others include Porter's Five forces, PESTLE(E), the balanced scorecard and the congruence models.

Finally, a systems diagnosis approach focuses on understanding the organization as a complex system made up of interconnected parts. This approach involves analysing how different elements of the organization, such as its culture, structure, and strategy, interact with each other to produce outcomes. Systems diagnosis can be done through Value stream mapping, business process modelling and root causes analysis are fine examples.

Overall, each of these approaches provides a unique perspective on the organization and its performance. Depending on the organization's needs and goals, one or more of these approaches may be used to diagnose and address any issues that may be impacting the organization's effectiveness and success.

Multiple Contingencies Framework

The multiple contingencies framework is a management theory that suggests that effective organizational practices depend on multiple factors, or contingencies, that interact with each other. According to this framework, there is no one-size-fits-all solution for managing organizations, and the best practices depend on the unique circumstances of each organization. The multiple contingencies framework considers various internal and external factors that affect organizational performance, including the organization's size, technology, strategy, culture, environment, and leadership. The multiple contingencies framework is a mapped out set of design parameters including organization configuration, specialisation, decision authority, information processing, coordination, control, and incentives. This is an established approach to diagnosing organizations that crosses the traditional borders of organization design and governance, offering a sound approach to diagnosing how an organization can become more efficient and effective (Burton & Obel, 2004).

Figure 10. Multiple contingency framework

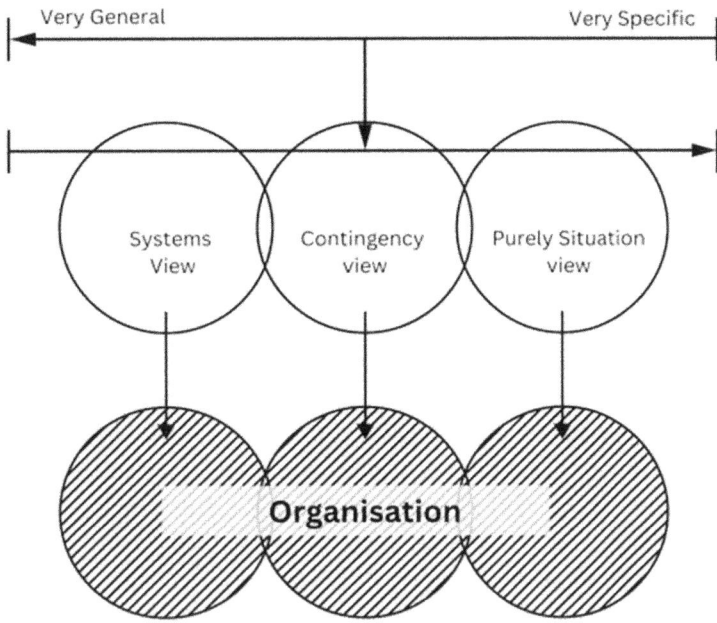

The framework proposes that the most effective organizational practices are those that fit the specific contingencies of the organization. For example, a small startup company with a flat organizational structure may benefit from a different management approach than a large multinational corporation with a complex hierarchy. Similarly, a company operating in a highly regulated industry may need to adopt different practices than one in a more flexible market.

The multiple contingencies framework suggests that managers should evaluate the various contingencies that affect their organization and adjust their practices accordingly (Amhalhal et al., 2021). By understanding the unique challenges and opportunities of their organization, managers can make informed decisions about strategy, structure, leadership, and other key aspects of management. The framework also emphasises the importance of flexibility and adaptability, as organizations may need to adjust their practices over time as their contingencies change.

Overall, the multiple contingencies framework provides a useful tool for managers to evaluate their organization's needs and design effective practices that align with its unique circumstances. By taking a contingency-based approach to management, managers can improve organizational performance and adapt to changing environments and challenges. A Known organizational diagnosis framework that fits with the concept of organizations being open adaptive systems, creating a firm foundation for how we visualise an organization and how we might choose to diagnose it. There is a myriad of tools for diagnosing organizations available and it's important to know what it is you are wanting to find out before beginning any diagnosis so one can choose the right tools for the job.

SOLUTIONS AND RECOMMENDATIONS

Everything is vague to a degree you do not realise till you have tried to make it precise. (Elkind & Landini, 2018). This phrase by Elkind and Landini sums up the very real reason to diagnose an organization and at the same time the starting point for many who begin assessing and realise what they didn't know was staring them in the face. It takes a formulated structured approach to then easily unearth basic information that can inform decisions and help organizations tackle problems before they get so big that they ask for a huge investment, or worse become part of the organizational debt creep that can so easily happen in unaware organizations. The simple act of starting to assess is already a giant step, and a necessary one if we are to truly understand our organizations enough to make further steps and explore some of the invitations held in this text. Measuring and questioning whether we measure the right things is the key to unlocking the way to a healthy organization.

With measurement comes information and with information often comes choices. Simply following blindly, the way it's always been done leaves us with very little to work with in terms of information and a lot to navigate in the unknown. Measuring allows us to create choices about the best step, or the right organizational design to strategically achieve our organization's purpose. Questioning what we measure and how it's defined already opens a huge area for innovation. One person's organization definition is another's structure gone wrong. Definitions and alignment with key stakeholders are key to a united effort toward realising purpose, organizational definition and design fit.

Organizational structures such as governance, operating systems and organizational design were explored in this chapter but only representative of the many types of structures we find in organizations. If these structures can be made to enable purpose while being more framework-like in nature that support continuous flex they can become the beating heart of any organization, particularly if technology and data collection is enabled to truly optimise and automate where appropriate. Besides this working with the realisation that static structure is old the moment it's established, and we need to build in the change maturity and capability to keep the parts moving. We also need the real time updating and centralised approach to data management in organizations to that technology enables. Organizations experiencing mass change often build up organizational and technical debt by simply making the necessary choices to survive events, the trick is to clean the wreckage up before we need to invest to simply maintain. Value chains and processes are natural structures of both change and flow that systematically link all parts of the organization if appropriately designed and maintained.

All these organizational structures are closely linked to the people who create, maintain and work within them. If well setup, processes and technology are easily updatable but when it comes to people, we need to take a closer look. People are an organization constant. What motivates them, makes them successful at value creation, that keeps them from leaving are also constants. But what is less known and mature is our knowledge of mass change that organizations need for survival in these times and how capable people are to work within the context of organizations meeting this change need. Building change maturity and other people motivators into the fabric of our organizations and the way they operate is key to supporting a healthy organization. But there is a very real chance this might not be enough if the extent of the change we need to manage keeps increasing to the degree we have seen in the last few years. So besides organizational health seen through the lens of structure and people, we need to build a lot more knowledge and best practice around building change maturity in organizations and the way we support people stay productive with mass change.

FUTURE RESEARCH DIRECTIONS

The furtherance of this work will be to naturally investigate the same topic to a much deeper level. With the aim of really looking at how key theories and best practices around Systems theory, multiple contingency frameworks, change maturity framework and open adaptive systems truly overlap and at the same time enable flow across organizations.

CONCLUSION

Diagnosing organizations is critical to realising long term strategic purpose fulfilment and health. Questioning the very definition of factors, we seek to measure will enable a far more profound development of both structure and how this facilitates an organizations people to create value. By understanding organizations as open systems that need to embrace their environments, competitors and partners in order to best serve both their employees and their customers. Understanding that no organization is the same although they might have recognisable attributes or factors is key enabling a multiple contingency understanding that can lead to aspirational new levels of approach to organizations and organising purpose. Building change maturity into will ensure that structures maintain vigour and are able to move with the demand of the times, which equals an increasing amount of change. Finally, embracing the powerful combination of all types of change whether its change as projects or change in the form of continuous improvement. Using this along with our understanding of the factors of diagnosis we harness the true power of systems thinking.

REFERENCES

Ajogwu, F., & King, M. (2020). *Outcomes-Based Governance: A Modern Approach to Corporate Governance*. Juta Limited.

Amabile, T., Conti, R., & Amabile, T. M. (n.d.). *Changes in the Work Environment for Creativity during Downsizing - Article - Faculty & Research*. Harvard Business School. https://www.hbs.edu/faculty/Pages/item.aspx?num=7435

Amhalhal, A., Anchor, J., Tipi, N., & Elgazzar, S. (2021, August 27). *The impact of contingency fit on organizational performance: an empirical study*. Emerald. https://www.emerald.com/insight/content/doi/10.1108/IJPPM-01-2021-0016/full/html

Bainbridge, S. M., & Henderson, M. T. (2018). *Outsourcing the Board: How Board Service Providers Can Improve Corporate Governance*. Cambridge University Press. doi:10.1017/9781108149792

Brown, J. (2012). *Systems Thinking Strategy: The New Way to Understand Your Business and Drive Performance*. iUniverse.

Buchanan, M. (2003). *Nexus: Small Worlds and the Groundbreaking Theory of Networks*. W. W. Norton.

Burton, R. M., & Obel, B. (2004). *Strategic Organizational Diagnosis and Design: The Dynamics of Fit*. Springer. doi:10.1007/978-1-4419-9114-0

Christensen, C. M. (2016). *The Innovator's Dilemma: When New Technologies Cause Great Firms to Fail*. Harvard Business Review Press.

Cuellar, R., Scheere, A., & Augustine, S. (2021). *From PMO to VMO: Managing for Value Delivery*. Berrett-Koehler Publishers.

De Kluyver, C. A. (2013). *A Primer on Corporate Governance*. Business Expert Press.

DeSchoolmeester, D. (2014). *Systems Thinking: A Blueprint for Success*. CreateSpace Independent Publishing Platform.

Development, O. f. E. C. a., & OECD. (2012). *Corporate Governance Corporate Governance, Value Creation and Growth: The Bridge Between Finance and Enterprise*. OECD Publishing.

Dignan, A. (2019). *Brave New Work: Are You Ready to Reinvent Your Organization?* Penguin Publishing Group.

Drucker, P. F. (1993). *Managing in Turbulent Times*. Butterworth-Heinemann.

Elkind, L. D. C., & Landini, G. (Eds.). (2018). *The Philosophy of Logical Atomism: A Centenary Reappraisal*. Springer International Publishing.

Financial Training, A. (2017). *CIMA BA4 Fundamentals of Ethics, Corporate Governance and Business Law Study Text*. CreateSpace Independent Publishing Platform.

Graaf, K. d., Malnight, T. W., & Keys, T. S. (2013). *Ready? The 3Rs of Preparing Your Organization for the Future*. Keys.

Gray, D. (2016). *Liminal Thinking: Create the Change You Want by Changing the Way You Think*. Rosenfeld Media.

Gunay, S. G. (2008). *Corporate Governance Theory: A COMPARATIVE ANALYSIS of STOCKHOLDER and STAKEHOLDER GOVERNANCE MODELS*. iUniverse.

Hamel, G., & Zanini, M. (2020). *Humanocracy: Creating Organizations as Amazing as the People Inside Them*. Harvard Business Review Press.

Hanson, B. G. (1995). *General Systems Theory Beginning with Wholes*. Taylor & Francis.

Herzberg, F. (2008). *One More Time: How Do You Motivate Employees?* Harvard Business Press.

Howe, J. (2014). *Unleashing the Power of People: A Guide to Organizing People and Systems*. Outskirts Press, Incorporated.

Hughes, L., & Brennan, R. (n.d.). Effective communication during organizational change. *Journal of Change Management. "Idea Generation and the Quality of the Best Idea" by Karan Girotra, Christian Terwiesch et al.* ScholarlyCommons. https://repository.upenn.edu/mgmt_papers/304/

Jaffee, D. (2000). *Organization Theory: Tension and Change*. McGraw Hill.

Jaques, E. (1997). *Requisite Organization: A Total System for Effective Managerial Organization and Managerial Leadership for the 21st Century*. Taylor & Francis Group.

Jensen, F. (2016). *Integrated Management System: Combining Other Standards with ISO 9001*. Lulu.com.

Johnson, T. (2020). *Lean Methodology Mastery Collection: 8 Books in 1: Lean Six Sigma, Startup, Enterprise, Analytics, Agile Project Management, Kanban, Scrum and Kaizen*. Amazon Digital Services LLC - KDP Print US.

Jones, G. R. (2007). *Organizational Theory, Design, and Change*. Pearson Prentice Hall.

Kanikani, I. (2023). Building Change maturity in organizations. In K. L. Tennin, (ed.) Change Management During Unprecedented Times. IGI Global.

Kanikani, I. (n.d.). Whitepaper Building organizational Change Maturity by FUTURE:CM. *Academia*. https://www.academia.edu/96132653/Whitepaper_Building_organizational_Change_Maturity_by_FUTURE_CM

King, D., Skelsey, D., Smith, R., Sidhu, R., & APMG (Eds.). (2014). *The Effective Change Manager's Handbook: Essential Guidance to the Change Management Body of Knowledge*. Kogan Page.

Koestler, A. (2015). *The Ghost in the Machine*. One 70 Press.

Konrad, M., Shrum, S., & Chrissis, M. B. (2003). *CMMI: Guidelines for Process Integration and Product Improvement*. Addison-Wesley.

Kotter, J. P. (2014). *Accelerate: Building Strategic Agility for a Faster-moving World*. Harvard Business Review Press.

Kraakman, R., Armour, J., & Davies, P. (2017). *The Anatomy of Corporate Law: A Comparative and Functional Approach* (R. Kraakman, Ed.). Oxford University Press. doi:10.1093/acprof:oso/9780198739630.001.0001

Leicester, G. (2020). *Transformative Innovation: A Guide to Practice and Policy for System Transition*. Triarchy Press.

Loudon, A. (2001). *Webs of Innovation: The Networked Economy Demands New Ways to Innovate*. FT.com.

Mansfield, R. (1986). *Company Strategy and Organizational Design*. Croom Helm.

McKinsey. (2008, March 1). *Enduring Ideas: The 7-S Framework*. McKinsey. https://www.mckinsey.com/capabilities/strategy-and-corporate-finance/our-insights/enduring-ideas-the-7-s-framework

Mella, P. (2018). *The Combinatory Systems Theory: Understanding, Modeling and Simulating Collective Phenomena*. Springer International Publishing.

Millstein, I. M., & MacAvoy, P. W. (2004). *The recurrent crisis in corporate governance*. Business Books.

Morgan, G. (2006). *Images of Organization*. SAGE Publications.

Morree, P. d., & Minnaar, J. (2020). *Corporate Rebels: Make Work More Fun*. Corporate Rebels Nederland B.V.

OECD. (2017). *Methodology for Assessing the Implementation of the G20/OECD Principles of Corporate Governance*. OECD.

Örtenblad, A., Putnam, L. L., & Trehan, K. (2016, April 5). Beyond Morgan's eight metaphors: Adding to and developing organization theory. *Sage Journals*. https://journals.sagepub.com/doi/full/10.1177/0 018726715623999#bibr3-0018726715623999

Orwell, G. (n.d.). ⇥*Taylorism in the 21st Century Essay Example*. GraduateWay. https://graduateway. com/taylorism-in-the-21st-century/

Peters, J., & Weggeman, M. C. D. P. (2019). *Het Grote Rijnlandboekje*.

Peters, S. C. A., & Frisart, R. (2000). *Network Organizations*. Lansa.

Pink, D. H. (2022). *Drive: de verrassende waarheid over wat ons motiveert* [V. V. Walsmit, Trans.].

Pirson, M. A., & Gazella, K. (n.d.). *(PDF) Developing the Langer Mindfulness Scale*. ResearchGate. https://www.researchgate.net/publication/291372253_Developin g_the_Langer_Mindfulness_Scale

Rice, D., & Galbraith, M. (2008, November 16). *Rewards, Intrinsic Motivation, and Creativity: A Case Study of Conceptual and Methodological Isolation*. Taylor and Francis Online. https://www.tandfonline. com/doi/abs/10.1080/10400419.2003.9651404

Rigazio-DiGilio, S. A., Ivey, A. E., & Grady, L. T. (2005). *Community Genograms: Using Individual, Family, and Cultural Narratives with Clients* (S. A. Rigazio-DiGilio, Ed.). Teachers College Press.

Robertson, B. J. (2016). *Holacracy: The Revolutionary Management System that Abolishes Hierarchy*. Penguin Books, Limited. doi:10.15358/9783800650880

Rogers, E. M. (2003). *Diffusion of innovations*. Free Press.

Ross, A. (2017). *The Industries of the Future*. Simon & Schuster, Limited.

Ruotolo, R. A. (1972, December). *Jstor*. A Diagnostic Model for Organizations. https://www.jstor.org/ stable/45392830

Schmidt, G. (n.d.). *New Technologies and Post-Taylorist Regulation Models. The Introduction and Use of Production Planning Systems in French, Italian, and German Enterprises (1)*. Academia.edu. https:// www.academia.edu/31338056/New_Technologies_and_Post_Taylorist_Regulation_Models_The_Intro-duction_and_Use_of_Production_Planning_Systems_in_French_Italian_and_German_Enterprises_1_

Scott, W. R. (1987). *Organizations: Rational, Natural, and Open Systems*. Prentice-Hall.

Senge, P. M. (2006). *The Fifth Discipline: The Art & Practice of The Learning Organization*. Crown.

Sinek, S. (2011). *Start with why: How Great Leaders Inspire Everyone to Take Action*. Portfolio / Penguin.

Skyttner, L. (2006). *General Systems Theory*. World Scientific. doi:10.1142/5871

Smedley, G., Purse, R., & Kariwala, A. (2017). *People - the Heart of Good Governance: A People-Centred Approach to Corporate Governance*. CreateSpace Independent Publishing Platform.

Stafford, B., & Schindlinger, D. (2019). *Governance in the Digital Age: A Guide for the Modern Corporate Board Director*. Wiley.

Sterman, J. (2010). *Business dynamics: systems thinking and modeling for a complex world*. McGraw-Hill Education (India) Pvt Limited.

Taylor, F. W. (2006). The Principles of Scientific Management. Taylor & Francis.

Tohidian, I., & Rahimian, H. (n.d.). Bringing Morgan's metaphors in organization contexts: An essay review. *Tandfonline*. https://www.tandfonline.com/doi/full/10.1080/23311975.2019.1587808

UKEssays. (2021, July 29). *Is Taylor's theory of scientific management still useful in today's business?* UKEssays. https://www.ukessays.com/essays/business/is-taylors-theory-of-scientific-management-still-useful-today-business-essay.php

Ulrich, D., Ashkenas, R., Jick, T., & Kerr, S. (1995). *The Boundaryless Organization: Breaking the Chains of Organizational Structure*. Wiley.

Van Haren Publishing (Ed.). (2017). It-Cmf - A Management Guide: Based on the It Capability Maturity Framework(tm) (It-Cmf(tm). Van Haren Publishing.

Viscio, A. J., Frank, A., & Pasternack, B. A. (1999). *The Centerless Corporation: A New Model for Transforming Your Organization for Growth and Prosperity*. Simon & Schuster.

Welch, J., & Byrne, J. A. (2003). *Jack: Straight from the Gut*. Headline.

Womack, J. P., Jones, D. T., & Roos, D. (2007). *The Machine that Changed the World*. Simon & Schuster.

KEY TERMS AND DEFINITIONS

Change Maturity: Change maturity refers to the degree of an individual or organization's readiness and ability to effectively navigate and adapt to change in a systematic and proactive manner.

Dual Operating System: The dual operating system refers to a management model that combines traditional hierarchical structures with a flexible and agile network of teams or initiatives. It involves maintaining the stability and efficiency of the traditional hierarchy while also fostering innovation, adaptability, and responsiveness through self-organising teams or projects.

Governance: Governance refers to the framework, processes, and structures that guide and control an organization, ensuring proper decision-making, accountability, and compliance with rules and regulations. It involves establishing and enforcing policies, procedures, and responsibilities to achieve organizational goals and protect stakeholders' interests.

Invitation: This refers to a possibility to measure organizational health or redefine vital parameters in order to set up the 'as is' state of organizations to be able to achieve organizational health.

Metaphor: A metaphor is a figure of speech that draws a comparison between two unrelated things or concepts to create a deeper understanding or evoke a certain imagery or emotion.

Open Adaptive System: This refers to a system that interacts with its environment, continuously adapting and adjusting its behaviour to external changes and inputs. It is characterised by its ability to receive information, feedback, and resources from its environment and use them to modify its structure, processes, and behaviours.

Operating System: An organization's operating system refers to the underlying principles, values, and practices that govern how the organization operates and functions. It encompasses the organization's culture, structure, processes, and strategies that shape how work is done, decisions are made, and goals are achieved. It provides a framework for coordinating activities, aligning resources, and driving performance across the organization.

Organizational Design: Organizational design refers to the deliberate arrangement of structures, roles, processes, and systems within an organization to achieve specific goals, optimise efficiency, enhance communication, and facilitate coordination. It involves shaping the overall framework and components of an organization to align with its strategy and support effective performance.

Organizational Diagnosis: Organizational diagnosis refers to the systematic assessment and analysis of an organization's functioning and performance across various dimensions. It involves evaluating the organization's structure, culture, processes, communication, leadership, and other relevant factors to identify strengths, weaknesses, opportunities, and threats.

People-Centric: People-centric refers to an approach or mindset that places individuals at the centre of organizational strategies, policies, and practices. It emphasises valuing and prioritising the well-being, development, and engagement of employees.

Process Flow: flow refers to the smooth and uninterrupted movement of tasks or activities from start to completion. It emphasises the seamless progression of work without delays, bottlenecks, or idle time between process steps.

Process: This refers to a series of interconnected activities or steps designed to achieve a specific outcome or produce a desired output. It involves systematically transforming inputs into valuable outputs through a defined set of actions and decisions.

Purpose: refers to the underlying reason or core mission that drives and guides the organization's activities and decisions.

Systems Theory: Systems theory is an interdisciplinary framework that studies the relationships, interactions, and interdependencies between components within a complex system. It views a system as a set of interconnected parts that work together to achieve a common goal or purpose.

Value Chain: A value chain represents the sequential set of activities and processes within an organization that add value to a product or service from its creation to its delivery to customers. It encompasses activities such as procurement, production, marketing, sales, and customer service, each contributing to the overall value-creation process.

Chapter 11
Institutionalized Organizational Internal, Environmental, and Interacting Variables and Perspectives.

José G. Vargas-Hernandez

Tecnológico Superior de Jalisco Mario Molina, Zapopan, Mexico

Omar C. Vargas-González

Tecnológico Nacional de México, Ciudad Guzmán, Mexico

ABSTRACT

The purpose of this study is to analyze the interacting internal and environmental variables of an institutionalized organizational perspective. It departs from the assumption that the institutional analysis of the interacting relations between the internal and environmental variables are critical to explain the coevolution development of organizations. The method employed originated in the conceptual, theoretical, and empirical literature review as the basis for the application of meta-cognitive and meta-analytical methods. The analysis concludes that the interactions between the internal and environmental variables using the institutional theory makes relevant contributions to the organizational studies.

INTRODUCTION

Debates and controversies on institutional perspectives permeate research on organizations and management. In the early 1990s, institutional discussions derived in criticisms despite the fact that organizations do not respond similarly to conflicting institutional processes (Greenwood et al., 2008). Organization studies have abundant research however not yet in transition studies. The analytical perspective of organizational institutionalism and transition studies diverge in epistemology to some degree. Institutional complexity cannot transpose these fields but provide boundary objects for integrative theoretical frameworks (Fuenfschilling, 2019).

DOI: 10.4018/978-1-6684-8392-3.ch011

The new organizational theory applied in organizational studies questions the variety of institutional concepts, theoretical arguments and applicability (Peci, 2006). Institutional organizationalism in transition studies has a complicated relationship with fundamental differences, complementarities and contradictions on basic epistemologies, ontologies and empirical issues concerning with the institutional logics enacted at macro and micro organizational levels aimed to manage strategically incompatible moral expectations (Greenwood et al., 2017; Fuenfschilling, 2019). Institutional logics and resource dependence motivate organizational actors (Furnari, 2016; Palmer et al., 2013).

An institution is a perennial social practice in any specific organizational field (Baratter, 2014; Baratter, et al., 2010). Embedded institutions and institutional embeddedness operate at global, nation-state organizational field, industry, organization and interpersonal levels of analysis (Scott, 1995; Scott, 2014). This concept of institution is like others developed in economics and organizational studies (Hodson, 2006; North, 1991).

Institutionalist theory has evolved into a dominant framework in management and organizational studies and becoming useful for researching the interactions between business and society interact (Greenwood et al., 2017; Brammer et al., 2012). Institutional analysis is a critical examination of conventional organizational models and development premises of management models more morally justifiable that the corporation as the voluntary association of shareholders who own the enterprise and that the only members that count (Selznick, 1996). An arrangement of the levels of analysis can separate the factors to exert force on each other, which count on the less force has over social interactions of an organizational authority or institution, the configurations is more loosely coupled. Institutional and organizational tight and loosely coupled to social interactions (Hallet & Hawbaker, 2021). Social interactions are loosely coupled to institutional and organizational commitments.

Business and society scholarship uses the theoretical framework of the institutional perspective to approach organizational research to values. The coevolution of organizational ethics from a descriptive approach does not assess the normative perspective (Haveman & Rao, 1997). Studies in organizational economics analyze the effects of formal and informal institutional distance on outcome variables and construct measures (Zhou et al., 2016; Sartor & Beamish, 2014; Schwens et al., 2011). The institutional distance construct develops the concepts of institutional embeddedness across borders and its institutional distance effects on organizational outcomes.

Analysis and synthesis of the theoretical and empirical literature review are aimed to identify robust findings in institutional distance on organizational outcomes including choices on locations, entry modes, performance, gaps, and problems, among others. Research on institutional theory should focus on the institutional forces leading organizations to be receptive to social needs. Institutional theory relies on a nested approach that conceptualizes nested individuals inside organizations nested inside institutions (Hallett & Hawbaker, 2021). Maintaining a critical view on intertwining institutions, organizations, and social interaction influencing social outcomes aimed to improve social life.

To achieve the purpose of this study, it is firstly analyzed the institutionalized organizational theoretical framework to be applied in the analysis of the organizational variables in the order of process, organizational behavior organized as the internal variables to continue with the environmental variables considering the complexity and uncertainty. The study of the interacting organizational variables between the internal and environmental, culture and strategy are then analyzed. Finally, the study offers some concluding remarks.

BACKGROUND: INSTITUTIONALIZED ORGANIZATIONAL THEORETICAL FRAMEWORK

Institutional theory is a dominant approach in organizational analysis. The institutional theory is a perspective useful for explaining the influence of institutions on increasing transaction costs and resources development, normative and regulatory aspects, and the quality of institutions at organizational field level (Meyer & Nguyen, 2005; North, 1990; Peng, et al., 2009). An organizational field is defined as the aggregated organizations that constitute a recognized area of the institutional life such as suppliers, consumers, regulatory agencies, resources, other organizations that produce similar goods and services (DiMaggio & Powell, 1983). Various kinds of institutions are operating at organizational field level with specific determinants for each organization shaped by their contexts.

The institutional perspective is a tool used to analyze organizational competitiveness considering the institutional, social, cultural, financial, technical, etc. context in which organizations are immersed (Machado-da-silva & Fonseca, 1996). Classic structuralism notion is embedded in a paradox of embedded agency in institutional structures simultaneously producing, reproducing, and transforming organizational practices (Battilana & D'aunno, 2009). Agency spaces may flourish despite institutional and organizational forces.

The institutional logics perspective is a framework to understand and analyze society incorporating the interplaying of institutions, organizations, culture, individuals, and cognitions in the shaping of social reality. From the institutional perspective, the institutional logics and frameworks emerge, are identified, and diffuse within and through the organizational field and organizations for a dynamic influencing the digitalization actions (Hinings et al., 2018). The concept of institutional logic relates to the institutional context, which is complex and uncertain, composed of competing needs and demands interpreted by the organizations and responding to in diverse ways.

Institutional logic is an integrated analytical tool that can be applied to all societies, fields, organizations, group, individuals, etc. (Blomgren & Waks, 2015). Institutional logics are available to organizations and individuals as bases for action (Friedland & Alford, 1991; Jackall, 1988). The institutional logics from social construction frameworks explains digitalization adoption in organizations at the field level that occurs when the collective awareness of opportunities and threats for the actors and their organizations (Rachinger et al., 2019).

Empirical data on organizations is tensioned with a theoretical approach leading to analytical categories of institutional entrepreneurship at the action level, institutions at institutional context and organizational field (Dimaggio, 1988; Greenwood et al., 2008; Dimaggio & Powell, 2005; Scott, 1994). The empirical work in institutional logics is significant to sensitize organizational studies on its complexity of broader interactive patterns (Smets et al. 2015).

Drawing from the institutional theory perspective, digitalization logic has emerged on a firm level in the 1960s, adopted, and manifested itself in the different organizational fields in 2020. Digitalization logic from the institutional perspective adopted in organizations structures and practices with the potential to further transform organizational processes.

The institutional perspective is an approach to explain better the emergence, adaptation, and manifestation of the digitalization in organizations, although other theoretical frameworks may provide a better analysis. The emergence, adoption of digital products and services, and manifestation of institutional digitalization in organizations linked to the institutional logics complexity in large sociotechnical systems at the firm and field levels. The complexity of institutional level cyber security to preserve the organizational data requires to protect server and computer mechanism, platforms, online services, etc. (Laterza & Duncan, 2021).

From an institutional perspective, the identification of mechanisms to facilitate field change advancing theory through the emergence and adoption of the digitalization logic in the context of organizational fields. Mechanisms of accreditation cause institutional contradictions leading to organizational change (Cooper et al., 2014). The emergence, adoption, and advance of digitalization by the organizational fields requires a construct of institutional logics (Scott, 1991; Thornton et al., 2012).

Institutional theory framework for organizational theories and studies is related to social and environmental components of supply chain sustainability performance (Seles et al., 2016). Institutional theory has influenced organizational studies. Understanding the role of institutions in the organizational field, the identification of themes such as isomorphism, legitimacy, etc., that may result in uncertainty reduction delimits the organizational mechanism and the theoretical fundaments of the institutional theory supported by theoretical debates on the development of institutional theory (Crubellate et al. 2004; Hall & Taylor, 1996).

Institutional legitimacy is an assumption of a desirable entity and actions properly to social construct system of values, norms, beliefs, and definitions experienced intersubjectively between and within the organizational field and actors (Suchman, 1995; Clark, 1985; Giddens, 1984). A model of corporate social performance integrates the social demands with an emphasis on institutional legitimacy and power to organizations (Wood, 1991). Institutional theory analyses the organizational embeddedness of organizations in institutional environments (Hall & Soskice, 2001; Whitley, 1999; Jackson & Deeg, 2008, 2019; North, 1990; Scott, 1995; Scott, 2014).

From another theoretical perspective, in any institutional analysis, organizations are the independent variables, meaning that the organizational actors change the institutions, a phenomenon known as institutional entrepreneurship (Greenwood et al., 2008). Institutional determinants of economic and institutional diversity analysis need for an institutional theory framework to study and analyze the effects on local institutions in organizational environments (Nielsen, 2017).

Categories of collected data are subdivided considering the precipitating events in institutional entrepreneurship actions, cultural-cognitive, normative, and regulatory elements supporting social actors and their practices at various stages of organizational field (Greenwood et al., 2002; Dorado, 2013; Scott, 2008; Dimaggio & Powell, 2005; Hardy & Maguire, 2008).

Theoretical frameworks approaches are used to analyze institutional determinants of local organizations in terms of arguments focusing on the relationship between the theoretical assumptions and the ownership, location and internationalization paradigm applied at local organizations. Studies based on the institutional theory applied to institutional dimensions of institutional determinants of organizations under the assumption on location advantages combines with the ownership, location, and internationalization paradigm. The dialectic perspective of organizational isomorphism analysis how to combat it through human action under pressures from institutional entrepreneurs and various actors from the field and at the same time the balance derived from legitimacy led to changes.

MAIN FOCUS OF THE CHAPTER

Organizational Processes

The institutional theory analyzes the institutional forces leading the organizations to become more receptive to the social needs. Institutional theory merged with resource base theory are the theoretical framework to analyze the institutional pressures leading to risk organizational management practices in supply management processes of firms. The concept of institutional work (IW) based on thematic and semantic analysis along with institutional theory has created a framework leading to the study of organizations and management (Forgues et al., 2012).

Eco-design, green information system, green purchases, and manufacturing have a positive impact on organizational sustainable performance. Institutional myths are the prevailing organizational practices and procedures to adopt and maintain legitimacy, resource systems and stability (Meyer & Rowan, 1977). The concept of institutional entrepreneurship perspective is an institutional microanalysis model that encompasses the concept of institutional work with a bottom-up logic to the creation and maintenance processes and the rupture of institutions in the organizational field considering the immersed action capacity of actors (Lawrence & Suddaby, 2006).

Institutional work is the intentionally performed actions aimed to trigger institutional creation, maintenance and rupture processes of institutions and organizations. The institutional work is prevalent in organizations, although individuals and actors are also relevant in the analysis in which power and institutional work take different forms (Hampel et al. 2017; Leximancer, 2018), such as the Church that remains a powerful institution even in secular societies (Styhre, 2014).

The institutional theory explains the institutional logics and mechanisms behind the emergence, adoption and manifestation processes of digitalization changes and shifts of perception and frames through the different organizational fields. The emergence and adoption of a digitalization logic in organizations to participate in economic globalization processes based on institutional logics supported by both symbolic and cognitive elements needed for the implementation of organizational practices (Thornton & Ocasio, 2008).

Organizational Structure

Structural components, organizational forms, and rules are institutionalized and taken for granted. Formal institutions are regulatory and organizational structures that have an impact on the framework from motivation to outcome likely to political institutional and organizational research while the informal institutions are norms and values (Purtik & Arenas, 2019; Scott, 2008; Helmke & Levitsky, 2004). Institutions provide legitimacy of structures and practices of organizational fields including similar and isomorphic organizations to conduct some functions in society in institutional environments (Meyer & Rowan, 1977; Powell & DiMaggio, 1991; Selznick, 1957; Scott, 1995).

Organizations are closely and hierarchically structured aligned in organizational fields. The organizational field results from interactions over time between institutions, organizations, and individuals in the context in which they are inserted. The socio-technical system transforms the structure with new agents and actors entering as regime incumbents de-institutionalizing and adjusting their organizational structures and roles, with new values and technologies being institutionalized, supported by collective action to mitigate institutional complexity.

A framework to build-up ideal trajectories for the settlement of institutional complexity in transitions are based on the structural preconditions, types of institutional complexity, organizational and field-level responses and settlements (Raynard, 2016). The new institutional arrangement is not always departing from prior situations but from field level commitments and compromises between different logics leading to new institutionalized organizational forms coexisting with organizational principles and practices (Schildt & Perkmann, 2017).

Organizational Behavior

Institutions have effects on organizational behavior (Greenwood et al., 2008). Organizations and individuals assume to seek approval within the social influence contexts. Institutionalized organizations are perceived as effective by individuals who end up as the causal source of behavior patterns (Zucker, 1977). Institution is a social form or template composed of conventions scripting behavior in given contexts to varying degrees (Barley, 2008). An institutional perspective of formal and informal organizations rules the behavior of social actors (Greenwood et al., 2017).

The institutional theory analyses the impact of institutional environment on organizational behavior (Hirsch, 2008). The Institutional theory explains the effects of behavioral incentives derived from organizational legitimacy for the adoption of organizational behaviors and technologies (DiMaggio & Powell, 1983). Individual actors inhabit institutions among social interactions with others to form a variety of organizations.

Institutions existing in organizational fields are collective frames and systems aimed to provide stability and meaning to social behavior and interaction taking on a rule-like status in social thought and action (Djelic & Quack, 2008). Institutional logic is the organizing principles between and within an organizational field aimed to shape cognition and behavior in an organizational field (Besharov & Smith, 2014). Functional differentiation theory does replace or integrate into institutional logics theory but find some theoretical support with potential development of an institutional perspective more attuned to the institutional analysis of organizations and empirical studies of conflicting hybrid behavioral patterns.

Institutional Context and Environment of Organizations

The object of study is the elements of the institutional context formed by the local interorganizational relationships between the institutional and technical environments within geography of a defined sector. The institutional context refers to macro environment with interacting and sharing elements in the space of organizational field. Contextual analysis is essential to study institutions and organizations, class syetms, gender in places (Dacin et al., 2010) gender in places, etc. (Karam & Jamali, 2013; Styhre, 2014).

The institutional contexts pressure specific organizations to adopt more appropriate and efficient management processes, practices, and activities (DiMaggio & Powell, 1991) through the mechanisms of cultural-cognitive or mimetic, regulatory or coercive and normative mechanisms. Institutional distance is linked to organizational and management sciences and practices such as transfer activities and headquarters control (Kostova & Roth, 2002; Dellestrand & Kappen, 2012). Institutions encompass the values, norms and rules governing the relationships between and within organizations and their relationships with stakeholders and the environment. Empirically, the environments are concomitant and overlap with each other influenced by the organizational reality (Machado-da-Silva & Fonseca, 1996).

The Institutional perspective on organizations has limited and restrictive capacity to capture the uncertainty, complexity and diversity of the context and environment constrained to local analysis. From this restrictive premise, institutional uncertainty, complexity, and diversity reduce the information flow increasing the barriers to create incentives aimed to establish ventures and get involved in organizational practices and activities in certain places and locations (Monaghan et al., 2017). Institutional work analyzes organizational complexity and ambiguity inherent to agent behavior of organizations in institutionalized fields (Pinheiro et al., 2016).

A conceptual model builds up and settlement of institutional complexity in transition trajectories developed and empirically studied to trace the emergence leading to the reorganization of local actors internally adapted to structures. Complexity of local variations of institutional dimensions have implications for organizations that are challenged to find the most favorable institutional profiles at local environments.

Institutions play a role in organizational movements and operations in a local context with implications of the traditional determinants such as the institutional assets not necessarily related to the quality of institutions. Institutional differences at local levels in relation to the national context and the effects on economic and institutional determinants should be further studied and analyzed to include different insights from the firm perspective in organizational dynamic capabilities leading to adapt to changing institutional determinants (Teece & Pisano, 1994).

Organizational variations in quality of the diverse types of institutions result in various levels of contextual stringency and enforcement (Kostova et al., 2008; Rottig, 2016). Institutions are not only exogenous constraints of organizations in an environment socially constituted by an evolving system of rules as the result of continuous processes of sensemaking, interaction, promulgation and political negotiation among economic agents and political actors (Kostova et al., 2008). Institutions influence organizations and thus, conducting an institutional analysis needs to base the research on an institutional theory (Scott, 1987).

Organizations seek alignment and adjustments for legitimacy with their contexts in which are inserted affecting their policymaking, actions in goods and services (Meyer & Rowan, 1977). Institutional environment is related to the norms and requirements of organizations to gain legitimacy, which differs from technical environmental that refers to the product or services exchanged in the market and rewarding organizations for the effective and efficient control of processes (Scott, 2008; Scott, 1992). From the technical environment follows the organizational economic logic with the organizations are evaluated according to their technical efficiency (Fonseca, 2003; Machado-da- Silva & Fonseca, 1996). Both types of environments are necessary elements to make up the institutional context.

Institutional environments in less developed markets have more institutional voids related to issues of formal and informal institutions, pressures from local governments, institutional transitions, and changes (Rottig, 2016) that challenge the organizational flexibility required by the development of international business (Mudambi et al., 2018)

In a coevolution process, formal and informal institutions have influence on organizational change by engaging in environmental and political activities and bargaining in location dynamics (Dunning & Lundan, 2011; Monaghan et al., 2017). The institutional eclectic paradigm identifies intangible elements such as the political factors that make it difficult to trace the sources and resources to improve the institutional conditions for organizations.

Institutional analysis extends the dynamic interaction of the ownership, location, and internationalization advantages in organizational learning competitive advantages, the institutional distance and institutional infrastructure that regions and local places may offer to organizations for various kinds of projects. The institutional distance construct is rooted on the organizational contextual embeddedness of economic activity in social structures (Dacin et al., 1999). Formal institutional distance is concerned with rules and lawys that influence organizational strategies and operatios. Informal institutional distance is concerned with rules embedded in values, beliefs and norms (Estrin et al., 2009).

Institutional distance in different countries have different legitimate institutions and functions, which may create external tensions between organizations and the external environment and internal between organizational units located in different territories under different institutional rules (Kostova & Zaheer, 1999). Organizational units located in different countries have internal tensions when working under external institutional arrangements (Kostova & Roth, 2002).

Institutions influence organizations in terms of their ownership, location and internationalization processes integrating macro and micro elements enabling to combine institutional and economic factors, which are the bases for making decisions on location choices, including institutional variations on organizational operations. The OLI paradigm enables analysis of the institutional environment in relation to the exploitation of economic endowments, transaction costs and competitive advantages of organizations which are developed and required for an entry to foreign markets through foreign direct investments.

The ownership, location, and internationalization (OLI) theoretical framework model of institutional rationale is a set of advantages for organizations to analyze cognition, motivations and behavior required to get involved in international business which can be acquired and consolidated considering the institutional environment and economic endowments of the location (Dunning & Lundan, 2008). The ownership, location, and internationalization (OLI) revisited paradigm broader the institutional perspective based on combining economic and institutional determinants at the different organizational levels, transactions costs theory and modes of entry, supporting the institutional influences on within and between the firm and the environment (Sethi et al., 2011; Jain et al., 2016).

Institutional pressures have insignificant moderation between factors of green supply chain management: eco-design, green purchases, and manufacturing and sustainability performance while institutional pressures have a significant moderation between cooperation with customers, green information systems and organizational sustainable performance as factors of green supply chain management (Ahmad et al., 2022). The moderating effects of institutional pressures examine the association between factors of green supply chain management and organizational sustainability performance growth (Ahmad et al., 2022).

Institutional pressure has a moderating impact on cooperation with customers and organizational sustainability performance. Institutional pressure has a moderating effect between green purchases, and sustainability performance. Institutional pressure on organizations shows that cannot lead to higher sustainability performance. Institutional pressure on organizations tends to deliver better performance in green manufacturing and production, etc. Institutional pressure in organizations has a moderating effect between green manufacturing and sustainability performance. Institutional pressures exerted by the institutional quality on firms to adopt green purchase, recycling waste and control of waste defecation (Habib et al., 2021). Institutional pressure on quality promotes cooperation with customers leading to sustainable performance with respect to institutional stake in the organizations (Zaid et al., 2018).

Institutional pressures on organizations to comply with environmental regulations strengthen green manufacturing and sustainability performance (Sarkis et al., 2011). Rodrigues et al. (2016) stated something similar, like institutional pressures on organizations to follow environmental regulations is a link between green manufacturing and sustainability performance. Institutional pressure has a moderating effect between green manufacturing and organizational sustainability performance. So, as a result, institutional pressure could not cause harm, but has made contributions toward win-win situations for some organizations.

The institutional perspective is strictly constrained to be able to capture the diversity and complexity of institutions and organizations at national level analysis and regional institutional complexity may reduce the information flow, may increase investment barriers, may create incentives for ventures, etc. (Monaghan et al., 2017). The context of locations for the establishment of organizations must enable adaptation to be considered more attractive and less- effort-intensive in terms of formal and informal institutions such as for example, the relationships and social norms (Mudambi et al., 2002). Between the location and organizations there is a symbiotic relationship alignment between the advantages offered and the drivers of value creation of organizational activities (Dunning & Lundan, 2008).

The Chinese institutional environment has peculiarities that reflect different challenges faced by organizations involved in international business, as well as emerging advanced economies differ in terms of economic, institutional, social, and political characteristics.

Culture

The principles of organization and action are based on cultural notions and material practices prevalent in different societal and institutional sectors (Thornton, 2004). Few studies have analyzed the performance of accreditation agencies from the perspective of institutional theory and its role in organizational values, decisions, and practices of business schools (dos Santos Teixeira & Maccari, 2018). Identification of the institutional role of accreditation agencies in global values, structures, and practices in the organizational dynamics of business schools. Institutional theory discusses the contradictory role that accreditation agencies have in the organizational field of business schools.

The analysis from institutional normative aspects to institutional cultural-cognitive and regulative elements of the organizational field (Suddaby, 2015). Institutional myth, social interaction and organizational practice influence each other leading to coupling configurations. Organizations tend to adopt and adhere to similar popular mythologies, but the ground practices may vary despite the contextual differences, enabling them to appear similar across the institutions. In anthropology, institutional myths are cultural explanations of the operating world and occasionally in inconsistent organizational operations (Hallett & Hawbaker, 2021). People in organizations inhabit institutions to have myths rather than assume formal structures homogenously implemented. Organizational rules, regulations and policies perpetuate institutional myths such as meritocracies, professionalism, etc. (Cobb, 2017).

Social interactions are related to local organizational constraints and institutional mythologies. Organizational myths and ceremonies progressively homogenize and embedded in organizations to adhere ceremonially to institutional myths to create an institutional isomorphism which maintains external credibility (DiMaggio & Powell, 1983). Loosely coupled to social interactions in organizations is committed to institutions, as the tight coupling between the institutional myth and social interactions (Ray, 2019; Winkle-Wagner & McCoy, 2018). Organizational loose couplings maintain institutional myths and ceremonies to provide legitimacy, while tight couplings stimulate uncertainty threatening institutional legitimacy and leading to conflicts and organizational disruptions (Hallett, 2010).

Accreditation agencies of institutions in the organizational field must identify themes delimiting the accreditation mechanisms, theoretical framework for the development of the institutional theory, methodology supported by theoretical debates promoted by Crubellate et al. (2004) and Hall and Taylor (1996). The benefits of accreditation are related to the context of pressures from the institutional isomorphism and the contingent strategies. An institutional perspective masks the ebb and actions of change affecting the organization and its institutional environment (McKee et al., 2005).

From a critical analysis, accreditation agencies as other organizations are not exempt from institutional normalization, homogenization and subject to cyclical effects of standardization by institutions concerned with obtaining legitimacy for ensuring compliance with management standards as the result of coercive pressures and isomorphic pressures. The institutional role of organizations such as the accreditation agency changes depending on the local market in which operate and the global context. Organizations subject to coercive institutional pressure dissociate more than those subject to normative pressure.

SOLUTIONS AND RECOMMENDATIONS

Strategy

The institutional processes in organizations lead to strategic responses (Oliver, 1991). Organizational strategic responses result from institutional pressures, as identified by Oliver (1991). Some elements of the formal and informal institutional environment, such as the dynamics of politics at the national, regional, and local levels, tend to relativize and moderate the traditional determinants and effects on organizations with implications in location strategies to manage on complex and heterogeneous socio-economic contexts. An organization engages in managing interactions in the context of corporate social responsibility due to normative reasons sustained in the values (Aguinis & Glavas, 2012).

Political strategy is related to government and organizations to analyze political dynamics leading to plan the actions of organizations aimed to reduce the uncertainty of market and minimize adverse effects of regulations and contract with governments, which have an impact on location strategies despite the cultural differences, types of institutions and dynamics of relationships with other levels.

Organizations respond with strategies to different forms of environmental complexity (Raynard, 2016; Jancsary et al., 2017). In restraining complexity organizations resist the dominant logic implementing decoupling strategies (Greenwood et al., 2011). Institutions produce different organizational environment quality and the place conditions to offer development through policies and strategies aimed at attracting new organizations capable of investing. However, sometimes the institutional quality is not always reflected in specific regions and locations leading to organizations to face barriers in terms of differing liabilities.

The eclectic paradigm in international business influence of institutional determinants at the level of organizations and organizational fields. The ownership, location, and internationalization (OLI) Paradigm is a comprehensive model aimed at capturing the effects of factors beyond economic endowments and quality of institutions. Institutional diversity and the dynamics of relationships between governmental institutions at various levels affect the location context of organizations. Organizations may choose specific locations determined by contextual factors such as the institutional, economic, and political factors in heterogeneous environments and institutional quality.

The dynamics of institutional and political factors have effects on location strategies and determinants at organizations and organizational field. Market innovations in logistics requires advances in digitalization processes to participate in economic globalization processes through the development of institutions with international standards regulated at the level of organizational field in market digitalization.

Organizations and corporations involve in international business are engaged in a co-evolution process that adjust to formal and informal institutions and engaging in socio-political activities and bargaining in a firm-location dynamic (Dunning & Lundan, 2011; Monaghan et al., 2017). Mature markets usually have consolidated institutions which may lead to weaknesses of organizations in international business enring to emerging markets (Chakrabarti, 2001; Buckley et al., 2017).

Corporate social responsibility becomes institutionalized in organizations while formal structures of corporate social responsibility disappear (Risi & Wickert, 2017).

FUTURE RESEARCH DIRECTIONS

Further research needs to be conducted in all the variables of organizations: Processes, human and organizational behaviors, structure, environmental uncertainty and complexity, organizational culture and strategy.

Future research on institutionalist theory must consider the dominant framework in management and organizational studies to becoming useful for the analysis of the interactions between business and society scholarship using a theoretical framework of the institutional perspective to approach organizational research to values.

Future research on institutional theory should focus on the institutional forces leading organizations to be receptive to social needs.

Further research is needed on the methodological implications of the clinical approach to institutional analysis with the involvement of research intervention on institutional theories in organizational practices.

CONCLUSION

The study analyzes the interacting internal (Processes, structure, and human behavior) with environmental (uncertainty, complexity), variables, including the interactive variables of culture and structure of an institutionalized organizational perspectives, considered to be critical to understand and explain the coevolution development of organizations. The analysis concludes that the interactions between the internal and environmental variables using the institutional theory makes relevant contributions to the organizational studies.

The clinical approach to institutional analysis has methodological implications with the involvement of research intervention on institutional theories in organizational practices. The institutional distance effects have not presented clear explanatory mechanisms of the different institutional variables, reiterating similar arguments of organizational outcomes leading to theoretical concerns. Formal and regulatory institutions, as well as informal institutions, cognitive and normative institutional approaches, have influence on different institutional and organizational outcomes based on similar explanations such as referring to increased costs of doing international business.

The institutional perspective to transition studies requires further analysis of institutional complexity at system and organizational levels in processes change leading to the development specified in various respects from dominant socio-technical configuration to another. The transition studies provide explanations of actors managing institutional complexity in transition process with potential future contributions institutional and organizational complexity mediated by the organizational reconfigurations and adapting field-level structures supported by collective system building and institutional activities.

Regulators and actors such as designed organizations, consultants and suppliers coordinate the system and managing competing institutional demands to stabilize a turbulent transition trajectory in places such as the network positions endowed with the needed resources to be sustained through institutional contestation as the mitigation of complexity. Institutional complexity subjects the organizations to power battles, uncertainty in planning, increase costs and lower the quality of service. Segregated complexity responds with the creation of organizational units structurally compartmentalized. Institutional complexity is not mitigated through organizational responses and organizational changes complemented with reconfigurations of incumbent socio-technical system configurations.

Challenges related to organizational ability are concerned with learning how to function under different institutional environments development with various levels of formal and informal institutions development. The institutional challenges for organizations moving from a more developed institutional environment relying on formal institutions to less developed institutional environment to conduct economic activities. Organizations from developed institutional environments expanding into less developed institutional economies requires understanding the functioning of informal institutions and to design and implement strategies based on a less institutional environment.

Social practices are institutionalized over time leading to configuring organizational practices.

Organizations to develop must face challenges to overcome barriers and make choices to find the right place based on the institutional transaction costs to determine the attractiveness of locations. Institutions must reduce transaction costs. Organizations may be analyzed if they engage in corporate social responsibility under certain regulative and cultural-cognitive institutional conditions.

REFERENCES

Aguinis, H., & Glavas, A. (2012). What we know and don't know about corporate social responsibility: A review and research agenda. *Journal of Management*, *38*(4), 932–968. doi:10.1177/0149206311436079

Ahmad, A., Ikram, A., Rehan, M. F., & Ahmad, A. (2022). Going green: Impact of green supply chain management practices on sustainability performance. *Frontiers in Psychology*, *13*, 973676. doi:10.3389/fpsyg.2022.973676 PMID:36457908

Baratter, M. A. (2014). *A influência da comunidade local na configuração do arranjo produtivo local de louças e porcelanas de Campo Largo/PR. Curitiba*, 2014. Tese. (Doutorado em Administração) – Setor de Ciências Sociais Aplicadas, Universidade Federal do Paraná, 2014.

Baratter, M. A., Ferreira, J. M., & Costa, M. C. (2010). Empreendedorismo institucional: características da ação intencional. Perspectivas Contemporâneas, Campo Mourão, Edição Especial, p. 237-266.

Barley, S. R. (2008). Coalface Institutionalism. In *The SAGE Handbook of Organizational Institutionalism* (pp. 491–518). SAGE Publications Ltd. doi:10.4135/9781849200387.n21

Battilana, J., & D'Aunno, T. (2009). Institutional work and the paradox of embedded agency. In T. B. Lawrence, R. Suddaby, & B. Leca (Eds.), *Institutional work: Actors and agency in institutional studies of organizations* (p. 3158). Cambridge University Press. doi:10.1017/CBO9780511596605.002

Besharov, M. L., & Smith, W. K. (2014). Multiple institutional logics in organizations: Explaining their varied nature and implications. *Academy of Management Review, 39*(3), 364–381. doi:10.5465/amr.2011.0431

Blomgren, M., & Waks, C. (2015). Coping with contradictions: Hybrid professionals managing institutional complexity. *Journal of Professions and Organization, 2*(1), 78–102. doi:10.1093/jpo/jou010

Brammer, S., Jackson, G., & Matten, D. (2012). Corporate social responsibility and institutional theory: New perspectives on private governance. *Socio-economic Review, 10*(1), 3–28. doi:10.1093er/mwr030

Buckley, P. J., Doh, J. P., & Benischke, M. H. (2017). Towards a renaissance in international business research? Big questions, grand challenges, and the future of IB scholarship. *Journal of International Business Studies, 48*(9), 1045–1064. doi:10.105741267-017-0102-z

Chakrabarti, A. (2001). The determinants of foreign direct investments: Sensitivity analyses of cross-country regressions. *Kyklos, 54*(1), 89–114. doi:10.1111/1467-6435.00142

Clark, P. A. (1985). *A Review of the Theories of Time and Structure for Organizational Sociology.* University of Aston.

Clegg, S. R., Hardy, C., Lawrence, T. B., & Nord, W. R. (2020). *Sage Handbook of organization studies,* 215-254. Sage. https://www.researchgate.net/publication/242437344_Instituti ons_and_institutional_work/link/550aa6900cf290bdc10fdad3/dow nload.

Cobb, J. S. (2017). Inequality frames: How teachers inhabit color-blind ideology. *Sociology of Education, 90*(4), 315–332. doi:10.1177/0038040717739612

Cooper, S., Parkes, C., & Blewitt, J. (2014). Can accreditation help a leopard change its spots? Social accountability and stakeholder engagement in business schools. *Accounting, Auditing & Accountability Journal, 27*(2), 234–258. doi:10.1108/AAAJ-07-2012-01062

Crubellate, J. M., Grave, P. S., & Mendes, A. A. (2004). A questão institucional e suas implicações para o pensamento estratégico. *RAC. Revista de Administração Contemporânea, 37*(spe), 37–60. doi:10.1590/S1415-65552004000500004

Dacin, M. T., Munir, K. & Tracey, P. (2010). Formal dining at Cambridge colleges: Linking ritual performance and institutional maintenance. *Academy of Management Journal, 53*(6), 1393–1418. https://doi.org/. 2010.57318388 doi:10.5465/amj

Dacin, T., Ventresca, M., & Beal, B. (1999). Contextual embeddedness of organizations: Dialogue and directions. *Journal of Management, 25*(3), 317–356. doi:10.1177/014920639902500304

Dellestrand, H., & Kappen, P. (2012). The effects of spatial and contextual factors on headquarters resource allocation to MNE subsidiaries. *Journal of International Business Studies, 43*(3), 219–243. doi:10.1057/jibs.2011.57

DiMaggio, P., & Powell, W. (1983). The iron cage revisited: Institutional isomorphism and collective rationality in organizational fields. *American Sociological Review, 48*(2), 147–160. doi:10.2307/2095101

Dimaggio, P. J. (1988). Interest and agency in institutional theory. In: ZUCKER, Lynne G. (ed.). Institutional patterns and organizations. Cambridge, MA: Ballinger.

Dimaggio, P. J., & Powell, W. W. (1983). A gaiola de ferro revisitada: Isomorfismo institucional e racionalidade coletiva nos campos organizacionais. *Revista de Administração de Empresas*, 45(2), 74–89.

DiMaggio, P. J., & Powell, W. W. (Eds.). (1991). *The new institutionalism in organizational analysis* (Vol. 17). University of Chicago Press.

Dimaggio, P. J. & Powell, W. W. (2005). A gaiola de ferro revisitada: isomorfismo institucional e racionalidade coletiva nos campos organizacionais. *Revista de Administração de Empresas, 45*(2), 74-89.

Djelic, M.-L., & Quack, S. (2008). Institutions and transnationalization. In R. Greenwood, C. Oliver, R. Suddaby, & K. Sahlin-Andersson (Eds.), *The SAGE Handbook of Organizational Institutionalism* (pp. 299–323). Sage. doi:10.4135/9781849200387.n12

Dorado, S. (2003). Small groups as context for institutional entrepreneurship: An exploration of the emergence of commercial microfinance in Bolivia. *Organization Studies*, *34*(4), 533–557. https://www.researchgate.net/publication/259285127_Small_Groups_as_Context_for. doi:10.1177/0170840612470255

dos Santos Teixeira, G. C., & Maccari, E. A. (2018). The institutional role of business school accreditation agencies: A systematic literature review. *Revista de Gestão*, *25*(3), 274–290. doi:10.1108/REGE-04-2018-035

Dunning, J. H., & Lundan, S. M. (2008). *Multinational enterprises and the global economy* (2nd ed.). Edward Elgar Publishing.

Dunning, J. H., & Lundan, S. M. (2011). The changing political economy of foreign investment: finding a balance between hard and soft forms of regulation. In J. E. Alvarez & K. P. Sauvant (Eds.), *The Evolving International Investment Regime: Expectations, Realities, Options* (pp. 125–152). Oxford Scholarship Online. doi:10.1093/acprof:oso/9780199793624.003.0011

Estrin, S., Baghdasaeyan, D., & Meyer, K. E. (2009). The impact of institutional and human resource distance on international entry strategies. *Journal of Management Studies*, 46(7), 1171–1196. doi:10.1111/j.1467-6486.2009.00838.x

Fonseca da Silva, V. A. (2003). Abordagem institucional nos estudos organizacionais: bases conceituais e desenvolvimentos contemporâneos. In *Vieira, M. M. F., Carvalho, C. A. (org.). Organizações, instituições e poder no Brasil*. Editora FGV.

Friedland, R., & Alford, R. R. (1991). Bringing society back in: Symbols, practices, and institutional contradictions. In W. W. Powell & P. J. DiMaggio (Eds.), *The new institutionalism in organizational analysis* (pp. 232–263). University of Chicago Press.

Fuenfschilling, L. (2019). *An Institutional perspective on sustainability transitions Handbook of Sustainable Innovation*. Edward Elgar Publishing. https://www.elgaronline.com/view/edcoll/9781788112567/9781788112567.00020.xml

Furnari, S. (2016). Institutional fields as linked arenas: Inter-field resource dependence, institutional work, and institutional change. *Human Relations*, *69*(3), 551–580. doi:10.1177/0018726715605555

Giddens, A. (1984). *The Constitution of Society: Outline of the Theory of Structuration*. University of California Press.

Greenwood, R., Oliver, C., Lawrence, T. B., & Meyer, R. (2017). Introduction. In R. Greenwood, C. Oliver, T. B. Lawrence, & R. Meyer (Eds.), *The SAGE handbook of organizational institutionalism* (2nd ed., pp. 1–49). SAGE. doi:10.4135/9781446280669.n1

Greenwood, R., Oliver, C., Lawrence, T. B., & Meyer, R. E. (2017). *The SAGE Handbook of Organizational Institutionalism*. SAGE Publications. doi:10.4135/9781526415066

Greenwood, R., Oliver, C., Sahlin, K., & Suddaby, R. (Eds.). (2008). *The Sage Handbook of Organizational Institutionalism*. SAGE. doi:10.4135/9781849200387

Greenwood, R., Raynard, M., Kodeih, F., Micelotta, E. R., & Lounsbury, M. (2011). Institutional complexity and organizational responses. *The Academy of Management Annals*, *5*(1), 317–371. doi:10.5465/19416520.2011.590299

Greenwood, R., Suddaby, R., & Hinings, C. R. (2002). Theorizing change: The role of professional associations in the transformations of institutionalized fields. *Academy of Management Journal*, *45*(1), 58–80. doi:10.2307/3069285

Habib, M. A., Bao, Y., Nabi, N., Dulal, M., Asha, A. A., & Islam, M. (2021). Impact of strategic orientations on the implementation of green supply chain management practices and sustainable firm performance. *Sustainability (Basel)*, *13*(1), 340. doi:10.3390u13010340

Hall, P. A., & Soskice, D. (2001). *Varieties of capitalism: The institutional foundations of comparative advantage*. Oxford University Press. doi:10.1093/0199247757.001.0001

Hall, P. A., & Taylor, R. C. (1996). Political science and the three new institutionalisms. *Political Studies*, *44*(5), 936–957. doi:10.1111/j.1467-9248.1996.tb00343.x

Hallett, T. (2010). The myth incarnate: Recoupling processes, turmoil, and inhabited institutions in an urban elementary school. *American Sociological Review*, *75*(1), 52–74. doi:10.1177/0003122409357044

Hallett, T., & Hawbaker, A. (2021). The case for an inhabited institutionalism in organizational research: Interaction, coupling, and change reconsidered. *Theory and Society*, *50*(1), 1–32. doi:10.100711186-020-09412-2

Hampel, C., Lawrence, T., & Tracey, P. (2017). Institutional work: Taking stock and making it matter. In R. Greenwood, C. Oliver, & T. B. Lawrence (Eds.), *The Sage handbook of organizational institutionalism* (pp. 558–590). Sage. doi:10.4135/9781446280669.n22

Hardy, C., & Maguire, S. (2008). Institutional Entrepreneurship. In R. Greenwood & ... (Eds.), *The Sage Handbook of Organizational Institutionalism* (1st ed.). Sage Publications. doi:10.4135/9781849200387.n8

Haveman, H. A., & Rao, H. (1997). Structuring a theory of moral sentiments: Institutional and organizational coevolution in the early thrift industry. *American Journal of Sociology, 102*(6), 1606–1651. doi:10.1086/231128

Helmke, G., & Levitsky, S. (2004). Informal institutions and comparative politics: A research agenda. *Perspectives on Politics, 2*(4), 725–740. doi:10.1017/S1537592704040472

Hinings, B., Gegenhuber, T., & Greenwood, R. (2018). Digital innovation and transformation: An institutional perspective. *Information and Organization, 28*(1), 52–61. doi:10.1016/j.infoandorg.2018.02.004

Hirsch, P. M. (2008). Been there, done that, moving on: Reflections on institutional theory's continuing evolution. In R. Greenwood, C. Oliver, R. Suddaby, & E. Andersson (Eds.), *Handbook of Organizational Institutionalism* (pp. 783–789). Sage., doi:10.4135/9781849200387.n34

Hodgson, G. M. (2006). What are institutions? *Journal of Economic Issues, 40*(1), 1–25. doi:10.1080/00213624.2006.11506879

Jackall, R. (1988). *Moral mazes: The world of corporate managers.* Oxford University Press.

Jackson, G., & Deeg, R. (2008). Comparing capitalisms: Understanding institutional diversity and its implications for international business. *Journal of International Business Studies, 39*(4), 540–561. doi:10.1057/palgrave.jibs.8400375

Jain, N. K., Kothari, T., & Kumar, V. (2016). Location choice research: Proposing new agenda. *MIR. Management International Review, 56*(3), 303–324. doi:10.100711575-015-0271-6

Jancsary, D., Meyer, R. E., Höllerer, M. A., & Barberio, V. (2017). Toward a structural model of organizational-level institutional pluralism and logic interconnectedness. *Organization Science, 28*(6), 1150–1167. doi:10.1287/orsc.2017.1160

Karam, C., & Jamali, D. (2013). Gendering CSR in the Arab Middle East: An institutional perspective. *Business Ethics Quarterly, 23*(1), 31–68. doi:10.5840/beq20132312

Kostova, T., & Marano, V. (2019). Institutional theory perspectives on emerging markets. In *The Oxford Handbook of Management in Emerging Markets* (Vol. 99). Oxford University Press.

Kostova, T., & Roth, K. (2002). Adoption of an organizational practice by subsidiaries of multinational corporations: Institutional and relational effects. *Academy of Management Journal, 45*(1), 215–233. doi:10.2307/3069293

Kostova, T., Roth, K., & Dacin, M. T. (2008). Institutional theory in the study of multinational corporations: A critique and new directions. *Academy of Management Review, 33*(4), 994–1006. doi:10.5465/amr.2008.34422026

Kostova, T., & Zaheer, S. (1999). Organizational legitimacy under conditions of complexity: The case of the multinational enterprise. *Academy of Management Review, 24*(1), 64–81. doi:10.2307/259037

Laterza, V., & Duncan, A. T. (2021, March). Studying edtech platforms as platforms: Some notes towards a theoretical framework. *Workshop, 1,* 30–31.

Lawrence, T. B., & Suddaby, R. (2006). *Institutions and institutional work.* doi:10.4135/9781848608030.n7

Leximancer Pty Ltd. (2018). *Leximancer user guide: Release 4.5*. Leximancer. doc.leximancer.com/doc/Leximancermanual.pdf

Machado-da-Silva, C. L., & Fonseca, V. S. (1996). Competitividade organizacional: Uma tentativa de reconstrução analítica. *Organizações & Sociedade, 4*(7), 97–114. doi:10.1590/S1984-92301996000400004

McKee, M. C., Mills, A. J., & Weatherbee, T. (2005). Institutional field of dreams: exploring the AACSB and the new legitimacy of Canadian business schools, *Canadian Journal of Administrative Sciences/Revue Canadienne des Sciences de l'Administration, 22*(4), 288-301.

Meyer, J. W., & Rowan, B. (1977). Institutionalized organizations: formal structure as myth and ceremony. *American Journal of Sociology*, [S. I], *83*(2), 340-363.

Monaghan, S., Gunnigle, P., & Lavelle, J. (2017). Firm-location dynamics and subnational institutions: Creating a framework for collocation advantages. *Industry and Innovation, 25*(3), 242–263. doi:10.1080/13662716.2017.1315562

Mudambi, R., Li, L., Ma, X., Makino, S., Qian, G., & Boschma, R. (2018). Zoom in, zoom out: Geographic scale and multinational activity. *Journal of International Business Studies, 49*(8), 929–941. doi:10.105741267-018-0158-4

Mudambi, R., Navarra, P., & Paul, C. (2002). Institutions and market reform in emerging economies: A rent seeking perspective. *Public Choice, 112*(1-2), 185–202. doi:10.1023/A:1015687527568

Nielsen, B. B., Asmussen, C. G., & Weatherall, C. D. (2017). The location choice of foreign direct investments: Empirical evidence and methodological challenges. *Journal of World Business, 52*(1), 62–82. doi:10.1016/j.jwb.2016.10.006

North, D. C. (1990). *Institutions, Institutional Change and Economic Performance*. Cambridge University Press. doi:10.1017/CBO9780511808678

North, D. C. (1991). Institutions. *The Journal of Economic Perspectives, 5*(1), 97–112. doi:10.1257/jep.5.1.97

Oliver, C. (1991). Strategic responses to institutional processes. *Academy of Management Review, 16*(1), 145–179. doi:10.2307/258610

Palmer, M., Simmons, G., & Hall, M. (2013). Textbook (non-) adoption motives, legitimizing strategies and academic field configuration. *Studies in Higher Education, 38*(4), 485–505. doi:10.1080/03075079.2011.583983

PeciA. (2006). A nova teoria institucional em estudos organizacionais: umaabordagem crítica. *Cadernos EBAPE*. BR, Rio de Janeiro, *4*(1), 1-12. https://doi.org/ doi:10.1590/S1679-39512006000100006

Pinheiro, R., Geschwind, L., Ramirez, F., & Vrangbæk, K. (2016). *Towards a comparative institutionalism: Forms, Dynamics and Logics Across the Organizational Fields of Health Care and Higher Education* (Vol. 45). Emerald.

Powell, W. W., & Dimaggio, P. J. (Eds.). (1991). *The new institutionalism in organizational analysis*. University of Chicago Press. doi:10.7208/chicago/9780226185941.001.0001

Purtik, H., & Arenas, D. (2019). Embedding social innovation: Shaping societal norms and behaviors throughout the innovation process. *Business & Society, 58*(5), 963–1002. doi:10.1177/0007650317726523

Rachinger, M., Rauter, R., Müller, C., Vorraber, W., & Schirgi, E. (2019). Digitalization and its influence on business model innovation. *Journal of Manufacturing Technology Management, 30*(8), 1143–1160. doi:10.1108/JMTM-01-2018-0020

Ray, V. A. (2019). Theory of Racialized Organizations. *American Sociological Review, 84*(1), 26–53. doi:10.1177/0003122418822335

Raynard, M. (2016). Deconstructing complexity: Configurations of institutional complexity and structural hybridity. *Strategic Organization, 14*(4), 310–335. doi:10.1177/1476127016634639

Risi, D., & Wickert, C. (2017). Reconsidering the "symmetry" between institutionalization and professionalization: The case of corporate social responsibility managers. *Journal of Management Studies, 54*(5), 613–646. doi:10.1111/joms.12244

Rodrigues, V. P., Pigosso, D. C. A., & McAloone, T. C. (2016). Process-related key performance indicators for measuring sustainability performance of ecodesign implementation into product development. *Journal of Cleaner Production, 139*, 416–428. doi:10.1016/j.jclepro.2016.08.046

Rottig, D. (2016). Institutions and emerging markets: Effects and implications for multinational corporations. *International Journal of Emerging Markets, 11*(1), 2–17. doi:10.1108/IJoEM-12-2015-0248

Sarkis, J., Zhu, Q., & Lai, K.-H. (2011). An organizational theoretic review of green supply chain management literature. *International Journal of Production Economics, 130*(1), 1–15. doi:10.1016/j.ijpe.2010.11.010

Sartor, M. A., & Beamish, P. W. (2014). Offshoring innovation to emerging markets: Organizational control and informal institutional distance. *Journal of International Business Studies, 45*(9), 1072–1095. doi:10.1057/jibs.2014.36

Schildt, H., & Perkmann, M. (2017). Organizational settlements: Theorizing how organizations respond to institutional complexity. *Journal of Management Inquiry, 26*(2), 139–145. doi:10.1177/1056492616670756

Schwens, C., Eiche, J., & Kabst, R. (2011). The moderating impact of informal institutional distance and formal institutional risk on SME entry mode choice. *Journal of Management Studies, 48*(2), 330–351. doi:10.1111/j.1467-6486.2010.00970.x

Scott, W. R. (1987). The adolescence of institutional theory. *Administrative Science Quarterly, 32*(4), 493–511. doi:10.2307/2392880

Scott, W. R. (1991). Unpacking institutional arguments. In W. W. Powell & P. J. DiMaggio (Eds.), *The New Institutionalism in Organizational Analysis* (pp. 164–182). University of Chicago Press.

Scott, W. R. (1992). *Organizations: rational, natural, and open systems* (3rd ed.). Prentice-Hall.

Scott, W. R. (1994). Conceptualizing organizational fields: Linking organizations and societal systems. In: Derlien, Hans-Ulrich.; Gerhardt, Uta.; Scharpf, Fritz W. (Eds.), Systems rationality and partial interests (pp. 203-221). Baden-Baden: Nomos.

Scott, W. R. (1995). *Institutions and Organizations*. Sage.

Scott, W. R. (1995). *Institutions and organizations*. Sage.

Scott, W. R. (2008). *Institutions and organizations: Ideas and interests* (3rd ed.). Sage Publications.

Scott, W. R. (2014). *Institutions and organizations* (4th ed.). Sage.

Seles, B. M. R. P., de Sousa Jabbour, A. B. L., Jabbour, C. J. C., & Dangelico, R. M. (2016). The green bullwhip effect, the diffusion of green supply chain practices, and institutional pressures: Evidence from the automotive sector. *International Journal of Production Economics, 182*, 342–355. doi:10.1016/j. ijpe.2016.08.033

Selznick, P. (1957). *Leadership in Administration*. Harper and Row.

Selznick, P. (1996). Institutionalism "old" and "new.". *Administrative Science Quarterly, 41*(2), 270–277. doi:10.2307/2393719

Sethi, D., Judge, W., & Sun, Q. (2011). FDI distribution within China: An integrative conceptual framework for analyzing intra-country FDI variations. *Asia Pacific Journal of Management, 28*(2), 325–352. doi:10.100710490-009-9144-5

Smets, M., Jarzabkowski, P., Burke, G. T., & Spee, P. (2015). Reinsurance trading in Lloyd's of London: Balancing conflicting-yet-complementary logics in practice. *Academy of Management Journal, 58*(3), 932–970. doi:10.5465/amj.2012.0638

Styhre, A. (2014). Gender equality as institutional work. *Gender, Work and Organization, 21*(2), 105–120. doi:10.1111/gwao.12024

Suchman, M. C. (1995). Managing legitimacy: Strategic and institutional approaches. *Academy of Management Review, 20*(3), 571–610. doi:10.2307/258788

Suddaby, R. (2015). Can institutional theory be critical? *Journal of Management Inquiry, 24*(1), 93–95. doi:10.1177/1056492614545304

Teece, D., & Pisano, G. (1994). The dynamic capabilities of firms: An introduction. *Industrial and Corporate Change, 3*(3), 537–556. doi:10.1093/icc/3.3.537-a

Thornton, P. (2004). *Markets from culture: Institutional logic and organizational decisions Organization, Theory in higher education publishing*. Stanford University Press. doi:10.1515/9781503619098

Thornton, P., & Ocasio, W. (2008). Institutional logics. In R. Greenwood, C. Oliver, K. Sahlin, & R. Suddaby (Eds.), *The Sage handbook of organizational institutionalism* (pp. 99–129). SAGE Publications. doi:10.4135/9781849200387.n4

Thornton, P. H., Ocasio, W., & Lounsbury, M. (2012). *The Institutional Logics Perspective: A New Approach to Culture, Structure, and Process*. Oxford University Press. doi:10.1093/acprof:o so/9780199601936.001.0001

Whitley, R. (1999). *Divergent capitalisms: The social structuring and change of business systems*. Oxford University Press.

Winkle-Wagner, R., & McCoy, D. L. (2018). Feeling like an "Alien" or "Family"? Comparing students and faculty experiences of diversity in STEM disciplines at a PWI and an HBCU. *Race, Ethnicity and Education, 21*(5), 593–606. doi:10.1080/13613324.2016.1248835

Wood, D. J. (1991). Corporate social performance revisited. *Academy of Management Review, 16*(4), 691–718. doi:10.2307/258977

Zaid, A. A., Jaaron, A. A., & Bon, A. T. (2018). The impact of green human resource management and green supply chain management practices on sustainable performance: An empirical study. *Journal of Cleaner Production, 204*, 965–979. doi:10.1016/j.jclepro.2018.09.062

Zhou, C., Xie, J., & Wang, Q. (2016). Failure to complete cross-border M&As: "To" vs. "From" emerging markets. *Journal of International Business Studies, 47*(9), 1077–1105. doi:10.105741267-016-0027-y

Zucker, L. G. (1977). The role of institutionalization in cultural persistence. *American Sociological Review, 42*(5), 726–743. doi:10.2307/2094862

KEY TERMS AND DEFINITIONS

Complexity: The quality of what is composed of various elements.

Organizational Behavior: is a kind of evaluative circle that seeks to clarify how people behave within an organization, why they act that way and what are the impacts of their ways of acting.

Organizational Culture: Those norms and values by which a company is governed. Some principles related to the structure of the company, with the methods of work performance, and even the way in which the staff is related. It is, in Roman Paladino, the psychology of the organization, its core.

Organizational Environment: Everything that surrounds the organization, and from which it can receive influences and, at the same time, on which it can act.

Organizational Structure: The way in which the functions and responsibilities that each member has to fulfill within a company are assigned to achieve the proposed objectives.

Organizational Variables: A qualitative nature, and a set of attributes, in time and space, which give significance to its raison d'être, its object that generates the administrative dynamics of the organization and its respective management philosophy.

Process: A process is a sequence of actions that are carried out to achieve a specific end.

Strategy: The art of projecting and directing military operations, especially those of war. A series of well-considered actions, directed towards a specific goal.

Uncertainty: Refers to epistemic anomalies involving imperfect or unknown information. Applies to predictions of future events.

Chapter 12
Training for Crisis Situations:
A Panoramic View of Theory and Practice Around the World

Helena Martins

https://orcid.org/0000-0002-0749-917X

ESCE, Polytechnic Institute of Setúbal, Portugal & CEOS, ISCAP, Polytechnic of Porto, Portugal & Nova School of Business and Economics, Lisbon, Portugal

Lisa Dollmann

Nova School of Business and Economics, Lisbon, Portugal

Melanie Lehmann

Nova School of Business and Economics, Lisbon, Portugal

Ana Cláudia Rodrigues

https://orcid.org/0000-0002-6238-1385

CEOS, Polytechnic of Porto, Portugal

ABSTRACT

Challenges like pandemics, technological breakthroughs, geopolitical instability, and climate change are making crisis an ever more present reality in the lives of people, organizations, and societies. This chapter examines how people around the world are being trained for crisis situations, focusing on skills and competencies being developed, as well as the training approaches and practices. Two complementary methodologies were used to address theory as well as practice. To grasp the perspective of researchers, a systematic crisis training literature review following the SPIDER approach was conducted; for the examination of training designs, a benchmarking of training websites on Google was completed. The analyses conducted, resulted in practical recommendations for future research and practice in the crisis training niche, ultimately aiming at facilitating crisis management and skills trainings worldwide to better prepare the society for inevitable critical events.

DOI: 10.4018/978-1-6684-8392-3.ch012

INTRODUCTION

High-impact and low-probability situations, or "crises" pose a genuine and serious threat to society by inflicting harm, spreading illness, or killing people (Daoudi, Chebil, Tranvouez, Chaari & Espinasse, 2017). Crises can emerge from environmental, and natural causalities, technological and human failures, malevolence, political tensions, organizational misdeeds, etc. As globalization is an element of everyday lives, so are crises becoming more global as evidenced by the worldwide effects of COVID-19 (Bhaduri, 2019) and the current Russia-Ukraine conflict (World Health Organisation, 2022). Therefore, businesses and organizations find themselves operating in a time of great uncertainty, as do individuals fighting for their own or other people's lives.

In order to prevent, de-escalate, and recover from deadly situations, crisis management training should be provided not only for first responders but also for professionals in general, especially when assuming leadership roles.

This chapter focuses on the practices of crisis management training in several fields, focusing on the addressed competencies as well as training methods. Hence, we aim to grasp an idea of how people around the world are being trained to deal with crisis situations and disasters, specifically regarding:

- What kind of competencies do these trainings seem to focus on the most? Which professional area is focusing on which competencies and skills?
- How are crisis trainings conducted in respect to types of delivery, content, and training strategies?

This chapter starts with basic definitions of crises, disasters, emergencies, and crisis management, explores the concepts of competences, competencies, and skills and presents basic concepts of training and development. Then an explanation of the methodology used for this chapter and main results are presented. Finally, a discussion is conducted both on the training design and competencies, while drawing comparisons to further crisis training literature and deriving recommendations for practice as well as research. Finally, an overall conclusion is drawn, providing an outlook for future research.

BACKGROUND

Crises, Disasters, Emergencies

The expression "crisis" stems from the Greek word "krisis", which can be translated to "decision" or "choice" (Paraskevas, 2006). Although scholars seem to have offered a variety of differing definitions for the term, crises refer to high-impact, low-probability, and disruptive events that come with uncertainty and risk, whereby decisions and choices must be made under time pressure (Gregory, 2005).

The expression is often used in combination with or as a replacement for the word disaster and emergency. Al-Dahash, Thayaparan and Kulatunga (2016) point out that, although they all share a sudden nature and represent the root cause for subsequent damage, they should not be understood as the same concepts. According to their analysis, many similarities could be found between crises and disasters, while emergencies did not share as many commonalities with the two, although, both could lead to disasters in cases of mismanagement or neglect. The relationship between the three is highly interdependent, interconnected, and complex, as illustrated in Figure 1.

Figure 1. Similarities and differences between crises, disasters, and emergencies
Source: Al-Dahash et al., 2016, pp.1197

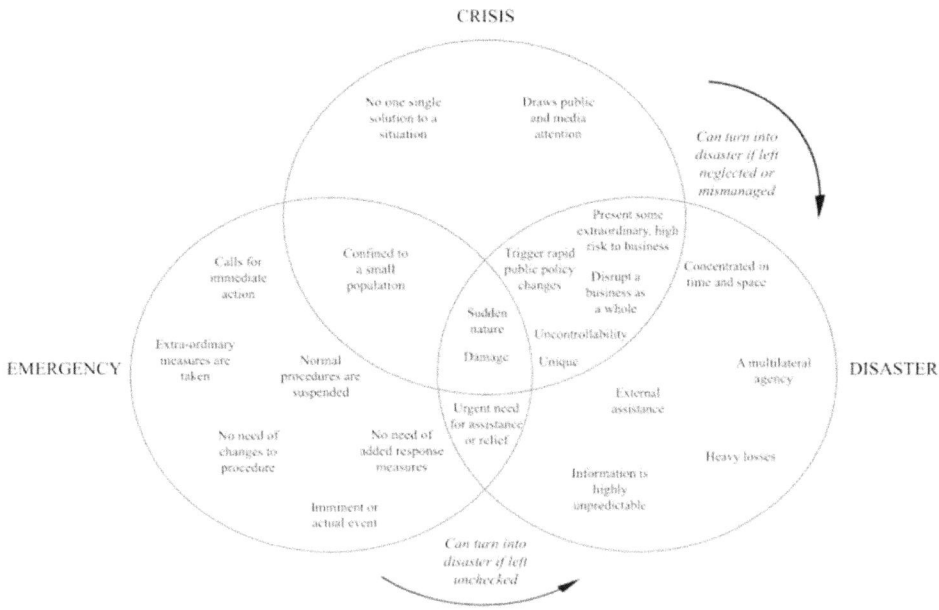

Considering the work in this chapter applies to the three circumstances, from here on we use the term "crises" as a representative of the three concepts, for simplicity.

Crisis Management

Crisis management is an activity whereby experiences and perceptions are shaped through interaction with stakeholders to prevent, rectify, recover, and learn from crises (Jankelová & Mišún 2021; Kim & Lim 2020). Although the commonsense view is that this discipline is merely reactive in response to a worst-case scenario, Jaques (2007) pledges a more holistic view of crisis management that emphasizes not only crisis response but also crisis prevention, preparedness, and recovery.

Attentiveness and preparedness are especially important in times of instability (Khodarahmi, 2009). Due to various elements that are environmental, political, technological and human, it is safe to say that the frequency of unprecedented situations is increasing with no signs of relenting in the near future (Mitroff & Alpaslan, 2003; Vargo & Seville, 2011). The world is facing more turbulence than before, which underscores the importance of managing crises holistically across industries and countries. Thus, people all around the world should be equipped with the right competencies to deal with unprecedented situations, and one of the ways of developing such knowledge, skills and attitudes is by undergoing efficient training programs. To form a common ground for the subsequent research, these basic concepts will be elaborated on next.

Competences, Competencies, and Skills

The words "*competency*" and "*competence*" are often seen as synonyms when referring to an individual's ability to achieve success or efficiency, whereas skill is a component of both constructs. The three constructs are closely related although they have different levels of complexity and will be presented from most to least complex.

Competence can be described as the capacity of an individual to consistently use the information, skill, and judgment necessary for safe, moral, and efficient practice (Moghabghab, Tong, Hallaran & Anderson, 2018, in some ways equated to the construct of practical wisdom, e.g. making the best use of one's knowledge skills and abilities while considering ethical values and the common good (Rocha, Kragujl & Pinheiro, 2022). Competence refers to the level of performance attained and can be developed through life (Garcia-Perez, Cegarra-Navarro, Bedford, Thomas & Wakabayashi, 2020), relating to an individual's mental or physical ability while considering context. Competence can affect one's capacity to work, succeed in education, participate in legal procedures, and interact with others; the aptitude to independently draw a logical conclusion is also referred to as "competence". A person may have to exhibit a certain degree of knowledge and skill in a given situation to establish his or her competence in order to successfully operate in that environment (Bullard 2022).

There are various definitions of competency (e.g., Cinque, 2016; Hendarman & Cantner, 2018; Garcia-Perez et al., 2018). It can be described as "the ability to do something well" (Moghabghab et al., 2018) and according to Mirabile (1997), it is a combination of knowledge, ability, and skill that is necessary for high levels of performance at work; examples include problem-solving, critical thinking, and leadership. Shortly, competency is related with the efficient behavior that is exhibited (Garcia-Perez et al., 2020).

Competencies may be generally categorized as either personal or corporate, although these two groups are not fully distinct from one another (Turner & Crawford, 1994; Bayley, Phipps, Batac & Stevens, 2018). According to Bayley and colleagues (2018), the categories for management competency clusters are: *intellectual* (such as analysis and judgment), *interpersonal* (like persuasiveness and decisiveness), *adaptability* (such as resilience), and *results-oriented* (like initiative and business sense).

Accordingly, skills are related to the level of an individual's performance on a certain activity or the capacity to accomplish a task that may be split into technical and behavioral components (Noe, Hollenbeck, Gerhart & Wright, 2020; Patacsil & Tablatin, 2017). As stated in the EUCEN Glossary (2008), "skills" refers to the capacity to put knowledge and expertise to use in completing tasks and resolving issues. They are sometimes viewed as the "visible" or "behavioral" parts of competence and are similar to competencies. However, while skills represent the learning abilities needed to execute tasks effectively, competencies are the knowledge and behaviors that help one succeed. To be effective, both must work together (McNeill, 2019). Skills can be gained through training or by doing the task at hand (Hendarman & Cantner, 2018).

In this chapter, these terms will be used synonymously for simplification.

Hard Skills vs. Soft Skills

Hard skills are technical abilities required to do certain activities while processing information.

They serve as a foundation for the creation of educational curricula, job profiles, and the technological functions most desired by the industry and the world (Patacsil & Tablatin, 2017) and are predominantly cognitive in nature (Page, Wilson & Kolb, 1993; Hendarman & Cantner, 2018).

Soft skills include intrapersonal and interpersonal abilities that are crucial for healthy interaction and cooperation in general (Heckman & Kautz, 2012), as well as for successfully navigating the challenges of a changing world (Deming, 2017). Numerous of these abilities are covered by the idea of emotional intelligence (Vaira, 2004), but depending on the situation and the influence of both global and local factors, soft skills can be clustered differently. According to Cinque (2016), some frequent elements are *people-related skills* (e.g., communication and teamwork), *conceptual and thinking skills* (e.g., problem-solving or creativity), *personal skills* (e.g., flexibility and having self-esteem), *skills related to the business world* (e.g., enterprise skills), and *skills related to the community* (e.g., civic or citizenship knowledge).

While social skills pertain to interactions with other people, personal skills primarily correspond to cognitive skills like knowledge and reasoning abilities. Overall, soft skills complement hard skills with the necessary flexibility to grow and stay agile in an ever-changing environment (Cimatti, 2016). Soft skills aid individuals in adapting and behaving positively so they can successfully navigate the challenges of their professional and everyday lives (Haselberger, Oberhuemer, Perez, Cinque & Capasso, 2012).

There are various approaches to labelling, defining, classifying, and clustering soft skills. The concept of *"soft skills"* or *"non-technical skills"* occasionally overlaps with previously established terms such as generic competences and key competencies (Cinque, 2016). Also tending to intersect with the soft skill concept are *life skills*, or *21st-century* skills, that refer to abilities relevant to deal with present and future issues (Joynes, Rossignoli & Amonoo-Kuofi, 2019).

In crisis situations, soft skills (especially emotional and social) have gained increasing recognition over the past few years and can be developed through education (Deming, 2017). These competencies are critical in a variety of industries and disciplines (Warin, 2017) and when dealing with inevitable or unusual circumstances, it is eminently essential to seize opportunities to develop agility. Leaders will need to reflect creatively and apply divergent thinking using higher cognitive skills in an increasingly VUCA (volatile, uncertain, complex and ambiguous) reality (Brooks, Curnin, Owen & Boldeman, 2019). Therefore, soft skills, such as the ability to communicate, handle a crisis, and operate under pressure, are extremely important for a quick and reasonable reaction (Dixon, Belnap, Albrecht & Lee, 2010). In a society dealing with issues brought on by terrorist attacks, extreme weather occurrences, technological revolutions, pandemics and geopolitical instability, crisis and paradigm-shifting change are destined to stay with us.

The topic of soft skills is likely to become even more of a priority in coping with nowadays' continual changes and crises, considering its potential benefits in terms of people's effectiveness in handling distressing and unexpected events individually as well as in groups (Coelho & Martins, 2022).

Training and Development

The terms *"training"* and *"development"* are often used collectively or interchangeably and allude to systematic processes that bring about relatively permanent changes in the KSAs (knowledge, skills and attitudes) of individuals (Kraiger, 2003; Salas, Tannenbaum, Kraiger & Smith-Jentsch, 2012). To be more precise, training serves the improvement of individuals', teams', or organizations' effectiveness (Goldstein & Ford, 2002), while development can be seen as a long-term investment in employees, aiming for personal growth (Aguinis & Kraiger, 2009); in the following text, the word "training" will be utilized for both realities, for simplicity's sake.

In order to provide practitioners with the correct training approaches that enable them to maximize learning potential, **training research** has advanced significantly since its beginning. In 1971, Campbell critiqued the training literature for being too "non-theoretical", "non-empirical" and "dull" (p. 565). After more than thirty years, Salas and Cannon-Bowers (2001) found that the research on training had made great strides, increased in size, and gained contributions in both empirical as well as theoretical areas. These advancements have enabled not only the industry but also other sectors such as aviation and the military to design and deliver appropriate and effective training systems (Salas, Wilson, Priest & Guthrie, 2006).

After decades of scrutinizing the training domain in detail, researchers agree on the fact that **well-designed trainings work** (cf. Powell & Yalcin, 2010; Salas et al., 2008; Salas, Nichols & Driskell, 2007) and that their effectiveness heavily hinges on the way they are designed and delivered (Salas et al. 2012). There are endless variations and combinations of tools and strategies used to create and implement training. However, each training should **cover the following four steps for it to be effective**: *instruction* of the targeted knowledge, skills, and attitudes; followed by a *demonstration* by the instructor, whereafter the trainee gets the opportunity to *practice;* and, finally, prompt, and constructive *feedback* about the trainee's performance (Salas & Cannon-Bowers, 2001).

Effective and potent training is not a once-over event: it represents an **iterative process**, where determinants leading up to and happening after the session should be considered as well (Salas et al., 2012). Training can be divided into 3 phases: 1) pre-training, 2) during training, and 3) post-training. The pre-training stage occurs before the actual training, including training needs analysis and creating the right learning climate. The training stage includes the delivery of training to trainees and the post-training includes the assessment of training, including trainee assessment, feedback as well as training transfer.

Training and Development of Soft Skills

Soft skill training has the potential to prevent worst-case scenarios and save lives across diverse areas (Carayon, Kleinschmidt, Hose, Salwei, 2021; Helmreich, Merritt, & Wilhelm, 2009; Kanki, Helmreich & Anca, 2010). Soft skill training can be viewed as a systematic process that allows for the development of interpersonal skills. Soft skills teaching is not sufficient: proper training must be completed (Choudary & Ponnuru, 2015).

It has long been debated whether it is even possible to develop soft skills. On the one hand, there is the point of view that categorizes soft skills as inherent and stagnant traits of humans, which therefore cannot be changed; on the other hand, there is the perspective that being skills that represent actions that were taken based on knowledge, they can be trained and developed (Heckman & Kautz, 2012). Therefore, by recognizing one's weakness regarding a skill, deciding to improve it (Schulz, 2008), and undergoing proper training, each skill can be improved (Matteson, Anderson & Boyden, 2016). Moreover, social learning theory supports the notion that skills are not simply innate in people but that they are learned socially through observation and modelling (Bandura, 1994). Likewise, John (2009) shows that students continuously undertaking soft skill training could significantly improve their transpersonal abilities, arguing that these competencies are available in every person, however, at diverse individual levels. By successfully undergoing soft skill training, barriers and blocks that inhibit people from using these skills can be abolished. Hence, though the development of these competencies starts in the earliest stages of childhood (Cimatti, 2016), proper training has proven to be able to aid in the development and improvement of soft skills, even in adults.

To prepare people for the demands of the 21st century, social-emotional skill development through different training methods becomes increasingly important (Naamati-Schneider, Meirovich & Dolev,

2020). Soft skills may be cultivated in formal and informal settings, including both within and outside of the "classroom" (Cinque, 2016). Mini-curricula, programs, workshops, training sessions, projects, study journeys, and individual or group assignments can all be used to enhance said skills. In general, there is a variety of teaching philosophies and educational contexts, which may result in a different set of learning outcomes. Examples can be cooperative learning, problem-based learning, action learning, experiential learning, or critical reflection (Cinque, 2016). Furthermore, skills and competencies are better learned and understood using simulation-based training methods (Wang, 2017).

During a crisis or disaster situation, it is frequently crucial to function as an educator, communicator, and sometimes even a consultant in any professional field to guarantee that teams can understand, for instance, the supplied emergency checklists and do the necessary activities to defend the business or organization. As a result, crisis and emergency circumstances require ongoing assessment and training to ensure the proper balance between soft skills and hard skills (Gladstone & Brown, 2022).

Since non-technical skills are more challenging to teach and assess than their technical equivalents, it takes more effort to develop a training curriculum for them (Naik & Brien, 2013).

In times of crisis, leaders are crucial for maintaining effective communication, creating trust, boosting productivity, or preserving brand value (Lockwood, 2005). Therefore, the success or failure of crisis management operations is highly determined by leadership competencies (Bhaduri, 2019), including the ability to make decisions, build organizational capacities, maintain an effective organizational culture, manage numerous constituencies, and grow human capital (James & Wooten, 2005).

Additionally, teams must assume further responsibility, but leaders must ensure that their group stays focused and engaged even when fatigue sets in. In order to guarantee that a team performs effectively while working under severe restrictions, especially during crises, important social skills are required. A variety of competencies must be possessed and comprehended by leaders in various crises or catastrophe circumstances to successfully manage different situations. These crisis demands could be the need for calm but strong leadership, the need for pragmatic decision-making under strict time and resource constraints, and the need for coordination and (re)organization, each with assigned competencies (Table 1). Consequently, training in soft skills is vital for crisis leaders (Van Wart & Kapucu, 2011).

Table 1. Crisis demands, including competency needs for leaders

Crisis Demand	Perceived Competency Needs
Need for calm but strong leadership	Self-confidence, motivating, resilience, communication skills, willingness to assume responsibility
Need for pragmatic decision making under severe time and resource constraints	Decision-making, decisiveness, flexibility, delegating, analytical skills
Need for coordination and (re)organization	Team building, social skills, operations planning, networking, and partnering

Source: Own elaboration, adapted from Van Wart & Kapucu (2011)

In their research, Flin and O'Connor (2017) developed a set of seven non-technical skill categories (Figure 2) for high-risk employees who could face different crises, including *situation awareness, decision-making, communication, teamwork, leadership, stress management*, and *fatigue tolerance*. Two of these abilities are cognition-based, namely situational awareness and decision-making, three are social, such as communication, leadership, and teamwork, and the other two are related to well-being, which would be managing stress and fatigue (Brooks et al., 2019).

Figure 2. Seven most important non-technical skills for crisis management
Source: Adapted from (Flin & O'Connor, 2017)

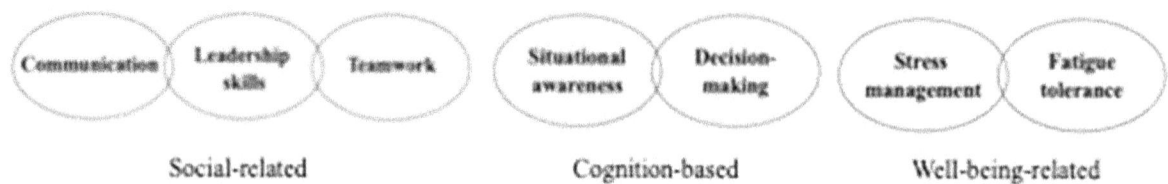

Gladstone and Brown (2022) have a similar perspective on **key competencies** that are necessary for crises and that should be trained. *Communication* is one of, if not the most critical, underdeveloped soft skill. It includes not just the spoken or written word but also how information is conveyed to an audience. People rely on it daily in their personal and professional lives. However, good communication is more difficult than many may acknowledge. *Flexibility*, or the capacity to respond to changing circumstances and handle a crisis, is almost as vital as communication. It is essential since flexibility enables individuals to make rational decisions, and it might be developed through repetition. Additionally, soft skills like *leadership and teamwork* should always be cultivated through instruction and individual practice when talking about disaster management. When trained, *problem-solving and decisiveness* can also positively affect crisis outcomes. Hereby, a proper issue-solving strategy involves identifying the problem, acquiring information, examining options, choosing one, and sticking with it (Gladstone & Brown 2022).

MAIN FOCUS OF THE CHAPTER

Methodology

In order to identify the methods of designing and delivering training for dealing with crisis situations as well as the competencies that said trainings aimed at developing, a systematic approach to the existing scientific literature was conducted, as well as a benchmarking analysis of training programs available online.

A systematic review of the literature was conducted to find out what the most relevant competencies in crisis training in the published scientific literature are. A **systematic review** can be defined as "a review that uses explicit, systematic methods to collate and synthesize the findings of studies that address a clearly formulated question" (Page et al., 2021). In a systematic analysis of the literature, researchers usually collect all the papers in one or more search engines using keywords or strings of words called "Boolean equations" (Donato & Donato, 2019). *Published papers and articles* dealing with crisis training and conveyed competencies and skills were searched in **Google Scholar**, whereby their selection was restricted by a time frame of the last 10 years. The keywords that were used alluded to programs and courses as well as teaching competencies and skills for crisis, emergency, and disaster management in diverse environments.

After examining whether to include or exclude a paper in this research, the information from the analyzed abstracts was systematized using the SPIDER approach (Methley, Campbell, Chew-Graham, McNally & Cheraghi-Sohi, 2014). The SPIDER approach was used to further narrow down and prioritize the previously selected papers by reading through their abstracts and determining their fit for this research's purpose according to the concerned area (**S**ample), the type and structure of the training (**P**henomenon of Interest), the conclusions of the paper (**E**valuation), and the **R**esearch type. In addition to the categories adapted from the SPIDER approach, the category "professional area" was added in order to facilitate further clustering.

Each of the suitable papers was scrutinized in detail, and all mentioned **competencies and skills** for crisis situations or competencies that are taught during trainings for disaster and emergency situations got summarized in a spreadsheet and grouped into generic terms like "teamwork", "communication", or "technical and job-related competencies" in order to find unified expressions for words with the same meaning to simplify further analysis. The groups were once again clustered into four subordinate areas that helped to distinguish between soft and hard skills: *Personal skills, social skills, content-reliant and methodological skills,* and *technical skills and knowledge*. For this purpose, the ModEs Framework for soft skills (Cinque, 2016) was used as a template and extended with the option for hard skills. The following table (Table 2) lists the four areas with their respective competencies.

Table 2. Clustered areas and their associated competencies

Area	Competencies
Personal skills	Learning skills, tolerance to stress, self-awareness, creativity/innovation, commitment
Social skills	Communication, contact network, conflict management, teamwork, leadership, culture adaptability
Content-reliant and methodological skills	Customer/user orientation, adaptability to change, decision making, results orientation
Technical skills and knowledge	General job-related skills, clinical skills, practical skill, nursing skills, common airway skills

Source: Adapted from Cinque (2016)

For benchmarking the courses being offered around the world, the **Google** search engine was used, where crisis and disaster training *websites* were sought after. Keywords met the same criteria as for the systematic literature review. Using a designated table for the websites found on Google, information on those training courses was broken down and systematized into training link, name, date of website access, origin country (i.e., the country that the training was created in), type (e.g., face-to-face, hybrid, etc.), objectives, addressed competencies, target audience, strategies used to convey the training content, duration, topics covered in the curriculum, instructor, and area.

What Kind of Competencies do Trainings for Crisis Situations Seem to Focus on the Most?

From a theoretical point of view, a total of 46 publications were selected for detailed analysis, with the use of the aforementioned SPIDER method; 228 competencies were identified and listed on a spreadsheet for further analysis; the practical standpoint was analyzed with reference to 54 trainings listed on websites, where 184 skills were mentioned in the training programs. The frequency analysis of the most referenced skills is presented in Figure 3.

Figure 3. Frequency of skills mentioned in papers (theory) and training websites (practice), clustered in 20 subordinate groups and presented in descending order of combined magnitude
Source: Adapted from (Flin & O'Connor, 2017)

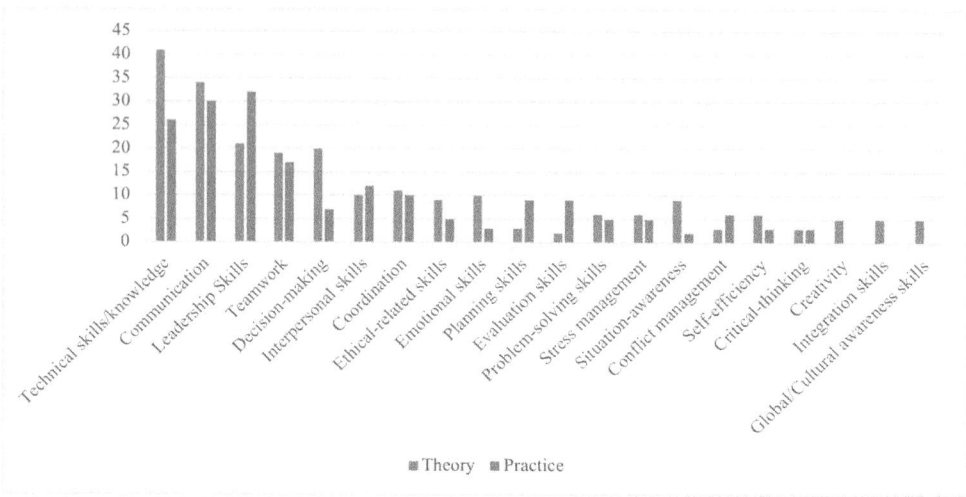

Interestingly, despite the theory's preference for technical skills (e.g. trainings that mostly focus a job related skill such as clinical skills) in practice, the trainings offered to the public has a stronger preference for leadership and communication skills, which led to the question that if in aggregate according to a known framework the two realities (theory and practice) would bear such big differences.

Thus, all identified skills were further organized into four broader skill categories adapted from Cinque's (2016) ModEs Framework. As a result, competencies were classified as *social skills* (e.g., communication, leadership, and teamwork skills), *content-reliant and methodological skills* (e.g., adaptability to change, analytical skills, and customer or user orientation), *technical skills and knowledge* (e.g., practical skills, clinical skills, and common airway skills), and *personal skills* (e.g., self-awareness, commitment, and creativity), as can be seen in Figure 4.

Figure 4. Frequency of skills mentioned in papers (theory) and training websites (practice) are clustered in 4 subordinated groups according to Cinque's (2016) ModEs Framework and presented in descending order of combined magnitude
Source: Adapted from (Flin & O'Connor, 2017)

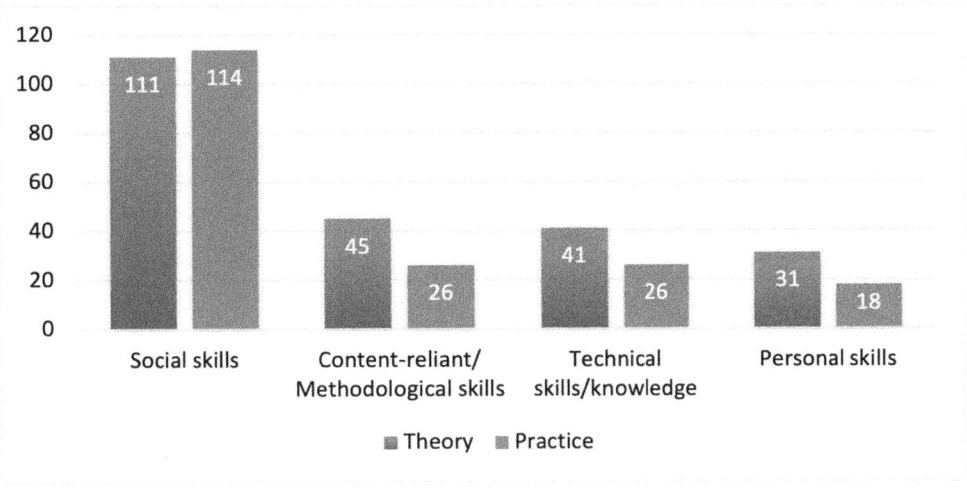

In all it seems clear that in theory as in practice social skills take the lead in terms of relevance in trainings for crisis situations.

Which Professional Field is Focusing on Which Competencies and Skills?

In the scientific literature, nine different occupational or professional areas addressing training for crisis situations could be identified: 1) health care, 2) education, 3) organizations, and businesses, 4) first responders and emergency response teams, 5) security, 6) government, 7) humanitarian and social work, 8) aviation, and 9) private.

As is visible in Figure 5, the majority of research caters towards the industries of health care and education, followed by security and first responders.

Figure 5. Frequency of addressed professional fields in all analyzed papers, presented in descending order of magnitude
Source: Adapted from (Flin & O'Connor, 2017)

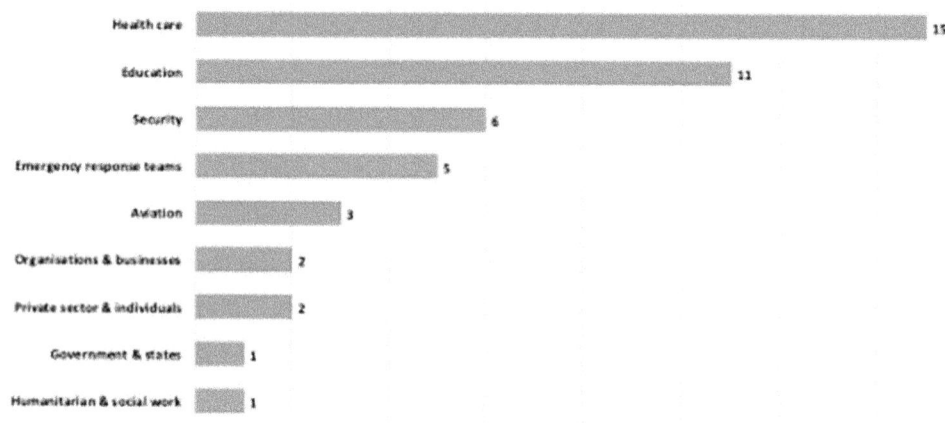

After gaining a first overview of the mentioned skills, the frequencies of all competencies indicated in the papers were analyzed across the nine different professional areas. Subsequently, and for the purpose of better characterizing the field, each sector was divided into subfields (Figure 6).

Figure 6. Training courses areas and subareas
Source: Adapted from (Flin & O'Connor, 2017)

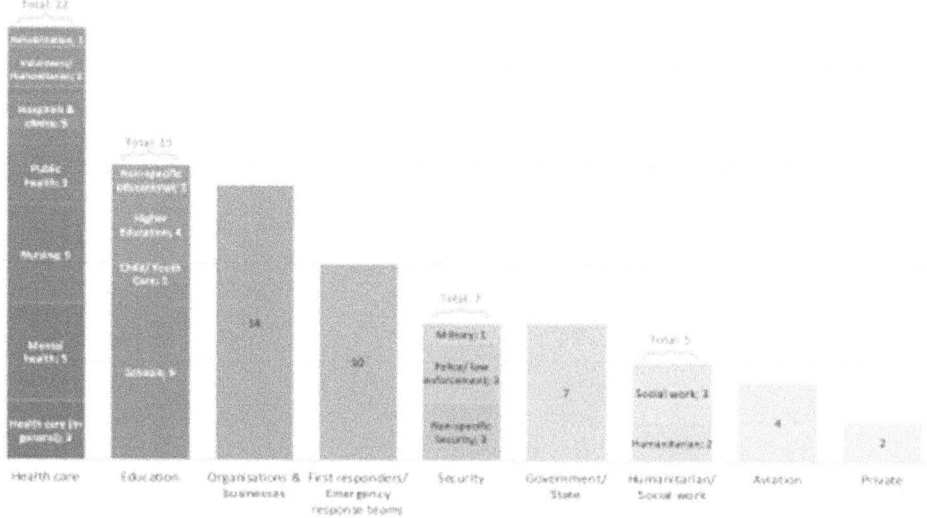

Competencies and Skills per Professional Sector

The primary focus of the next section is on competencies in the fields of *health care*, *education*, *security*, and *civil aviation*, the ones most frequently mentioned in the theoretical and practical sources.

Health Care Sector

In this sample, the competencies of nursing staff, health care professionals in general, medical residents, and telemental health workers for crisis and emergency situations were primarily examined. In order to handle crisis situations effectively, nurses, in particular, must demonstrate appropriate non-technical abilities in addition to their hard skills as initial responders. The occurrence of mistakes and adverse events in hospitals is strongly correlated with inadequate teamwork, leadership, decision-making, and collaboration between individuals and teams in the field of health care (Ong & Tan, 2018). Therefore, the American Psychological Association (2006) suggests common clinical competencies be emphasized throughout doctoral trainings. These should include research, ethical and legal standards, individual and cultural diversity, professional values, attitudes, and behaviors, communication and interpersonal skills, assessment, intervention, supervision, and consultation (Desai, Lankford & Schwartz, 2020).

The sample in this work makes frequent reference to general emergency response skills, technical abilities, including clinical skills, as well as soft skills for all facets of the healthcare industry, with results from theory and practice visible in Figure 7.

Figure 7. Frequency of skills mentioned in papers (theory) and training websites (practice) in the Health care sector, clustered in 20 subordinate groups and presented in descending order of combined magnitude
Source: Adapted from (Flin & O'Connor, 2017)

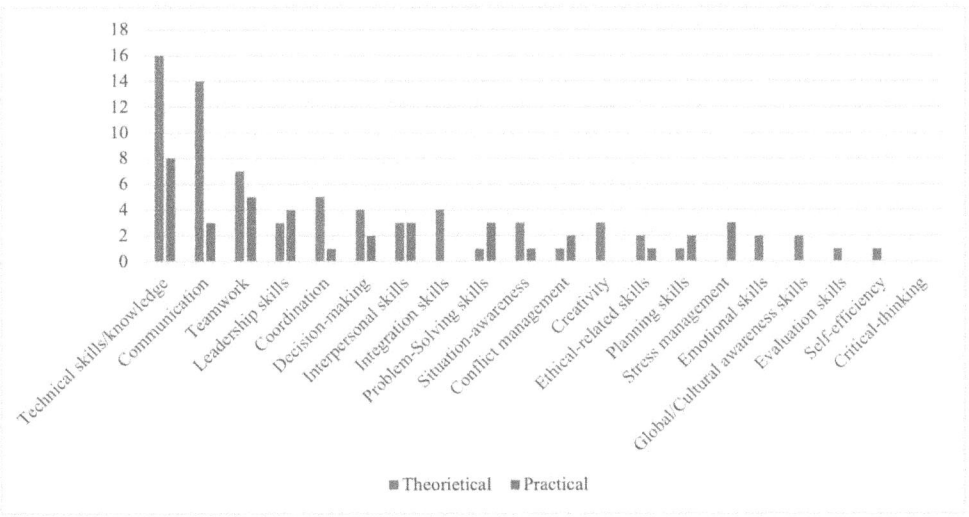

Therefore, it is evident that both hard skills and soft skills, such as teamwork and communication, are crucial for crisis management in the healthcare industry and that acquired abilities align with the suggested competencies in the literature.

Education Sector

Schools are among the safest places for children, but crisis situations such as student suicide, natural disasters, staff deaths, or shootings pose threats to every educational institution and can have serious and long-lasting effects on those who are exposed to them (Nickerson, Cook, Cruz & Parks, 2019). Therefore, school staff, educators, and students must be trained to avoid and respond to a variety of crisis situations. The PREPaRE training program, which instructs school staff in crisis *prevention and readiness* as well as crisis *intervention and recovery*, is one potential option for crisis management training in this sector. The crisis *prevention and preparedness* part concentrates instruction on preventative and readiness skills while providing a thorough overview of duties and responsibilities related to school safety. In cooperation with mental health specialists, the crisis *intervention and recovery* part focus on a variety of soft skills, including conducting psychological triage and attending to specific group needs (Nickerson et al. 2019).

The most addressed competencies in theory, as well as practice in Education, are presented in Figure 8.

Figure 8. Frequency of skills mentioned in papers (theory) and training websites (practice) in the Education sector, clustered in 20 subordinate groups and presented in descending order of combined magnitude
Source: Adapted from (Flin & O'Connor, 2017)

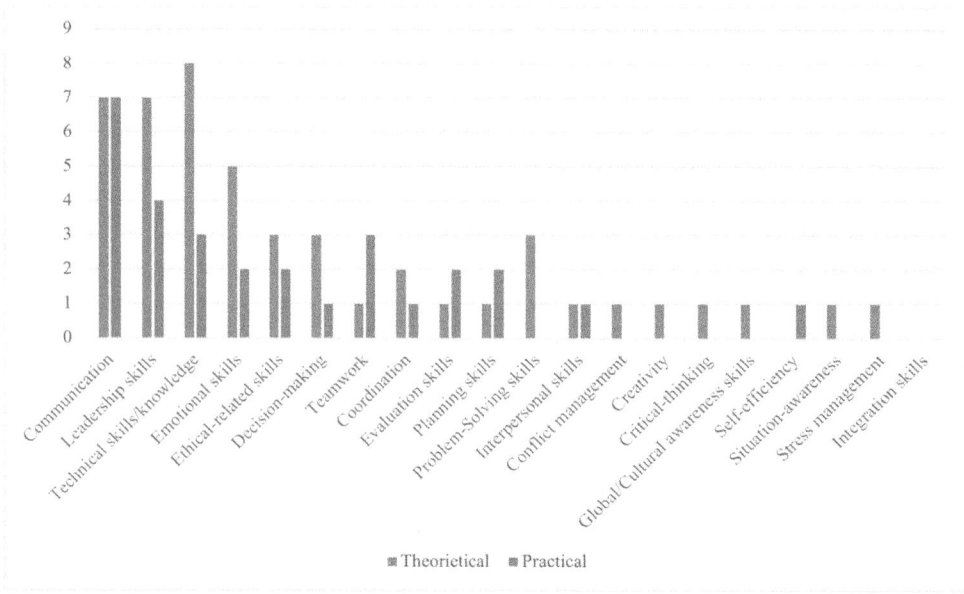

Security Sector

The majority of publications in this sector discuss the Crisis Intervention Team (CIT) program curriculum for police employees, which is meant to train officers in dealing with people with mental illness. In addition to teaching de-escalation techniques and basic soft skills, particularly social ones, the training also educates about mental illness, its origins, and its symptoms (Hassell, 2020). There are no further papers on more general operations and crisis training of police officers for disasters or emergency situations, which could be due to secrecy.

Furthermore, only one paper, which examines theme-based training techniques for emergency responders to large-scale crisis occurrences, specifically targets the military or army sector. A key part of a successful crisis response in this area is the ability of agents to work as coordinated teams in a collaborative setting. The U.S. Army Training and Doctrine Command (TRADOC) places a strong emphasis on the *human factor* in future military operations. TRADOC stresses the necessity for soldiers to have higher cognitive abilities, such as the capacity to quickly synthesize information, make correct situational assessments, and adapt to changing operations (Zimmerman et al. 2012).

The most commonly addressed competencies in theory as well as practice in the Security sector are presented in Figure 9.

Figure 9. Frequency of skills mentioned in papers (theory) and training websites (practice) in the Security sector, clustered in 20 subordinate groups and presented in descending order of combined magnitude
Source: Adapted from (Flin & O'Connor, 2017)

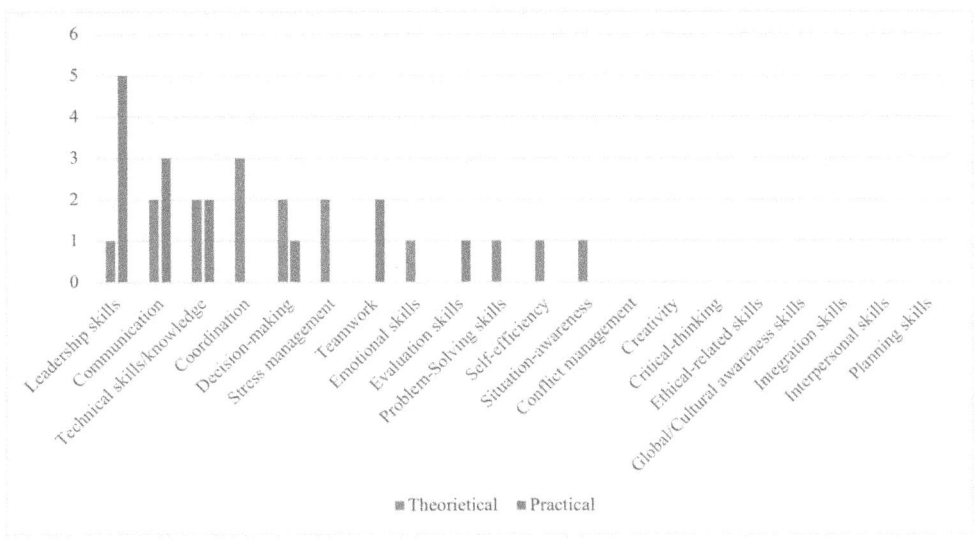

Civil Aviation Sector

The civil aviation industry is another significant field that offers training for crisis and emergency situations. Human error has been repeatedly recognized as one of the primary causes of aviation disasters since the late 1970s. This makes it a crucial topic for research. As a result, it is necessary to teach flight crews, pilots, inspectors, and general staff in this field to be prepared for any kind of crisis (Aguinis & Kraiger, 2009).

For more than 40 years, simulation has been used as a training tool for hard skills in the field of airway management. This creates an opportunity for trainees to actively participate in the aviation sector. Through a variety of airway management training addressing common airway skills, difficult aviation management strategies, and crisis management skills, it can efficiently improve and upgrade the knowledge and skills, which will ultimately decrease errors and improve patients' outcomes and safety.

However, in the airway industry, simulation training for crisis situations is not only a useful tool for technical skills like medical knowledge and procedural competencies but also for non-technical abilities like crisis management skills. The majority of these are behavior-based and involve teamwork, communication, leadership, situation awareness, decision-making, and awareness of stress and exhaustion (Yang, Wei, Xue, Deng & Zhi, 2016).

Looking at the aviation sector, three papers were analyzed in more detail in this sample with regard to the competencies taught in training courses. Many of them concentrated on developing safety skills, general first aid competencies, de-escalation skills, and emergency response training abilities, which were noted as technical skills and knowledge; the most frequently addressed competencies in theory as well as practice in the Civil Aviation sector are presented in Figure 10.

Figure 10. Frequency of skills mentioned in papers (theory) and training websites (practice) in the Civil Aviation sector, clustered in 20 subordinate groups and presented in descending order of combined magnitude
Source: Adapted from (Flin & O'Connor, 2017)

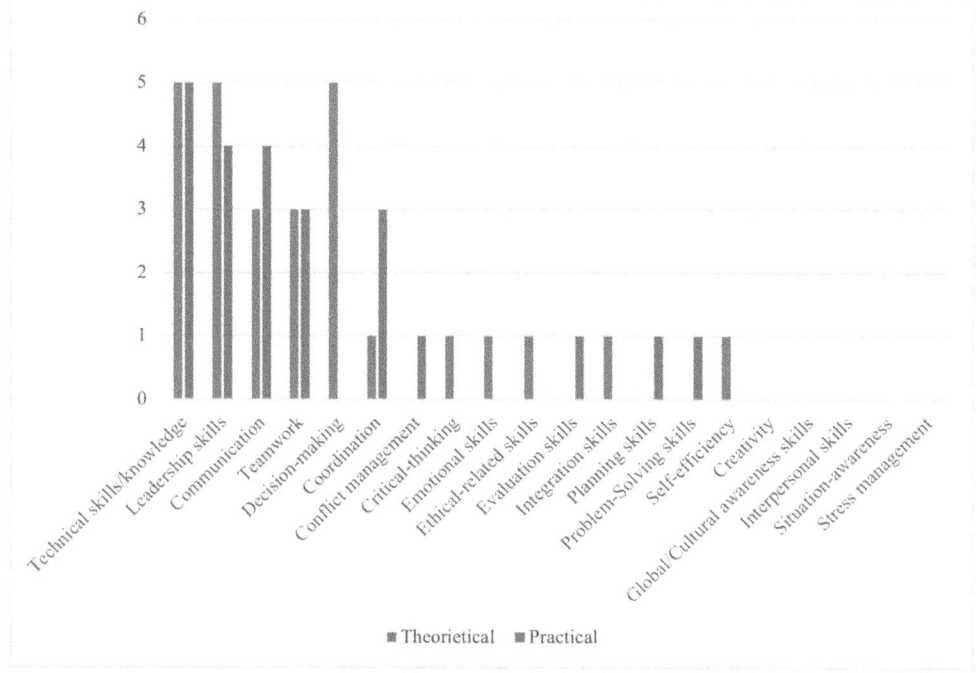

How Are Crisis Trainings Conducted in Respect to Types of Delivery, Content, and Training Strategies?

Ten different **types of training delivery** could be identified across all occupational areas, as can be seen in Figure 11. Hereby, face-to-face courses lead the way (21 trainings). Training programs that are conducted fully online, whether in the form of self-paced online courses (13 trainings) or virtual live classes (11 trainings), follow.

Figure 11. The training sample's types of training delivery, presented in descending order of magnitude
Source: Adapted from (Flin & O'Connor, 2017)

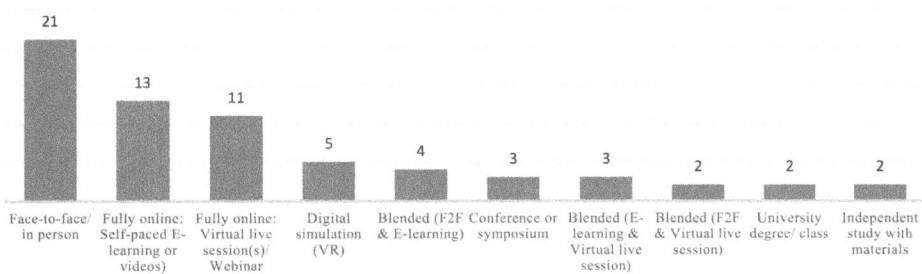

To get a full picture of strategies used to deliver the training, 28 diverse methods were first identified and then clustered according to the training phases alluded to in Chapter 2.3.3. (Figure 12).

When it comes to *Step 1: Conveying information*, presentations are on top of the list (19 trainings). Simulations are the leading strategy used for *Step 3: Practice* (14 trainings). (Further explanation follows in discussion section 4.2).

Concerning the training courses' curricula, they were thoroughly studied and distinguished based on noticeable foci taken (see Appendix 10). As such, different *timeframes* (pre-crisis, during, or post-crisis) are addressed, while a major emphasis is laid on the de-escalation of critical situations (49 trainings). By examining the *specificity of the content*, meaning whether crisis management in general is addressed (29 trainings) or whether the content is adapted and tailored towards a particular area (35 trainings), one can observe balanced proportions. Only two trainings also devoted some time to delivering content specific to the training provider (e.g., an explanation of the history of the Red Cross). Moreover, six curricula could be adapted according to training needs, and 10 curricula involved tools, frameworks, or models, either adopted from others or created by the training provider.

To attain the possibility of approximately determining whether there has been any progress in the domain of crisis training, the results of Ingrassia and colleagues' (2014) study will be compared to this paper's findings. Whereas the researchers have also conducted an internet-based qualitative search to scrutinize disaster management training programs based on the same criteria, their study was solely focused on the European Union back in 2012. Hence, it will be possible to point out similarities and differences between their sample of 140 EU trainings and this thesis' global sample at different points in time. Before the three diverse phases of training will be scrutinized, a common ground regarding this thesis' sample will be built by first covering two of the training benchmarking graphs.

Figure 12. Strategies used across the different phases of training
Source: Adapted from (Flin & O'Connor, 2017)

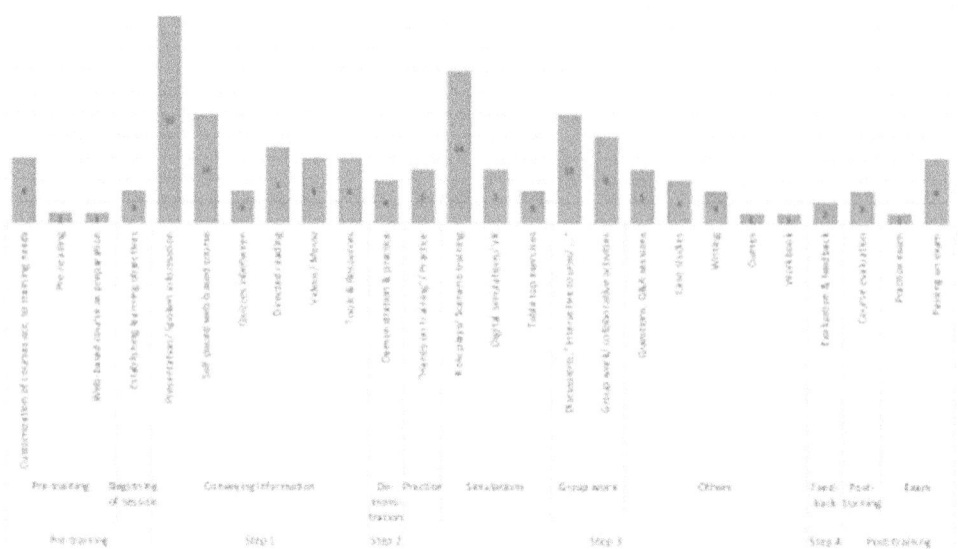

SOLUTIONS AND RECOMMENDATIONS

Considering the potential benefits in terms of people's performance in dealing with crises, emergencies, and disasters on an individual level as well as in groups, the topic of soft skills is certain to become even more of a priority in order to deal with ongoing changes (Coelho & Martins, 2022). When it comes to preparing for crisis and catastrophe circumstances, however, hard skills should not be overlooked. In the next section, the various training approaches for soft and hard skills will be further examined, according to the 3 stages of training: pre-training, during training and post-training.

Pre-Training

Regarding the phase before training in this sample, the initial training needs analysis (TNA) suggested by research does not seem to be conducted in most cases. As backed up by research, taking TNA results into account when creating trainings would maximize training outcomes and should, therefore, be considered by crisis training program managers across industries.

The **types of delivery** can also be chosen according to the group's capabilities and demands. Judging from this work's sample, face-to-face classes (F2F) are still deemed the most effective type training delivery. This finding also coincides with Ingrassia and colleagues (2014) results, where 84% of trainings consisted of F2F classes. This makes sense since human beings are naturally inclined to interact with other people and are used to learning in this manner.

However, courses that are offered fully online have gained immense popularity. These findings can be backed up by research stating that the COVID-19 pandemic boosted and forced the global usage of the Internet for training and, thus, has helped modernize this domain (Marinoni, Land, & Jensen, 2020).

So much so that top-ranked universities have been partnering with specialized online education providers to deliver curricula in the form of self-paced e-learnings. With passing time and accumulating experience both from the side of e-learning training providers as well as trainees, this fairly novel format of learning will be adjusted to meet the learning needs ingrained in human nature more adequately. In this way, it will represent a more valid alternative to live training, which is especially important for the crisis training niche. Since the benefits of e-learning lie in its immense potential to supply instant training to whomever and from the comfort of any place, people in need that might otherwise have no access to trainers or no time to wait can reap these courses' benefits.

Following the notion of increased popularity of online trainings, self-paced web courses are closely succeeded by *virtual online sessions and webinars*. Though F2F courses will most probably remain the courses best perceived by participants, both live formats (either F2F or virtual ones) prove to be efficient according to Ganesh, Paswan, and Sun (2015). By making sure to incorporate human interaction in online live courses, they could also be rated higher by future participants and still foster soft skills that are required during times of crisis.

Blended formats seem to be used to prepare learners for live sessions with the help of preparation material beforehand to save time during class and to prepare learners for the upcoming course (possibly also as part of the preparation of the right learning climate).

The fact that *several trainings are offered in multiple deliveries* might indicate that training providers try to appeal to as many trainees as possible by offering their programs in differing forms. Through this self-selection by the trainees, training needs get indirectly taken care of, even if a TNA by the training providers hasn't necessarily been conducted before.

Among professional sectors, there seem to be differences in types of delivery. For instance, the health care industry prefers not only *face-to-face options* (14 trainings) and those that are offered fully online (8 *virtual live classes*, 5 *e-learnings*), but also makes the most use of the delivery type "c*onference/ symposium*" (6 trainings), whereas organizations and businesses, offer training in almost every delivery type other than *conference/symposium, independent study,* and the *blended option, including F2F and virtual live classes.* All in all, as literature and practice have shown, diversification pays off. This phenomenon also applies to the types of delivery used in different areas. Hence, program managers and participants could try to switch up their common modes of delivery in order to determine whether there might be other options that work, too.

As a last step of the preparation phase, it is up to the trainers to **prepare the right learning climate,** hereby, one can observe that two trainings in this study require the trainees to finish a reading or a web-based course before the day of the training. This technique might not only equip participants with information but also spark their learning motivation for the training and can be recommended for other programs as well.

Furthermore, it can be assumed that some of the training program managers could stay in close contact with the trainees before the training and prepare the learning climate without stating so in their training descriptions on the websites. Likewise, there are some training programs that require leaders or a responsible person to get in contact with the program managers in order to schedule a training session. Perhaps some conversations between the program manager and group leader might follow, where the date of the training, the training objectives, or the attendance policy could be discussed. However, these are just assumptions, mitigating the fact that the setting of the right learning climate is not mentioned in any of the training descriptions. According to training literature, integrating the setting of the right learning climate ahead of the session would positively influence trainees' learning progress.

During the Training

Right at the beginning of the session, before the actual training starts, trainees should be clear on the objectives of training. In this sample, although most courses disclosed learning objectives on their websites, only three indicated that there would be a discussion regarding learning objectives. Practitioners should keep in mind that trainees' mindsets represent the cornerstone of training, ultimately determining whether learning content can be attained and transferred or not, including trainees' sense of self-efficacy, goals as well as learning orientation, or motivation to learn.

Therefore, ensuring the right trainee attitude from the beginning should not be neglected. Relating to crisis training, trainers could, for instance, emphasize that each and every person will probably deal with a crisis at some point in time (stressing the relevance of training), and that every single individual could play an important role in saving lives (fostering goal and learning orientation), and that the skills and knowledge have already been acquired by others and, therefore, surely can be learned by the course's participants as well (boosting a sense of self-efficacy and motivation to learn).

Regarding **imparting information**, trainings courses' *timeframe foci* clearly show that there's a tremendous emphasis on the de-escalation of crisis, while pre- and post-crisis management are less addressed elements of crisis management although properly educated workers should be trained on all three crucial phases (Hošková-Mayerová, 2016). Hence, training program managers should make sure to take a more wholesome approach to covering the entire lifecycle of crisis management.

Regarding *content foci*, general crisis management aspects as well as crisis management tailored to specific areas, e.g., medical emergency procedures for health care professionals, are present in the training sample's curriculum. Moreover, Ingrassia and colleagues (2014) found that more than 80% of their sample offered not only multi- but also cross-disciplinary disaster management content. Hence, in general, crisis management trainings seem to successfully cover a broad range of content, a practice that should be maintained.

The courses' curriculum analysis shows that there are 10 trainings that include *own frameworks, models, and tools,* supporting claims that this type of training is mostly don in an unstandardized manner (Ingrassia et al., 2014). While the notion that standardization could help ensure that all important aspects of curricula content are covered and that suiting strategies would be utilized can be supported, it must repeatedly be stressed that tailoring the trainings according to the needs of each individual trainee cohort leads to maximized learning outcomes, according to the literature. Both sentiments could be adhered to, for instance, by creating trainings with standardized building blocks that will be assembled based on the results of the initial TNA.

Having only a brief look at the curricula's *skill focus* (for a deeper analysis, refer to the previous discussion), it becomes evident that this chapter's findings follow the trend set by Ingrassia and colleagues (2014), where a "competency-based approach" was used in the majority of training interventions. Keeping the previously alluded importance of soft skills in crisis training in mind, a strong recommendation to put more effort into teaching of inter-personal skills can be derived. People from virtually any sector in any given situation could yield benefits in this way.

Regarding training **strategies**, *presenting* the content in the form of spoken information seems to be the most preferred way to convey training content. Still, self-paced web-based courses (also addressed in types of delivery) and therewith *strategies used in these e-learnings*, such as breakout rooms and digital whiteboards, have strongly caught up. In both cases, it's important to remember that trainees must be actively involved in the process to keep them interested and listening, ultimately guaranteeing that they really integrate the content. Nevertheless, only three trainings in the sample disclose that they make use of *quizzes during the transmission of information* to incrementally check trainees' understanding. Since many studies have already proven the effectiveness of chapter quizzes during readings on learning outcomes (e.g., Johnson & Kiviniemi, 2009; Pape-Lindstrom, Eddy & Freeman, 2018), one can imagine that this practice would prove as helpful in the crisis training niche, too. These quizzes would engage the group of learners more, keep up their concentration, confirm their understanding, or enable them to ask questions in case of any misunderstanding. After all, the literature on error management shows repeatedly that failure embodies the best teacher (Keith & Frese, 2008).

A more traditional way of conveying information, namely *directed reading*, was mentioned in at least 12.5% of the sample. Regardless, this strategy isn't and shouldn't be seen as a stand-alone method to convey content, rather, it should be a complementary measure alongside a joint discussion about the reading with the whole group, considering the importance of soft skill development in crisis training.

In this thesis' sample, *videos and movies* are used almost as much as directed reading to impart information. Since most people have rarely or never been in a crisis situation, showing participants real-life footage could better prepare them for such scenarios. Moreover, visual learners (i.e., people who build new brain connections the easiest by using their visual senses) get a better chance at understanding and remembering the content in this way (Rogowsky, Calhoun & Tallal, 2015). Lastly, not many of the sample's trainings seem to work with helpful *tools and materials* (e.g., handouts), despite the immense benefits for the crisis management niche in training: Skill and knowledge retention of the crisis training can easily be impeded by the fact that crises do not occur regularly. Materials that were used during training and can be used afterwards are able to stimulate trainees' recall of the training content post-training.

Thus, when considering which strategies to use when conveying the crisis training content, trainers should strive to operate with many different interactive methods to engage the crowd instead of opting for the plain presentation of information. The acquisition of information in every learning type (Rogowsky et al., 2015) that exists among the training cohort according to the TNA as well as the group's attention are guaranteed by activating their corresponding senses in various ways.

After all the content has been fully studied, it is the trainers' turn to **demonstrate the desired behavior in Step 2** of the training. This action gets merely enough attention, at least according to the training descriptions, where only four trainings specifically indicate this step. On the other hand, there are many strategies referenced for the subsequent step. As such, it could be the case that the desired behavior is demonstrated at the beginning of the practice strategies and is simply not mentioned on the websites. If that is not the case, crisis trainings must integrate demonstrations in their sessions before moving on to the next step.

In fact, there are plenty of **practice** opportunities provided during the sample's sessions. Hereby, *simulations* represent the most frequently used form. Bernstein and Rakowitz (2012) acknowledge the relevance of simulations in crisis training, as they mimic and offer the opportunity to experience scenarios where command, communication, coordination, and control are required. They see simulations not only as a beneficial exercise but as a necessity for any individual likely to face a crisis over the course of their life. Simulations are either deployed in the traditional way as roleplays or scenario trainings or in a digitalized manner, e.g., through computers. Some even resort to a more recent computer technology: virtual reality (VR). By this means, enormous potential can be tapped into due to the possibility of replicating real life as closely as possible without endangering any of the participants. With further advancements in VR, the training domain should incrementally improve their digital simulations as well, especially in the crisis training niche.

There are also traditional and digital versions of a special type of simulation that emerged in the *health emergency* training area, namely "tabletop exercises" (also TTX). They refer to imitations of emergencies where individuals practice their behaviors within a stress-free and informal group discussion (Frégeau et al., 2020). Traditionally, they have been used to assess an organization's readiness level to deal with a disaster and to train health care professionals on their roles during the de-escalation phase. Hence, other areas could analyze these long-used tabletop exercises and adopt aspects they deem beneficial for their trainee cohort and their corresponding training needs in their own simulations or group works, which tabletop exercises can be classified as, too.

Within *group works*, discussions among participants get highly valued by program managers, as do collaborative activities. Both are essential to foster the already mentioned soft skills that are needed in crisis scenarios. For that reason, crisis training programs all around the world should keep up their practice of letting their trainees work out tasks as an ensemble.

Other practice strategies are led by *case studies*, which are used to "help students connect to the variety of emergencies that may arise and develop knowledge of how organizations have worked through previous emergencies." (Shaw, 2018: 310) According to Barnes, Christensen and Hansen (1994), one can distinguish between several types of case studies. While *descriptive case studies* draw a full picture of the causalities leading up to the catastrophic event, the responding phase, as well as the results of crisis management and the aftermath, *decision case studies* explain the crisis scenario in detail, subsequently putting the readers in the position to determine how to deal with the situation. Since the importance of the development of soft skills has already been established, one can propose that program managers should incorporate more of the latter type of case studies, enabling participants to discuss and foster their group work competencies by solving the case collectively.

In addition, there's only one further training that describes the utilization of games, despite research affirming the effectiveness of 'serious games' in the domain of disaster risk management (Solinska-Nowak et al., 2018). Thus, this method can be considered more often, also in adult education and in the case of crisis training.

Furthermore, writing essays and filling out workbooks belong to common techniques in crisis trainings. Nevertheless, it must be stressed that these strategies might prove helpful in the first step of the training, when information is conveyed. However, writing alone will not equip learners with the skills needed to deal with a crisis as do group discussions, nor do they let them feel similar emotions and imitate actions as do simulations. Therefore, these writing activities should not be categorized as stand-alone practice procedures but rather as add-ons.

After the trainees have displayed their conversion to the desired behavior, the trainer should deliver immediate and constructive **feedback in the last step of the training** so that each trainee has a chance to correct potential mistakes. Especially in procedures concerning crisis situations, where high-risk scenarios are involved, confident implementation of the knowledge is of utter importance. Unfortunately, only two of the examined trainings specifically register feedback in their descriptions. It is likely that more trainers integrate feedback as part of the practice unit. But for the courses that don't allot time for feedback, this procedure certainly must be revised. Trainees can only reap the full benefits of the acquisition of new information and demonstration of desired behavior if these steps are accompanied by practice and, lastly, timely and diagnostic feedback.

Post-Training

After the training has been conducted, there are also some training programs that require their participants to pass an exam which is often a formality, making sure that the participants are eligible to be granted a certificate; assessing trainee satisfaction with training is important to receive feedback and improve crisis trainings.

To guarantee that the training transfer really takes place, crisis trainings should reoccur after a set time. For instance, they could be revised every two years for people to retain their knowledge and skills and to feel more confident to act in the manner taught during training. Also, supervisors and leaders should promote the application of newly acquired skills and eliminate any hurdles that may be present. In the sample, these measures are not emphasized in the training descriptions. Since training transfer is the fundamental goal, managers of crisis training program still must enhance their efforts to counteract skill atrophy, in line with Ingrassia and colleagues' (2014) work.

Figure 13 summarizes the solutions and recommendations in this book chapter.

Figure 13. Summary of recommendations for crisis training practitioners
Source: Adapted from (Flin & O'Connor, 2017)

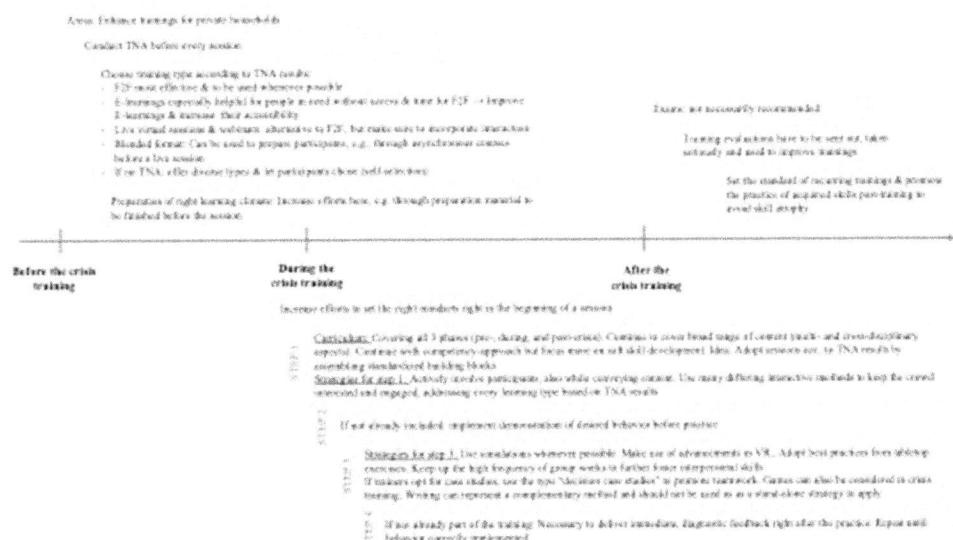

FUTURE RESEARCH DIRECTIONS

The frequency analyses conducted in this paper already yielded interesting insights into the current practices of crisis trainings all around the world. Thus, the procedures chosen can be imitated in future research to draw comparisons and derive further recommendations. To increase a sample's explanatory power over all the crisis trainings available, the sample size should be increased. Furthermore, more keywords for already used or even additional areas could be employed. To collect a more diverse sample, the keywords should also be composed in languages other than English. In contrast to this sample, where *health care* is the primary sector catered to, Ingrassia et al. (2014) noticed that *emergency responders* were the main target group in their research: this because results are highly dependent on the keywords searched for. If researchers in the future aim to identify the area most addressed, diversifying keywords in terms of the different fields, and comparing the search engines' numbers of findings could pose a helpful strategy.

Furthermore, as already mentioned, one can note that military and security staff are less present in this chapter's sample. It can be assumed that they have developed their own training programs so that they are not dependent on exterior training providers and that their programs are not publicly shared for safety reasons. If that belief is true, getting insights into these trainings, which are built on long-term experience, could offer valuable best practices for other areas as well. Therefore, future research could aim to scrutinize unknown programs.

Moreover, one may notice that all the areas represent professions. When it comes to crisis training, private households', or workers' behaviors in case a crisis hits in their free time are hardly addressed (i.e., two trainings). However, it could be advisable to train private households for unprecedented times so that society as a whole is prepared for any case that might come.

Aside from this paper's proceedings, scientific literature, and evidence-based approaches to soft skills development in crisis training are merely existent although their importance is widely accredited. The relatively new realm of digital training promises notably colossal potential. All in all, the crisis training field offers an abundance of yet unresearched aspects. Nonetheless, their exploration would aid not only practitioners but our whole society in coping with the inevitable but still unforeseeable future.

CONCLUSION

In the future, crises like the recent COVID-19 pandemic and natural disasters are expected to occur with a higher frequency. Therefore, the main purpose of this chapter was to find out how people all around the world are being prepared for critical situations. To examine which training methods are used and what competencies are thereby conveyed, a systematic approach to the literature and a frequency analyses of crisis training websites and papers were conducted. The results of both studies showed that training program managers should try to tailor their courses more to participants' training needs while using a plethora of interactive group activities (preferably simulations) to develop the competencies needed most during crises – soft skills.

To be specific, implications for practitioners resulting from the training website analysis include that too few programs conduct a training needs analysis beforehand. However, based on TNA results, the four steps of training – conveyance of information, demonstration of desired behavior, practice, and feedback – including type of training delivery, content, as well as strategies used can be adapted to maximize learning outcomes. Moreover, face-to-face classes are still deemed the most efficient format, while online courses quickly catch up. With time and experience, this type of delivery gains more and more efficiency and can be seen as valid approach by practitioners. Furthermore, simulations are a specifically powerful tool in order to let participants feel similar emotions as in crises situations without endangering them. They can be conducted digitally, or in the form of role plays. If possible, practitioners should try to integrate them into their programs. In general, no matter the training design, interactions among the trainee cohort must be included to develop their interpersonal skills.

On the other hand, the analysis of the crisis training literature also yielded valuable implications for practitioners. As such, it showed that hard skills are frequently taught using simulators in industries like health care and civil aviation. However, soft skills are highly relevant when it comes to unprecedented scenarios. Although they may also be learned through simulators, this chapter's analysis of the literature still implies that practitioners should make trainees study and practice these skills face-to-face with other applicants. In all fields, communication, leadership, and technical knowledge are taught as the three most crucial competencies that are required for various crisis scenarios. With the current pace of change, soft skills become more and more important in all areas as a source of sustainable competitive advantage. Thus, practitioners should prioritize this type of skills' development to benefit individuals, organizations and societies alike in the three stages of the crisis management lifecycle: prevention, de-escalation and recovery.

REFERENCES

Aguinis, H., & Kraiger, K. (2009). Benefits of training and development for individuals and teams, organizations, and society. *Annual Review of Psychology*, *60*(1), 451–474. doi:10.1146/annurev.psych.60.110707.163505 PMID:18976113

Al-Dahash, H., Thayaparan, M., & Kulatunga, U. (2016). Understanding the terminologies: Disaster, crisis, and emergency. *Association of Researchers in Construction Management (ACROM)*, 1191-1200.

American Psychological Association. (2006). *Guidelines and principles for accreditation of programs in professional psychology*. APA. http://www.apa.org/ed/accreditation/about/policies/guiding-principles.Pdf

Bandura, A. (1994). Self-efficacy. In V. S. Ramachaudran (Ed.), *Encyclopedia of human behavior, 4, 71-81*. Academic Press.

Barnes, L. B., Christensen, C. R., & Hansen, A. J. (1994). *Teaching and the case method: Text, cases, and readings*. Harvard Business Press.

Bayley, J. E., Phipps, D., Batac, M., & Stevens, E. (2018). Development of a framework for knowledge mobilisation and impact competencies. *Evidence & Policy*, *14*(04), 725–738. doi:10.1332/174426417X14945838375124

Bernstein, A. B., & Rakowitz, C. (2012). *Emergency public relations: Crisis management in a 3.0 world*. Xlibris Corporation.

Bhaduri, R. M. (2019). Leveraging culture and leadership in crisis management. *European Journal of Training and Development*, *43*(5/6), 554–569. doi:10.1108/EJTD-10-2018-0109

Brooks, B., Curnin, S., Owen, C., & Boldeman, J. (2019). New human capabilities in emergency and crisis management: From non-technical skills to creativity. *Australian Journal of Emergency Management*, *34*(4), 23–30. https://knowledge.aidr.org.au/resources/ajem-october-2019-new-human-capabilities-in-emergency-and-crisis-management-from-non-technical-skills-to-creativity/

Bullard, E. (2022). *Competence*. Salem Press Encyclopedia, Research Starters.

Campbell, J. P. (1971). Personnel training and development. *Annual Review of Psychology*, *22*(1), 565–602. doi:10.1146/annurev.ps.22.020171.003025

Carayon, P., Kleinschmidt, P., Hose, B. Z., & Salwei, M. (2021). Human Factors and Ergonomics in Health Care and Patient Safety from the Perspective of Medical Residents. In L. Donaldson, W. Ricciardi, S. Sheridan, & R. Tartaglia (Eds.), *Textbook of Patient Safety and Clinical Risk Management*. Springer. doi:10.1007/978-3-030-59403-9_7

Choudary, D. V., & Ponnuru, M. (2015). The importance of soft-skills training for MBA students and managers. *Abhinav International Monthly Refereed Journal of Research*, *4*(11), 6–14.

Cimatti, B. (2016). Definition, development, assessment of soft skills and their role for the quality of organizations and enterprises. *International Journal of Qualitative Research*, *10*(1), 97. doi:10.18421/IJQR10.01-05

Cinque, M. (2016). *"Lost in translation". Soft skills development in European countries*. Tuning Journal for Higher Education. doi:10.18543/tjhe-3(2)-2016pp389-427

Coelho, M.J. & Martins, H. (2022). The future of soft skills development: a systematic review of the literature of the digital training practices for soft skills. *Journal of e-Learning and Knowledge Society*, *18*(2), 78-85.

Daoudi, I., Chebil, R., Tranvouez, E., Chaari, W. L., & Espinasse, B. (2017). Towards a grid for characterizing and evaluating crisis management serious games. *International Journal of Information Systems for Crisis Response and Management*, *9*(3), 76–95. doi:10.4018/IJISCRAM.2017070105

Deming, D. (2017). The growing importance of social skills in the labor market. *The Quarterly Journal of Economics*, *132*(4), 1593–1640. https://EconPapers.repec.org/RePEc:oup:qjecon:v:132:y:2017:i:4:p:1593-1640. doi:10.1093/qje/qjx022

Desai, A., Lankford, C., & Schwartz, J. (2020). With crisis comes opportunity: Building ethical competencies in light of COVID-19. *Ethics & Behavior*, *30*(6), 401–413. doi:10.1080/10508422.2020.1762603

Dixon, J., Belnap, C., Albrecht, C. & Lee, K. (2010). The importance of soft skills. *Corporate finance review*, *14*(6), 35.

Donato, H. & Donato, M. (2019). Steps in conducting a systematic review. *Portuguese Medical Act*, *32*(3).

EUCEN. (2008). *Glossary*. Recommendation of the European Parliament and of the Council on the Establishment of the European Qualifications Framework for Lifelong Learning. http://www.eucen.eu/EQFpro/GeneralDocs/FilesFeb09/GLOSSARY.pdf

Flin, R., & O'Connor, P. (2017). *Safety at the sharp end: a guide to non-technical skills*. CRC Press. doi:10.1201/9781315607467

Frégeau, A., Cournoyer, A., Maheu-Cadotte, M.-A., Iseppon, M., Soucy, N., Bourque, J. S.-C., Cossette, S., Castonguay, V., & Fleet, R. (2020). Use of tabletop exercises for healthcare education: A scoping review protocol. *BMJ Open*, *10*(1), e032662. doi:10.1136/bmjopen-2019-032662 PMID:31915165

Ganesh, G., Paswan, A., & Sun, Q. (2015). Are face-to-face classes more effective than online classes? An empirical examination. *Marketing Education Review*, *25*(2), 67–81. doi:10.1080/10528008.2015.1029851

Garcia-Perez, A., Cegarra-Navarro, J. G., Bedford, D., Thomas, M., & Wakabayashi, S. (2020). *Critical Capabilities and Competencies for Knowledge Organizations*. Emerald Publishing Limited.

Gladstone, M., & Brown, S. (2022). Soft skills in a hard world: Why emergency management and business continuity leaders must update their professional toolbox. *Journal of Business Continuity & Emergency Planning*, *15*(3), 225–236. https://www.ingentaconnect.com/contentone/hsp/jbcep/2022/00000015/00000003/art00003 PMID:35190015

Goldstein, I. L., & Ford, J. K. (2002). *Training in organisations*. Wadsworth.

Gregory, A. (2005). Communication dimensions of the UK foot and mouth disease crisis, 2001. *Journal of Public Affairs*, *5*(3–4), 312–328. doi:10.1002/pa.31

Haselberger, D., Oberhuemer, P., Perez, E., Cinque, M., & Capasso, F. (2012). *Mediating Soft Skills at Higher Education Institutions. ModEs project: Lifelong Learning Program*. GEA College. https://gea-college.si/wp-content/uploads/2015/12/MODES_handbook_en.pdf

Hassell, K. D. (2020). The impact of crisis intervention team training for police. *International Journal of Police Science & Management*, *22*(2), 159–170. doi:10.1177/1461355720909404

Heckman, J. J., & Kautz, T. (2012). Hard evidence on soft skills. *Labour Economics*, *19*(4), 451–464. doi:10.1016/j.labeco.2012.05.014 PMID:23559694

Helmreich, R. L., Merritt, A. C., & Wilhelm, J. A. (2009). The evolution of crew resource management training in commercial aviation. In R. Key Dismukes (Ed.), *Human Error in Aviation* (pp. 275–288). Routledge.

Hendarman, A. F., & Cantner, U. (2018). Soft skills, hard skills, and individual innovativeness. *Eurasian Business Review*, *8*(2), 139–169. doi:10.100740821-017-0076-6

Hošková-Mayerová, S. (2016). Education and training in crisis management. In Z. Bekirogullari, M. Y. Minas, & R. X. Thambusamy (Eds.), *ICEEPSY 2016: Education and Educational Psychology* (pp. 849–856)., doi:10.15405/epsbs.2016.11.87

Ingrassia, P., Foletti, M., Djalali, A., Scarone, P., Ragazzoni, L., Corte, F., & Fisher, P. (2014). Education and training initiatives for crisis management in the European Union: A web-based analysis of available programs. *Prehospital and Disaster Medicine*, *29*(2), 115–126. doi:10.1017/S1049023X14000235 PMID:24642198

James, E. H., & Wooten, L. P. (2005). Leadership as (Un)usual: How to display competence in times of crisis. *Organizational Dynamics*, *34*(2), 141–152. doi:10.1016/j.orgdyn.2005.03.005

Jankelová, N., & Mišún, J. (2021). Key competencies of agricultural managers in the acute stage of the COVID-19 crisis. *Agriculture*, *11*(1), 59. doi:10.3390/agriculture11010059

Jaques, T. (2007). Issue management and crisis management: An integrated, non-linear, relational construct. *Public Relations Review, 33*(2), 147–157. doi:10.1016/j.pubrev.2007.02.001

John, J. (2009). Study on the nature of impact of soft skills training programme on the soft skills development of management students. *Pacific Business Review*, 19-27.

Johnson, B. C., & Kiviniemi, M. T. (2009). The effect of online chapter quizzes on exam performance in an undergraduate social psychology course. *Teaching of Psychology, 36*(1), 33–37. doi:10.1080/00986280802528972 PMID:20046908

Joynes, C., Rossignoli, S., & Amonoo-Kuofi, E. F. (2019). *21st century skills: Evidence of issues in definition, demand, and delivery for development context. K4D Emerging Issues Report.* Institute of Development Studies., https://opendocs.ids.ac.uk/opendocs/handle/20.500.12413/14674

Kanki, B. G., Helmreich, R. L., & Anca, J. (2010). *Crew resource management* (2nd ed.). Academic Press. doi:10.1016/B978-0-12-374946-8.10004-4

Keith, N., & Frese, M. (2008). Effectiveness of error management training: A meta-analysis. *The Journal of Applied Psychology, 93*(1), 59–69. doi:10.1037/0021-9010.93.1.59 PMID:18211135

Khodarahmi, E. (2009). Crisis management. *Disaster Prevention and Management, 18*(5), 523–528. doi:10.1108/09653560911003714

Kim, Y., & Lim, H. (2020). Activating constructive employee behavioural responses in a crisis: Examining the effects of pre-crisis reputation and crisis communication strategies on employee voice behaviours. *Journal of Contingencies and Crisis Management, 28*(2), 141–157. doi:10.1111/1468-5973.12289

Kraiger, K. (2003). Perspectives on training and development. In W. C. Borman, D. R. Ilgen, & R. J. Klimoski (Eds.), *Industrial and organizational psychology, 12* (pp. 171–192). Handbook of psychology. John Wiley & Sons, Inc., doi:10.1002/0471264385.wei1208

Lockwood, N. R. (2005). *Crisis management in today's business environment: HR's strategic role.* Society for Human Resource. https://www.shrm.org/hr-today/news/hr-magazine/documents/120 5rquartpdf.pdf

Marinoni, G., Land, H.V. & Jensen, T. (2020). The impact of Covid-19 on higher education around the world. *IAU global survey report,* 23.

Matteson, M. L., Anderson, L., & Boyden, C. (2016). "Soft skills": A phrase in search of meaning. *portal. Portal (Baltimore, Md.), 16*(1), 71–88. doi:10.1353/pla.2016.0009

McNeill, J. (2019). Skills vs. competencies – What's the difference, and why should you care? *Hays Social Worldwide.* https://social.hays.com/2019/10/04/skills-competencies-whats -the-difference/

Methley, A. M., Campbell, S., Chew-Graham, C., McNally, R., & Cheraghi-Sohi, S. (2014). PICO, PICOS and SPIDER: A comparison study of specificity and sensitivity in three search tools for qualitative systematic reviews. *BMC Health Services Research, 14*(1), 579. doi:10.118612913-014-0579-0 PMID:25413154

Mirabile, R. J. (1997). Everything you wanted to know about competency modeling. *Training & Development, 51*(8), 73+. https://link.gale.com/apps/doc/A20021823/AONE?u=anon~f2a0c5d4&sid=googleScholar&xid=aa3c51fe

Mitroff, I., & Alpaslan, M. C. (2003). Preparing for evil. *Harvard Business Review, 81*(4), 109–115. PMID:12687925

Moghabghab, R., Tong, A., Hallaran, A., & Anderson, J. (2018). The difference between competency and competence: A regulatory perspective. *Journal of Nursing Regulation, 9*(2), 54–59. doi:10.1016/S2155-8256(18)30118-2

Naamati Schneider, L., Meirovich, A., & Dolev, N. (2020). Soft skills on-line development in times of crisis. *Revista Romaneasca Pentru Educatie Multidimensionala, 12*(1Sup2), 122-129. doi:10.18662/rrem/12.1sup2/255

Naik, V. N., & Brien, S. E. (2013). Review article: Simulation: A means to address and improve patient safety. *Canadian Journal of Anesthesia/Journal Canadien d'anesthésie, 60*(2), 192–200. doi:10.1007/s12630-012-9860-z

Nickerson, A. B., Cook, E. E., Cruz, M. A., & Parks, T. W. (2019). Transfer of school crisis prevention and intervention training, knowledge, and skills: Training, trainee, and work environment predictors. *School Psychology Review, 48*(3), 237–250. doi:10.17105/SPR-2017-0140.V48-3

Noe, R. A., Hollenbeck, J., Gerhart, B., & Wright, P. (2020). *Fundamentals of Human Resource Management* (8th ed.). McGraw-Hill.

Ong, Y. H., & Tan, Y. H. (2018). The development of a skills taxonomy for nursing crisis management. *Clinical Simulation in Nursing, 25*, 6–11. doi:10.1016/j.ecns.2018.09.003

Page, C., Wilson, M., & Kolb, D. (1993). *Managerial competencies and New Zealand managers: On the inside, looking in*. University of Auckland.

Page, M. J., McKenzie, J. E., Bossuyt, P. M., Boutron, I., Hoffmann, T. C., Mulrow, C. D., Shamseer, L., Tetzlaff, J. M., Akl, E. A., Brennan, S. E., Chou, R., Glanville, J., Grimshaw, J. M., Hróbjartsson, A., Lalu, M. M., Li, T., Loder, E. W., Mayo-Wilson, E., McDonald, S., & Moher, D. (2021). The PRISMA 2020 statement: An updated guideline for reporting systematic reviews. *BMJ (Clinical Research Ed.), 372*(71), n71. doi:10.1136/bmj.n71 PMID:33782057

Pape-Lindstrom, P., Eddy, S., & Freeman, S. (2018). Reading quizzes improve exam scores for community college students. *CBE Life Sciences Education, 17*(2), ar21. doi:10.1187/cbe.17-08-0160 PMID:29749839

Paraskevas, A. (2006). Crisis management or crisis response system? A complexity science approach to organizational crises. *Management Decision, 44*(7), 892–907. doi:10.1108/00251740610680587

Patacsil, F., & Tablatin, S., C. (. (2017). Exploring the importance of soft and hard skills as perceived by IT internship students and industry: A gap analysis. *Journal of Technology and Science Education, 7*(3), 347–368. doi:10.3926/jotse.271

Powell, K. S., & Yalcin, S. (2010). Managerial training effectiveness: A meta-analysis 1952-2002. *Personnel Review, 39*(2), 227–241. doi:10.1108/00483481011017435

Rogowsky, B. A., Calhoun, B. M., & Tallal, P. (2015). Matching learning style to instructional method: Effects on comprehension. *Journal of Educational Psychology*, *107*(1), 64–78. doi:10.1037/a0037478

Salas, E., & Cannon-Bowers, J. A. (2001). The science of training: A decade of progress. *Annual Review of Psychology*, *52*(1), 471–499. doi:10.1146/annurev.psych.52.1.471 PMID:11148314

Salas, E., DiazGranados, D., Klein, C., Burke, C. S., Stagl, K. C., Goodwin, G. F., & Halpin, S. M. (2008). Does team training improve team performance? A meta-analysis. *Human Factors*, *50*(6), 903–933. doi:10.1518/001872008X375009 PMID:19292013

Salas, E., Nichols, D. R., & Driskell, J. E. (2007). Testing three team training strategies in intact teams: A meta-analysis. *Small Group Research*, *38*(4), 471–488. doi:10.1177/1046496407304332

Salas, E., Tannenbaum, S. I., Kraiger, K., & Smith-Jentsch, K. A. (2012). The science of training and development in organizations: What matters in practice. *Psychological Science in the Public Interest*, *13*(2), 74–101. doi:10.1177/1529100612436661 PMID:26173283

Salas, E., Wilson, K. A., Priest, H. A., & Guthrie, J. W. (2006). Training in organizations: The design, delivery and evaluation of training systems. In G. Salvendy (Ed.), *Handbook of human factors and ergonomics* (3rd ed., pp. 472–512). John Wiley. doi:10.1002/0470048204.ch18

Schulz, B. (2008). The importance of soft skills: Education beyond academic knowledge. *Journal of Language and Communication*, *2*, 146–154.

Shaw, M. (2018). Teaching campus crisis management through case studies: Moving between theory and practice. *Journal of Student Affairs Research and Practice*, *55*(3), 308–320. doi:10.1080/1949659 1.2018.1399894

Solinska-Nowak, A., Magnuszewski, P., Curl, M., French, A., Keating, A., Mochizuki, J., Liu, W., Mechler, R., Kulakowska, M., & Jarzabek, L. (2018). „An overview of serious games for disaster risk management–Prospects and limitations for informing actions to arrest increasing risk. *International Journal of Disaster Risk Reduction*, *31*, 1013–1029. doi:10.1016/j.ijdrr.2018.09.001

Turner, D., & Crawford, M. (1994). Future competitive. *Competence-Based Competition*, *4*, 241.

Vaira, M. (2004). Globalization and higher education organizational change: A framework for analysis. *Higher Education*, *48*(4), 483–510. doi:10.1023/B:HIGH.0000046711.31908.e5

Van Wart, M., & Kapucu, N. (2011). Crisis management competencies: The case of emergency managers in the USA. *Public Management Review*, *13*(4), 489–511. doi:10.1080/14719037.2010.525034

Vargo, J., & Seville, E. (2011). Crisis strategic planning for SMEs: Finding the silver lining. *International Journal of Production Research*, *49*(18), 5619–5635. doi:10.1080/00207543.2011.563902

Wang, M. (2017). Using crisis simulation to enhance crisis management competencies: The role of presence. *Journal of Public Relations Education*, *3*(2), 96–109.

Warin, J. (2017). Creating a whole school ethos of care. *Emotional & Behavioural Difficulties*, *22*(3), 188–199. doi:10.1080/13632752.2017.1331971

World Health Organization. (2022). *Coronavirus disease (COVID-19) pandemic*. World Health Organization. https://www.who.int/europe/emergencies/situations/covid-19#:~:text=This%20led%20WHO%20to%20declare,have%20died%20from%20the%20disease

Yang, D., Wei, Y. K., Xue, F. S., Deng, X. M., & Zhi, J. (2016). Simulation-based airway management training: Application and looking forward. *Journal of Anesthesia*, *30*(2), 284–289. doi:10.100700540-015-2116-7 PMID:26671260

Zimmerman, L. A., Sestokas, J. M., Burns, C. A., Bell, J., & Manning, D. (2012). *Methods and Tools for Training Crisis Response*. U.S. Army Research Institute for the Behavioral and Social Sciences. doi:10.1037/e643372013-001

KEY TERMS AND DEFINITIONS

Competence: The capacity of an individual to consistently use the information, skill, and judgment necessary for safe, moral, and efficient practice, that is akin to practical wisdom.

Competency: a combination of knowledge, ability, and skill that is necessary for proficient task or job performance.

Crisis Management: An activity whereby experiences and perceptions are shaped through interaction with stakeholders to prevent, rectify, recover, and learn from crises.

Crisis: A high-impact, low-probability, disruptive event that comes with uncertainty and risk, whereby decisions and choices must be made under time pressure.

De-escalation: The second stage of crisis management aims at defusing the intensity of a crisis aiming to reduce the likelihood of greater damages or the aggravation of the situation.

Hard Skills: Technical abilities required to do certain activities while processing information; these skills are predominantly cognitive in nature.

Prevention: The first step in crisis management, prevention aims to mindfully avoid crisis situations, including for example, establishing procedures for a range of crisis situations or monitoring risks.

Recovery: The last step in crisis management, recovery happens in the aftermath of the crisis situation aiming to help individuals, organizations and societies return to their baseline and mitigate the potential effects of other similar and deriving crises.

Skill: The ability to put knowledge and expertise to use in completing tasks and resolving issues.

Soft Skills: Intrapersonal and interpersonal abilities that are crucial for healthy interaction and cooperation in general as well as successfully navigating the challenges of a changing world.

Chapter 13
Taming the HiPPO (Highest Paid Person's Opinion) With Agile Metrics and Value Management

Chabi Gupta

https://orcid.org/0000-0002-1927-4349

School of Commerce, CHRIST University, India

ABSTRACT

If the organisation's ecosystem has an excess of HiPPOs, data, measured analytics, and other real-time information that minimises uncertainty can help them mitigate the consequences. They disregard the wisdom of the crowd, overlook the front-line staff's abilities, and risk disengaging the workforce. This research advocates agile metrics and value management to tame the HiPPO. The authors posit to reign in opinions with metrics. The corporate enlightenment brought about a revolutionary idea over three centuries ago: to elevate science and knowledge above magical thought and mysticism. When the authors convert this into modern terms, they are referring to data-driven management, analytics, and hypothesis validation. In fact, the idea of applying science in the form of true evidence, confirmed data, etc. to production processes underlies much of the industrial revolution.

INTRODUCTION

In the fast-paced world of business, it is imperative to make informed decisions based on reliable data rather than relying solely on instincts. Data provides a solid foundation for decision-making by offering an objective and analytical perspective that considers various factors affecting the organization's performance. Contrary to popular belief, making quick assumptions without considering all aspects can prove detrimental in the long run. However, instincts play a vital role too as they are often shaped by years of experience and knowledge gained through working in different environments or dealing with diverse challenges. Successful leaders have honed their intuition over time and trust their gut feeling when faced with complex situations. It allows them to take calculated risks while avoiding pitfalls that could negatively impact organizational growth.

DOI: 10.4018/978-1-6684-8392-3.ch013

Thus, using both data-driven analysis and instinctual judgment can lead organizations towards success as they complement each other perfectly - one providing insights into hard numbers while others offer invaluable insight gleaned from personal experiences and professional acumen. By integrating these two approaches seamlessly within the workplace culture, companies can improve retention and engagement of employees. Achieving the ideal balance between art and science is a complex process that requires an individual to possess astute judgment, intuition, and skillful interpretation of data. Knowing when to rely on statistics or trust one's gut feeling entails grappling with the intricacies of human decision-making which demands both humility and open-mindedness towards potential errors in judgement. Being able to navigate ambiguity deftly is essential for making informed decisions whilst weighing all available options carefully. Such nuanced understanding underscores the importance of harmonizing analytical prowess with emotional intelligence for effective leadership in any field or endeavor.

A well-crafted analogy possesses the unique ability to bridge seemingly disconnected concepts and transform abstract ideas into easily understandable ones. The sheer power of an effective comparison is undeniable, as it can leave a lasting impression on our minds that proves hard to shake off. For instance, when we come across the term "business ecosystem," what follows is an immediate mental image of a vast savanna teeming with life - majestic gazelles keeping watchful eyes over their younglings while cunning predators lay in wait for unsuspecting prey (Beinart & Coates, 2002). We envision murky ponds where crocodiles lurk beneath its surface, oblivious to the presence of giant hippos nearby. Such vivid imagery not only simplifies comprehension but also aids memory retention by offering visual cues that stimulate imagination and creativity within us all. Many species of this corporate ecosystem congregate in these "ponds." Some people arrive quietly, taking notes and without speaking unless spoken to. Some people make their presence known by raising their voices over others; their argument is based on volume.

Others seize control of the meeting and "facipulate" (manipulate) it; they rise and take notes or draw, promising to transmit a summary of what was agreed upon to sway the message closer to their goals. Then there are the hippos, who appear serene and asleep until they open their mouths, capsize the tourists' boat, and turn everything upside down.

According to the HiPPO effect, the opinion of the individual who makes the most money is given more weight in a judgement because it has a greater innate value. The worth of an opinion is thus proportional to the income of the person who expresses it. The higher the salary, the more the opinion gains perspective in the decision-making process.

The HiPPO effect is a fascinating phenomenon that sheds light on how human judgment operates. At its core, this concept suggests that when it comes to decision-making, the opinion of individuals with higher incomes holds more sway than those who earn less. This implies that there is an inherent value associated with wealth and status - qualities which are assumed to translate into expertise, credibility, or better information. In practice, what this means is that opinions expressed by high earners tend to be given more weight in important matters because they carry greater perceived merit. The idea here being that the amount one earns reflects their level of competence or knowledge in a particular area – as though income serves as some sort of proxy for wisdom or insight. However problematic such thinking may be from an ethical standpoint (and make no mistake; many critics have pointed out flaws in the logic), it remains true that our judgments can often hinge on factors beyond pure reason alone. Indeed, studies show time and again how biases related to identity markers like race.

In the cutthroat world of corporate business, it is an undeniable truth that HiPPOs - or highest-paid person's opinions - reign supreme in high-level meetings. These individuals, often occupying top management positions, hold a level of authority and decision-making power unparalleled by their peers. Their influence can make, or break deals worth millions of dollars and shape the future trajectory of entire companies. The mere presence of a HiPPO in a boardroom commands attention and respect from those present. Their word is law, and few are brave enough to challenge their ideas for fear of retribution or professional consequences. The result? A culture where innovation takes second place to conformity; where employees are discouraged from expressing dissenting views; where diversity is stifled under the weighty hand of hierarchy (Shin et al., 2020). While some may argue that HiPPOs bring invaluable expertise to the table, others see them as obstacles hindering progress towards more inclusive decision-making processes. To truly thrive in today's rapidly evolving market landscape, businesses must move towards data driven decision making (Shin et al., 2020).

People with a specific level of status (and authority) inside an organisation have a super-strong capacity for conviction, allowing them to weigh in on issues far more than others. (Lefebvre et al., 2022). These important positions are attained by specific managerial skills, knowledge, assertiveness, and personal talents, or by working longer hours than anyone else... always complimented by being in the right place at the right time. They all, however, have a strong confirmation bias, believing that they are not in that position by accident and that their judgement and intuition, which have led them there, are infallible and must be acknowledged by others. (Vedejová et al., 2022). Individuals who hold a certain level of status and authority within an organization possess an immensely powerful ability to influence others through their unwavering conviction. This unyielding sense of purpose allows them to have greater impact when expressing their opinions and perspectives on complex issues, far surpassing the weight that those with lesser status might carry in similar situations. Such individuals are often seen as pillars of leadership, revered for their exceptional confidence and capacity for decisive action.

The following are the characteristics of a suitable metric:

- They make sense on their own and don't need any more clarification.
- Like other things of the same kind.
- In the form of a ratio, percentage, or index, rather than an absolute number.
- The measure is strengthened and supplemented by another parameter, maybe one that relates to size or effort, Speed, for instance in relation to distance/time.
- and affect how individuals think, behave, and do things, as in the examples given.

Because evil never quits, the metrics, or data, can be infused with irrational thinking. Vanity metrics, for example, enhance the ego while providing little information or value. A team may be extremely happy of having completed a huge number of integrations or rectified several faults, but this tells us nothing about the value they provide, which is what matters. Vanity metrics are a bug in businesses; they pervade processes, distorting perceptions of reality, providing a false sense of certainty, and diverting attention away from what is genuinely essential (Carillo et al., 2019).

There are various sorts of metrics that can be used to assess value:

(Nazarenko et al., 2022) highlighted in their research that decisions can be made with actionable metrics. Vanity metrics are the exact opposite of them. Commuting time saved by building a new road is an example of an actionable metric. The "vanity" variant of this statistic is the length of the new road in miles.

The distinction between qualitative and quantitative metrics is that the former is based on observation and subjective evaluation, whilst the latter is obtained empirically.

Lagging and leading metrics are recordings of what happened, while the latter tells us where the data we're tracking is going. The number of speeding citations obtained on a long trip, for example, is a lagging signal that cannot be changed.

There are various sorts of measures that can be used to assess value:

By keeping an eye on our speed to prevent exceeding the speed limit, we can predict the speeding penalties we will receive at the end and take appropriate action.

Metrics that are connected and causal: With causal metrics, one variable causes the other (for example, spending capacity and income, quality/UX investment and customer satisfaction, rash judgments and company risks, and so on). The variables in correlated metrics are related in some way, but one does not cause the other. For example, just because ice cream consumption and geyser sales both rise at the same time does not suggest that people eat ice cream because of geyser. Both are connected, but not causally.

BACKGROUND

Literature Review

Although there is some evidence that using business analytics may be beneficial, the claim that "business analytics leads to value" must be further investigated (Sharma et al., 2014).

Because better decision-making processes often result in greater organisational performance, Sharma et al. (2014) argue that firms need to have a deeper understanding of their decision-making processes to identify how value may be gained via the use of business analytics. Using Business Data Analytics, businesses may collect their data, analyse it, and then utilise the findings to inform a number of strategic decisions (Pandey et al., 2022). When compared to modest sized data analytics, which aid in the decision-making process from the inside of a company, this method enables businesses to not only uncover new opportunities to provide high-value goods and services to consumers, but it also supports the internal decision-making process (Latan et al., 2018).

For example, LinkedIn's founder and current chairman, Reid Hoffman, together with his company's data scientists, have developed such features as Who's Viewed, and People You May Know. My Linkedin Page (Barton & Court, 2012). Because of the efficient analytics systems they have in place, a number of companies, like Amazon (with their recommendation systems) and Netflix (with their consumer choice modelling), have grown more productive and competitive in recent years (Fosso Wamba et al., 2018). Predictive analytics refers to a group of strategies that use current and historical data to forecast future outcomes. When it comes to making strategic choices, combining analytical thinking with intuitive analysis may provide longer-term outcomes that are more successful than those generated by using either method alone (Ransbotham et al. 2016).

The HiPPO effect is a common occurrence in many organizations, where even the most well-meaning leader can lose touch with their customers or forget to consider input from their own staff. This phenomenon often occurs when the highest-paid employee assumes that they are always the person in the room with the best idea due to their past successes, numerous promotions, and support from other decision-makers within the company (Gazdula, 2017). However, this belief can be dangerous as it may lead to an overreliance on one individual's perspective and prevent diverse viewpoints from being considered (Carillo, 2019). As a result of this narrow-minded approach, important insights may go unnoticed and potential opportunities for growth could be missed (Barton & Court, 2012). To overcome such challenges posed by HiPPO effect leaders must remain vigilant about considering all available information sources including feedbacks of employees at various levels while making critical decisions. By doing so they will ensure that no voice goes unheard, and every opportunity is explored fully before any course of action taken resulting in better outcomes for everyone involved (Gazdula, 2017).

Figure 1. Various challenges of agile metrics

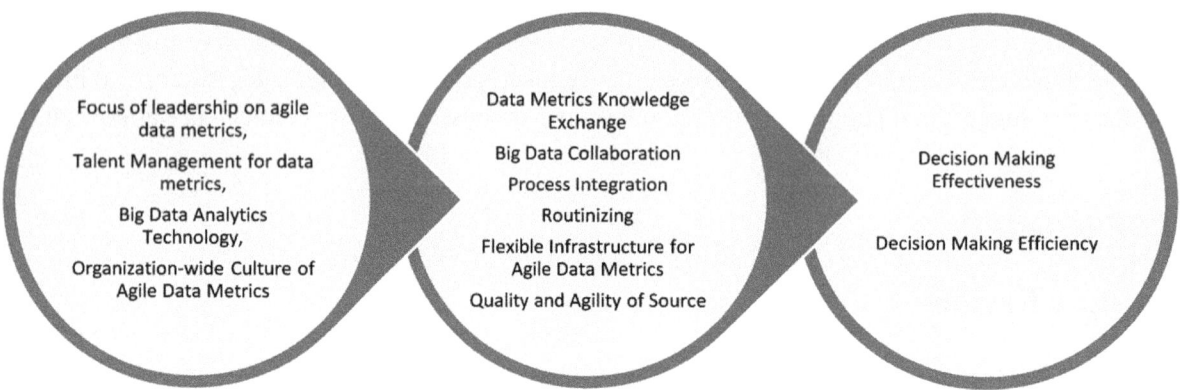

Research Methodology

This study used qualitative data collection methods because the research was exploratory in nature (Saunders et al., 2012). The complexity of the research issues necessitated the use of qualitative approaches in this study (Saunders et al., 2012). Because the goal of the study was to learn about the obstacles and potential of using agile metrics and value management in decision-making, non-numerical responses could help to gain a better grasp of the respondents' perspectives. According to Saunders et al. (2012), for researchers to use purposive sampling, they have to pick their examples with extreme caution so that they may obtain meaningful insights and contribute to the answers to the research questions. Because of this, the author made a choice to conduct interviews with individuals who had prior experience working with information systems and making decisions based on data. The author also sought for participants who had prior experience managing the incorporation of corporate data analytics into organisational decision-making processes. This is because the primary emphasis of this research is on the management viewpoint. The questionnaire survey was sent to 650 of the organisations that were discovered via a search conducted on LinkedIn and Google for businesses that base their decisions on agile criteria.

Interviews with participants, some of which were planned and others of which were produced during the course of the interviews, were used to collect the primary data for this study (Collis & Hussey, 2014). The semi-structured interviews created a setting that allowed for further questions to be asked (Saunders et al. 2012). To put it another way, the author was able to have questions that guided the interviews while also having the ability to reorganise the questions and alter them based on the replies of the respondents thanks to the framework that this kind of interview provided. Because of this, the people responding were able to influence the discourse in a direction that was first unexpected or unanticipated, but which may turn out to be crucial (Saunders et al., 2012).

Due to the exploratory goal of the study, semi-structured interviews were helpful in analysing the trend because respondents were given the opportunity to elaborate on their responses regarding problems and factors affecting the adoption of data metrics in decision making. This allowed the analysis of the trend to be more accurate. Because of this, the adaptability of semi-structured and in-depth interviews proved to be useful in extracting interviewees' opinions and knowledge regarding the challenges and opportunities presented by big data, as well as its use in enhancing the quality of decision-making. The study of the data included interpretations according to such views (Saunders et al. 2012). To elicit more in-depth replies from interviewees, both open-ended and in-depth questions were formulated as part of the interview process.

90% managers from a variety of global firms expressed increasing dissatisfaction with faulty decision-making procedures, the slow pace of decision-making deliberations, and the variable quality of decision-making outputs. Fewer than half of survey respondents believed decisions are made on time. A significant proportion of individuals, constituting 61% of the sample population, hold a firm belief that an excessive amount of time spent in the creation process goes to waste due to the involvement and influence of HiPPOs. These high-ranking personnel are deemed responsible for obstructing progress by imposing their own opinions and decisions without considering or incorporating valuable insights from other team members. Consequently, this detrimental practice results in subpar outcomes and missed opportunities for optimizing productivity levels within organizations.

MAIN FOCUS OF THE CHAPTER

What Really is the Vulnerability of the HiPPO Effect?

The HiPPO Effect, also known as the Highest Paid Person's Opinion, refers to a common phenomenon in which decision-making within an organization is heavily influenced by the opinions and input of senior-level executives or individuals who hold high-ranking positions (Brynjolfsson et al., 2011).

However, this vulnerability goes much deeper than just relying on one person's opinion. At its core, the HiPPO Effect can lead to a lack of diversity in ideas and perspectives being considered during important decisions. This can result in missed opportunities for innovation or potentially harmful outcomes if critical information is overlooked due to deference towards those with more authority. Moreover, the influence wielded by those at higher levels may not always align with what is best for the company. Personal biases or limited understanding of certain aspects of operations could cloud judgments and ultimately hinder growth. In essence, organizations must be mindful of how they approach decision-making processes and ensure that multiple voices are heard so that well-informed choices can be made based on collective knowledge rather than individual power dynamics (Brynjolfsson et al., 2011).

First, Milgram experiment of 1963 demonstrated and confirmed in subsequent investigations, that humans have an authority bias. This experiment looked at the tension between obeying an authoritative figure and following one's own conscience. 97% respondents were aware of the HiPPO effect and 33% admitted having been consciously a part of it in the decision-making process sometime in the recent past. 80% of the respondents of this research were of a strong opinion that most people tend to trust "experts", people with years of rich experience and follow their advice. Of course, this tendency benefits mostly in various tough situations, but it can also shut out disagreeing and quite valuable opinions in the workplace. Around 75% of them highlighted that sometimes the most astonishing ideas come from freshers in the organisation. They may be more in line with the latest trends and technologies but if their opinion is not outcome oriented, they become demotivated. Majority (around 80%) strongly advocated that the organisations are at risk of becoming obsolete and out of touch with market reality if the boardrooms are dominated with HiPPO's.

Rotterdam School of Management studied projects spear headed by senior executives and posit they fail more frequently than ones led by junior executives. Employees didn't feel comfortable giving critical input to high-status executives. On the other hand, lower managers profited from the criticisms of their project related plans that were provided by others, which assisted them in developing a more robust strategy. 70% of respondents pointed to occasions in which other decision makers in the boardroom accepted the view of the highest-paid person without inquiry. When this occurred, it gave the highest-paid individual a greater feeling of self-assurance and superiority. As a direct consequence of this, an endless loop arose, which was very hard to interrupt.

Once they have expressed their view, 77% of respondents believe that it is difficult for organisations to go against the opinion of the highest-paid individual without data. In the process of reaching a decision, the voice of the HiPPO will be given more consideration than the consideration given to any other voice. Employees are quite eager to please and readily implement what the leader wants done; consequently, well-intentioned leaders who want to connect with the team and be present in the dialogue do not primarily want their viewpoint to have a greater perspective. Employees are quite eager to implement please and readily do what the leader wants done.

Examining the results of the survey, it was discovered that a staggering 65 percent of respondents held fast to their belief that HiPPO opinions were purely subjective, even when presented with concrete proof. This revelation is quite concerning as it brings attention to the fact that many plans do not prioritize the wishes and desires of individuals who hold higher salaries. In situations where research studies or established facts are lacking, this can pose a significant challenge across various contexts and domains (Carillo, 2019). Clearly, there exists an urgent need for greater awareness and sensitivity towards diverse perspectives in decision-making processes. The HiPPO effect kicks in when a well-meaning leader loses his Midas touch with the firm's customers or forgets that his or her staff provide significant information. Because the highest-paid employee has typically had previous successes, numerous promotions, and consensus building from other decision makers in the organisation, they may really believe they are always without exception, the person in the room with the best idea.

Agile Metrics and Value Management

Agile enterprises, much like any other business out there, have the same overarching goal of ensuring profitability and compliance while maintaining a thorough level of traceability. Despite being an outstanding framework in itself, it begs the question - why bother with Agile if it fails to deliver value? To make certain that expectations are not just met but exceeded, organisations must employ both qualitative and quantitative evaluations to continuously improve their practices. These assessments allow for a more comprehensive understanding of performance indicators which then can be used as insights towards making informed decisions on areas needing further development or improvement within their agile frameworks. However, with a framework that is based on flexibility rather than processes, determining its performance can be difficult, especially when contrasted to typical top-down, ROI-type measurements. An agile bottom-up organisation structure necessitates a distinct measurement method, one that places a premium on what drives the priorities of the organisation. Additionally, agile techniques such as story points, the backlog, and business value should be used to build a robust measurement framework.

In today's data-centric world, making informed and accurate decisions has become more critical than ever before. Traditional opinion-based decision-making processes have been replaced with a modern approach that prioritizes using hard facts to guide business strategies - this is where Data-Driven Decision Making (DDDM) comes in. Organizations around the globe are increasingly turning to DDDM due to its ability to provide clear insights into customer behaviors, preferences, and buying patterns through systematic collection of relevant data points (Ludbrook et al., 2019). By utilizing various analytical tools like big-data analytics, machine learning algorithms and artificial intelligence models among others; it becomes possible for businesses not only make sense of large chunks of complex datasets but also identify trends or opportunities hidden therein. With data-driven decision-making now at the forefront of many successful companies' methodologies towards progress there are multiple benefits associated with taking such an evidence-based approach including increased accuracy levels in forecasting sales revenues as well as minimizing risk factors when launching new products/services which might fail without proper analysis beforehand (Ludbrook et al., 2019).

The integration of data metrics in decision making processes has been faced with a multitude of challenges and barriers, which have hindered its successful adoption. These problems and factors are diverse in nature, ranging from technical issues to organizational culture, human behaviors and cognitive biases. One major issue that affects the implementation of data metrics is inadequate infrastructure or lack of technological resources. In addition to this, there may be limited access to relevant information sources as well as insufficient skills among staff members responsible for handling these tools. This can lead to inaccurate results being generated or difficulty interpreting them correctly. Another crucial factor impeding the uptake of data analytics is resistance from individuals within an organization who prefer traditional methods over new technology-driven approaches. There might also be reluctance towards change due to fear associated with potential risks such as financial losses. Furthermore, there are inherent psychological tendencies that may impact how people use data metrics when making decisions. For instance confirmation bias where individuals tend seek out information that confirms their pre-existing beliefs rather than objective evidence can distort perceptions.

Establishing Business Value and KPIs

KPIs are metrics that are established to assess and analyse a firm's progress toward achieving certain aims and objectives regularly. They are also formed to contrast the firm's overall performance to that of other similar firms in the sector. 80% respondents highlighted that the problem for business executives and managers who evaluate offers is to choose the most valuable investments for their companies. They must choose challenges that are both important to tackle and will yield significant rewards. When pitching a proposal or building a business case, it's not enough to merely assert those two elements; they must be supported by thorough business analysis.

85% of the people were of the strong opinion that to establish whether the stated problem is a problem and whether the advantages of the solution are sufficient given the investment required, critical thinking must be used. The "correct" solution – one that is uniquely intended to solve the problem and generate the expected business value – requires further investigation.

Around 78% of the people favoured KPIs and other measurements that are well-crafted and can help demonstrate value. The organisations are aware that the teams are overworked and overburdened, supporting clients across the organisation. But how can they be sure that the teams are working and, more importantly, that the efforts are focused on the issues that matter most to the clients and the company as a whole? KPIs that are well-designed can aid this by clearly and easily displaying not only what the teams do, but also the value of that work. 95% people felt that KPIs should be part of a team's overall performance management strategy. The organisation can use a variety of performance models, but the main goal is to (1) define the purpose of each team and (2) connect the team's objectives, targets, and activities with the major goals of the business teams, units, and the overall organisation. 78% respondents highlighted that with limited resources and pressure to demonstrate value, the teams must focus on the most strategic aspects of the company's operations. These are likely to be the most critical and crucial areas for achieving the organization's long-term goals.

Prioritizing specific value requires a multi-faceted approach that delves deeper into the intricacies of the process. To add activities effectively, it is essential to ensure that all necessary resources are in place and readily available for use. This involves a comprehensive evaluation of client requests, as well as an assessment of any additional or alternate team resource requirements that may arise during implementation. Only through such meticulous planning can we guarantee successful outcomes and ultimately provide optimal value to our clients.

Fostering Communication Channels to Mitigate the HiPPO Effect

The HiPPO effect is a phenomenon that arises when the opinion of the highest paid individual in an organization holds greater significance compared to other viewpoints and evidence-based insights. It can have significant ramifications for businesses, as it may result in decisions being made solely since one person's subjective judgment rather than objective data analysis. This tendency towards relying on the opinions of those with higher compensation exists across various industries, including but not limited to management consulting firms and financial institutions. For instance, during strategy formulation sessions or project reviews where several stakeholders are involved, this dynamic may lead decision-makers to place disproportionate emphasis on what their most highly compensated executives suggest. In such situations where status hierarchy plays a crucial role in determining who has influence over important business decisions, alternative perspectives based on facts and figures could potentially be overlooked. Consequently, companies should aim at fostering open communication channels so that diverse viewpoints get heard while making critical strategic choices affecting their organizations' futures.

However, some argue that the HIPPO effect is not necessarily a bad thing as it brings in leadership and decision-making skills to an organization. A leader's experience and expertise should be respected, especially when making critical decisions for the company. While data-driven insights are important, they do not always consider intangible factors such as relationships with clients or industry trends that only experienced leaders may have knowledge of. Therefore, the HIPPO effect can serve as a balance between hard facts and human intuition for effective decision making.

Can the HiPPO be Tamed With Agile Metrics and Value Management?

92% respondents pointed out that to depersonalise decision-making, agile metrics work well. Although the process of decision-making in enterprises will continue to depend, at least partially, on internal gut feelings or instincts, data-driven insights have to be leveraged in order to help judgements. Even though data plays a significant role in the decision-making process for most professionals, as reported by eighty percent of survey respondents, it is noteworthy that management judgement still holds great sway over crucial decisions. The findings reveal that seventy-three percent of individuals rely on data to make informed judgments; however, this does not diminish the influence of leadership's perspective and expertise. Surprisingly enough, an overwhelming majority (86%) indicated that management judgement remains a critical factor when navigating complex choices. Evidently, according to research participants' feedback in this study- while data analytics can inform decision making - sound managerial judgment serves as an equally powerful tool in achieving favorable outcomes amidst dynamic circumstances. 82% people advocated those statistics can delete emotion and opinion from the decision-making process. According to their experience, the presence of reliable data metrics will help to make a decisive conclusion. Any fact-based foundation can also be used to assist decision making.

In the contemporary world of business, where competition is at its peak and every organization strives to stay ahead in the game, incorporating end-users' feedback can be considered a cardinal rule. The significance of paying attention to these inputs cannot be emphasized enough as they serve as valuable insights into improving user experience and customer satisfaction levels. Moreover, while evaluating performance metrics, businesses need to take external benchmarks and competitive data into account. This allows them to assess their position relative to others in the market and identify potential areas for growth or improvement. By gaining an understanding of industry trends through this comparative analysis, organizations can make informed decisions that will have far-reaching implications on their future success. In short, adopting such strategies with depth goes beyond simply surviving but thriving in today's fast-paced business landscape. A recent survey found that a staggering 74% of companies are keen on incorporating these factors in their decision-making process, indicating their commitment towards achieving long-term success by basing decisions on facts rather than assumptions. By delving deeper into user needs and combining them with industry standards, organizations can gain valuable insights into market trends, enabling them to stay ahead of the competition and foster customer loyalty through enhanced product offerings.

An overwhelming 84% of survey respondents have recommended the development of a comprehensive data warehouse that addresses crucial corporate issues, which are typically centered around bottom-line profits and performance evaluation. These insightful individuals firmly believe in the positive impact that factual and reliable data can have on decision-making processes, especially when it comes to addressing top concerns raised by key decision-makers known as HiPPOs. By providing accurate information on critical metrics related to profitability, such a data repository could prove instrumental in ensuring effective strategic planning and timely corrective actions where necessary - something that would ultimately drive business growth for organizations across different sectors.

Research findings reveal that a substantial proportion of individuals, precisely 61%, hold the view that establishing a consensus within a team before delving into discussions related to decision-making during conferences is an efficacious strategy for restraining HiPPO. This approach enables the larger group to be well-informed and equipped with comprehensive knowledge and relevant facts concerning any given choice or issue at hand. As such, they become more empowered and likely to challenge even the highest paid person within their organization Redman, T. C. (2008). The ability of teams to make informed decisions through consensus-building underscores the importance of fostering collaborative environments where all members have equal opportunities to contribute ideas without fear or intimidation from authority figures. This approach not only empowers all members of the team but also helps in fostering an environment where critical thinking and healthy debate prevail over mere hierarchical authority (Redman, 2008).

SOLUTIONS, RECOMMENDATIONS, AND FUTURE RESEARCH DIRECTIONS

A highly effective strategy, recommended by a significant majority of 60% respondents, is to undertake pilot testing for the HiPPO. This approach entails conducting thorough evaluations prior to allocating 100% of the organization's budget and resources towards an initiative. In this manner, it is suggested that approximately 10% of available funding be dedicated towards carrying out several tests to ascertain whether proceeding with the proposed course of action would yield optimal outcomes or not. By adopting such meticulous measures, organizations can guarantee superior results while mitigating any potential risks involved in investing substantial sums into untested projects. If that's the case, they are already 10% there. If it isn't, they will still have 90% of the budget to spend in a different way, as well as market feedback to assist them figure out what that path should be.

CONCLUSION

It is invariably that there are true HiPPOs in the corporate world, and more specifically, in top level business meetings. After all, ignoring reality to establish one's own point of view over others' is a leadership style that isn't easy to come by. It can be therefore concluded that having a strong representation of reality in the form of agile metrics that assist processes and reduce ambiguity while giving users a solid basis for decision making is a good approach to avoid the consequences that come with relying exclusively on instinct, intuition, and opinion.

Agile metrics are defined benchmarks that allow a business team to track how productive they are at various levels and stages of the process. They are a priority in the entire development process (Provost & Fawcett, 2013). Agile metrics support teams using the agile methodology in analysing system functionalities, in keeping a realistic and data-driven perspective of progress for each of the company's projects, ensuring more productivity, better quality, and enhanced customer happiness (Hedgebeth, 2007). Metrics should ideally be both leading and causal. They should enable us to predict the eventual result, and they should look at aspects that have genuine impact (that is, factors that add value to our customers, company, and even employees and colleagues; they shouldn't merely boost someone's ego).

Indeed, this research advocates that the HiPPO effect is undoubtedly one of the most significant bottlenecks to enhanced evidence-based and data-driven decision-making. In today's age, the abundance of data available to businesses is nothing short of astounding.

To ignore such a valuable resource in favor of subjective decisions made solely based on what the highest paid person's opinion (HiPPO) may be, would be a grave mistake for any company. Instead, modern organizations must approach decision-making with much more sophistication and nuance. This means identifying risks associated with potential choices while simultaneously establishing clear success criteria. It also involves adopting a culture that encourages trial and error as well as continuous iteration - all backed by solid evidence derived from reliable data sources. In short, relying exclusively on an individual or individuals within management who hold seniority without regard for objective information will only hinder growth and limit long-term success prospects. It therefore behooves forward-thinking companies to leverage advanced analytical tools alongside their human expertise when making key strategic decisions impacting everything from product development to market expansion initiatives. By embracing this mindset and staying ahead of the curve regarding emerging technologies in this arena; businesses can excel and be sustainable.

REFERENCES

Barton, D., & Court, D. (2012). Making advanced analytics work for you. *Harvard Business Review*, *90*(10), 78–83. PMID:23074867

Beinart, W., & Coates, P. (2002). *Environment and history: The Taming of Nature in the USA and South Africa*. Routledge. doi:10.4324/9780203133552

Bond, A., Morrison-Saunders, A., & Pope, J. (2012). Sustainability assessment: The state of the art. *Impact Assessment and Project Appraisal*, *30*(1), 53–62. doi:10.1080/14615517.2012.661974

BrynjolfssonE.HittL. M.KimH. H. (2011). Strength in numbers: How does data-driven decisionmaking affect firm performance? *Available at* SSRN 1819486. doi:10.2139/ssrn.1819486

Carillo, K. D. A., Galy, N., Guthrie, C., & Vanhems, A. (2019). How to turn managers into data-driven decision makers: Measuring attitudes towards business analytics. *Business Process Management Journal*, *25*(3), 553–578. doi:10.1108/BPMJ-11-2017-0331

Collis, J., & Hussey, R. (2014). *Business Research: Understanding Research*. Palgrave Macmillan. doi:10.1007/978-1-137-03748-0

Fosso Wamba, S., Gunasekaran, A., Dubey, R., & Ngai, E. W. (2018). Big data analytics in operations and supply chain management. *Annals of Operations Research*, *270*(1), 1–4. doi:10.100710479-018-3024-7 PMID:36687515

Gazdula, J. (2017). Can teaching critical reflexivity be improved using metaphors? The hippo in the room. *Educational Futures*, *8*(1), 35–50.

Hedgebeth, D. (2007). Data-driven decision making for the enterprise: An overview of business intelligence applications. *Vine*, *37*(4), 414–420. doi:10.1108/03055720710838498

Latan, H., Jabbour, C. J. C., de Sousa Jabbour, A. B. L., Wamba, S. F., & Shahbaz, M. (2018). Effects of environmental strategy, environmental uncertainty and top management's commitment on corporate environmental performance: The role of environmental management accounting. *Journal of Cleaner Production*, *180*, 297–306. doi:10.1016/j.jclepro.2018.01.106

Lefebvre, G., Summerfield, C., & Bogacz, R. (2022). A normative account of confirmation bias during reinforcement learning. *Neural Computation*, *34*(2), 307–337. doi:10.1162/neco_a_01455 PMID:34758486

Ludbrook, F., Michalikova, K. F., Musova, Z., & Suler, P. (2019). Business models for sustainable innovation in industry 4.0: Smart manufacturing processes, digitalization of production systems, and data-driven decision making. *Journal of Self-Governance and Management Economics*, *7*(3), 21–26.

Nazarenko, A., Vishnevskiy, K., Meissner, D., & Daim, T. (2022). Applying digital technologies in technology roadmapping to overcome individual biased assessments. *Technovation*, *110*, 102364. doi:10.1016/j.technovation.2021.102364

Pandey, S., DeHart-Davis, L., Pandey, S., & Ahlawat, S. (2022). Fight or flight: How gender influences follower responses to unethical leader behaviour. *Public Management Review*, 1–21.

Provost, F., & Fawcett, T. (2013). Data science and its relationship to big data and data-driven decision making. *Big Data*, *1*(1), 51–59. doi:10.1089/big.2013.1508 PMID:27447038

Ransbotham, S., Kiron, D., & Prentice, P. K. (2016). Beyond the hype: The hard work behind analytics success. *MIT Sloan Management Review*, *57*(3).

Redman, T. C. (2008). *Data driven: Profiting from your most important business asset*. Harvard Business Press.

Sharma, R., Mithas, S., & Kankanhalli, A. (2014). Transforming decision-making processes: A research agenda for understanding the impact of business analytics on organisations. *European Journal of Information Systems*, *23*(4), 433–441. doi:10.1057/ejis.2014.17

Shin, A., Kim, D. Y., Jeong, J. S., & Chun, B. G. (2020). Hippo: Taming hyper-parameter optimization of deep learning with stage trees. *arXiv preprint arXiv:2006.11972*.

Vedejová, D., & Čavojová, V. (2022). Confirmation bias in information search, interpretation, and memory recall: Evidence from reasoning about four controversial topics. *Thinking & Reasoning*, *28*(1), 1–28. doi:10.1080/13546783.2021.1891967

KEY TERMS AND DEFINITIONS

Authority Bias: Authority bias refers to the tendency of individuals to blindly accept and defer to those in positions of authority, regardless of whether their opinions or actions are justified. This cognitive bias can manifest itself in a variety of situations, such as workplaces, educational institutions or even social groups where there is an established hierarchy.

Big Data Analytics: Big Data Analytics refers to the process of extracting valuable insights and knowledge from large sets of complex data using sophisticated analytical tools. It involves analyzing massive volumes of structured, unstructured, or semi-structured information generated by various sources.

Confirmation Bias: Confirmation bias is a psychological phenomenon where individuals tend to search for, interpret and remember information in a way that confirms their pre-existing beliefs. This leads them to ignore or discredit evidence that contradicts their views.

Fallacy: A fallacy is a type of error in reasoning that occurs when an argument or belief is based on faulty logic. It involves making assumptions without sufficient evidence, ignoring counterarguments, and using emotional appeals rather than rational ones to persuade others.

HiPPO effect: The HiPPO (Highest Paid Person's Opinion) effect is a phenomenon where the opinion or decision of the highest-paid person in an organization carries significant weight, regardless of its validity or feasibility. This can lead to a lack of innovation and stifled creativity within the company.

Conclusion

Within the context of the publication some authors discussed institutional theory and its importance in measuring the effectiveness of organizational development (OD) strategies during unprecedented times. An important concept to look at for the conclusion of the publication and what's next.

Briefly, institutional theory regards how external pressures to an organization or system causes impact or some sort of change (Davidsson et al., 2006). Comparably, Newenham-Kahindi (2015) performed a qualitative study on multinational companies' sustainability efforts within 18 communities in Tanzania exercising institutional theory. Data collection tools were of archival documents and semi-structured interviews. Newenham-Kahindi (2015) explicated institutional theory, in general, is about organizations behaviors, culture, and setting. Hence, environmental surrounding, both societal and social (Newenham-Kahindi, 2015).

Institutional theory is about how leaders in companies make decisions (Newenham-Kahindi, 2015). Too, based on deep practitioner knowledge and experience of institutional theory, the theory regards companies obtain methods and even form similar enterprises. As a result, companies become a part of an organizational field (Kostova et al., 2008). The establishment of shared values, rules, expectations, and regulations for *members* to adhere to, is an organizational field (Greenwald, 2008). Similarly, DiMaggio and Powell (1983) claimed businesses that sell services and products similar to one another belong to the same organizational field, just like regulatory agencies and suppliers. Companies might even tailor leadership teams or departments within the institution like other enterprises in their organizational field. Also, Valente (2018) argued regulatory systems can be institutional forces, something organizations have no choice, but to conform to, or else be fined. In addition to this, debarments, suspensions, and even dissolution can occur when firms do not conform.

Overall, institutional theory provides a logical account for comprehending how institutions within the same industry develop and operate businesses. Specifically, the chapter herein regards institutional theorist Roy Suddaby's (2013) and (2015) institutional theories. Developed in 2013 and refined in 2015. Suddaby (2015) and Greenwald (2008) argued institutional theory arose between the 20th and 21st centuries, to provide understanding on phenomena that happen in large firms. In comparison to Kostova et al. (2008), institutional theory also regards businesses are created and operate according to how similar institutions in the same industry are constructed and operate (Suddaby, 2015; Greenwald, 2008). Leading to becoming a part of an organizational field (Greenwald, 2008; Suddaby, 2015).

From the 2013 Roy Suddaby institutional theory, Suddaby et al. (2013) contended norms and social structures are equivalent and are expected in companies. Plus, institutionalization happens in companies. To compare, Selznick (1996) argued a business is composed of norms, values, and rules with norms coming from norms and social architectures external to the company. As a result, Selznick (1996) argued company's rules and structure are institutionalized, but not the firms themselves.

Moreover, Davidsson et al. (2006) performed a qualitative study using structured telephone interviews on 321 new (young) knowledge-intensive companies that participated in a training program at Linkoping University in Sweden, to study institutional forces (external pressures). Particularly regarding young firms in economies, when launching a venture ideas and how pressures sometimes cause startups to change the venture idea because of the external market pressures (Davidsson et al., 2006). Data from 167 enterprises were collected (Davidsson et al., 2006).

DiMaggio and Powell (1983) stated institutional forces can be coercive, normative, and or mimetic (mimic) forces. DiMaggio and Powell (1983) advised all three forces can cause organizations to struggle when looking for ways to combat uncertainty and even gain legitimacy in a market. To compare, and to report the outcomes of the examination, Davidsson et al. (2006) claimed coercive forces can be informal or formal and are derived from *regulated expectations* societies place on the organization, and from pressures other companies that provide legal or other resources exert on institutions receiving the aid or resources. Also, regulated systems can be institutional voids. Normative forces which are also called normative pressures come about because of professionalization (Davidsson et al., 2006). For example, moving from abilities to formal titles like in professional associations that harness, improve, and defend organizational member's skills (Davidsson et al., 2006). Perhaps formal titles could be for subordinate employees, leaders, or departments. All forces are relevant for OD initiatives. Institutions can either conform, resist, avoid, comprise, or even manipulate or be manipulated when external market pressures arise.

So, organizational fields exist, as DiMaggio and Powell (1983) discussed. Firstly, to quickly touch on mimetic forces, Davidsson et al. (2006) claimed mimetic in markets means for an institution to copy what is thought to be best practice, due to uncertainty in the economy or environment. Davidsson et al. (2006) seemed to imply organizations practice this, whether large or small, to protect the company. To compare to Davidsson et al. (2006) and regarding firms being large or small, Suddaby (2015) and Greenwald (2008) claimed institutional theory applies to phenomena that occur in large or small firms versus Suddaby (2015) and Greenwald's (2008) claim of institutional theory applies to phenomena that occur only in large firms. Davidsson et al. (2006) did state this towards the end of the study. Organizations practice mimetic behaviors for survival, but also for success. What is of concern in emerging markets is if startups copy other startups, because multinationals operate on a different dimension? What is needed to be successful (scale) from level zero to level five, per se, is not necessarily a technique a firm can use to survive or scale from level 10 to 20, open regional offices, subsidiaries, and bring on 20 new team members for the enterprise. While also considering financial status.

Last, institutional theory regards companies obtain methods and even their form from similar enterprises. As a result, companies that acquire such from and methods become a part of an organizational field (Kostova et al., 2008). Like, Suddaby (2015) and Greenwald (2008) stated. The establishment of shared values, rules, expectations, and regulations for *members* to adhere to, is an organizational field (Greenwald, 2008). Similarly, DiMaggio and Powell (1983) claimed businesses that sell services and products similar to one another belong to the same organizational field, just like regulatory agencies and suppliers. Businesses might even tailor leadership teams or departments within the institution like other enterprises in their organizational field.

Nevertheless, institutional theory is not always seen as negative. DiMaggio and Powell (1983) argued institutions are assumed to create leadership structures. For instance, similar to firms in their industry. Yet, Greenwald (2008) and Jones (2013) claimed such design appropriateness depends on the firm's purpose, and even capabilities, not on mimicking other organizations. Plus, markets, industries, organizational fields, and even societies are distinct. However, what is still unsettled amongst institutional scholars is, what part of markets, societies, industries, and even organizational fields make them different from one another. As an example, Suddaby and Greenwood (2001) and Greenwald (2008) advised an organizational field contains shared rules, expectations, values, and companies, as abovementioned. Furthermore, Hotho and Saka-Helmhout (2017) and Zheng (2012) argued elements of organizational fields are educational, political, financial, and other systems, necessary for the operation of the field and can impact the company's individual entry and exit modes, and operations. This is paramount when considering firm resilience, during crises and when seeking OD solutions. The speculations of Hotho et al. (2017) and Zheng's (2012) definition of an organizational field seems to imply *institutionalization* exists, as previously discussed.

So, how does this apply to organizational development (OD)? DiMaggio and Powell (1983) seemed to imply institutional theory regards pressures in companies arise from societal expectations the firm operates within. This causes those firms to adopt similar or exactly the same economic behaviors, response, and events. Which should be considered when applying OD strategies to companies, especially during unprecedented times. What is working in one organization, within a particular organizational field, could work as a solution for another, after aspects like diagnosis, feedback, and strategy recommendations, for example. Components of OD initiatives (see Figure 1 below).

Comparable to DiMaggio and Powell (1983) and Love and Roper (2004), Wang (2014) conducted a longitudinal study to explore the association between the innovation competence and quality management practices of 607 high technology companies exercising the resource-based views of firms in contemporary literature and institutional theory. Wang (2014) argued institutional theory is about enterprises functions in social settings. Also, the social pressures of company's external surroundings and public's viewpoint of the company are capable of shaping the entities behaviors (Wang, 2014). Additionally, institutional forces, for example external institutional forces, as Love and Roper (2004) claimed, can be rules and customs. This is typically seen with nations, which are discrete institutional environments with different social standards, *like rules and customs.*

To conclude, with all of the commentary mentioned above in mind, overall, this text was written to provide the perspectives of various leaders, practitioners, and academics from around the world. Who come from organizations of all sizes that operate in various industries? Further, organizational development (OD) consulting improves firms operations, culture, systems, processes, and structures that are a part of human resources (HRs) responsibility, which chapter authors wrote about, respectively. Each improvement can be qualitatively and quantitatively measured, for effectiveness. Measurements can occur via assessments or tools, like *"The Qualitative Measurement of Organizational Culture", "The Corporate Culture Survey", instruments to measure organizational performance, "The Organizational Culture Scale", "The Organizational Culture Inventory", "The Organizational Culture Assessment Instrument (OCAI)",* and many others based on the organizational development initiative area. See examples in Figure 1. Too, OD initiatives can involve an ongoing systematic long range process of driving organizational effectiveness, solving problems, and improving organizational performance. Like some of the components show in Figure 1, discussed by chapter authors, and in conjunction with models/frameworks conversed by chapter authors.

Figure 1. What are some organizational development initiatives?
Source: (td.org, 2023)

Inclusive, OD consulting provides a variety of solutions enterprises can implement. Available OD frameworks/models from practicing practitioners, leaders, and academics, like the authors of each chapter of this publication. Including the Editor-in-Chief. So, if we can assist your firm with an OD initiative (e.g. planning, diagnosis/ assessment, feedback, strategy, or solution/implementation, or follow-up/ evaluation) please contact sales@LadyMirageGlobal.com .

Additional Resources: IGI Global publication – *"Change Management during Unprecedented Times"* https://www.igi-global.com/book/change-management-during-unprecedented-times/308290

REFERENCES

Association for Talent Development. (2023). *What is organization development?* Association for Talent Development. https://www.td.org/talent-development-glossary-terms/what-is-organization-development

Davidsson, P., Hunter, E., & Klofsten, M. (2006). Institutional forces: The invisible hand that shapes venture ideas? *International Small Business Journal*, *24*(2), 115–131. doi:10.1177/0266242606061834

DiMaggio, P., & Powell, W. (1983). The iron cage revisited: Institutional isomorphism and collective rationality in organizational fields. *American Sociological Review*, *48*(2), 147–160. doi:10.2307/2095101

Greenwald, H. P. (2008). *Organizations: Management without control*. Sage Publications. doi:10.4135/9781483329635

Hotho, J., & Saka-Helmhout, A. (2017). In and between societies: Reconnecting comparative institution-alism and organizational theory. *Organization Studies*, *38*(5), 647–666. doi:10.1177/0170840616655832

Jones, G. R. (2013). *Organizational theory, design, and change* (7th ed.). Prentice Hall.

Kostova, T., Roth, K., & Dacin, M. T. (2008). Institutional theory in the study of multinational corpora-tions: A critique and new directions. *Academy of Management Review*, *33*(4), 994–1006. doi:10.5465/amr.2008.34422026

Love, J. H., & Roper, S. (2004). The organisation of innovation: Collaboration, cooperation and multi-functional groups in UK and German manufacturing. *Cambridge Journal of Economics*, *28*(3), 379–395. doi:10.1093/cje/28.3.379

Newenham-Kahindi, A. (2015). Managing sustainable development through people: Implications for multinational enterprises in developing countries. *Personnel Review*, *44*(3), 388–407. doi:10.1108/PR-07-2013-0121

Selznick, P. (1996). Institutionalism "old" and "new". *Administrative Science Quarterly*, *41*(2), 270–277. doi:10.2307/2393719

Suddaby, R. (2013). Institutional theory. In E. Kessler (Ed.), *Encyclopedia of management theory* (pp. 379–384). Sage.

Suddaby, R. (2015). Can institutional theory be critical? *Journal of Management Inquiry*, *24*(1), 93–95. doi:10.1177/1056492614545304

Suddaby, R., & Greenwood, R. (2001). Colonizing knowledge: Commodification as a dynamic of jurisdictional expansion in professional service firms. *Human Relations*, *54*(7), 933–953. doi:10.1177/0018726701547007

Valente, M. (2018). *Home*. Organizing for sustainability. https://www.organizingforsustainability.com

Wang, C.-H. (2014). A longitudinal study of innovation competence and quality management on firm performance. *Innovation (North Sydney, N.S.W.)*, *16*(3), 392–403. doi:10.1080/14479338.2014.11081995

Zheng, C. (2012). Isomorph isomorphic influences and aspiration: Reference group choice in entry mode decisions. *Journal of International Business Research*, *11*(2), 129–141.

Compilation of References

Abbasia, M.S., Ahmeda, N., Sajjadb, B., Alshahranic, A., Saeedd, S., Sarfaraze, S., Alhamdanf, R.S., Vohrac,F. & Abduljabbarc, T. (2020). *E-Learning perception and satisfaction among health sciences students amid the COVID-19 pandemic*. IOS Press. doi:10.3233/WOR-203308

Abed, E. K. (2019). Electronic learning and its benefits in education. *Eurasia Journal of Mathematics, Science and Technology Education*, *15*(3), 1–8. doi:10.29333/ejmste/102668

Abimbola, T., Lim, M., Hillestad, T., Xie, C., & Haugland, S. A. (2010). Innovative corporate social responsibility: The founder's role in creating a trustworthy corporate brand through "green innovation.". *Journal of Product and Brand Management*, *19*(6), 440–451. doi:10.1108/10610421011085758

Abuhassàn, A., & Bates, T. C. (2015). Grit: Distinguishing effortful persistence from conscientiousness. *Journal of Individual Differences*, *36*(4), 205–214. doi:10.1027/1614-0001/a000175

Adam, M., Wessel, M., & Benlian, A. (2021). AI-based chatbots in customer service and their effects on user compliance. *Electronic Markets*, *31*(2), 427–445. doi:10.100712525-020-00414-7

Agrawal, A., Gans, J., & Goldfarb, A. (2018). *Prediction Machines: The Simple Economics of Artificial Intelligence*. NY: Harvard Business Review.

Aguilera, R. V. (2005). Corporate governance and director accountability: An Institutional comparative perspective. *British Journal of Management*, *16*(s1), S39–S53. doi:10.1111/j.1467-8551.2005.00446.x

Aguinis, H., & Glavas, A. (2012). What we know and don't know about corporate social responsibility: A review and research agenda. *Journal of Management*, *38*(4), 932–968. doi:10.1177/0149206311436079

Aguinis, H., & Kraiger, K. (2009). Benefits of training and development for individuals and teams, organizations, and society. *Annual Review of Psychology*, *60*(1), 451–474. doi:10.1146/annurev.psych.60.110707.163505 PMID:18976113

Ahmad, A., Ikram, A., Rehan, M. F., & Ahmad, A. (2022). Going green: Impact of green supply chain management practices on sustainability performance. *Frontiers in Psychology*, *13*, 973676. doi:10.3389/fpsyg.2022.973676 PMID:36457908

Ahmad, S. A. (2012). Essentialities for E-Learning: The Nigerian tertiary Institutions in question. *Academic Research International*, *2*(2), 286–219.

Ahmed, M. (2020). COVID-19 Hinders Progress in U.S. Renewable Energy Job Growth. *American Council of Renewable Energy*. https://acore.org/covid-19-hinders-progress-in-u-s-renewable-energy-job-growth/

Ahmed, A., Arshad, M. A., Mahmood, A., & Akhtar, S. (2016). Holistic human resource development: Balancing the equation through the inclusion of spiritual quotient. *Journal of Human Values*, *22*(3), 165–179. doi:10.1177/0971685816650573

Ahumada, L. (2001). *Teoría y cambio en las organizaciones: Un Acercamiento desde los modelos de aprendizaje organizacional*. Ediciones Universitarias de Valparaíso.

AIHR (Jayla Cosentino). (2023). *15 OD interventions every HR practitioner should know.* AIHR. https://www.aihr.com/blog/od-interventions/#:~:text=As%20stated%20above%2C%20there%20are,from%20each%20of%20the%20groups

Aithal, P. S. & Shubhrajyotsna Aithal. (2018). Nanotechnology based Innovations and Human Life Comfortability –Are we Marching towards Immortality? *International Journal of Applied Engineering and Management Letters*, *2*(1), 1–8. doi:10.5281/zenodo.1485048

Ajogwu, F., & King, M. (2020). *Outcomes-Based Governance: A Modern Approach to Corporate Governance*. Juta Limited.

Akbari, M., Mehrali, M., SeyyedAmiri, N., Rezaei, N., & Pourjam, A. (2019). Corporate social responsibility, customer loyalty and brand positioning. *Social Responsibility Journal*, *16*(5), 671–689. doi:10.1108/SRJ-01-2019-0008

Alahdab, F., Halvorsen, A. J., Mandrekar, J. N., Vaa, B. E., Montori, V. M., West, C. P., Murad, M. H., & Beckman, T. J. (2020). How do we assess resilience and grit among internal medicine residents at the Mayo Clinic? A longitudinal validity study including correlations with medical knowledge, professionalism, and clinical performance. *BMJ Open*, *10*(12), e040699. doi:10.1136/bmjopen-2020-040699 PMID:33323437

Alameda, C., Sanabria, D., & Ciria, L. F. (2022). The brain in flow: A systematic review on the neural basis of the flow state. *Cortex*, *154*, 348–364. doi:10.1016/j.cortex.2022.06.005 PMID:35926367

Alanezi., & Azwani, A. (2020). Future of mobile learning during and after global (covid-19) pandemic: College of basic education as case. *Journal of Education and Practice, 11*.

Alawattage, C., & Fernando, S. (2017). Postcoloniality in corporate social and environmental accountability. *Accounting, Organizations and Society*, *60*, 1–20. doi:10.1016/j.aos.2017.07.002

Al-Dahash, H., Thayaparan, M., & Kulatunga, U. (2016). Understanding the terminologies: Disaster, crisis, and emergency. *Association of Researchers in Construction Management (ACROM)*, 1191-1200.

Aldianto, L., Anggadwita, G., Permatasari, A., Mirzanti, I., & Williamson, I. (2021). Toward a Business resilience framework for startups. *Sustainability (Basel)*, *13*(6), 3132. doi:10.3390u13063132

Alhouti, S., Wright, S. A., & Baker, T. L. (2021). Customers need to relate: The conditional warm glow effect of CSR on negative customer experiences. *Journal of Business Research*, *124*, 240–253. doi:10.1016/j.jbusres.2020.11.047

Alibašić, H. (2018). *Sustainability and resilience planning for local governments: The quadruple bottom line strategy*. Springer International Publishing. doi:10.1007/978-3-319-72568-0

Alipio, M. (2021). Education during Covid-19 era: Are learners in a less-economically developed country ready for E-Learning? *IMCC Journal of Science*, *1*(2), 94–101.

Alipour, F., & Karimi, R. (2018). Creating and developing learning organization dimensions in educational settings; Role of human resource development practitioners. *International Journal of Management. Accounting & Economics*, *5*(4), 197–213.

Almomani, E. Y., Qablan, A. M., Atrooz, F. Y., Almomany, A. M., Hajjo, R. M., & Almomani, H. Y. (2019). *The influence of Coronavirus diseases (COVID-19)*. National Institute of Health.

Al-Shamlan, H. M., & Al-Mudimigh, A. S. (2011, March). The change management strategies and processes for successful ERP implementation: A case study of MADAR. *International Journal of Computer Science Issues*, *8*(2), 399–407.

Alturise, F. (2020). Evaluation of the blackboard learn learning management system for full online courses in Western Branch Colleges of Qassim University. *International Journal of Emerging Technologies in Learning*, 15(15), 33–50. doi:10.3991/ijet.v15i15.14199

Amabile, T., Conti, R., & Amabile, T. M. (n.d.). *Changes in the Work Environment for Creativity during Downsizing - Article - Faculty & Research*. Harvard Business School. https://www.hbs.edu/faculty/Pages/item.aspx?num=7435

Amanchukwu, R. N., Stanley, G. J., & Ololube, N. P. (2015). A review of leadership theories, principles and styles and their relevance to educational management. *Management*, 5(1), 6–14. doi:10.5923/j.mm.20150501.02

Ambrose, J. (2020). Investors fear there ' ll be no bright post Covid dawn for oil majors. *Observer Business Agenda*. https://www.theguardian.com/business/2020/oct/25/investors-fear-therell-be-no-bright-post-covid-dawn-for-oil-majors

Amburgey, T. L., & Rao, H. (1996). Organizational ecology: Past, present and future directions. *Academy of Management Journal*, 39(5), 1265–1286. doi:10.2307/256999

American Psychological Association. (2006). *Guidelines and principles for accreditation of programs in professional psychology*. APA. http://www.apa.org/ed/accreditation/about/policies/guiding-principles.Pdf

Amhalhal, A., Anchor, J., Tipi, N., & Elgazzar, S. (2021, August 27). *The impact of contingency fit on organizational performance: an empirical study*. Emerald. https://www.emerald.com/insight/content/doi/10.1108/IJPPM-01-2021-0016/full/html

Amini, A., Shirvani, H., & Bazgir, B. (2021). Effectiveness of guided visualization and mental imagery on perceived stress, psychological well–being and sleep quality in Armed Forces retirement. *Journal Mil Med*, 23(12), 913–924.

Ammanath, B., Jarvis, D., & Hupfer, S. (2020). *Thriving in the era of pervasive AI*. Deloitte Consulting LLP.

Amoah, J., Belas, J., Dziwornu, R., & Khan, K. A. (2022). SMEs contribution to economic development: A perspective from an emerging economy. *Journal of International Students*, 15(2), 63–76. doi:10.14254/2071-8330.2022/15-2/5

Anderson, R., Amodeo, M., & Harzfeld, J. (2010). Changing business cultures from within. The World watch Institute.

Applebaum, S. H., Degbe, M. C., MacDonald, O., & Nguyen-Quang, T. S. (2015). Organizational outcomes of leadership style and resistance to change (part two). *Industrial and Commercial Training*, 47(3), 134–144. doi:10.1108/ICT-07-2013-0045

Aragon-Correa, J. A., Hurtado-Torres, N. E., Sharma, S., & García-Morales, V. J. (2008). Environmental strategy and performance in small firms: A resource-based perspective. *Journal of Environmental Management*, 86(1), 88–103. doi:10.1016/j.jenvman.2006.11.022 PMID:17239519

Aravamudhan, N. R., & Krishnaveni, R. (2014). Spirituality at workplace–an emerging template for organization capacity building? *PURUSHARTHA—A Journal of Management. Ethics, and Spirituality*, 7(1), 63–78.

Arkorful, V., & Abaidoo, N. (2014). The role of E-Learning, the advantages and disadvantages of its adoption in Higher Education. *International Journal of Education and Research*, 2(12), 397–410.

Armenakis, A. A., & Bedeian, A. G. (1999). Organizational change: A review of theory and research in the 1990s. *Journal of Management*, 25(3), 293–315. doi:10.1177/014920639902500303

Armstrong-Mensah, E., Ramsey-White, K., Yankey, B., & Self-Brown, S. (2020). covid-19 and distance learning: Effects on Georgia State University School of Public Health Students. *Public Health*, 8, 576227. doi:10.3389/fpubh.2020.576227 PMID:33102425

Asahak, S., Albrecht, S. L., Sanctis, M. D., & Barnett, N. S. (2018). Boards of directors: Assessing their functioning and validation of a multi-dimensional measure. *Frontiers in Psychology*, 9, 2425. doi:10.3389/fpsyg.2018.02425 PMID:30564176

Association for Talent Development. (2023). *What is organization development?* Association for Talent Development. https://www.td.org/talent-development-glossary-terms/what-is-organization-development

Astin, H. S. (2004). Some thoughts on the role of spirituality in transformational leadership. *Spirituality in Higher Education Newsletter*, 1(4), 1–5.

Ates, A., & Umit, B. (2011). Change process: A key enabler for building resilient SMEs. ("Change process: a key enabler for building resilient SMEs"). *International Journal of Production Research*, 49(18), 5601–5618. doi:10.1080/002075 43.2011.563825

Athar, H. S. (2020). The influence of organizational culture on organizational commitment post-pandemic Covid-19. *International Journal of Multicultural and Multireligious Understanding*, 7(5), 148–157.

Atkins, B. (2022, Jun 16). Into the metaverse: Use cases for directors. *Forbes.* https://www.forbes.com/: sites/betsyatkins/2022/06/16/into-the-metaverse-use-cases-for-directors/?sh=47d9b863dc89

Atwater, D. C., & Bass, B. M. (1994). Transformational leadership in teams. In B. M. Bass & B. J. Avolio (Eds.), *Improving Organizational Effectiveness Through Transformational Leadership*. Sage Publications, Inc.

Austin, J. R., & Bartunek, J. M. (2003). Theories and practices of organizational Development. W. Borman, D. Ilgen, R. Klimoski, and I.Weiner (ed.). Handbook of Psychology. John Wiley and sons, Inc, New York.

Avolio, B. J., Sosik, J. J., Jung, D. L., & Berson, Y. (2003). *Leadership models, methods, and applications: Small steps and giant leaps* (Vol. 12). Handbook of Psychology. John Wiley & Sons. doi:10.1002/0471264385.wei1212

Bachman, D. (2020). The economic impact of COVID-19 (novel coronavirus). *Deloitte Insight.* https://www2.deloitte.com/us/en/insights/economy/covid-19/economic-impact-covid-19.html

Bainbridge, S. M., & Henderson, M. T. (2018). *Outsourcing the Board: How Board Service Providers Can Improve Corporate Governance*. Cambridge University Press. doi:10.1017/9781108149792

Baldacchino, P. J., Camilleri, A., Schembri, B., Grima, S., & Thalassinos, Y. E. (2020). Performance evaluation of the board of directors in listed companies: A small state perspective. *International Journal of Finance. Insurance and Risk Management*, 10(1), 99–119.

Bandura, A. (1994). Self-efficacy. In V. S. Ramachaudran (Ed.), *Encyclopedia of human behavior, 4, 71-81*. Academic Press.

Bansal, P. (2005). Evolving sustainably: A longitudinal study of corporate sustainable development. *Strategic Management Journal*, 26(3), 197–218. doi:10.1002mj.441

Bapuji, H., Patel, C., Ertug, G., & Allen, D. G. (2020). Corona crisis and inequality: Why management research needs a societal turn. *Journal of Management*, 46(7), 1205–1222. doi:10.1177/0149206320925881

Baratter, M. A. (2014). *A influência da comunidade local na configuração do arranjo produtivo local de louças e porcelanas de Campo Largo/PR. Curitiba*, 2014. Tese. (Doutorado em Administração) – Setor de Ciências Sociais Aplicadas, Universidade Federal do Paraná, 2014.

Baratter, M. A., Ferreira, J. M., & Costa, M. C. (2010). Empreendedorismo institucional: características da ação intencional. Perspectivas Contemporâneas, Campo Mourão, Edição Especial, p. 237-266.

Barbier, E. B., & Burgess, J. C. (2020). Sustainability and development after COVID-19. *World Development, 135,* 105082. doi:10.1016/j.worlddev.2020.105082 PMID:32834381

Barley, S. R. (2008). Coalface Institutionalism. In *The SAGE Handbook of Organizational Institutionalism* (pp. 491–518). SAGE Publications Ltd. doi:10.4135/9781849200387.n21

Barnes, L. B., Christensen, C. R., & Hansen, A. J. (1994). *Teaching and the case method: Text, cases, and readings.* Harvard Business Press.

Barnet, M. L. (2007). Stakeholder influence capacity and the variability of financial returns to corporate social responsibility. *Academy of Management Review, 33*(3), 794–816. doi:10.5465/amr.2007.25275520

Barney, J. (1991). Firm Resources and Sustained Competitive Advantage. *Journal of Management, 17*(1), 99–120. doi:10.1177/014920639101700108

Barron, D. N., West, E., & Hannan, M. T. (1994). A time to grow and a time to die: Growth and mortality of credit unions in New York City, 1914-1990. *American Journal of Sociology, 100*(2), 381–421. doi:10.1086/230541

Barroso-Castro, C., Villegas-Periñan, M. M., & Dominguez, M. (2017). Board members' contribution to strategy: The mediating role of board internal processes. *European Research on Management and Business Economics, 23*(2), 82–89. doi:10.1016/j.iedeen.2017.01.002

Bartik, A. W., Bertrand, M., Cullen, Z., Glaeser, E. L., Luca, M., & Stanton, C. (2020). The impact of COVID-19 on small business outcomes and expectations. *Proceedings of the National Academy of Sciences of the United States of America, 117*(30), 17656–17666. doi:10.1073/pnas.2006991117 PMID:32651281

Barton, D., & Court, D. (2012). Making advanced analytics work for you. *Harvard Business Review, 90*(10), 78–83. PMID:23074867

Baticulon, R. E., Sy, J. J., Alberto, N. R. I., Baron, M. B. C., Mabulay, R. E. C., Rizada, L. G. T., & Reyes, J. C. B. (2021). Barriers to online learning in the time of COVID-19: A national survey of medical students in the Philippines. *Medical Science Educator, 31*(2), 615–626. doi:10.100740670-021-01231-z PMID:33649712

Battilana, J., & D'Aunno, T. (2009). Institutional work and the paradox of embedded agency. In T. B. Lawrence, R. Suddaby, & B. Leca (Eds.), *Institutional work: Actors and agency in institutional studies of organizations* (p. 3158). Cambridge University Press. doi:10.1017/CBO9780511596605.002

Bauer, H. H., Grether, M., & Leach, M. (2002). Building customer relations over the Internet. *Industrial Marketing Management, 31*(2), 155–163. doi:10.1016/S0019-8501(01)00186-9

Bauer, H. H., Grether, M., & Leach, M. (2002). Customer relations through the Internet. *Journal of Relationship Marketing, 1*(2), 39–55. doi:10.1300/J366v01n02_03

Bayham, J., & Fenichel, E. P. (2020). Impact of school closures for COVID-19 on the US health-care workforce and net mortality: A modelling study. *The Lancet. Public Health, 5*(5), 271–278. doi:10.1016/S2468-2667(20)30082-7 PMID:32251626

Baykal, E. (2019). Creating organizational commitment through spiritual leadership: Mediating effect of meaning at work. *Business & Management International Journal, 7*(2), 837–855. doi:10.15295/bmij.v7i2.1113

Bayley, J. E., Phipps, D., Batac, M., & Stevens, E. (2018). Development of a framework for knowledge mobilisation and impact competencies. *Evidence & Policy, 14*(04), 725–738. doi:10.1332/174426417X14945838375124

Baysinger, B. D., & Butler, H. N. (2019). Corporate governance and the board of directors: Performance effects of changes in board composition. *Journal of Law Economics and Organization, 1*, 101–121.

BBC News. (2020). *Worldwide cases overtake 2003 Sars outbreak.* BBC News. https://www.bbc.com/news/world-51322733

Beck, U. (1986). Risikogesellschaft: Auf dem weg in eine Andere Moderne. Frankfurt a M: Suhrkamp.

Beckhard, R., & Pritchard, W. (1992). *Changing the essence: The art of creating and leading fundamental change in organizations.* Jossey-Bass Publishers.

Beer, M., & Nohria, N. (2000, May). Cracking the code of change. *HBR's Ten Must Reads on Change Management, 78*(3), 137–154. PMID:11183975

Beinart, W., & Coates, P. (2002). *Environment and history: The Taming of Nature in the USA and South Africa.* Routledge. doi:10.4324/9780203133552

Bell-Ellis, R. (2013). Integrating spirit at work: A ripple of hope for healthy organizational cultures. In *Handbook of Faith and Spirituality in the Workplace* (pp. 333–343). Emerging Research and Practice. doi:10.1007/978-1-4614-5233-1_21

Bell, G. G., & Dyck, B. (2011). Conventional resource-based theory and its radical alternative: A less materialist-individualist approach to strategy. *Journal of Business Ethics, 99*(1), 121–130. doi:10.100710551-011-1159-4

Bell, M. (2004). *Farming for us all: Practical agriculture & the cultivation of sustainability.* The Pennsylvania State University Press.

Benefiel, M. (2008). *The soul of a leader: Finding your path to fulfillment and success.* The Crossroad Publishing Company.

Bengtsson, M., & Raza-Ullah, T. (2016). A systematic review of research on coopetition: Toward a multilevel understanding. *Industrial Marketing Management, 57*, 23–39. doi:10.1016/j.indmarman.2016.05.003

Bennis, W. (2021). *On becoming a leader.* Perseus Books Group.

Bennis, W. G. (1959). Leadership theory and administrative behavior: The problem of authority. *Administrative Science Quarterly, 4*(3), 259–301. doi:10.2307/2390911

Berardi, U., GhaffarianHoseini, A. H., & GhaffarianHoseini, A. (2014). State-of-the-art analysis of the environmental benefits of green roofs. *Applied Energy, 115*, 411–428. doi:10.1016/j.apenergy.2013.10.047

Berger, P., & Luckmann, T. (1966). *The social construction of reality.* Anchor Books.

Berkes, F., & Folke, C. (Eds.). (1998). *Linking social and ecological systems: Management practices and social mechanisms for building resilience.* Cambridge University Press.

Berlin, G. (2020). *Capital of Green Trends: How Berlin leads the Way in Urban Sustainability.* Visit Berlin. https://about.visitberlin.de/en/green berlin

Berlin, N. (2020). *Stadt der grünen Trends-Wie Berlin den Weg der urbanen Nachhaltigkeit geht.* Visit Berlin. https://about.visitberlin.de/nachhaltiges-berlin

Bernardini, C, & Irvine, K. (2007). The 'nature' of urban sustainability: private or public green spaces? *Transactions on Ecology and the Environment,* 661-673.

Berndt, A., & Brink, A. (2004). *Customer relationship management and customer service.* Juta and company Ltd.

Bernstein, A. B., & Rakowitz, C. (2012). *Emergency public relations: Crisis management in a 3.0 world.* Xlibris Corporation.

Besharov, M. L., & Smith, W. K. (2014). Multiple institutional logics in organizations: Explaining their varied nature and implications. *Academy of Management Review*, *39*(3), 364–381. doi:10.5465/amr.2011.0431

Bettencourt, L. A., Blocker, C. P., Houston, M. B., & Flint, D. J. (2015). Rethinking customer relationships. *Business Horizons*, *58*(1), 99–108. doi:10.1016/j.bushor.2014.09.003

Bhaduri, R. M. (2019). Leveraging culture and leadership in crisis management. *European Journal of Training and Development*, *43*(5/6), 554–569. doi:10.1108/EJTD-10-2018-0109

Bilginoğlu, E., & Yozgat, U. (2021). The impact of sparking leadership on creating work passion and job satisfaction in organizations - An empirical study. Anadolu University. *Journal of Social Sciences*, *21*(1), 43–58. doi:10.18037/ausbd.902549

Birol, F. (2020). Put clean energy at the heart of stimulus plans to counter the coronavirus crisis. In *IEA*. https://www.iea.org/commentaries/put-clean-energy-at-the-heart-of-stimulus-plans-to-counter-the-coronavirus-crisis

Bissing-Olson, M. J., Iyer, A., Fielding, K. S., & Zacher, H. (2013). Relationships between daily affect and pro-environmental behavior at work: The moderating role of pro-environmental attitude. *Journal of Organizational Behavior*, *175*(2), 156–175. doi:10.1002/job.1788

Blanchard, K. H., & Hersey, P. (1997). Situational leadership. In: *Dean's Forum, 12*(2), 5.

Blau, P. M., & Schoenherr, R. (1971). *The structure of organizations*. Basic Books.

Blomgren, M., & Waks, C. (2015). Coping with contradictions: Hybrid professionals managing institutional complexity. *Journal of Professions and Organization*, *2*(1), 78–102. doi:10.1093/jpo/jou010

Bloomsburg report. (2020). *Scale-up of Solar and Wind Puts Existing Coal, Gas at Risk*. Bloomsberg. https://about.bnef.com/blog/scale-up-of-solar-and-wind-puts-existing-coal-gas-at-risk/

BMC Software. (2023). *Lewin's 3-stage model of change explained*. BMC Software. https://www.bmc.com/blogs/lewin-three-stage-model-change/

Boatwright, A., & Wynne, M. A. (2020). Record Global GDP Contraction Indicative of COVID-19's Cross-Country Effect. *Dallas Federal Economics*, *30*, 1–3.

Bock, G. W., Zmud, R. W., Kim, Y. G., & Lee, J. N. (2005). Behavioral intention formation in knowledge sharing: Examining the roles of extrinsic motivators, social-psychological forces, and organizational climate. *Management Information Systems Quarterly*, *2005*(29), 87–112. doi:10.2307/25148669

Bogers, M., & West, J. (2012). Managing distributed innovation: Strategic utilization of open and user innovation. *Creativity and Innovation Management*, *21*(1), 61–75. doi:10.1111/j.1467-8691.2011.00622.x

Boiral, O., Brotherton, M.-C., Rivaud, L., & Guillaumie, L. (2021). Organizations' management of the COVID-19 pandemic: A scoping review of business articles. *Sustainability (Basel)*, *13*(7), 3993. doi:10.3390u13073993

Boiral, O., & Paillé, P. (2012). Organizational citizenship behaviour for the environment: Measurement and validation. *Journal of Business Ethics*, *109*(4), 431–445. doi:10.100710551-011-1138-9

Bolisani, E., & Bratianu, C. (2017). Knowledge strategy planning: An integrated approach to manage. *Journal of Knowledge Management*, *21*(2), 233–253. doi:10.1108/JKM-02-2016-0071

Bolman, L. G., & Deal, T. E. (2011). *Leading with soul: An uncommon journey of the spirit*. Jossey-Bass Publishers. doi:10.1177/1071799199600300117

Bommer, W. H., Rich, G. A., & Rubin, R. S. (2005). Changing attitudes about change: Longitudinal effects of transformational leader behavior on employee cynicism about organizational change. *Journal of Organizational Behavior, 26*(7), 733–753. doi:10.1002/job.342

Bonacini, L., Gallo, G., & Scicchitano, S. (2021). Working from home and income inequality: Risks of a 'new normal' with Covid-19. *Journal of Population Economics, 34*(1), 303–360. doi:10.100700148-020-00800-7 PMID:32952308

Bond, A., Morrison-Saunders, A., & Pope, J. (2012). Sustainability assessment: The state of the art. *Impact Assessment and Project Appraisal, 30*(1), 53–62. doi:10.1080/14615517.2012.661974

Boons, F., & Lüdeke-Freund, F. (2013). Business models for sustainable innovation: State of the art and steps towards a research agenda. *Journal of Cleaner Production, 45*, 9–19. https://www.sciencedirect.com/science/article/pii/S095965261 2003459. doi:10.1016/j.jclepro.2012.07.007

Boutaud, N., Agarwal, A., Postel, E. A., & Pericak-Vance, M. A. (2005). Complement factor H variant increases the risk of age-related macular degeneration. *Science, 308*(5720), 419–421. doi:10.1126cience.1110359 PMID:15761120

Boyatzis, R. E., Smith, M., & Blaize, N. (2006). Developing sustainable leaders through coaching and compassion. *Academy of Management Learning & Education, 5*(1), 8–24. doi:10.5465/amle.2006.20388381

Boyd, E. (2017, February). Holistic thinking beyond technology. *Nature Climate Change, 7*(2), 97–98. doi:10.1038/nclimate3211

Brammer, S., Jackson, G., & Matten, D. (2012). Corporate social responsibility and institutional theory: New perspectives on private governance. *Socio-economic Review, 10*(1), 3–28. doi:10.1093er/mwr030

Brands, R. A., & Fernandez-Mateo, I. (2017). Leaning out: How negative recruitment experiences shape women's decisions to compete for executive roles. *Administrative Science Quarterly, 62*(3), 405–442. doi:10.1177/0001839216682728

Brauer, M., & Schmidt, S. L. (2008). Defining the strategic role of boards and measuring boards' effectiveness in strategy implementation. *Corporate Governance (Bradford), 8*(5), 649–660. doi:10.1108/14720700810913304

Bremer, M. (2018). *Developing a positive culture where people and performance thrive.* Motivational Press, Inc.

Brooks, B., Curnin, S., Owen, C., & Boldeman, J. (2019). New human capabilities in emergency and crisis management: From non-technical skills to creativity. *Australian Journal of Emergency Management, 34*(4), 23–30. https://knowledge.aidr.org.au/resources/ajem-october-2019-new-human-capabilities-in-emergency-and-crisis-management-from-non-technical-skills-to-creativity/

Brown, J. (2012). *Systems Thinking Strategy: The New Way to Understand Your Business and Drive Performance.* iUniverse.

Brown, B. (2010). *The gifts of imperfection: Let go of who you think you're supposed to be and embrace who you are.* Hazelden.

Brown, B. (2019a). *Braving the wilderness: The quest for true belonging and the courage to stand alone.* Penguin Random House LLC.

Brown, J. (2019b). *How to be an inclusive leader: Your role in creating cultures of belonging where everyone can thrive.* Berrett-Koehler Publishers.

Brudermann, T., & Sangkakool, T. (2017). Green roofs in temperate climate cities in Europe - An analysis of key decision factors. *Urban Forestry & Urban Greening, 21*, 224–234. doi:10.1016/j.ufug.2016.12.008

Brundtland, G. (1987). *Our Common Future: The World Commission on Environment and Development.* Oxford University Press.

BrynjolfssonE.HittL. M.KimH. H. (2011). Strength in numbers: How does data-driven decisionmaking affect firm performance? *Available at* SSRN 1819486. doi:10.2139/ssrn.1819486

Buchanan, M. (2003). *Nexus: Small Worlds and the Groundbreaking Theory of Networks*. W. W. Norton.

Buckley, P. J., Doh, J. P., & Benischke, M. H. (2017). Towards a renaissance in international business research? Big questions, grand challenges, and the future of IB scholarship. *Journal of International Business Studies*, *48*(9), 1045–1064. doi:10.105741267-017-0102-z

Buckley, P., & Bachman, D. (2017). Meet the US workforce of the future: Older, more diverse, and more educated. *Deloitte Review*, *21*, 47–61.

Budiharta, P., & Kacaribu, H. E. (2020). The influence of board of directors, managerial ownership, and audit committee on Carbon Emission Disclosure: A study of non-financial companies listed on BEI. *Review of Integrative Business and Economics Research*, *9*(3), 75–87.

Bullard, E. (2022). *Competence*. Salem Press Encyclopedia, Research Starters.

Burnes, B. (2004). Kurt Lewin and the planned approach to change: A re-appraisal. *Journal of Management Studies*, *41*(6), 977–1002. doi:10.1111/j.1467-6486.2004.00463.x

Burnes, B. (2020). The origins of Lewin's three-step model of change. *The Journal of Applied Behavioral Science*, *56*(1), 32–59. doi:10.1177/0021886319892685

Burns, J., & Steele, A. (2020). *Blockchain and internal control The COSO perspective*. Durham: Committee of sponsoring organizations of the treadway commission.

Burns, R. B. (1981). *The self-concept*. Longman.

Burszta-Adamiak, E., & Fiałkiewicza, W. (2019). Review of green roof incentives as motivators for the expansion of green infrastructure in European cities. *Scientific Review – Engineering and Environmental Sciences* (2019), *28* (4), 641–652.

Burszta-Adamiak, E., Stańczyk, J., & Łomotowski, J. (2019). Hydrological performance of green roofs in the context of the meteorological factors during the 5-year monitoring period. *Water and Environment Journal : the Journal / the Chartered Institution of Water and Environmental Management*, *33*(1), 144–154. doi:10.1111/wej.12385

Burton, R. M., & Obel, B. (2004). *Strategic Organizational Diagnosis and Design: The Dynamics of Fit*. Springer. doi:10.1007/978-1-4419-9114-0

Bushe, G. R. (2011). Appreciative inquiry: Theory and critique. *The Routledge Companion to Organizational Change*, 87-102.

Busienss leaders. (2020). *Clean Energy & COVID-19 Crisis*, *2*(November). https://e2.org/reports/clean-jobs-covid-economic-crisis-april-2020/

Cameron, K. S. (1984). The effectiveness of ineffectiveness. In B. M. Staw & L. L. Cummings (Eds.), *Research in organizational behaviour* (Vol. 6, pp. 235–285). JAI Press.

Cameron, K. S. (1986). Effectiveness as a paradox: Consensus and conflict in conceptions of organisational effectiveness. *Journal of Management Science*, *32*(5), 539–553.

Cameron, K. S., & Quinn, R. E. (2006). *Diagnosing and changing organizational culture: Based on the competing values framework*. Jossey-Bass Publishers.

Cameron, K. S., & Whetton, D. A. (1983). *Organisational effectiveness: A comparison of multiple models*. Academic Press.

Campbell, B. (2018). Biodiversity, livelihoods and struggles over sustainability in Nepal. *Landscape Research*, *43*(8), 1056–1067. doi:10.1080/01426397.2018.1503241

Campbell, J. P. (1971). Personnel training and development. *Annual Review of Psychology*, *22*(1), 565–602. doi:10.1146/annurev.ps.22.020171.003025

Cantista, I., & Tylecote, A. (2008). Industrial innovation, corporate governance and supplier-customer relationships. *Journal of Manufacturing Technology Management*, *19*(5), 576–590. doi:10.1108/17410380810877267

Cantrell, J. E., Kyriazis, E., & Noble, G. (2015). Developing CSR giving as a dynamic capability for salient stakeholder management. *Journal of Business Ethics*, *130*(2), 403–421. doi:10.100710551-014-2229-1

Capital Group. (2020). 2021 Outlook : Turning points on the road to recovery. In *Capital Group*. https://www.capital-group.com/advisor/insights/articles/2021-outlook.html

Carayon, P., Kleinschmidt, P., Hose, B. Z., & Salwei, M. (2021). Human Factors and Ergonomics in Health Care and Patient Safety from the Perspective of Medical Residents. In L. Donaldson, W. Ricciardi, S. Sheridan, & R. Tartaglia (Eds.), *Textbook of Patient Safety and Clinical Risk Management*. Springer. doi:10.1007/978-3-030-59403-9_7

Carder, B., & Monda, M. (2013). *Deming's profound knowledge and leadership: We are still not out of the crisis*. ASQ Quality Press.

Carder, B., & Ragan, P. (2005). Measurement matters. *Professional Safety*, *50*(4), 17.

Carillo, K. D. A., Galy, N., Guthrie, C., & Vanhems, A. (2019). How to turn managers into data-driven decision makers: Measuring attitudes towards business analytics. *Business Process Management Journal*, *25*(3), 553–578. doi:10.1108/BPMJ-11-2017-0331

Carolan, M. S. (2006). Social change and the adoption and adaptation of knowledge claims: Whose truth do you trust regarding sustainable agriculture? *Agriculture and Human Values*, *23*(3), 325–339. doi:10.100710460-006-9006-4

Castro, A. J. L., & Orellana, F. (2019). Green roofs as a strategy for urban green innovation spaces. *Sustainable Cities and Society*, *44*, 697–705. doi:10.1016/j.scs.2018.10.034

Cekada, T. L. (2018). Salesmanship for change: Utilizing WIIFM and understanding employee needs. *Professional Safety*, *63*(03), 44–47.

Chakrabarti, A. (2001). The determinants of foreign direct investments: Sensitivity analyses of cross- country regressions. *Kyklos*, *54*(1), 89–114. doi:10.1111/1467-6435.00142

Chakrabortty, R. K., Abdel-Basset, M., & Ali, A. M. (2023). A multi-criteria decision analysis model for selecting an optimum customer service chatbot under uncertainty. *Decision Analytics Journal*.

Chakraborty, O. (2023). Theories and application of organisational change management during the COVID-19 era. In K. L. Tennin (Ed.), *Change management during unprecedented times* (pp. 155–185). IGI Global. doi:10.4018/978-1-6684-7509-6.ch008

Chambers, R. (2019). *Development*, *22*(7), 953–969.

Chang, N. J., & Fong, C. M. (2010). Green product quality, green corporate image, green customer satisfaction, and green customer loyalty. *African Journal of Business Management*, *4*(13), 2336–2344.

Chang, T. W., Chen, Y. S., Yeh, Y. L., & Li, H. X. (2020). Sustainable consumption models for customers: Investigating the significant antecedents of green purchase behavior from the perspective of information asymmetry. *Journal of Environmental Planning and Management*, *2020*, 1–21.

Chang, V. (2016). Review and discussion: E-Learning for academia and industry. *International Journal of Information Management*, *36*(3), 476–485. doi:10.1016/j.ijinfomgt.2015.12.007

Chaturvedi, S., Rizvi, I. A., & Pasipanodya, E. T. (2019). How can leaders make their followers to commit to the organization? The importance of influence tactics. *Global Business Review*, *20*(6), 1462–1474. doi:10.1177/0972150919846963

Chaubey, A., & Sahoo, C. K. (2021). Assimilation of business intelligence: The effect of external pressures and top leaders' commitment during pandemic crisis. *International Journal of Information Management*, *59*, 102344. doi:10.1016/j.ijinfomgt.2021.102344

Chawla, V. (2014). The effect of workplace spirituality on salespeople's organizational deviant behaviors: Research propositions and practical implications. *Journal of Business and Industrial Marketing*, *29*(3), 199–208. doi:10.1108/JBIM-08-2012-0134

Chen, Y. S. (2008). The driver of green innovation and green image–green core competence. *Journal of Business Ethics*, *81*(3), 531–543. doi:10.100710551-007-9522-1

Chen, Y. S., & Chang, C. H. (2013). The determinants of green product development performance: Green dynamic capabilities, green transformational leadership, and green creativity. *Journal of Business Ethics*, *2013*(116), 107–119. doi:10.100710551-012-1452-x

Chen, Y. S., Lai, S. B., & Wen, C. T. (2006). The influence of green innovation performance on corporate advantage in Taiwan. *Journal of Business Ethics*, *2006*(67), 331–339. doi:10.100710551-006-9025-5

Chen, Y. S., Lin, S. H., Lin, C. Y., Hung, S. T., Chang, C. W., & Huang, C. W. (2020). Improving green product development performance from green vision and organizational culture perspectives. *Corporate Social Responsibility and Environmental Management*, *2020*(27), 222–231. doi:10.1002/csr.1794

Chen, Y., Wang, Q., Chen, H., Song, X., Tang, H., & Tian, M. (2019). An overview of augmented reality technology. *Journal of Physics: Conference Series*, *1237*(2), 022082. doi:10.1088/1742-6596/1237/2/022082

Cheri, L., & Abdullahi, M. (2018). E-governance: Illusion or opportunity for Nigerian university's administration. *Global Journal of Political Science and Administration*, *6*(3), 33–43.

Cherns, A. (1976). The principles of sociotechnical design. *Human Relations*, *29*(8), 783–792. doi:10.1177/001872677602900806

Chesbrough, H. W. (2003). *Open innovation: The new imperative for creating and profiting from technology*. Harvard Business School Press.

Chiou, T. Y., Chan, H. K., Lettice, F., & Chung, S. H. (2011). The influence of greening the suppliers and green innovation on environmental performance and competitive advantage in Taiwan. *Transportation Research Part E, Logistics and Transportation Review*, *2011*(47), 822–836. doi:10.1016/j.tre.2011.05.016

Choudary, D. V., & Ponnuru, M. (2015). The importance of soft-skills training for MBA students and managers. *Abhinav International Monthly Refereed Journal of Research*, *4*(11), 6–14.

Christensen, C. M. (2016). *The Innovator's Dilemma: When New Technologies Cause Great Firms to Fail*. Harvard Business Review Press.

Christensen, M. (2005). The third hand: Private sector consultants in public sector accounting change. *European Accounting Review*, *14*(3), 447–474. doi:10.1080/0963818042000306217

Christie, R. (2013). Why Machiavelli? In: Christie, R., & Florence, L. G. (Eds.), Studies in Machiavellianism. Academy Press.

Christopher, M. (1983). Creating effective policies for customer service. *International Journal of Physical Distribution & Materials Management*, *13*(2), 3–24. doi:10.1108/eb014555

Christopher, M., & András, T. (2013). Imprinting: Toward a multilevel theory. *The Academy of Management Annals*, *7*(1), 195–245. doi:10.5465/19416520.2013.766076

Cimatti, B. (2016). Definition, development, assessment of soft skills and their role for the quality of organizations and enterprises. *International Journal of Qualitative Research*, *10*(1), 97. doi:10.18421/IJQR10.01-05

Cinque, M. (2016). *"Lost in translation". Soft skills development in European countries.* Tuning Journal for Higher Education. doi:10.18543/tjhe-3(2)-2016pp389-427

Cipresso, P., Giglioli, I. A., Raya, M. A., & Riva, G. (2018). The past, present, and future of virtual and augmented reality research: A network and cluster analysis of the literature. *Frontiers in Psychology*, *9*, 2086. doi:10.3389/fpsyg.2018.02086 PMID:30459681

Clark, P. A. (1985). *A Review of the Theories of Time and Structure for Organizational Sociology.* University of Aston.

Clegg, S. R., Hardy, C., Lawrence, T. B., & Nord, W. R. (2020). *Sage Handbook of organization studies,* 215-254. Sage. https://www.researchgate.net/publication/242437344_Institutions_and_institutional_work/link/550aa6900cf290bdc10fdad3/download.

Clemen, J. C., Ali, H., Abdulmadid, A., & Jabbar, J. H. (2021). Education during covid-19 era: Readiness of students in a less-economically developed country for E-Learning. *IMCC Journal of Science*, *1*(2), 94–101.

Cobb, J. S. (2017). Inequality frames: How teachers inhabit color-blind ideology. *Sociology of Education*, *90*(4), 315–332. doi:10.1177/0038040717739612

Coelho, M.J. & Martins, H. (2022). The future of soft skills development: a systematic review of the literature of the digital training practices for soft skills. *Journal of e-Learning and Knowledge Society, 18*(2), 78-85.

Coghlan, D., & Brannick, T. (2014). *Doing action research in your own organization.* Sage.

Colbert, A. E., Judge, T. A., Choi, D., & Wang, G. (2012). Accessing the trait theory of leadership using self and observer ratings of personality: The mediating role of contributions to group success. *The Leadership Quarterly*, *23*(4), 670–647. doi:10.1016/j.leaqua.2012.03.004

Collis, J., & Hussey, R. (2014). *Business Research: Understanding Research.* Palgrave Macmillan. doi:10.1007/978-1-137-03748-0

Commission on Higher Education [CHEd]. (2020). *Guidelines on the implementation of flexible learning.* CHED. https://ched.gov.ph/wp-content/uploads/CMO-No.-4-s.-2020-Guidelines-on-the-Implementation-of-FlexiblE-Learning.pdf

Conger, J. A. (1994). *Spirit at work: Discovering the spirituality in leadership* (1st ed.). Jossey-Bass Publishers.

Contractor, N. S., DeChurch, L. A., Carson, J., Carter, D. R., & Keegan, B. (2012). The topology of collective leadership. *The Leadership Quarterly*, *23*(6), 994–1011. doi:10.1016/j.leaqua.2012.10.010

Coolen, H., & Meesters, J. (2012). Private and public green spaces: Meaningful but different settings. *Journal of Housing and the Built Environment*, *27*(1), 49–67. doi:10.100710901-011-9246-5

Cooperrider, D. L., & Godwin, L. N. (2022). Strengths-based megacommunities and the Appreciative Inquiry's complete convention: Creating wholepower, willpower and waypower for our world's Earthshot moment. *AI Practitioner, 24*(1), 94–106. doi:10.12781/978-1-907549-50-2-8

Cooperrider, D. L., Peter, F. S. Jr, Whitney, D., & Yaeger, T. F. (2000). Appreciative inquiry: Rethinking human organization toward a positive theory of change. *Team Performance Management, 6*(7-8), 140–140.

Cooperrider, D. L., & Srivastva, S. (1987). Appreciative inquiry in organizational life. *Research in Organizational Change and Development, 1*(1), 129–169.

Cooper, S., Parkes, C., & Blewitt, J. (2014). Can accreditation help a leopard change its spots? Social accountability and stakeholder engagement in business schools. *Accounting, Auditing & Accountability Journal, 27*(2), 234–258. doi:10.1108/AAAJ-07-2012-01062

Cork, S. (2010). *Resilience and transformation: Preparing Australia for uncertain futures.* CSIRO Publishing. doi:10.1071/9780643098138

Covello, C., & Iatridis, K. (2021). On the challenges and drivers of implementing responsible innovation in foodpreneurial SMEs. In E. Yaghmaei, & I. v. (eds), Assessment of Responsible Innovation (pp. 98-116). London: Taylor & Francis.

Cox, T., Kuk, G., & Leiter, M. P. (1993). Burnout, health, work stress, and organizational healthiness. In: W. B. Schaufeli, C. Maslach, & T. Marek (Eds.), *Series in applied psychology: Social issues and questions, Professional Burnout: Recent Developments in Theory & Research* (pp. 177–193). Taylor & Francis.

Craig, W. (2007). *Overview of the E-Learning capital programme.* JISC. https://www.jisc.ac.uk/media/documents/programmes/capital/elearningprogramme_craigwentworth

Crane, A. (2020). *Is COVID-19 changing the face of corporate social responsibility?* BATH. https://blogs. bath.ac.uk/business-and-society/2020/09/09/is-covid-19-changing-the-face-of-corporate-social-responsibility/

Crossman, J. (2016). Alignment and misalignment in personal and organizational spiritual identities. *Identity, 16*(3), 154–168. doi:10.1080/15283488.2016.1190726

Crubellate, J. M., Grave, P. S., & Mendes, A. A. (2004). A questão institucional e suas implicações para o pensamento estratégico. *RAC. Revista de Administração Contemporânea, 37*(spe), 37–60. doi:10.1590/S1415-65552004000500004

Cuellar, R., Scheere, A., & Augustine, S. (2021). *From PMO to VMO: Managing for Value Delivery.* Berrett-Koehler Publishers.

Cummings, T., & Worley, G. (2009). *Organization development & change* (9th ed.). South Western Cengage Learning.

Cuyper, L. D., Kucukkeles, B., & Reuben, R. (2020). *Discovering the real impact of COVID-19 on entrepreneurship.* World Economic Forum. https://www.weforum.org/agenda/2020/06/how-covid-19-will-change-entrepreneurial-business/

Czifra, G., & Molnár, Z. (2020). Covid-19 and Industry 4.0. *Research Papers: Faculty of Materials Science and Technology, 28*(46), 36-45. Slovak University of Technology. doi:10.2478/rput-2020-0005

Dabla-Norris, E., Ji, Y., Townsend, R. M., & Filiz Unsal, D. (2015). Distinguishing constraints of financial inclusion and their impact on GDP and inequality. *NBER Working Paper 20821.* Cambridge, MA: National Bureau of Economic Research.

Dacin, M. T., Munir, K. & Tracey, P. (2010). Formal dining at Cambridge colleges: Linking ritual performance and institutional maintenance. *Academy of Management Journal, 53*(6), 1393–1418. https://doi.org/. 2010.57318388 doi:10.5465/amj

Dacin, T., Ventresca, M., & Beal, B. (1999). Contextual embeddedness of organizations: Dialogue and directions. *Journal of Management*, 25(3), 317–356. doi:10.1177/014920639902500304

Dale, V. H., Brown, S., Haeuber, R. A., Hobbs, N. T., Huntly, N., Naiman, R. J., Riebsame, W. E., Turner, M. G., & Valone, T. J. (2000). Ecological principles and guidelines for managing the use of land. *Ecological Applications*, 10(3), 639–670. doi:10.2307/2641032

Danter, K. J., Griest, D. L., Mullins, G. W., & Norland, E. (2000). Organizational change as a component of ecosystem management. *Society & Natural Resources*, 13(6), 537–547. doi:10.1080/08941920050114592

Daoudi, I., Chebil, R., Tranvouez, E., Chaari, W. L., & Espinasse, B. (2017). Towards a grid for characterizing and evaluating crisis management serious games. *International Journal of Information Systems for Crisis Response and Management*, 9(3), 76–95. doi:10.4018/IJISCRAM.2017070105

Daud, Y. M. (2020). Self-leadership and its application to today's leader-A review of literature. *Strategic Journal of Business & Change Management, 8*(1), 1-11.

Davidson, R., Goodwin-Stewart, J., & Kent, P. (2005). Internal governance structures and earnings management. *Accounting and Finance*, 45(2), 241–267. doi:10.1111/j.1467-629x.2004.00132.x

Davidsson, P., Hunter, E., & Klofsten, M. (2006). Institutional forces: The invisible hand that shapes venture ideas? *International Small Business Journal*, 24(2), 115–131. doi:10.1177/0266242606061834

Day, D. V., & Sin, H. P. (2011). Longitudinal tests of an integrative model of leader development: Charting and understanding developmental trajectories. *The Leadership Quarterly*, 22(3), 545–560. doi:10.1016/j.leaqua.2011.04.011

de Geus, A. (1997). *The Living Company - habits for survival in a turbulent environment*. Harvard Business School Press.

de Geus, A. (1998). *Planning as learning*. Harvard Business School Press.

De Kluyver, C. A. (2013). *A Primer on Corporate Governance*. Business Expert Press.

de Melo, M. A. C. (1997). *Processo de planejamento e as inovações tecnológicas e sociais: Uma perspectiva sócio-ecológica*. Anais do 5o. Seminário de Modernização Tecnológica.

de Melo, M. A. C. (2002). Inovação e modernização tecnológica e organizacional nas MPMEs: O domínio interorganizacional. *Seminário Internacional: Políticas para Sistemas Produtivos Locais de MPME*: 2002.

de Melo, M. A. C., & de Melo, L. C. P. (1985). Os agentes reticuladores e o processo de planejamento: um estudo de caso. Anais do X simpósio nacional de pesquisa de administração em C&T. FEA/USP.

de Melo, M. A. C. (1991). *Innovatory planning: Antecipating social and technological innovation. Resumo. Anais do "3e Congrés International in France:Le Génie Industriel: facteur de Competitivité des enterprises"*. Groupement de Génie Industriel-GGI.

de Melo, M. A. C. (2002). *Enriquecendo a atuação de incubadora de emrpesas.Tecnologia e inovação: experiências de gestão nas micro e pequenas empresas*. PGT/USP.

de Rue, D. S., Nahrgang, J. D., Wellman, N. E. D., & Humphrey, S. E. (2011). Trait and behavioral theories of leadership: An integration and meta-analytic test of their relative validity. *Personnel Psychology*, 64(1), 7–52. doi:10.1111/j.1744-6570.2010.01201.x

de Smet, A., & Vogel, T. (2021, January 21). *McKinsey Live: Reenergizing the workforce: How leaders can overcome pandemic fatigue*. COVID Response Center. McKinsey & Company.

Deal, T. E., & Kennedy, A. A. (1982). *Corporate cultures*. Addison-Wesley.

Dealy, M. D., & Thomas, A. R. (2007). *Managing by accountability: What every leader needs to know about responsibility, integrity—and results*. Praeger Publishers.

Delaunay, C. D., Augusto, A., & Santos, M. (2020). Invisible vulnerabilities: Ethical practical, and methodological dilemmas in conducting qualitative research on the interaction with IVF embryos. *Societies, 10*(1). *Article, 7*, 1–15. doi:10.3390oc10010007

Dellestrand, H., & Kappen, P. (2012). The effects of spatial and contextual factors on headquarters resource allocation to MNE subsidiaries. *Journal of International Business Studies, 43*(3), 219–243. doi:10.1057/jibs.2011.57

Deloitte. (2020). *The board's role in the COVID-19 crisis*. Deloitte Touche Tohmatsu Limited.

Deming, D. (2017). The growing importance of social skills in the labor market. *The Quarterly Journal of Economics, 132*(4), 1593–1640. https://EconPapers.repec.org/RePEc:oup:qjecon:v:132:y:2017:i:4:p:1593-1640. doi:10.1093/qje/qjx022

Demirci, İ., & Ekşi, H. (2018). Keep calm and be happy: A mixed method study from character strengths to well-being. *Educational Sciences: Theory & Practice, 18*(2).

Denzin, N. K. (2012). Triangulation 2.0. *Journal of Mixed Methods Research, 6*(2), 80–88. doi:10.1177/1558689812437186

DePietro, A. (2020). Impact of Coronavirus (COVID-19) on Colleges and Universities in the U.S. *Forbes*. https://www.forbes.com/sites/andrewdepietro/2020/04/30/impact-coronavirus-covid-19-colleges-universities/#6ecab23661a6

Desai, A., Lankford, C., & Schwartz, J. (2020). With crisis comes opportunity: Building ethical competencies in light of COVID-19. *Ethics & Behavior, 30*(6), 401–413. doi:10.1080/10508422.2020.1762603

Desai, P. (2009). Spiritual psychology: A way to effective management. *African Journal of Marketing Management, 1*(7), 165–171.

DeSchoolmeester, D. (2014). *Systems Thinking: A Blueprint for Success*. CreateSpace Independent Publishing Platform.

Development, O. f. E. C. a., & OECD. (2012). *Corporate Governance Corporate Governance, Value Creation and Growth: The Bridge Between Finance and Enterprise*. OECD Publishing.

Dhawan, S. (2020). Online learning: A panacea in the time of COVID-19. Crisis. *Journal of Educational Technology Systems, 49*(1), 5–22. doi:10.1177/0047239520934018

Diefenbach, S., & Deelmann, T. (2016). Organizational approaches to answer a VUCA world. In O. Mack, A. Khare, A. Krämer, & T. Burgartz (Eds.), *Managing in a VUCA World*. Springer Nature. doi:10.1007/978-3-319-16889-0_13

Dignan, A. (2019). *Brave New Work: Are You Ready to Reinvent Your Organization?* Penguin Publishing Group.

Dilmaghani, M. (2019). Deep-level religious diversity and work-life balance satisfaction in Canada. *Applied Research in Quality of Life, 16*(1), 315–350. Advance online publication. doi:10.100711482-019-09768-3

Dimaggio, P. J. & Powell, W. W. (2005). A gaiola de ferro revisitada: isomorfismo institucional e racionalidade coletiva nos campos organizacionais. *Revista de Administração de Empresas, 45*(2), 74-89.

Dimaggio, P. J. (1988). Interest and agency in institutional theory. In: ZUCKER, Lynne G. (ed.). Institutional patterns and organizations. Cambridge, MA: Ballinger.

Dimaggio, P. J., & Powell, W. W. (1983). A gaiola de ferro revisitada: Isomorfismo institucional e racionalidade coletiva nos campos organizacionais. *Revista de Administração de Empresas, 45*(2), 74–89.

DiMaggio, P. J., & Powell, W. W. (Eds.). (1991). *The new institutionalism in organizational analysis* (Vol. 17). University of Chicago Press.

DiMaggio, P., & Powell, W. (1983). The iron cage revisited: Institutional isomorphism and collective rationality in organizational fields. *American Sociological Review*, *48*(2), 147–160. doi:10.2307/2095101

Dixon, J., Belnap, C., Albrecht, C. & Lee, K. (2010). The importance of soft skills. *Corporate finance review, 14*(6), 35.

Djelic, M.-L., & Quack, S. (2008). Institutions and transnationalization. In R. Greenwood, C. Oliver, R. Suddaby, & K. Sahlin-Andersson (Eds.), *The SAGE Handbook of Organizational Institutionalism* (pp. 299–323). Sage. doi:10.4135/9781849200387.n12

Dolan, S. L., & Altman, Y. (2012). Managing by values: The leadership spirituality connection. *People & Strategy*, *35*(4), 20–26.

Donato, H. & Donato, M. (2019). Steps in conducting a systematic review. *Portuguese Medical Act, 32*(3).

Donelly, R., Patrinos, H. A., & Gresham, J. (2021). *The impact of COVID-19 on education – recommendations and opportunities for Ukraine*. World Bank.

Dorado, S. (2003). Small groups as context for institutional entrepreneurship: An exploration of the emergence of commercial microfinance in Bolivia. *Organization Studies, 34*(4), 533–557. https://www.researchgate.net/publication/259285127_Small_Groups_as_Context_for. doi:10.1177/0170840612470255

dos Santos Teixeira, G. C., & Maccari, E. A. (2018). The institutional role of business school accreditation agencies: A systematic literature review. *Revista de Gestão*, *25*(3), 274–290. doi:10.1108/REGE-04-2018-035

Drucker, P. F. (1993). *Managing in Turbulent Times*. Butterworth-Heinemann.

Duckworth, A. L. (2016). *Grit: The power of passion and perseverance*. Simon and Schuster.

Duckworth, A. L. (2021). *Strengths of will playbooks*. Character Lab.

Due, A., Ellingrud, D., Lazar, M., Luby, R., Srinivasan, S., & Van Aken, T. (2021). *Achieving an inclusive US economic recovery*. McKinsey & Company. https://www.mckinsey.com/~/media/McKinsey/Industries/Public%20and%20Social%20Sector/Our%20Insights/Achieving%20an%20incl usive%20US%20economic%20recovery/Achieving-an-inclusive-US-e conomic-recovery.pdf?shouldIndex=false

Duncan, D. L. (2020). What the Covid-19 pandemic tells us about the need to develop resilience in the nursing workforce. *Nursing Management*, *27*(3). PMID:32400142

Dunning, J. H., & Lundan, S. M. (2008). *Multinational enterprises and the global economy* (2nd ed.). Edward Elgar Publishing.

Dunning, J. H., & Lundan, S. M. (2011). The changing political economy of foreign investment: finding a balance between hard and soft forms of regulation. In J. E. Alvarez & K. P. Sauvant (Eds.), *The Evolving International Investment Regime: Expectations, Realities, Options* (pp. 125–152). Oxford Scholarship Online. doi:10.1093/acprof:oso/9780199793624.003.0011

Dvořáková, L., & Faltejsková, O. (2016). Development of corporate performance management in the context of customer satisfaction measurement. *Procedia: Social and Behavioral Sciences*, *230*, 335–342. doi:10.1016/j.sbspro.2016.09.042

Dweck, C. S. (2015). Carol Dweck revisits the growth mindset. *Education Week*, *35*(5), 20–24.

Earth.org. (2020). *Renewable Energy Hits Record Growth in 2020- Report*. Earth.org. https://earth.org/renewable-energy-hits-record-growth-in-2020/#:~:text=Solar power capacity has increased 18-fold since 2010,renewable energy is becoming increasingly appealing to investors.

Elkind, L. D. C., & Landini, G. (Eds.). (2018). *The Philosophy of Logical Atomism: A Centenary Reappraisal*. Springer International Publishing.

Elkington, J. (1994). Towards the sustainable corporation: Win-win-win business strategies for sustainable development. *Cal. Manag. Rev. 36* (3), 90e100.

Elkington, J. (1997). The triple bottom line. *Environmental Management: Readings and Cases*, 2, 49–66.

Ellis, J. (2022). *What is the board's role regarding strategy?* The Corporate Governance Institute. https://www.thecorporategovernanceinstitute.com/: insights/guides/what-is-the-boards-role-regarding-strategy/

Emmons, R. A. (2000a). Is spirituality an intelligence? Motivation, cognition, and the psychology of ultimate concern. *The International Journal for the Psychology of Religion, 10*(1), 3–26. doi:10.1207/S15327582IJPR1001_2

Emmons, R. A. (2000b). Spirituality and intelligence: Problems and prospects. *The International Journal for the Psychology of Religion, 10*(1), 57–64. doi:10.1207/S15327582IJPR1001_6

Ergen, M. (2019). What is artificial intelligence? Technical considerations and future perception. *The Anatolian Journal of Cardiology, 22*, 5–7. doi:10.14744/AnatolJCardiol.2019.79091 PMID:31670719

Ericsson, A., & Pool, R. (2016). *Peak: Secrets from the new science of expertise*. Houghton Mifflin Harcourt.

Eroğlu, H. (2020). Effects of Covid-19 outbreak on environment and renewable energy sector. *Environment, Development and Sustainability, 0123456789*. doi:10.100710668-020-00837-4 PMID:32837274

Errida, A., & Lotfi, B. (2020). Measuring change readiness for implementing a project management methodology: An action research study. *Academy of Strategic Management Journal, 19*(1), 1–17.

Estrin, S., Baghdasaeyan, D., & Meyer, K. E. (2009). The impact of institutional and human resource distance on international entry strategies. *Journal of Management Studies, 46*(7), 1171–1196. doi:10.1111/j.1467-6486.2009.00838.x

EUCEN. (2008). *Glossary*. Recommendation of the European Parliament and of the Council on the Establishment of the European Qualifications Framework for Lifelong Learning. http://www.eucen.eu/EQFpro/GeneralDocs/FilesFeb09/GLOSSARY.pdf

Evan, W. (1966). Organizational lag. *Human Organization, 25*(1), 51–53. doi:10.17730/humo.25.1.v7354t3822136580

Fairholm, G. W. (1996). Spiritual leadership: Fulfilling whole-self needs at work. *Leadership and Organization Development Journal, 17*(5), 11–17. doi:10.1108/01437739610127469

Fenwick, M., & Vermeulen, E. P. (2018). *Technology and corporate governance: Blockchain, Crypto, and Artificial Intelligence*. Ecgi Global.

Ferguson, L. (2009). Working spiritually: Aligning gifts, purpose, and passion. *The Workplace and Spirituality: New Perspectives on Research and Practice*, 23-33.

Fernandes, A. A. R., & Solimun. (2017). The mediating effect of strategic orientation and innovations on the effect of environmental uncertainties on the performance of business in the Indonesian aviation industry. *International Journal of Law and Management, 59*(6), 1269–1278. doi:10.1108/IJLMA-10-2016-0087

Fernández-del-Río, E., Ramos-Villagrasa, P. J., & Escartín, J. (2021). The incremental effect of dark personality over the Big Five in workplace bullying: Evidence from perpetrators and targets. *Personality and Individual Differences, 168*, 110–291. doi:10.1016/j.paid.2020.110291

Fernandez, S., & Rainey, H. G. (2017). Managing successful organizational change in the public sector. In: *Debating Public Administration Review* (pp. 7–26). Routledge. doi:10.4324/9781315095097-2

Fernet, C., Trépanier, S. G., Austin, S., Gagné, M., & Forest, J. (2015). Transformational leadership and optimal functioning at work: On the mediating role of employees' perceived job characteristics and motivation. *Work and Stress, 29*(1), 11–31. doi:10.1080/02678373.2014.1003998

Fialkiewicz, W., Burszta-Adamiak, E., Kolonko-Wiercik, A., Manzardo, A., Loss, A., Mikovits, C., & Scipioni, A. (2018). Simplified direct water footprint model to support urban water management. *Water (Basel), 10*(5), 630. doi:10.3390/w10050630

Financial Training, A. (2017). *CIMA BA4 Fundamentals of Ethics, Corporate Governance and Business Law Study Text*. CreateSpace Independent Publishing Platform.

Finnegan, M., & O'Donoghue, B. (2019). Rethinking vulnerable groups in clinical research. *Irish Journal of Psychological Medicine, 36*(1), 63–71. doi:10.1017/ipm.2017.73

Fischer-Kowalski, M., Haas, W., Wiedenhofer, D., Weisz, U., Pallua, I., & Possanner, N. (2012). Socio-ecological transitions: definition, dynamics and related global scenarios. Institute of Social Ecology - AAU, Centre for European Policy Studies, Vienna, Brussels.

Flin, R., & O'Connor, P. (2017). *Safety at the sharp end: a guide to non-technical skills*. CRC Press. doi:10.1201/9781315607467

Følstad, A., & Skjuve, M. (2019, August). Chatbots for customer service: user experience and motivation. In *Proceedings of the 1st international conference on conversational user interfaces* (pp. 1-9). ACM. 10.1145/3342775.3342784

Fong, C. M., & Chang, N. J. (2012). The impact of green learning orientation on proactive environmental innovation capability and firm performance. *African Journal of Business Management, 6*(32), 727–735.

Fonseca da Silva, V. A. (2003). Abordagem institucional nos estudos organizacionais: bases conceituais e desenvolvimentos contemporâneos. In *Vieira, M. M. F., Carvalho, C. A. (org.). Organizações, instituições e poder no Brasil*. Editora FGV.

Forschungsanstalt Landschaftsentwicklung Landschaftsbau [FLL] (2002). *Dachbegrünungsrichtlinie. Richtlinien für die Planung, Ausführung und Pfl ege von Dachbegrünungen [Green roof policy. Guidelines for theplanning, execution, and maintenance ofgreen roofs]*. Bonn: Forschungsanstalt Landschaftsentwicklung Landschaftsbau.

Fosso Wamba, S., Gunasekaran, A., Dubey, R., & Ngai, E. W. (2018). Big data analytics in operations and supply chain management. *Annals of Operations Research, 270*(1), 1–4. doi:10.100710479-018-3024-7 PMID:36687515

Fottrell, Q. (2020). Will COVID-19 push more employees to work remotely after the pandemic? This economist says yes. *Market Watch*. https://www.marketwatch.com/story/does-covid-19-have-the-power-to-revolutionize-work-this-economist-says-yes-2020-12-11

Fox-Penner, P. (2020). Will the COVID-19 Pandemic Slow The Global Shift to Renewable Energy? In *The Brink, Boston University*. https://www.bu.edu/articles/2020/will-the-covid-19-pandemic-slow-the-global-shift-to-renewable-energy/

Franchi, T. (2019). The impact of the covid-19 pandemic on current anatomy education and future careers: A student's perspective. *Anatomical Sciences Education*. doi:10.1002/ase.1966 PMID:32301588

Franklin, M. (2014). *Agile change management: A practical framework for successful change planning and implementation*. Kogan Page Limited.

Frégeau, A., Cournoyer, A., Maheu-Cadotte, M.-A., Iseppon, M., Soucy, N., Bourque, J. S.-C., Cossette, S., Castonguay, V., & Fleet, R. (2020). Use of tabletop exercises for healthcare education: A scoping review protocol. *BMJ Open*, *10*(1), e032662. doi:10.1136/bmjopen-2019-032662 PMID:31915165

Friedland, R., & Alford, R. R. (1991). Bringing society back in: Symbols, practices, and institutional contradictions. In W. W. Powell & P. J. DiMaggio (Eds.), *The new institutionalism in organizational analysis* (pp. 232–263). University of Chicago Press.

Frosch, R. A. (1996). The customer for R&D is always wrong! *Research Technology Management*, 22–27.

Fry, L. W., & Matherly, L. L. (2007). *Workplace spirituality, spiritual leadership, and performance excellence. Encyclopedia of Industrial/Organizational Psychology*. Sage Publications, Inc.

Fuenfschilling, L. (2019). *An Institutional perspective on sustainability transitions Handbook of Sustainable Innovation*. Edward Elgar Publishing. https://www.elgaronline.com/view/edcoll/9781788112567/9781788112567.00020.xml

Fung, K. L. (2018). *Expanding the green network on rooftops: A study of integrating green roofs as a part of urban green innovation space planning* (Order No. 10932095). ProQuest One Academic. http://wdg.biblio.udg.mx:2048/login?url=https://www.proquest.com/dissertations-theses/expanding-green-network-on-rooftops-study/docview/2124999351/se-2?accountid=28915 https://www.proquest.com/docview/2124999351?pqorigsite=gscholar&fromopenview=true

Furnari, S. (2016). Institutional fields as linked arenas: Inter-field resource dependence, institutional work, and institutional change. *Human Relations*, *69*(3), 551–580. doi:10.1177/0018726715605555

Galdeano-Gómez, E., Céspedes-Lorente, J., & Martínez-del-Río, J. (2008). Environmental performance and spillover effects on productivity: Evidence from horticultural firms. *Journal of Environmental Management*, *88*(4), 1552–1561. doi:10.1016/j.jenvman.2007.07.028 PMID:17825476

Gallos, J. (2006). *Organization development: A jossey bass reader*. Jossey-Bass.

Gallup. (2023). *Global indicator: Hybrid work*. Gallup. https://www.gallup.com/401384/indicator-hybrid-work.aspx

Gamble, P. R. (2006). *Up Close & Personal?: Customer relationship marketing@ Work*. Kogan Page Publishers.

Gamidullaeva, L., Vasin, S., & Wise, N. (2020). Increasing small-and medium-enterprise contribution to local and regional economic growth by assessing the institutional environment. *Journal of Small Business and Enterprise Development*, *27*(2), 259–280. doi:10.1108/JSBED-07-2019-0219

Ganatra, S., Hammond, S. P., & Nohria, A. (2020). The novel coronavirus disease (COVID-19) threat for patients with cardiovascular disease and cancer. *JACC. CardioOncology*, *2*(2), 350–355. doi:10.1016/j.jaccao.2020.03.001 PMID:32292919

Ganesh, G., Paswan, A., & Sun, Q. (2015). Are face-to-face classes more effective than online classes? An empirical examination. *Marketing Education Review*, *25*(2), 67–81. doi:10.1080/10528008.2015.1029851

Garcia-Perez, A., Cegarra-Navarro, J. G., Bedford, D., Thomas, M., & Wakabayashi, S. (2020). *Critical Capabilities and Competencies for Knowledge Organizations*. Emerald Publishing Limited.

Gargi, B. (2019). Financial inclusion, women empowerment, and entrepreneurship: A special emphasis to India. *Malaysian E-commerce Journal*, *3*(3), 18–21. doi:10.26480/mecj.03.2019.18.21

Gazdula, J. (2017). Can teaching critical reflexivity be improved using metaphors? The hippo in the room. *Educational Futures*, *8*(1), 35–50.

Geh, E. Z. (2014). Organizational spiritual leadership of worlds "made" and "found": An experiential learning model for "feel." *Leadership and Organization Development Journal*, *35*(2), 137–151. doi:10.1108/LODJ-04-2012-0052

George, A. S., & George, A. H. (2023). A review of ChatGPT AI's impact on several business sectors. *Partners Universal International Innovation Journal*, *1*(1), 9–23.

George, G., Haas, M. R., McGahan, A. M., Schillebeeckx, S. J., & Tracey, P. (2021). Purpose in the for-profit firm: A review and framework for management research. *Journal of Management*. doi:10.1177/01492063211006450

Geraie, M. S., & Rad, F. M. (2015). Mediator role of the organizational identity green in relationship between total quality management and perceived innovation with sustainable competitive advantage. *International Journal of Biology, Pharmacy and Allied Sciences*, *2015*(4), 266–276.

Geroski, P. A., & Mazzucato, M. (2001). Modelling the dynamics of industry populations. *International Journal of Industrial Organization*, *19*(7), 1003–1022. doi:10.1016/S0167-7187(01)00060-1

Giblin, E. J. (1981). Bureaupathology: The denigration of competence. *Human Resource Management*, *20*(4), 22–25. doi:10.1002/hrm.3930200405

Giddens, A. (1984). *The Constitution of Society: Outline of the Theory of Structuration*. University of California Press.

Giddens, A. (1984). *The construction of society*. University of California Press.

Giorgi, G., Lecca, L. I., Alessio, F., Finstad, G. L., Bondanini, G., Lulli, L. G., Arcangeli, G., & Mucci, N. (2020). Covid-19-Related mental health effects in the workplace: A narrative review. *International Journal of Environmental Research and Public Health*, *17*(21), 7857. doi:10.3390/ijerph17217857 PMID:33120930

Gladstone, M., & Brown, S. (2022). Soft skills in a hard world: Why emergency management and business continuity leaders must update their professional toolbox. *Journal of Business Continuity & Emergency Planning*, *15*(3), 225–236. https://www.ingentaconnect.com/contentone/hsp/jbcep/2022/00000015/00000003/art00003 PMID:35190015

Goldstein, I. L., & Ford, J. K. (2002). *Training in organisations*. Wadsworth.

Golestanipour, M. (2016). Simple and multiple relationships between ethical leadership, transformational leadership and ethical climate and organizational spirituality among the employees of the Iran national steel industrial. *Review of European Studies*, *8*(2), 355–363. doi:10.5539/res.v8n2p183

Gong, Y., Li, X., & Li, Z. (2020). How to design green roofs to enhance urban green innovation space? Evidence from Beijing. *Habitat International*, *107*, 102–113. doi:10.1016/j.habitatint.2020.102113

Goodman, P. S., & Pennings, J. M. (1977). *New perspectives on organisational effectiveness*. Jossey-Bass.

Goulden, M., Mason, M. A., & Frasch, K. (2011). Keeping women in the science pipeline. *The Annals of the American Academy of Political and Social Science*, *638*(1), 141–162. doi:10.1177/0002716211416925

Gouverneur, J., & Netzer, N. (2014). Take the wheel and steer! Trade unions and the just transition. In *State of the World 2014. State of the World*. Island Press. doi:10.5822/978-1-61091-542-7_21

Graaf, K. d., Malnight, T. W., & Keys, T. S. (2013). *Ready? The 3Rs of Preparing Your Organization for the Future*. Keys.

Gravenhorst, K. M. B., Werkman, R. A., Boonstra, J. J., Gravenhorst, K. M. B., Werkman, R. A., & Boonstra, J. J. (2003). Questionnaire to assess the change capacity of organizations. *Applied Psychology*, *52*, 83–105. doi:10.1111/1464-0597.00125

Gray, D. (2016). *Liminal Thinking: Create the Change You Want by Changing the Way You Think.* Rosenfeld Media.

Greene, J. C., Caracelli, V. J., & Graham, W. F. (1989). Toward a conceptual framework for mixed-method evaluation designs. *Educational Evaluation and Policy Analysis*, *11*(3), 255–274. doi:10.3102/01623737011003255

Greenwald, H. P. (2008). *Organizations: Management without control.* Sage Publications. doi:10.4135/9781483329635

Greenwood, R., Oliver, C., Lawrence, T. B., & Meyer, R. (2017). Introduction. In R. Greenwood, C. Oliver, T. B. Lawrence, & R. Meyer (Eds.), *The SAGE handbook of organizational institutionalism* (2nd ed., pp. 1–49). SAGE. doi:10.4135/9781446280669.n1

Greenwood, R., Oliver, C., Lawrence, T. B., & Meyer, R. E. (2017). *The SAGE Handbook of Organizational Institutionalism.* SAGE Publications. doi:10.4135/9781526415066

Greenwood, R., Oliver, C., Sahlin, K., & Suddaby, R. (Eds.). (2008). *The Sage Handbook of Organizational Institutionalism.* SAGE. doi:10.4135/9781849200387

Greenwood, R., Raynard, M., Kodeih, F., Micelotta, E. R., & Lounsbury, M. (2011). Institutional complexity and organizational responses. *The Academy of Management Annals*, *5*(1), 317–371. doi:10.5465/19416520.2011.590299

Greenwood, R., Suddaby, R., & Hinings, C. R. (2002). Theorizing change: The role of professional associations in the transformations of institutionalized fields. *Academy of Management Journal*, *45*(1), 58–80. doi:10.2307/3069285

Gregory, A. (2005). Communication dimensions of the UK foot and mouth disease crisis, 2001. *Journal of Public Affairs*, *5*(3–4), 312–328. doi:10.1002/pa.31

Greuning, H. V., & Bratanovic, S. B. (2020). *Analyzing banking risk: a framework for assessing corporate governance and risk management.* World Bank Group.

Grove, H., Clouse, M., & Xu, T. (2020). Trategies for boards of directors to respond to the Covid-19 pandemic. *Corporate Board: Role. Duties and Composition*, *5*(1).

Gunarathne, P., Rui, H., & Seidmann, A. (2018). When social media delivers customer service: Differential customer treatment in the airline industry. *Management Information Systems Quarterly*, *42*(2), 489–520. doi:10.25300/MISQ/2018/14290

Gunay, S. G. (2008). *Corporate Governance Theory: A COMPARATIVE ANALYSIS of STOCKHOLDER and STAKEHOLDER GOVERNANCE MODELS.* iUniverse.

Gunn, A., & Mintrom, M. (2016). Higher Education Policy Change in Europe: Academic Research Funding and the Impact Agenda. *European Education*, *48*(4), 241–257. doi:10.1080/10564934.2016.1237703

Güntürkün, P., Haumann, T., Edinger-Schons, L. M., & Wieseke, J. (2023). How attributions of coproduction motives shape customer relationships over time. *Journal of the Academy of Marketing Science*, 1–29. PMID:36684408

Guo, Y., Fan, D., & Zhang, X. (2020). Social media–based customer service and firm reputation. *International Journal of Operations & Production Management*, *40*(5), 575–601. doi:10.1108/IJOPM-04-2019-0315

Gupta, J., & Vegelin, C. (2016). Sustainable development goals and inclusive development. *International Environmental Agreement: Politics, Law and Economics*, *16*(3), 433–448. doi:10.100710784-016-9323-z

Habib, M. A., Bao, Y., Nabi, N., Dulal, M., Asha, A. A., & Islam, M. (2021). Impact of strategic orientations on the implementation of green supply chain management practices and sustainable firm performance. *Sustainability (Basel)*, *13*(1), 340. doi:10.3390u13010340

Hadavi, S. (2017). Direct and indirect effects of the physical aspects of the environment on mental well-being. *Environment and Behavior*, *2017*(49), 1071–1104. doi:10.1177/0013916516679876

Hall, A., Rasheed Sulaiman, V., Clark, N., & Yoganand, B. (2003). From measuring impact to learning institutional lessons: An innovation systems perspective on improving the management of international agricultural research. *Agricultural Systems*, *78*(2), 213–241. doi:10.1016/S0308-521X(03)00127-6

Hallett, T. (2010). The myth incarnate: Recoupling processes, turmoil, and inhabited institutions in an urban elementary school. *American Sociological Review*, *75*(1), 52–74. doi:10.1177/0003122409357044

Hallett, T., & Hawbaker, A. (2021). The case for an inhabited institutionalism in organizational research: Interaction, coupling, and change reconsidered. *Theory and Society*, *50*(1), 1–32. doi:10.100711186-020-09412-2

Hall, P. A., & Soskice, D. (2001). *Varieties of capitalism: The institutional foundations of comparative advantage*. Oxford University Press. doi:10.1093/0199247757.001.0001

Hall, P. A., & Taylor, R. C. (1996). Political science and the three new institutionalisms. *Political Studies*, *44*(5), 936–957. doi:10.1111/j.1467-9248.1996.tb00343.x

Hamad, A., & Jia, B. (2022). How virtual reality technology has changed our lives: An overview of the current and potential applications and limitations. *International Journal of Environmental Research and Public Health*, *19*(18), 11278. doi:10.3390/ijerph191811278 PMID:36141551

Hamel, G., & Zanini, M. (2020). *Humanocracy: Creating Organizations as Amazing as the People Inside Them*. Harvard Business Review Press.

Hampel, C., Lawrence, T., & Tracey, P. (2017). Institutional work: Taking stock and making it matter. In R. Greenwood, C. Oliver, & T. B. Lawrence (Eds.), *The Sage handbook of organizational institutionalism* (pp. 558–590). Sage. doi:10.4135/9781446280669.n22

Hannah, S. T., Avolio, B. J., & Walumbwa, F. O. (2011). Authentic leadership and effects on follower moral courage, psychological capital, and performance. *Business Ethics Quarterly*, *21*, 555–557. doi:10.5840/beq201121436

Hanson, B. G. (1995). *General Systems Theory Beginning with Wholes*. Taylor & Francis.

Hao, G. (2022). Research on the agency problem, corporate governance and firm value. *7th International Conference on Financial Innovation and Economic Development (ICFIED 2022)* (pp. 2917-2923). NY: Atlantis Press. 10.2991/aebmr.k.220307.475

Hardison, C. M. (2017). Three hundred sixty-degree assessment. In A. Farazmand (Ed.), *Global Encyclopedia of Public Administration, Public Policy, and Governance*. Springer. doi:10.1007/978-3-319-31816-5_2744-1

Hardy, C., & Maguire, S. (2008). Institutional Entrepreneurship. In R. Greenwood & … (Eds.), *The Sage Handbook of Organizational Institutionalism* (1st ed.). Sage Publications. doi:10.4135/9781849200387.n8

Harraf, A., Wanasika, I., Tate, K., & Talbott, K. (2015). Organizational agility. [JABR]. *Journal of Applied Business Research*, *31*(2), 675–686. doi:10.19030/jabr.v31i2.9160

Hart, S. L. (1995). A natural-resource-based view of the firm. *Academy of Management Review*, *20*(4), 986–1014. doi:10.2307/258963

Hart, S. L. (2007). *Capitalism at the crossroads: Aligning business, earth, and humanity.* Wharton School Publishing.

Hart, S. L., & Dowell, G. (2011). A natural-resource-based view of the firm: Fifteen years after. *Journal of Management,* *37*(5), 1464–1479. doi:10.1177/0149206310390219

Haselberger, D., Oberhuemer, P., Perez, E., Cinque, M., & Capasso, F. (2012). *Mediating Soft Skills at Higher Education Institutions. ModEs project: Lifelong Learning Program.* GEA College. https://gea-college.si/wp-content/uploads/2015/12/MODES_handbook_en.pdf

Hassanein, N. (1999). *Changing the way America farms: Knowledge and community in the sustainable agriculture movement.* University of Nebraska Press.

Hassell, K. D. (2020). The impact of crisis intervention team training for police. *International Journal of Police Science & Management,* *22*(2), 159–170. doi:10.1177/1461355720909404

Haveman, H. A., & Rao, H. (1997). Structuring a theory of moral sentiments: Institutional and organizational coevolution in the early thrift industry. *American Journal of Sociology,* *102*(6), 1606–1651. doi:10.1086/231128

Healing, D. (2020). Big Oil's interest in renewable energy investments expected to waver, report says. In *The Globe and Mail.* https://www.theglobeandmail.com/business/article-big-oils-interest-in-renewable-energy-investments-expected-to-waver/

Heckman, J. J., & Kautz, T. (2012). Hard evidence on soft skills. *Labour Economics,* *19*(4), 451–464. doi:10.1016/j.labeco.2012.05.014 PMID:23559694

Hedgebeth, D. (2007). Data-driven decision making for the enterprise: An overview of business intelligence applications. *Vine,* *37*(4), 414–420. doi:10.1108/03055720710838498

Heinonen, K. (2014). Multiple perspectives on customer relationships. *International Journal of Bank Marketing,* *32*(6), 450–456. doi:10.1108/IJBM-06-2014-0086

Helmke, G., & Levitsky, S. (2004). Informal institutions and comparative politics: A research agenda. *Perspectives on Politics,* *2*(4), 725–740. doi:10.1017/S1537592704040472

Helmreich, R. L., Merritt, A. C., & Wilhelm, J. A. (2009). The evolution of crew resource management training in commercial aviation. In R. Key Dismukes (Ed.), *Human Error in Aviation* (pp. 275–288). Routledge.

Hemsley-Brown, T., & Laing, A. (2019). Green roofs and sustainable urban development: An exploratory review of potential barriers to adoption. *Sustainable Cities and Society,* *50,* 101648. doi:10.1016/j.scs.2019.101648

Hendarman, A. F., & Cantner, U. (2018). Soft skills, hard skills, and individual innovativeness. *Eurasian Business Review,* *8*(2), 139–169. doi:10.100740821-017-0076-6

Hendry, C. (1996). Understanding and creating whole organizational change through learning theory. *Human Relations,* *48*(5), 621–641. doi:10.1177/001872679604900505

Henry, P. S., & Luo, H. (2002). WiFi: What's next? *IEEE Communications Magazine,* *40*(12), 66–72. doi:10.1109/MCOM.2002.1106162

Herbst, P. G. (1974). *Socio-technical design: Strategies in multi-disciplinary research.* Tavistock Publications.

Herzberg, F. (2008). *One More Time: How Do You Motivate Employees?* Harvard Business Press.

Hesse-Biber, S. N. (2010). *Mixed methods research: Merging theory with practice.* Guilford Press.

Hiatt, J. M. (2006). *ADKAR: A model for change in business, government, and our community—How to implement successful change in our personal lives and professional careers*. Prosci Learning Center Publications.

Hiatt, J. M., & Creasey, T. J. (2012). *Change management: The people side of change*. Prosci Learning Center Publications.

Hinings, B., Gegenhuber, T., & Greenwood, R. (2018). Digital innovation and transformation: An institutional perspective. *Information and Organization*, *28*(1), 52–61. doi:10.1016/j.infoandorg.2018.02.004

Hirsch, P. M. (2008). Been there, done that, moving on: Reflections on institutional theory's continuing evolution. In R. Greenwood, C. Oliver, R. Suddaby, & E. Andersson (Eds.), *Handbook of Organizational Institutionalism* (pp. 783–789). Sage., doi:10.4135/9781849200387.n34

Hodge, T. (1997). Toward a conceptual framework for assessing progress toward sustainability. *Social Indicators Research*, *1997*(40), 5–98. doi:10.1023/A:1006847209030

Hodgson, G. M. (2006). What are institutions? *Journal of Economic Issues*, *40*(1), 1–25. doi:10.1080/00213624.2006.11506879

Holmes, B., & Gardner, J. (2006). *E-Learning: concepts and practice*. SAGE Publications. doi:10.4135/9781446212585

Hong, B. L., & Minor, D. (2016). Corporate governance and executive compensation for corporate social responsibility. *Journal of Business Ethics*, *136*(1), 199–213. doi:10.100710551-015-2962-0

Hope, N., Koestner, R., & Milyavskaya, M. (2014). The role of self-compassion in goal pursuit and well-being among university freshmen. *Self and Identity*, *13*(5), 579–593. doi:10.1080/15298868.2014.889032

Hošková-Mayerová, S. (2016). Education and training in crisis management. In Z. Bekirogullari, M. Y. Minas, & R. X. Thambusamy (Eds.), *ICEEPSY 2016: Education and Educational Psychology* (pp. 849–856)., doi:10.15405/epsbs.2016.11.87

Hosseini, S. E., & Wahid, M. A. (2016). Hydrogen production from renewable and sustainable energy resources: Promising green energy carrier for clean development. *Renewable & Sustainable Energy Reviews*, *57*, 850–866. doi:10.1016/j.rser.2015.12.112

Hotho, J., & Saka-Helmhout, A. (2017). In and between societies: Reconnecting comparative institutionalism and organizational theory. *Organization Studies*, *38*(5), 647–666. doi:10.1177/0170840616655832

Howe, J. (2014). *Unleashing the Power of People: A Guide to Organizing People and Systems*. Outskirts Press, Incorporated.

Howell, K. R. (2018). Fiedler & Chemers Revisited: Understanding the implications of the least preferred co-worker scale. *Journal of Business & Management Sciences*, *6*(3), 82–85. doi:10.12691/jbms-6-3-3

Huang, Y. M., & Chiu, P. S. (2015). The effectiveness of a meaningful learning-based evaluation model for context-aware mobile learning. *British Journal of Educational Technology*, *46*(2), 437–447. doi:10.1111/bjet.12147

Hughes, L., & Brennan, R. (n.d.). Effective communication during organizational change. *Journal of Change Management*. *"Idea Generation and the Quality of the Best Idea" by Karan Girotra, Christian Terwiesch et al.* ScholarlyCommons. https://repository.upenn.edu/mgmt_papers/304/

Hussain, S. T., Lei, S., Akram, T., Haider, M. J., Hussain, S. H., & Ali, M. (2018). Kurt Lewin's change model: A critical review of the role of leadership and employee involvement in organizational change. *Journal of Innovation & Knowledge*, *3*(3), 123–127. doi:10.1016/j.jik.2016.07.002

IAASTD. (2008). *About*. International assessment of agricultural knowledge, science and technology for Development. https://www.agassessment.org/.

IEA. (2020). *Exploring the impacts of the Covid-19 pandemic on global energy markets, energy resilience, and climate change.* IEA.

Ihnatenko, M., & Novak, N. (2018). Development of regional programs for the development of agrarian enterprises with organic production based on the European and international experience. *Baltic Journal of Economic Studies*, 4(4), 126–133. doi:10.30525/2256-0742/2018-4-4-126-133

Ilies, R., Morgeson, F. P., & Nahrgang, J. D. (2005). Authentic leadership and eudaemonic well-being: Understanding leader-follower outcomes. *The Leadership Quarterly*, 16(3), 373–394. doi:10.1016/j.leaqua.2005.03.002

ILO. (2015). *News.* ILO. https://www.ilo.org/global/topics/green-jobs/news/WCMS_42257 5/lang--en/index.htm

Imperial, M. T. (1999). Institutional analysis and ecosystem-based management: The institutional analysis and development framework. *Environmental Management*, 24(4), 449–465. doi:10.1007002679900246 PMID:10501859

Ingrassia, P., Foletti, M., Djalali, A., Scarone, P., Ragazzoni, L., Corte, F., & Fisher, P. (2014). Education and training initiatives for crisis management in the European Union: A web-based analysis of available programs. *Prehospital and Disaster Medicine*, 29(2), 115–126. doi:10.1017/S1049023X14000235 PMID:24642198

International Energy Agency [IEA]. (2020). *Renewables 2020 – Analysis and forecast to 2025* (Issue November). IEA. https://www.iea.org/reports/renewables-2020

International Renewable Energy Agency (IRENA). (2020). *Renewable Capacity Statistics 2020.* IRENA. https://www.irena.org/publications/2020/Mar/Renewable-Capacity-Statistics-2020

Irawanto, D. W. (2020). Unexpected and habit driven: Perspectives of working from home during the Covid-19 Pandemic. [Asia Pacific Management and Business Application]. *APMBA*, 8(3), 165–168. doi:10.21776/ub.apmba.2020.008.03.1

IRENA. (2020). *Renewables Account for Almost Three Quarters of New Capacity in 2019.* IRENA.

Jabbour, C. J. C., Santos, F. C. A., Fonseca, S. A., & Nagano, M. S. (2013). Green teams: Understanding their roles in the environmental management of companies located in Brazil. *Journal of Cleaner Production*, 2013(46), 58–66. doi:10.1016/j.jclepro.2012.09.018

Jackall, R. (1988). *Moral mazes: The world of corporate managers.* Oxford University Press.

Jackson, G., & Deeg, R. (2008). Comparing capitalisms: Understanding institutional diversity and its implications for international business. *Journal of International Business Studies*, 39(4), 540–561. doi:10.1057/palgrave.jibs.8400375

Jaffee, D. (2000). *Organization Theory: Tension and Change.* McGraw Hill.

Jain, S. K., & Kaur, G. (2004). Green marketing: an Indian perspective. *Decision* (0304-0941), 31(2), 161–209.

Jain, N. K., Kothari, T., & Kumar, V. (2016). Location choice research: Proposing new agenda. *MIR. Management International Review*, 56(3), 303–324. doi:10.100711575-015-0271-6

James, E. H., & Wooten, L. P. (2005). Leadership as (Un)usual: How to display competence in times of crisis. *Organizational Dynamics*, 34(2), 141–152. doi:10.1016/j.orgdyn.2005.03.005

Jancsary, D., Meyer, R. E., Höllerer, M. A., & Barberio, V. (2017). Toward a structural model of organizational-level institutional pluralism and logic interconnectedness. *Organization Science*, 28(6), 1150–1167. doi:10.1287/orsc.2017.1160

Jandik, T., & Salikhova, T. (2023). The effect of social connections on capital structure in supplier-customer relationships. *Journal of Corporate Finance*, 79, 102352. doi:10.1016/j.jcorpfin.2023.102352

Jankelová, N., & Mišún, J. (2021). Key competencies of agricultural managers in the acute stage of the COVID-19 crisis. *Agriculture*, *11*(1), 59. doi:10.3390/agriculture11010059

Jaques, E. (1997). *Requisite Organization: A Total System for Effective Managerial Organization and Managerial Leadership for the 21st Century*. Taylor & Francis Group.

Jaques, T. (2007). Issue management and crisis management: An integrated, non-linear, relational construct. *Public Relations Review*, *33*(2), 147–157. doi:10.1016/j.pubrev.2007.02.001

Jaruzelski, B., & Dehoff, K. (2008). Customer connection: The innovation 1000. *Strategic Finance*, *89*(8), 17.

Jensen, F. (2016). *Integrated Management System: Combining Other Standards with ISO 9001*. Lulu.com.

John, J. (2009). Study on the nature of impact of soft skills training programme on the soft skills development of management students. *Pacific Business Review*, 19-27.

Johnson, S. K. (2017). What 11 CEOs have learned about championing diversity. *Harvard Business Review*.

Johnson, S. K. (2019) *Leaking Talent How People of Color are Pushed Out of Environmental Organizations. Diverse Green*. diversegreen.org/research/leaking-talent/

Johnson, B. C., & Kiviniemi, M. T. (2009). The effect of online chapter quizzes on exam performance in an undergraduate social psychology course. *Teaching of Psychology*, *36*(1), 33–37. doi:10.1080/00986280802528972 PMID:20046908

Johnson, T. (2020). *Lean Methodology Mastery Collection: 8 Books in 1: Lean Six Sigma, Startup, Enterprise, Analytics, Agile Project Management, Kanban, Scrum and Kaizen*. Amazon Digital Services LLC - KDP Print US.

Jones, G. R. (2007). *Organizational Theory, Design, and Change*. Pearson Prentice Hall.

Jones, G. R. (2013). *Organizational theory, design, and change* (7th ed.). Prentice Hall.

Joshua, D., Obille, K., John, E., & Shuaibu, U. (2016). E-Learning platform system for the department of library and information science, Modibbo Adama University of Technology, Yola: A Developmental plan. *Journal of Information and Knowledge Management*, *7*(1), 51–69.

Joynes, C., Rossignoli, S., & Amonoo-Kuofi, E. F. (2019). *21st century skills: Evidence of issues in definition, demand, and delivery for development context. K4D Emerging Issues Report*. Institute of Development Studies., https://opendocs.ids.ac.uk/opendocs/handle/20.500.12413/14674

Jung, C. G. (1973). *Synchronicity: An acausal connecting principle*. Princeton University Press.

Kalandides, A., & Grésillon, B. (2021). The Ambiguities of "Sustainable" Berlin. *Sustainability (Basel)*, *2021*(13), 1666. doi:10.3390u13041666

Kalogiannidis, S. (2020). Covid impact on small business. *International Journal of Social Science and Economics Invention*, *6*(12), 387–391. doi:10.23958/ijssei/vol06-i12/257

Kamal, M. M. (2020). The triple-edged sword of COVID-19: Understanding the use of digital technologies and the impact of productive, disruptive, and destructive nature of the pandemic. *Information Systems Management*, *37*(4), 310–317. doi:10.1080/10580530.2020.1820634

Kam-Sing Wong, S. (2012). The influence of green product competitiveness on the success of green product innovation: Empirical evidence from the Chinese electrical and electronics industry. *European Journal of Innovation Management*, *2012*(15), 468–490. doi:10.1108/14601061211272385

Kanikani, I. (2023). Building Change maturity in organizations. In K. L. Tennin, (ed.) Change Management During Unprecedented Times. IGI Global.

Kanikani, I. (n.d.). Whitepaper Building organizational Change Maturity by FUTURE:CM. *Academia*. https://www.academia.edu/96132653/Whitepaper_Building_organizational_Change_Maturity_by_FUTURE_CM

Kanki, B. G., Helmreich, R. L., & Anca, J. (2010). *Crew resource management* (2nd ed.). Academic Press. doi:10.1016/B978-0-12-374946-8.10004-4

Karam, C., & Jamali, D. (2013). Gendering CSR in the Arab Middle East: An institutional perspective. *Business Ethics Quarterly*, *23*(1), 31–68. doi:10.5840/beq20132312

Karlin, M. (2020). Slow Job Growth in November Leaves 446,000 Clean Energy Workers Unemployed as COVID Cases, Shutdowns Surge. *American Council on Renewable Energy [ACORE]*. https://goodmenproject.com/featured-content/slow-job-growth-in-november-leaves-446000-clean-energy-workers-unemployed-as-covid-case

Kaur, M., Malik, K., & Sharma, S. (2021). A note on boardroom challenge, board effectiveness and corporate stewardship during COVID-19. *Vision (Basel)*, *25*(2), 131–135. doi:10.1177/0972262920987326

Kaushik, M., & Guleria, N. (2020). The impact of pandemic COVID -19 in workplace. *European Journal of Business and Management*, *12*(5), 9–18.

Kavanagh, M. H., & Ashkanasy, N. M. (2006). The impact of leadership and change management strategy on organizational culture and individual acceptance of change during a merger. *British Journal of Management*, *17*(S1), S81–S103. doi:10.1111/j.1467-8551.2006.00480.x

Kazemi, F., Khan, M. S., & Shafique, M. (2018). Green roofs as an innovative urban infrastructure for environmental sustainability: A case study of Calgary, Canada. *Environmental Science and Pollution Research International*, *25*(27), 27411–27423. doi:10.100711356-018-2649-6

Kazmi, S. A. Z., & Naarananoja, M. (2013, January). Comparative approaches of key change management models—a fine assortment to pick from as per situational needs. In: International Conference on Business Strategy and Organizational Behavior (BizStrategy), *Proceedings*, 217-224. Global Science and Technology Forum.

Keith, N., & Frese, M. (2008). Effectiveness of error management training: A meta-analysis. *The Journal of Applied Psychology*, *93*(1), 59–69. doi:10.1037/0021-9010.93.1.59 PMID:18211135

Keller, T. (2021). *Hope in times of fear: The resurrection and the meaning of Easter*. Penguin Publishing Group. 9780525560807.

Kelly, D., & Amburgey, T. L. (1991). Organizational inertia and momentum: A dynamic model of strategic change. *Academy of Management Journal*, *34*(3), 591–612. doi:10.2307/256407

Kemp, E., Porter, M. III, Anaza, N. A., & Min, D. J. (2021). The impact of storytelling in creating firm and customer connections in online environments. *Journal of Research in Interactive Marketing*, *15*(1), 104–124. doi:10.1108/JRIM-06-2020-0136

Khari, C., & Sinha, S. (2018). Organizational spirituality and knowledge sharing: A model of multiple mediation. *Global Journal of Flexible Systems Managment*, *19*(4), 337–348. doi:10.100740171-018-0197-5

Khodarahmi, E. (2009). Crisis management. *Disaster Prevention and Management*, *18*(5), 523–528. doi:10.1108/09653560911003714

Kim, Y., & Lim, H. (2020). Activating constructive employee behavioural responses in a crisis: Examining the effects of pre-crisis reputation and crisis communication strategies on employee voice behaviours. *Journal of Contingencies and Crisis Management, 28*(2), 141–157. doi:10.1111/1468-5973.12289

King, D., Skelsey, D., Smith, R., Sidhu, R., & APMG (Eds.). (2014). *The Effective Change Manager's Handbook: Essential Guidance to the Change Management Body of Knowledge.* Kogan Page.

Kiron, D., Kruschwitz, N., Haanaes, K., Reeves, M., & Gho, E. (2013). The innovation bottom line. research report. *MIT Sloan Management Review, 54*(2), 69–73.

Klemm, W., Zinngrebe, Y., & Heidenreich, S. (2019). Green roofs as part of urban green infrastructure for innovative cities. *Environmental Innovation and Societal Transitions, 31*, 50–56. doi:10.1016/j.eist.2018.11.003

Kodama, M. (2019). Business innovation through holistic leadership-developing organizational adaptability. *Systems Research and Behavioral Science, 36*(4), 365–394. doi:10.1002res.2551

Koestler, A. (2015). *The Ghost in the Machine.* One 70 Press.

Kökalan, Ö. (2019). The effect of organizational cynicism on job satisfaction. *Management Research Review, 42*(5), 625–640. doi:10.1108/MRR-02-2018-0090

Kokubun, K., Ogata, Y., Koike, Y., & Yamakawa, Y. (2020). Brain condition may mediate the association between training and work engagement. *Scientific Reports, 10*(1), 6848. doi:10.103841598-020-63711-3 PMID:32321951

Kolomiets T.V., Tomashuk I.V. (2021). Entrepreneurship and development of rural areas in Ukraine. *Colloquium-journal, 9*(96).

König, A., Graf-Vlachy, L., Bundy, J., & Little, L. M. (2020). A blessing and a curse: How CEOs' trait empathy affects their management of organizational crises. *Academy of Management Review, 45*(1), 130–153. doi:10.5465/amr.2017.0387

Konrad, M., Shrum, S., & Chrissis, M. B. (2003). *CMMI: Guidelines for Process Integration and Product Improvement.* Addison-Wesley.

Kostova, T., & Marano, V. (2019). Institutional theory perspectives on emerging markets. In *The Oxford Handbook of Management in Emerging Markets* (Vol. 99). Oxford University Press.

Kostova, T., & Roth, K. (2002). Adoption of an organizational practice by subsidiaries of multinational corporations: Institutional and relational effects. *Academy of Management Journal, 45*(1), 215–233. doi:10.2307/3069293

Kostova, T., Roth, K., & Dacin, M. T. (2008). Institutional theory in the study of multinational corporations: A critique and new directions. *Academy of Management Review, 33*(4), 994–1006. doi:10.5465/amr.2008.34422026

Kostova, T., & Zaheer, S. (1999). Organizational legitimacy under conditions of complexity: The case of the multinational enterprise. *Academy of Management Review, 24*(1), 64–81. doi:10.2307/259037

Kotrba, L. M., Gillespie, M. A., Schmidt, A. M., Smerek, R. E., Ritchie, S. A., & Denison, D. R. (2012). Do consistent corporate cultures have better business performance? Exploring the interaction effects. *Human Relations, 65*(2), 241–262. doi:10.1177/0018726711426352

Kotter, J. P. (1990). *A force for change: How leadership differs from management.* Free Press.

Kotter, J. P. (1996). *Leading change.* Harvard Business School Press.

Kotter, J. P. (2014). *Accelerate: Building Strategic Agility for a Faster-moving World.* Harvard Business Review Press.

Kotter, J. P. (2019). *Accelerate!: Building strategic agility for a faster-moving world.* Harvard Business Review Press.

Kozcu, G. Y., & Timurcanday Özmen, Ö. N. (2021). Effects of transformational leadership on organizational change management and organizational ambidexterity. *Global Journal of Economics & Business Studies, 10*(20), 15–25.

Kožená, M., & Mlázovský, M. (2021). The impact of customer behaviour on the corporate competitiveness in the European environment. In *SHS Web of Conferences* (*Vol. 129*, p. 07003). EDP Sciences.

Kraakman, R., Armour, J., & Davies, P. (2017). *The Anatomy of Corporate Law: A Comparative and Functional Approach* (R. Kraakman, Ed.). Oxford University Press. doi:10.1093/acprof:oso/9780198739630.001.0001

Kraiger, K. (2003). Perspectives on training and development. In W. C. Borman, D. R. Ilgen, & R. J. Klimoski (Eds.), *Industrial and organizational psychology, 12* (pp. 171–192). Handbook of psychology. John Wiley & Sons, Inc., doi:10.1002/0471264385.wei1208

Kramarchuk, R., Klein, D., Brunetti, B., Joseph, I., Schiavo, M., Georges, P., Redmond, S., Anankina, E., Prabhu, A., Lu, G., Huang, D., Amiot, M., & Roache, S. (2020). How is COVID-19 Impacting the Energy Transition? *SP Global.* https://www.spglobal.com/en/research-insights/featured/how-is-covid-19-impacting-the-energy-transition

Kritsonis, A. (2005). Comparison of change theories. *International Journal of Scholarly Academic Intellectual Diversity, 8*(1), 1–7.

KucherA. (2019), *Sustainable soil management in the formation of competitiveness of agricultural enterprises.* Academic Publishing House «Talent», Plovdiv, Bulgaria. doi:10.13140/RG.2.2.19554.07366

KucherL.HeldakM.OrlenkoA. (2018). Project management in organic agricultural production. *Agricultural and Resource Economics, 4*(3), pp. 104–128. doi:10.22004/ag.econ.281753

Kumaran, L. A., & Hemalatha, J. (2023). E-business enabled customer service management and its performance: Evidence from Indian micro, small and medium enterprises. *International Journal of Business Forecasting and Marketing Intelligence, 8*(1), 1–12. doi:10.1504/IJBFMI.2023.127700

Kumar, V., & Christodoulopoulou, A. (2014). Sustainability and branding: An integrated perspective. *Industrial Marketing Management, 43*(1), 6–15. doi:10.1016/j.indmarman.2013.06.008

Kurtz, A. (2021). The US economy lost 140,000 jobs in December. All of them were held by women. *CNN Business.*

Kurucz, E. C., Colbert, B. A., & Marcus, J. (2014). Sustainability as a provocation to rethink management education: Building a progressive educative practice. *Management Learning, 45*(4), 437–457. doi:10.1177/1350507613486421

Kwan, L. Y., Hung, Y. S., & Lam, L. (2021). How can we reap learning benefits for individuals with growth and fixed mindsets?: Understanding self-reflection and self-compassion as the psychological pathways to maximize positive learning outcomes. *Frontiers in Education.* doi:10.3389/feduc.2022.800530

Lacey, M. Y. (1995). Internal consulting: Perspectives on the process of planned change. *Journal of Organizational Change Management, 8*(3), 75–84. doi:10.1108/09534819510090178

Lalkaka, R., & Abetti, P. (1999). Business incubation and enterprise support systems in restructuring countries. *Creativity and Innovation Management, 8*(3), 197–209. doi:10.1111/1467-8691.00137

Lamprinakis, L. (2019). Improving business resilience through organizational embeddedness in CSR. *Development and Learning in Organizations, 33*(1), 24–27. doi:10.1108/DLO-06-2018-0071

Larwood, L., Falbe, C. M., Kriger, M. P., & Miesing, P. (1995). Structure and meaning of organizational vision. *Academy of Management Journal, 1995*(38), 740–769. doi:10.2307/256744

Lasek, M., & Jessa, S. (2013). Chatbots for customer service on hotels' websites. *Information Systems Management*, 2.

Latan, H., Jabbour, C. J. C., de Sousa Jabbour, A. B. L., Wamba, S. F., & Shahbaz, M. (2018). Effects of environmental strategy, environmental uncertainty and top management's commitment on corporate environmental performance: The role of environmental management accounting. *Journal of Cleaner Production*, *180*, 297–306. doi:10.1016/j.jclepro.2018.01.106

Laterza, V., & Duncan, A. T. (2021, March). Studying edtech platforms as platforms: Some notes towards a theoretical framework. *Workshop*, *1*, 30–31.

Lawrence, P. (2015). Leading change – Insights into how leaders actually approach the challenge of complexity. *Journal of Change Management*, *15*(3), 231–252. doi:10.1080/14697017.2015.1021271

Lawrence, T. B., & Suddaby, R. (2006). *Institutions and institutional work*. doi:10.4135/9781848608030.n7

Leach, A., Wandmacher, R., Ayres, J., & Gobran, L. (2013, April). Change management: Creating an internal change capacity—What's the right organizational model? [Accenture.]. *Outlook Point of View*, *1*, 1–2.

Lee, H. Y., & Kamarul, Z. B. A. (2009). The moderating effects of organizational culture on the relationships between leadership behavior and organizational commitment and between organizational commitment and job satisfaction and performance. *Leadership and Organization Development Journal*, *30*(1), 53–86. doi:10.1108/01437730910927106

Lee, S. M., & Lee, D. (2020). "Untact": A new customer service strategy in the digital age. *Service Business*, *14*(1), 1–22. doi:10.100711628-019-00408-2

Lefebvre, G., Summerfield, C., & Bogacz, R. (2022). A normative account of confirmation bias during reinforcement learning. *Neural Computation*, *34*(2), 307–337. doi:10.1162/neco_a_01455 PMID:34758486

Leicester, G. (2020). *Transformative Innovation: A Guide to Practice and Policy for System Transition*. Triarchy Press.

Leiter, M. P., Maslach, C., & Frame, K. (2014). Burnout. Encyclopedia of Clinical Psychology, 1-7.

Leiter, M. P. (1992). Burnout as a crisis in professional role structures: Measurement and conceptual issues. *Anxiety, Stress, and Coping*, *5*(1), 79–93. doi:10.1080/10615809208250489

Leiter, M. P., & Harvie, P. (1997). The correspondence of supervisor and subordinate perspectives on major organizational change. *Journal of Occupational Health Psychology*, *2*(4), 1–10. doi:10.1037/1076-8998.2.4.343 PMID:9552302

Leiter, M. P., & Maslach, C. (1988). The impact of interpersonal environment on burnout and organizational commitment. *Journal of Organizational Behavior*, *9*(4), 297–308. doi:10.1002/job.4030090402

Lencioni, P. M. (2012). *The advantage: Why organizational health trumps everything else in business*. John Wiley & Sons.

Le, T. T., & Behl, A. (2022). Role of corporate governance in quick response to Covid-19 to improve SMEs' performance: Evidence from an emerging market. *Operations Management Research : Advancing Practice Through Research*, *15*(1-2), 528–550. doi:10.100712063-021-00238-4

Lewin, K. (1946). Action research and minority problems. In G. W. Lewin (Ed.), *Resolving social conflict*. Harper & Row. doi:10.1111/j.1540-4560.1946.tb02295.x

Lewin, K. (1947). Frontiers in group dynamics II. Channels of group Life; Social Planning and Action Research. *Human Relations*, *1*(2), 143–153. doi:10.1177/001872674700100201

Lewis, S., Passmore, J., & Cantore, S. (2008). Using appreciative inquiry in sales team development. *Industrial and Commercial Training*, *40*(4), 175–180. doi:10.1108/00197850810876217

Lewis, S., Passmore, J., & Cantore, S. (2016). *Appreciative inquiry for change management: Using AI to facilitate organizational development.* Kogan Page Publishers.

Lewitt, B., & March, J. G. (1988). Organizational learning. *Annual Review of Psychology, 14*, 319–340.

Leximancer Pty Ltd. (2018). *Leximancer user guide: Release 4.5.* Leximancer. doc.leximancer.com/doc/Leximancer-manual.pdf

Li, C., & Lalani, F. (2020). *The COVID-19 pandemic has changed education forever.* World Economic Forum.

Li, J., Ghosh, R., & Nachmias, S. (2020). In a time of Covid-19 pandemic, stay healthy, connected, productive, and learning: Words from the editorial team of HRDI. *Human Resources Development Institute*, 199-207.

Liao, S. H., Chang, J. C., Cheng, S. C., & Kuo, C. M. (2004). Employee relationship and knowledge sharing: A case study of a Taiwanese finance and securities firm. *Knowledge Management Research and Practice, 2004*(2), 24–34. doi:10.1057/palgrave.kmrp.8500016

Li, J., Yin, Z., Li, Y., Sun, S., Li, M., & Li, Y. (2021). The application of green roofs in urban green innovation spaces: A case study in Jinan City, China. *Environmental Science and Pollution Research International, 28*(3), 3525–3537. doi:10.100711356-020-11544-2 PMID:32892283

Lin, Y. H., & Chen, Y. S. (2017). Determinants of green competitive advantage: The roles of green knowledge sharing, green dynamic capabilities, and green service innovation. *Quality & Quantity, 51*(4), 1663–1685. doi:10.100711135-016-0358-6

Liu, D., Jiang, K., Shalley, C. E., Keem, S., & Zhou, J. (2016). Motivational mechanisms of employee creativity: A meta-analytic examination and theoretical extension of the creativity literature. *Organizational Behavior and Human Decision Processes, 2016*(137), 236–263. doi:10.1016/j.obhdp.2016.08.001

Liu, J., Chen, J., & Tao, Y. (2015). Innovation Performance in New Product Development Teams in China's Technology Ventures: The Role of Behavioral Integration Dimensions and Collective Efficacy. *Journal of Product Innovation Management, 2015*(32), 29–44. doi:10.1111/jpim.12177

Li, W. D., Arvey, R. D., & Song, Z. (2011). The influence of general mental ability, self-esteem and family socio-economic status on leadership role occupancy and leader advancement: The moderating role of gender. *The Leadership Quarterly, 22*(3), 520–534. doi:10.1016/j.leaqua.2011.04.009

Llonch, P., Haskell, M. J., Dewhurst, R. J., & Turner, S. P. (2017). Current available strategies to mitigate greenhouse gas emissions in livestock systems: An animal welfare perspective. *Animal, 2017*(11), 274–284. doi:10.1017/S1751731116001440 PMID:27406001

Lockwood, N. R. (2005). *Crisis management in today's business environment: HR's strategic role.* Society for Human Resource. https://www.shrm.org/hr-today/news/hr-magazine/documents/1205rquartpdf.pdf

López-Gamero, M. D., Claver-Cortés, E., & Molina-Azorín, J. F. (2008). Complementary resources and capabilities for an ethical and environmental management: A qual/quan study. *Journal of Business Ethics, 82*(3), 701–732. doi:10.100710551-007-9587-x

LoPucki, L. M. (2018). Algorithmic entities. *Washington University Law Review, 95*(4), 887–951.

Loudon, A. (2001). *Webs of Innovation: The Networked Economy Demands New Ways to Innovate.* FT.com.

Love, J. H., & Roper, S. (2004). The organisation of innovation: Collaboration, cooperation and multifunctional groups in UK and German manufacturing. *Cambridge Journal of Economics, 28*(3), 379–395. doi:10.1093/cje/28.3.379

Lucire, Y. (1986). Neurosis in the workplace. *The Medical Journal of Australia, 145*(7), 323–327. doi:10.5694/j.1326-5377.1986.tb113838.x PMID:2945081

Ludbrook, F., Michalikova, K. F., Musova, Z., & Suler, P. (2019). Business models for sustainable innovation in industry 4.0: Smart manufacturing processes, digitalization of production systems, and data-driven decision making. *Journal of Self-Governance and Management Economics, 7*(3), 21–26.

Luhmann, N. (1991). *Soziologie des risikos*. De Gruyter.

Maas, C. J., & Hox, J. J. (2005). Sufficient sample sizes for multilevel modeling. *Methodology: European Journal of Research Methods for the Behavioral and Social Sciences, 2005*(1), 86–92. doi:10.1027/1614-2241.1.3.86

Macdonald, S. (1995). Too close for comfort?: The strategic implications of getting close to the customer. *California Management Review, 37*(4), 8–27. doi:10.2307/41165808

Machado-da-Silva, C. L., & Fonseca, V. S. (1996). Competitividade organizacional: Uma tentativa de reconstrução analítica. *Organizações & Sociedade, 4*(7), 97–114. doi:10.1590/S1984-92301996000400004

Mack, O., Khare, A., Krämer, A., & Burgartz, T. (2015). *Managing in a VUCA world*. Springer Nature.

Madsen, T. L., & Mckelvey, B. (1996). Darwinian dynamic capability: Performance effects of balanced intrafirm selection processes. *Proceedings - Academy of Management, 1996*(1), 149. doi:10.5465/ambpp.1996.4978158

Mahyoob, M. (2020). Challenges of E-Learning during the COVID-19 Pandemic Experienced by EFL Learners. *Arab World English Journal, 11*(4), 351–362. doi:10.24093/awej/vol11no4.23

Majorro, N. (2020). COVID-19 is a game-changer for renewable energy. Here's why. In *World economic forum*. https://www.weforum.org/agenda/2020/06/covid-19-is-a-game-changer-for-renewable-energy/

Mansfield, R. (1986). *Company Strategy and Organizational Design*. Croom Helm.

Marchi, V. D. (2012). Environmental innovation and R&D cooperation: Empirical evidence from Spanish manufacturing firms. *Research Policy, 41*(3), 614–623. doi:10.1016/j.respol.2011.10.002

Marinoni, G., Land, H.V. & Jensen, T. (2020). The impact of Covid-19 on higher education around the world. *IAU global survey report, 23.*

Marques, I. C., Marques, P., Serrasqueiro, Z., & Nogueira, F. (2021). Covid-19 and organisational development: Important signs of a new pillar for sustainability. *Social Responsibility Journal*. doi:10.1108/SRJ-10-2020-0415

Maruani, T., & Amit-Cohen, I. (2007). Open Space planning models: A review of approaches and methods. *Landscape and Urban Planning, 81*(1-2), 1–13. doi:10.1016/j.landurbplan.2007.01.003

Maslow, A. H. (1954). *Motivation and personality*. Harper & Row.

Mason, M. A. (2015). *What is a learning organization?* Moyak. https://www.moyak.com/papers/learning-organization.html

Massey, D., Quintas, P., & Wield, D. (1992). *High tech fantasies: Science parks in society, science, and space*. Routledge.

Matteson, M. L., Anderson, L., & Boyden, C. (2016). "Soft skills": A phrase in search of meaning. *portal. Portal (Baltimore, Md.), 16*(1), 71–88. doi:10.1353/pla.2016.0009

Maxwell, J. C. (2017). *The power of your leadership: Making a difference with others*. Hachette Book Group, Inc.

Mazur, K. V., & Tomashuk, I. V. (2019). Governance, and regulation as an indispensable condition for developing the potential of rural areas. *Baltic Journal of Economic Studies*, *5*(5), 67–78. doi:10.30525/2256-0742/2019-5-5-67-78

McAlearney, A. S., Gregory, M., Walker, D. M., & Edwards, M. (2021). Development and validation of an organizational readiness to change instrument focused on cultural competency. *Health Services Research*, *56*(1), 145–153. doi:10.1111/1475-6773.13563 PMID:33025602

McElroy, B. (2020). How COVID-19 is impacting renewable energy. *Renewable Energy World*. https://www.renewableenergyworld.com/2020/04/29/how-covid-19-is-impacting-renewable-energy/.

McKee, M. C., Mills, A. J., & Weatherbee, T. (2005). Institutional field of dreams: exploring the AACSB and the new legitimacy of Canadian business schools, *Canadian Journal of Administrative Sciences/Revue Canadienne des Sciences de l'Administration, 22*(4), 288-301.

McKibbin, W. J., & Fernando, R. (2020). The Global Macroeconomic Impacts of COVID-19: Seven Scenarios. SSRN *Electronic Journal, 1*–43. doi:10.2139/ssrn.3547729

McKibbin, W., & Fernando, R. (2021). The global macroeconomic impacts of covid-19: Seven scenarios. *Asian Economic Papers*, *20*(2), 1–30. doi:10.1162/asep_a_00796

McKinsey. (2008, March 1). *Enduring Ideas: The 7-S Framework*. McKinsey. https://www.mckinsey.com/capabilities/strategy-and-corporate-finance/our-insights/enduring-ideas-the-7-s-framework

McLean, G. (2005). *Organization development: Principles, processes, performance*. Berrett-Koehler Publishers.

McNeill, J. (2019). Skills vs. competencies – What's the difference, and why should you care? *Hays Social Worldwide*. https://social.hays.com/2019/10/04/skills-competencies-whats-the-difference/

Mell, I. C. (2010). *Green infrastructure: concepts, perceptions, and its use in spatial planning*. [Doctoral Thesis, School of Architecture, Planning and Landscape Newcastle University].

Mella, P. (2018). *The Combinatory Systems Theory: Understanding, Modeling and Simulating Collective Phenomena*. Springer International Publishing.

Melnychenko, O. (2020). Is artificial intelligence ready to assess an. *Journal of Risk and Financial Management*, *13*(191), 1–19.

Melville, R., & Merendino, A. (2019). The board of directors and firm performance: Empirical evidence from listed companies. *Corporate Governance (Bradford)*, *19*(3), 508–551. doi:10.1108/CG-06-2018-0211

Menguc, B., Auh, S., Yeniaras, V., & Katsikeas, C. S. (2017). The role of climate: Implications for service employee engagement and customer service performance. *Journal of the Academy of Marketing Science*, *45*(3), 428–451. doi:10.100711747-017-0526-9

Mentens, J., Raes, D., & Hermy, M. (2006). Green roofs as a tool for solving the rainwater runoff problem in the urbanized 21st century? *Landscape and Urban Planning*, *77*(3), 217–226. doi:10.1016/j.landurbplan.2005.02.010

Mesimaki, M., Hauru, K., Kotze, D. J., & Lehvavirta, S. (2017). Neo-spaces for urban livability? Urbanities' versatile mental image of green roofs in the Helsinki metropolitan area, Finland. *Land Use Policy*, *61*, 587–600. doi:10.1016/j.landusepol.2016.11.021

Methley, A. M., Campbell, S., Chew-Graham, C., McNally, R., & Cheraghi-Sohi, S. (2014). PICO, PICOS and SPIDER: A comparison study of specificity and sensitivity in three search tools for qualitative systematic reviews. *BMC Health Services Research*, *14*(1), 579. doi:10.118612913-014-0579-0 PMID:25413154

Meyer, J. W., & Rowan, B. (1977). Institutionalized organizations: formal structure as myth and ceremony. *American Journal of Sociology*, [S. I], *83*(2), 340-363.

Meyer, E. (2016). *The culture map: Decoding how people think, lead, and get things done across cultures* (International Ed.). Public Affairs.

Milliman, J., Czaplewski, A. J., & Ferguson, J. (2003). Workplace spirituality and employee work attitudes: An exploratory empirical assessment. *Journal of Organizational Change Management, 16*(4), 426–447. doi:10.1108/09534810310484172

Milliman, J., Gatling, A., & Kim, J. S. (2018). The effect of workplace spirituality on hospitality employee engagement, intention to stay, and service delivery. *Journal of Hospitality and Tourism Management, 35*, 56–65. doi:10.1016/j.jhtm.2018.03.002

Millstein, I. M., & MacAvoy, P. W. (2004). *The recurrent crisis in corporate governance*. Business Books.

Miñon, C. G. (2017). Workplace spirituality, work ethics, and organizational justice as related to job performance among state university educators. *Journal of Teaching and Education, 7*(1), 407-418.

Mirabile, R. J. (1997). Everything you wanted to know about competency modeling. *Training & Development, 51*(8), 73+. https://link.gale.com/apps/doc/A20021823/AONE?u=anon~f2a0c5d4&sid=googleScholar&xid=aa3c51fe

Mitroff, I., & Alpaslan, M. C. (2003). Preparing for evil. *Harvard Business Review, 81*(4), 109–115. PMID:12687925

Miyagawa, Y., Taniguchi, J., & Niiya, Y. (2018). Can self-compassion help people regulate unattained goals and emotional reactions toward setbacks? *Personality and Individual Differences, 134*, 239–244. doi:10.1016/j.paid.2018.06.029

Mladenova, I. (2022). Relation between organizational capacity for change and readiness for Change. *Administrative Sciences (2076-3387), 12*(4), 135. doi:10.3390/admsci12040135

Modlin, H. C. (1986). Compensation neurosis. *The Bulletin of the American Academy of Psychiatry and the Law, 14*(3), 263–271. PMID:2945605

Moghabghab, R., Tong, A., Hallaran, A., & Anderson, J. (2018). The difference between competency and competence: A regulatory perspective. *Journal of Nursing Regulation, 9*(2), 54–59. doi:10.1016/S2155-8256(18)30118-2

Mohamed, T., Singh, J. S. K., & Subramaniam, S. (2020). Social ontelligence, spiritual intelligence, and emotional intelligence: Job satisfaction among public sector employees in a high-risk country. *Global Business and Management Research, 12*(3), 104–117.

Mohd, H. A. and Norhidayah, S. (2016), Sustainable food production: insights of Malaysian halal small and medium sized enterprises. *International Journal of Production Economics, 181*, 303–314. . doi:10.1016/j.ijpe.2016.06.003

Mohr, L. B. (1971). Organisational technology and organisational structures. *Administrative Science Quarterly, 16*(4), 444–459. doi:10.2307/2391764

Mojarro, N. (2020). *COVID-19 is a game-changer for renewable energy. Here's why.* World Economic Forum. https://www.weforum.org/agenda/2020/06/covid-19-is-a-game-changer-for-renewable-energy

Moloi, T., & Marwala, T. (2020). The agency theory. In *Artificial Intelligence in Economics and Finance Theories. Advanced Information and Knowledge Processing* (pp. 95–102). Springer. doi:10.1007/978-3-030-42962-1_11

Monaghan, S., Gunnigle, P., & Lavelle, J. (2017). Firm-location dynamics and subnational institutions: Creating a framework for collocation advantages. *Industry and Innovation, 25*(3), 242–263. doi:10.1080/13662716.2017.1315562

Moon, J. (2021). Effect of emotional intelligence and leadership styles on risk intelligent decision making and risk management. *Journal of Engineering. Project & Production Management, 11*(1), 71–81. doi:10.2478/jeppm-2021-0008

Morgan, G. (2006). *Images of Organization*. SAGE Publications.

Morgan, K. (2017). Nurturing novelty: Regional innovation policy in the age of smart specialization. *Environment and Planning C. Politics and Space, 35*(4), 569–583.

Morree, P. d., & Minnaar, J. (2020). *Corporate Rebels: Make Work More Fun*. Corporate Rebels Nederland B.V.

Mouawad, M., & Kleiner, B. H. (1996). New developments in customer service training. *Managing Service Quality, 6*(2), 49–56. doi:10.1108/09604529610109774

Muchemi, A., & Wakonyo, E. N. (2020). Change management practices and performance of the national police service in Uasin Gishu County, Kenya. *International Journal of Current Aspects, 4*(1), 1–21. doi:10.35942/ijcab.v4i1.95

Mudambi, R., Li, L., Ma, X., Makino, S., Qian, G., & Boschma, R. (2018). Zoom in, zoom out: Geographic scale and multinational activity. *Journal of International Business Studies, 49*(8), 929–941. doi:10.105741267-018-0158-4

Mudambi, R., Navarra, P., & Paul, C. (2002). Institutions and market reform in emerging economies: A rent seeking perspective. *Public Choice, 112*(1-2), 185–202. doi:10.1023/A:1015687527568

Mulili, B. M., & Wong, P. (2011). Continuous organizational development (COD). *Industrial and Commercial Training, 43*(6), 377–384. doi:10.1108/00197851111160513

Murphy, M. P. (2020). COVID-19 and emergency eLearning: Consequences of the securitization of higher education for post-pandemic pedagogy. *Contemporary Security Policy, 1*(3), 1–4. doi:10.1080/13523260.2020.1761749

Murray, N. (2017). Urban disaster risk governance. A systemic review. UCL Institute of Education.

Mystakidis, S. (2022). Metaverse. *Encyclopedia, 2*(1), 486–497. doi:10.3390/encyclopedia2010031

Naamati Schneider, L., Meirovich, A., & Dolev, N. (2020). Soft skills on-line development in times of crisis. *Revista Romaneasca Pentru Educatie Multidimensionala, 12*(1Sup2), 122-129. doi:10.18662/rrem/12.1sup2/255

Naik, V. N., & Brien, S. E. (2013). Review article: Simulation: A means to address and improve patient safety. *Canadian Journal of Anesthesia/Journal Canadien d'anesthésie, 60*(2), 192–200. doi:10.1007/s12630-012-9860-z

Nam, D., Lee, J., & Lee, H. (2019). Business analytics adoption process: An innovation diffusion perspective. *International Journal of Information Management, 49*, 411–423. doi:10.1016/j.ijinfomgt.2019.07.017

Namkung, Y., & Jang, S. (2013). Effects of restaurant green practices on brand equity formation: Do green practices really matter? *International Journal of Hospitality Management, 33*(2), 85–95. doi:10.1016/j.ijhm.2012.06.006

Naplyokov, Y. V. (2018). Changing of mental models for effective decision-making. *Public Management, 1*(11), 209–228. doi:10.31618/vadnd.v1i11.28

Nazarenko, A., Vishnevskiy, K., Meissner, D., & Daim, T. (2022). Applying digital technologies in technology roadmapping to overcome individual biased assessments. *Technovation, 110*, 102364. doi:10.1016/j.technovation.2021.102364

Nedeva, V., & Dimova, E. (2010). Some advantages of E-Learning in English language training. *Trakia Journal of Sciences, 8*, 21–28.

Neff, K. D. (2003). The development and validation of a scale to measure self-compassion. *Self and Identity, 2*(3), 223–250. doi:10.1080/15298860309027

Nelson, J. (2020). Staying Resilient During and Post Covid-19—Research Findings and Resources for Entrepreneurs and Governments: Interview with Jane Nelson (Harvard Kennedy School by Susann Tischendorf). *Inclusive Business*. https://www.inclusivebusiness.net/ib-voices/staying-resilient-during-and-post-covid-19-research-findings-and-resources-entrepreneurs

Nelson, R. R., & Winter, S. G. (1982). *An evolutionary theory of economic change*. Belknap Press.

Newenham-Kahindi, A. (2015). Managing sustainable development through people: Implications for multinational enterprises in developing countries. *Personnel Review*, *44*(3), 388–407. doi:10.1108/PR-07-2013-0121

Nguyen, M. H. (2021). Factors influencing home-based telework in Hanoi (Vietnam) during and after the Covid-19 era. *Transportation*, *48*(6), 1–32. doi:10.100711116-021-10169-5 PMID:33518829

Nickerson, A. B., Cook, E. E., Cruz, M. A., & Parks, T. W. (2019). Transfer of school crisis prevention and intervention training, knowledge, and skills: Training, trainee, and work environment predictors. *School Psychology Review*, *48*(3), 237–250. doi:10.17105/SPR-2017-0140.V48-3

Nicola, M., Alsafi, Z., Sohrabi, C., Kerwan, A., Al-Jabir, A., Iosifidis, C., Agha, M., & Agha, R. (2020). The socio-economic implications of the coronavirus pandemic (COVID-19): A review. *International Journal of Surgery*, *78*, 185–193. doi:10.1016/j.ijsu.2020.04.018 PMID:32305533

Nicolescu, L., & Tudorache, M. T. (2022). Human-Computer Interaction in Customer Service: The Experience with AI Chatbots—A Systematic Literature Review. *Electronics (Basel)*, *11*(10), 1579. doi:10.3390/electronics11101579

Nielsen, B. B., Asmussen, C. G., & Weatherall, C. D. (2017). The location choice of foreign direct investments: Empirical evidence and methodological challenges. *Journal of World Business*, *52*(1), 62–82. doi:10.1016/j.jwb.2016.10.006

Nilsson, N. (2010). *The quest for artificial intelligence: A history of ideas and achievements*. Cambridge University Press.

Noe, R. A., Hollenbeck, J., Gerhart, B., & Wright, P. (2020). *Fundamentals of Human Resource Management* (8th ed.). McGraw-Hill.

Nogué, S., & Sala, M. (2018). The use of green roofs in urban green innovation spaces: A case study in Barcelona. *Urban Forestry & Urban Greening*, *33*, 19–29. doi:10.1016/j.ufug.2018.02.008

Nolan-Arañez, S. I., & Ludvik, M. B. (2018). Positing a framework for cultivating spirituality through public university leadership development. *Journal of Research in Innovative Teaching & Learning*, *11*(1), 94–109. doi:10.1108/JRIT-08-2017-0018

Nordheim, C. B. (2018). *Trust in chatbots for customer service–findings from a questionnaire study* [Master's thesis, University of Oslo].

Nordheim, C. B., Følstad, A., & Bjørkli, C. A. (2019). An initial model of trust in chatbots for customer service—Findings from a questionnaire study. *Interacting with Computers*, *31*(3), 317–335. doi:10.1093/iwc/iwz022

North, D. C. (1990). *Institutions, Institutional Change and Economic Performance*. Cambridge University Press. doi:10.1017/CBO9780511808678

North, D. C. (1991). Institutions. *The Journal of Economic Perspectives*, *5*(1), 97–112. doi:10.1257/jep.5.1.97

Norton, T. A., Parker, S. L., Zacher, H., & Ashkanasy, N. M. (2015). Employee green behavior: A theoretical framework, multi-level review, and future research agenda. *Organization & Environment*, *2015*(28), 103–125. doi:10.1177/1086026615575773

Nortvig, A. M., Petersen, A. K., & Balle, S. H. (2018). A literature review of the factors influencing E-Learning and blended learning in relation to learning outcome, student satisfaction and engagement. *Electronic Journal of e-Learning*, *16*, 46–55.

NRC. (2010). *Toward sustainable agricultural systems in the 21ˢᵗ century*. National Academic Press. [National Research Council]

Obrenovic, B., Du, J., Godinic, D., Khan, M. A., & Jakhongirov, I. (2020). Sustaining enterprise operations and productivity during the COVID-19 pandemic: "Enterprise effectiveness and sustainability model". *Sustainability (Basel)*, *12*(15), 5981. doi:10.3390u12155981

OECD. (1999). *Boosting innovation: The cluster approach*. OECD.

OECD. (2001a). *Innovative Clusters: drivers of national innovation systems*. OECD.

OECD. (2001b). *Innovative Networks: co-operation in national innovation systems*. OECD.

OECD. (2017). *Methodology for Assessing the Implementation of the G20/OECD Principles of Corporate Governance*. OECD.

OECD. (2020). *SMEs are major employers and particularly vulnerable to the impact of the Covid-19 crisis*. OECD.

OECD. (2021). *Recommendation of the council on artificial intelligence*. OECD.

Oleś, P., & Jankowski, T. (2018). Positive orientation—A common base for hedonistic and eudemonistic happiness? *Applied Research in Quality of Life*, *13*(1), 105–117. doi:10.100711482-017-9508-9 PMID:29492164

Oliver, C. (1991). Strategic responses to institutional processes. *Academy of Management Review*, *16*(1), 145–179. doi:10.2307/258610

Olsson, P., Folke, C., & Hahn, T. (2004). Social-ecological transformation for ecosystem management: the development of adaptive co-management of a wetland landscape in southern Sweden. *Ecology and Society, 9*(4), 2. https://www.ecologyandsociety.org/vol9/iss4/art2

Omer, A. M. (2008). Energy, environment and sustainable development. *Renewable & Sustainable Energy Reviews*, *12*(9), 2265–2300. doi:10.1016/j.rser.2007.05.001

Ones, D. S., & Dilchert, S. (2012a). Employee green behaviors. In D. S. S. E. Jackson (Ed.), *Managing human resource for environmental sustainability* (pp. 85–116). Jossey-Bass.

Ong, Y. H., & Tan, Y. H. (2018). The development of a skills taxonomy for nursing crisis management. *Clinical Simulation in Nursing*, *25*, 6–11. doi:10.1016/j.ecns.2018.09.003

Organisation for Economic Cooperation and Development [OECD] (2020a). *The territorial impact of COVID-19: Managing the crisis across levels of government*. OECD. https://www.read.oecd-library.org/view/?ref=128_128287-5agkk ojaaa&title=The–territorial-impact-of-covid-19-managing-the-crisis-across-levels-of-government

Organisation for Economic Cooperation and Development [OECD] (2020b). *Strategic foresight for the COVID-19 crisis and beyond: Using futures thinking to design better public policies*. OECD. https://www.oecd.org/coronavirus/policy-responses/strategic-foresight-for-the-covid-19-crisis-and-beyond-using-futures-thinking-to-design-better-public-policies-c3448fa5/

Organisation for Economic Cooperation and Development [OECD] (2020c). *The territorial impact of covid-19: Managing the crisis across levels of government.* OECD. https://www.oecd.org/cfe/leed/COVID-19-Italian-regions-SME-policy-responses.pdf

Organisation for Economic Cooperation and Development [OECD]. (2020d). *OECD Economic Outlook: Interim report.* OECD. doi:10.1787/34ffc900-en

Organization Development Network. (2023). *What is organization development?* OD Network. https://www.odnetwork.org/page/what-is-od

Örtenblad, A., Putnam, L. L., & Trehan, K. (2016, April 5). Beyond Morgan's eight metaphors: Adding to and developing organization theory. *Sage Journals.* https://journals.sagepub.com/doi/full/10.1177/0018726715623999#bibr3-0018726715623999

Orwell, G. (n.d.). ⇉*Taylorism in the 21st Century Essay Example.* GraduateWay. https://graduateway.com/taylorism-in-the-21st-century/

Oswald, S. L., Mossholder, K. W., & Harris, S. G. (1994). Vision salience and strategic involvement: Implications for psychological attachment to organization and job. *Strategic Management Journal, 1994*(15), 477–489. doi:10.1002mj.4250150605

OziliP. K.ArunT. (2020). *Spillover of Covid-19: Impact on the global economy.* doi:10.2139/ssrn.3562570

Page, C., Wilson, M., & Kolb, D. (1993). *Managerial competencies and New Zealand managers: On the inside, looking in.* University of Auckland.

Page, M. J., McKenzie, J. E., Bossuyt, P. M., Boutron, I., Hoffmann, T. C., Mulrow, C. D., Shamseer, L., Tetzlaff, J. M., Akl, E. A., Brennan, S. E., Chou, R., Glanville, J., Grimshaw, J. M., Hróbjartsson, A., Lalu, M. M., Li, T., Loder, E. W., Mayo-Wilson, E., McDonald, S., & Moher, D. (2021). The PRISMA 2020 statement: An updated guideline for reporting systematic reviews. *BMJ (Clinical Research Ed.), 372*(71), n71. doi:10.1136/bmj.n71 PMID:33782057

Palmer, M., Simmons, G., & Hall, M. (2013). Textbook (non-) adoption motives, legitimizing strategies and academic field configuration. *Studies in Higher Education, 38*(4), 485–505. doi:10.1080/03075079.2011.583983

Palomino, J. C., & Durán, P. (2020). The influence of green roofs on the urban heat island effect: A review of the current state of knowledge. *Urban Climate, 34*, 100696. doi:10.1016/j.uclim.2020.100696

Pandey, S., DeHart-Davis, L., Pandey, S., & Ahlawat, S. (2022). Fight or flight: How gender influences follower responses to unethical leader behaviour. *Public Management Review*, 1–21.

Papageorge, N. W., Zahn, M. V., Belot, M., Van den Broek-Altenburg, E., Choi, S., Jamison, J. C., & Tripodi, E. (2021). Socio-demographic factors associated with self-protecting behavior during the Covid-19 pandemic. *Journal of Population Economics, 34*(2), 691–738. doi:10.100700148-020-00818-x PMID:33462529

Pape-Lindstrom, P., Eddy, S., & Freeman, S. (2018). Reading quizzes improve exam scores for community college students. *CBE Life Sciences Education, 17*(2), ar21. doi:10.1187/cbe.17-08-0160 PMID:29749839

Papke-Shields, K. E., & Boyer-Wright, K. M. (2017). Strategic planning characteristics applied to project management. *International Journal of Project Management, 35*(2), 169–179. doi:10.1016/j.ijproman.2016.10.015

Paraskevas, A. (2006). Crisis management or crisis response system? A complexity science approach to organizational crises. *Management Decision, 44*(7), 892–907. doi:10.1108/00251740610680587

Paskaleva, K. (2011). The smart city: A nexus for open innovation? *Intelligent Buildings International, 3*(3), 153–171. doi:10.1080/17508975.2011.586672

Patacsil, F., & Tablatin, S., C. (. (2017). Exploring the importance of soft and hard skills as perceived by IT internship students and industry: A gap analysis. *Journal of Technology and Science Education*, *7*(3), 347–368. doi:10.3926/jotse.271

PeciA. (2006). A nova teoria institucional em estudos organizacionais: umaabordagem crítica. *Cadernos EBAPE*. BR, Rio de Janeiro, *4*(1), 1-12. https://doi.org/ doi:10.1590/S1679-39512006000100006

Pell, A. N. (1996). Fixing the leaky pipeline: Women scientists in academia. *Journal of Animal Science*, *74*(11), 2843–2848. doi:10.2527/1996.74112843x PMID:8923199

Pennings, J. M. (1975). The relevance of the structure-contingency model for organisational effectiveness. *Administrative Science Quarterly*, *20*(3), 393–410. doi:10.2307/2391999

Pereira, Á., & Vence, X. (2012). Key business factors for eco-innovation: An overview of recent firm-level empirical studies. *Cuadernos de Gestión*, *12*, 73–103. doi:10.5295/cdg.110308ap

Peters, J., & Weggeman, M. C. D. P. (2019). *Het Grote Rijnlandboekje.*

Peters, S. C. A., & Frisart, R. (2000). *Network Organizations.* Lansa.

Pinheiro, R., Geschwind, L., Ramirez, F., & Vrangbæk, K. (2016). *Towards a comparative institutionalism: Forms, Dynamics and Logics Across the Organizational Fields of Health Care and Higher Education* (Vol. 45). Emerald.

Pink, D. H. (2022). *Drive: de verrassende waarheid over wat ons motiveert* [V. V. Walsmit, Trans.].

Pirson, M. A., & Gazella, K. (n.d.). *(PDF) Developing the Langer Mindfulness Scale.* ResearchGate. https://www.researchgate.net/publication/291372253_Developing_the_Langer_Mindfulness_Scale

Pokhrel, S., & Chhetri, R. (2021). A literature review on impact of COVID-19 pandemic on teaching and learning. *Higher Education for the Future*, *8*(1), 133–141. doi:10.1177/2347631120983481

Porter, M. (2001). Clusters of Innovation: regional foundations of U. S competitiveness. Council on Competitiveness. Washington, D.C.: Monitor Group.

Pourmansouri, R., Mehdiabadi, A., Shahabi, V., Spulbar, C., & Birau, R. (2022). An investigation of the link between major shareholders' behavior and corporate governance performance before and after the COVID-19 Pandemic: A case study of the companies listed on the Iranian stock market. *J. Risk Financial Manag*, *5*(5), 208. doi:10.3390/jrfm15050208

Pourmola, M., Bagheri, M., Alinezhad, P., & Nejad, P. (2019). Investigating the impact of organizational spirituality on human resources productivity in manufacturing organizations. *Management Science Letters*, *9*(1), 121–132. doi:10.5267/j.msl.2018.10.011

Powell, D. (2020). Autonomous systems as legal agents: Directly by the recognition of personhood or indirectly by the alchemy of algorithmic entities. *Duke Law & Technology Review*, *18*(1), 306–331.

Powell, K. S., & Yalcin, S. (2010). Managerial training effectiveness: A meta-analysis 1952-2002. *Personnel Review*, *39*(2), 227–241. doi:10.1108/00483481011017435

Prahalad, C. K. (2010). The fortune at the bottom of the pyramid: Eradicating poverty through profits (Revised and Updated 5th Anniversary Edition). Upper Saddle River, N.J.: Wharton School Pub.

Price, J. L. (1968). *Organisational effectiveness.* Richard D. Irwin, Inc.

Price, J. L. (1972). The study of organisational effectiveness. *The Sociological Quarterly*, *13*(3), 3–15. doi:10.1111/j.1533-8525.1972.tb02100.x

Price, R. M. (1996). Technology and strategic advantage. *California Management Review*, *38*(3), 38–56. doi:10.2307/41165842

Prosci, Inc. (2023). *Definition of change management*. Prosci Inc. https://www.prosci.com/resources/articles/definition-of-change-management#:~:text=Change%20management%20is%20the%20application,adopt%20and%20use%20a%20change

Provost, F., & Fawcett, T. (2013). Data science and its relationship to big data and data-driven decision making. *Big Data*, *1*(1), 51–59. doi:10.1089/big.2013.1508 PMID:27447038

Purtik, H., & Arenas, D. (2019). Embedding social innovation: Shaping societal norms and behaviors throughout the innovation process. *Business & Society*, *58*(5), 963–1002. doi:10.1177/0007650317726523

Quinn, R. E., Spreitzer, G. M., & Brown, M. V. (2000). Changing others through changing ourselves: The transformation of human systems. *Journal of Management Inquiry*, *9*(2), 47–164. doi:10.1177/105649260092010

Rachinger, M., Rauter, R., Müller, C., Vorraber, W., & Schirgi, E. (2019). Digitalization and its influence on business model innovation. *Journal of Manufacturing Technology Management*, *30*(8), 1143–1160. doi:10.1108/JMTM-01-2018-0020

Rago, W. V. (1996). Struggles in transformation: A study in TQM, leadership, and organizational culture in a government agency. *Public Administration Review*, *56*(3), 227–234. doi:10.2307/976445

Rahouti, A., Lovreglio, R., Datoussaïd, S., & Descamps, T. (2021). Prototyping and validating a non-immersive virtual reality serious game for healthcare fire safety training. *Fire Technology*, *57*(6), 3041–3078. doi:10.100710694-021-01098-x

Rajab, M. H., Gazal, A. M., & Alkattan, K. (2020). Challenges to online medical education during the covid-19 pandemic. *Cureus*, *12*(7). doi:10.7759/cureus.8966 PMID:32766008

Rajagopalan, N., & Spreitzer, G. M. (1996). Towards a theory of strategic change: A multi-lens perspective and integrative framework. *Academy of Management Review*, *22*(1), 48–79. doi:10.2307/259224

Ramachandaran, S. D., Krauss, S. E., Hamzah, A., & Idris, K. (2017). Effectiveness of the use of spiritual intelligence in women's academic leadership practice. *International Journal of Educational Management*, *31*(2), 160–178. doi:10.1108/IJEM-09-2015-0123

Ramakrishnan, P. S. (2000). Biodiversity, land use and traditional ecological knowledge: the context. In: Ramakrishnan, P.S., Chandrashekara, U.M., Elouard, C., Guilmoto, C.Z., Maikhuri, R.K., Rao, K.S., Sankar, S., Saxena, K.G. (eds). Mountain biodiversity, land use dynamics and traditional ecological knowledge. Oxford & IBH Publication, India (P) Ltd.

Ransbotham, S., Kiron, D., & Prentice, P. K. (2016). Beyond the hype: The hard work behind analytics success. *MIT Sloan Management Review*, *57*(3).

Raspopovic, M., Cvetanovic, S., & Jankulovic, A. (2016). Challenges of transitioning to E-Learning system with learning objects capabilities. *International Review of Research in Open and Distance Learning*, *17*(1). doi:10.19173/irrodl.v17i1.2172

Raynard, M. (2016). Deconstructing complexity: Configurations of institutional complexity and structural hybridity. *Strategic Organization*, *14*(4), 310–335. doi:10.1177/1476127016634639

Ray, V. A. (2019). Theory of Racialized Organizations. *American Sociological Review*, *84*(1), 26–53. doi:10.1177/0003122418822335

Redman, C. (2014). Should sustainability and resilience be combined or remain distinct pursuits? *Ecology and Society*, *19*(2), 190–202. doi:10.5751/ES-06390-190237

Redman, T. C. (2008). *Data driven: Profiting from your most important business asset*. Harvard Business Press.

Rees, W. E. (2002). Globalization and sustainability: Conflict or convergence? *Bulletin of Science, Technology & Society*, *22*(4), 249–268. doi:10.1177/0270467602022004001

Rehman, A. (2022). With the mediation of internal audit, Can artificial intelligence eliminate and mitigate fraud? In S. S. Kamwani, E. S. Vieira, M. Madaleno, & G. A. (eds), Handbook of Research on the Significance of Forensic Accounting Techniques in Corporate Governance (pp. DOI:). NY: IGI Global. doi:10.4018/978-1-7998-8754-6.ch012

Rehman, A., & Hashim, F. (2018). Forensic accounting on corporate governance maturity mediated by internal audit: A conceptual overview. *1st Economics and Business International Conference 2017 (EBIC 2017)* (pp. 161-168). NY: Atlantis Press. 10.2991/ebic-17.2018.26

Rehman, A., & Hashim, F. (2022). Can internal audit function impact artificial intelligence? Case of public listed companies of Oman. *The 5th Innovation and Analytics Conference & Exhibition (IACE 2021)* (pp. 040024-1–040024-7). AI.). .10.1063/5.0092755

Rehman, A., & Hashim, F. (2020). Impact of fraud risk assessment on good corporate governance: Case of public listed companies in Oman. *Business Systems Research*, *11*(1), 16–30. doi:10.2478/bsrj-2020-0002

Reisinger, A., & Clark, H. (2018). How much do direct livestock emissions contribute to global warming? *Global Change Biology*, *2018*(24), 1749–1761. doi:10.1111/gcb.13975 PMID:29105912

Rengkung, L. R. (2022). Exploration and exploitation: Driving organizational capability and organizational change toward competitive advantage. *Management Theory and Studies for Rural Business and Infrastructure Development*, *44*(1), 39–51. doi:10.15544/mts.2022.05

Renwick, D. W. S., Redman, T., & Maguire, S. (2008). Green human resource management: A review and research agenda. *International Journal of Management Reviews*, *10*(1), 1–18. doi:10.1111/j.1468-2370.2011.00328.x

Restubog, S. L. D., Ocampo, A. C. G., & Wang, L. (2020). *Taking control amidst the chaos: Emotion regulation during the Covid-19 pandemic*.

Rice, D., & Galbraith, M. (2008, November 16). *Rewards, Intrinsic Motivation, and Creativity: A Case Study of Conceptual and Methodological Isolation*. Taylor and Francis Online. https://www.tandfonline.com/doi/abs/10.1080/10400419.2003.9651404

Richard, B. (2020, Oct 30). *The effects of Covid-19 on boards and governance*. Spencer Stuart. https://www.spencerstuart.com: https://www.spencerstuart.com/research-and-insight/the-effects-of-covid-19-on-boards-and-governance

Richard, J. E., Thirkell, P. C., & Huff, S. L. (2007). An examination of customer relationship management (CRM) technology adoption and its impact on business-to-business customer relationships. *Total Quality Management & Business Excellence*, *18*(8), 927–945. doi:10.1080/14783360701350961

Rigazio-DiGilio, S. A., Ivey, A. E., & Grady, L. T. (2005). *Community Genograms: Using Individual, Family, and Cultural Narratives with Clients* (S. A. Rigazio-DiGilio, Ed.). Teachers College Press.

Risi, D., & Wickert, C. (2017). Reconsidering the "symmetry" between institutionalization and professionalization: The case of corporate social responsibility managers. *Journal of Management Studies*, *54*(5), 613–646. doi:10.1111/joms.12244

Robertson, B. J. (2016). *Holacracy: The Revolutionary Management System that Abolishes Hierarchy*. Penguin Books, Limited. doi:10.15358/9783800650880

Rocha, R. G., & Pinheiro, P. G. (2020, February 21). Organizational spirituality: Concept and perspectives. [Springer Nature Switzerland.]. *Journal of Business Ethics*, 1–12.

Rodrigues, V. P., Pigosso, D. C. A., & McAloone, T. C. (2016). Process-related key performance indicators for measuring sustainability performance of ecodesign implementation into product development. *Journal of Cleaner Production*, *139*, 416–428. doi:10.1016/j.jclepro.2016.08.046

Rogers, E. M. (2003). *Diffusion of innovations*. Free Press.

Rogowsky, B. A., Calhoun, B. M., & Tallal, P. (2015). Matching learning style to instructional method: Effects on comprehension. *Journal of Educational Psychology*, *107*(1), 64–78. doi:10.1037/a0037478

Ronteltap, F., & Eurelings, A. (2002). Activity and interaction of students in an electronic learning environment for problem-based learning. *Distance Education*, *23*(1), 11–22. doi:10.1080/01587910220123955

Rosenberg, M. J. (2001). *E-Learning*. McGraw-Hill.

Ross, A. (2017). *The Industries of the Future*. Simon & Schuster, Limited.

Rossmann, A., Zimmermann, A., & Hertweck, D. (2020). The impact of chatbots on customer service performance. In *Advances in the human side of service engineering: Proceedings of the AHFE 2020 Virtual Conference on The Human Side of Service Engineering,* (pp. 237-243). Springer International Publishing. 10.1007/978-3-030-51057-2_33

Rotas, E. E., & Cahapay, M. B. (2020). Difficulties in remote learning: Voices of Philippine university students in the wake of COVID-19 crisis. *Asian JDE*, *15*, 147–158.

Rottig, D. (2016). Institutions and emerging markets: Effects and implications for multinational corporations. *International Journal of Emerging Markets*, *11*(1), 2–17. doi:10.1108/IJoEM-12-2015-0248

Rowe, D. B. (2011). Green Roofs as a means of pollution abatement. *Environmental Pollution*, *159*(8-9), 2100–2110. doi:10.1016/j.envpol.2010.10.029 PMID:21074914

Ruotolo, R. A. (1972, December). *Jstor*. A Diagnostic Model for Organizations. https://www.jstor.org/stable/45392830

S&P Global Market Intelligence. (2020). *As market expands, renewable energy unemployment barely budges*. SP Global. https://www.spglobal.com/marketintelligence/en/news-insights/latest-news-headlines/as-market-expands-renewable-energy-unemployment-barely-budges-60666681

S., S., & Newell, J. P. (2017). Detroit, Spatial planning for multifunctional green infrastructure. *Landscape and Urban Planning* 62-75.

Salas, E., & Cannon-Bowers, J. A. (2001). The science of training: A decade of progress. *Annual Review of Psychology*, *52*(1), 471–499. doi:10.1146/annurev.psych.52.1.471 PMID:11148314

Salas, E., DiazGranados, D., Klein, C., Burke, C. S., Stagl, K. C., Goodwin, G. F., & Halpin, S. M. (2008). Does team training improve team performance? A meta-analysis. *Human Factors*, *50*(6), 903–933. doi:10.1518/001872008X375009 PMID:19292013

Salas, E., Nichols, D. R., & Driskell, J. E. (2007). Testing three team training strategies in intact teams: A meta-analysis. *Small Group Research*, *38*(4), 471–488. doi:10.1177/1046496407304332

Salas, E., Tannenbaum, S. I., Kraiger, K., & Smith-Jentsch, K. A. (2012). The science of training and development in organizations: What matters in practice. *Psychological Science in the Public Interest*, *13*(2), 74–101. doi:10.1177/1529100612436661 PMID:26173283

Salas, E., Wilson, K. A., Priest, H. A., & Guthrie, J. W. (2006). Training in organizations: The design, delivery and evaluation of training systems. In G. Salvendy (Ed.), *Handbook of human factors and ergonomics* (3rd ed., pp. 472–512). John Wiley. doi:10.1002/0470048204.ch18

Samuel, A. I. (2021). The concept of E-Learning amid coronavirus (covid-19) pandemic in Nigeria: Issues, benefits, challenges, and way forward. *International Journal of Education and Evaluation*, 7(3), 23–33.

Sarad, N. J., Alexander, M. J., & Donovan, L. P. (2020). COVID-19 Impact on US Renewable Energy Projects Article By. *The National Law Review*, 10(363), 1–5.

Sarkis, J., Zhu, Q., & Lai, K.-H. (2011). An organizational theoretic review of green supply chain management literature. *International Journal of Production Economics*, 130(1), 1–15. doi:10.1016/j.ijpe.2010.11.010

Sarrazin, H., & Willmott, P. (2016, July 13). *Adapting your board to the digital age.* McKinsey. https://www.mckinsey.com/: https://www.mckinsey.com/capabilities/mckinsey-digital/our-i nsights/adapting-your-board-to-the-digital-age

Sartor, M. A., & Beamish, P. W. (2014). Offshoring innovation to emerging markets: Organizational control and informal institutional distance. *Journal of International Business Studies*, 45(9), 1072–1095. doi:10.1057/jibs.2014.36

Savickiene, J., & Miceikiene, A. (2018). *Sustainable economic development assessment model for family farms* (Vol. 64). Agricultural Economics – Czech. doi:10.17221/310/2017-AGRICECON

Scharenbroch, B. C., & Bucci, M. (2017). Green roofs as an ecosystem service provider in the Chicago Wilderness region. *Ecological Engineering*, 99, 240–251. doi:10.1016/j.ecoleng.2016.11.010

Schein, E. H. (1996). *Organizational learning: What is new?* MIT. http://dspace.mit.edu/bitstream/handle/1721.1/2628/SWP-3912-35650568.pdf

Schein, E. H. (1968). Organizational socialization and the profession of management. *Industrial Management Review*, 9, 1–15.

Schein, E. H. (1978). *Career dynamics: Matching individual and organizational needs.* Addison-Wesley.

Schein, E. H. (1992). *Organizational culture and leadership* (2nd ed.). Jossey-Bass Publishers.

Scherer, M. (2019). *International arbitration 3.0 – How artificial intelligence will change dispute resolution.* Austrian Yearbook of International Arbitration.

Schildt, H., & Perkmann, M. (2017). Organizational settlements: Theorizing how organizations respond to institutional complexity. *Journal of Management Inquiry*, 26(2), 139–145. doi:10.1177/1056492616670756

Schmidt, G. (n.d.). *New Technologies and Post-Taylorist Regulation Models. The Introduction and Use of Production Planning Systems in French, Italian, and German Enterprises (1).* Academia.edu. https://www.academia.edu/31338056/New_Technologies_and_Post_Taylorist_Regulation_Models_The_Introduction_and_Use_of_Production_Planning_Systems_in_French_Italian_and_German_Enterprises_1_

Schmidt, E., Groeneveld, S., & van de Walle, S. (2017). A change management perspective on public sector cutback management: Towards a framework for analysis. *Public Management Review*, 19(10), 1538–1555. doi:10.1080/14719037.2017.1296488

Schon, D. A. (1973). A study of field experience. [Unpublished memorandum, Massachusetts Institute of Technology].

Schuemie, M. J., Straaten, P. V., & Krijn, M. (2001). Research on presence in virtual reality: A survey. *Cyberpsychology & Behavior*, 4(2), 183–202. doi:10.1089/109493101300117884 PMID:11710246

Schulz, B. (2008). The importance of soft skills: Education beyond academic knowledge. *Journal of Language and Communication*, *2*, 146–154.

Schumpeter, J. (1934). *The Theory of Economic Development: An inquiry into profits, capital, credit, interest and the business cycle*. Transaction Publishers.

Schumpeter, J. A. (1942). *Capitalism, Socialism and Democracy*. HarperCollins.

Schwendicke, F., & Krois, J. (2021). Better reporting of studies on artificial intelligence: CONSORT-AI and beyond. *Journal of Dental Research*, *100*(7), 677–680. doi:10.1177/0022034521998337 PMID:33655800

Schwens, C., Eiche, J., & Kabst, R. (2011). The moderating impact of informal institutional distance and formal institutional risk on SME entry mode choice. *Journal of Management Studies*, *48*(2), 330–351. doi:10.1111/j.1467-6486.2010.00970.x

Scott, W. R. (1994). Conceptualizing organizational fields: Linking organizations and societal systems. In: Derlien, Hans-Ulrich.; Gerhardt, Uta.; Scharpf, Fritz W. (Eds.), Systems rationality and partial interests (pp. 203-221). Baden-Baden: Nomos.

Scott, R. W. (1987). *Organisations: Rational, natural, and open systems* (2nd ed.). Prentice Hall.

Scott, W. R. (1987). *Organizations: Rational, Natural, and Open Systems*. Prentice-Hall.

Scott, W. R. (1987). The adolescence of institutional theory. *Administrative Science Quarterly*, *32*(4), 493–511. doi:10.2307/2392880

Scott, W. R. (1991). Unpacking institutional arguments. In W. W. Powell & P. J. DiMaggio (Eds.), *The New Institutionalism in Organizational Analysis* (pp. 164–182). University of Chicago Press.

Scott, W. R. (1992). *Organizations: rational, natural, and open systems* (3rd ed.). Prentice-Hall.

Scott, W. R. (1995). *Institutions and organizations*. Sage.

Scott, W. R. (1995). *Institutions and Organizations*. Sage.

Scott, W. R. (2008). *Institutions and organizations: Ideas and interests* (3rd ed.). Sage Publications.

Seashore, S. E., & Yutchman, E. (1967). Factor analysis of organisational performance. *Administrative Science Quarterly*, *12*(3), 377–395. doi:10.2307/2391311

Segal, T. (2020, Mar 27). *Evaluating the board of directors*. Marottao Money. www.marottaonmoney.com/wp-content/uploads/2020/07/Evaluating-the-Board-of-Directors.pdf: www.marottaonmoney.com/wp-content/uploads/2020/07/Evaluating-the-Board-of-Directors.pdf

Seles, B. M. R. P., de Sousa Jabbour, A. B. L., Jabbour, C. J. C., & Dangelico, R. M. (2016). The green bullwhip effect, the diffusion of green supply chain practices, and institutional pressures: Evidence from the automotive sector. *International Journal of Production Economics*, *182*, 342–355. doi:10.1016/j.ijpe.2016.08.033

Selznick, P. (1957). *Leadership in Administration*. Harper and Row.

Selznick, P. (1996). Institutionalism "old" and "new.". *Administrative Science Quarterly*, *41*(2), 270–277. doi:10.2307/2393719

Senge, P. M. (2006). *The Fifth Discipline: The Art & Practice of The Learning Organization*. Crown.

Sethi, D., Judge, W., & Sun, Q. (2011). FDI distribution within China: An integrative conceptual framework for analyzing intra-country FDI variations. *Asia Pacific Journal of Management*, *28*(2), 325–352. doi:10.100710490-009-9144-5

Shafi Que, M., Kim, R. & Rafi Q. M. (2018). Green roof benefits, opportunities, and challenges– A review. *Renewable and Sustainable Energy Reviews, 90*, 757-773.

Shanafelt, T. D., West, C. P., Sinsky, C., Trockel, M., Tutty, M., Satele, D. V., Lindsey, E., Carlasare, F., Lotte, N., & Dyrbye, L. N. (2019, September). Changes in burnout and satisfaction with work-life integration in physicians and the general US working population between 2011 and 2017. *Mayo Clinic Proceedings, 94*(9), 1681–1694. doi:10.1016/j.mayocp.2018.10.023 PMID:30803733

Sharma, R., Mithas, S., & Kankanhalli, A. (2014). Transforming decision-making processes: A research agenda for understanding the impact of business analytics on organisations. *European Journal of Information Systems, 23*(4), 433–441. doi:10.1057/ejis.2014.17

Shaw, M. (2018). Teaching campus crisis management through case studies: Moving between theory and practice. *Journal of Student Affairs Research and Practice, 55*(3), 308–320. doi:10.1080/19496591.2018.1399894

Shearer, C. S., Hames, D. S., & Runge, J. B. (2001). How CEOs influence organizational culture following acquisitions. *Leadership and Organization Development Journal, 22*(3), 105–113. doi:10.1108/01437730110389256

Shevchenko, A., & Petrenko, O. (2020). Current state of micro and small agribusiness in Ukraine. *Agricultural and Resource Economics, 6*(1), 146–160. doi:10.51599/are.2020.06.01.10

Shin, A., Kim, D. Y., Jeong, J. S., & Chun, B. G. (2020). Hippo: Taming hyper-parameter optimization of deep learning with stage trees. *arXiv preprint arXiv:2006.11972*.

Shoeb, A., & Nisar, T. (2015). Green Human Resource Management: Policies and practices. *Cogent Business & Management*. https://www.tandfonline.com/doi/full/10.1080/23311975.2015.1030817 doi:10.1080/23311975.2015.1030817

Silvestre, B. S. (2015). Sustainable supply chain management in emerging economies: Environmental turbulence, institutional voids, and sustainability trajectories. *International Journal of Production Economics, 167*, 156–169. doi:10.1016/j.ijpe.2015.05.025

Sinclair, R. R., Allen, T., Barber, L., Bergman, M., Britt, T., Butler, A., Ford, M., Hammer, L., Kath, L., Probst, T., & Yuan, Z. (2020). Occupational Health Science in the Time of Covid-19: Now more than ever. *Occupational Health Science, 4*(1-2), 1–22. doi:10.100741542-020-00064-3 PMID:32838031

Sinek, S. (2011). *Start with why: How Great Leaders Inspire Everyone to Take Action*. Portfolio / Penguin.

Singh, S. K., Del Giudice, M., Chierici, R., & Graziano, D. (2020). Green innovation and environmental performance: The role of green transformational leadership and green human resource management. *Technological Forecasting and Social Change, 150*, 119762. doi:10.1016/j.techfore.2019.119762

Sintema, E. J. (2020). Effect of COVID-19 on the performance of grade 12 students: Implications for stem education. *Eurasia Journal of Mathematics, Science and Technology Education, 16*(7), 1–6. doi:10.29333/ejmste/7893

Skydan, O., Nykolyuk, O., Pyvovar, P., & Martynchuk, I. (2020). Methodological approach to the evaluation of agricultural business system flexibility. *Management Theory and Studies for Rural Business and Infrastructure Development, 41*(4), 444–462. doi:10.15544/mts.2019.36

Skyttner, L. (2006). *General Systems Theory*. World Scientific. doi:10.1142/5871

Smedley, G., Purse, R., & Kariwala, A. (2017). *People - the Heart of Good Governance: A People-Centred Approach to Corporate Governance*. CreateSpace Independent Publishing Platform.

Smets, M., Jarzabkowski, P., Burke, G. T., & Spee, P. (2015). Reinsurance trading in Lloyd's of London: Balancing conflicting-yet-complementary logics in practice. *Academy of Management Journal, 58*(3), 932–970. doi:10.5465/amj.2012.0638

Smith, J. M., & Halligan, C. L. (2021). *Making meaning without a maker: Secular consciousness through narrative and cultural practice. Sociology of Religion, 82(1), 85-110.* Oxford University Press. doi:10.1093ocrelraa016

Solinska-Nowak, A., Magnuszewski, P., Curl, M., French, A., Keating, A., Mochizuki, J., Liu, W., Mechler, R., Kulakowska, M., & Jarzabek, L. (2018). „An overview of serious games for disaster risk management–Prospects and limitations for informing actions to arrest increasing risk. *International Journal of Disaster Risk Reduction, 31*, 1013–1029. doi:10.1016/j.ijdrr.2018.09.001

Solomon, D., & Weller, C. E. (2018). *Systematic inequality: how America's structural racism helped create the black-white wealth gap.* Center for American Progress. https://www.americanprogress.org/issues/race/reports/ 2018/0 2/21/447051/systematic-inequality/

Sorensen, P. F., Yaeger, T. F., Savall, H., Zardet, V., Bonnet, M., & Peron, M. (2022). A review of two major global and international approaches to organizational change: SEAM and Appreciative Inquiry. *Organization Development Journal, 40*(2), 21–27.

Sorenson, B. (2020). Renewable Power Generation Costs in 2019. *IRENA.* https://irena.org/publications/2020/Jun/Renewable-Power-Costs-in-2019

Stafford, B., & Schindlinger, D. (2019). *Governance in the Digital Age: A Guide for the Modern Corporate Board Director.* Wiley.

Stemmler, H. (2022). The effects of COVID-19 on businesses: Key versus non-key firms. Geneva: International Labor Organization (ILO).

Stephan, U., Zbierowski, P., Perez-Luno, A., & Klausen, A. (2021). *Entrepreneurship during the COVID-19 pandemic: A global study of entrepreneurs challenges, resilience, and well-being.* King's Business School. https://www.kcl.ac.uk/business/assets/pdf/research- papers/global-report-entrepreneurship-during-the-covid-19-pandemic-a-global-study-of-entrepreneurs'-challenges-resilience-and-well-being.pdf

Sterman, J. (2010). *Business dynamics: systems thinking and modeling for a complex world.* McGraw-Hill Education (India) Pvt Limited.

Stubbs, W. & Cocklin, C. (2008). Conceptualizing a sustainability business model. *Org.Env. 21* (2), 103e127.

Styhre, A. (2014). Gender equality as institutional work. *Gender, Work and Organization, 21*(2), 105–120. doi:10.1111/gwao.12024

Suchman, M. C. (1995). Managing legitimacy: Strategic and institutional approaches. *Academy of Management Review, 20*(3), 571–610. doi:10.2307/258788

Suddaby, R. (2013). Institutional theory. In E. Kessler (Ed.), *Encyclopedia of management theory* (pp. 379–384). Sage.

Suddaby, R. (2015). Can institutional theory be critical? *Journal of Management Inquiry, 24*(1), 93–95. doi:10.1177/1056492614545304

Suddaby, R., & Greenwood, R. (2001). Colonizing knowledge: Commodification as a dynamic of jurisdictional expansion in professional service firms. *Human Relations, 54*(7), 933–953. doi:10.1177/0018726701547007

Sukhdev, P. (2013). Transforming the corporation into a driver of sustainability. In *State of the World 2013*. Island Press. doi:10.5822/978-1-61091-458-1_12

Sultana, U. S., Tarofder, A. K., Darun, M. R., Haque, A., & Sharief, S. R. (2020). Authentic leadership effect on pharmacists' job stress and satisfaction during Covid-19 Pandemic: Malaysian perspective. *Journal of Talent Development and Excellence, 12*(3s) 1824-1841, and ISSN: 1869-2885.

Sun, Z., Wu, L. Z., Ye, Y., & Kwan, H. K. (2023). The impact of exploitative leadership on hospitality employees' proactive customer service performance: A self-determination perspective. *International Journal of Contemporary Hospitality Management, 35*(1), 46–63. doi:10.1108/IJCHM-11-2021-1417

Sutton, R. (2014). Aesthetics for green roofs and green walls. *The Journal of Living Architecture, 1*(2), 1–20. doi:10.46534/jliv.2014.01.02.001

Swanepoel, D. (2021). Does artificial intelligence have agency? In R. G. Clowes, *The Mind-Technology Problem.* [Cham: Springer.]. *Studies in Brain and Mind, 18*, 1–2. doi:10.1007/978-3-030-72644-7_4

Tan, P. Y., Wong, N. H., Tan, T. K., & Wong, K. W. (2019). Green roof innovation in Singapore: Policies, performance, and potential. *Journal of Environmental Management, 233*, 128–135. doi:10.1016/j.jenvman.2018.12.060

Taylor, F. W. (2006). The Principles of Scientific Management. Taylor & Francis.

Team LightBox. (2020). *The Effects of COVID-19 on the Renewable Energy Industry, and How this Industry is Important to Economic Recovery*. Dig Map. https://www.digmap.com/blog/the-effects-of-covid-19-on-the-renewable-energy-industry-and-how-this-industry-is-important-to-economic-recovery/

Teece, D., & Pisano, G. (1994). The dynamic capabilities of firms: An introduction. *Industrial and Corporate Change, 3*(3), 537–556. doi:10.1093/icc/3.3.537-a

Teece, D., Pisano, G., & Shuen, A. (1997). Dynamic capabilities and strategic management. *Strategic Management Journal, 18*(7), 509–533. doi:10.1002/(SICI)1097-0266(199708)18:7<509::AID-SMJ882>3.0.CO;2-Z

TEP. (2005). *Advancing the delivery of green infrastructure Targeting Issues in England's Northwest*. Issue Paper, England Northwest.

Terziev, V., & Georgiev, M. (2018). Organizational development strategies. *Knowledge – . International Journal (Toronto, Ont.), 28*(1), 315–322.

Thakur, K., & Singh, J. (2016). Spirituality at workplace: A conceptual framework. *International Journal of Applied Business and Economic Research, 14*(7), 5181–5189.

The Economic Times. (2021). Definition of E-Learning. *The Economic Times.* https://economictimes.indiatimes.com/definition/E-Learning

The Economist. (2020). *Covid-19 to send almost all G20 countries into a recession - Economist Intelligence Unit*. EIU. https://www.eiu.com/n/covid-19-to-send-almost-all-g20-countries-into-a-recession/

The Lancet. (2020). Redefining vulnerability in the era of COVID-19. *Lancet, 395*, 1089.

Thornhill, S., & Amit, R. (2001). A dynamic perspective of internal fit in corporate venturing. *Journal of Business Venturing, 16*(1), 25–50. doi:10.1016/S0883-9026(99)00040-3

Thornton, P. (2004). *Markets from culture: Institutional logic and organizational decisions Organization, Theory in higher education publishing*. Stanford University Press. doi:10.1515/9781503619098

Thornton, P. H., Ocasio, W., & Lounsbury, M. (2012). *The Institutional Logics Perspective: A New Approach to Culture, Structure, and Process*. Oxford University Press. doi:10.1093/acprof:oso/9780199601936.001.0001

Thornton, P., & Ocasio, W. (2008). Institutional logics. In R. Greenwood, C. Oliver, K. Sahlin, & R. Suddaby (Eds.), *The Sage handbook of organizational institutionalism* (pp. 99–129). SAGE Publications. doi:10.4135/9781849200387.n4

Tidd, C. (2016). *Staff perceptions of the effect of the leader in me on student motivation and peer relationships in elementary school*. Walden University.

Tidd, J. (1997). *Managing innovation: Integrating technological, market and organizational change*. John Wiley & Sons.

Tierney, T. J. (2006). Understanding the nonprofit sector's leadership deficit. *Leader to Leader*, *1*, 13S–19S.

Tohidian, I., & Rahimian, H. (n.d.). Bringing Morgan's metaphors in organization contexts: An essay review. *Tandfonline*. https://www.tandfonline.com/doi/full/10.1080/23311975.2019.1587808

Tomashuk I.V. & Baldynyuk V.M., (2021). Identification of problems and prospects of rural infrastructure development of Ukraine. *Economic sciences*, *13* (100). doi:10.24412/2520-6990-2021-13100-58-70

Tomich, T. P., Brodt, S., Ferris, H., Galt, R., Horwath, W. R., Kebreab, E., Leveau, J. H. J., Liptzin, D., Lubell, M., Merel, P., Michelmore, R., Rosenstock, T., Scow, K., Six, J., Williams, N., & Yang, L. (2011). Agroecology: A review from a global-change perspective. *Annual Review of Environment and Resources*, *36*(1), 193–222. doi:10.1146/annurev-environ-012110-121302

Torch. (2023). *Research Report: Leveraging coaching and mentoring to create more effective leaders*. Harvard Business School Publishing.

Trist, E. L. (1976a). A Concept of Organizational Ecology: an invited address to the three Melbourne universities. Melbourne, AU: xxx.

Trist, E. L. (1981). Evolution of socio-technical systems. *Occasional Paper, 02*. Ontario: Quality of Working Life Center.

Trist, E. L. (1971). Critique of scientific management in terms of socio-technical theory. *Prak-seologia*, (39-40), 159–174.

Trist, E. L. (1976b). Action research and adaptative planning. In A. W. Clark (Ed.), *Experimenting with Organizational Life: The Action Research Approach*. Plenum Press. doi:10.1007/978-1-4613-4262-5_17

Trougakos, J. P., Chawla, N., & McCarthy, J. M. (2020). Working in a pandemic: Exploring the impact of Covid-19 health anxiety on work, family, and health outcomes. *The Journal of Applied Psychology*, *105*(11), 1234–1245. doi:10.1037/apl0000739 PMID:32969707

Tsai, W., & Ghoshal, S. (1998). Social capital and value creation: The role of intrafirm networks. *Academy of Management Journal*, *1998*(41), 464–476. doi:10.2307/257085

Tumwebaze, Z., Bananuka, J., Alinda, K., & Kalembe, D. (2021). Intellectual capital: Mediator of board of directors' effectiveness andadoptionof International Financial Reporting Standards. *Journal of Financial Reporting and Accounting*, *19*(2), 272–298. doi:10.1108/JFRA-03-2020-0076

Turner, D., & Crawford, M. (1994). Future competitive. *Competence-Based Competition*, *4*, 241.

U.S. Bureau of Labor Statistics. (2019). *Women in the labor force: a databook*. BLS. https://www.bls.gov/opub/reports/womens-databook/2019/home.htm

U.S. Bureau of Labor Statistics. (2020). *Usual weekly earnings of wage and salary workers fourth quarter 2019, Table 1*. BLS. https://www.bls.gov/news.release/archives/wkyeng_01172020.pdf

U.S. Census Bureau. (2021). *Current population survey: PINC-05. Work experience-people 15 years old and over, by total money earnings, age, race, Hispanic origin, sex, and disability status: 2018*. USCB. https://www.census.gov/data/tables/time-series/demo/income-poverty/cps-pinc/pinc-05.html

U.S. Energy Information Administration [EIA]. (2019). *Renewable energy explained: Portfolio standards*. US EIA. https://www.eia.gov/energyexplained/renewable-sources/portfolio-standards.php

Ugai, T. (2016). Evaluation of sustainable roof from various aspects and benefits of agriculture roofing in urban core. *Procedia: Social and Behavioral Sciences, 216*, 850–860. doi:10.1016/j.sbspro.2015.12.082

UKEssays. (2021, July 29). *Is Taylor's theory of scientific management still useful in today's business?* UK Essays. https://www.ukessays.com/essays/business/is-taylors-theory-of-scientific-management-still-useful-today-business-essay.php

Ulrich, D., Ashkenas, R., Jick, T., & Kerr, S. (1995). *The Boundaryless Organization: Breaking the Chains of Organizational Structure*. Wiley.

UNDP. (2020). *Environmentally Sustainable Operations*. UNDP. https://www.undp.org/accountability/social-and-environmental-responsibility/sustainable-operations

United Nations Educational, Scientific and Cultural Organization [UNESCO]. (2020). *COVID-19 educational disruption and response*. UNESCO. https://en.unesco.org/themes/education-emergencies/coronavirus-school-closures

Vaira, M. (2004). Globalization and higher education organizational change: A framework for analysis. *Higher Education, 48*(4), 483–510. doi:10.1023/B:HIGH.0000046711.31908.e5

Valente, M. (2018). *Home*. Organizing for sustainability. https://www.organizingforsustainability.com

Van de Ven, A. H., & Poole, M. S. (1995). Explaining development and change in organizations. *Academy of Management Review, 20*(3), 510–540. doi:10.2307/258786

van der Voet, J. (2016). Change leadership and public-sector organizational change: Examining the interactions of transformational leadership style and red tape. *American Review of Public Administration, 46*(6), 660–682. doi:10.1177/0275074015574769

van der Voet, J., & Vermeeren, B. (2017). Change management in hard times: Can change management mitigate the negative relationship between cutbacks and the organizational commitment and work engagement of public-sector employees? *American Review of Public Administration, 47*(2), 230–252. doi:10.1177/0275074015625828

Van Haren Publishing (Ed.). (2017). It-Cmf - A Management Guide: Based on the It Capability Maturity Framework(tm) (It-Cmf(tm). Van Haren Publishing.

Van Holt, T., Statler, M., Atz, U., Whelan, T., van Loggerenberg, M., & Cebulla, J. (2020). The cultural consensus of sustainability-driven innovation: Strategies for success. *Business Strategy and the Environment, 29*(8), 3399–3409. doi:10.1002/bse.2584

van Vulpen, E. (2023) *What is organizational development? A complete guide*. AIHR. https://www.aihr.com/blog/organizational-development/

Van Wart, M., & Kapucu, N. (2011). Crisis management competencies: The case of emergency managers in the USA. *Public Management Review, 13*(4), 489–511. doi:10.1080/14719037.2010.525034

Vargo, J., & Seville, E. (2011). Crisis strategic planning for SMEs: Finding the silver lining. *International Journal of Production Research, 49*(18), 5619–5635. doi:10.1080/00207543.2011.563902

Vasconcelos, A. F. (2018). Workplace spirituality: Empirical evidence revisited. *Management Research Review, 41*(7), 789–821. doi:10.1108/MRR-07-2017-0232

Vázquez-de-Príncipe, J. (2021). *Investigating leadership and human-intelligences during public-sector organizational change: A mixed methods study* [Doctoral dissertation, University of Phoenix]. ProQuest Dissertations & Theses (PQDT) Global – ProQuest Publishing.

Vedejová, D., & Čavojová, V. (2022). Confirmation bias in information search, interpretation, and memory recall: Evidence from reasoning about four controversial topics. *Thinking & Reasoning, 28*(1), 1–28. doi:10.1080/13546783.2021.1891967

Vedovello, C. (2001). Perspectivas e limites da interação entre universidades e MPMEs de base tecnológica localizadas em incubadoras de empresas. *Revista do bndes, 16*(8), 281-316.

Velev, D., & Zlateva, P. (2017). Virtual reality challenges in education and training. *International Journal of Learning and Teaching, 3*, 33–37. doi:10.18178/ijlt.3.1.33-37

Vijayaraghavan, K. (2016). Green roofs: A critical review on the role of components, benefits, limitations, and trends. *Renewable & Sustainable Energy Reviews, 57*, 740–752. doi:10.1016/j.rser.2015.12.119

Virginia Commonwealth University. (2015). *Education and health: The return on investment*. Virginia Commonwealth University. https://societyhealth.vcu.edu/work/the-projects/education- a nd-health-the-return-on-investment.html

Viscio, A. J., Frank, A., & Pasternack, B. A. (1999). *The Centerless Corporation: A New Model for Transforming Your Organization for Growth and Prosperity*. Simon & Schuster.

VisitBerlin (2017). *12 mal Berliner Leben, 12 mal Berlin Erleben. Konzept für einen stadtverträglichen Berlin-Tourismus 2018+;* VisitBerlin: Berlin, Germany. https://about.visitberlin.de/tourismuskonzept-2018

Vroman, S. R., & Danko, T. (2020, June 8). Against what model? Evaluating women as leaders in the pandemic era. *Gender, Work and Organization, 27*(5), 860–867. doi:10.1111/gwao.12488

Vu, M. C., & Nguyen, L. A. (2022). Mindful unlearning in unprecedented times: Implications for management and organizations. *Management Learning, 53*(5), 797–817. doi:10.1177/13505076211060433

Vygotsky, L. S. (1962). *Thought and language*. MIT Press. doi:10.1037/11193-000

Walske, J. (2013). Exploring theoretical fit of the resource-based view and human capital theory. In Social entrepreneurship and broader theories: Shedding new light on the 'bigger picture. *Journal of Social Entrepreneurship, 4*(1), 88–107. doi:10.1080/19420676.2012.725422

Walumbwa, F. O., Lawler, J. J., Avolio, B. J., & Wang, P. (2003). *Relationship between transformational leadership and work-related attitudes: The moderating effects of collective and self-efficacy across cultures* (Working paper). University of Nebraska-Lincoln.

Walumbwa, F. O., & Lawler, J. J. (2003). Building effective organizations: Transformational leadership, collectivist orientation, work-related attitudes, and withdrawal behaviors in three emerging economies. *International Journal of Human Resource Management, 14*(7), 1083–1101. doi:10.1080/0958519032000114219

Wang, C.-H. (2014). A longitudinal study of innovation competence and quality management on firm performance. *Innovation (North Sydney, N.S.W.), 16*(3), 392–403. doi:10.1080/14479338.2014.11081995

Wang, M. (2017). Using crisis simulation to enhance crisis management competencies: The role of presence. *Journal of Public Relations Education, 3*(2), 96–109.

Wang, Y., Hu, H., Dai, W., & Burns, K. (2021). Evaluation of industrial green development and industrial green competitiveness: Evidence from Chinese urban agglomerations. *Ecological Indicators*, *124*, 107371. doi:10.1016/j.ecolind.2021.107371

Ward, S. J., & King, L. A. (2018). Moral self-regulation, moral identity, and religiosity. *Journal of Personality and Social Psychology*, *115*(3), 495–525. doi:10.1037/pspp0000207 PMID:30024183

Warin, J. (2017). Creating a whole school ethos of care. *Emotional & Behavioural Difficulties*, *22*(3), 188–199. doi:10.1080/13632752.2017.1331971

Warren, R. L. (1967). The interorganizational field as a focus for investigation. *Administrative Science Quarterly*, *12*(3), 396–419. doi:10.2307/2391312

Watzlawick, P., Weakland, J. H., & Fisch, R. (1974). *Change: principles of problem formation and problem resolution.* W. W. Norton.

Wayland, R. E., & Cole, P. M. (1997). *Customer connections: New strategies for growth.* Harvard Business Press.

Weick, K. E. (1995). *Sensemaking in organizations.* Sage.

Weick, K. E., & Quinn, R. E. (1999). Organizational change and development. *Annual Review of Psychology*, *50*(1), 361–386. doi:10.1146/annurev.psych.50.1.361 PMID:15012461

Weiss, P. G., & Li, S. T. T. (2020). Leading change to address the needs and well-being of trainees during the Covid-19 Pandemic. *Academic Pediatrics*, *20*(6), 735–741. doi:10.1016/j.acap.2020.06.001 PMID:32512054

Welch, J., & Byrne, J. A. (2003). *Jack: Straight from the Gut.* Headline.

Wendong, L., Wei, Y., & Li, X. (2019). What dimension of CSR matters to organizational resilience? Evidence from China. *Sustainability (Basel)*, *11*(6), 1561. doi:10.3390u11061561

Westley, F. (1995). Governing design: The management of social systems and ecosystems management. In L. H. Gunderson & C. S. Holling (Eds.), *Barriers and Bridges to the Renewal of Ecosystems and Institutions.* Columbia University Press.

Whitler, K. A., & Puto, C. P. (2020). The influence of the board of directors on outside-in strategy. *Industrial Marketing Management*, *90*, 143–154. doi:10.1016/j.indmarman.2020.07.007

Whitley, R. (1999). *Divergent capitalisms: The social structuring and change of business systems.* Oxford University Press.

Wicks, P. G., & Reason, P. (2009). Initiating action research challenges and paradoxes of opening communicative space. *Action Research*, *7*(3), 243–262. doi:10.1177/1476750309336715

Wieman, J. M., & Giles, H. (1997): Azinterperszonáliskommunikáció In: Szociálpszichológiaszerk. KJK, Budapest.

Wiering, M., Liefferink, D., Boezeman, D., Kaufmann, M., Crabbé, A., & Kurstjens, N. (2020). The Wicked Problem the Water Framework Directive Cannot Solve. The Governance Approach in Dealing with Pollution of Nutrients in Surface Water in the Netherlands, Flanders, Lower Saxony, Denmark, and Ireland. *Water (Basel)*, *12*(5), 1240. doi:10.3390/w12051240

Wigert, B., & Agrawal, S. (2022). *Returning to the office: The current, preferred and future state of remote work.* Gallup.

Wilson, J. Q. (1989). *Bureaucracy: What government agencies do and why they do it.* Basic Books.

Winkle-Wagner, R., & McCoy, D. L. (2018). Feeling like an "Alien" or "Family"? Comparing students and faculty experiences of diversity in STEM disciplines at a PWI and an HBCU. *Race, Ethnicity and Education*, *21*(5), 593–606. doi:10.1080/13613324.2016.1248835

Wire, F. (2020). Oil and Coronavirus Shocks Add Pressure for MEA Sovereigns. In *FitchRatings*. https://www.fitchratings.com/research/sovereigns/oil-coronavirus-shocks-add-pressure-for-mea-sovereigns-10-03-2020

Wirtenberg, J., Harmon, K. D., Russell, W. G., & Fairfield, K. D. (2007). HR's role in building a sustainable enterprise. *Human Resource Planning*, *30*, 10–20.

Wohlgenannt, I., Simons, A., & Stieglitz, S. (2020). Virtual reality. *Business & Information Systems Engineering*, *62*(5), 455–461. doi:10.100712599-020-00658-9

Wolf, S., & Primmer, E. (2006). Between incentives and action: A pilot study of biodiversity conservation competencies for multifunctional forest management in Finland. *Society & Natural Resources*, *19*(9), 845–861. doi:10.1080/08941920600835601

Womack, J. P., Jones, D. T., & Roos, D. (2007). *The Machine that Changed the World*. Simon & Schuster.

Wood, D. J. (1991). Corporate social performance revisited. *Academy of Management Review*, *16*(4), 691–718. doi:10.2307/258977

World Economic Forum (WEF). (2020). *Discovering the real impact of COVID-19 on entrepreneurship*. WEF. https://www.weforum.org/agenda/2020/06/how-covid-19-willchange-entrepreneurial-business/

World Economy. (2020). *5 charts show what the global economy looks like heading into 2021*. CNBC. https://www.cnbc.com/2020/12/28/5-charts-show-covid-impact-on-the-global-economy-in-2020.html

World Health Organization. (2022). *Coronavirus disease (COVID-19) pandemic*. World Health Organization. https://www.who.int/europe/emergencies/situations/covid-19#:~:text=This%20led%20WHO%20to%20declare,have%20died%20from%20the%20disease

Worldometer. (2020). *COVID-19 CORONAVIRUS PANDEMIC*. World Meter. https://www.worldometers.info/coronavirus/

Wu, W., & Jim, C. Y. (2021). Urban green infrastructure and sustainable urbanization: A comprehensive review of the roles of green roofs. *Landscape and Urban Planning*, *212*, 104097. doi:10.1016/j.landurbplan.2021.104097

Wysocki, J. (2021). Innovative green initiatives in the manufacturing SME sector in Poland. *Sustainability (Basel)*, *13*(4), 2386. doi:10.3390u13042386

Xu, A., Liu, Z., Guo, Y., Sinha, V., & Akkiraju, R. (2017, May). A new chatbot for customer service on social media. In *Proceedings of the 2017 CHI conference on human factors in computing systems* (pp. 3506-3510). 10.1145/3025453.3025496

Yang, B., Sun, Y., & Shen, X. L. (2023). Understanding AI-based customer service resistance: A perspective of defective AI features and tri-dimensional distrusting beliefs. *Information Processing & Management*, *60*(3), 103257. doi:10.1016/j.ipm.2022.103257

Yang, D., Wei, Y. K., Xue, F. S., Deng, X. M., & Zhi, J. (2016). Simulation-based airway management training: Application and looking forward. *Journal of Anesthesia*, *30*(2), 284–289. doi:10.100700540-015-2116-7 PMID:26671260

Yardeni, E., Johnson, D., & Quintana, M. (2020). *Global Economic Briefing: Industrial Production*. Global Economic Briefing: Industrial Production. www.yardeni.com

Yukl, G. (1999). An evaluation of conceptual weaknesses in transformational and charismatic leadership theories. *The Leadership Quarterly*, *10*(2), 285–305. doi:10.1016/S1048-9843(99)00013-2

Zaid, A. A., Jaaron, A. A., & Bon, A. T. (2018). The impact of green human resource management and green supply chain management practices on sustainable performance: An empirical study. *Journal of Cleaner Production*, *204*, 965–979. doi:10.1016/j.jclepro.2018.09.062

Zainun, N. F. H., Johari, J., & Adnan, Z. (2021). Machiavellianism, locus of control, moral identity, and ethical leadership among public service leaders in Malaysia: The moderating effect of ethical role modeling. *International Journal of Sociology & Social Policy*. Emerald Publishing Limited. doi:10.1108/IJSSP-07-2020-0289

Zhang, S., Sun, J., & Gao, X. (2020). The effect of fatigue on brain connectivity networks. *Brain Science Advances*, 6(2), 120–131. doi:10.26599/BSA.2020.9050008

Zhang, Z., & Sundaresan, S. (2010). Knowledge markets in firms: Knowledge sharing with trust and signalling. *Knowledge Management Research and Practice*, *2010*(8), 322–339. doi:10.1057/kmrp.2010.22

Zhao, J. (2021). Reimagining corporate social responsibility in the Era of COVID-19: Embedding resilience and promoting corporate social competence. *Sustainability (Basel)*, *13*(12), 6548. doi:10.3390u13126548

Zheng, C. (2012). Isomorph isomorphic influences and aspiration: Reference group choice in entry mode decisions. *Journal of International Business Research*, *11*(2), 129–141.

Zhou, C., Xie, J., & Wang, Q. (2016). Failure to complete cross-border M&As: "To" vs. "From" emerging markets. *Journal of International Business Studies*, *47*(9), 1077–1105. doi:10.105741267-016-0027-y

Zimmerman, L. A., Sestokas, J. M., Burns, C. A., Bell, J., & Manning, D. (2012). *Methods and Tools for Training Crisis Response*. U.S. Army Research Institute for the Behavioral and Social Sciences. doi:10.1037/e643372013-001

Zohar, D., & Marshall, I. N. (2004). *Spiritual capital: Wealth we can live by*. Berrett-Koehle Publishers, Inc.

Zolkiewski, J., Lewis, B., Yuan, F., & Yuan, J. (2007). An assessment of customer service in business-to-business relationships. *Journal of Services Marketing*, *21*(5), 313–325. doi:10.1108/08876040710773624

Zucker, L. G. (1977). The role of institutionalization in cultural persistence. *American Sociological Review*, *42*(5), 726–743. doi:10.2307/2094862

About the Contributors

Kyla L. Tennin has both an DM, and MBA - Doctor of Management in Organizational Leadership; PhD Fellow, Global Peace Institute UK/Singapore. Chairwoman, President, Global CEO (LMG) World Business Angels Investment Forum (WBAF)-G20.

***

Ashok Kumar Asthana is an alumni and a gold medallist from Jiwaji University, Gwalior. He is a highly motivated, organized and a versatile person with a passion for inculcating innovative methods in teaching. He has done his PGDBM (Approved by AICTE and Eqv. to MBA by AIU) in Marketing and International Business from NDIM and MBA in HRM form Alagappa University. He has qualified UGC-NET in management. He has over 13 years of rich teaching experience. He has done his doctoral research in the area of OB and HR from ICFAI University, Ranchi. His topic of research was related to Attitude and Performance of teachers in higher educational institutions. He is currently working as Assistant professor in Faculty of Commerce and Management, Sarala Birla University, Ranchi, Jharkhand and also holding an additional responsibility of "Dean Student`s Welfare". Earlier he was associated with New Delhi Institute of Management (Affiliated to GGSIP University), New Delhi. To his credit there are several national, international publications in journal of repute. He has also presented many papers in National and international seminar and conferences. His research areas of interest are Organization Behaviour and HR. He has received many awards and recognition including "Best Teacher Award", "Chairman`s Appreciation Award for Outstanding Performance", "Researcher of the Year Award" etc. He has also participated in FDP`S and MDP`s. He is a life time member of TERA. He has been actively mentoring Undergraduates and as well as Post Graduates students so that they can build their career.

Oindrila Chakraborty is a gold medalist in her MBA programme from University of Calcutta. She has 14 years of teaching experience in management education. She has completed her PhD from University of Calcutta and has several publications to furnish in National and International Journals of high repute.

Lisa Dollmann is a Master in Management student; Master Thesis Nova SBE. (Portugal)

Helena Martins is a lecturer in Human Resources Management at the Instituto Politécnico de Setúbal and the Nova School of Business and Economics in Portugal. She is an integrated member of the CEOS.PP research centre and her research interests focus the development of soft skills for crisis situations especially for leaders and managers. She holds a PhD in Management (University of Porto,

Portugal), a Masters in Work, Organizational and Personnel Psychology (University of Coimbra, Portugal and University of Valencia, Spain) and a Bachelors in Psychology (University of Minho, Portugal). Member of the Scientific Committee in several international and national conferences and congresses, and international journals. Extensive experience in guiding master's theses/projects and participation in juries of public examinations. Author and co-author of several scientific articles and book chapters and reviewer in several journals.

Joanne Principe is a Doctor of Management in Organizational Leadership; Fellow in Residence, Center of Leadership Studies & Organizational Research College of Doctoral Studies affiliated with the University of Phoenix.

Ali Rehman received Ph.D from Universiti Sains Malaysia in 2020 in the area of Risk and Corporate Governance and MSc from Birmingham City University in the area of Audit Risk and Consultancy. He is currently working in A'Sharqiyah University as Director of Internal Audit and is also Board Member for Institute of Internal Auditors (IIA) Oman Chapter. He is knowledgeable Auditing and accounting professional bringing more than 21 years of experience in academic, research, audit, finance and corporate governance. As a holder of professional certifications such as Fellow Chartered Management Accountant (FCMA – UK), Chartered Global Management Accountant (CGMA), Certified Internal Auditor (CIA) and Certified Risk Assurance Management (CRMA) he have successfully revamped and strengthened controls and implemented Corporate Governance Maturity Framework in various organisations. He is champion in reorganising processes and simplifying procedures to maximise efficiency and accuracy of accounting and operational records. He was also awarded with World Top 100 "Driver of Audit Excellence" by Dilligent. He is performing part time teaching in various Universities. He has written several book chapters and research articles which are published in esteemed journals and books indexed in Scopus and WOS.

Ana Cláudia Rodrigues holds a PhD in Human Resources Management and Development (ISCTE-Instituto Universitário de Lisboa), teaching in this area at undergraduate and masters level, at Porto Accounting and Business School (ISCAP-P.Porto) and in the postgraduate course in People Management at Porto Business School (University of Porto). She is also director of the Bachelor Degree in Human Resources at ISCAP-P.Porto. She is an integrated member of the Center for Organizational and Social Studies of the Polytechnic of Porto (CEOS.PP) and participates in national and international research projects. Participates in international conferences as author, reviewer and guest speaker. She published in different indexed international journals on organizational culture, competencies, human resources relationship with performance, virtual/augmented reality applications and virtual teams.

Teresa Salazar-Echeagaray is a research professor.

Swati Srivastava is an assistant professor in the Department of Commerce and Management, K R Mangalam University, India.

Omar Vargas-González is Professor and Head of Systems and Computing Department at Tecnologico Nacional de Mexico Campus Ciudad Guzman, professor at Telematic Engineering at Centro Universitario del Sur Universidad de Guadalajara with a master degree in Computer Systems. Has been trained in Innovation and Multidisciplinary Entrepreneurship at Arizona State University (2018) and a Generation of Ecosystems of Innovation, Entrepreneurship and Sustainability for Jalisco course by Harvard University T.H. Chan School of Health. At present conduct research on diverse fields such as Entrepreneurship, Economy, Statistics, Mathematics and Information and Computer Sciences. Has colaborated in the publication of over 20 scientific articles and conducted diverse Innovation and Technological Development projects.

José Vargas-Hernandez is a research professor.

Index

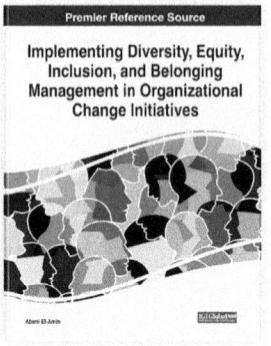

Ingram Content Group UK Ltd.
Milton Keynes UK
UKHW050821210723
425555UK00012B/459